Using
Turbo C++®

David S. Linthicum
Larry Klein

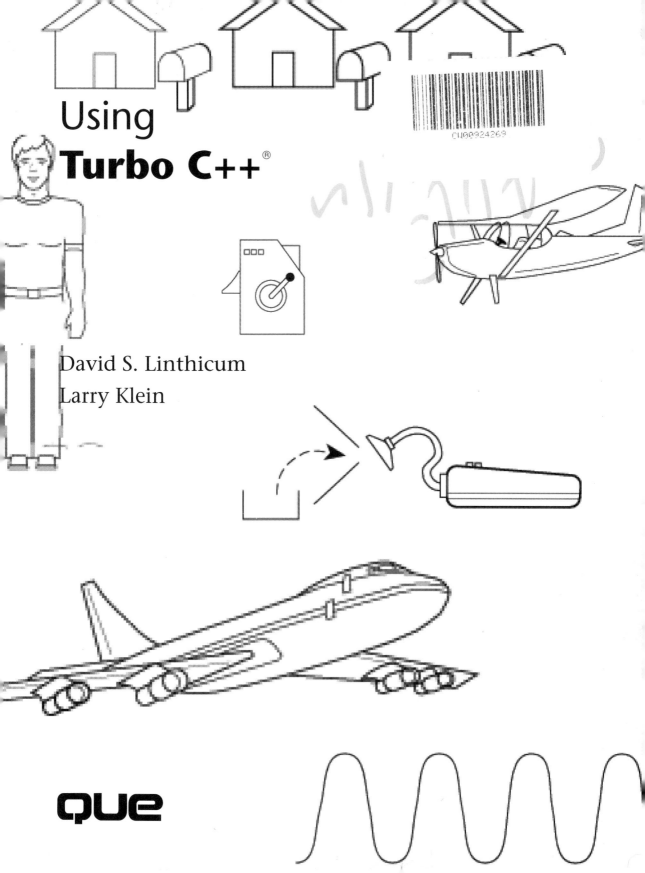

que

Using Turbo C++

Library of Congress Catalog No.: 93-086416

ISBN: 1-56529-471-8

96 95 94 93   4 3 2 1

Interpretation of the printing code: the rightmost double-digit number is the year of the book's printing; the rightmost single-digit number, the number of the book's printing. For example, a printing code of 93-1 shows that the first printing of the book occurred in 1993.

Publisher: David P. Ewing

Director of Publishing: Michael Miller

Managing Editor: Corinne Walls

Marketing Manager: Ray Robinson

Credits

Publishing Manager

Joseph B. Wikert

Acquisitions Editor

Nancy Stevenson

Product Directors

Bryan Gambrel

Greg Guntle

Production Editor

Mike La Bonne

Copy Editors

Lorna Gentry

Chuck Hutchinson

Susan Pink

Andy Saff

Mary Anne Sharbaugh

Midge Stocker

Technical Editor

Greg Guntle

Book Designer

Amy Peppler-Adams

Graphic Image Specialists

Teresa Forrester

Tim Montgomery

Dennis Sheehan

Sue VandeWalle

Production Team

Angela Bannan

Claudia Bell

Danielle Bird

Paula Carroll

Anne Dickerson

Karen Dodson

Brook Farling

Bob LaRoche

Joy Dean Lee

Nanci Sears Perry

Michael Thomas

Tina Trettin

Jennifer Willis

Donna Winter

Michelle Worthington

Indexer

Michael Hughes

Dedication:

To my Mom and Dad, Ronald and Joan Linthicum. Thanks for the love, support, and persistent encouragement. David S. Linthicum

To Cheryl: I love you allways. Larry Klein

About the Authors

David Linthicum is a 10-year veteran of the computer industry. He currently works for the Computer Services Division of Mobil Oil in Fairfax, Va., as a Senior Software Engineer. Dave also is an associate professor of computer science at Northern Virginia Community College in Sterling, Va., where he teaches courses in systems analysis and design, and database design. He has published more than 100 articles for a variety of popular technical publications, and speaks at computer conferences throughout the country. You can contact him through CompuServe at 72740,2016.

Larry Klein is the principal of a technology consulting company, LCK Consulting, which develops software products.

Acknowledgments:

Thanks to all the people at Que who worked so hard "behind the scenes" to make this book possible. Thanks also to the Publishing Relations Department at Borland for supporting this effort, and providing software to me and Larry. And a special thanks to my wife, Celeste, for putting up with me and my absences as I pursued "just one more book." David S. Linthicum

Thanks to everyone for their kind words of encouragement and for their support in making this book become a reality. Larry Klein

Trademarks

Que Corporation has made every attempt to supply trademark information about company names, products, and services mentioned in this book. The following trademarks are derived from various sources. Que Corporation cannot attest to the accuracy of this information.

Turbo C and Turbo C++ are registered trademarks of Borland International, Inc.

UNIX is a trademark of AT&T

ANSI is a registered trademark of American National Standards Institute.

Intel is a registered trademark of Intel Corporation.

Microsoft and MS-DOS are registered trademarks of Microsoft Corporation.

Contents at a Glance

Part I

Part II

Part III

Part IV

Part V

Part VI

Contents

10 Introduction to String Constants and String Arrays   223

11 Understanding Variable Scope   243

12 Using the Preprocessor   265

13 Using Functions   285

Introduction

Hailed by many as the "people's compiler," Turbo C++ is an inexpensive but powerful C and C++ development tool for small and large application programs. Turbo C and C++ have won many awards, including praise from many technical publications. The number of Turbo C++ books written over the years is a testament to its sustained popularity, quality, and value.

More than 20 years have passed since the C programming language was introduced to the programming world. Over the years, C has evolved into a popular, powerful computer programming language used worldwide. C and C++ are the programming languages of choice for Microsoft DOS, Microsoft Windows, IBM OS/2, and UNIX applications.

Borland International has played the most significant role in furthering the popularity of C and C++ on Intel-based computers. The Borland line of C/C++ development environments is considered the benchmark of excellence for other competing products. The Borland products provide sophisticated programming tools at an affordable price. This affordable power is the credo of Borland International.

Borland introduced Turbo C in the mid-1980s as an inexpensive alternative to MS-DOS C compilers such as the popular, but expensive, Microsoft C. At the time, Borland was an up-and-coming software company with other successful products such as Sidekick, a memory-resident personal manager; and Turbo Pascal, a Pascal language compiler. The $100 price of Turbo C was revolutionary.

Soon after the release of Turbo C++, it became a hit with students, hobbyists, and even professional programmers. Most considered Turbo C++ a practical software development tool that gave the developer real bang for the buck.

Magazines dedicated to Turbo C++ filled the newsstands, Turbo C++ programs clogged the disks of bulletin board systems (BBSs), and an abundance of Turbo C++ books were on the shelves of major book stores and libraries. A legend was born.

Today, Turbo C++ provides an integrated development environment (IDE), a source code debugger, on-line help facilities, and one of the fastest C compilers available (see the section "Features of Turbo C++ 3.0" later in this introduction). The price remains under $100. Don't let the low price fool you; it is a full-blown C and C++ compiler. Turbo C++ can create full-fledged business programs, utilities, and other MS-DOS applications the same as compilers costing five times the price.

Why You Should Read This Book

This book provides the beginner and intermediate C/C++ programmer with an excellent usage guide to Turbo C++ and the C/C++ programming language. It teaches concepts and techniques related to C and C++ programming, and builds on this knowledge as the chapters progress. This book also enables the more advanced Turbo C++ user or programmer to go directly to chapters of interest; reading previous chapters is not required. Also, included at the end of the book, is a handy ASCII chart.

Who Should Read This Book?

This book was created for the following groups:

- *Students* who are taking a class in C and C++, including college students who may have purchased Turbo C++ in the campus bookstore as a requirement for a computer science or management information systems class. When trying to learn the practical aspects of the language, the Borland documentation that comes with Turbo C++, or the book selected by an instructor, may leave much to be desired. Most students want understandable, "no-nonsense" explanations and examples that use numerous sample code listings and illustrations. *Using Turbo C++* uses easy-to-follow examples that correspond to concepts presented in each chapter, making learning C and C++ easy and fun.

■ *Self-taught programmers*—those who are trying to "go it on their own." This group includes anyone who wants to learn C/C++, but must do so with only this book as a guide. The writers have designed this book so that beginning C/C++ programmers are guided through the learning process step by step, topic by topic, and program by program. Other than interactive training, there is no better way to learn Turbo C++.

■ *Hobby programmers* who want to create C and C++ applications just for the fun of it, but don't want to spend an arm and a leg for a compiler and development environment. This book is especially helpful to the programmer/hobbyist, because the reader "learns by example," using some fairly complex sample programs. The programmer/hobbyist gets a "quick start" with C and C++ programming, building on concepts already learned. Most important, the explanation moves quickly enough to hold the interest of someone more technical than a beginning programmer.

■ *C/C++ converts* who know one or several other programming languages such as COBOL or FORTRAN, and want to add C and C++ to their list of programming skills. This decision is often a career move, because C/C++ programmers are in great demand, and demand usually results in higher salaries. *Using Turbo C++* gives professional programmers enough basic information to get them up and running with C/C++, and enough advanced material to add significantly to experienced programmers' skills.

How to Use This Book

Your own level of C/C++ expertise determines the way you approach this book. If you are a beginner, moving sequentially through the chapters will provide the greatest benefit. The most elementary concepts are presented in the first half of the book, and the most complex topics are presented in the second half. For example, discussion moves from the basic Turbo C++ concepts, such as using the IDE and the *debugger*, to the most complex object-oriented programming facilities of the C++ language.

If you already have some C/C++ experience, feel free to go directly to the chapters that interest you. For example, if you have a good understanding of C, but not the C++ object-oriented concepts, you could skip to the middle of the book where these concepts are first presented. However, even the most experienced programmer can stand some review. Make sure you understand the concepts presented in the earlier chapters.

The chapters are short, but there are many of them. Short chapters work better because concepts are more easily absorbed when a chapter can be read from beginning to end in one sitting. The chapters are also self-contained, so you don't have to read several sections just to understand one point. This "bite-size" method has been proven effective with previous "learning" books.

Conventions Used in This Book

Chapters contain bulleted lists, numbered lists, italicized text, figures, program listings, code fragments, and tables of information. Each has its own purpose. These design features should help you understand the material presented in each chapter.

Bulleted lists have the following characteristics:

- Bulleted items draw your attention to the concept being presented.

- The information in the bulleted list is not necessarily sequential.

- Items in a bulleted list contain explanations, not simple actions. The text is often longer than text found in other types of lists.

Numbered lists contain actions to be performed in a particular sequence. When you see a numbered list, you should do the following:

1. Start at the beginning of the list. Remember, the order is important. Don't skip ahead without completing the previous steps.

2. Take time to understand each item as you encounter it. Ask yourself whether you know exactly what's going on. Can you explain it?

3. Make sure that you read all items in the list, because no single item is designed to stand on its own. You must understand the "big picture."

Italic text stresses an important word or phrase. Pay close attention to text presented in italics. Italics are also used to introduce new technical terms. When you see a new term presented in italics, the definition or explanation follows. Code lines, variables names, and any text you see on-screen appear in a special monospace typeface. User input following a prompt appears in **bold monospace**.

Figures illustrate a point being made in the text. Illustrations bring a topic to life by borrowing from the adage, "A picture is worth a thousand words." Moreover, this book includes many screen images (screen shots) as you would view them on your computer monitor. This feature allows you to check the image you see on your monitor with the image in the book."

Program listings are complete C or C++ program listings. They can be compiled as a complete program. The code listings help illustrate concepts presented in the text. You may review the code in the book, or enter the code into Turbo C++ to create a complete sample program. For example, the following is a sample program listing:

Listing 0.1. HELLO.C—a sample program listing.

```
1    #include <stdio.h>
2    void main()
3    {
4         printf("Hello there\n");
5    }
```

Notice that the line numbers are included on the left side of the listing. *Do not* enter them into Turbo C++. They are not a part of the C languages, and would cause compiler errors. If, for some reason, a line of program code is so long that it goes beyond the limits of the page, code-continuation characters draw attention to this. If a code-continuation character is present, the next line of code is actually part of the line containing the code-continuation character.

Code fragments show C or C++ source code, as with a program listing; however, only portions of the program are presented. This is not a complete program and it can't be compiled. Code fragments are inserted directly into the text. They don't have headings, reference numbers, or line numbers. They illustrate a point made in the text.

Syntax form is a code fragment that shows the general form used when writing particular C statements or declarations. *Placeholders*—terms used in code lines to hold the place for text you will substitute, appear in *italic monospace*. A code fragment looks like the following:

```
type ( * function-pointer ) ( parameter-List );
```

Tables have their own headings and reference numbers. They present lists and columns of information for any number of reasons. For example, the book may use a table to present the available options of a particular Turbo C++ feature, such as command line switches, compiler options, and so on.

Organization of This Book

As mentioned earlier, *Using Turbo C++* is designed to be a learning tool and, to a lesser extent, a reference manual. Although the needs of the beginning student programmer were considered when organizing the information, this book also meets the needs of the more advanced C/C++ programmer.

The book is divided into the following parts:

- The first part covers the ins and outs of the Turbo C++ product itself. These chapters cover installation of Turbo C++, use of the IDE, editor, and debugger. The chapter also compiles a simple C program.

- The next portion of the book covers the standard (older) C language, including the basics of C programming.

- In the next portion of the book, you get into advanced C programming by creating your own C functions, and by using the program logic control facilities of C++. Then you look at how pointers and arrays are put to use by using C++, as well how to use structures and unions.

- In this section, you explore the world of object-oriented programming by introducing object-orientation as a concept, then explaining how these concepts work by using the C++ programming language. The use of C++ classes, objects, and member functions are just a few of the object-oriented C++ facilities that are explored. In addition, this section provides information on overloading and using object constructors and destructors.

- In the last portion of the book, you learn how to use the object-oriented concept of inheritance to maximize program power with fewer lines of code. Then, you learn about the Container Class Library, and how to use templates when creating your program. Finally, you learn about building, compiling, debugging, and testing your C++ program, and making the most of your Turbo C++ experience.

Again, the chapters are designed to contain just the right amount of information. This approach makes the information easily digestible. The chapters stand on their own. Previous chapters are not prerequisites, and information presented in subsequent chapters does not rely on previously presented information. The information is presented in a graduating scale of topic complexity. The basic topics are at the beginning of the book, and the more advanced are at the end.

Learning by Doing

Using Turbo C++ takes a hands-on approach because doing something yourself is the best way to learn. As examples are presented, you should take the time to enter and execute them in Turbo C++. When you do, make sure that the output is what you expected, and that the program is functioning correctly. After you try the examples, go a step further. Modify the program, change a line of code, or change the Turbo C++ options. See how these changes affect the overall function of the program. In other words, play with the program and Turbo C++, have fun, and learn.

Don't worry if you make a mistake. Your computer will not blow up. At worst, you'll have to reset or turn off your computer. Even the best professional C/C++ programmers are intimate with the Reset button. Errors are part of the process. Gain knowledge from your errors; never dread them.

Buying Turbo C++

You can buy Turbo C++ through a software distributor or directly from Borland. Prices range from $75 to $100, depending on the discount Borland or your software vendor is willing to extend. Most college bookstores sell educational versions of the compiler at a reduced price. Make sure that you purchase version 3.0 or later.

Use the following information to contact Borland directly:

> Borland International
> 1800 Green Hills Road
> P.O. Box 660001
> Scotts Valley, CA 95067-0001
> (800) 331-0877

Moving to Other C++ Compilers

Now that several new and improved versions of Borland C++ compilers are available, you might be wondering whether the skills you learn in this book can be applied to other, more advanced Borland C++ development products. The answer is yes. All of what you learn in *Using Turbo C++* can be applied to other C++ products from Borland, and other non-Borland C++ development products from companies such as Microsoft and Zortech.

Programmers can move from product to product in the Borland product line with little or no additional training. The IDEs are similar among the Borland products, even between the DOS and Windows versions.

These advanced Borland language products are basically enhanced versions of Turbo C++. These versions provide advanced "add-ons" such as Microsoft Windows application development facilities and stand-alone debuggers, which provide additional features besides the debugger that comes with Turbo C++. Other development aids are also included, such as class libraries and quick application generators.

In addition to Turbo C++, Borland currently offers the following C++ products:

Turbo C++ Visual Edition for Windows

The *Turbo C++ Visual Edition for Windows* is the Microsoft Windows version of the Turbo C++ compiler. It provides an IDE based on the Windows graphical user interface (GUI) and allows basic Windows application development by using the C++ programming language.

The product includes the following:

- Full ANSI C and AT&T CFRONT C++ 3.0 support for Windows

- A Windows IDE that can be used to edit, compile, and run programs from within Windows

- A visual ObjectBrowser

- The ObjectWindows application framework for a ready-made user interface

- Resource Workshop for the creation of a Windows user interface

- Turbo Debugger

- Protogen, a visual code generator for C and C++

Borland C++ for OS/2

Borland C++ for OS/2 allows its users to build true 32-bit OS/2 applications. This compiler is true Borland, providing a new graphical debugger and Borland's visual tools for use with OS/2's Presentation manager. This product provides a 32-bit code generation facility and optimization features customized for the OS/2 operating system. The compiler is compatible with ANSI C and AT&T C++ standards, and applications are portable to and from other Borland C++ compilers.

Borland C++

This is a complete compiler for both DOS and Windows, based on Turbo C++ for Windows. Borland C++ provides both a DOS and Windows-based IDE, *Turbo Debugger* (a stand-alone symbolic debugger), and a *Windows Resource Workshop* that enables you to create Windows resources such as dialog boxes, icons, and so on, for use with Windows applications.

The product includes the following:

- A standard C and C++ development system for creating Windows and DOS applications

- ObjectBrowser

- Global optimization

- Turbo Drive protected-mode compiler and environment

- Turbo Debugger and Turbo Profiler for Windows and DOS

- Resource Workshop

- Turbo Assembler

Borland C++ and Applications Frameworks

This product comes with everything included in Borland C++, but also includes a set of class libraries called the *ObjectWindows Library (OWL)* and *ObjectVision* application generator. The OWL class library allows the program to reuse functions provided by Borland, such as dialog boxes, buttons, and so on.

The product includes the following features in addition to the ones listed for Borland C++:

■ ObjectWindows Library for Windows

■ Turbo Vision for DOS

■ Source code for ObjectWindows and Turbo Vision

■ Runtime Library Source Code

Features of Turbo C++

Following are the major features of Turbo C++ 3.0. These features are explained in greater detail in the first portion of the book:

■ Full support for AT&T's C++ CFRONT 3.0 specification and 100 percent ANSI C-compliant C compiler

■ Precompiled header files used to speed up recompilation of programs

■ Inline assembly

■ Response files and multiple configuration files

■ Support for six memory models

■ 80286 code generation

■ Stack checking

■ Programs to set command-line options in source code, save registers, and add startup and exit functions

■ A macro-based editor that supports full undo and redo, as well as editing of large files

■ Multiple overlapping windows with mouse support

■ Transfer options that allow integration with other editors and third-party software

■ Automatic dependency checking for header files

■ Smart Project Manager

- Color syntax highlighting

- Integrated debugger with data and object inspectors

- Debug VROOMM overlays

- The ability to view stacks, evaluate expressions, modify variables, and watch expressions as you step through a program

- Automatic desktop save and restore

- DPMI (DOS extender), which allows loading of huge programs

- The ability to use 25-, 43-, and 50-line mode

- Dynamic segment overlay manager

- Support for a cache overlay to EMS, extended memory and disk

- Support for an overlay manager in the runtime library

- Support for a math coprocessor with runtime detection

- UNIX compatibility functions

- More than 450 programming functions

Turbo C++ 3.0 System Requirements

Turbo C++ runs on most Intel-based computers, and its resource requirements are reasonable. Before buying the product, take some time to review the following requirements and determine whether your computer or the computer you have access to is able to run Turbo C++.

- An IBM personal computer (PC) or a 100 percent compatible

- 80286 or greater Intel processor

- PC-DOS/MS-DOS 3.31 or later

- 1M of extended memory

- 5M minimum of disk space

How to Contact the Authors

Should you want to contact the authors of *Using Turbo C++*, electronic mail is the best way to do so, either through CompuServe information service or Internet.

Please address your comments and questions to the following:

David Linthicum	CompuServe:	72740,2016
	Internet:	72740.2016@compuserve.com

or

Larry Klein	CompuServe:	76330,2525
	Internet:	76330.2525@compuserve.com

Part I

Familiarizing Yourself with Turbo C++

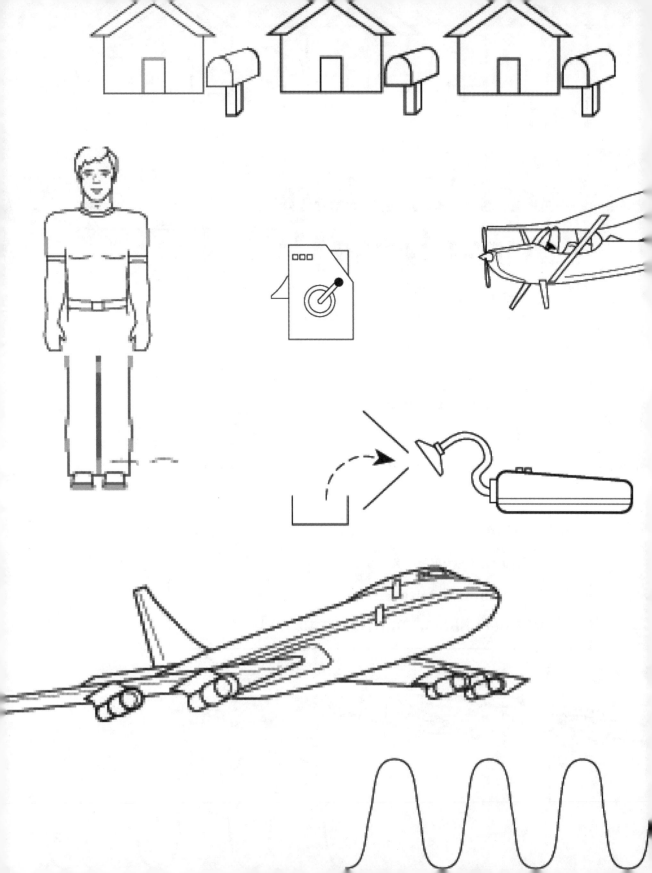

## Chapter 1

Understanding the Basics

In this chapter, you learn about Turbo C++ and basic PC programming concepts. On the Turbo C++ side, you learn about the differences between C and C++, why C++ was created, and what advantages C++ offers a programmer. You also learn about structured programming and object-oriented programming. And you learn about the types of software you can create by using Turbo C++. On the PC side, you learn about the MS-DOS operating system, the BIOS, device drivers, memory, disk drives, and the CPU.

The C Language

In the late 1960s, Brian Kernighan and Dennis Ritchie at AT&T Bell Labs developed the C language. C was an evolution of two earlier languages, BCPL and B, which also were developed at AT&T Bell Labs.

C is the native language of the UNIX operating system. (UNIX is written in the C programming language.) The C programming language's ties to operating system development and its capability to perform high-level and low-level (operating system) operations have lead to its wide acceptance as a system programming language. Many MS-DOS device drivers and terminate-and-stay resident (TSR) programs that interact with the operating system use the C programming language.

In the years after the introduction of C, many derivations of the language were developed on different computing platforms. The problem of *portability*, or the capability to move source code from one platform to the next, was addressed in 1983, when the American National Standards Institute (ANSI) created a committee to provide standard definitions of the C programming language. This committee defined the functions and facilities to be supported by C program compilers and certified them as ANSI C-compliant.

Today, most C and C++ compilers (Turbo C++ included) are ANSI C-compliant and can—in theory—compile all C programs written in ANSI C with few or no modifications to the source code. However, many have found that this sounds better than it works. Although many C compilers are ANSI C-compliant, moving and recompiling complex systems developed in C from one compiler to another is no simple task.

C is the preferred development tool for MS-DOS, OS/2, Microsoft Windows, Microsoft Windows NT, and the UNIX operating systems. Most popular MS-DOS and Windows programs are written in C or C++, including dBASE IV, Lotus 1-2-3, Paradox, Microsoft Excel, and Microsoft Word for Windows. Most computer platforms have C compilers, and as compilers and standards progress, the degree of portability is increasing. Many foresee the day when software developed in C can be moved from MS-DOS to Windows to NT to UNIX and to other operating system and hardware platforms, with few or no modifications.

The C++ Language

C++ is the new superset of the C programming language. The C++ programming language supports all the features of earlier C compilers and the new features introduced in the C++ language. Classes are the most important feature of C++ and are the basis of object-oriented programming.

Object-oriented programming enables the programmer to reuse code that is already written. Code reusability is the underlying concept also of structured programming; however, object-oriented programming does it much better.

Object-oriented programming is not new. It was developed in the late 1960s but remained on the bookshelves, a topic of academic discussion. In the 1980s, researchers wanted to incorporate object-oriented features into a programming language. C was gaining popularity on many hardware and operating system platforms, and it was selected as the language to receive the object-oriented functionality. C with Classes was the result. Because

C with Classes had roots in the C programming language, it was adopted easily by C programmers who needed to use the new object-oriented features but didn't want to learn an entirely new language.

The C with Classes language was extended in 1984, and the result was called C++. In 1985, C++ was being discussed at academic forums, universities, and technical conferences throughout the United States. Articles detailing the advantages of the C++ programming language filled magazines. It made a big splash in the software development world, and programmers went back to school to learn the object-oriented features of C++. New analysis and formal program design methods were developed to follow the object-oriented constructs.

Although there are other object-oriented programming languages (such as Smalltalk, Actor, Objective C, Ada, and Pascal with Classes), C++ dominates the world of object-oriented programs. Much of this popularity is due to the success of the Turbo C++ compiler.

The Turbo C++ Language

Back in 1983, a little-known company called Borland International introduced a product that became an overnight hit: Turbo Pascal. Turbo Pascal was so successful that Borland came out with a similar compiler for C in 1987 called Turbo C. Many colleges and universities adopted Turbo C as a standard development and education environment for students learning C. Many hobby programmers adopted Turbo C as their preferred development environment. The public bulletin board systems were (and are) filled with thousands of megabytes of Turbo C application programs.

Like Turbo Pascal, Turbo C has an editor, a linker, and a compiler in an all-inclusive package called the *Integrated Development Environment*, or *IDE*. Turbo C was introduced at less than $100, which was a fraction of the price of other C compilers. The combination of low price and high functionality made Turbo C the compiler value of the decade. This is still true today.

In 1990, Borland began shipping Turbo C++. This C and C++ compiler offers features such as ANSI C and C++ compiler compatibility, a revamped IDE, and a new project management tool. By supporting the C++ language, Borland brought the compiler into the world of object-oriented programming.

In 1992, Borland released Turbo C++ 3.0, which is the current version of the product and the topic of this book. Called the next-generation programming environment for the PC, Turbo C++ 3.0 is a DOS development tool that you can use to create C and C++ applications quickly and efficiently for less than $100.

Although Microsoft Windows programming support is not provided with Turbo C++ 3.0, all the concepts learned by using Turbo C++ are upwardly compatible with the new Borland Windows development systems: Borland C++ and Turbo C++ Visual Programming.

Programming

Programming is a process that involves defining the problem, planning the steps to solve the problem, collecting the tools to solve the problem, and finally creating a working program or programs to meet the requirements. Many jobs, such as the construction of a house or the creation of a book, can be defined in a similar way.

A *program* is a set of instructions that tell the computer what to do. A program can be as simple as a one-line program that prints to the screen or as complex as Lotus 1-2-3 or the Microsoft Windows operating environment.

Before a Turbo C++ program can be executed, it must be compiled and linked. A *compiler* processes the instructions, or *source code,* created by the programmer in the IDE editor. The compiler evaluates the source code statements, makes sure the syntax is correct, and then creates an *object file* (with an OBJ extension). The object file is then linked into an executable program file (with an EXE extension) by using a *linker.* After this is accomplished, the program can be executed (see fig. 1.1).

Fig. 1.1.
The process of making a source file into an executable file.

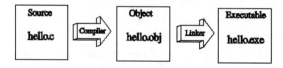

Another way to execute a program is by using an interpreter. An *interpreter* processes each program statement directly from the source code file. As the interpreter reads each line of code, that line of code is executed. Then the interpreter moves to the next line. This method eliminates the process of creating an object file and linking the object file into an executable file.

An example of an interpreter is dBASE III Plus. (Some interpreters, such as dBASE IV and FoxPro, can create an object file and decipher the program instructions from the object code rather than the source file. This increases the performance of the interpreter.)

Using an interpreter is not as complicated as using a compiler. Many consider interpreters an easier development environment than compilers such as Turbo C++ because you do not have to wait for the program to compile and link, and errors can be handled interactively.

However, interpreters do not run programs as fast as compilers. For example, a complex sort program compiled by using Turbo C++ would run faster than running the same program by using a C++ interpreter. Using an interpreter also means that the interpreter and program must be present on the computer where the program will run. When using a compiler, only the executable file is required to run the program.

Now that you know how programs are run on a computer, it's time to dive into the concepts of programming.

Structured Programming versus Object-Oriented Programming

This section is only an introduction to structured and object-oriented programming. Chapter 21, "Introducing Object-Oriented Programming," looks at these topics in more detail.

Structured programming is a modular form of programming. The programmer breaks a large program into small, easy-to-understand modules, or *subroutines*, that each perform a specific task. The main program calls these modules, which in turn may call other modules. In addition, modules may be shared. A module to clear the screen and change the screen color, for example, might be called by more than one program.

Most high-level languages (such as COBOL, FORTRAN, and Pascal) support structured programming techniques. C and C++ both support structured programming constructs; however, a few languages, such as GW-BASIC, do not.

Object-oriented programming combines structured programming techniques and sophisticated data structures. It offers developers the ability to combine data and processes (called *methods*) into one component called an *object*. In other words, an object contains, or encapsulates, everything required to perform a set of functions or behaviors, including data.

Object-oriented programming is a new way to approach programming. It was designed to save time and money by giving the programmer an enhanced ability to reuse program code. This reusability is accomplished through *inheritance*, which makes it possible for objects to inherit characteristics (methods and data) from other objects. For example, an object that performs a basic set of functions to display a menu can have its properties inherited by another object that is also required to perform a menu operation. Instead of writing the menu display routines again, the programmer simply invokes the inherited method.

Generally, object-oriented programming enables the programmer to modify the properties of the inherited object. In structured programming, the called module performs one function, and you must accept the function as it is written, or you can copy code and modify it to meet your needs.

In structured programming, all data is passive; a record of data is passed from one subroutine to another. To modify the data in the record, the programmer must create an external subroutine and pass the record to the module as a parameter.

Object-oriented programming enables you to create objects that can be stored in a library and reused in other programming tasks. This reduces the time programmers spend rewriting routines. Many software development companies sell object libraries that help the programmer create object-oriented programs using OPC (Other People's Code). For example, Borland's ObjectWindows Library (OWL) comes with the Borland C++ Applications Frameworks product. This library gives the Microsoft Windows programmer several standard Windows features such as file dialog boxes, user dialog boxes, and menus. The programmer needs only to inherit the properties required to perform an operation and invoke them.

Developing Software

The idea behind a product such as Turbo C++ is to develop application programs to meet a particular requirement. Software is the exciting aspect of computer technology. Take a tour through your local software store and notice the variety of computer programs to help you in all types of work and recreational activities. There are four basic types of software: business applications, games, utilities, and device drivers.

Business applications include any program that was written to solve a business problem. An abundance of software products can be found in this category, including word processors, desktop publishing packages, spreadsheets, databases, drawing programs, computer-aided design packages, and accounting programs.

If programming is your career or you are planning a programming career, you'll probably develop at least one business application. Many organizations need their own version of a business application. For example, some businesses have special inventory processing requirements that cannot be addressed by inventory programs sold by software vendors. These businesses develop a custom application using a software development tool such as Turbo C++. Game programs are fun. These types of applications include flight simulators, action games, and other arcade type programs. Although many people consider game programs a novelty, many successful computer companies such as Nintendo, employing many programmers, do nothing but create game programs.

Utility programs perform a low-level operation, usually at the operating system level. Programs that defragment a disk drive, copy a file, or delete a directory are examples of utility programs. Norton Utilities, one of the most famous utility programs, can undelete MS-DOS files, search the disk for data, and recover information from a hard disk that has gone bad.

Turbo C++ is valuable when creating utility programs due to its capability to mix high-level and low-level operations. Not only can you design an effective user interface, but also you can make low-level operating system calls to perform operations such as direct disk or memory manipulation. Many helpful utility programs found on bulletin board systems are created by using Turbo C++. Its capability to integrate C/C++ and assembly language allows the programmer to perform low-level operations such as manipulating CPU registers, controlling a printer, or manipulating memory directly.

Device drivers facilitate the interface with a hardware device such as a printer, a network interface card, or a disk drive. You can create device drivers with Turbo C++ because it can provide both low-level and high-level operations.

There are two basic types of device control programs. One type of device driver is the one you load in your CONFIG.SYS file; this is usually a SYS file such as ANSI.SYS. The second type of device driver is a terminate-and-stay-resident (TSR) program. This program remains in memory after execution, such as MS-DOS MOUSE.COM. Both types of device drivers, although loading into memory by using different methods, perform the same basic function of providing the interface with hardware. For example, you may load a driver for your mouse by using MOUSE.SYS in your CONFIG.SYS, or by using MOUSE.COM as a TSR. Both work just as well. One works as well as the other.

For Fun

Programmers are a strange lot. Many write programs just for the fun of it. These types of programmers are called *hobby programmers*. You would be surprised to see the variety and number of people who program computers just to prove that they can do it. These programmers create the majority of freeware or shareware programs on BBSs and other public networks. *Freeware* is software that is provided free of charge, but the programmer still maintains the copyright. Although *shareware* is usually provided at no charge, the programmer generally requests a small fee for use of the software. Some of the better software in use today is (or was initially) shareware or freeware.

As a Career

Programming is a great occupation, if you find programming interesting and enjoyable. C and C++ programmers are in demand. Remember, C and C++ are not only an MS-DOS phenomenon; these languages are found on many hardware and software platforms, especially UNIX.

If you are an experienced programmer, moving from one programming language to C and C++ is not difficult. Reading this book is the first step toward teaching yourself the proper usage of the language. After you learn the basics, the next step is to gain hands-on C/C++ experience. This might be as simple as changing projects at your current job, or it might mean looking for a company that has C and C++ programming requirements.

If you are a beginning programmer, getting a job may take longer. From an employer's perspective, you have yet to prove yourself as a programmer and are therefore something of a risk. Based on your relevant experience, your education, and your willingness to learn, you can probably find an entry-level position. After you've had a few years of programming experience, getting subsequent jobs becomes significantly easier.

The PC

To program a PC effectively, you must first understand the components of the Intel-based personal computer, because many C/C++ functions manipulate these components directly. This section examines the PC in detail. You explore the operating system, the BIOS, devices, drivers, memory, the disk drive, and the CPU (see fig. 1.2).

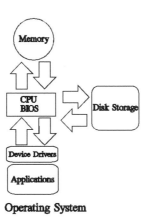

Fig. 1.2.
The components of a computer.

The Operating System

The PC is the most widely used computer in the world. Many different operating systems now work with the Intel series of PC-compatible processors. These operating systems include Windows NT, UNIX, and OS/2, but none are more popular than MS-DOS (Microsoft Disk Operating System). MS-DOS was developed as the operating system for the original IBM PC; after five major revisions, it is still providing advanced operating system facilities for most PC users.

Operating systems such as MS-DOS are the most complex and intricate computer programs ever developed. Operating systems manage the operation of the computer directly, including memory, disk, and program execution and control. In addition, MS-DOS provides *command processing*, or the ability to accept and take action on commands from the user. This is the task of the MS-DOS command processor, which is called COMMAND.COM. COMMAND.COM is normally found in the root directory of the boot drive (usually the C drive) on a PC.

MS-DOS also provides the ability to process *batch files*. Batch files carry out commands in an ordered sequence that are entered into a special batch-type file with the BAT extension. MS-DOS users use batch files to perform repetitive tasks such as compiling a program, deleting files, or performing database-like operations.

The *operating system* provides the best means of controlling the PC hardware. You can program the PC through the operating system, or DOS, calls. This is usually the most reliable method of manipulating PC hardware. The operating system provides services to the application programs. These services are invoked by using common operating system calls from the application. Virtually hundreds of types of DOS services can be requested from a Turbo C++ application program. Generally, this is advanced programming for drivers, TSRs, and other programs that invoke low-level MS-DOS services.

The BIOS

The BIOS (Basic Input/Output System) is another program that interfaces directly to the hardware components of the PC. You can program the PC by using the BIOS in the same manner as when you use MS-DOS system calls. The resulting program is usually faster than a program performing the same function by using MS-DOS system calls. This fact has driven many programmers to use BIOS calls.

Devices and Drivers

Programs, including those created by using Turbo C++, use devices. For example, the facilities of the programming language can be used to direct program output to a printer. A *device* is any component, connected to or residing in the computer, that performs a certain function. Programs are used to control devices.

A *driver* is a program loaded at boot time that becomes an integral part of MS-DOS. Generally, device drivers are loaded in the CONFIG.SYS file of a PC and facilitate communication between applications and a particular hardware device. Some drivers must use particular hardware add-ons, such as certain disk drive controllers, or pointing devices, such as a mouse. The manufacturer of the device usually provides the driver. MS-DOS comes standard with some drivers. Table 1.1 lists and defines a few of these drivers.

Table 1.1. Standard MS-DOS device drivers.	
File Name	**Description**
ANSI.SYS	Used to make the PC screen and keyboard emulate an ANSI terminal.
RAMDRIVE.SYS	Allows use of extended or expanded memory (covered next) as a RAM disk. A RAM disk is just a portion of memory that can be used to store files. It is noted for its speed, because it only uses memory.
DRIVER.SYS	Used to inform DOS of the characteristics of more than two floppy drives, or floppy drives that are nonstandard.
MOUSE.SYS	Facilitates communications between your mouse and your applications program.

Memory

Other than the CPU, memory is the most important component of a computer. It is the work area of the operating system and the application programs. All of the computer's other components are responsible for transferring the information among the processor, RAM, and the disk drive.

Memory is divided into small units called *bytes*. A byte is 8 bits, or one character. A byte may contain data or program information. A byte allows the application program to maintain a unique address in memory. It allows you to access memory directly by using this address. Memory can be written to, read from, or erased at the will of a computer program.

Memory is volatile. If the power is turned off, the information stored in memory is lost forever. This is in contrast to a disk drive, which is nonvolatile. When the power is turned off, the information on a disk remains intact.

Two bytes together (also called a *word*) can hold two characters or numbers. Logically, larger portions of memory bytes can hold even more information, including decimal or floating-point numbers (real numbers that have both an integer and a fractional portion).

When programming the PC, you must be careful not to overwrite information stored in memory that is required to complete the program. Poorly written programs have been known to overwrite pieces of themselves, usually by misaddressing memory, or having a data block expand beyond the area reserved for the program, thus overwriting instructions. When the processor attempts to execute the overwritten instructions, the result is a program that does not function correctly. The program can also cause some strange things to take place on the computer, or worst of all, lock up the computer, requiring you to turn off the computer or reset it (by pressing Ctrl-Alt-Delete or pressing the Reset button). Although it is not unusual to find between 4M to 32M of memory on a PC, MS-DOS only cares about the first 1M of memory. This memory limitation of MS-DOS is a function of the limitation imposed on the operating system when it was created. The original designers did not see the need to address memory above 1M. This limitation had to live on in the OS to maintain compatibility with MS-DOS applications, although there are ways around this.

In the MS-DOS operating system, memory is complex. Because of the 640K program execution limitation on application programs, several "schemes" are used to gain access to additional memory above 640K. A few of these schemes are examined later in this chapter; for now, let's take a look at the architecture of MS-DOS memory.

Basically, MS-DOS memory looks like figure 1.3. Application programs and operating system processes use the bottom portion of memory, below 640K. The *upper memory area* sits between 640K and the 1024K memory mark. Programs are loaded into the upper memory area to allow more room for the application programs bound to the 0 to 640K portion of memory. The blocks of memory in this area are called *upper memory blocks*, or *UMBs*. The small portion of memory just above the 1024K line is called the *high memory area (HMA)*. All potential megabytes of memory above the HMA are called *extended memory*. The upper memory area and the HMA are discussed next. Extended memory and its uses are discussed in the "XMS" and "EMS" sections of this chapter.

Fig. 1.3.
MS-DOS memory

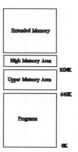

Upper Memory and High Memory Areas. The upper memory area contains adapter addresses for devices such as network cards, and video and disk adapters. You can load programs such as drivers and TSRs into this area by using programs called *high loaders*. MS-DOS uses LH.EXE (**L**oad **H**igh, an internal DOS command) as its high loader (shipped with MS-DOS 6.0). Others are also available.

More adapters in upper memory mean fewer programs are able to load into that area. Packing upper memory has become a skill. MS-DOS 6.0 comes with a program called *Memory Maker* that automates and maximizes the amount of memory in a system by loading TSRs and drivers in the upper memory area using a kind of trial-and-error method.

The high memory area (HMA) is also able to store programs loaded into its 64K size. It requires an *extended memory system (XMS)* driver (covered later) to gain access to this area of memory, and works only on 286 or greater processors that have 24 address lines, a device called the A20 gate. This gate ensures that attempts to access memory above the 1024K line are mapped to the bottom of the address range. The A20 gate allows programmers to access memory above the 1024K line. This is a true memory management trick where memory above the 1024K line is mapped to the bottom of the memory address range, allowing legal access by an application program. The A20 gate is only supported by 286 and greater computers.

XMS service is usually provided by the HIMEM.SYS driver that comes with MS-DOS 5.0 and 6.0, and Microsoft Windows. In figure 1.4, you can see that XMS sits above the upper memory area. HMA can be used by only one program at a time, and is usually employed as the loading location for parts of the MS-DOS kernel in MS-DOS 5.0 and 6.0, using the DOS=HIGH command in the CONFIG.SYS file.

Extended Memory. *Extended memory* is the addressable memory above the HMA area (see fig. 1.3). Using today's advanced computers, this memory may be well over 100M in size. It is directly accessible when you are running an advanced operating system such as UNIX, OS/2, or Windows NT; however, this memory cannot be used by programs running under DOS as an application execution area.

The real mode of the Intel processor is the mode that most programmers use when running standard MS-DOS applications. It basically works like an older 8086 Intel CPU, with the normal 1M memory restriction. Protect mode is supported by 286 and greater Intel processors. It allows many applications to run at the same time while protecting applications from each other, including real mode applications.

When running DOS programs, the CPU runs in *real mode*. It emulates an 8086 process and is therefore subject to 8086 addressing restrictions. You can address extended memory only in the protected mode of the Intel 286 and 386 processors.

Extended memory stores data in its "raw" form under MS-DOS; however, the most efficient way to use extended memory is to employ EMS or XMS *memory managers*. These memory managers do not extend the 640K limit of DOS. They do allow MS-DOS programs to make ordered calls to the extended memory of the computer, using this memory for program or data storage.

EMS. To solve the memory shortage problem of the MS-DOS operating system's 640K limit, the industry responded with a method of accessing extended memory well above the 640K line. Lotus, Intel, and Microsoft joined forces to create a memory specification that provided expanded memory, hence the name *expanded memory specification (EMS)*. Some call EMS *LIM memory* after the initials of its creators; **L**otus, **I**ntel, and **M**icrosoft. It is an ordered method for using the installed extended memory.

In the early days, expanded memory was provided by using a memory board such as the Intel AboveBoard. Because the pre-386 PCs could address only 1M of memory physically, the creators of EMS designed a board that provided additional memory outside the PC's range, which is addressed by using a 64K buffer area called a *page frame*.

The user selects the location of the page framer. Most locate the page in the upper memory area, although it can exist anywhere in conventional memory (0 to 1M). This page frame is a window into the expanded memory. Through the frame, the program can access EMS memory by swapping 16K pages of data to and from expanded memory.

If you use an older version of Lotus or another product that uses EMS, you can see the benefits of expanded memory. Lotus places portions of a spreadsheet into expanded memory, saving the memory below the 640K line for the actual Lotus program. Before expanded memory, spreadsheet size was limited. The dreaded `"Memory Full"` error message was finally eliminated or at least delayed by using EMS. Other programs use EMS in much the same way as

Lotus does. In most cases, you may not even be aware that EMS is being used. The programs detect it and use it automatically.

To use expanded memory, you must first load an *expanded memory manager (EMM)*. On 386 or faster PCs, the MS-DOS program EMM386.EXE is an example of an expanded memory manager that can be loaded at boot time to provide EMS services. Other EMS programs (such as *386 to the Max* and *QEMM 386*) work fine as well.

EMS is important because well-written programs make use of EMS memory when it is available. Using Turbo C++, EMS memory can be allocated for use as data storage, freeing up precious MS-DOS memory for other purposes.

XMS. Like EMS, *extended memory specification (XMS)* provides a set of predefined functions for allocating and transferring data to and from extended memory. Because allocated memory is protected, "XMS-aware" DOS programs can allocate extended memory without conflicting with other programs.

This specification also allows access to the HMA (High Memory Area), located just above the 1024K line in DOS memory. The XMS driver normally used is HIMEM.SYS, which comes with Microsoft Windows and DOS 5.0 and 6.0 and above. Other memory drivers also provide XMS services. Microsoft Windows 3.X uses XMS as the primary means of memory management. Other application programs are moving toward using XMS as well as EMS. Using Turbo C++, XMS memory can be appropriated and used by data, thus freeing precious MS-DOS memory for other purposes. Note that under Windows, the operating environment handles the XMS management. The programmer does not need to interface directly with the driver.

Memory Addressing. With the earlier Intel microprocessors, you can access memory up to 1M. When you think of memory, you must think in terms of simple units that contain either a 1 or a 0. We call these units *binary digits*, or *bits*. There are 8 bits to a *byte*. The CPU manipulates memory in 16-bit units (2 bytes). When processing memory using MS-DOS, it's just a matter of addressing portions of memory using these 16-bit values.

You use *segmented addressing* to achieve 1M of addressable memory. In segmented addressing, an address is made up of two parts: a segment number that indicates where a block of memory begins, and the offset that indicates how far the address is from the beginning of the segment. Generally, the address is represented in hexadecimal notation, for example:

1234:0005

The standard notation is to place a colon between the segment address and the offset. When working with the MS-DOS debug utility, this information becomes handy. The *segment:offset* notation is helpful for C++ programmers because programs handle segments and offsets individually. Many debugging operations require that the segment and the offset addresses examine and manipulate memory.

DOS Extenders

You may be wondering whether DOS will ever access memory above the 1M line as easily as it uses memory under the 640K line. It is not likely in the near future; however, certain facilities called *DOS extenders* do exist. DOS extenders allow programs to run in the protected mode of the processor, and therefore have access to all installed memory. For example, Turbo C++ 3.0 uses a DOS extender to speed up the compiler.

Basically, DOS extenders overcome the DOS and BIOS functions' inability to run in protected mode by switching to real mode when a DOS or BIOS function needs to be executed. When a call is executed, the extender copies the required portion of the program from extended memory, the code is executed, and then you return to extended memory.

Turbo C++ applications can use DOS extenders. You can purchase these extenders as program libraries that your software can use. There are two major types of DOS extenders: the Virtual Control Program Interface (VCPI), produced by Phar Lap Software, and Quarter-deck Office Systems. As the popularity of Windows and the need to operate a DOS extender under Windows became apparent, Microsoft developed its own version of a DOS extender standard. The *DOS Protected Mode Interface (DPMI)* is friendly with Windows.

The Disk Drive

The disk drive is the mass storage device that holds both the program and the data used by the program. Information held on a disk drive is nonvolatile; when the power is removed, the information remains intact. Many different types of disk drives are available.

Generally, disk drives should not be of concern unless you run out of space or experience the dreaded *head crash*. This means that the head that reads and writes the disk has dug into the physical disk platter. If this happens, the drive needs to be repaired or replaced, and the information stored on the disk is usually lost. Remember: Make backup copies of your files often. This security measure avoids loss of data if disaster occurs.

There are four popular disk interfaces. The operating system uses the disk interface to talk to a disk drive. The major disk interfaces are Modified Frequency Modulation (MFM), Enhanced Small Device Interface (ESDI), Small Computer System Interface (SCSI—pronounced "Scuzzy"), and Integrated Drive Electronics (IDE). IDE and SCSI are the most popular disk interfaces.

The CPU

The most important component of the computer is the *central processing unit* or the *CPU*. The CPU is the brain of the computer. It does most of the work a computer performs, including reading the program instructions held in memory and carrying out the instructions quickly. The CPU on a PC is a microprocessor chip. The chip is usually the size of a half dollar, but can process information as well as mainframes did just a few years ago.

The PC uses Intel or compatible microprocessors. The original IBM PC used the 8088 or the 8086 line of processors. Those processors operated at only 4.77 MHz, but they were the fastest PCs around. Today, the new advanced processors, such as the Intel Pentium, are operating up to 120 MIPS (million instructions per second), rivaling most mini and mainframe computers currently in service.

Computer programs instruct the CPU to move data from one memory location to another. Other operations may load information into on-chip local storage or a CPU register, and then add, subtract, multiply, or divide the information. Sometimes the program instructs the CPU to perform some test and then move to a new portion of the program if the test succeeds. These instructions are called *machine code*. Machine code is very primitive, and it takes dozens of instructions of machine code just to display a single character on the terminal. It's a good thing computers are getting faster.

Summary

This chapter introduced the basics of Turbo C++ and the PC. You learned where Turbo C++ came from, what programming is, and the history of the C and C++ programming languages. You also learned about structured and object-oriented programming, how programming types differ, and the advantages and disadvantages of each. In addition, you learned about software, its types, why it is developed, and who develops it. This chapter also discussed the PC, the operating system, BIOS, device drivers, the concepts and management of memory, the disk drive, and the very important CPU.

The following topics were covered in this chapter:

- Turbo C++ was developed by Borland. It is an inexpensive but powerful compiler.

- Programming is an art form, much like writing, painting, or sculpting. It requires skill, experience, and creativity.

- The C language was developed at AT&T Bell Labs by Dennis Ritchie and Brian Kernighan.

- The C++ language was an object-oriented version of the C language, and is the most popular object-oriented language in use today. The biggest improvement is the addition of classes. Classes form the basis of object-oriented programming.

- Structured programming allows programmers to break larger programs into smaller "bite-size" modules. A program stands on its own as an independent program, and each can be called more than once, by more than one other module.

- Object-oriented programming provides facilities to maximize the reuse of program code. The concept of inheritance, in which properties from other objects are absorbed into new objects, is the basis of object-oriented programming. You can use the code from "parent" objects without having to copy program code from one program to another.

- Software development includes all types of applications, such as business application software that solves a business problem, utilities for low-level management of the operating system, device controllers (such as printer and mouse management), and programming just for the fun of it.

- Programming in C/C++ using compilers such as Turbo C++ is a great career in which opportunities abound.

- The personal computer is made up of several components: the operating system, the Basic Input/Output System (BIOS), devices, drivers, memory, the disk drive, and the central processing unit (CPU).

- The operating system (such as MS-DOS) manages the hardware of the computer.

■ The BIOS is another program stored on a chip that interfaces directly with the hardware components of the PC. You can program the PC using the BIOS in the same manner as you do when using MS-DOS system calls, although it is considered less reliable.

■ Devices are used by programs, including programs created using Turbo C++. A device is any component connected to or residing in the computer that performs a certain function. Programs assist other programs by controlling devices for them.

■ A driver is a program loaded at boot time that becomes an integral part of MS-DOS. Generally, device drivers are loaded into the CONFIG.SYS file of a PC, and facilitate communication between programs and a particular hardware device.

■ Memory is the working area of the CPU. MS-DOS memory management is complex. The area between 0K and 640K is the program area. This is where the programs are executed. The area between 640K and 1M is called the upper memory area. This area is used to locate adapters and load locations for device drivers or TSRs. The high memory area (HMA) is a small area of memory above the 1M memory line. HMA is a valid load location for a program, although it can be used by only one program at a time. To use the HMA area, you must obtain an XMS driver such as HIMEM.SYS.

■ The extended memory is all of the memory above HMA. MS-DOS cannot use it directly; however, EMS and XMS memory managers, as well as DOS extenders, can use it.

■ The Expanded Memory Specification (EMS) was developed by Lotus, Intel, and Microsoft as the ordered method to access extended memory. Programs can utilize EMS using a 64K page frame that resides in the memory area below 1M.

■ Microsoft developed the Extended Memory Specification (XMS) as a better means of using extended memory. Like EMS, it is an ordered method of access. XMS memory is primarily used by Microsoft Windows, although other programs use it as well.

- DOS extenders extend the execution area of an MS-DOS program beyond the 640K line. Turbo C++ applications can use DOS extenders. You can purchase these extenders as program libraries that your software can use. Microsoft developed its own version of a DOS extender standard. The DOS Protected Mode Interface (DPMI) does not conflict with Windows.

- Disk drives are used for nonvolatile storage of programs and data. There are four popular disk interfaces. The major disk interfaces are Modified Frequency Modulation (MFM), Enhanced Small Device Interface (ESDI), Small Computer System Interface (SCSI—pronounced "Scuzzy"), and Integrated Drive Electronics (IDE). Today, IDE and SCSI are the most popular.

- The Central Processing Unit (CPU) is the brain of the computer; it does most of the work a computer performs. This includes reading the program instruction held in memory and carrying out the instructions quickly.

Chapter 2

Installing Turbo C++

This chapter guides you through the installation and configuration of Turbo C++. In addition, you examine the system requirements of Turbo C++, you learn how to test the installation after it is complete, and finally, you learn how to solve common problems and get technical assistance from Borland.

In the early days of the PC, installing most software packages was a chore because few installations were automated. Manuals guided you through the DOS commands that were required to install and configure the software. Many users found this type of "read and do" installation process frustrating and ineffective.

The software industry responded with installation batch files. These batch programs provided an automated installation process, saving the user from much of the drudgery of manual software installation and configuration. Although installation batch files worked fine in most cases, many users experienced some shortcomings with them. For instance, these batch files could not respond well to the inevitable problems that arise during the installation process.

As the software industry progressed, manufacturers developed software to automate installation procedures. These stand-alone programs install and configure software, and they handle such problems as enforcing disk space and memory requirements.

Today you expect software to come with an automated installation procedure that guides you through the software installation process. Most of the time you don't even need to read the installation manuals to install and configure the software. You simply enter

```
A:>INSTALL
```

The remainder of the procedure is automatic. This is the idea behind the Turbo C++ installation procedures.

With Borland's installation program, INSTALL, you can easily install Turbo C++.

System Requirements

The system requirements for installing Turbo C++ change with each version. The current version, Turbo C++ 3.0, requires the following:

- An IBM PC or compatible computer

- An 80286 or greater processor

- DOS 3.1 or later version

- 1M of extended memory

- 5M minimum of disk space (10.5M is required if all options are installed)

Turbo C++ cannot be installed if your system does not meet these requirements.

Turbo C++ can make use of an 80x87 math coprocessor. A coprocessor is a chip that is optionally installed on the motherboard of your computer. Turbo C++ is able to see a coprocessor and take advantage of it, allowing your programs to run faster. The speed is gained because the math operations execute on a separate processor, freeing up the main CPU for other activities. If you do not happen to have a coprocessor, Turbo C++ does fine without one. If you have an Intel 486DX processor in your PC, there is no need to install a coprocessor. It comes built into the main processor.

Although the *mouse* and the *mouse driver* are not required, they can be quite beneficial. As you discover in the next chapter, the IDE (Integrated Development Environment) is "mouse aware"—that is, it recognizes the presence of a mouse and uses it. Although using a mouse to interact with the IDE may be awkward at first, it does enhance productivity.

Installing Turbo C++

Before beginning the installation procedure, now is a good time to back up the Turbo C++ disks. Use the

    DISKCOPY A: A:

DOS command to copy each program disk. Enter the DISKCOPY command at the MS-DOS prompt (see your DOS manual for the details, or enter HELP DISKCOPY from the DOS 5.0 or 6.0 prompt). Mark each disk with the disk numbers printed on the originals.

To make sure that the backup works, use your new backup copies for the installation. Put the disks that came with Turbo C++ in a safe place. If your backup disks go bad, you are going to need the originals.

Since this may take a few minutes, now is a good time to fill out your product registration card. This card provides Borland with your name and address so they can send you information about upgrade deals, bug fixes, and so on.

The INSTALL program is on the first program disk. Most of the Turbo C++ files are archived—that is, the files are compressed to save space on the program disks. The installation program decompresses the files as the software is installed. You can find the complete list of distribution files in the README file on the installation disk.

Running the INSTALL Program

Before you run INSTALL, check the amount of free space available on your hard disk. To do this, enter from the MS-DOS prompt

    C:>CHKDSK

The CHKDSK DOS command returns the number of bytes available on the disk. Remember that you need as much as 10.5M to install all Turbo C++ options. If you don't have enough space available, now is the time to inventory the software installed on your hard drive and find candidates for deletions.

To install Turbo C++, insert the installation disk into drive A or B of your PC. Then, at the DOS prompt, enter

    A:INSTALL

Turbo C++ comes with both 5.25-inch floppy disks (1.2M high density), and 3.5-inch floppy disks (720K). You may use either, depending on your available floppy drive.

The initial screen, displayed in figure 2.1, welcomes you to the Turbo C++ installation program. Notice that it also displays the amount of space INSTALL requires for a full system installation. If you have more than the amount required, press Enter. If you do not, press Escape (Esc) to return to the DOS prompt.

Fig. 2.1.
The Turbo C++
INSTALL welcome
screen.

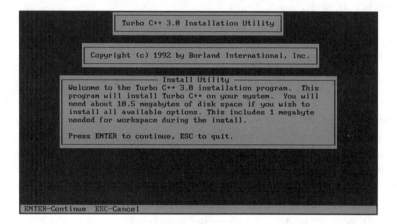

After you press Enter, the Source Drive Prompt screen (see fig. 2.2) appears. This screen allows you to let the installation program know what source drive you're inserting the Turbo C++ program disk into during installation. Usually, the source drive is either A or B.

Fig. 2.2.
The Source Drive
Prompt screen.

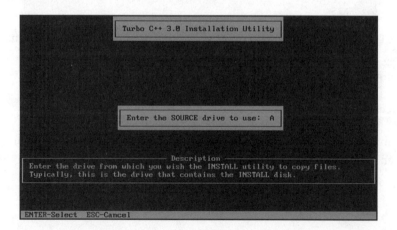

The Main INSTALL Menu

Like all INSTALL menus, the Main INSTALL menu (shown in fig. 2.3) uses a *highlight bar* type menu to select menu options. You use the highlight bar menu by moving the cursor up, down, or side to side with the arrow keys, highlighting various menu options by placing them in reverse video (where black is now white, and white is now black). Move your cursor up and down on your computer to see how this works. You'll see a prompt for Directories... on the top menu option that can be reached with the highlight bar. When this option is selected, you can enter the drive letter and destination directory name where you desire for the Turbo C++ files to be installed. You use the next option, Option... (shown in fig. 2.4.). When selected, it allows you to customize several Turbo C++ installations.

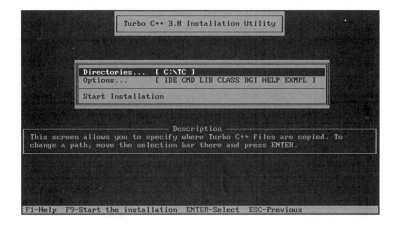

Fig. 2.3.
The Directories menu.

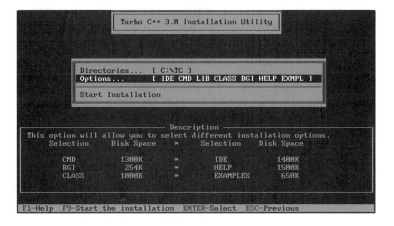

Fig. 2.4.
The Options menu.

Selecting Directories. If you press Enter when the Directories... option is highlighted, a dialog box appears in which you can modify the installation directories for Turbo C++ (as shown in fig. 2.5). The Turbo C++ directory (usually C:\TC) is the root directory for the other Turbo C++ subdirectories. If you want to load Turbo C++ on a different drive or directory, modify the defaults in this selection box. Simply highlight the Turbo C++ Directory... option and press Enter. Another Directories dialog box appears and allows you to set the default drive and path name where the Turbo C++ files are to be installed (C:\TC by default).

Fig. 2.5.
Installation
Directories
dialog box.

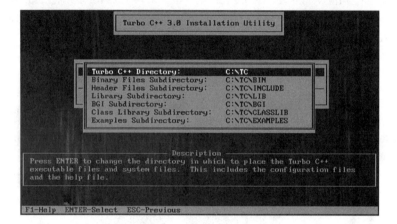

When you modify the default, the other directories change accordingly. Remember that in order to install all of Turbo C++, at least 10.5M of disk space is required. If there isn't enough disk space, you can count on a Disk Full error message during the installation.

Selecting Options. The next option on the main menu is titled Options..., as shown in figure 2.4. With the Options... option you can pick out the Turbo C++ components you want to install and the components you want to leave out. Press Enter and the Options submenu appears, as shown in figure 2.6. If you have a limited amount of disk space, you may want to leave some Turbo C++ components out of the installation. If disk space is not a problem, you may install all the options.

As the highlight bar is moved down the Options submenu, you can toggle between "Yes" and "No" by pressing Enter. Move the highlight bar by pressing the up- or down-arrow keys. "Yes" does install the selected option, and "No" does not.

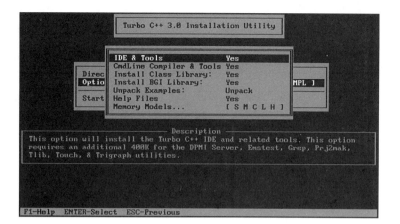

Fig. 2.6.
The Options
submenu.

The Unpack Examples option includes Unpack, Pack, and No. If Unpack is selected, INSTALL decompresses the Turbo C++ Example programs for immediate use. Again, if disk space is not a problem, this is the best choice. If Pack is selected, INSTALL will leave the Example programs in a compressed state to conserve disk space. If the Example programs remain packed, you will have to decompress them later using the decompression program. If No is selected, INSTALL will not install the Examples. Unless you are a strong C++ programmer, install the Example programs. They come in handy as examples of types of programming operations that you may refer to at any time.

Selecting Memory Models. The last Options... submenu option on the main menu is Memory Models.... After you highlight this option, press Enter. The Memory Models menu is displayed, as shown in figure 2.7. Now you can select the memory models for installation. As with the previous menu you select each option by toggling between "Yes" and "No."

Turbo C++ provides six *memory models*. Briefly, each model is suited for different program and code sizes for the types of applications that can be developed using Turbo C++. Each model uses memory differently, for different purposes. For information on memory models, refer to Chapter 4.

Memory models work with the segmented architecture of the 8086, 286, 386, and 486 processors. The processor has a total addressable memory of 1M, but the processors are designed to directly address only 64K of memory at one time. The 64K piece is known as a *segment* of memory; thus, you have *segmented memory*. Refer to Chapter 4 for more information on memory models.

Fig. 2.7.
The Memory
Model options
submenu.

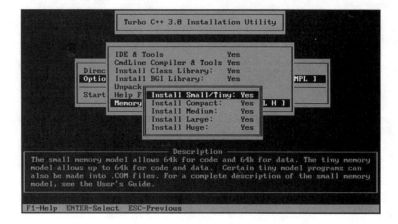

A program consists of a combination of code and data. When the code or the data fits in a single segment, it executes quickly. When the code or the data is larger than the size of a segment, it is invoked differently. The result is slower execution of the program.

You need to select a memory model large enough to accommodate the program you are developing, but it is not advisable to select a memory model that is too large. Larger models reduce the speed of execution. Part of the programming task involves selecting the best memory model to execute your program.

The INSTALL program copies the files containing the appropriate routines from the C and C++ library routine files that support the particular models that you selected. Again, if disk space is a concern, install only the models you want to use. If disk space isn't a problem, install all the memory models; you're probably going to need them. Press Escape (Esc) twice to return to the main INSTALL menu.

Starting Installation. After all the desired options are selected, you can begin the installation of Turbo C++. Press F9 or position the highlight bar on the Start Installation option in the main INSTALL menu, and press Enter (see fig. 2.8).

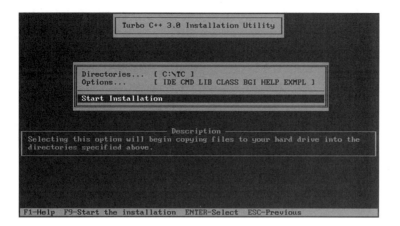

Fig. 2.8.
Starting the
Installation by
selecting the Start
Installation
option.

Familiarizing Yourself

When the installation begins, INSTALL displays a window at the bottom of
the screen that shows the Turbo C++ files decompressing to the hard drive
(see fig. 2.9).

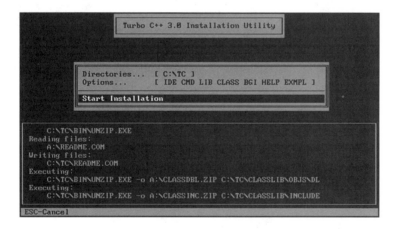

Fig. 2.9.
Decompressing
files to the hard
drive.

After the selected files have been decompressed to the hard drive from the
first disk, INSTALL displays a window prompting you to insert Disk 2 (see
fig. 2.10). After you insert Disk 2, press any key.

If you do not have enough disk space, a Disk Full error message appears (see
fig. 2.11) during the installation procedure. If this happens, you must exit
INSTALL, locate or create additional disk space, and try again.

If disk space is not a problem, the INSTALL program continues through the
Turbo C++ installation process. After the second disk is inserted, INSTALL
prompts you to place the next disk in the source drive.

Fig. 2.10.
The prompt for
Disk 2.

Fig. 2.11.
The Disk Full
error message.

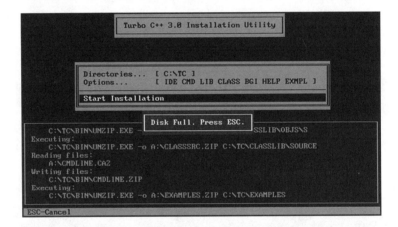

If you inadvertently place the incorrect disk in the source drive during the
"disk swapping" procedure, the INSTALL program responds with a Wrong Disk
error message. If this occurs, locate the correct disk, place it in the source
drive, and continue the installation process.

After Installation

If you had enough disk space, and the installation worked, the Installation
Complete message appears, as shown in figure 2.12. If you selected the
command-line version of the compiler, INSTALL reminds you to set a path to
the Turbo C++ program directory (usually C:\TC\BIN) and to make sure that
FILES is set to a number greater than 20 in your CONFIG.SYS file.

After you press any key, the README file is displayed, as shown in figure
2.13. Read this file and learn about any last minute changes to the Turbo C++
product and documentation.

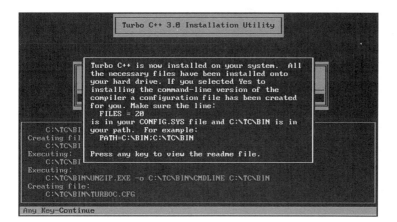

Fig. 2.12.
The Installation
Complete message.

Familiarizing Yourself

Fig. 2.13.
The README file.

That's it! You are ready to program in Turbo C++. Now is a good time to add your selected Turbo C++ program directory (for example, PATH=C:\TC\BIN) to your AUTOEXEC.BAT file. You can make changes to the CONFIG.SYS and the AUTOEXEC.BAT files using the MS-DOS EDIT command that comes with DOS 5.0 or 6.0. For information on EDIT, refer to your MS-DOS manual.

Also, make sure that the FILES setting in your CONFIG.SYS file is correct:

FILES=20

After making changes to your CONFIG.SYS and AUTOEXEC.BAT files, you're going to have to reboot your computer in order for the changes to take effect.

Solving Minor Problems

Most Turbo C++ installations go smoothly. If a problem arises, however, it's usually because of a hardware failure, but it can also be because of a configuration problem. For example, the floppy disks shipped with Turbo C++ occasionally go bad in the box. If this occurs, DOS or INSTALL will let you know that there is an error in reading your source drive. At this point, see if you can install Turbo C++ on another computer. If you can install it, without the same error message, then your system's floppy drive may need repair or replacement.

If your 5.25-inch disks are bad, try the 3.5-inch disk as an alternative, and visa versa. If another size floppy drive is not available, then it's time to call Borland and request replacement disks (see the section titled, "Getting Help").

Testing Your Installation

Does it work? It's time to find out . . .

If your path is properly set, you can enter the following from your DOS prompt:

    tc

If you receive a `File not found` message, check your path. Make sure that the path is set to your Turbo C++ binary directory:

    PATH=C:\TC\BIN

When you invoke Turbo C++, the About box appears (see fig. 2.14) in which you can find the version information. From here, either press Enter or use your mouse to click the OK button.

You are now in the Turbo C++ IDE. The Integrated Development Environment is the user interface program that will create, edit, compile, and link a C++ program. The IDE is covered in detail in Chapter 3, but for testing purposes, you are going to perform a simple compile operation. The IDE displays a set of pull-down menu options across the top of the screen, as shown in figure 2.15. You can either press Enter to display the menu options, or you can use your mouse.

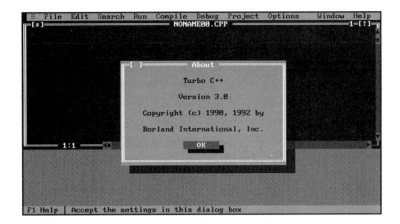

Fig. 2.14.
The About box.

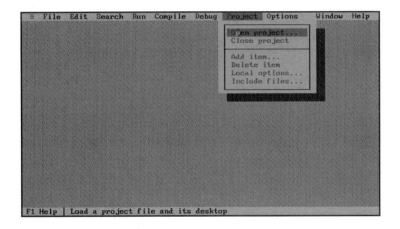

Fig. 2.15.
The IDE main
menu.

From the IDE, choose Project, Open Project. The IDE displays the Open
Project File dialog that allows you to navigate through the MS-DOS directory structure using a user interface to locate Turbo C++ project (.PRJ) files
(see fig. 2.16). If you have elected to install your example files, you're going
to see subdirectories for the example programs and projects, usually
C:\TC\EXAMPLES. These are the sample programs and projects that Turbo
C++ provides for your reference. Among these project files is TCALC.PRJ,
which is the project file you're going to use to test your installation. The
TCALC demonstration application is a simple spreadsheet program, much
like Lotus 1-2-3.

Use your arrow keys or your mouse with the file dialog to navigate through
the MS-DOS directory structure. When selecting a new directory, the file
dialog box automatically lists all of the available files and subdirectories in

that particular directory. You can select the directory or file by highlighting it
and pressing Enter or by clicking it with your mouse.

Fig. 2.16.
The Open Project
File dialog box.

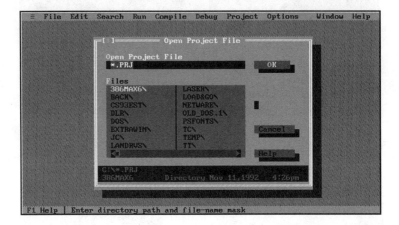

Use the file dialog box to locate the TCALC directory. When you find the
TCALC directory, the TCALC project file (TCALC.PRJ) should be displayed in
the Files box of your Open Project File dialog box. Select the TCALC.PRJ file,
as shown in figure 2.17.

Fig. 2.17.
Selecting the
TCALC.PRJ file in
the Open Project
File dialog box.

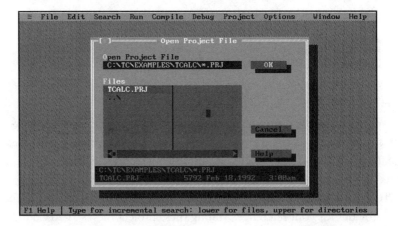

If you opened the TCALC.PRJ file correctly, you see a screen that looks like
figure 2.18. Notice that the window at the bottom of the screen contains all
the files that are required to build the TCALC application.

To compile and execute the TCALC application, select Run from the Main IDE
menu. Then select the Run option from the Run submenu (see fig. 2.19).

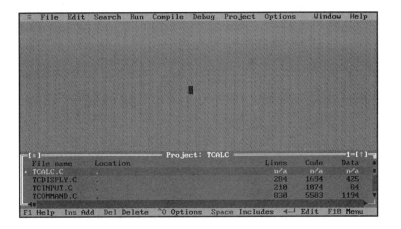

Fig. 2.18.
The TCALC project work area.

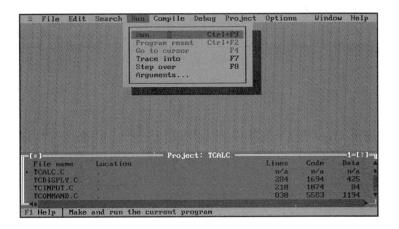

Fig. 2.19.
Selecting the Run option from the Run submenu.

Turbo C++ starts to compile the TCALC application. A Compiling information box appears on-screen that lets you know what is going on during the compile operation, such as lines compiled (see fig. 2.20). If the compile operation completes without errors, Turbo C++ automatically runs the program. After the compile is completed successfully, it invokes the application automatically (see fig. 2.21).

Congratulations! You have just compiled a rather complex C++ program by using Turbo C++! You are now ready to develop your own programs by using Turbo C++.

Fig. 2.20.
The Compiling
information box.

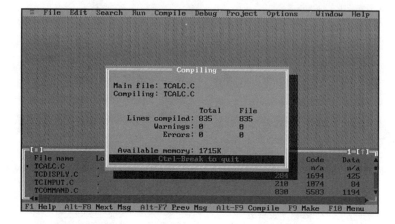

Fig. 2.21.
The TCALC
Application
welcome menu.

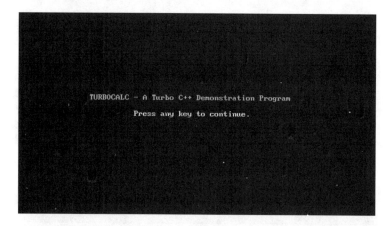

Fig. 2.22.
The TCALC
application.

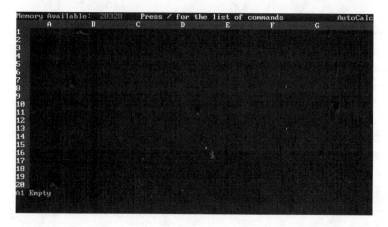

Getting Help

You're not alone when you use a Borland product. Borland has an excellent technical support system that includes voice access to Turbo C++ technical support representatives, and other very creative methods of receiving assistance for your Borland product. Support is provided to help with the installation of the Turbo C++ product and the actual C++ programming language.

Before you decide to use this service, make sure that you have already attempted to solve the problem yourself. You can use the documentation provided with Turbo C++, the Turbo C++ help system, or this book. Remember, the experience of solving problems on your own will make you a better programmer. If this is not possible, however, it's nice to know that help is available.

Phone Support

If you can't solve a particular problem on your own, call Borland's technical support. Although you may have to spend some time in the phone queue, eventually you'll be able to discuss your problem with a Borland technical support professional. Borland's technical support line is (408) 438-5300. It is open from 6:00 a.m. to 5:00 p.m. PST, Monday thru Friday, seven days a week.

Before you call, make sure you are near your computer and have the following information available:

- Product name
- Serial number
- Version number
- Make and model of your computer
- DOS version number
- AUTOEXEC.BAT printout
- CONFIG.SYS printout
- Your phone number

TechFax

TechFax is another technical service offered by Borland. TechFax, which requires that you have a Fax machine or Fax modem, is a 24-hour automated service that can send free technical information to your fax machine or PC (using a fax modem). The TechFax phone number is (800) 822-4269. To use TechFax, you must have and use a touch-tone phone to enter the commands for the voice prompts to send a Fax. You are allowed to send up to three documents per call.

Borland File Download BBS

The Borland File Download Bulletin Board System (BBS) offers sample files, applications, bug fixes, and technical information to those users with modems. The number is (408) 439-9096, and it operates at 2400 bits per second (BPS).

Public Networks

In the last 10 years, the use of public information services has risen greatly. People who use these services are able to access detailed information on virtually any topic, including Turbo C++ programming. These services are available to anyone with a computer and a modem. If you are a subscriber to CompuServe, GEnie, or BIX information services you're already set up to receive technical support for Turbo C++.

When you use CompuServe enter

> **GO BORLAND**

When you use BIX enter

> **JOIN BORLAND**

When you use GEnie enter

> **BORLAND**

No matter what service you use, if you address your electronic message to Sysop (System Operator) or All, a Borland representative should respond to the problem. Include as much information in the message as you can, and be patient; it may take some time before your message is answered.

Summary

In this chapter you were introduced to the Turbo C++ installation procedure. You learned about the system requirements for Turbo C++; you examined the installation process; and you learned how to find help. The following topics were covered.

- Installing Turbo C++ is easy using the INSTALL program supplied by Borland.

- To install Turbo C++, you need at least a 286 processor with 5M or more of free disk space, MS-DOS 3.1 or greater, and at least 1M of extended memory.

- When you install Turbo C++, several installation options are available. You can set the directory where the Turbo C++ files are to be installed, and you can select installation options (such as whether to install the Example programs).

- Turbo C++ supports several memory models that are used by different types of programs. You can pick and choose the memory models you want to load with Turbo C++.

- You can test your Turbo C++ installation by loading the Example application TCALC project file and running it. If it compiles and runs successfully, you installed Turbo C++ successfully.

- There are several ways to get technical support from Borland. You can call them directly, use a Fax-back service, a BBS, or a public information network.

Chapter 3

Using the Integrated Development Environment

The Integrated Development Environment, or IDE, includes all the facilities required to create, edit, compile, link, and debug Turbo C or C++ programs. The IDE is so important to the overall operation of Turbo C++ that several chapters are devoted to mastering it. This chapter uses a step-by-step approach to cover the following topics:

- Starting the IDE

- The IDE Main menu

- The IDE hotkeys and cursor-movement keys

- The IDE Help system

Starting the IDE

To start the IDE, enter **tc** at the DOS prompt and press Enter. Several IDE command-line options are available. Command line options are passed to Turbo C++ after naming the program from the MS-DOS prompt. You pass these options to Turbo C++ by using the following syntax:

```
tc [option [option...]] [program name¦ project name [program name]]
```

The *option* is a method of controlling the IDE. The IDE command-line options are described in table 3.1. The *program name* is any program (ASCII) file. The *project name* is any Turbo C++ project (.PRJ) file. When you see "...," that means the menu option has additional options.

The following is a list of IDE command line options. As the book progresses, you'll become more familiar with them. For now, read through the table and survey the options available.

Table 3.1. The IDE command-line options.	
Option	**Description**
/b	Recompile and link (build) all the files in your project file, display the results of the compilation, then return to DOS. You must pass in the name of the project file. Passing options in means placing the options after tc on the MS-DOS command line.
/d	Operates in dual monitor mode. (This mode works only if Turbo C++ detects two video cards in your computer.) The /d option is used for program debugging.
/e[=n]	Swaps to expanded memory. This option is on by default. *n* is the number of 16K expanded memory pages to be used for swapping. Use /e- to turn off the swap to expanded memory.
/h	List all command-line options that the IDE supports.
/l	Use the lowercase option when running Turbo C++ on an LCD screen.
/m	Turbo C++ does a make rather than a build. Therefore, only the older source code is compiled and linked. Using the make facility, the IDE checks the executable program with the date and time stamp of the source files only compiling source files that have changed.
/p	Controls palette registers and palette swapping on EGA video adapters.
/rx	Specify a swap drive, where *x* is the drive letter. The swap drive is usually a RAM disk. Use this option when virtual memory is filled.
/s	Use the majority of installed memory for the internal tables (a place where the compiler stored its information) of the compiler. This option is on by default. Use /s- to turn off this option.
/x[=n]	This option designates how much memory will be used for its heap space (similar to /e). *n* is the number of kilobytes of memory. If you use /x with no amount specified, Turbo C++ uses all available memory.

The IDE Screen

The first time you start the IDE, the Welcome screen appears. Thereafter, the program goes directly to the IDE screen, which is shown in figure 3.1.

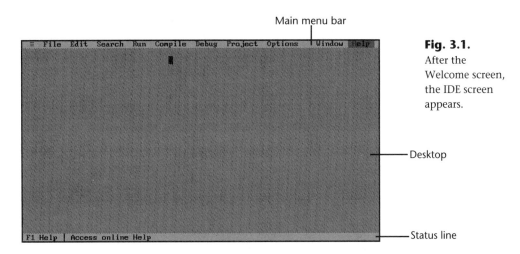

Main menu bar

Fig. 3.1.
After the Welcome screen, the IDE screen appears.

Desktop

Status line

The main menu bar provides access to the Turbo C++ tools used to create, edit, compile, and link C and C++ programs. The desktop is your work area. The status line tells you what Turbo C++ is up to, such as opening a program file or compiling a program, and also displays the shortcut keys for carrying out several popular commands.

You can open windows that contain programs, help information, project file information, and more. You can display, resize, and move windows. An editor window appears on the desktop when you edit programs. (Editing is covered in detail in Chapter 6.)

Using the Main Menu

From the main menu, you can load programs, save programs, configure the IDE, and compile and link applications. Also, built into the IDE, is an integrated Help facility, an interactive debugging facility, and many other features.

You can access the commands on the IDE main menu in three ways:

- Press F10 to make the menu bar selection active; meaning that you're now able to use the menus on the top of the screen. Then, use the arrow keys to move left and right along the main menu and press Enter to choose a menu command.

- Press Alt and the first letter of the main menu name. Note that the first letter in each menu command is highlighted.

- Click the main menu command.

All main menu commands display a submenu. Some submenu entries themselves display dialog boxes or other menus. A submenu entry, followed by an ellipsis (...) displays a dialog box. A submenu entry, followed by a downward pointing arrow, displays another type of menu called a popup. A popup menu is a little menu that appears on the screen for a particular purpose.

Several menu commands are *context-sensitive*, which means that you can use them only while you are performing certain operations. For example, if you are not editing a program, the editing options (Copy, Cut, Paste, and so on) cannot be selected. Menu commands that cannot be selected are shown in gray.

The following sections introduce each main menu command.

The System Menu (=)

The system menu is represented by the = entry on the left end of the IDE menu bar. You use the system menu to launch external utility or application programs. Borland provides the following commands in the system menu by default:

Command	Action
Repaint desktop	Redisplays the desktop
GREP	Searches for a string in a group of files
Turbo Assembler	Executes the Turbo Assembler
Turbo **D**ebugger	Executes the Turbo Debugger
Turbo **P**rofiler	Executes the Turbo Profiler

> **Note**
>
> Although Turbo Assembler, Turbo Debugger, and Turbo Profiler appear on the menu, you must purchase them separately.

In addition to the programs Borland provides, you can add programs to the system menu. You learn how to do this later on in the book.

The File Menu

When you select **F**ile from the IDE main menu, the **F**ile menu shown in figure 3.2 appears.

Fig. 3.2.
After you select File from the main menu, the File menu appears.

The **F**ile menu has the following options:

Option	Action
New	Creates a program file
Open	Opens an existing program file
Save	Saves the current program file
Save as...	Saves the program file and gives it a different name
Save all	Saves all files that are open in the work area
Change dir...	Changes the current default directory
Print	Prints an open program
DOS shell	Go to the DOS prompt; to return to Turbo C++, type **EXIT**
Quit	Exits from Turbo C++

The Edit Menu

The Edit menu is similar to the Edit menu in a Windows application. You use the Edit menu to do clipboard operations (cut, copy, and paste) and perform other editing tasks. When you select the **E**dit option, the menu in figure 3.3 appears. Note that most Edit commands are grayed (unselectable) unless you are editing a program.

Fig. 3.3.
When you select the Edit option, the Edit menu appears.

The **E**dit menu contains the following options:

Option	Action
Undo	Undoes the last editing operation
Redo	Re-executes the last editing operation
Cu**t**	Cuts a selected portion of text from the program and places it in the clipboard
Copy	Copies a selected portion of text from the program and place it in the clipboard
Paste	Pastes the information from the clipboard into the program
C**l**ear	Clears all of the text from the work area so you can start fresh
C**o**py example	Copies the example you are viewing in the Help system to the program being edited
Show clipboard	Displays the information that is in the clipboard

The Search Menu

The Search menu, shown in figure 3.4, contains other commands related to editing.

Fig. 3.4.
The Search menu contains commands related to editing.

The Search menu options are the following:

Option	Action
Find...	Finds a string in a program
Replace...	Finds and replaces a string in a program
Search again	Repeats the last search operatation
Go to line number	Moves the current line to a particular line number
Previous error	Moves cursor or pointer from the current line to the first compile error before the current line
Next error	Moves the cursor or pointer from the current line to the next compile error
Locate function...	Locates a function in a program

The Run Menu

You use the Run menu options to run and debug your programs. The debug stage is when you test and correct your programs (see fig. 3.5).

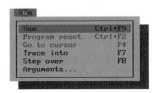

Fig. 3.5.
The Run menu options run and debug your programs.

The Run menu commands include the following:

Option	Action
Run	Compiles, links, and runs the program currently on the desktop
Program reset	Reloads the program and starts from the beginning

(continues)

(continued)

Option	Action
Go to cursor	Executes the program to the current location of the cursor
Trace into	When you are debugging a program, this option steps through a function, if it is accessible to the debugger
Step over	Steps over functions when you are debugging
Argument...	Passes arguments to a C++ program

The Compile Menu

You use the Compile menu to actually create a stand-alone application program (an EXE or COM file). Here is where you compile and link your C++ programs (see fig. 3.6).

Fig. 3.6.
You can create a stand-alone application program by using the Compile menu.

The Compile menu commands include the following:

Option	Action
Compile	Compiles the current program
Make	Using a project file, compiles only the programs that are not current
Link	Links object files to an executable file
Build all	Builds all of the files in the project, regardless of the data status
Information...	Provides information pertaining to the operation of Turbo C++, such as the current directory, memory usage, and compiler information
Remove messages	Clears the current compiler messages

The Debug Menu

Several facilities are available to perform debugging operations such functions as keeping an eye on program variables, modifying variables as the program executes, and setting breakpoints or places to stop in the program while debugging (see fig. 3.7).

Fig. 3.7.
Use the Debug menu to debug your programs.

The Debug menu commands include the following:

Option	Action
Inspect...	Inspects a program variable
Evaluate/modify...	Looks at and modifies a program's variables
Call stack...	Shows the sequence of functions that your program called to reach the function that is now being executed
Watches	Watches a variable as a program executes to monitor how that particular variable is affected by your program
Toggle breakpoint	Turns on or off a breakpoint
Breakpoints...	Lists all of the breakpoints you have set

The Project Menu

The purpose of the Project menu is the management of Turbo C++ projects. Here is where you maintain project files, or a catalog of all the files that make up your Turbo C++ program, such as program (.C or .CPP) files. This feature is so important that we have devoted Chapter 5, "Working with Project Files," to the topic. Using the Project menu, you can open and close projects, add and delete items, and perform other project file management operations (see fig. 3.8).

Fig. 3.8.
The Project menu
manages your
Turbo C++
projects.

The Project menu commands include the following:

Option	Action
Open project	Opens an existing project file
Close project	Closes an existing project file
Add item...	Adds a program file or other items to a project
Delete item	Deletes an item from a project
Local options...	Sets project options for a specific project that overrides the predefined options
Include files...	Lists the `include` files currently in use for a project

Options

You can use the commands on the **O**ptions menu to customize your Turbo
C++ work environment (see fig. 3.9). The commands include options to set
such things as screen color, screen size, memory models to use when compiling, and many other options. Again, this topic is so complex that we have
devoted a chapter to it (Chapter 4, "Customizing the Integrated Development
Environment").

Fig. 3.9.
The Options
menu helps
customize your
Turbo C++ work
environment.

The **O**ptions menu contains the following commands:

Option	Action
Application...	Sets application options such as memory model, output, overlay options, and so on
Compiler	Sets compiler options such as Code generation, C++ options, Optimization, and so on
Transfer...	Adds or deletes utilities from the System menu (=)
Make...	Sets options for the MAKE utility
Linker	Sets options for the linker
Li**b**rarian...	Sets options for the Librarian
De**b**ugger...	Sets options for the debugger
Directories...	Sets the default directories for the header files, libraries, and so on
Environment	Sets preferences for the editor, mouse, colors, and so on
Save...	Saves the options permanently

The Window Menu

The options on the Window menu provide for the maintenance and management of the windows that Turbo C++ supports. Using these menu commands, you can do such things as move and size windows, zoom in to see a window more closely, arrange the windows in a tile or a cascade formation, or other typical window operations.

You can handle many of these window operations with a mouse (see fig. 3.10). Using a mouse to manage windows is generally easier than using these menu commands or other Turbo C++ hotkeys.

Fig. 3.10.
The Window menu options help maintain and manage the windows that Turbo C++ supports.

The Window menu contains the following commands:

Option	Action
Size/Move	Changes the size of a window or move it on the screen
Zoom	Zooms in to a window
Tile	Arranges the windows in a tile formation
Cascade	Arranges the windows in a cascade formation
Next	Goes to the next window in the windows list
Close	Closes the current window
Clos**e** all	Closes all windows
Message	Opens the messages window
Output	Opens the output window
Watch	Opens the watch window
User screen	Displays the user screen
Register	Displays the CPU registers
Project	Displays the project window
Project notes	Opens the project notes window, in which you can store comments
List all...	Lists all of the current windows on the desktop

The help system, which is the menu option on the right, is covered later.

Shortcut Keys

Turbo C++ provides a set of *shortcut keys* (also called hotkeys) that you can use to select menu commands. Although it makes no difference whether you use the shortcut keys, access the menu directly, or click and drag with a mouse, many prefer the shortcut keys because with them you can invoke a menu option in one or two key strokes, versus using several for a typical menu selection operation. Using shortcut keys, you can access the menu bar, select a menu command, or bring up dialog boxes instantly.

For example, if you want to open a program file, you can press Alt-F from the main menu and then the first letter of the next menu command you would like to invoke, in this case **O** for **O**pen. You can invoke other menu selections in the same manner. Notice that some of the menu commands have the hotkeys displayed next to the selection. For example, the menu selection Edit ¦ Undo (meaning select the Edit menu option, then select Undo) can be invoked by Alt+BkSp (Backspace). That is an example of an *edit hotkey*.

Window management hotkeys, *On-line Help hotkeys*, *Menu hotkeys*, and *General hotkeys*, as well *Debugging/Running hotkeys* also exist. General hotkeys and Menu hotkeys are defined in table 3.2 and table 3.3. If you find you are using the menu to select the same menu options repeatedly, using a hotkey should save you some time.

Command Set Selection

Turbo C++ supports two hotkey command sets:

- The Common User Access (CUA) command set

- The Alternate Command set

The Common User Access (CUA) command set is the standard interface as defined by the IBM CUA standard. The Alternate Command set is a supported set of hotkeys from previous Borland products.

The General hotkeys (CUA and Alternate) are described in table 3.2. The Menu hotkeys are described in table 3.3. You can select the command set you want to use by selecting Options ¦ Environment ¦ Preferences and then selecting the command set you want.

Table 3.2. General hotkeys.

CUA	Alternate	Menu Selection	Function
F1	**F1**	Help	Displays the help screen
	F2	File ¦ Save	Saves the active file
	F3	File ¦ Open	Brings up the Open File dialog box

(continues)

Table 3.2. Continued.

CUA	Alternate	Menu Selection	Function
	F4	Run ¦ Go to cursor	Runs your program to the cursor
	F5	Window ¦ Zoom	Zooms the active window
Ctrl+F6	**F6**	Window ¦ Next	Cycles through all open windows
F7	**F7**	Run ¦ Trace into	Traces into functions
F8	**F8**	Run ¦ Step over	Steps over functions
F9	**F9**	Compile ¦ Make	Invokes the Project Manager
F10	none	none	Takes you to the menu bar

Table 3.3. General hotkeys.

CUA	Alternate	Menu Selection	Invokes
Alt+Spacebar	Alt+Spacebar	= menu	The (System) menu
Alt+C	Alt+C	Compile menu	The Compile menu
Alt+D	Alt+D	Debug menu	The Debug menu
Alt+E	Alt+E	Edit menu	The Edit menu
Alt+F	Alt+F	File menu	The File menu
Alt+H	Alt+H	Help menu	The Help menu
Alt+O	Alt+O	Options menu	The Options menu
Alt+P	Alt+P	Project menu	The Project menu
Alt+R	Alt+R	Run menu	The Run menu
Alt+S	Alt+S	Search menu	The Search menu
Alt+W	Alt+W	Window menu	The Window menu
Alt+F4	Alt+X	File ¦ Exit	Exits from Turbo C++

Using Dialog Boxes

As referred to in the preceding section, menu commands with ellipses (...) after them are used to access a *dialog box*. A dialog box, as the name implies, carries on a dialog with the user (see fig. 3.11). It can gather information such as Turbo C++ configuration options, or assist the user with the selection of a program file.

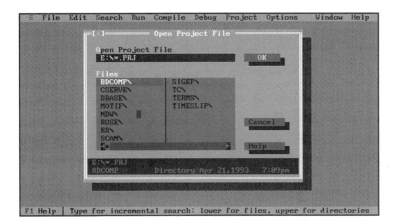

Fig. 3.11.
The Open Project File dialog box.

When you are working with dialog boxes, you use five basic types of on-screen controls:

- Action buttons

- Radio buttons

- Check boxes

- Input boxes

- List boxes

Action buttons cause some immediate action to take place when selected. Some examples of action buttons are the OK, Cancel, and Help buttons. OK is an example of a *default action button* (see fig. 3.13). That means you need only press Enter to select that button, or click it with the mouse. The default button is usually highlighted, and you can use Tab key to change the default button.

Radio buttons are options that are mutually exclusive, meaning that only one option can be selected at a time—like the old-style car radio selection buttons. In figure 3.13, the memory model portion of the dialog box is an example of radio buttons. You can select a radio button by using the Tab key to move to the list. Use the arrow keys to move to the desired selection, or click the selection with the mouse.

Check Boxes enable you to turn on or off an option. Unlike the radio buttons, you can check or uncheck as many boxes as you want. The Options portion of the Code Generation dialog box in figure 3.12 is an example of check boxes. You can change the state of the check boxes by using the Tab key to move to the box, and then by using the arrow keys to select a desired check box. Use the space bar to change the state of the selection. You may also use the mouse to turn off or on an option by clicking the mouse on the particular check box.

Input Boxes enable you to enter text into a box. Sometimes a down arrow is near the input box where the previously entered entries are listed. You can select an old entry or create a new one. The Defines portion of the dialog box in figure 3.12 is an example of an input box.

Fig. 3.12.
The Code Genera-
tion dialog box,
which contains
examples of action
buttons, radio
buttons, input
boxes, and check
boxes.

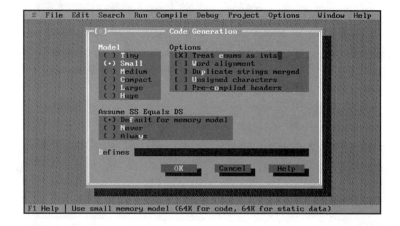

List boxes display a list of items from which you may select. Using the Tab key, you can move to the box and press Enter to display the list. Select an item and press Enter again. Alternatively, you can use the mouse to click on the list box to display the list, and you can then click on your selection.

Using Windows

The Turbo C++ IDE is based on windows. A program displays in a window, compiler messages are placed in a window, and the project files are managed from windows, as well. The number of windows you can have open on the desktop at one time is limited only by the amount of memory you have installed.

The window in which you are working is called the *active window*, or sometimes the *current window*. The active window usually is displayed on top of the other open windows, and it is enclosed in a double border.

The best way to manage windows is with a mouse; however, you can perform all window functions with the keyboard. To make a window active, you need only click it with the mouse. If you are using a keyboard, select from the **W**indow menu (described earlier) the windows you want to make active.

The active window always has a close box, a zoom box, and a set of scroll bars, as does the Help window. Turbo C++ uses many types of windows, but they have the following in common:

- Window number

- Title bar

- Close box

- Set of scroll bars

- Zoom box

The *window number* is at the top right of the window. You can identify open editor windows by these numbers. Use the Alt key and the window number to make that particular window active. If more than nine windows are open, use Alt-0 to display a selection of available windows.

The *title bar* is across the top of the window. Generally, it describes what the window is used for. Figure 3.15 is a Help window, therefore Help is on the window title bar. If you are editing a file, the window that you are using has the file name displayed in the title bar.

The *close box* is located in the top left corner of the window. It is the small square enclosed in brackets. If you click it, the window closes; it is removed from the desktop.

The *scroll bars* are displayed on the bottom of the window (the horizontal scroll bar), as well as on the right side (the vertical scroll bar). They enable you to use the mouse to navigate through a window by clicking the up or down arrows on the vertical scroll bar, and the right or left arrows on the horizontal scroll bar.

The *zoom box* is located in the top right corner of the window. It is an up-arrow character. When you click the zoom box, the window is enlarged; it becomes a *maximized* window. If the window is already enlarged or maximized, a double-sided arrow appears in the zoom box. If you click this arrow, the window returns to its previous size.

Using Help

The Turbo C++ Help system has set the industry standard. Using the help system, you can get information about any Turbo C++ topic, including how to use the IDE, hotkeys, editor commands, and the C/C++ programming language.

To enter the Turbo C++ Help system, select Help from the main menu (see fig. 3.13). The following menu commands are available:

- **Contents**

- **Index**

- **Topic search**

- **Previous topic**

- **Help on help**

- **About**

Help Contents

When you select **Contents**, a window is displayed with the Help contents (see fig. 3.14).

From here, you can tab to, or click on, a topic, and then move to subtopics. Help works much like a book, but it is much faster.

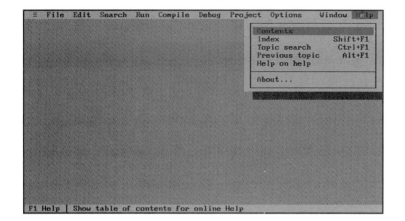

Fig. 3.13.
The options on
the Help menu.

Close box   Title bar   Window number
                                      Zoom box

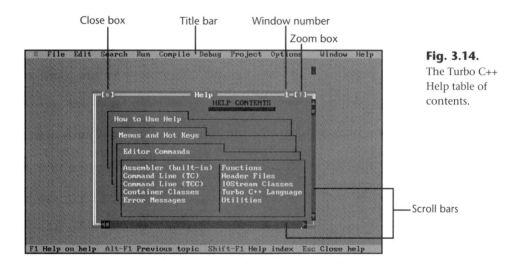

Fig. 3.14.
The Turbo C++
Help table of
contents.

Scroll bars

The Turbo C++ Help screens usually contain highlighted keywords. The high-lighting means that you can double-click the highlighted word, or tab to it and press Enter, to get further information. The Help system moves down a hierarchy of topics, from the most general to the most detailed.

Finding a Topic

The Help Index menu command displays a list of help topics (see fig. 3.15). You can move through the list by using the scroll bars and the mouse, or by using the cursor. To find topics instantaneously, simply begin typing the topic. The Help index moves directly to the word that matches the letters you are enter-ing. The more you type, the more the help index narrows the topic search. If for some reason the topic you are seeking help on is not in the index, Help displays the closest match. After you have selected the topic about which you would like information, press Enter, or double-click it with the mouse.

Fig. 3.15.
The Turbo C++
Help Index.

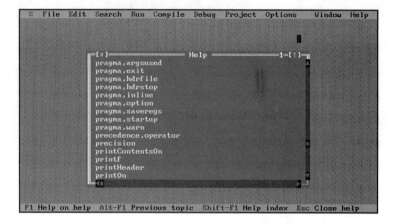

As you may have guessed, several hotkeys are available for use with the Turbo C++ help system. They are

F1	Displays the Help window
Shift+F1	Displays the Help index
Ctrl+F1	Displays a topic search
Alt+F1	Redisplays the Help information you viewed previously

Help on Help

The Help system is complex, and from time to time you may need assistance with using it. Turbo C++ has provided a Help facility that gives you information about using Help (see fig. 3.16). This window is brought up by selecting "Help on Help" from the Help menu.

Fig. 3.16.
Getting help from
the Help System.

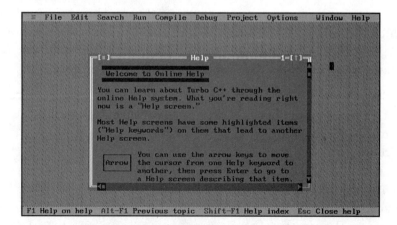

Using the Examples

The real power for programmers is the examples that are available from the Help system. Not only can the programmer access information about functions and commands, but actual program examples are available as well. The programmer even has the option of incorporating the examples into the current program file using the clipboard facility.

For example, say you want to receive information about the `printf()` function. Using the Help index, you can locate the Help window for `printf()`, as shown in figure 3.17.

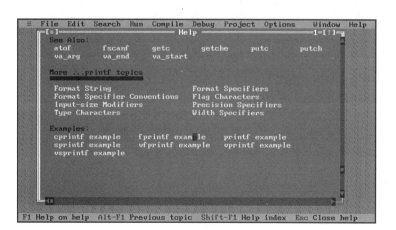

Fig. 3.17.
The Help window for `printf()`.

You can find a list of examples by scrolling to the bottom of this Help window. The highlighted text means that additional information exists on the topic, in this case program examples (see fig. 3.18). To see this additional information, move the cursor to the `printf()` example and press Enter, or double-click it.

Fig. 3.18.
A list of high-lighted examples.

In figure 3.19, the sample program using `printf()` appears. From this point, you can learn from the example, or better yet use it.

Fig. 3.19.
An example program that uses `printf()`.

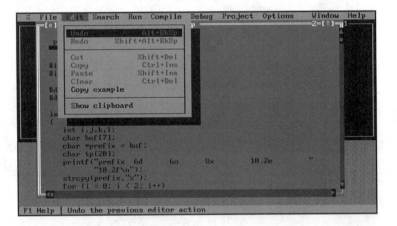

From here, you can pull down the **E**dit menu from the main menu bar. The Edit menu contains the Copy **e**xample command, which you can use to copy the sample program in the Help window to the clipboard (see fig. 3.20).

Fig. 3.20.
The Copy example command can be chosen from the Edit menu.

The sample program should now be in the Clipboard. You can check this by displaying the Clipboard by using the **S**how Clipboard command from the Edit menu (see fig. 3.21).

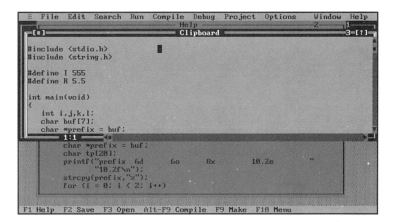

Fig. 3.21.
Displaying the sample program on the Clipboard.

You can then use the **E**dit menu's **P**aste command to place the program in an existing C or C++ program, or create a new program file using the **N**ew command from the **F**ile menu. When the new program window is displayed, you can paste the example program into the window (see fig. 3.22).

```
 ≡  File  Edit  Search  Run  Compile  Debug  Project  Options    Window  Help
┌─[■]───────────────────────── C:\NONAME00.CPP ────────────────────────1=[↑]┐
│#include <stdio.h>                                                          ▲
│#include <string.h>                                                         ▒
│                                                                            ▒
│#define I 555                                                               ▒
│#define R 5.5                             █                                 ▒
│                                                                            ▒
│int main(void)                                                              ▒
│{                                                                           ▒
│   int i,j,k,l;                                                             ▒
│   char buf[7];                                                             ▒
│   char *prefix = buf;                                                      ▒
│   char tp[20];                                                             ▒
│   printf("prefix  6d       6o      8x       10.2e        "                 ▒
│         "10.2f\n");                                                        ▒
│   strcpy(prefix,"x");                                                      ▒
│   for (i = 0; i < 2; i++)                                                  ▒
│   {                                                                        ▒
│      for (j = 0; j < 2; j++)                                               ▼
│═══ 1:1 ═══◄■───────────────────────────────────────────────────────►     │
└────────────────────────────────────────────────────────────────────────────┘
 F1 Help  F2 Save  F3 Open  Alt-F9 Compile  F9 Make  F10 Menu
```

Fig. 3.22.
Pasting the sample program from the Clipboard to a program.

To see how the program works, you can compile and run it using the Run command from the **R**un menu (see fig. 3.23). The Compiling message window appears. If everything goes okay, the program compiles and runs, and in this case displays the program output (see fig. 3.24). This portion of the Help system gives you access to thousands of lines of code that you can learn from or incorporate into your program.

Fig. 3.23.
Compiling the
sample program.

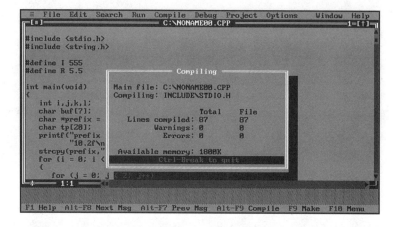

Fig. 3.24.
The output of the
sample program.

The About Box

The last command on the Help menu is **A**bout..., which displays the About
dialog box on-screen (see fig. 3.25). The About dialog box displayed when
you first executed Turbo C++, and you can see it whenever you want using
this command. Notice the version number. You can refer to this version
number to make sure that the Turbo C++ version you are using is up-to-date.
You can invoke an amusing feature of the About box by pressing Alt+I while
the About box is being displayed. A scrolling list of the names of the Turbo
C++ programmers appears.

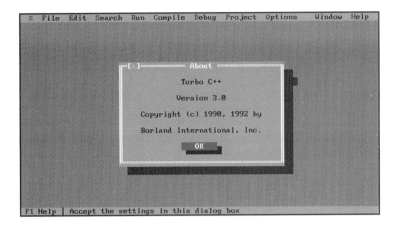

Fig. 3.25.
The About dialog box.

Using Microsoft Windows and the IDE

Many computers use Microsoft Windows. If you are a Windows user, you can run Turbo C++ from the DOS compatibility box of Windows without a conflict. You can either run the DOS box and then invoke Turbo C++, or you can actually add it as an icon in any group using the Program Manager's **F**ile **N**ew command and selecting the Program **I**tem radio button in the New Program Object dialog box. You can run Turbo C++ in full-screen mode or as a window (see fig. 3.26). Both options maintain support for the mouse.

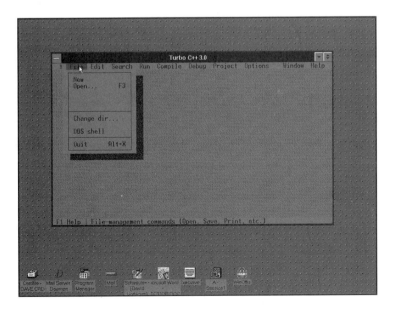

Fig. 3.26.
Running Turbo C++ under Microsoft Windows.

Summary

This chapter introduced the Turbo C++ IDE. The discussion covered the basics, including the features of the IDE, start-up options, the architecture of the screen, the main menu structure, using windows and dialog boxes, and using the Help facility.

- The IDE includes all of the facilities you need to edit, create, compile, link, and debug your program.

- Several start-up options exist for the IDE. They control the amount and type of memory to be utilized, automated operations, and using custom hardware setups.

- The IDE screen is made up of a menu bar, a status bar, a desktop, and a series of windows.

- The main menu contains menus that have options for file operations, program editing, searching for information, running a program, building a stand-alone executable file, debugging a program, managing programming projects, customizing the IDE, managing the windows of the IDE, and getting help.

- There are shortcut keys and hotkeys that enable Turbo C++ users to gain access to menu commands, dialog boxes, and other facilities using few keystrokes.

- The Turbo C++ user has a choice of using two different hotkey command sets: the industry-standard Common User Interface and Borland's Alternate Command set. Both work equally well.

- Dialog boxes are used to talk with the user. They can contain action buttons, radio buttons, check boxes, input boxes, and list boxes.

- Windows are maintained by the IDE. An IDE window contains many parts, including the window number, the title bar, the close box, the scroll bars, and a zoom box.

- The Borland Help system is the best in the business. It allows programmers to locate help on topics using a table of contents, an index, and a topics search facility.

- The Help facility provides help about using the Help facility, as well as an About box that displays version and copyright information.

- The Turbo C++ IDE can be run under Microsoft Windows, and even maintains full-screen and reduced-screen mouse support.

Chapter 4

Customizing Turbo C++

Turbo C++ is configurable. Through configurable options you can tell the compiler, linker, and debugger how to build and debug your current or future Turbo C++ programs. In addition, you can use configurable options to define other features such as screen colors, screen size, mouse behavior, and the default directories used by Turbo C++.

Borland always has understood the benefits of an application development environment that adapts to the ever-changing needs of programmers and the applications they construct. For that reason, Borland made Turbo C++ and other Borland development environments extremely adaptable by including in these environments the extensive options settings of the Integrated Development Environment, called the IDE. The Turbo C++ IDE is customizable through the facilities and features of the main menu command, **O**ptions.

Many beginning Turbo C++ programmers are overwhelmed by the number of Turbo C++ compiler, linker, debugger, and other options available in the **O**ptions area of the IDE. The following are some of the questions frequently raised by beginning Turbo C++ programmers:

- What are memory models?

- What memory models are used? Where? Why?

- What is the difference between an Overlay, Standard, and Library standard output?

- What are C++ Options?

The purpose of this chapter is to take the mystery out of setting and resetting the configurable options of Turbo C++. In this chapter, you explore each option, the meaning of each available setting, the role each option plays in the overall operation of Turbo C++, and the options' effects on your application. As in previous chapters, you are walked through these operations step by step, option by option, screen by screen. This chapter is designed as a reference chapter. Each option is laid out in the order in which it appears in the Options menus. Each heading refers to a configurable Turbo C++ option.

As you read through this chapter, you can use your copy of Turbo C++ to follow along as each option is addressed. But be careful—many of these options are for advanced Turbo C++ programmers, and you have not yet reached the sections of this book that explain the underlying concepts behind these options. This chapter provides basic information about a particular option or options. As you progress through later chapters of this book that explain in more detail the concepts behind these advanced options, you can refer back to this chapter.

You might inadvertently make changes to your compiler configuration that could cause problems when programming, linking, and compiling with Turbo C++. Configuration problems take a lot of time to correct.

Setting IDE Options

The **O**ptions menu command is on the main Turbo C++ menu (see fig. 4.1). You may recall from Chapter 3 that you can choose **O**ptions by using your mouse, by pressing Alt-O, or by pressing F10 and moving the lightbar over the **O**ptions main menu command. Chapter 3 also discusses the use of radio buttons, check boxes, and so on to select menu commands and options; as you progress through this chapter, you can refer back to Chapter 3 when necessary to refresh your memory on using these selection methods.

Fig. 4.1.
The Turbo C++ IDE Options pull-down menu.

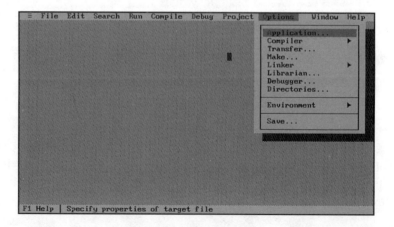

You set many configurable options only once. Most of the defaults provided by Borland's INSTALL program may be fine for your current application development needs, especially if you're a beginning programmer. As a rule, alter a default only if you are absolutely sure what that option setting affects. A change in just one option can cause countless problems.

When you choose **O**ptions, a pull-down menu appears and offers the following menu selections:

- **A**pplication

- **C**ompiler

- **T**ransfer

- **M**ake

- **L**inker

- Li**b**rarian

- De**b**ugger

- **D**irectories

- **E**nvironment

- **S**ave

The following sections describe each of these options in greater detail.

Application Generation Options

When you choose **O**ptions, **A**pplication, you see a dialog box similar to that shown in figure 4.2.

Fig. 4.2.
The Set Application Options dialog box.

Tip
Remember: A
menu command
followed by (. . .)
displays a dialog
box when the
command option
is invoked.

The Set Application Options dialog box is fairly simple and offers only three
selections: **S**tandard, **O**verlay, and **L**ibrary. These selections are mutually
exclusive; you can select only one of them at a time. Because you use only
one option to define a number of compiler and linker settings, you can set up
the application generation environment quickly with this dialog box.

When you select **S**tandard, **O**verlay, or **L**ibrary from the Set Application
Options dialog box, changes occur automatically to the Linker/Output,
Prolog/Epilog, and Memory Model settings used by the program (see table
4.1). Memory models are configurable both here and in the Code Generation
options area, which is covered later. Memory models are examined briefly in
this section; however, they are examined in detail in the Code Generation
options section.

Table 4.1 describes the application settings (**S**tandard, **O**verlay, and **L**ibrary),
and the effects on Linker/Output, Prolog/Epilog, and Memory Model.
You may use this table now or in the future to select the proper application
settings.

Table 4.1. Application Settings.			
Setting	**Standard**	**Overlay**	**Library**
Linker/Output	Standard	Overlaid	Standard
	EXE	EXE	Library
Prolog/Epilog	Standard	Overlay	Standard
Memory Model	Small	Medium	Small

The Linker/Output setting determines the type of executable created by the
Turbo C++ linker. With this setting, you tell the compiler to create a Standard
EXE file, an Overlaid EXE file, or a Library.

For typical programs, especially those you first create as a programmer, use
the Standard Linker/Output option. This option is the default Turbo C++
selection. When you create a program using the Standard Linker/Output
option, Turbo C++ creates an executable program with an EXE extension.
You can run this program from the DOS operating system in the same way
that you run the Turbo C++ compiler program.

Typical applications, such as the example programs included in this book, are simple enough to run within the available RAM memory of a typical computer running DOS. Remember, however, that DOS has a size limitation. Most older XT-based PCs had RAM memory limited to 256K (the K designation is a shorthand notation for *kilobytes*; a kilobyte is approximately 1,000 bytes). The largest program these PCs could run was around 200K (the remaining RAM was required by DOS). Today's DOS computers generally have 640K of RAM and can run programs as large as 550K (the rest of RAM memory is occupied by DOS). A program cannot run if it is larger than the available RAM memory.

The example programs in this book give you an idea of the size of a simple program; most of these example programs, when compiled and linked by using the Standard option, are between 10K and 20K. You need very sophisticated applications to create programs larger than 550K. Many programs are larger than 550K, however—especially those programs that use graphics, such as CAD (Computer Aided Design) applications.

The Overlay option in the Set Application Options dialog box helps you break your very large program into smaller pieces, each of which you safely can load and run on your target PCs.

Overlays allow a program to swap portions of the program to and from a common portion of memory, reducing the amount of memory a program requires. Programs using overlays use less memory because only a piece of the program uses the memory at any given time. By using overlays, you can execute large programs that would not normally fit into available memory. This overlay processing is handled by an overlay manager.

Turbo C++ uses an overlay manager known as VROOMM (Virtual Runtime Object-Oriented Memory Manager) that does the overlay work for you. VROOMM becomes part of the program. You set the Overlay option of the Application Set Options dialog box and the compiler automatically creates programs that use VROOMM.

When using VROOMM overlay manager, if a portion of the program is called that is not currently in memory, it is read from disk to a buffer set up by VROOMM. Once executed, that portion of code is taken out of memory, freeing that memory for the next portion of code that needs processing. Although this feature reduces the amount of memory required to run your application, all the extra work can slow your application down.

In Turbo C++, a *library* function is a set of routines that are precompiled and usable by any program. A library function is not a program; it cannot run from the DOS prompt. A library function is a series of specialized code that you write and package in a library file so that the code can be shared by other applications. You use a library function when you need specialized functions that are shared across many applications.

Turbo C++ comes with a complete set of library functions that handle math, disk access, and other typical programming tasks. These libraries are described in later chapters. In addition to the libraries provided by Turbo C++, you may want to create specialized libraries of functions that are specific to your application. For example, you may want to create a graphics library that draws different shapes on the screen.

To create a library, select **L**ibrary in the Set Application Options dialog box; instead of creating a program with an EXE extension, Turbo C++ creates a library file with an LIB extension. The LIB file can then be linked into any other program that requires the functionality programmed in the library.

The Prolog/Epilog setting specifies how the program is started and stopped. To the code that you write, the compiler and linker add code that interacts with the operating system to start up and shut down your program.

Slight differences occur in the ways that Standard programs and Overlay programs are started and stopped. The Prolog/Epilog setting reflects these differences. When you use the Library setting, no Prolog/Epilog setting applies, because a library is not a program.

The Model setting tells the compiler how the program is going to use DOS memory during execution. The choices include Small when Standard is selected, Medium when Overlay is selected, and Small when Library is selected (memory models are explained later in the chapter).

Compiler Configuration Options

Choosing **O**ptions, **C**ompiler produces a drop-down menu of commands (see fig. 4.3). Choosing a command from the Compiler drop-down menu produces a dialog box containing options that affect code compilation. The Compiler submenu includes the following options:

- Code generation...

- **A**dvanced code generation...

- **E**ntry/Exit Code...

- **C**++ options...

- **O**ptimizations...

- **S**ource...

- **M**essages

- **N**ames...

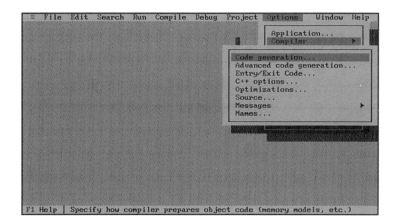

Fig. 4.3.
The Compiler
menu commands.

You can use the Compiler options to customize the compiler's evaluation and generation of your program. You rarely need to alter these settings, because Turbo C++ does a good job of providing the proper defaults. If you do need to alter these settings, please remember that many problems experienced by beginning Turbo C++ programmers can be traced to improper Compiler option settings. You need to pay special attention to what each option means, how each option is set, when it should be set, and why it is set. The following sections explore each option in considerable detail.

Code Generation. When you select **O**ption, **C**ompiler, **C**ode generation, a dialog box appears (see fig. 4.4). You can set several options in the Code Generation dialog box; these options are included in the Model, Options, and Assume SS Equals DS list boxes, and the **D**efines text box. The following sections detail each of these options.

Fig. 4.4.
The Code
Generation dialog
box.

Models. A number of memory models are available in the Model option list box. You select a model by clicking its radio button. Memory models, by definition, are mutually exclusive, and your selection of a memory model represents an important decision. If you select the wrong model, your program may not function as efficiently as possible, or may not function at all. The following memory models are available:

- **T**iny

- **S**mall

- **M**edium

- **C**ompact

- **L**arge

- **H**uge

In general the names of the memory models correspond in meaning to their use in common English; a **T**iny memory model is meant to be used for tiny programs, and a **H**uge memory model is meant to be used for huge programs. For most programs, the differences between these settings are negligible. In general, you can maintain the default Turbo C++ setting, **S**mall. If you need to optimize your program for speed or size, however, you may benefit from selecting an appropriate memory model. The following paragraphs describe the memory models and general reasons for their use.

The Tiny memory model is the smallest of the memory models supported by Turbo C++. Select **T**iny when you want to generate a program using the smallest amount of memory. A utility program is one example of a program to which you may want to apply this model. When you use the Tiny model, all of the segment registers are set to the same values and you can use only

64K for all of your program code and data. As a result, your program fits into a small package under 64K. Although all the example programs in this book fit this description, they do not need to be optimized and, therefore, use the default memory setting. Programmers generally apply the Tiny model to small utility programs where using the smallest amount of memory is a beneficial feature. The Tiny model uses the smallest amount of memory and therefore is a good fit for programs that need to run in an environment where memory is scarce, or when it is desirable for a program to use the smallest possible amount of memory.

The **S**mall memory model enables you to break your code and data into two separate areas of memory, each of which is less than 64K in size. Unlike the **T**iny memory model, the data in the **S**mall memory model has its own 64K area, separate from the code. The maximum size of program using the Small memory model is 128K. **S**mall is the default memory model setting for the compiler; most application programs are compiled using the Small model.

Select the **M**edium memory model when you need more than 64K of memory to accommodate your program's code. The Medium model provides 1M (*M* is an abbreviation for *megabyte*, approximately one million bytes) of available memory space for code and 64K of available memory space for data. Remember, the Medium model data segment is no larger than that of the Small memory model—both are limited to 64K.

The **C**ompact memory model is the reverse of the Medium model and is well suited for programs with small portions of code and large amounts of data. Selecting **C**ompact makes 64K of memory available to your code and 1M of memory available for your data.

The **L**arge memory model is a combination of the Medium and the Compact models. The **L**arge model uses multiple segments and can accommodate up to 1M of code and 1M of data. Select **L**arge when both your code and data require more than 64K of memory.

The **H**uge memory model is similar to the Large memory model, but it allows for a single data item (such as an array) that is larger than 64K. Use the Huge memory model only when required. The compact model provides 1M for data; however, it cannot accommodate a single data item larger than 64K. The Huge model is a necessity when using a single data item that exceeds 64K, which is too big for the compact model. When using the compact model, a single data item cannot exceed 64K, even if there is 1M reserved for data. When using very large data items, such as arrays exceeding 64K, the Huge model is your only option.

Table 4.2 lists each memory model and the sizes and segments of memory each uses. When selecting a memory model, remember that every model offers a tradeoff in speed, memory usage, and executable size. Programs compiled using memory models other than Tiny or Small are slower, and these programs' EXE file sizes are larger. Of course, on today's faster processors, the speed difference may be unnoticeable. Take a look at your program. What are its data and code requirements? When you answer that question, you can make a reasonable assumption as to the correct memory model to use.

Note

You can use only those memory models you installed with Turbo C++ (see Chapter 2, "Installing Turbo C++"). If you installed only the Small and Tiny models during installation, only those models are available. If you need to access a memory model that you didn't install, you can reinstall Turbo C++ and install all memory models during the reinstallation.

Table 4.2. Memory model options.

Memory	Segments	
Model	Code	Data
Tiny	64K	
Small	64K	64K
Medium	1M	64K
Compact	64K	1M
Large	1M	1M
Huge	1M	64K
(Default) Small		

Options. The Options selections in the Code Generation Options dialog box turn various code generation options off or on. For most application purposes, the default Options settings are correct. Notice that you use check boxes to select these options (an X appears in the check box when the option is selected). You can select as many options as you want. The available options include the following:

- Treat **e**nums as ints

- **W**ord alignment

- Du**p**licate strings merged

- **U**nsigned characters

- Pre-**co**mpiled headers

As with the Model settings, beginning programmers usually find the default Options settings to be adequate. The discussions that follow introduce you to the various options that you may need when your programming requirements become sophisticated or highly specialized.

The Treat **e**nums as ints option tells Turbo C++ to treat enumerators as integers. An *enumerator* is a type of data used in programming (enumerators are discussed later in this book). The Treat **e**nums as ints option enables you to choose to have enumerated data use one or two bytes of storage space. Set the Treat **e**nums as ints option to on when you want the compiler to allocate a whole word for enumerated data (a *word* is two bytes of storage space in the computer's memory). Turbo C++ stores enumerators as single bytes when Treat **e**nums as ints is off.

Make sure the **W**ord alignment option is selected if you want to align non-character data at even addresses. *Word-aligned* data is aligned to even bytes in memory; for example, byte 30,000 rather than byte 30,001. Deselect this option when you want to use *byte-aligning*. Byte-aligned data can be aligned at either odd or even addresses.

The computer has an easier time reading and writing data into word-aligned memory. Selecting **W**ord alignment, therefore, increases the speed with which the processor retrieves and stores data. Using word-aligning, however, may force the computer to waste some odd addresses. As a result, selecting **W**ord alignment increases speed, but also increases program storage requirements; deselecting **W**ord alignment has the reverse effect. As with most of these Code Generation options, you notice a difference in wither speed or storage requirements in small programs, such as the examples in this book. If this option is selected, the program is able to make better use of memory because identical strings that take space in memory are merged into only one string. This eliminates redundant strings residing in memory, thus using memory more efficiently. For example, if "Programming is fun" exists twice in memory, taking up 32 bytes for both, the compiler would merge each instance of that string into one string, only taking up 18 bytes.

If the Du**p**licate strings merged option is selected, two strings are merged together when they match, and are deselected when merging is not required.

Selecting the **U**nsigned characters option tells Turbo C++ to treat all *char* data types as if they are *unsigned char types*. Data types are discussed in greater detail in Chapter 9, but, in brief, unsigned characters can contain only positive values; signed characters can contain both positive and negative values. This distinction generally is of no significance to you as a programmer, unless you happen to be using the *char* data type for special purposes that are too detailed for this book.

When this setting is on, all char variable declarations are treated as if they were declared as unsigned char types. This treatment allows your char variable types to contain only positive values (0 to 255). When using unsigned types, you're limited to storing only small numbers and the full PC ASCII character set. If off (default), the char variables can contain both positive and negative values (-128 to 127). This allows storage of very small numbers and ASCII characters, the normal use of the char type. You should never change this option from the default unless (for some strange reason) your application needs to declare all chars as unsigned chars, which is rarely done.

Select the Pre-c**o**mpiled headers option when you want the IDE to generate and utilize pre-compiled headers. Pre-compiled headers are used by Turbo C++ to save on compile time. The header files are compiled once during the first build operation. Unless the header files are altered, they are not re-compiled during subsequent compiles. The IDE does not generate or use pre-compiled headers if this option is deselected.

Assume SS Equals DS. The selections in the Assume SS Equals DS list box specify how the compiler considers the stack segments (SS) and data segments (DS) of the program. You can select these items by using radio buttons, but you can make only one selection at a time. The Assume SS Equals DS list box contains the De**f**ault for memory model, **N**ever, and Alwa**y**s settings.

Selecting De**f**ault for memory model enables the memory model to decide whether the stack segment (SS) is the same as the data segment (DS). By default, this option is selected. This option is helpful when you are porting (moving programs from one type of computer system to another) code originally written for a compiler that makes the stack part of the data segment. When De**f**ault for memory model is selected, the compiler links in an alternate startup module. This module (C0Fx.OBJ) places the stack in the data segment. The compiler automatically assumes that the stack segment is equal to the data segment when using **T**iny, **S**mall, and **M**edium memory models. The stack segment is a portion of memory used for holding short-term data such as subroutine parameters and results. The data segment is a portion of memory reserved for data that doesn't execute while a program is running.

Selecting **N**ever instructs the compiler to assume that the stack segment is not equivalent to the data segments. Selecting Alwa**y**s instructs the compiler to assume the reverse—that the stack segment is equivalent to the data segments. Unless you have a specific reason to change the setting, leave this option set to De**f**ault for memory model.

Defines. The **D**efines text box in the Code Generation dialog box enables you to enter macro definitions to the preprocessor. You would use this option to pass information to your program that changes such things as operating system versions, names of variables, and formulas. For example:

```
VERSION = 2.0
OS = MS_DOS
TAX = ((INCOME-20000)*.20)
```

Using this option is functionally equivalent to making edits to your source code file before submitting it to the compiler. This option is convenient because you can make the change without having to change a source file. You can separate several defines with a semicolon (;) or assign values by using the equals sign (=). Chapter 12, "Using the Preprocessor," explains the preprocessor and preprocessor macros in detail.

Advanced Code Generation. Using the **A**dvanced code generation menu command, you can set several compiler options. Choosing **O**ptions, **C**ompiler, **A**dvanced code generation produces the Advanced Code Generation dialog box shown in figure 4.5. This dialog box enables you to set several compiler options. You can select Floating Point and Instruction Set settings, and the Options list box contains check boxes for Advanced Code Generation options. This dialog box also provides a Far Data **T**hreshold text box. The following paragraphs discuss the elements of the Advanced Code Generation dialog box in detail.

As the name of this dialog box implies, these settings are provided for advanced application developers. As a beginning programmer, you may have little need to change the Advanced Code Generation default settings; you benefit, however, from an understanding of their use.

Fig. 4.5.

The Advanced
Code Generation
dialog box.

Floating Point. The Floating Point setting tells the compiler how to handle floating point numbers. *Floating point* numbers are those that contain a fractional part of a number. For example,

$ 100.25

is an example of a floating point number.

The four Floating Point selections are **N**one, **E**mulation, **8**087, and 80287.

If you select **N**one, the compiler assumes that your program contains no floating point calculations. If your program does contain floating point calculations and you select **N**one, you get linker errors. Selecting **N**one creates a smaller, more efficient executable if no floating point calculations are required.

When you click the **E**mulation radio button, Turbo C++ detects whether your computer has an 80x87 math coprocessor (see information on math coprocessors in Chapter 1, "Understanding the Basics"). If your computer has the math coprocessor, Turbo C++ makes use of it. If no coprocessor is present in your computer, Turbo C++ emulates a coprocessor. Selecting **8**087 generates direct 8087 inline code, allowing the program to use the coprocessor directly. Moreover, when selecting 80287, the compiler generates code that allows the program to use the 80287 math coprocessor directly. When using a coprocessor directly, such as an 80287, that particular coprocessor must reside in the computer where the program is executed. For example, if you compiled a program by using the 80287 directly, that program would not run on a computer, such as an IBM XT, that did not contain an 80287. For most applications, you would not want to make your program dependent on the presence of a coprocessor that many PCs may not contain.

Instruction Set. The Instruction Set settings tell the compiler to create executable code for a particular CPU. Code generated for an 80286 CPU, for example, does not work on an 8088/8086 processor. The selections in this list box are 8088/808**6**, 80**1**86, and 80**2**86. The 8088/808**6** selection directs the compiler to generate code for the 8088/8086 CPU. Selecting 80**1**86 tells the compiler to generate code for the 80186; selecting 80**2**86 generates code for the 80286 CPU.

In most situations, keep 8088/808**6** selected in Instruction Set, because you can run 8088/8086 instructions on all old and new Intel processors. If you are generating code for an 80286 processor, make sure the program is executed on a computer with an 80286 or greater processor.

Options and the Far Data Threshold Text Box. The Options settings enable advanced programmers to fine-tune the generation of their code. This list box includes these options:

- **G**enerate underbars

- **L**ine numbers debug info

- **D**ebug info in OBJs

- **F**ast floating point

- Fast huge po**i**nters

- Generate CO**M**DEFs

- **A**utomatic far data

Select **G**enerate underbars when you want Turbo C++ to automatically put an underbar character (_) in front of all global identifiers (this option is selected by default). Using underbars for C/C++ identifiers is optional; however, underbars are required if you are using the standard Turbo C++ libraries. Unless you are using non-standard libraries, therefore, leave this option at its default setting.

Select the **L**ine numbers debug info option when you want the compiler to include line numbers in the object and object MAKE files. These line numbers are used by the symbolic debugger, a program that enables you to monitor the execution of your program. The line numbers are helpful points of reference.

Select the **D**ebug info in OBJs option if you want debugging information included in the object files for use with Turbo Debugger (the Turbo Debugger program is included with Turbo C++). This option places debugging information in the executable file that tells the debugger where to find the equivalent line of source code for a particular program instruction. By using this setting, you will notice that the executable program increases in size. For this reason, you would want to recompile the program with the source debugging option off before sending it to a user.

Selecting **F**ast floating point optimizes floating-point operations (operations on portions of a number). Selecting Fast huge pointers lets the compiler know that when huge pointers are encountered in a program, the compiler should alter them in such a way as to make the program run faster. Pointers are pieces of data that point to areas of memory. The **F**ast floating point and Fast huge pointers options have the effect of speeding up computations of huge pointer expressions. A definition of a variable appears in the header files if Generate COMDEFs is selected.

Using the Fast huge pointers option may cause problems for huge arrays. Array elements sometimes cross a segment boundary.

The **A**utomatic far data option and the Far Data **T**hreshold text box work together. If **A**utomatic far data is selected, the compiler automatically generates far objects using the value you specify in the Far Data **T**hreshold text box to specify the size option required for the command. A far object generates function code for a far call and a far return. The Far Data **T**hreshold is the size portion required to complete the **A**utomatic far data option (the default=32767). If this option is deselected, the size value is ignored.

Entry/Exit Code. Choosing **O**ptions, **C**ompiler, **E**ntry/Exit Code produces the dialog box shown in figure 4.6. You use the options in this dialog box to determine how the compiler configures your application. The following list boxes appear in this dialog box:

- Prolog/Epilog Code Generation

- Calling Convention

- Stack Options

The Prolog/Epilog Code Generation list box enables you to select either **S**tandard or **O**verlay. Selecting **S**tandard generates code that is not for use with overlays; selecting **O**verlay generates code that is for use with overlays.

Fig. 4.6.
The Entry/Exit
Code Generation
dialog box.

Familiarizing Yourself

The Calling Convention setting tells the compiler which calling sequence to create for the function calls. The options in this list box are **C** or **P**ascal. A detailed explanation of these options is beyond the scope of this book. Never alter the Calling Convention setting unless you are an expert programmer and have read and understand the Borland Language Guide.

The Stack Options settings enable you to select a Standard stack **f**rame or a Test stack o**v**erflow. If Standard stack **f**rame is selected, the compiler creates a standard stack frame using standard function entry and exit code. Always leave Standard stack **f**rame selected when you are compiling a program for debugging. If the option is deselected, any function not using local variables and not using parameters is compiled using abbreviated entry and return code. This use of abbreviated entry and return code has the effect of making the code shorter and faster, but it prevents the debugger from accessing the function.

Selecting Test stack o**v**erflow instructs the compiler to generate code used to check for stack overflow at time of execution. If this option is deselected (the default setting), this functionality is not included in the compiler. Usually this option is deselected to save memory required for execution and to improve program performance.

Although selecting the Test stack o**v**erflow option requires additional memory and reduces performance of your program, this option can save many hours of debugging time. In most cases, a stack overflow bug is difficult to spot.

C++ options. The **O**ptions, **C**ompiler, C++ Options menu command displays a dialog box that enables you to tell the compiler how to prepare the object code when you use C++ (see fig. 4.7). The C++ Options dialog box includes the following list boxes:

■ Use C++ Compiler

■ Template Generation

■ Options

■ C++ Virtual Tables

Fig. 4.7.
The C++ Options
dialog box.

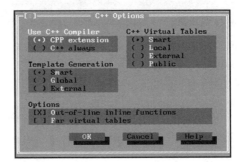

The Use C++ Compiler list box includes settings for CPP Extension or **C**++ Always. Select CPP Extension if all your programs are to be compiled as C code even if the file has a CPP (C Plus Plus) extension. Select **C**++ Always if your programs always compile as C++ code. Code compiled as C++ code looks different internally than does regular C code. This difference is not important unless you need to use third-party libraries that use C++ code. The compiler needs to know what type of code is in those libraries in order for them to be included correctly in your program during compile operations.

The options in this list box are **S**mart, **G**lobal, and Ex**t**ernal. The Template Generation setting determines how templates are managed in the program. Templates are discussed in Chapter 31, "Using Templates." As a rule, leave this setting at the default of **S**mart.

The C++ Virtual Tables settings enable you to control C++ virtual tables and the expansion of inline functions used when debugging. A discussion of virtual tables is beyond the scope of this book; for now, leave this setting at the default, **S**mart.

The last item in the C++ Options dialog box is the Options list box. In this list box, you can enable **O**ut-of-line inline functions and **F**ar virtual tables. Selecting **O**ut-of-line inline functions (described in Chapter 23) enables you to step through or set breakpoints on inline functions during debugging.

Inline functions are described in a later chapter. Selecting **F**ar virtual tables causes virtual tables to be placed in the code segment instead of the data segment. Leave this option deselected.

Optimizations. When you select the **O**ptions, **C**ompiler, **O**ptimization Compiler menu command, you see the dialog box shown in figure 4.8. The options in this dialog box enable you to optimize program performance. The Optimization Options include the following:

■ Optimizations

■ Register Variables

■ Optimize For

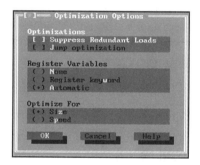

Fig. 4.8.
The Optimization Options dialog box.

Keep the Optimizations and Register Variables options at their default settings. These settings either improve the performance or decrease the space required for your programs in certain circumstances. In most programs, differences achieved by changing these settings are negligible.

The Optimize For options enable you to control the Turbo C++ compiler code-generation strategy, either for Si**z**e or S**p**eed. As their names imply, selecting Si**z**e directs the compiler to find the smallest possible code sequence. Selecting S**p**eed generates the fastest executable possible. A full explanation of the way a compiler generates code to optimize for either size or speed is beyond the scope of this book and, similar to other optimization options, changes to these settings produce negligible differences.

Source. Selecting **O**ptions, **C**ompiler, **S**ource menu command produces the dialog box shown in figure 4.9. Options in this dialog box enable you to instruct the compiler to expect certain types of programs. The Source Options dialog box options are as follows:

- Keywords

- Source Options

- Identifier Length

Fig. 4.9.
The Source
Options dialog
box.

Setting the Keyword option tells the compiler how to recognize keywords in your source code. Keywords are reserved words that have special meanings to various types of compilers such as Turbo C++. Turbo C++ allows you to set Turbo C++ to use keywords for other types of compilers. You can set the compiler for **T**urbo C++, **A**NSI, **U**NIX V, or Kernighan and **R**itchie. Unless you have a particular need to change the Keywords setting, leave **T**urbo C++ selected, to instruct the compiler to expect Turbo C++ keywords. Selecting **A**NSI instructs the compiler to accept ANSI compliant keywords (for a detailed discussion of the ANSI standard, see Chapter 1, "Understanding the Basics"). Selecting **U**NIX in the Keywords list box tells the compiler to expect only UNIX V keywords; selecting Kernighan and **R**itchie instructs the compiler to expect Kernighan-and-Ritchie-style keywords.

The selections in the Keywords list box are of little importance to you as a beginning programmer, because you are likely to be using Turbo C++ keywords. An understanding of these selections is useful to you, however, if you recompile a program that was first written in Unix or if you use another compiler with different keywords. You also may use this information if you are learning C++ by using an instruction book that uses a non-Turbo C++ standard.

The Source Options list box contains a check box for only one option, **N**ested Comments. If you select this option, you can nest comments in Turbo C++ source files. Nested comments are not standard C. Only Turbo C++ uses this format. Therefore, if you decide to use nested comments, you cannot port your C program to other C compilers without first deleting the nested comments from the source files.

In the **I**dentifier Length text box, you can specify the number of signficant characters in an identifier. An *identifier* is a word that you can define within your code to represent a number or a set of characters. Instead of using numbers that represent significant values within your program (such as setting the length of a line to 10), you use the identifier to represent the number (the identifier LINE_LENGTH, for example, may represent the number 10). C++ can recognize identifiers of unlimited length. The default maximum length of the identifier word is 32; as a rule, you have little need to change this setting.

Messages. Choosing **O**ptions, **C**ompiler, **M**essages produces the drop-down menu shown in figure 4.10. You use the command options in this menu to select error-message reporting for several categories of errors. Those command options are as follows:

- **D**isplay...

- **P**ortability...

- **A**NSI violations...

- **C**++ warnings...

- **F**requent errors...

- **L**ess frequent errors...

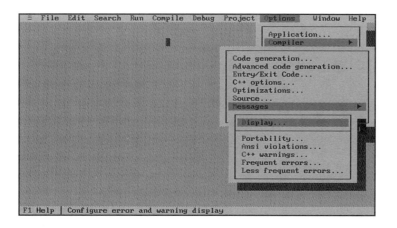

Fig. 4.10.
The Messages menu selections.

Here you can select what errors you would like to display on your screen when the errors are detected by the compiler. There are a variety of them. Some of these errors, such as portability errors, are not that important unless you're planning to move your source code from Turbo C++ to another compiler. Displaying all warning messages using the **D**isplay menu command is important so you can see if the program is correct.

You use the **D**isplay menu command to tell the compiler whether or not to display error messages and how to display those messages when translating a program. The **P**ortability menu command enables you to specify how and when to display C and C++ portability warnings, or warnings about problems that may occur later when porting your code to other compilers. The **A**nsi violations menu command specifies how and if warnings of ANSI errors are to be displayed. The **C**++ warnings menu command specifies how you want C++ warnings to display. The **F**requent errors and **L**ess frequent errors menu selections enable you to control how and when each type of error is displayed on your terminal.

Maintain the default settings for these messages unless you have a reason to either ignore errors or check for specific errors that require settings other than the default settings.

Names. The last menu command under the **O**ptions **C**ompiler menu is **N**ames. Use this command if you want to specify what segment names the compiler is to use when it compiles programs. When you choose **O**ptions, **C**ompiler, **N**ames, the Segment Names dialog box appears (see fig. 4.11).

Fig. 4.11.
The Segment
Names dialog box.

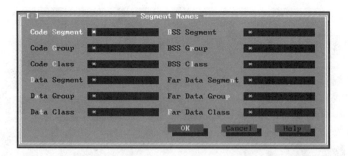

A *segment* is a portion of your program that is designated for a specific type of information. Your program uses code and data segments for information storage. The *code segment* of a program is designated for the program's code; that is, the program's logic as expressed in a form that the computer can execute. The *data segment* is the portion of the program that stores all data that is to be used by the program's code. For example, if you write a program to display the word Hello on the screen, that program's code—the logic that tells the computer to display something—is placed in the program's code segment. The word "hello"—the data that is to be displayed—is placed in the program's data segment.

As a C++ programmer, you need not be aware of segments or even know that they exist. Turbo C++ is designed to manage all the behind-the-scenes work of naming and managing segments; therefore, you can leave these options at their default settings.

Transfer Options

When you choose the **O**ptions, **Transfer** menu command, the Transfer dialog box appears (see fig. 4.12). This dialog box enables you to add or delete programs in the System menu of the IDE.

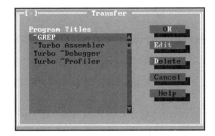

Fig. 4.12.
The Transfer dialog box.

As you recall from Chapter 3, "Using the Integrated Development Environment," the System menu is on the extreme left side of the main menu. You can enter items in the Transfer dialog box that then appear on the System menu and can be invoked without exiting Turbo C++.

The System menu is merely a convenience provided by the Turbo C++ IDE, so that you can run another program without exiting Turbo C++. For example, you may have a Rolodex program that you want to use while you are in the process of developing an application. Rather than close the Turbo C++ IDE and open the Rolodex program, you can use the Options Transfer dialog box to add the Rolodex program to the System menu's list of callable external programs. Thereafter, you can run the Rolodex program simply by selecting that option from the System menu.

When you execute an external program from within the IDE, you must exit the external program to return to the Turbo C++ IDE. In addition to the defaults displayed in the menu box (GREP, Turbo Assembler, Turbo Debugger, and Turbo Profiler), you can enter several other programs. These programs include the (ASCII) editors of your choice, utility programs, and even electronic mail packages.

To enter a new program in the Program Titles list box, select the blank line after the last entry in the list box. After selecting a blank line, you can use the **E**dit button to set the attributes for the program. When you select the **E**dit button, a dialog box appears in which you can enter the title to appear in the System menu, the default DOS path, the DOS command line necessary to execute the program, and (optionally) a hotkey, such as **F12**, to directly execute the program. After you enter this information, you can run the program by choosing it from the System menu of the IDE or by using the hotkey associated with the entry.

Choosing the **D**elete button in the Transfer dialog box removes an item from the System menu. To delete an item, select the item to be deleted and choose the **D**elete button.

Make Options

Using the **O**ptions, **M**ake menu command, you can display the Make dialog box shown in figure 4.13. In this dialog box you can set options such as what types of compile problems (including warnings, errors, or fatal errors) you would consider serious enough to stop the make (compile and link) process. You may also tell the compiler whether you would like to run the linker after a successful compile. In this dialog box, you can set certain conditions for Turbo C++ project management (see Chapter 5, "Working with Project Files," for further details on managing Turbo C++ projects). The Make dialog box enables you to customize what happens when you select the **C**ompile, **M**ake menu option. Until you begin working with advanced Turbo C++ programming, you need not change the default settings in this dialog box.

Fig. 4.13.
The Make dialog box.

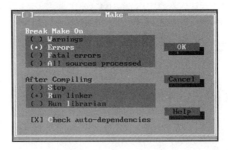

The Break Make On list box in the Make dialog box enables you to select on which types of errors the Project Manager (compile and link) is to stop. This list box contains four selections: **W**arnings, **E**rrors, **F**atal errors, and **A**ll sources processed. Selecting the **W**arnings option causes the make operation to stop if warning messages are displayed. If the **E**rrors option is selected, the make operation stops if errors are displayed. If the **F**atal errors option is selected, Project Manager stops only on fatal errors, and if **A**ll sources processed is selected, Project Manager continues to compile and link your project regardless of what warnings and errors occur during the process.

The settings in the After Compiling list box instruct the compiler to perform an action—**S**top, **R**un linker, or Run l**i**brarian—after the program compile is complete.

At the bottom of the Make dialog box is the **C**heck auto-dependencies check box. If this check box is selected, the Project Manager tells the compiler to check dependencies automatically. When checking dependencies, the compiler matches OBJ files located on the disk drive with corresponding C or CPP program files. The OBJ and source files are dependent upon one another (see Chapter 1 for more information on object and source files). If source files have changed due to normal program file editing, the compiler knows this and rebuilds the corresponding OBJ file. A *dependency* is any file that is required to support another file in the compile or link process.

Linker Options

The **O**ptions, **L**inker menu command is used to set options for the link process. The **O**ptions, **L**inker menu command produces two submenu options: **S**ettings and **L**ibraries. Selecting **S**ettings displays the Linker dialog box shown in figure 4.14. You can use the options in the Linker dialog box to configure the linker program (the program that links the code into executable form, in effect, as an EXE program). The Linker dialog box options are as follows:

- Options

- Map File

- Output

The Options list box contains selections that enable you to control specific areas of the linker's behavior. If you select the **I**nitialize segments check box, the linker initializes uninitialized segments (this initialization usually is unnecessary and has the effect of making your executable larger).

Fig. 4.14.
The Linker dialog
box.

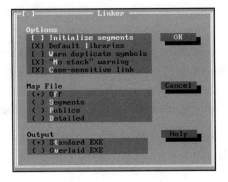

Selecting Default **l**ibraries tells the linker that undefined functions within
your program are to be found in a set of default libraries. Turbo C++ comes
with a set of default libraries containing functions that, for example, display
information to the screen, read and write files, and compute mathematical
equations. You may use third-party libraries, or libraries that did not come
with Turbo C++ to provide special functions for your application. When Default **l**ibraries is selected, the linker looks for all non-Turbo C++ as well as
Turbo C++ libraries; when deselected, the linker searches only the Turbo C++
libraries.

Selecting the **W**arn duplicate symbols option directs the linker to warn you if
you define a symbol more than once. A *symbol* is a word you define as a replacement for code or values. For example, you can define the word NUM-
BER_10 to represent the value of 10 in your code. Using defined symbols can
make your code easier to read.

Selecting "**N**o stack" warning directs the linker to warn you if the linker finds
no program stack. You usually get a No program stack message when working
with the **T**iny memory model.

Selecting **C**ase-sensitive link directs the linker to be case-sensitive to upper-
and lowercase characters when linking your program; for example, to find a
function typed as "dosomething" only if it is defined in a library as lowercase. If this option is deselected, the linker automatically registers all functions internally as uppercase.

You can use the selections in the Map File list box to select the type of map
file to be produced by the linker. A *map file* is a file that itemizes symbols and
functions used in your program. Selecting **O**ff tells the linker not to create a
map file. Selecting **S**egments instructs the linker to produce a map file that

includes a list of segments, the program start addresses, and any warning error messages produced during the link. Selecting **P**ublics instructs the linker to produce the same map file as that produced by selecting the **S**egments option, but with a list of public symbols added. Selecting **D**etailed tells the linker to create the same map file that selecting the **P**ublics option creates, but with a detailed segment map added.

The Linker dialog box Output list box contains two options, **St**andard EXE and O**v**erlaid EXE, with which you can specify your application type for linking purposes. Selecting **St**andard EXE produces a standard executable that runs under DOS. Selecting O**v**erlaid EXE creates an executable that can be overlaid, or swapped to and from the disk into memory.

Library Options

Choosing the **O**ptions, **L**inker, **L**ibrary menu commands displays the Libraries dialog box shown in figure 4.15. This dialog box contains all the available Turbo C++ libraries that you can use within your program. As mentioned earlier in this chapter, a library is a set of functions provided by Turbo C++ to do a specific type of task; for example, the graphics library contains functions that do graphics displays.

Turbo C++ enables you to select which library you want to link into your program. Although you can select all the Turbo C++ libraries, linking each library adds extra code to your program. Unless you are using the functions within the library, you have no reason to link it with your code. Using only the libraries you need minimizes the size of your program file.

You can include the following libraries in your program:

- **C**ontainer Class
- Turbo **V**ision
- **G**raphics library
- **S**tandard Run Time

To include a library, select the check box that precedes the library's name in the Libraries list box; the linker then automatically links that library. Each library has its own set of facilities that can be accessed by your application. For a further description of using libraries, see Chapter 14, "Using Library Functions."

Fig. 4.15.
The Libraries
dialog box.

Librarian Options

Choosing the **O**ptions, **Li**brarian menu command displays a dialog box that enables you to configure your Librarian options (see fig. 4.16). The Turbo C++ Librarian combines the OBJ files in your project with an LIB file. This dialog box includes the following selections:

- **G**enerate list file

- **C**ase-sensitive library

- **P**urge comment records

- Create **e**xtended dictionary

Fig. 4.16.
The Librarian
Options dialog
box.

If you select the **G**enerate list file option, the Librarian creates a list file (LST). This file lists the contents of your library as it is produced. Selecting **C**ase-sensitive library directs the Librarian to discern between upper- and lowercase letters. Selecting **P**urge comment records directs the Librarian to delete all comment records from the modules as they are added to the library. Selecting Create **e**xtended dictionary directs the Librarian to provide information that helps the linker process libraries at a greater speed.

Debugger Options

Choosing the **O**ptions, De**b**ugger command brings up the Debugger dialog box shown in figure 4.17. You can use the options in this dialog box to customize the integrated debugging facility of the IDE. You can set the compiler for Source Debugging, Display Swapping, Inspectors, and **P**rogram Heap Size.

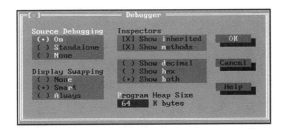

Fig. 4.17.
The Debugger
dialog box.

The Source Debugging option consists of three radio buttons with which you can select which debugger is to be used to debug your program. Selecting the **O**n radio button activates source debugging. Selecting **S**tandalone limits you to using the Turbo Debugger to debug your program. If you select the **N**one radio button, you can't use either debugging program.

You use the Display Swapping option to control when the debugger alters display windows during program execution. Selecting the Non**e** radio button tells the debugger never to swap the displays. Selecting the Sma**r**t radio button directs the debugger to display only code being executed. Selecting **A**lways tells the debugger to display debugging information every time a statement executes.

The Inspectors option contains two check boxes and a set of three radio buttons. These settings enable you to define how program objects are inspected.

The two check boxes, Show **i**nherited and Show **m**ethods, control how the debugger displays and summarizes methods used to inspect an object. Selecting Show **i**nherited tells the integrated debugger to display all member functions and methods. Selecting Show **m**ethods instructs the debugger to display member functions when a class is inspected.

You use the Inspectors radio buttons to control how the debugger displays values in the Inspector window. Selecting Show **d**ecimal directs the Inspector to display values as decimals; Show **h**ex displays values in hexadecimal format; Show **b**oth displays both Decimal and Hex. The value in the **P**rogram Heap Size text box specifies how much memory is used by a program when it is being debugged; 64K is the standard heap size.

Default Directory Settings

Choosing the **O**ptions, **D**irectories menu command produces the Directories dialog box shown in figure 4.18. In this dialog box, you can tell Turbo C++ where to look for include files, source files, or library files. This dialog box also allows you to set the directories where the compiler places EXE and OBJ files after compile operations.

Fig. 4.18.
The Directories
dialog box.

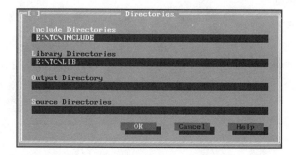

Environment Settings

By choosing the **O**ptions, **E**nvironment menu command you can set a variety of user preferences and configure the IDE to meet your individual needs. When you choose **O**ptions, **E**nvironment, another drop-down menu appears, as shown in figure 4.19. The options in this menu include:

- **P**references
- **E**ditor
- **M**ouse
- **D**esktop
- **S**tartup
- **C**olors

Fig. 4.19.
The Environment
menu selections.

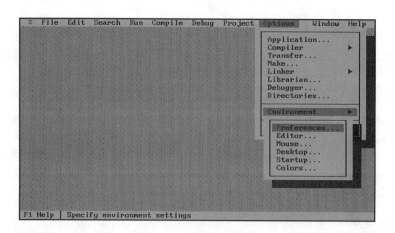

Choosing **P**references produces the dialog box shown in figure 4.20. In this dialog box you can specify the *screen size*, or the number of lines that display on your screen at one time. Programmers increase screen size to display additional information on the same screen, but many find the characters smaller and more difficult to read.

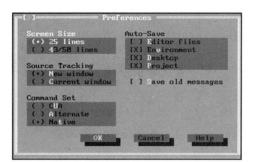

Fig. 4.20.

The Preference dialog box.

The Source Tracking option enables you to specify whether Turbo C++ opens an Edit window or uses the current window as you step through each line of your program; the corresponding options are **N**ew window and **C**urrent window.

The Command Set options enable you to select the Command set (hotkeys) to be used. Chapter 3 contains more information about hotkeys. Hotkeys let you perform menu commands by pressing one key or a set of keys, thus avoiding more time-consuming menu selections made with the keyboard or the mouse.

The Auto-Save options enable you to specify what parts of the current environment are to be saved to disk for use in the next IDE session. You can select to save **E**ditor files, En**v**ironment, **D**esktop, and **P**roject.

The last option, **S**ave old messages, specifies whether Turbo C++ is to add messages to the message window as successive compiles are performed.

Choosing the **O**ptions, **E**nvironment, **E**ditor menu commands displays the Editor Options dialog box (see fig. 4.21). In this dialog box you can customize the functionality of the IDE editor (refer to Chapter 6). The settings in this dialog box control user preferences that Turbo C++ uses as defaults.

Choosing the **O**ptions, **E**nvironment, **M**ouse menu commands produces the Mouse Options dialog box shown in figure 4.22. Using this dialog box, you can customize the way your mouse operates; you can specify the actions of the right mouse button, the amount of time that can elapse between clicks in order for the action to count as a double-click, and you can reverse the functionality of the mouse buttons. The Reverse mouse buttons option typically is used by left-handed mouse users who find that the reversed functionality makes the mouse easier to use.

Fig. 4.21.
The Editor Options dialog box.

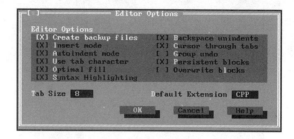

Fig. 4.22.
The Mouse Options dialog box.

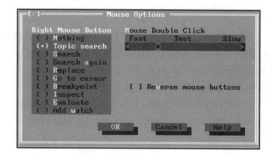

The Desktop Preferences dialog box appears when you choose the **O**ptions, **E**nvironment, **D**esktop menu commands (see fig. 4.23). You can use this dialog box to set options that tell the IDE what to save after the IDE quits. Here you can tell the IDE to save the Environment, Desktop, and the Project. The Environment includes information such as editor macros, color tables, and mouse preferences. The Desktop includes information on history lists for input boxes, the location of a window on a screen, and layout of the windows on the desktop. The Project includes information on the Compiler, Linker, and Make options.

Fig. 4.23.
The Desktop Preferences dialog box.

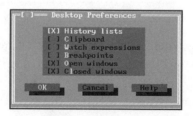

Choosing **O**ptions, **E**nvironment, **S**tartup produces the Startup Options dialog box (see fig. 4.24). In this dialog box you can specify how you want your desktop to look when the IDE is invoked. The Video Startup Options box allows you to set three options: Save Entire Palette, **S**now Checking, and **D**ual Monitor Mode. The Save Entire Palette option tells the IDE to save the entire EGA or VGA video palette into a buffer when switching between graphics and text mode. The **S**now Checking option is turned on to correct problems with snow on your monitor (little dots flashing on the screen). The **D**ual Monitor mode option allows you to run your program on one monitor and debug it on another. You can also select Swap **F**ile Drive, use EMS Memory, or use Extended Memory for use by the IDE. When selecting Swap **F**ile Drive you specify a disk drive that Turbo C++ will use as a temporary storage file if Turbo C++ runs out of memory during compile and link operations. Selecting **E**MS (Expanded Memory Specification) or E**x**tended Memory tells the IDE the amount of Extended or EMS memory to use during compile and link operations. (See Chapter 1 for more information on EMS and Extended memory.) The Video Mode options enable you to specify the type of monitor you are using, or to direct the IDE to detect your monitor type automatically as the IDE is invoked.

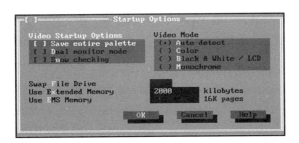

Fig. 4.24.
The Startup Options dialog box.

The Colors dialog box appears when you choose **O**ptions, **E**nvironment, **C**olors (see fig. 4.25). Using the options in this dialog box, you can customize the colors of menus, windows, selection bars, and other IDE features.

Saving Your Options

When you are happy with the options you have selected, you can save them using the **O**ptions, **S**ave menu command. When you choose this command, the Save Options dialog box appears, as shown in figure 4.26. By selecting check boxes in this dialog box, you can save to permanent storage your option settings, the search dialog boxes, and the settings in the **O**ptions menu and dialog boxes.

Fig. 4.25.
The Colors dialog
box.

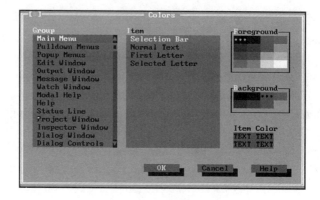

Fig. 4.26.
The Save Options
dialog box.

When you save these settings, Turbo C++ stores the options in three files:

- Your customized environment (TCCONFIG.TC)

- Your desktop (*.DSK)

- Your project (*.PRJ)

These files are only useful for the Turbo C++ IDE and cannot be read as a text
file.

Summary

In this chapter, you learned about the IDE configuration settings. You learned
that by using the **O**ptions area of the IDE, you can establish how the compiler, debugger, and linker work with your program. You learned that you can
customize such things as screen colors, screen sizes, mouse settings, and System menu selections.

In this chapter, you learned the following:

- How to use the Standard, Overlay, and Library options in the Application Generation Options dialog box to set your compiler and linker
defaults quickly and easily.

■ How to use the Compiler configuration options to customize the way in which the Turbo C++ compiler creates your application. With these options you can set such things as code generation options, entry/exit code configuration, C++ options, and application optimization settings.

■ How the Make options enable you to customize the methods in which the Project Manager creates your applications, such as by determining how the IDE breaks on errors, and whether the linker is run automatically after a successful compile.

■ To use the Linker options to configure how your application program is linked.

■ How to use the Library and Librarian options to specify the libraries you want to use with your application and how the Librarian is to use these files.

■ How using the Debugger options can help you configure such things as source debugging and object inspectors.

■ How other option settings enable you to set user preferences such as default directories used by Turbo C++, and how things like the editor, mouse, desktop, and screen colors are customized in the IDE.

■ How to save your configuration for use in later IDE sessions.

Chapter 5

Working with Project Files

Anyone who has ever written or edited a book can tell you that a difficult part of the process is keeping track of chapters, topics, appendixes, indexes, table of contents, and so on. These components of a book must be managed as the book progresses. For example, as a chapter or topic changes during the editing process, other components such as the index or table of contents must change as well. Making sure that these changes are made is difficult at best.

To help track changes in manuscripts and control how each change affects the final product, writers and editors use word processors, document managers, and other such tools. This ability to manage groups of related items, and the effects each item has on the entire product, is the idea behind Turbo C++ project files.

Applications usually grow in size and, as they do, you need to separate the source code into more manageable files. After you separate the code, you need a tool to help you manage the multiple source files. Project files is that tool. Project files are managed by using the Project menu selection from the main IDE menu. The options in that menu enable you to do the following:

- Create a new project file

- Open an existing project file

- Add or delete files from your project file

- Customize your project file by setting available project file options

- Define which application compiler is used for compiling your source code

The purpose of this chapter is to introduce you to project files and how they are used in building an application, and the Project Manager facilities of the IDE. You will walk through each project file operation as the concepts are presented. You should try to perform each operation as you go through it. In this chapter, you learn about the following:

- Working with project files

- Setting project file options

- Auto-dependency checking using project files

- Recording information about a project

- Setting linker, library, or debugger options

- Creating applications

What is a Project File?

A *project file* is a database of source files and other information you need when your application uses more than one source file. Most complex applications are made up of many source files. Programmers prefer to use many files to make their applications more modular. When building an application, the compiler translates each source file into an object module by using a translator such as the Turbo C++ compiler, or Turbo Assembler. After the translation, the linker links each module into one single executable. Invoking this executable file runs the program.

The project manager built into the IDE manages this process by using project files as a kind of "blueprint" for your application. A project file includes the following information:

- The location of source files on your hard disk

- The location where you would like the executable file placed when the compile and link operation is complete

- Source file dependencies, meaning information included about which file should be compiled before other files are compiled

- Data size, code size, and file sizes information from the latest compile and link operation used to figure out which modules must be recompiled because of changes in the source file

- Instructions the compiler uses when building the executable file

Working with Projects

Programmers manage project files by using the Project menu of the IDE (see fig. 5.1). As you can see, the following menu commands are available:

- **O**pen project

- **C**lose project

- **A**dd item

- **D**elete item

- **L**ocal options

- **I**nclude files

From this menu you can create, open, close, add items, delete items, and set options for your project file.

Fig. 5.1.
Using the Project menu of the IDE.

Creating and Opening Projects

You can open an existing project file by using several methods:

- The first two methods are self-explanatory. For example, from the DOS prompt enter the following command. If only one project file is in the current directory, the Turbo C++ assumes that it is the project file you want to use, and opens it.

    tc YOURPROJ.PRJ

- Load the project file from the IDE Project menu by invoking the Open menu command

The first two methods are self-explanatory. The most popular method of locating and opening an existing project file is to use the IDE. When you invoke the Open Project menu command, the Open Project File dialog box appears, as shown in figure 5.2. Change directories by using the file dialog box. Selecting "..\" from the list of files changes your current directory to the parent directory in the MS-DOS directory hierarchy. If you need to move to a directory below your current directory, select the directory name from the file list. Directory names end with a "/".

To create a project file, select the same menu command (Open Project) from the Project menu. Using the same file dialog box used to open an existing project file, you can provide a new project name. If you type in a file name that doesn't already exist, a new project file will be created.

Fig. 5.2.
Opening a project by using the Project File dialog box.

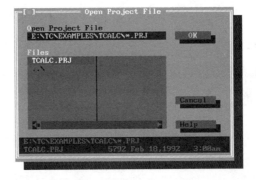

After you've opened an existing project, or created a new one, the Project Window appears and should look similar to figure 5.3. At this point, you are ready to add source files to the project by using the Project menu commands. Of course, what you see in your project file may differ, but the basic concepts are the same.

Fig. 5.3.
Viewing the project file windows from the IDE.

Table 5.1 summarizes the actions you can perform from the IDE project window.

Table 5.1. Actions that can be performed from the project window.	
Key	**Description**
F1	Invokes the IDE help facility for project file management
Ins	Same effect as invoking the Project Add menu command, adding an item to a project window
Del	Deletes from the project list
^O	Opens the dialog box, allowing you to set options for a particular item in the list
Space bar	Displays include file information
F10	Takes you to the Project menu selection from the main menu

To edit a file listed in an existing project file, select the source file by using your keyboard or your mouse then press Enter, or double-click the mouse. The file you selected is placed in an IDE editor window (see fig. 5.4) where you can make changes to the source code and save the file back to disk. Many programmers who manage large projects and several source files find this method of editing program files convenient.

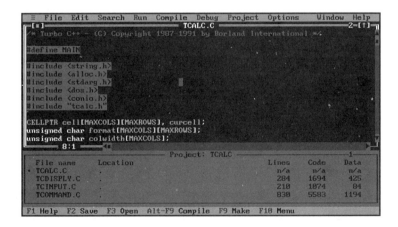

Fig. 5.4.
Editing a source file in the Project Window.

Adding and Deleting from Project Files

Now that you've created or opened a project file, you can begin adding or deleting source files from the project. To Add an item, access the Add item menu command and the Add to Project List dialog box appears as shown in figure 5.5. When highlighting a source file from the file dialog (using the cursor or your mouse), use the Add button to place a required source file into the project file's list.

Fig. 5.5.

The Add to Project List dialog box.

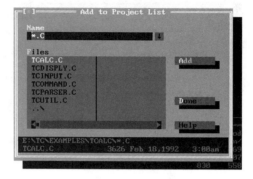

You can select these files in one of two ways: enter the file name in the Name input box, or choose a file from the file list box by using your keyboard or your mouse. After you've added the files you need, press the Done button, which closes the dialog and saves your selections.

Desktop Files

Each project file has a desktop file associated with it. The file has the same file name as the project you are working on, with the file extension DSK. This file is loaded and saved automatically as you enter and leave a project. It contains miscellaneous information about the project such as:

- Breakpoints

- The context information for the desktop, such as positions in files, bookmarks, and so on

- Contents of the Clipboard

- Watch information

A project file uses its own private desktop file, which belongs to that project file. When a project file changes, it causes the layout you see on your screen to change. When creating a new project file, the IDE uses the current state of your desktop as the default for that project file. In other words, the new project file inherits the characteristics of the existing desktop.

Default Files

If a project file is not loaded, then two default files are used as the global place holders for project information. The default files are as follows:

- TCDEF.DPR

- TCDEF.DSK

Generally, these files can be found in the \BIN directory of Turbo C++. If the IDE is executed from a directory that does not contain these files and no project file is loaded, these files set up your desktop as the default. When you exit the IDE, these files are updated with the current project-related options. When the IDE is invoked again, the options you set in your previous project are put into effect automatically.

Using Local Options

By default, Turbo C++ builds projects that use Turbo C++ and Turbo Assembler as the language translators. Programmers have the option to create projects by using both C++ and assembler code.

Generally, if you are planning to program only with Turbo C++ and sometimes with Turbo Assembler, there is no need to alter the Local Options for your project. More complex projects may require support for third-party or stand-alone translators that can be applied to the modules included in your project. This type of customization is reserved for only the advanced Turbo C++ programmers. Make sure you understand the options completely before making changes.

By using the Local Options menu command for every source file you have included in your project file, you can select or determine the following:

- The project to use as a target file

- Whether the module is an overlay

- The command line options to pass to the program

- What to call the module produced and where it should be placed

- Whether the modules should contain debug information

- Whether the module is included in the link operation

To set these options, access the Local Options menu command and the Local Options dialog box appears (see fig. 5.6). This dialog box contains a listing of the transfer programs defined by default. You can use the arrow keys or your mouse to select items in the Project File Translators list. The options area also contains areas where you can define Command Line Options for the translators, the Output Path, and overlay, debugging, and link settings.

Turbo C++ by default uses the following for each module:

- No command-line override options

- The Output directory is used for output

- No overlays

- Debug information is included (the default)

Fig. 5.6.
Using the Local
Options dialog
box.

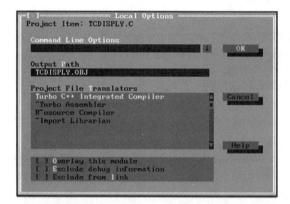

Using Your Own Translators

To modify a module that uses stand-alone tools or translators in lieu of the defaults (Turbo C++ and Turbo Assembler), you should first define the tool or translator as a valid Project File Translator in the Transfer dialog box of the Options menu.

To define a stand-alone translator, you need to enter your Tool Name in the Program Path input box, update the Program title information, and sometimes enter a macro such as $EDNAME (the name of the file in the active editor) for the Command line information. Now select the Translator check box and press New. Your tool is now listed in the Program Titles list box.

Your tool or translator may require different options. Consult your documentation or technical support for details.

By using the Project menu, select the Local options menu command. Your tool is now listed as a valid choice in the Project File Translator list and you can select your translator name from the Project File Translator list box for a particular module. Your own translator is now used in the same manner as the other translators listed. Again, this type of customization is for advanced Turbo C++ programmers. Usually, there is not a need to make changes to Local options unless an application explicitly requires it.

Viewing Header Files

As you will discover in subsequent chapters, *header files* (.H or .HPP files that contain C source code called by the preprocessor) are placed in C/C++ programs

```
#include <filename.h>
```

to include functions that may be required in your source files. As you will discover in subsequent chapters, header files are called from within your source files to bring in additional source code into your program. Using this option, you can display all of the header files that your source files call in your project.

Of course, the purpose of the project file is to control the construction of an application program. You can build an application by using a project file with the Compiler section of the IDE.

The first four menu commands listed under Compile are as follows:

- Compile

- Make

- Link

- Build all

The Compile menu command compiles the program in the active editor window. The Make menu command uses the project file to make a project target. The Make menu command only compiles the files that have been changed since the last Make operation. If you are working with project files, the Make menu command is the best choice to build and rebuild your application.

The Build All menu command recompiles all the files in your project file regardless of whether they have been changed. This option is the best if you want to process all your source files in the project file simultaneously, but it does require additional compile time.

Auto-Dependency Checking

The Project file manager collects auto-dependency information at compile time. The Project Manager automatically checks dependencies between source files listed in the project file and the corresponding object files. During the application programming task, it is common for C/C++ programs to include several header files (.H or .HPP). If these files change, you want the Make facility to understand this and recompile the routines and link them into the executable.

If you have selected the Auto-Dependencies option from the Options menu and the Make menu command, the Make facility gathers date and time information for all source files included in the project. When Make is invoked, the date and time information is compared with the date and time of the last compile. If the dates and times are different, that particular module is recompiled and linked into the executable.

If the auto-dependency option is not selected, the Make facility checks the object files with the source files. The program is recompiled if any differences are detected.

If you change compiler options (Memory Models, and so on), you might assume the Make facility recognizes the change and recompiles that file. This is not true. If a compiler option is altered, you must invoke the Build All menu command to recompile all the files.

Making Notes

Many programmers use pads of paper to make notes about a particular programming project. This process certainly is effective, but not automated. The IDE provides you with a Project Notes window (see fig. 5.7) as a selection under the Windows menu that can keep electronic text records of your project. In that window you can record details such as the following:

- To-do lists

- Maintenance logs

- Records of bug fixes

- Anything you feel you need to record

This information is stored along with your other project information. This window is basically a normal IDE editor window and all the normal editing functions are applicable. You can print your project notes by accessing the main menu and selecting File, then the Print menu command.

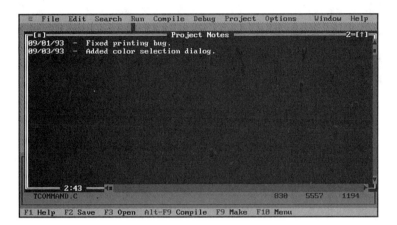

Fig. 5.7.
Using the Project Notes window to record information about a project.

Tracking Errors

Syntax errors are generated when the compiler locates problems with the program. Errors messages display in a Message window, usually at the bottom of the screen. Remember that you can select the type of message you want the Make operation to stop on by setting the Break Make On options. These settings are located by accessing the Options menu and selecting the Make menu command, which brings up the Make dialog box.

When you compile a project by selecting the Make menu command, the Compiling window displays the files currently being compiled. If errors or warnings are found, they are totaled for the entire Make operation in the Compiling window. If errors or warning messages occur, you'll see a message like that shown in figure 5.8.

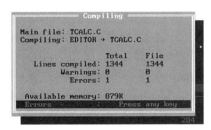

Fig. 5.8.
Viewing Compiler error messages.

After the Compiler message error appears on your screen, then press any key? You can scroll up and down the message window to browse through the errors and warnings as shown in figure 5.9.

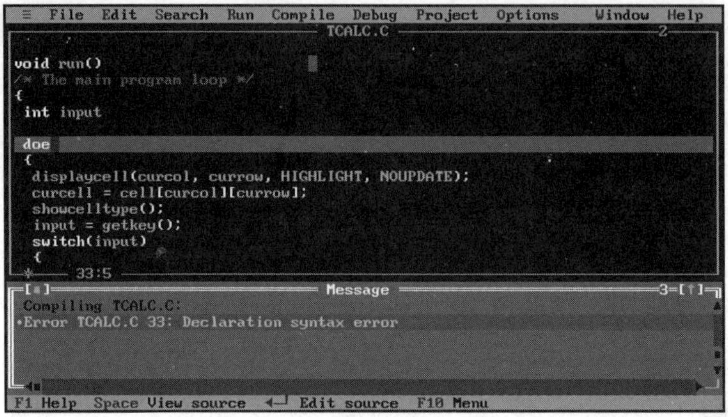

Fig. 5.9.
Locating the error by using the Message window.

```
≡  File  Edit  Search  Run  Compile  Debug  Project  Options      Window  Help
┌──────────────────────────────── TCALC.C ──────────────────────────────2─┐
│void run()                            █                                    │
│/* The main program loop */                                                │
│{                                                                          │
│  int input                                                                │
│                                                                           │
│  doe                                                                      │
│  {                                                                        │
│    displaycell(curcol, currow, HIGHLIGHT, NOUPDATE);                      │
│    curcell = cell[curcol][currow];                                        │
│    showcelltype();                                                        │
│    input = getkey();                                                      │
│    switch(input)                                                          │
│    {                                                                      │
│─── 33:5                                                                   │
├─[■]─────────────────────────── Message ────────────────────────3─[↑]─┐   │
│Compiling TCALC.C:                                                      ▲  │
│•Error TCALC.C 33: Declaration syntax error                               │
│                                                                          ▼ │
│◄■                                                                    ►     │
└──────────────────────────────────────────────────────────────────────────┘
 F1 Help  Space View source  ◄─┘ Edit source   F10 Menu
```

By double-clicking your mouse, or pressing Enter, you can automatically load the offending program file into the IDE editor causing the problem, and the suspect line that contains the error is highlighted.

If the program file is already loaded into the IDE editor, the first line that caused the program error or warning is highlighted. This saves time, because the IDE informs you of the error or warning that a programming mistake was generated, but also it automatically invoked the editor, and placed the cursor at the location of the problem. A Clear advantage when developing applications.

You can clear your messages by accessing the main menu and selecting Compile, then Remove Message. This step deletes all the current messages displayed in the message window.

Project Files versus Make Files

Besides using project files to control your multiple source file applications, the MAKE.EXE program of the Turbo C++ command line compiler is functionally equivalent to using project files with the IDE compiler.

Make files are created either by programmers using ASCII editors such as the Turbo C++ IDE editor, or by converted project files (explained later in this section). Make files resemble programs unto themselves. Because the IDE and project files are used in this book, you'll learn about only the major features of Make. For more information on Make, consult your Turbo C++ documentation.

MAKE.EXE and make files perform the following tasks:

■ Interpret a special file called a make file. This file contains information on source files, object files, the location of the library files, and so on, used to build an executable file.

■ Check the time and date of each object file with the time and date of the source files to perform selective recompiles. If a difference is noted, the files are recompiled.

■ Invoke the linker to process object files

■ Invoke the compiler to process source files

These tasks can be performed by both the Turbo C++ command line compiler and IDE Make facilities by using project files or make files, respectively. Make files were the original means of constructing executable files from multiple source files. While some programmers find that make files are much more flexible for large programming projects, others find that project files are much easier to learn and use.

As with the project files, make files rely on the time and date stamps that DOS places on each file as it changes. To compile an application with a make file, enter the following from the DOS prompt:

make -f myprogrm.mak

MYPROGRM.MAK is the name of the make file being passed in on the command line. Many command line options are associated with make, and the make files use a "pseudo" programming language, allowing such things as conditional compiles and error handling procedures.

Make file, like project file, depends on the time and date stamps of DOS. If your clock battery is dead, the time and date may be incorrect. An incorrect time and date confuses both the command line and IDE Make facilities. Always check your time and date before using the Turbo C++ Make facilities.

If you're a project file user but want to use make files instead, you can use the utility PRJ2MAKE.EXE (Project to Make) to convert Turbo C++ project files to make files. The utility is located in the /BIN directory of Turbo C++. For example, to convert the Turbo C++ project file MYPROJ.PRJ to a make file, enter the following command:

prj2mak myproj.prj myproj.mak

If the utility works, you're returned to the DOS prompt. In your current directory, you should see a new file named MYPROJ.MAK. Try one on your own. Refer to the TCALC example project that comes with your Turbo C++ example programs. By invoking prj2mak, you can create a TCALC.MAK file for TCALC.PRJ that looks like listing 5.1. If the utility doesn't work, error messages are generated and the make file is not created.

Listing 5.1. The TCALC.MAK Make file.

```
#          *Translator Definitions*
CC = tcc +TCALC.CFG
TASM = TASM
TLIB = tlib
TLINK = tlink
LIBPATH = ..\..\LIB
INCLUDEPATH = ..\..\INCLUDE

#       *Implicit Rules*
.c.obj:
  $(CC) -c {$< }

.cpp.obj:
  $(CC) -c {$< }

#       *List Macros*


EXE_dependencies =  \
 tcalc.obj \
 tcdisply.obj \
 tcinput.obj \
 tcommand.obj \
 tcparser.obj \
 tcutil.obj

#       *Explicit Rules*
tcalc.exe: tcalc.cfg $(EXE_dependencies)
  $(TLINK) /v/x/c/L$(LIBPATH) @&&¦
c0s.obj+
tcalc.obj+
 tcdisply.obj+
tcinput.obj+
tcommand.obj+
tcparser.obj+
tcutil.obj
tcalc
        # no map file
graphics.lib+
emu.lib+
maths.lib+
cs.lib
¦
¦
```

```
#        *Individual File Dependencies*
tcalc.obj: tcalc.cfg tcalc.c
    IMPLIB TCALC.LIB TCALC.EXE

tcdisply.obj: tcalc.cfg tcdisply.c

tcinput.obj: tcalc.cfg tcinput.c

tcommand.obj: tcalc.cfg tcommand.c

tcparser.obj: tcalc.cfg tcparser.c

tcutil.obj: tcalc.cfg tcutil.c

#        *Compiler Configuration File*
tcalc.cfg: tcalc.mak
  copy &&¦
-v
-vi-
-w-ret
-w-nci
-w-inl
-wpin
-wamb
-wamp
-w-par
-wasm
-wcln
-w-cpt
-wdef
-w-dup
-w-pia
-wsig
-wnod
-w-ill
-w-sus
-wstv
-wucp
-wuse
-w-ext
 -w-ias
-w-ibc
-w-pre
-w-nst
-I$(INCLUDEPATH)
-L$(LIBPATH)
-P-.C
¦ tcalc.cfg
```

You can create TCALC.EXE by using the TCALC.PRJ project file and the IDE,
or by entering the following command at the DOS prompt:

make -f tcalc.mak

Take a few minutes to study this make file. Notice how the directories are set, the translators defined, and the object files tracked. If you need to make changes in this make file, you have to use an ASCII editor. If you make a mistake in the make file, you cannot alter Make settings by using dialog boxes; instead, you have to debug the make file in much the same way you debug a program.

Maintaining and Saving Projects

Each time you use project files they are automatically saved to your hard disk; there is no formal save procedure. To close a project file, access the Project menu, then choose Close project.

Other handy project file management tips include the following:

- Keep your project file in the same directory as your source code. This procedure will help you find the file on the hard drive when you need it.

- Back up your project files with your source code. If lost, you can spend hours attempting to reconstruct all the correct source file lists and options that project files contain.

- Use the Project Notes window to maintain information on the project. Many programmers work on several projects at once, and many important details can be forgotten. Also, if you're a consultant, the Project Notes windows can be used to maintain a list of hours worked on a particular project.

- If several programmers work on the same file, make sure that the project file options are coordinated. If one programmer changes an object, that action that changes the object could very well change the functionality of the entire application. Generally, these types of problems occur when programmers share files on networks.

- Convert your project files to make files only if you prefer to use the Turbo C++ command line compiler. Converting back to project files can be troublesome.

- Make use of the help system. Its ability to assist you with any type of project file management function makes it an invaluable resource.

Summary

In this chapter you learned how to use Turbo C++ project files effectively. You learned that project files are useful tools for controlling large applications that use many source files or require other specialized options. Project files also allow flexibility in how these large applications are built, and save time by selectively compiling only the files that need to be recompiled. The topics covered in this chapter include the following:

- Project files control multi-source file applications.

- Project files are used to maintain the location for source code and executable files, source file dependencies, size information, and compiler instructions.

- Project files are managed in much the same way you manage source code.

- Desktop files are associated with project files and maintain desktop attributes from session to session.

- Default files are used to provide a template for new projects, or a default desktop.

- Local Options can be set to control the translator used to translate source files in the project list.

- You are allowed to use your own language translators in a project by configuring the project by using Local Options.

- You can browse through all the include files associated with a project by accessing the Project menu and selecting Include files.

- You can use your own libraries by including them in the project file.

- The Auto-dependency facility controls how the Make facility checks the dates and times of source files and their relationships to one another to control compile operations.

- You can use the Project Notes window to record any information about the project.

- Errors are tracked in a message window that allows you to edit and locate problems in source files that are causing errors and warnings.

- Make files are the functional equivalent of project files for the Turbo C++ command line compiler.

- The PRJ2MAKE.EXE utility is used to convert a project file to a make file.

Chapter 6

Using the Editor

An editor enables you to enter and modify source code in a program file. The Turbo C++ IDE supports program editing through the IDE editor window. This window is created when the editor is invoked from the IDE. The IDE editor is a complete and powerful editor that can create and edit any program or ASCII file.

The IDE editor is simple to use; most programmers pick it up quickly. Yet the IDE editor is rich in features and can handle all of the text manipulation operations that programmers require, such as the following:

- Creating a program

- Adding information to the program

- Deleting information from the program

- Moving code

- Copying code

- Searching the file

- Searching and replacing strings in the file

Learning the ins and outs of the editor now can save you loads of programming time later. For example, instead of replacing several program variable names one at a time, you simply can invoke the search-and-replace facility of the IDE editor; rather than retype several lines of program code, you can use a cut-and-paste operation. As a rule, the best programmers are those that are most skilled with their program editors. A few minutes spent learning the editor is bound to payoff several times over when you are programming in Turbo C++.

This chapter introduces you to the editor that comes with the Turbo C++ IDE and walks you through several editor operations, including those just listed. If possible, use the IDE editor to try out what you learn, as you learn it.

Hundreds of editors are available to edit Turbo C++ source code. Many programmers prefer to use their own editor. Turbo C++ can use third-party editors, and their use also is described in this chapter. Remember, however, that IDE's built-in editor is powerful enough to meet most, if not all, of your Turbo C++ programming needs.

Using the Editor Keyboard Commands

If you use a word processor, you are familiar with *keyboard commands*. Keyboard commands perform operations such as deleting text, moving the curser, scrolling the editor window, inserting a line, and many other operations. To perform these editing operations quickly, Turbo C++ provides a set of cursor keyboard commands, shown in table 6.1.

Table 6.1. Cursor keyboard commands.

Function	Key
Character left	Left arrow
Character right	Right arrow
Word left	Ctrl+Left arrow
Word right	Ctrl+Right arrow
Line up	Up arrow
Line down	Down arrow
Scroll up one line	Ctrl+W
Scroll down one line	Ctrl+Z
Page up	PgUp
Page down	PgDn
Beginning of line	Home

Function	Key
End of line	End
Top of window	Ctrl+Q+E
Bottom of window	Ctrl+Q+X
Top of file	Ctrl+Q+R
Bottom of file	Ctrl+Q+C
Move to previous position	Ctrl+P

Using the block of text you entered earlier, try some of the operations just mentioned. Notice how each command affects the text. For example, to move a character to the left or right, you can use the left and right arrows respectively. To move one word to the left or right, you use Ctrl+left arrow or Ctrl+right arrow. You can move the cursor to the beginning of the line by pressing the Home key, and can move to the end of the line by pressing the End key.

Other keyboard commands are not so obvious. For example, Ctrl+Q+E moves the cursor to the top of the editor window, Ctrl+Q+R moves the cursor to the top of the file, and Ctrl+P moves the cursor to the previous position in the window.

Of course, using these keyboard commands takes practice. You may want to keep a copy of the preceeding table nearby until you get the hang of it. Remember: Help F1 is always available to guide you through keyboard commands. Try each command, if you have a chance, to see how each affects the program you are editing. You need not worry about "ruining" your program by experimenting with these commands: the changes you make in the file are only permanent if you choose to save the file (covered later).

Deleting Lines and Text

From time to time, you may need to remove several characters or several lines from the program file. To accomplish this task, the Turbo C++ editor provides several keyboard commands that you can use to perform delete operations. Table 6.2 summarizes these commands.

Table 6.2. Delete commands.	
Command	**Key**
Delete character	Del
Delete character to left	Backspace
Delete line	Ctrl+Y
Delete to end of line	Ctrl+Q+Y
Delete word	Ctrl+T

Using the keyboard commands to delete text is a simple operation. For example, you press the Del key to delete the character where the cursor is located. To delete an entire line, use Ctrl+Y. To delete all text to the end of the line, press Ctrl+Q+Y, and to delete a word where the cursor is located, press Ctrl+T.

Creating a Program with the IDE Editor

You learn by doing. One of the best ways to learn to use the IDE editor is to create a program. This way, you'll understand the basics of the editor quickly, since program file editing usually entails a wide range of edit operations. To begin this task, you simply choose the **F**ile option from the main menu, then choose **N**ew from the File drop-down menu (see fig. 6.1). When you choose this option, the default program window NONAME00.CPP becomes the active window (see fig. 6.2). For now, don't worry about whether or not you like this window's name. You can change it later.

At the bottom-left corner of the editor window you can see the number of the current line and the number of the cursor's column position. If you modify the file at any time, an asterisk (*) appears to the left of the line numbers.

Adding Text

If the editor window is active, and you are not currently in a menu or a dialog box, you can begin entering program code. You enter text in the IDE editor window in much the same manner as you enter words into a word processor. The text appears at the current cursor position, usually at the upper-left portion of the editor window (see fig. 6.3).

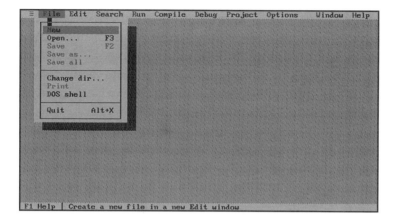

Fig. 6.1.
Creating a new program by using the New menu command.

Familiarizing Yourself

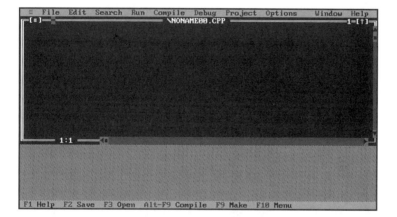

Fig. 6.2.
The default program editor window (NONAME00.CPP).

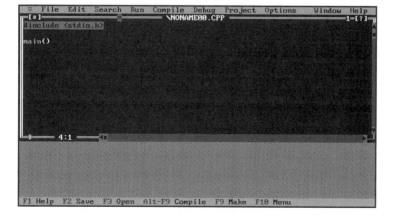

Fig. 6.3.
Inserting text into the editor window.

Using the editor is intuitive to most beginners. When the editor begins, it is in *insert* mode—as you enter program code, the code is placed at the location of the cursor. Any existing text to the right of the cursor position is "pushed" ahead to make room for inserted text. You can switch to *overwrite* mode if you want to overwrite existing text. You switch back and forth from insert to overwrite mode by pressing the Insert key. Notice how the cursor changes from an underline (_ = insert) to a block (n = overwrite,) denoting the current mode. Give it a try. Enter a block of text to get the feel of it. Enter the following:

```
This is the way we
insert information
into a program file.
```

Now try to change the text by using the insert mode, then the overwrite mode. The editor is now ready to begin entering code into a program file.

Using Undo

Made a mistake? Well, Turbo C++ comes to the rescue. In the Edit pull-down menu, you find a menu command called Undo. As its name implies, this menu command has the power to undo your last operation. If you unintentionally delete a line of your program, you can use Undo to recover it. If you performed a copy or move operation on the wrong portion of text, Undo can put things back the way you found the file.

You can choose **E**dit, **U**ndo to execute the Undo command, or you can simply press Alt+Backspace. You can undo most editing operations by invoking Undo. The command undoes one operation at a time only for the last altered or deleted line. Each operation is undone in reverse chronological order. Therefore, not only can you undo your last mistake, but your last several mistakes as well.

The Undo command does have a few limits, however:

- Undo cannot undo any toggle setting that has a global effect, such as Ins/Ovr.

- Undo can work only on the last changed or deleted line.

Adding Lines and Text

To add a line in the program you need only press Enter. The cursor moves to the first column of the new line and is ready to for you to enter new code. As described in the keyboard commands table, you can move your cursor around the screen by pressing the up, down, right, or left arrows. You can move quickly up and down the editor windows by pressing the PageUp or PageDown keys respectively. Table 6.3 describes the keyboard commands that can add lines or text in your file.

Table 6.3. Insert Commands.	
Command	**Key**
Insert line	Ctrl+N
Insert mode on/off	Ins

To insert a new line in your program file, press Ctrl+N. As mentioned previously, you can toggle the insert mode on and off by pressing Ins. When insert mode is on, text that you enter is placed in front of the text currently in the file. As you enter information, the text moves to the right. It is not overwritten. If the insert mode is off, anything you enter overwrites information already in the file.

Using Other Commands

In addition to the basic keyboard commands listed in table 6.1, Turbo C++ has several keyboard commands that perform other, more specialized operations. Table 6.4 describes these keyboard commands. Many of these commands invoke menu commands that also can be selected through standard menu operations. If one or more of these operations are common in your editing routine, you can save time by invoking them with the keyboard commands. Your personal preference, however, can determine whether you invoke these commands through the menus or with the keyboard commands.

Table 6.4. Other keyboard commands.	
Command	**Keys**
Auto indent mode on/off	Ctrl+O+I
Cursor through tabs on/off	Ctrl+O+R
Find place marker	Ctrl+Q+n*
Help	F1

(continues)

Table 6.4. Continued.

Command	Keys
Help index	Shift+F1
Insert control character	Ctrl+P
Optimal fill mode on/off	Ctrl+O+F
Pair matching	Ctrl+Q+[Ctrl+Q+]
Save file	Ctrl+K+S
Search	Ctrl+Q+F
Search and replace	Ctrl+Q+A
Set marker	Ctrl+K+n*
Tabs mode on/off	Ctrl+O+T
Topic search help	Ctrl+F1
Undo	Alt+Backspace
Unindent mode on/off	Ctrl+O+U

* n is a number from 0 to 9.

These keyboard commands work in the same manner as those discussed earlier in this chapter. For example, the Ctrl+K+S keyboard command performs a file save operation (described below), Ctrl+F1 brings up a topic search help screen, and Ctrl+P enables you to insert a control character into your program.

Moving and Copying Text

The IDE editor, like most editors, supports block *copy* and *move* operations on text in your program file. Programmers find themselves using these facilities often to relocate portions of program code, copy a useful function from one program to another, or to delete a segment of the program that is no longer needed.

If you are a Windows user, you already are familiar with many of the concepts about to be presented. The Turbo C++ Edit menu options resemble the Edit menu options of many Windows programs (see fig. 6.4). When you

choose the **E**dit main menu command, the Edit pull-down menu appears.
This menu contains the following commands:

- **U**ndo

- **R**edo

- **C**ut

- **C**opy

- **P**aste

- **C**lear

- **C**opy example

- **S**how clipboard

Fig. 6.4.
The Edit drop-
down menu.

To move or copy text in your program file, you first must mark the text. You
can use your mouse or keyboard and any of several methods to mark a block
of text.

To use the keyboard to mark text, move the cursor to the beginning of the
text you want to mark. Hold down the Shift key and move the cursor across
the text. When you reach the end of the text you want to move or copy,
release the Shift key. The marked text, called a *block*, is highlighted on your
screen. Table 6.5 summarizes all of the keyboard block commands.

Table 6.5. Borland-style block commands.

Command	Keys
Set beginning of block	Ctrl+K+B
Set end of block	Ctrl+K+K

(continues)

Table 6.5. Continued.	
Command	**Keys**
Hides/shows selected text	Ctrl+K+H
Copy selected text to the cursor.	Ctrl+K+C
Move selected text to the cursor.	Ctrl+K+V

To perform the same operation using your mouse, simply use the mouse to move the mouse cursor to the beginning of the area you want to mark, press and hold down the left mouse button, drag down to the end of the text you want to mark, and let go of the mouse button. Again, the marked area is highlighted on your screen.

The Clipboard. Now that you have highlighted an area of text, you can perform, copy, or move operations. By choosing **E**dit from the main menu, you have access to the menu commands Cu**t** or **C**opy. When you use these commands, the editor copies the marked text into the editor's *clipboard*. The clipboard is a temporary storage location in memory that holds text you have cut or copied from the file you are editing.

The Cu**t** command removes the selected area of the file and places it on the clipboard. The **C**opy command makes a copy of the text and places it on the clipboard. The C**l**ear menu command deletes highlighted text. You can choose the Edit drop-down menu command, **S**how clipboard, to see what text is in the clipboard (see fig. 6.5).

Fig. 6.5.
Contents of the clipboard.

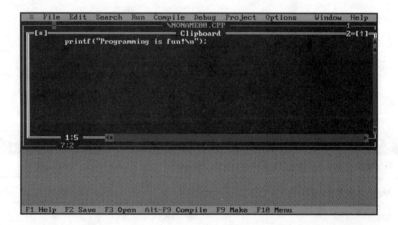

When you move or copy text onto the clipboard, you can place that text anywhere within the file you currently are editing, or into another file if desired. To insert text from the clipboard into an editor window, position the cursor at the location in the window where you the inserted text to begin. Choose **E**dit, **P**aste. When you choose these commands, the editor inserts into the editor window a copy of all of the text on the clipboard. The text remains on the clipboard as well, and you can repeat the Paste operation as many times as you choose.

Figure 6.6 illustrates the Paste operation. The information on the clipboard shown in figure 6.5 has been pasted into the current editor window. The copied program is placed directly after the original line. The program line is duplicated. Try these operations yourself by using the block of text you entered earlier.

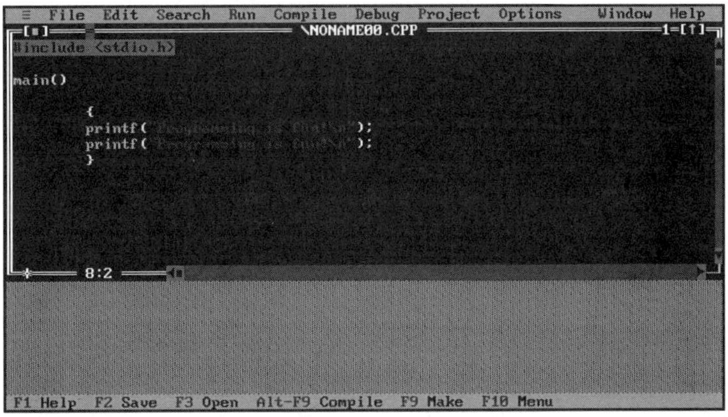

Fig. 6.6.
The Paste operation.

To paste the text into another file, simply copy or cut the desired block of text to the clipboard, and use the **F**ile, **O**pen menu commands to open an existing file, or create a new one. After the new editor window is active, use the **E**dit, **P**aste menu commands to insert the text from the clipboard into the active window. This type of operation is helpful when moving or copying several lines of program code from one program to another.

Searching

In many Turbo C++ programming situations, you need to find a particular string of text within the file. Variable names, commands, and functions, are just a few things you may need to search for within your program. A program file can be large, and visually scanning it to locate strings of text can be a difficult and time consuming task. To make this task quicker and easier, Turbo C++ provides facilities for locating text information inside the file you are currently editing.

Choosing **S**earch from the main menu produces the list of menu commands shown in figure 6.7. From this list of commands, you can select **F**ind, to produce the Find dialog box shown in figure 6.8.

Fig. 6.7.
The Search menu.

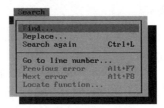

Fig. 6.8.
The Find dialog box.

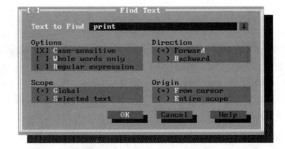

In the Find dialog box is a text box labeled Text to Find. In this text box you can enter any alphanumeric (letter or numbers) string that you want to locate in the file. Other options in the Find dialog box also affect the search operation. Those options are:

- Options

- Scope

- Direction

- Origin

In the **O**ptions portion of the dialog box, you can specify how you want to search for text. A **C**ase-sensitive search distinguishes between upper- and lowercase letters. If you conduct a case-sensitive search for the string pRintf, for example, the search does not locate the word printf, because the lettercases of the two words do not match. If you want to locate word strings regardless of the case, do not select this option.

If you select the **W**hole words only option, the Find operation locates only complete words, and does not locate strings that occur within larger strings. If you conduct a Whole words only search for the string print, for example, the search locates just the word print, but does not locate printf or printing.

You also can further define the search by selecting the **R**egular expressions option. *Regular expressions* are GREP-like (Unix command that finds strings within files) wild cards. Table 6.6 briefly defines Regular expressions available for use.

Table 6.6. Regular Expressions.

Expression	Definition
^	Matches the start of a line.
$	Matches the end of a line.
.	Matches any character.
*	Matches any number of occurrences of a character.
+	Matches one or more occurrences
[ ]	Matches any character that appears in the brackets.
[^]	Means not to match.
[-]	A Range of characters.
\	Treats that character literally.

For example, [cot] matches c, o, or t.

The Scope option of the Find dialog box enables you define the area of the search. If you select **G**lobal, the search encompasses the entire editing window. Selecting Selected text confines the search to a block of marked text.

In the Direction portion of the Find dialog box, you can designate the search direction as either Forward or Backward. You also can set the Origin options to specify the point from which the search is to begin. Selecting From the cursor searches from the cursor either backward or forward (depending on your Direction selection). Selecting Entire scope directs the search to include the entire window.

The Find operation locates the first occurrence in the editor window and highlights it (see fig. 6.9). If Find cannot locate the string, you receive an error message saying the operation was unsuccessful. If you perform subsequent searches by using the Search again menu command, the Find operation begins the search after the string you just located. Using repeated Find operations, you locate each occurrence of the string until you receive a `string not found` error message. When executing the Find operation or Search again several times, you'll locate each occurrence of the string until you receive a `[string not found]` message.

Fig. 6.9.

Find locates and highlights a string.

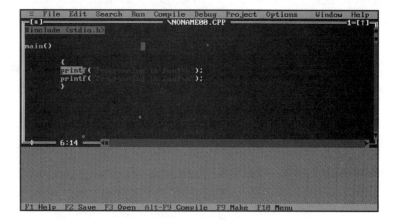

Searching and Replacing. By far the most productive use of the editor is the performance of search-and-replace operations. By *searching and replacing*, you not only can locate strings, but you also can replace them with other strings. If you want to alter the name from `totalnumber` to `total_number` you can do so throughout the file with just a single search-and-replace operation. Obviously, this feature comes in quite handy.

You can do a search-and-replace operation by choosing the **R**eplace menu command on the **S**earch menu. Choosing this command displays a dialog box that enables you to define your search-and-replace criteria (see fig. 6.10). In the example shown in this figure, you are attempting to replace all instances of the text string `programming` with the text string `editing`.

Most of the options in the **R**eplace **T**ext dialog box have the same names and meaning as those in the Find dialog box. The **R**eplace **T**ext dialog box, however, also includes a New Text box. In the New Text text box, you enter the text with which you want to replace the located text. Select the Prompt on replace option if you want to be prompted each time your search string has located a target and is about to replace it with new text. This prompt enables you to replace only selected finds within the file, rather than replacing all occurrences of the located text. The prompt is a dialog box, shown in figure 6.11.

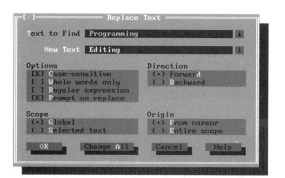

Fig. 6.10.
The Replace Text dialog box replacing one word with another.

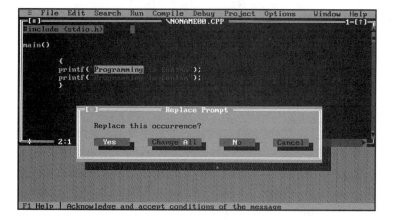

Fig. 6.11.
Replace Prompt dialog box.

The Replace Prompt dialog box offers four options. Choosing these options has the following effect: **Y**es replaces the text; Change **A**ll replaces all occurrences of the text; **N**o leaves this occurrence and moves to the next; Cancel cancels the entire operation.

The OK button at the bottom of the Replace Text dialog box invokes the search-and-replace operation, locating and changing the first occurrence of the Text to Find string. Remember: If the Prompt on replace box is not checked, the string is automatically replaced and the operation stops.

Tip
Remember: You can use the Undo menu command to undo most mistakes you make using the Turbo C++ search-and-replace operations.

Next to the OK button is the Change All button. The Change All button also invokes the search-and-replace operation, but this time the operation locates all occurrences of the string, one after the other. Again, if you selected the Prompt on replace option, the user is prompted at each occurrence of the located text as to whether to complete the replacement. If you did not select Prompt on replace, the search-and-replace operation performs without interruption.

Figure 6.12 shows the results of our search-and-replace operation. The word editing replaces all instances of the word programming. Now is a good time to try a few search and replace operations on your own. When programming Turbo C++, these operations are invaluable.

Fig. 6.12.
The changed text.

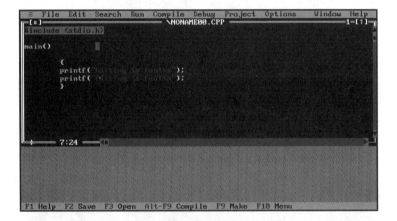

Finding Line Numbers. Another command in the Search menu is **G**o to line number. This command takes you directly to a specific line of your choice in the file. To go to line 5, for example, invoke the **G**o to line number menu command; a small dialog box appears (see fig. 6.13). In this dialog box, enter the line number **5**, and press OK. The cursor moves directly to line 5 in the file. This command is helpful for managing large program files, locating syntax errors reported by the compile, or for just moving up and down in the program.

Fig. 6.13.
The go to Line Number dialog box.

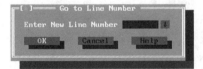

Getting Help

You may be overwhelmed by all the information about the IDE editor presented in this chapter. But remember, you have no need to memorize editor commands. If you get lost, simply press F1 (Help). Help is on the way in the Turbo C++ help systems. These systems offer help for editor commands, block commands, insert and delete commands, and special commands that you may need only once or twice in a lifetime of programming. The help system already knows where you are in the editor, and provides assistance for whatever operation you are currently performing.

Using Your Favorite Editor

What if you have your own favorite editor that you would like to use in place of the IDE editor? No problem. As you recall from chapter 4, "Customizing the Integrated Development Environment," selecting **O**ptions on the main menu produces a list of menu commands that includes **T**ransfer. With this command you can define external programs, including program editors, that you then can invoke from the Turbo C++ System menu.

After you invoke the **T**ransfer menu command, the dialog box shown in figure 6.14 prompts you for external program (item) information. Turbo C++ defines several programs/items by default, but you can move the lightbar to a blank line and press the Edit button to define your own.

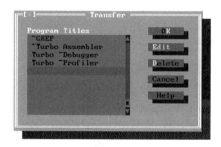

Fig. 6.14.
The Transfer dialog box.

When you press the Edit button, the Modify/New Transfer Item dialog box appears (see fig. 16.15). In this dialog box, you must provide several pieces of information to enable Turbo C++ to invoke your editor. This information includes:

- Program Title

- Program Path

- Command Line

Fig. 6.15.
The Modify/New
Transfer Item
dialog box.

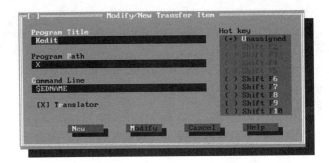

In the Modify/New Transfer Item dialog box, Program Title refers to the name of the program as it is to appear on the System menu. Program Path refers to the way your editor program is executed from the DOS command line, and Command Line defines parameters passed to your editor. In the Command Line text box, you can use a strange parameter, $EDNAME. This parameter is a Turbo C++ macro that defines the name of the program you are currently editing, using the IDE editor, and passes that name to your editor program.

When you invoke your editor from the System menu, the name of the file that you were editing by using the IDE editor is loaded automatically into your external editor. Although most ASCII editors allow you to pass in file names to the editing program, some do not. Check with your documentation to see whether this works.

The program presented in figure 6.15, for example, is Mansfield Software's Kedit program editor. The Program Title is Kedit, the Program Path is X (X.EXE), and the Command Line (the file name to pass to the editor) is $EDNAME. Your own editor may have different characteristics. You also can define hot-keys that can invoke your external editor using the hot-key configuration options on the right-hand side of the Modify/New Transfer Item dialog box.

Press New at the bottom of the dialog box and you return to the Transfer dialog box, as shown in figure 6.16. In this figure, notice that Kedit is now listed in the Program Titles listing.

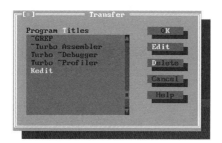

Fig. 6.16.
The Transfer dialog
with the Kedit
editor defined.

After you have defined your editor, when you invoke the System (∫) menu,
your editor is listed as a menu selection. In the example, Kedit is listed as a
menu selection (see fig. 6.17). When you select your editor from the System
menu, the Turbo C++ IDE invokes your editor and your editor loads the program that was in the active IDE editor window (see fig. 6.18). To return to the
IDE, you exit from your editor; you return to the IDE automatically. The IDE
automatically transfers the information in the active IDE editor windows to
the external program, in this case, your editor. Remember, using your own
editor is optional. For most programmers, the IDE editor is more than
sufficient.

Fig. 6.17.
The System Menu
with the Kedit
editor listed.

Of course, much of this depends on your editor. Most program editor software vendors are aware of the Turbo C++ IDE, and can help you configure
Turbo C++ to utilize your editor. Make sure you save your program before
returning to the IDE, or your changes may be lost forever.

Of course, the ability to integrate your editor with the IDE depends on your
editor. Editors have aspects such as large memory requirements, or the inability to work off the command line that may make them unable to function
with the IDE. A TSR (Terminate and Stay Resident) program comes with

Turbo C++ (THELP.COM) that can provide access to the Turbo C++ Help facility while in an external program (such as program editors). To load this program, enter the following at the DOS prompt:

```
thelp
```

The THELP.COM TSR is loaded into memory. Pressing the number 5 on the numeric keypad brings up Turbo C++ Help's main selection screen.

Figure 6.18.
The Kedit program editor.

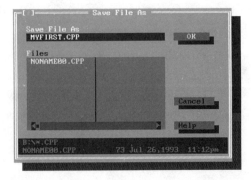

Saving Your Program File

After a program file edit operation is complete, it's time to save it to disk for later use. To do this, choose **F**ile from the main menu and then invoke the File menu command Save **A**s; the Save As dialog box appears (see fig. 6.19). In this dialog box you can enter a new name for the program file name, or replace an existing file on the disk.

Fig. 6.19.
Save File As dialog box.

If you are replacing a previous file with the file you are saving, Turbo C++ responds with a warning message that informs you the file is being overwritten (see fig. 6.20). The warning message is accompanied by Yes and No selections. If you select Yes, the previous file is replaced. If you press No, the save file operation is abandoned. The **S**ave menu command performs the same operation, but it uses the default file name. You are not prompted for a file name.

Fig. 6.20.
Overwrite existing file warning message.

Summary

This chapter introduced the IDE program editor. The IDE editor is a powerful program editing facility accessed through the Turbo C++ IDE. The IDE editor can perform operations such as creating a program file, adding code, copying code, moving code, and other specialized operations. Topics covered in this chapter include:

■ The IDE editor can create and modify a Turbo C++ program.

■ Several keyboard commands are available to perform all editing operations such as adding text and lines, deleting text and lines, and moving around the program file.

■ The **U**ndo menu command can correct one or more mistakes by invoking Undo.

■ The IDE editor can move and copy text around the same file, or to and from several files. The editor uses a block, move, and copy operation to select the area of the file to be moved or copied to a clipboard. You can copy text to the clipboard, and then paste the into an editor window using the Paste menu command.

■ The IDE editor can find text in a program file by using the search facility. By using the search-and-replace facility, the programmer can locate and replace strings within the program.

■ The Go to line number menu command enables you to move the cursor directly to a particular line in the program.

■ The Save As, and Save menu commands enable you to save your program to the disk for use later.

Chapter 7

Programming with Turbo C++

Now that you know about the IDE and other relevant components of Turbo C++, it's time to get down to the real business of creating applications using Turbo C++. In this chapter and the next you become acquainted with the following:

- Program design concepts

- Use of the IDE compiler and linker

- Use of the command line compiler linker

- Correcting errors

The information presented in this chapter provides a foundation for the C++ programming concepts you read and learn about in subsequent chapters of this book. Before you take on a complex language such as C++, you need to understand the fundamentals of working with the language. As you read these next two chapters, keep in mind that you soon may be employing in your own application each concept the chapters discuss.

This chapter introduces the basics of designing your Turbo C++ application. The chapter discusses application design concepts, design tools such as flow charts, structure charts, and CASE tools, and the role these tools play in designing a Turbo C++ application, or any application.

This chapter also discusses the compile and link operations. Previous chapters touched upon the techniques of compiling and linking from the Turbo C++ IDE. This chapter expands upon that discussion, then goes on to cover using the Turbo C++ command line compiler. In the final sections of this chapter, you learn how to handle program errors.

Understanding Application Design

Most books about C or C++ programming omit any details about how to design your application. This omission leaves a void in your understanding of the application development process, because application design is such an important part of the *Software Development Life Cycle* (SDLC). The SDLC is the process an application goes through from its inception to its final retirement. Programming is but one step in that process.

The construction of a system involves detailed specifications. Programs are like any other complex system, whether that system is mechanical (such as an automobile), electrical (such as a VCR), or structural (such as a house). The construction of a system requires a plan for the best uses of the resources that make up the finished product. In an information system, *construction* means *programming*. Program commands are a sizable portion of the resources required to develop a new system; as such, program commands represent a resource that programmers must manage effectively. The best way to manage this resource is through effective application design.

In the past, many programmers used a kind of "design-as-you-go" method of creating an application, or neglected the design entirely. The applications were simple, and programmers saw few obvious benefits to using the formal application design process.

Today's systems are complex, because users have demanded more and more performance from software applications. Systems that once could be constructed with 1000 lines of C++ code, now require a hundred times that number to meet user-demands. The graphical interfaces required to construct Microsoft Windows applications offer one example of such an expanded system.

Since applications have become more complex, the design process has taken on a greater role in software development organizations. Software analysts and software engineers make up a growing segment of the software development work force. These professionals exist to gather system requirements from the user, and translate the requirements into a formal application design specification. Programmers, including those that use Turbo C++, translate the application design into program code to create the finished application.

A detailed description of application design and other system design concepts is beyond the scope of this book. (For additional information on application design, see your local computer book store.) The following sections of this chapter, however, briefly introduce you to design concepts. You can employ these concepts when you create your first program.

Although programming is the actual construction of the software used to solve a particular problem, the information-gathering and design phases of the SDLC are critical to the overall process. In many projects, these tasks require the largest portion of development time. The most successful software development projects employ a meticulous design process that occurs before even one line of program code is written.

Steps in Creating an Application

As with any procedure, you can follow a logical sequence of steps to create an application program. These steps are as follows:

1. Define the problem.

2. Gather information about the problem.

3. Design the application.

4. Write the code.

5. Compile and run the new application.

6. Test and debug the program.

The amount of effort required to design an application depends on the type and complexity of the target application. For example, you may be able to define the problem addressed by your application during your lunch hour, using only a pencil and the back of your lunch bag. Alternatively, you may spend many months and many hours moving through this first step in the application design process. The following paragraphs discuss each of the steps for creating an application and how you accomplish them:

Step 1. Define the problem. To accomplish this step you need to develop a clear idea of what the application must do. Generally, most applications are created to solve some sort of problem. The problem could be a lack of inventory control for a business, a need for better sales accounting at the local car dealer, or a need for a program to operate an air conditioner that currently is manually controlled. The types of problems that can be solved by an application are almost limitless in number. When you attempt to define the problem your application must address, make sure you consider the type of input the program requires, and the type of output the application is required to produce.

Step 2. Gather information. When you have defined the problem, you're ready to gather information to help solve the problem. As a rule, during this step you are in contact with the person who is going to use your application. The *user* is the person who can provide reports, forms, statements, and other information relevant to the application you are creating.

Step 3. Design the application. The problem is defined, the information is gathered; now you must determine how the application is to work. In this step, you design the application's user interfaces, logic, output, input, and other program aspects. You employ design tools (such as those discussed in the "Design Tools" section later in this chapter) to automate this process.

Step 4. Write the code. Now that you know how the application should look and function, you can write the code. This phase is where Turbo C++ comes into the picture, and where you really use the information presented in this book.

Step 5. Compile and run the new application. When you have written all the code, you're ready to compile and run your new application. In this step, you see how well the computer executes your code and how well the code solves the original problem. This compile-and-link process enforces the rules of programming, grammar, and structure that are maintained by the programming language.

Step 6. Test and debug the program. Even a program that compiles and links correctly may not function as designed. To determine how well the program functions you have to test and debug it. You run the new application through its paces and test to see if it meets the design specifications (and thus, meets the demands of the user). After you find the program's bugs, you isolate and correct them.

The first releases of new software applications often are called *beta* releases. If you read software-related publications, you know that most companies call their new or revised applications "beta" until all of the bugs have been located and corrected. The beta release represents a valuable period in the life of software, because the testing period produces the following benefits:

- Provides feedback from users as to how the initial application design succeeds or fails in meeting their requirements

- Assures that few if any bugs remain at the time the official version of the software is released

- Introduces the software to users before the software is placed into an organization as a means to solve a problem

- Involves the user in the software development process

As a rule, the longer the testing period, the better the quality of the final application software. Software development companies who rush software to market without an adequate test period usually are plagued with complaints about bugs—bugs discovered by users who thought the software was a finished product. This leads to a loss of credibility for the software development company. A programmer who makes the mistake of inadequate testing risks the same loss of credibility.

Structured versus Object-Oriented Design

This portion of the chapter primarily presents structured design concepts. *Structured design* refers to the manner in which you approach a particular problem. Structured design and structured design methods provide a procedure that you employ when you design an application. The usual programming language of choice is a *structured language* such as C or COBOL.

Turbo C++ is a structured programming language as well as an object-oriented programming language. Therefore, structured design is relevant.

Many structured design concepts are difficult to apply to object-oriented programming and object-oriented languages such as C++. The advent of these programming languages has lead to the rise of a new approach to software design and development; object-oriented design. *Object-oriented* design methods approach the problems of application design in many of the same ways used by structured design methods, but with the target development language being an *object-oriented programming language* such as C++. Object-oriented design methods approach the problems of application design by employing the object-oriented model. The object-oriented model makes best use of the benefits of object-oriented programming languages such as C++. For instance, object-oriented programming languages such as C++ are able to reuse program code through a concept known as inheritance where one object can inherit and use characteristics of another object. In order to make the best use of inheritance, the programmer must carefully plan out an application using object-oriented design methods.

Of course, the structured versus object-oriented debate rages on, and properly addressing these concepts is beyond the scope of this book. While you read the following information on structured design concepts, keep in mind that an object-oriented approach to programming also exists (see Part IV for more details on object-oriented programming and object-oriented concepts).

Using Design Tools

To facilitate the application design process, systems analysts employ tools. *Design tools* are design techniques or software packages that can assist in the application design process. A few of these design tools include:

- Formal design methods that provide a step-by-step approach to application design

- Graphical tools such as flow charts, data flow diagrams, and structure charts

- Computer Aided Software Engineering (CASE) tools that automate the application design process

What purpose do these design tools serve? Generally, they exist to aid the programmer/analyst in planning how each program is going to be implemented as a module in the application, and how the modules relate to other modules in the structure of the application. An application design tool must meet the following several objectives:

- Convey adequate details to the programmer, without over-specifying

- Convey the design in an understandable manner

- Present logic at the primitive level (the level of greatest detail)

- Convey the design in a generic manner, not specific to any programming language and

- Create distinct, yet cohesive, modules

The next few sections introduce you to a few design tools and their practical applications. Take care in selecting your design tool. It should meet your design requirements and be relatively easy to use and understand. The design tools discussed in this chapter include the following:

- Flow Charts

- Structure Charts

- CASE Tools

Using Flow Charts

A *flow chart* is a diagram that outlines the logical flow of operations within a program. Generally, a flow chart depicts only one program or module. Flow charts use standard block shapes to represent the different operations within a program (see fig. 7.1). The ANSI flow chart symbols have become the standard among program designers.

- A diamond represents a decision that needs to be made in the program

- A rectangle represents a process that takes place in the program

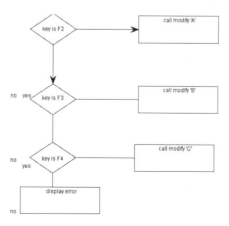

Fig. 7.1.
A flow chart.

■ Lines and arrows depict the program's logical flow

Using Structure Charts

A *structure chart* depicts the hierarchy of software modules and the intercon-
nections between modules. In addition, structure charts sometimes display
execution information, such as calling sequences and iterations (an *iteration* is
the repetition of a command or program statement). Where a flowchart depicts the inner workings of program modules, a structure chart depicts how
several modules function together.

A structure chart displays how programs/modules are hooked together to
create an actual application program. In the structure chart shown in figure
7.2, for example, the Pie Order Processing module calls three modules: Fill
Out Order Form, Check Customer Acct Info, and Reserve Stock. Those modules call additional modules which, in turn, can call even other modules.

Fig. 7.2.
A structure chart.

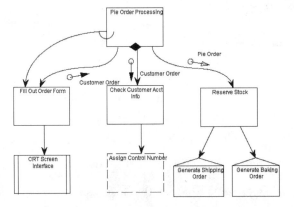

A structure chart assists the developer in planning out how modules are
placed in an application. You need only arrange each module in a hierarchy.
The modules are linked together where one module calls another, thus
creating the structure of an application.

A structure chart minimizes coupling and maximizes cohesion among the
modules. *Coupling* refers to the tightness of the interconnection from module
to module. A high degree of coupling, meaning lots of connections between
the modules, often is an indication of a poorly designed application. *Cohesion*
is a measure of how well a module's code and data structures belong together

in the application. You want your program to demonstrate a high degree of cohesion.

A structure chart is able to assist the developer in planning out the implementation of an application and thus is able to assist in the minimization of coupling and maximizing of cohesion.

CASE Tools

Computer Aided Software Engineering tools, or *CASE* tools, are software packages that provide a set of graphical and information storage tools to assist in the formal software analysis and design process. CASE tools support formal design methodologies, meaning formal step-by-step procedures that programmers follow to create a formal application design. You use a CASE tool to create charts such as the flow and structure charts discussed in the previous section (see fig. 7.3).

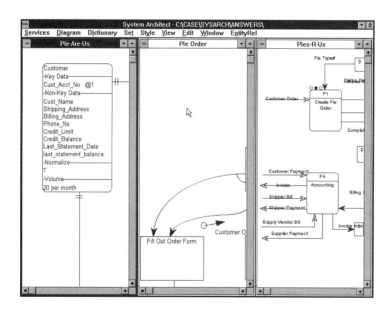

Fig. 7.3.
A Typical CASE tool.

Figure 7.3 shows a typical CASE tool for windows. This CASE tool is displaying an Entity Relationship Diagram (ERD) for database design, a structure chart, and a data flow diagram for process design.

Not only can CASE tools graphically depict an application, but they can store other features of that application such as information about data, the data structures, and other design information about the module. This information is stored in the repository of the CASE product. The *repository* is a database for all aspects of the software being developed.

Many CASE tools can generate program code or data structures for development environments such as Turbo C++ after the data structures have been defined in the tool. Some CASE tools can read, understand, and make use of existing program code, allowing the developer to redesign from the existing application.

CASE tools vary in cost and functionality. They benefit the software designers as a means of automating their application design tasks and enforcing design rules. Programmers realize the benefits of CASE through the code or the data structures that some CASE products can generate. If your organization is involved in software design, or plans such involvement for the future, you may benefit from investigating CASE tools; they're an easier means of designing applications than using paper and pencil.

Compiling and Linking

Now that you have been introduced to application design concepts, you must learn how to compile and link your program properly before you can get to the task of programming. Although compiling and linking have been touched on briefly in previous chapters, the following sections walk you through typical compile and link operations step by step and explain how you can solve problems that typically arise during the operation.

The two methods of compiling and linking an application are as follows:

- Using the facilities of the Turbo C++ Compile menu selection of the IDE

   or

- Using the command line Turbo C++ compiler from the DOS prompt

You can use either of these methods to compile and link a program; both methods produce the same executable files. Using the IDE is a bit easier than using the command line compiler because Turbo C++ can walk you through the steps. The Turbo C++ IDE helps you create the application with the editor, compile and link the program, and handle any errors that may appear. If you are a beginning Turbo C++ or C/C++ programmer, using the IDE is your best bet.

The command line compiler provides many of the same messages from the IDE compiler; but because you use the command line compiler from DOS and not in the IDE, you are required to locate and correct the problems without the assistance of Turbo C++. As mentioned earlier, your choice of methods is a matter of personal preference.

Remember to load THELP.COM when you run the command line compiler. THELP.COM is a memory resident program (Terminate and Stay Resident, see Chapter 1) that provides Turbo C++ help from the DOS prompt or another application outside the IDE, such as a program editor. Afer you load THELP.COM, press the **5** on your numeric key pad and the main help menu appears.

Using the IDE Compiler

To compile, link, and run a program using the IDE, follow this procedure:

1. Create a new application or load an existing one from the disk.

2. Choose **R**un from the main IDE menu and choose the **R**un menu command if you want to run the program as well as compile and link it.

   or

   Choose **C**ompile from the main IDE menu and choose the **C**ompile menu command if you want to compile the program, but not execute it.

These steps demonstrate that compiling, linking, and running a program from the IDE is a very simple process. The IDE automates this procedure and takes many of the detailed steps out of your hands.

To practice this procedure, load the example program GAME.CPP from disk. If you installed and unpacked your examples, GAME.CPP is located in the /TC/EXAMPLES directory. Use the **F**ile, **O**pen menu commands to locate and load the file using the Open a File dialog box (see fig. 7.4).

When you finish loading the program, it appears in an editor window with the name of the program listed at the top of the window (see fig. 7.5). From this point, you can edit the file, or compile and run it.

To compile, link, and run this program, choose the **R**un, **R**un menu commands. When you choose these commands, the compile process begins. The IDE displays a compiler status box in the middle of the screen, as shown in figure 7.6. This box tells how much progress the compiler is making on the program as it is compiling. The compiler then passes the program off to the linker (if no errors are present). The linker first builds then invokes an executable.

Fig. 7.4.
The Open a File
dialog.

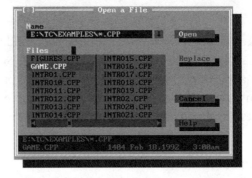

Fig. 7.5.
The GAME.CPP
program.

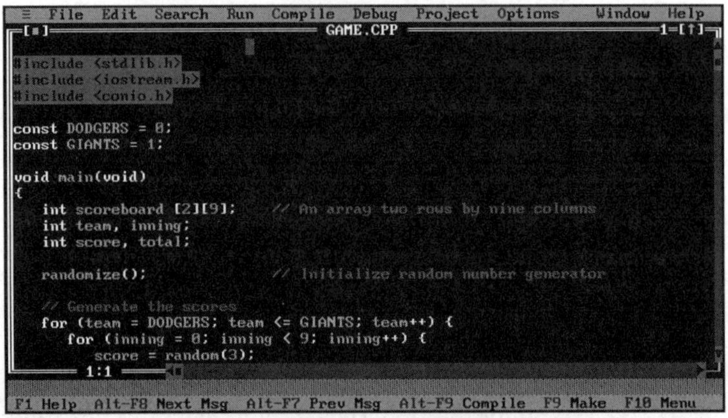

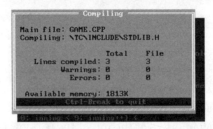

Fig. 7.6.
Compiler status
box.

You may notice that 1293 lines compiled displays on the compiler information screen, although GAME.CPP contains only about 50 lines. This discrepancy is due to the fact that the header files (files with H or HPP extensions) also are counted in the number of lines compiled. A small program that just prints one line on the terminal may require the compiler to read over a thousand lines of code.

Because you chose the **R**un command, the program automatically executes when the compile and link operation successfully concludes. You are thrown directly into the application and the IDE puts itself aside until your application program returns control to the IDE or you press the Esc key. You always can return to the application screen by selecting **W**indows from the main IDE menu then invoking the User screen menu command.

When the GAME.CPP program is run, it generates the screen shown in figure 7.7. In this figure you see a baseball scoreboard-type of output. After you return to the IDE, you can return to the user screen at any time by invoking the User screen menu command. Programmers use the Windows facility to "pop up" the screen that the user would see when running the C++ program.

If your program does not ask for input from the program user, it's going to execute and return to the IDE menu. If you're running on a fast computer, this is going to happen so fast that it's tough to see. If this is the case, you're going to need to use the Alt-F5 key to view the program output.

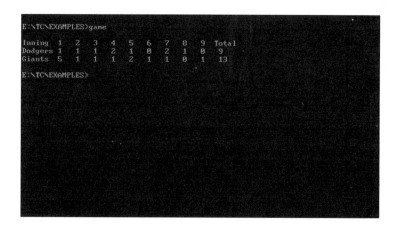

Fig. 7.7.
Running the
GAME.CPP user
window.

Your computer may lock up and require a reboot (turning the computer off and on, or pressing Ctrl-Alt-Del) procedure if the program you are running is somehow destructive to memory or other important aspects of the system. Be careful when testing a program for the first time; save your program to disk before running it. A mishap could result in hours of lost work.

Other facilities also are available to compile and link your program. Those facilities can be found in the **C**ompile menu from the Main IDE menu. As you may recall from Chapter 4, "Customizing the Integrated Development Environment," the compile menu offers the Compile, Make, Link, Build all, Information, and Remove messages command options.

The **C**ompile command works in a way similar to **R**un, but **C**ompile does not attempt to run the application. In most cases, you should use this option to first compile a new application. Many errors and warnings commonly occur during compiling, and you can correct them before the program is executed. When using compile, the IDE only compiles the program, it does not attempt to link it.

When the program is ready to go, use **R**un to execute it from the IDE. Alternatively, you can run the program from the DOS prompt, because the executable RUN.EXE has been built and saved to your disk automatically by the IDE. To run the GAME.CPP program after it has been compiled and linked, for example, enter the name of the program from the DOS prompt in the directory where the program (GAME.EXE) is located, as follows:

C:\TC\EXAMPLES>game

If all goes well, the program executes normally and returns you to the DOS prompt.

The **C**ommand, **M**ake menu commands are helpful when you are compiling project files (see Chapter 5, "Working with Project Files," for more information on this command). Using **C**ompile, **M**ake checks such things as source file date and time stamps to selectively compile a system made up of many source files. If you invoke **M**ake after you have compiled and linked the application, a window similar to that shown in figure 7.8 appears. This window tells you that the executable is up to date and does not require a compile and link operation.

The make facility is helpful in determining if an executable module matches the source file exactly. If the files do not match, the Make facility calls the compiler and linker to create a new executable by using the source files that may have changed.

Fig. 7.8.
Running Make.

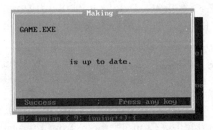

The **C**ompile, **L**ink menu commands call the linker only and do not compile the application. The object files must be present in order for the link operation to occur.

Familiarizing Yourself

Choosing the **C**ompile, **I**nformation menu commands displays a screen full of information (see fig. 7.9). On this screen, you see the current directories in use, the current program file loaded, the type of memory being used by Turbo C++, and compile information such as lines compiled, total errors, and warnings.

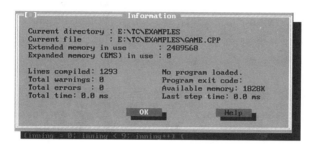

Fig. 7.9.
Compiler
Information.

Using the Command Line Compiler

The Turbo C++ compiler can perform all the operations of the IDE's Compile menu command, and even calls the linker automatically when the compile is complete. To use the Turbo C++ compiler from the DOS command line, type at the DOS prompt **tcc** followed by the name of the program to be compiled. To compile the GAME.CPP program, for example, type at the DOS prompt

tcc game.cpp

As figure 7.10 illustrates, the compiler compiles the program and then calls the linker. If no errors appear, the compile-and-link operation was successful. You now can execute the GAME.EXE executable by entering

game

at the DOS prompt (see fig. 7.10).

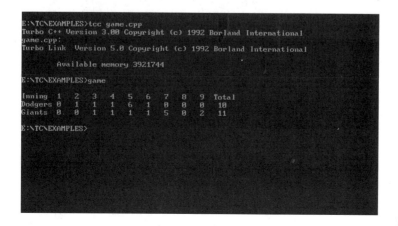

Fig. 7.10.
Output from
running
GAME.EXE.

Correcting Program Errors

This section introduces you to the basic techniques for solving common problems and staying out of trouble. Return to your GAME.CPP example to see what happens if you intentionally create a bug in the GAME.CPP program, then compile it. When you compile a program that contains a bug, the compiler status window informs you that an error has been found and the compile process stops (see fig. 7.11). This error was placed in the program intentionally; however, most are simply programmer mistakes.

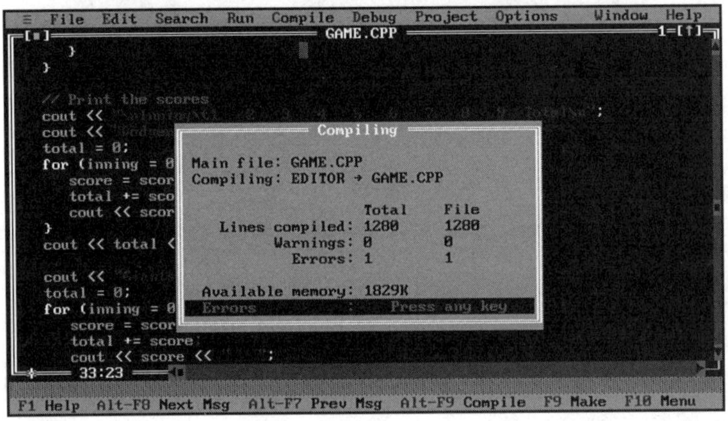

Fig. 7.11.
The compiler status window reports an error.

After the compile process locates an error and stops, you automatically are placed in the IDE editor if you press a key. An error message window containing the error message you received from the compiler appears at the bottom of the screen. The suspect line of code is highlighted in the editor, as shown in figure 7.12.

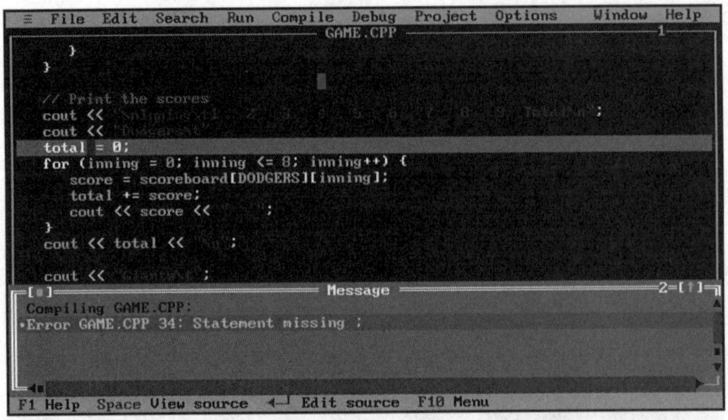

Fig. 7.12.
The editor and message window displaying a compiler error.

In the editor window, you can fix the problem (a missing semicolon [;] at the end of a program line) and recompile. You can perform this procedure repeatedly until the compile-and-link procedures produce no errors and the program can execute correctly.

You can use an entire debugging system from the IDE. The debugging menu system, shown in figure 7.13, displays several debugging operations that you can perform on a source file to locate errors in the code.

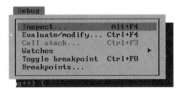

Figure 7.13.
The Debug menu.

Summary

This chapter has introduced you to application design concepts you can employ to design an effective application program. You walked through the procedures involved in the program compile and link processes for the command line Turbo C++ compiler, and you learned to use the compiler through the IDE. This chapter also discussed the following concepts:

- The application design process is required to gain a clear understanding of how the application should function.

- To create an application, you follow these specific steps: define the problem, gather relevant information, design the application, write the code, and debug and test.

- Object-oriented C++ programs may be designed a bit differently than structured programs, but the underlying concepts are basically the same.

- Design tools are used to help the application designer create the application designs. Flow charts, structure charts, and CASE tools are examples of design tools.

- The process of compiling and linking a Turbo C++ application is the same using the IDE as it is using the command line compiler. The IDE, in general, is easier to use.

- Using the IDE, you quickly and easily can correct problems in a program that you have just compiled. The IDE automates this process by automatically displaying the error message and the location in the source file where the problem can be found and corrected.

## Chapter 8

Writing Your First Program

The structure of a C++ program is like the structure of a book. You need a beginning to set the mood for the book and define the characters that conduct the action. You need a main body where the action occurs, and even subplots to maintain interest. Finally, you need an ending to conclude the plot. Although this analogy may be reaching, you can see the similarity with a C++ program, which has the following:

- At the beginning of the program where the variables, functions, and macros are defined.

- The main body of the program (called the main( ) function), where the variables, functions, and macros actually perform the action.

- User-defined functions, which perform certain discrete tasks, separate from the main body of the program.

- An end of the program, where execution stops.

> **Note**
>
> Although C++ is an object-oriented as well as a structured programming language, at first you're only going to exploit the non-object-oriented structured aspects of the language supported by C++'s predecessor, C. However, to avoid confusion, C++ refers to both C and C++ programs.

Until now, you have been exposed specifically to Turbo C++ (the IDE, editor, compiler, and so on), with less emphasis on the actual programming language. In this chapter, you create your first Turbo C++ program. Proper programming grammar is essential to create program code that others can understand. This chapter is the first of many chapters that instruct you on the ins and outs of the C/C++ programming language. This chapter also is the last introductory chapter before you learn the down and dirty programming concepts.

From time to time, you should refer to subsequent chapters for the details of a particular concept when appropriate. At the end of this chapter, you write and run a sample program to get the feel of programming. Creating a program of your own is a skill you need as you progress to the subsequent chapters. As always, hands-on experience is the best way to get going in Turbo C++ programming.

The Structure of a C Program

Like sentences, the C++ language also has a certain basic structure to which you must adhere. In this section, you learn the basic components that are required to create a C++ program, including the following:

- Preprocessor directives

- Global declarations

- The `main( )` function

- User-defined functions

- Program comments (used throughout the program)

First, look at the structure of a typical C++ program. Listing 8.1 shows a program named SAMPLE1.CPP.

Listing 8.1. SAMPLE1.CPP—A simple C++ program.

```
1.    /* SAMPLE1.CPP -- Our first C++ Program */
2.    #include <stdio.h>
3.    int main()
4.    {
5.    printf("Programming is fun\n");
6.    return 0;
7.    }
```

I

As you can see, this simple program really does nothing more than print a line on-screen by using the `printf( )` library function (which you examine later in this chapter). Understanding the structure of a program is helpful, however. In the next several sections, you walk through each program component.

Preprocessor Directives

You can include compiler instructions in your C++ program. These instructions are called preprocessor directives. *Preprocessor directives* are not part of the C language, but they enable you to expand the scope of the language, customizing each application. These directives provide instruction to the compiler before the main program compiles. Using preprocessor directives, you can define logic, set macros, include additional source files, and more. In this chapter, you get a basic introduction to the preprocessor, and Chapter 12, "Using the Preprocessor," discusses it in detail; you need some knowledge of the preprocessor here so that you can address topics in upcoming chapters.

You introduce preprocessor directives to a program by using the following:

- `#include`

- `#define`

The following sections provide more information about these directives.

#include. Consider listing 8.1 again. In that listing, the preprocessor directive is on line 2 of the program:

```
#include <stdio.h>
```

All preprocessor directives begin with the pound (#) sign, which tells the compiler to read the directives before compiling the main portion of the program. The `#include` directive tells the Turbo C++ compiler to include another source file in your main program and read that file before compiling your application. Usually, this file is called a *header file* (*header* for short), or it may be called an *include file*.

Most C++ programmers place the preprocessor directives at the beginning of the program, although this placement is not required. Usually, you group the directives together so that other programmers do not have to search through the code for all the preprocessor commands that are present.

In listing 8.1, the #include line calls stdio.h, which provides the compiler with information about the standard Input/Output library that is required to compile and run the following printf( ) function properly in the main function of the program:

```
printf("Programming is fun\n");
```

If the header file is not included, the compiler cannot handle this function and therefore reports errors.

If you edit the stdio.h file (usually located in the \TC\INCLUDE subdirectory), you see that it is actually a source code file that contains information about many library functions, including printf( ).

The angle brackets (< and >) denote that a particular header file is found in the default INCLUDE directory. Here is where the header files that come with Turbo C++, such as stdio.h and string.h, are kept for your use in your C++ programs. Sometimes, you may want to use header files in another directory or in your local directory. To do this, place the header file in quotation marks ("") instead of brackets. Using this method, you can create your own header files, or use header files that you may purchase, or ones created by other users.

Caution

Although you can edit and alter stdio.h and other include files that come with Turbo C++, it is not a good idea to do so. You may affect the instructions as presented to the compiler and therefore cause your programs to function incorrectly. If you must pass preprocessor directives to the compiler, place them in the source file directly or place them in a file of your own making. For example:

```
#include "myfile.h"
```

You discover how to include preprocessor directives in Chapter 12.

Header files are made up of function declarations, variable declarations, and macro definitions. These components are covered in more detail later in the book, but briefly:

■ *Function declarations* tell the compiler how to handle all functions, such as printf( ) or scanf( ).

- *Variable declarations* tell the compiler what variables you are using in your program and what type of information that variable can hold.

- *Macro definitions* provide the replacement text found in the macro definition (for example, using `#define`, presented next). When the preprocessor finds a macro name, it replaces that macro name with a string previously defined by using a macro definition.

#define. The `#define` preprocessor command directive signals the beginning of a macro definition. A *macro definition* allows the program to substitute one string for another during normal program operation. On lines 7 and 8 of listing 8.2, for example, you see how `#define` can specify percentages or weights:

```
#define MIDPERC 0.40
#define FINPERC 0.60
```

When `MIDPERC` or `FINPERC` is encountered, the compiler substitutes 0.40 and 0.60, respectively. The macros, therefore, are put to use on line 23 of the program:

```
Class_grade = ((Midterm_grade*MIDPERC)+(Final_grade*FINPERC));
```

The macro is evaluated by the precompiler, not the compiler. The program actually sees the following instead:

```
Class_grade = ((Midterm_grade*0.40)+(Final_grade*0.60));
```

Listing 8.2. SAMPLE2.CPP—A simple C++ program to calculate a grade.

```
1.     // This program prompts the user for a midterm exam, and
2.     // a final exam grade.  It then calculates the final
3.     // grade.

4.  // Header file
5.  #include <stdio.h>

6.  // Define Macros
7.  #define MIDPERC 0.40
8.  #define FINPERC 0.60

9.  // Global declarations
10. int Class_grade;

11. main()
```

(continues)

Listing 8.2. Continued.

```
12.  {

13.      // Initialize the variables
14.      int Midterm_grade;
15.      int Final_grade;

16.      // Prompt for the midterm grade
17.      printf("What is your grade for the Midterm?");
18.      scanf(" %d", &Midterm_grade);

19.      // Prompt for the final grade
20.      printf("What is your Final grade?");
21.      scanf(" %d", &Final_grade);

22.      // Calculate the grade and store the value to 'Fin_grade'
23.      Class_grade = ((Midterm_grade*MIDPERC)+(Final_grade*FINPERC));

24.      // Evaluate the grade
25.      if (Class_grade > 89)
26.  {
27.          printf("You got an A!\n");
28.  }

29.      if ((Class_grade < 90) && (Class_grade > 79))
30.  {
31.          printf("You got a B\n");
32.  }

33.       if ((Class_grade < 80) && (Class_grade > 69))
34.  {
35.          printf("You got a C\n");
36.  }

37.       if ((Class_grade < 70) && (Class_grade > 59))
38.  {
39.          printf("You got a D\n");
40.  }

41.       if (Class_grade < 60)
42.  {
43.          printf("You got an F\n");
44.  }

45.      // Return 0
46.      return 0;

47.  }
```

As you might recall from the discussion of header files earlier in this chapter, you can place macro definitions in include files. Most C++ programs have at least one include file that accompanies the program file. Using include files, you can keep all the macro definitions, function, and variable declarations in one file. Using a separate header file maintains better program organization by keeping these types of commands in one location, a header file.

Global Declarations

You usually define variables or functions that can be utilized by any function in your C++ application. You can introduce a variable that defines a tax rate in an accounting application, for example, to a program using a global declaration, and it therefore is available to all functions within the application, including `main( )`. Refer to Chapter 11 for more details about using global variables.

To use any function in your C++ application, you use global declarations. *Global declarations* tell the compiler about user-defined functions or variables that are common to all functions in your application. You can make global declarations before the `main( )` function of the program and in include files as well.

In listing 8.2, for example, the variable `Class_grade` is declared globally on line 10:

```
int Class_grade;
```

Now, any function in your application, including `main( )`, can access the `Class_grade` variable as it is defined. It does not need to be redefined in each function that uses it. You can declare other functions the same way. The following line, for example, lets the compiler know that `printme( )` is a valid function:

```
void printme();
```

The actual function is defined in another portion of the source file but called inside any function in the application, including `main( )`. Chapters 13-17 cover functions in more detail.

main( ) Function

Every C++ program has a `main( )` function, which is the initial entry point into the program. In listing 8.2, the `main( )` function begins on line 11. Immediately after `main( )`, the function is defined with the program code between braces (`{` and `}`). These braces tell the compiler where the function begins and ends (see fig. 8.1).

Tip

Global variable declarations can be troublesome in larger programs. You can forget that you have altered the value of a global variable in another function in the application. It is easy to lose track of the value placed inside a global variable. Try to use the fewest number of global variables possible when you're creating a program.

Fig. 8.1.
Outline of a
simple C++
program using
main( ) only.

```
#include <stdio.h>   <----    preprocessor commands
   main()            <----    main
{                    <----    beginning of function
     .
     .                <----    program goes here
     .
}                    <----    end of function
```

A program can have only one main( ) function. If you attempt to place two
in a C++ program, the compiler produces an appropriate error.

You define other functions besides main( ) in exactly the same way. You simply use main( ) to define the first area of code that executes. From main( ) you
may call additional functions, and they in turn may call others. From that
point, you can branch to other functions defined in the application and run
in the main( ) function. Functions also include ready-to-run functions that
ship with Turbo C++. Another type of function is a user-defined function, or
a function that you create to perform a certain task. Library functions and
user-defined functions are explained in the following sections.

Library Functions

In listing 8.1, the program calls the printf( ) function. The printf( ) function takes a string in quotation marks and prints it on-screen:

```
printf("Programming is fun\n");
```

This example is a library function, or ready-to-run function, that comes with
the C++ language. Another example of a-library function is scanf( ), which
receives input from the user and places that input into a variable, as on line
18 of listing 8.2:

```
scanf(" %d", &Midterm_grade);
```

The printf( ) and the scanf( ) library functions are defined in the stdio.h file
that is included at the top of the programs. Virtually hundreds of functions
are defined in several library header files that you can include in your C++
programs.

Library functions save time because you do not have to write them yourself.
You even can purchase additional library functions to perform certain specialized activities such as database operations, graphics creation, or screen
painting. Library functions are defined in more detail in Chapter 14, "Using
Library Functions," and Chapter 15, "Using the C Library."

User-Defined Functions

In some programs (such as the ones presented in listings 8.1 and 8.2), the program contains only one function, main( ). This setup is fine for small programs, but in most larger applications, it makes sense to place most of the code in *user-defined functions*, or functions that the user defines in conjunction with the program to accomplish a particular task. In a sense, you are creating your own custom library function.

You can put these user-defined functions in other portions of the main source file, outside the main( ) function, or even place them in other source files. The execution is the same. Chapter 13, "Using Functions," presents the details of using functions in your C++ program, but here you learn the basic concepts you need to create a program. See Chapter 16 for more information on creating your own functions.

User-defined functions are invoked the same way C++ library functions are invoked. Anywhere in the main( ) function, the user-defined function can be run simply by naming the function. After the function is run, the code associated with that particular function executes, and then returns to the function that called it (see fig. 8.2). This aspect of C makes it a *structured* programming language because you can divide discrete tasks into modules or, in this case, functions.

```
      #include <stdio.h>   <----     preprocessor commands
                           <----     prototype information
      main( )              <----     main
   {                       <----     beginning of function
           .               <----     program goes here
           function();     <----     call to a function
   }                       <----     end of function
      function()
   {                       <----     beginning of function
           .               <----     program for function goes here
           return;         <----     return from the function
   }                       <----     end of function
```

Fig. 8.2.
Outline of a simple C++ program using a user-defined function.

A C program is a collection of functions. All programs are made up of one or more functions that have been integrated to create an application. All functions contain one or more C++ statements, and generally are created to perform a single task, such as printing to the screen, writing to a file, or changing the color of a screen. You can declare and run an almost unlimited number of functions in a C++ program.

All functions have names and a list of values that the function receives. You can assign any name to your function, but usually the name describes the purpose of the function. In listing 8.3, for example, the program in listing 8.1 is rewritten, this time defining the portion of the program that prints to the screen in a user-defined function called `printme()`.

Notice that `printme()` requires a prototype or a function declaration in the program:

```
void printme();
```

A *function declaration* tells the compiler the name of the function that is invoked in the program. If the function is not defined, the compiler reports an error. The keyword `void` lets the compiler know that the function does not, at least in this case, return a value.

Listing 8.3. SAMPLE3.CPP—A C++ program with a user-defined function.

```
1.    /* SAMPLE3.C -- Our first C++ Program
using a user-defined function */
2.    #include <stdio.h>
3.    void printme();
4.    int main()
5.        {
6.               printme();
7.               return 0;
8.        }
9.    void printme()
10.   {
11.        printf("Programming is fun\n");
12.   }
```

Now that you're well on the way to understanding programming in C++, you might want to spend some time looking at the proper way to create a C++ program.

Programming Grammar

As mentioned in the writing analogy presented in the introduction to this chapter, writing a C++ program is much like writing a book. You must follow certain rules of proper grammar so that others can read and interpret your book. In the same light, when you're creating a C++ program, you also should follow some grammatical rules, called programming grammar. *Programming grammar*, like English grammar, is a set of predefined formatting rules with which you should comply to make your program easy to follow.

Following are the advantages of using good program grammar:

■ You can read and understand your programs.

■ Other programmers can read and understand your programs easily.

■ You make fewer errors because proper programming grammar enables you to recognize problems before you send the program to the compiler.

Other programming languages such as COBOL strictly enforce program formatting rules. Unlike COBOL, C++ is a *free-form* programming language that provides you with the freedom to structure a program as you want. Program statements, for example, can begin in any column of any line, and blank lines can exist virtually anywhere. This freedom has lead to programs that are virtually unreadable, however, even by the programmers who created them. Consider listing 8.1, for example. You can rewrite it as follows:

```
#include <stdio.h>
int main() {printf("Programming is fun\n");return 0;}// SAMPLE1.C -- Our
➥first C++ Program
```

Turbo C++ does not know the difference between the program you see here and the program in listing 8.1. Both programs do the same thing, but one with only two lines of programming code.

Other programmers who read the preceding program may be confounded by its lack of adherence to the grammatical rules of programming. Making the required programming changes to this program takes a bit longer than if the program were properly formatted from the beginning, as it is in listing 8.1.

If you are new to the world of C++ programming, developing good programming grammar now is helpful, rather than trying to break old habits later. In the following sections, you learn:

■ How to make your C++ program readable

■ How to use spaces and lines to your best advantage

■ How to place comments into your program

■ How to use the case-sensitivity of the C++ language to your best advantage

■ How to use the C character set

Readability

Programs are functional in that they define the logical flow and operation of a program. A program can be functional but not readable, however. *Readability* is the concept of creating a program that others can understand and modify. Generally, the more readable a program is, the faster you can make changes to it or correct errors.

Most programmers work in organizations in which other programmers are bound to read each other's program code. You may be required to modify someone else's code, and others may make modifications to yours. Given this situation, effective programmers are not only those who solve a problem with their computer program, but those who write programs that have a straightforward structure, that are understandable, and that contain many separating lines and spaces. A program that contains hard-to-read and convoluted program statements results in a program that is difficult and costly to maintain.

Spaces and Lines

Make sure you place several separating lines and spaces in your program. As you can see in listing 8.2, the program uses blank lines and spaces to separate the code, so you can evaluate the program more effectively, locating the important sections with just a glance. Also note that the program contains several sections called *blocks*, or portions of the code that perform some discrete function. On line 24, for example, a block begins as follows:

```
    // Evaluate the grade
    if (Class_grade > 89)
{
        printf("You got an A!\n");
}
```

This type of formatting helps you move from block to block in the program listing, locating the exact portion of the program that performs a particular task. In the preceding example, the block determines whether the grade is greater than 89, and thus an A. If you do not consider readability of the program and utilize lines and spaces effectively, you may end up with the following:

```
    if(Class_grade>89){printf("You got an A!\n")};//Evaluate the grade
```

This statement is certainly concise, but it is not as understandable as the original block of code.

Comments

A *comment* is any information that you add to your source file to provide information for any reason. The compiler ignores comments; they do not perform any program-related tasks. The use of comments is completely optional, but commenting a program is usually desirable. Comments do not add to the size of the executable, nor do they affect execution speed of the program.

Using comments within your source file is an easy way to document exactly what is taking place in your program. Generally, it is considered good programming practice to comment your source file as much as possible because other programmers who read your comments in the future should be better able to understand the details of your program rapidly. You may even benefit from your comments in the future because they refresh your memory if you have forgotten the purpose of a particular application.

Commenting your program at the top of each source file also is a good practice, providing information that makes its use by others much easier. Provide information such as the file name, the programmer, a brief description, the date the program was created, and revision information.

Using C++, you can enter comments in your program in two ways:

- Standard C style

- C++ style

If you are using only a C++ compiler, it makes no difference which comment style you use. If you need to run your program under another standard C compiler for some reason, the C++ style comments usually are not recognized and errors occur. Therefore, it makes sense to use only the standard C style comments if your program is to be run with non-C++ compilers.

The following sections on the two types of commenting styles explain each more thoroughly.

Standard C Style. Standard C comments begin with the sequence /* and are terminated with the sequence */. All the text placed between the two sequences is ignored. Refer to listing 8.1; the comment on line 1 is an example of a standard C style comment:

```
/* SAMPLE1.C -- Our first C++ Program */
```

Familiarizing Yourself

Tip

It is a good idea to place comments in your program as you create the program. Many programmers wait until the program is completed before adding comments, but this practice leads to a program that is not commented well, or even at all. Get into the habit of adding comments to your program as you write it.

If you need to use several lines of the program for comments, you can do the following:

```
/*
     Program:      SAMPLE1.C
     Programmer:   David S. Linthicum
     Description:  Our first C++ Program
     Date Created: 09/09/94
     Revision Info: None yet
*/
```

You also can place the comment on the program line as follows:

```
printf("Programming is fun\n"); /* print to the screen */
```

C++ Style. With the introduction of C++, a new type of program comment was introduced. You can define a single line comment by prefacing the comment with a double slash (//). When you use a double slash, the compiler ignores anything after it until the end of the line. For example:

```
//   SAMPLE1.C -- Our first C++ Program
```

If you need to use several lines of the program for comments, you can do the following:

```
//
//    Program:      SAMPLE1.C
//    Programmer:   David S. Linthicum
//    Description:  Our first C++ Program
//    Date Created: 09/09/94
//    Revision Info: None yet
//
```

You cannot nest C++ comments, meaning you cannot put a comment in another comment. If you nest comments, the compiler produces errors because it cannot discern between the comments.

The comment can begin anywhere on the line, such as after a program statement. For example:

```
// SAMPLE1.C -- Our first C++ Program
#include <stdio.h>                  // header file
int main()                          // main function
{
printf("Programming is fun\n");     // print to the screen
return 0;                           // end the function and return 0
}
```

Many programmers prefer this style of program comment because they do not need to terminate this type of comment (*/) as they do with the standard

C style. The standard C style also takes up more space on the line. The style you decide to use makes absolutely no difference in the operation of Turbo C++.

Case-Sensitivity

The C++ programming language is case-sensitive. Uppercase and lowercase letters mean different things to the Turbo C++ compiler. Generally, the entire C++ programming language is in lowercase. In listing 8.1, for example, if you capitalize any of the program commands such as int, printf, or return, the resulting program produces several program errors. All the C/C++ commands are in lowercase and are presented as such in the programs.

This case-sensitivity comes from the C language's roots in the Unix operating system, which is case-sensitive and requires that the operating system commands be in the correct case. Usually, uppercase characters are reserved for special words and messages you use to send output to a screen, printer, or a disk file. This use enables you to locate these special words or messages because they stand out among the lowercase words in the program.

The C Character Set

The C++ programming language has a character set. A character set is a set of letters and numbers that C++ recognizes. The set uses the following:

■ Uppercase letters *A* to *Z*

■ Lowercase letters *a* to *z*

■ Digits *0* to *9*

The C++ character set also uses the following special characters:

[	]	{	}	<	>	(	)
~	|	;	:	,	@	$	
!	*	+	+	"	'	.	?
#	/	\	&	%	-	_	^

Sometimes a combination of the special characters represents a special operation such as the following:

>>=	&=	^=	|=	,	#	##
%	<<	>>	<	>	<=	>=

```
[]      ()      .       ->      ++      —       &

==      !=      ^       |       &&      ||      ?:

=       *=      /=      %=      +=      -=      <<=

*       +       -       ~       !       /
```

You learn about each of the operators later in the book. For now, note how the special characters in combinations create entirely new meanings.

MYFIRST.CPP

In this section, you create and run your first Turbo C++ program by using the information already presented in this chapter and the first portion of this book. There is simply no better way to learn C++ programming than to just dive right in and do it. You create your program by using the following steps:

1. Define your program.

2. Define preprocessor directives.

3. Define global declarations.

4. Create main( ).

5. Create the body of the program.

6. Create your own user-defined functions.

7. Test your program.

8. Use proper program grammar and comments.

It is assumed that you understand how to use the IDE editor to create a new program. If you do not, you should read Chapter 6, "Using the IDE Editor." It also is assumed that you know how to compile and debug a program. If you do not, refer to Chapter 7, "Programming with Turbo C++."

You'll be taken down this path of programming step by step. A complete program listing combining all of the steps is forthcoming. Starting with something simple, your first program counts from one 1 to 100.

Defining Preprocessor Directives

Use the IDE to create a new program file. After you create the program by using the IDE editor, you need to define the preprocessor directives. You usually create them at the top of the file (see fig. 8.3).

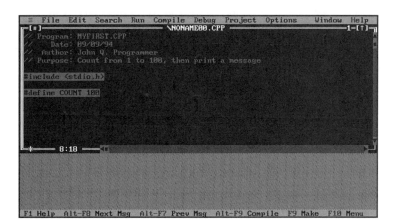

Fig. 8.3.
Entering the preprocessor directives.

In the program, the #include directive calls in the stdio.h header file, which is required to place the printf( ) library function. The #define directive defines the COUNT macro as 100. This macro sets the number where the counting stops.

Defining Global Declarations

After you define the preprocessor directives, you can define global declarations (see fig. 8.4). Recall from the previous discussion that a global declaration is a variable or a function that is defined as being accessible to the entire program.

Fig. 8.4.
Entering the global declarations.

In this program, you define two global declarations:

```
int counter;
void countall();
```

The first declaration is the variable (counter), used as the counter for this counting program. As the program prints the count on-screen, the counter variable is incremented by one. The countall( ) function is declared as a user-defined function that is available to the entire program. After the function is declared, it can be called from anywhere in the program. The program invokes countall( ) from the main( ) function. The program then is saved to disk and given the name MYFIRST.CPP. It is a good idea to save your program frequently in case of loss of power or other system problems. Although some of this is new, each command is covered in greater detail in subsequent chapters.

Creating *main( )*

After you define the preprocessor directives and make all the global declarations you need, it is time to create your main( ) function (see fig. 8.5).

Fig. 8.5

Creating main( ).

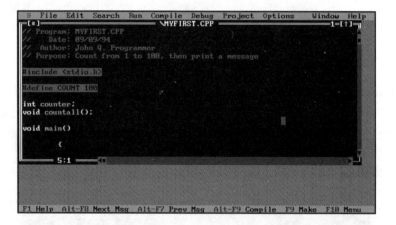

In the program, you declare main as follows:

```
void main()
```

In this case, you do not require main to return a value.

If instead you use

```
int main()
```

the compiler expects the main function to return a value. If this is the case, return is added to the main function, returning a value from the function.

You declare all C/C++ functions in the same manner, as you can see in the user-defined function described later in this chapter.

Creating the Body of the Program

After you create the main( ) function, you can enter the body of the program. The body is made up of all the programming commands you need to place in the main function. In this program, you include program commands that call library functions as well as your own user-defined functions. You can enter any valid C/C++ program command into the body of the program.

Creating Your Own User-Defined Function

Remember that you can use user-defined functions to perform a certain task. You can run this user-defined function from the main( ) function or from other functions in your application.

In the sample program, you create a function called countall( ). You declare countall( ) as a global function at the top of the program. The program commands executed by this function are defined at the bottom of the program outside the main( ) function (see fig. 8.6). Note that countall also is declared as follows:

```
void countall()
```

Therefore, a value is not expected from this function either.

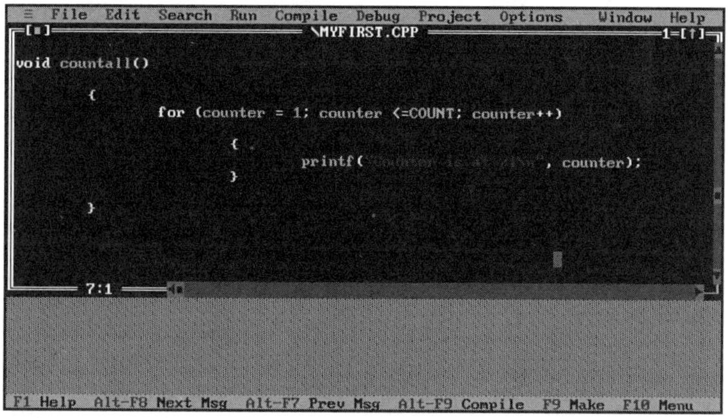

Fig. 8.6
Creating your own user-defined function, countall( ).

As you can see, the countall( ) function counts from 1 to the value of the COUNT macro, displaying the results on-screen. Note the use of the for command to loop through the code below it a predefined number of times:

```
for (counter = 1; counter <=COUNT; counter++)
```

The `for` command (which is covered in greater detail in upcoming chapters) executes a loop using a counter. After the counter condition is reached, the looping stops. In the user-defined function, after the count is complete, it returns to the function that called it, in this case, `main( )`.

Testing Your Program

After you complete your program, you are ready to test it. Compiling, linking, and running a program are defined in the preceding chapter, but as you may recall, selecting Run from the Run menu is the fastest method of compiling, linking, and running your program.

If you made a mistake, the compiler reports the errors in the message windows at the bottom of the screen. Usually, these errors are no more than problems with your syntax and can be corrected easily. After you execute the program, the output should look much like figure 8.7.

Fig. 8.7
Testing your
program.

The program counts from 1 to 100 and then prints a `Count is complete` message.

If everything goes okay, you have just created your first program by using Turbo C++. This program is just the beginning. As you discover in the upcoming chapters, you have only scratched the surface of programming with Turbo C++. Now complete the program by making sure that the program is commented properly.

Using Proper Grammar and Comments

You should have commented your program as you created it. If you did not, now is the time to go over the program and add comments to make it more understandable. In this program, comments at the top of the program define information such as program name, the programmer, the data, and the purpose of the program. Throughout the rest of the program, you should give each activity a comment as it is performed in the programming code.

You may find it difficult to see the benefit in commenting a small program such as this one, but in larger programs, comments provide a distinct advantage. Suppose you are asked to maintain a program with over 5,000 lines of code. Now suppose that the programmer who wrote the program did so without the use of comments. The task of maintaining the program would be considerable because you would have to decipher the code line by line, block by block, function by function.

Listing 8.4 is the finished program.

Listing 8.4. MYFIRST.CPP—Your first Turbo C++ program.

```
1.   // Program: MYFIRST.CPP
2.   //    Date: 09/09/94
3.   /???Dave: John Q. Programmer
4.   // Purpose: Count from 1 to 100, then print a message

5.   // Define preprocessor directives
6.   // Use the standard input/output header file
7.   #include <stdio.h>

8.   // Define the count macro as 100
9.   #define COUNT 100

10.  // Define global declarations
11.  int counter;
12.  void countall();

13.  // Main function
14.  void main()

15.  {

16.      countall();  // Call the user-defined function to count
from 1 to 100

17.      // Print the complete message
18.      printf("\nCount is complete!\n");

19.  }

20.  // User defined function to count from 1 to 100
21.  void countall()
```

(continues)

> **Listing 8.4. Continued.**
>
> ```
> 22.  {
>
> 23.      for (counter = 1; counter <=COUNT; counter++)
>
> 24.          {
> 25.              printf("Counter is at %i\n", counter);
> 26.          }
>
> 27.  }
> ```

Notice how the use of spaces and blank lines makes your program more readable than if you had left them out. You easily can spot where the user-defined function is specified and where the main( ) function begins. If you follow this basic structure for future C++ programs, you may find yourself well on the way to becoming a valuable asset to any software development organization.

Summary

In this chapter, you wrote your first Turbo C++ program. First, you learned about the correct structure of a C++ program including the use of the preprocessor and global declaration of functions as variables. You learned what the main( ) function does and how you declare and add user-defined functions to your application. You also discovered how to write grammatically correct C++ programs that other programmers can understand and maintain easily. This chapter covered the following topics:

- A typical C++ program is structured with preprocessor directives, global declarations, the main( ) function, user-defined functions, and program comments.

- Preprocessor directives expand the scope of the language and are read before the main program is compiled. The #include and #define commands are examples of preprocessor directives.

- You include files in a C program by using the #include statement, which is read before compiling your applications. Usually, these files are called header files, or headers for short. They contain such things as macro definitions, and variable and function declarations.

- The #define command signals the beginning of a macro definition. A macro definition allows the program to substitute one string for another during normal program operations.

- Global declarations instruct the compiler about user-defined functions or variables that are passed to and from functions in your application. You make global declarations before the `main()` function.

- The `main()` function is the entry point into the program, or the first function called when the program is run.

- Library functions are ready-to-run functions that come with the C++ language. They save you time because you do not need to write them. Functions such as `printf()` and `scanf()` are examples of library functions.

- User-defined functions are functions that you define to accomplish a particular task. For user-defined functions to be run from a program, they first must be declared.

- Programming grammar is a set of structure rules that make a program more understandable and maintainable by other programmers. Correct programming grammar includes the use of many lines and spaces, block structure of the program, and comments.

- You place comments inside the program to describe the operations of the program. Compilers ignore the comments, and the comments do not affect performance or executable size. You can use two types of C++ program comments: standard C and C++. You can use either type when you're using Turbo C++.

- The C++ language is case-sensitive. Uppercase and lowercase letters mean different things to the Turbo C++ compiler. Most C++ commands are in lowercase.

- The C character set uses uppercase letters *A* to *Z*, lower case letters *a* to *z*, and digits *0* to *9*. A special set of characters that C understands also is available.

- You created the program MYFIRST.CPP step by step to learn how a C++ program is constructed properly.

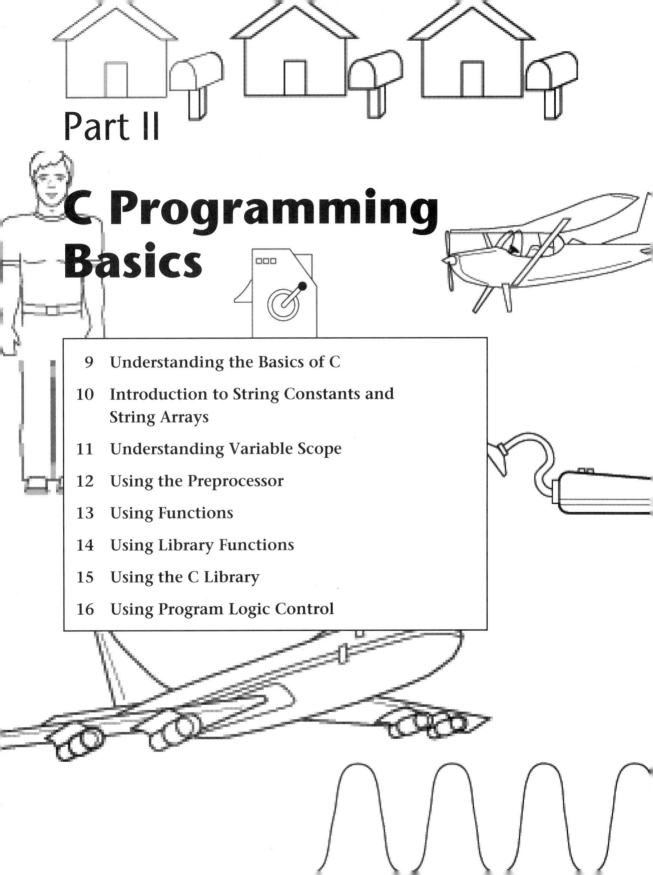

Part II

C Programming Basics

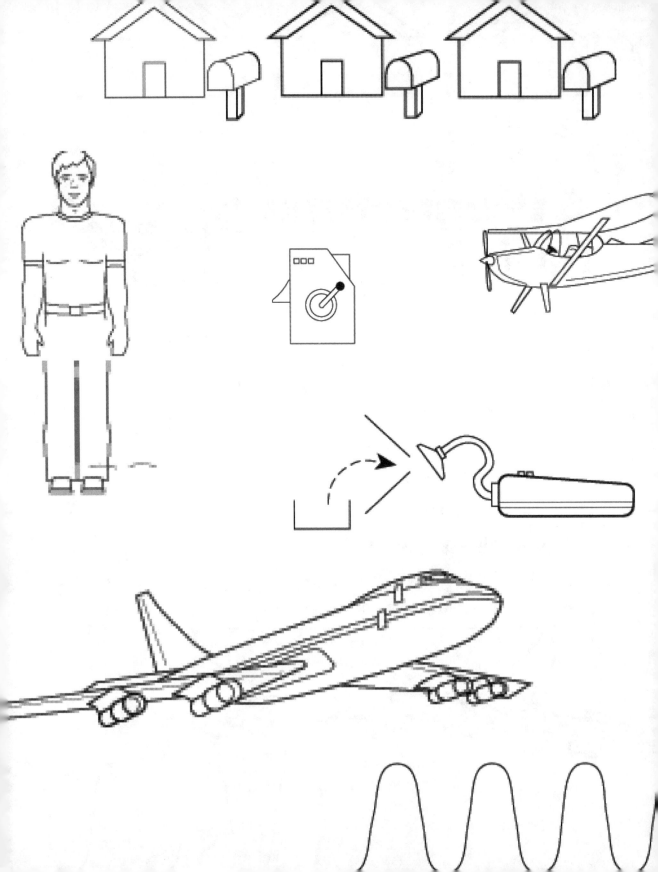

Chapter 9

Understanding the Basics of C

Now that you can create programs on your own, you can get down to the business of learning the details of the programming language. This chapter concentrates on the foundations of the C and C++ programming languages, including the following details:

- How to control program logic and flow

- How to declare data types

- How to compile and run programs

- How to convert data types when required

This chapter sets the stage for the upcoming programming chapters because you build on the information here as the book progresses. You need to know the details of data types, for example, to master the use of the `printf()` and the `scanf()` library functions. Additionally, you need to know how to control the logical flow of a program to effectively create an application that uses data files. Take time to understand each topic and discover how it fits into the overall goal of creating an effective application program, in this chapter and the rest.

Many concepts in this chapter have been presented in example programs contained in earlier chapters. Most of these concepts (program statements, for example) have not yet been explained in enough detail for you to use them effectively. Here and in upcoming chapters, you finally get to fill in the blanks.

When you read the upcoming chapters, you may find it useful to refer to the appendixes, particularly the library function reference sections. There you quickly can find information that you need, without having to read through supercilious information.

Program Logic and Flow

In this section, you learn how C/C++ programs evaluate certain conditions. Then, based on those conditions, the programs perform certain operations such as program branching, looping, or other logical actions.

Programs execute one line at a time, from the top of the source file to the bottom. But if your program were able to execute through each statement only once, then creating a usable application certainly would be difficult. The C language provides several program statements that control program flow.

You can control the order of program line execution by using conditional statements such as the following:

- `if`

- `if-else`

- `switch`

To perform repetitive tasks, you can use looping statements such as the following:

- `do-while`

- `while`

- `for`

These commands are covered in the following sections. It is helpful to try a program using the commands presented as you move along. Several example program listings provide the resources you need to get going quickly.

Making Decisions

When you're programming, sometimes your program needs to deal with certain situations and execute different program instructions based on predefined conditions. You can use the `if`, `if-else`, and `switch` statements for this purpose. The `if` statement can handle one or two conditions you set to specify whether a line or a block of code should execute. The `if-else` statement selects

one line or a block of code over another, and the `switch` command can deal
with several conditional expressions at once, as with menu selection processing
or database operations. Each statement is explained more thoroughly in the
following sections.

if. The syntax of the `if` command is as follows:

```
if( expression is true )
      execute a program statement;
    or
if( expression is true )
{
      execute a group of statements;
}
```

If the expression in the parentheses is found true, the statement or group
of statements that follow execute. Consider the following example (from
listing 8.2 in Chapter 8):

```
    // Evaluate the grades
    if (Class_grade > 89)
{
    printf("You got an A!\n");
}


    if ((Class_grade < 90) && (Class_grade > 79))
{
    printf("You got a B\n");
}
```

If the variable `Class_grade` is greater than 89 in the first `if` statement, then
the commands enclosed within the braces execute. The second `if` statement
evaluates two conditions, and if both are true, the command enclosed within
the braces directly below the command executes. If none of the predefined
conditions are met, none of the `printf()` commands are executed, and the
program continues processing.

Expressions are complex unto themselves. They are evaluated using the
following two groups of tools:

- Relational operators

- Logical operators

Tables 9.1 and 9.2 define relational operators and logical operators, respectively. You may find that a few of the relational operators are similar to
mathematical expressions you learned in school.

Table 9.1. Relational operators.

Operator	Description
>	Greater than
<	Less than
==	Equal to
!=	Not equal to
>=	Greater than or equal to
<=	Less than or equal to

Relational operators enable you to compare two values. If you rewrite the preceding code fragment, for example, and change the expression from greater than to less than, the expression looks like the following:

```
if (Class_grade < 89)
```

If you want to check whether the variable and the number are equal, then try this expression:

```
if (Class_grade == 89)
```

Caution

Note that double equal signs (==) mean equal to in an expression, but the single equal sign sets values in the normal processing of variables. You easily can become confused.

If you want to check whether the variable and the number are not equal, then try the following expression:

```
if (Class_grade != 89)
```

Table 9.2. Logical operators.

Operator	Description
&& (AND)	True if both expressions are true
¦¦ (OR)	True if either expression is true
! (NOT)	Reverses the true or false condition of an expression

Logical operators enable you to evaluate more than one condition at one time. As an expression is stated in the parentheses, it is evaluated and the result logically compared using an operator:

```
(( expression ) logical operator ( expression ))
```

Consider, for example, the program code presented earlier:

```
if ((Class_grade < 90) && (Class_grade > 79))
{
    printf("You got a B\n");
}
```

Both expressions in the parentheses on the right and left side of the double ampersand (&&) are evaluated. If both expressions are true, then the entire expression is true.

If you want the expression to return true if either expression is true, then rewrite the expression using the double pipes (¦¦), which mean *or*:

```
if ((Class_grade < 90) ¦¦ (Class_grade > 79))
{
    printf("You got a B\n");
}
```

If you want to evaluate an expression as false if it is actually true, then you can redo the expression by using the !, which means *not*:

```
if (!(Class_grade < 90))
{
    printf("You got a B\n");
}
```

Using expressions takes some practice before you understand each logical and relational operator and its use. Take the time now to enter listing 8.2 into Turbo C++ and then alter the expressions in the program to see how the logical flow of the program is affected.

if-else. Sometimes you need to deal with more than two conditions at once. If so, you should find the if-else command useful. It is an extension to the if command you learned in the preceding section. The syntax is as follows:

```
if( expression is true )
      execute this program statement;
else
      execute this program statement;
```

Consider the following example:

```
if (!(Class_grade < 90))
   printf("You got an A\n");
else
   printf("You did not get an A\n");
```

Here, if the grade is not less than 90, print You got an A; else, print You did not get an A.

If several program statements are required for each alternative, consider the following example:

```
if (!(Class_grade < 90))
  {
   clrscr();            // Clear the screen
   printf("Great!\n\n");
   printf("You got an A\n");
  }
else
  {
   printf("Sorry\n\n");
   printf("You did not get an A\n);
  }
```

As you can see, if-else makes sense when you have two alternatives. If you have more than two alternatives, consider using the switch statement (which is covered next).

Caution

Generally, nesting if-else statements is not a good idea. For example:

```
if (expression)
    if (expression)
            if (expression
            .
            else
            .

    else
else
```

If you must do this sort of nesting, consider using the switch statement as an alternate. This type of program is legal but confusing. You easily can lose track of what is going on in the program logic.

---

switch. The switch statement is effective when you're evaluating several alternatives within a program. Instead of evaluating only one or two expressions, switch, unlike if and if-else, can evaluate as many expressions as you want. The syntax is as follows:

```
switch( value )
{
      case value1:
          program statement;
          .

          .
```

```
        case value2:
            program statement;
                .
                .
                .
        default:
            program statement;
                .
                .
                .
    }
```

As you can see, this statement has several components:

- The `value` is the value of the variable condition to be evaluated

- The `case` signals the beginning of the code that is to execute when a particular conditional value is met

- The `default` signals the beginning of the code that is executed by default, if no case values match the conditional value

- The `break` signals when the code that is executed for each case statement stops and then jumps to the end of the `switch` statement

Examine listing 9.1, which shows a `switch` statement.

Listing 9.1. SWTDEMO.CPP— Switch demo program.

```
1.   //     Name:  SWTDEMO.CPP
2.   // ???Dave:  David Linthicum
3.   //   Purpose:  Demonstrates the use of the switch statement

4.   #include <stdio.h>
5.   #include <conio.h>  //Needed for the clrscr() (clear screen)
     statement

6.   void main()

7.   {

8.       char selection;
9.       clrscr();

10.      printf("  ***  Menu  ***\n\n");
11.      printf(" 1.  Option One\n");
12.      printf(" 2.  Option Two\n");
13.      printf(" 3.  Option Three\n");
14.      printf(" 4.  Option Four\n\n");
15.      printf("Enter your selection\n");

16.      scanf ("%c", &selection);     //Receive input from the
         user
```

(continues)

Listing 9.1. Continued.

```
17.        switch (selection)

18.        {
19.            case '1':
20.                printf("Option %c selected\n", selection);
21.                break;
22.            case '2':
23.                printf("Option %c selected\n", selection);
24.                break;
25.            case '3':
26.                printf("Option %c selected\n", selection);
27.                break;
28.            case '4':
29.                printf("Option %c selected\n", selection);
30.                break;
31.            default:
32.                printf("You must enter 1,2,3, or 4");
33.        }

34.    }
```

In this program, the user is presented with several menu selections. After the user makes a selection, the value is stored in a variable called selection. Then the value is evaluated using the switch statement and the code between lines 17 and 33. Then the appropriate message displays on-screen (see fig. 9.1).

Fig. 9.1.
The switch demo program results.

Looping

Sometimes you need a program statement or statements to execute several times. You can copy each line over and over in the editor, of course, but there is a better way. Several looping statements that are supported by C enable you to execute a block of code repeatedly until a predefined condition is met.

They are

- do-while

- while

- for

Although each statement provides looping, note the differences and when it is appropriate to use each.

do-while. An example of a *post checked loop*, or a loop that checks for a condition after a loop occurs, is the do-while statement. You can use do-while to execute a block of code while a defined condition is true. The do-while statement uses the following syntax:

```
do
      program statement
      while (expression is true);
```

See how do-while can count from 1 to 10, for example:

```
int number = 1;

do
      {
            ++number;
            printf(" %i ", number);
      }
      while (number < 10)
```

In the preceding example, the variable number, once declared, is set to 1. After the do-while loop is entered, the number variable is incremented by one (++number) and then the current number contained in the variable is printed on-screen. After it reaches the bottom of the loop, the program checks the condition set in the while statement, and if not true, the loop is repeated. If the expression is true after any loop operation, the looping is terminated and the program continues.

while. The while statement enables you to define a *prechecked loop*, in which a condition is checked before a loop instead of after the loop, as happens with do-while. The while statement has the following syntax:

```
while ( expression )
      program statement
```

Now rewrite the previous example using `while`:

```
int number = 1;

while (number < 10)

        {
                ++number;
                printf(" %i ", number);
        }
```

Here the condition is checked before the statements in the loop execute. If the condition is not true when the `while` statement is read, the loop never executes. If true, the looping proceeds, but once the condition is not true, the loop terminates.

Take some time now to note the similarities with examples presented previously. When the `do-while` example is run with the condition checked at the end of the loop, the output is as follows:

```
2 3 4 5 6 7 8 9 10
```

When the `while` example is executed with the condition checked at the beginning of the loop, the output is as follows:

```
2 3 4 5 6 7 8 9 10
```

Both examples count from 2 to 10, although the loop condition is checked at the beginning of the loop in one example and at the end of the loop in another. If you increment the counter after the `printf()` statement, the program counts from 1 to 9 because the `printf()` occurs before the variable is checked by the loop condition.

As you may have guessed, you can use either the `while` or `do-while` statement to perform the same sort of looping operations. In many situations, however, your loop may need to check a condition at the beginning rather than at the end of the loop. One example is if you need to check whether your data file is not at the end of the file marker before its contents are processed. You also may have situations that call for a condition to be checked at the end of the loop. Your choice of statement depends on your particular application. Many programmers prefer using the `while` statement because the condition is stated at the beginning of the loop, thus making the program more readable.

for. Another looping statement is `for`. As with `do-while` and `while`, this command enables you to loop until a predetermined condition is met. The format of the `for` statement is as follows:

```
for ( initial expression; loop condition; loop expression)
    program statement
```

The expressions enclosed in parentheses set up the environment for your program loop. They include the following:

- The `initial expression` sets the beginning values

- The `loop condition` sets the condition that must be true in order for the looping to continue

- The `loop expression` is evaluated each time the body of the loop is executed and usually increments a value

Consider the following example:

```
int i;

for (i=0; i<10; i++)
    printf(" %i ", i);
```

This example is similar to the counting examples you used previously when learning `do-while` and `while`. It counts from 1 to 10, printing the contents of the `i` variable on-screen during each loop operation.

The `for` statement is functionally equivalent to the `while` statement, and you can use either one to produce the same results. Many programmers prefer the `for` statement because the entire looping logic, including the counter, exists on one line of the program.

Listing 9.2 demonstrates how each type of looping statement is utilized in an actual program. Each loop basically performs the same process (see figure 9.2). Enter this program and give looping a try.

Listing 9.2. LOOPDEMO.CPP—Looping demo program.

```
1.  //      Name:   LOOPDEMO.CPP
2.  // ???Dave:  David Linthicum
3.  //   Purpose:  Demonstrates the use of looping statements

4.  #include <stdio.h>
5.  #include <conio.h>

6.  void main()

7.  {
```

(continues)

Listing 9.2. Continued.

```
8.      char selection;
9.      int counter = 1;

10.     clrscr();

11.     printf("  ***  Menu  ***\n\n");
12.     printf(" 1.  Count using do-while\n");
13.     printf(" 2.  Count using while\n");
14.     printf(" 3.  Count using for\n");

15.     printf("Enter your selection\n");

16.     scanf ("%c", &selection);

17.     switch (selection)

18.     {
19.         case '1':
20.             do
21.             {
22.                 printf(" %i ", counter);
23.                 ++counter;
24.
            }
25.             while( counter < 10);
26.             break;

27.         case '2':
28.             while( counter < 10)
29.             {
30.                 printf(" %i ", counter);
31.                 ++counter;
32.             }
33.             break;

34.         case '3':
35.             for (counter=1; counter < 10; ++counter)
36.                 printf(" %i ", counter);
37.             break;

38.         default:
39.                 printf("You must enter 1,2,3, or 4");
40.     }

41.  }
```

Figure 9.2 shows the results of this looping program.

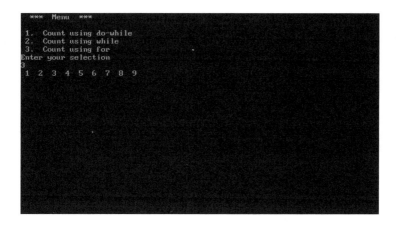

Fig. 9.2.
The looping demo
program results.

Data Types

In the C programming language, *variables* are temporary storage areas for numeric and character information as it is processed in a program. All variables are not created equally. Each is categorized by variable *types*, or the type of information that a variable can contain, and the ranges of values the variable can contain. As a programmer, you declare the type when you create the variable.

Using the proper data type is important. This section examines the use of basic data types, including how, when, and why you use each type in a program. Many data types have appeared already in previous sample programs. This section should help you understand them.

Applications that you develop manage data. The data that the application works with comes in diverse sizes and types. The program needs to know what type of data is being manipulated so that it can appropriate the correct amount of memory; therefore, the program must know the data types.

Following are three basic data types:

- Integers
- Floating-point numbers
- Characters

Each of these data types comes in many forms, offering you many options about how you can store data during the execution of the program. Table 9.3 lists all data types, their sizes, and the range of values each can store. Use this table as a point of reference as you learn the data types in this chapter.

Tip
When you're planning your application, take some time to determine what the variables are to contain and declare them as such. It is a good idea to keep notes about which variables are declared as what and whether they are declared as local or global variables. As you write your program, you can refer to your variable reference as needed. This system should save you time and reduce your number of programming errors.

Table 9.3. Available data types.

Type	Length	Range
unsigned char	8 bits	0 to 255
char	8 bits	–128 to 127
enum	16 bits	–32,768 to 32,767
unsigned int	16 bits	0 to 65,535
short int	16 bits	–32,768 to 32,767
int	16 bits	–32,768 to 32,767
unsigned long	32 bits	0 to 4,294,967,295
long	32 bits	–2,147,483,648 to 2,147,483,647
float	32 bits	$3.4 * (10^{-38})$ to $3.4 * (10^{38})$
double	64 bits	$1.7 * (10^{-308})$ to $1.7 * (10^{308})$
long double	80 bits	$3.4 * (10^{-4932})$ to $1.1 * (10^{4932})$

Integers

When you're working with numeric data, you use an *integer* data type. If your program requires a variable for the storage of a whole number, you can use the reserved word int and then a list of variables you want to declare as integers with a value between –32,768 and 32,767. (You have seen integer data types often in example programs already presented.)

Variables you want to declare with the following value, for example, declare a single variable (value) as an integer:

```
int value;
```

You can declare several variables at once by listing each value on the same line separated by commas, as in the following example:

```
int value1, value2;
```

Or you can declare a value and assign a value to it as well, as in the following example:

```
int value = 99;
```

From table 9.3, you can see three different modifiers that work with `int` to alter the range of values that can be stored in your variables:

- `unsigned`

- `short`

- `int`

An `unsigned` data type is for numbers between 0 and 65,535. The `long` data type is for large numbers between –2,147,483,648 and 2,147,483,647. The `short` data type is for a number between –32,768 and 32,767. Note how much memory is allocated when you declare different data types. You should allocate memory only as required; otherwise, your application is going to be a memory hog.

Floating-Point Numbers

Sometimes you may need to use integer data types that use fractions. *Floating-point numbers* (sometimes called real numbers) are C data types that can store values to several places beyond the decimal point. You use these numbers when you're expressing an exact quantity. You can use floating-point data types for financial or scientific applications where precision is a requirement. Floating-point data types can represent larger or smaller value ranges than integer data types.

You declare floating-point variables in the same way you declare integers. The reserved `float` word, when read, allocates enough memory to store a floating-point number. To declare a simple floating-point variable, for example, you enter the following:

```
float value;
```

To declare several floating-point values, use the following line:

```
float value1, value2;
```

Or to assign a value when the variable is declared, use the following:

```
float value=9.999;
```

II

C Programming Basics

As with integers, floating-point variables come in larger sizes, offering better precision and range. The types of floating-point variables are as follows:

- `float`

- `double`

- `long double`

As you can see from table 9.3, the `float` data type declares variables that can store values from 3.4 * (10^{-38}) to 3.4 * (10^{38}) and have 7 digits of precision. The `double` and `long double` data types can store even larger numbers and provide 15 digits and 19 digits of precision, respectively. The length header in table 9.3 is the amount of memory required by each data type.

Listing 9.3 demonstrates how the different variable declarations affect variables in a program. Notice how the same number is stored in `value1`, `value2`, and `value3`, but how each is affected by its data type. The `float` declaration is the only data type in this program that can store the number (`9.999900`) as displayed in figure 9.3. Try integer or floating-point data types on your own.

Tip

When you're allocating a floating-point variable, remember that always using the larger data types, such as `double` and `long double`, may cause memory problems. Both data types allocate more than twice the memory required by the smaller `float` and several times the memory allocated by `int`. Make sure the variables defined as larger floating-point data types are variables that actually require and use the additional memory.

Listing 9.3. INTTEST.CPP—Integer and floating-point demo program.

```
1.    //      Name:   INTTEST.CPP
2.    // ???Dave:  David Linthicum
3.    //   Purpose:  Demonstrates the use of integers and floating-
      point numbers

4.    #include <stdio.h>
5.    #include <conio.h>

6.    void main()

7.    {

8.        clrscr();

9.        int value1   = 9.9999;
10.       printf("Integer    = %i\n", value1);

11.       long value2  = 9.9999;
12.       printf("Long       = %lu\n", value2);

13.       float value3 = 9.9999;
14.       printf("Float      = %f\n", value3);

15.   }
```

Fig. 9.3.
Integer and floating-
point demo program
output.

Now that you have mastered the difficult task of using numbers in C++, it's time to move on to using characters. Notice how many of the concepts differ from integers to characters, and how you must take care in selecting the proper data type for a particular situation.

Characters

Now that you know how Turbo C++ handles numeric data, you can explore how C handles character data. Storing characters into variables is a common programming activity. As you may have guessed, a data type for declaring variables that can store characters also exists (see table 9.3).

In earlier programs, you may have noticed that the reserved word char declared a variable able to hold a single letter. For example:

```
char char_data;
char_data = 'Y';
printf(" %c\n", char_data);
```

The output is as follows:

```
Y
```

This example illustrates how a variable (char_data) is declared as a character data type and how a letter (Y) is stored in the variable and then printed on-screen using printf(). From listing 9.1, lines 8 through 16 demonstrate how you can declare a variable with a character data type and then use the scanf() function to store a menu selection entered by the user:

```
char selection;
clrscr();

    printf(" ***  Menu  ***\n\n");
    printf(" 1.  Option One\n");
```

```
printf(" 2.  Option Two\n");
printf(" 3.  Option Three\n");
printf(" 4.  Option Four\n\n");
printf("Enter your selection\n");

scanf ("%c", &selection);      //Receive input from the
user
```

It is interesting to note that your computer maintains all of its information in binary code, which means that letters are not stored in the variables directly, and an ASCII number reference represents each letter in the variables declared by char. (See Appendix A, "ASCII Charts.")

Each variable of type char uses one byte of memory, but only 7 bits actually store the information about the character. The last bit is a sign bit. Both the ASCII and the extended character sets can be stored in type char variables.

Data Type Conversions

Sometimes when you're programming, you may need to convert data types, such as an integer data type converted to a character data type or vice versa. Usually, you convert data types when you're performing the following operations:

- Converting user input into a usable type

- Facilitating precision calculations

- Displaying data

You have learned about data types and that type determines the data that is associated with a variable. In this section, you learn how data types can be changed from one type to another through automatic conversion or through a forced type conversion. A *type conversion* is the conversion of data types of an object (variable). There are two types:

- Implicit type conversions

- Explicit type conversion

These type conversions are explained more fully in the following sections.

Implicit Type Conversions
Sometimes type conversions are performed automatically by Turbo C++. If the compilers perform the conversion, it is called an *implicit* type conversion.

An implicit type conversion usually occurs in mathematical operations where objects of two different types are involved. Objects of lower or less precise data types, for example, are converted to more precise data types automatically in a math operation. As with anything associated with math, a set of predefined rules governs implicit type conversions.

Table 9.4 describes the implicit type conversion process for integers. When a character is altered implicitly, the character is a single byte, but when a char type is converted to an int type, two bytes are required. The value of the low-order byte of the new integer is identical to the original char, but the value of the high-order byte depends on whether the char object is signed or unsigned. If unsigned, the high-order byte of the integer is zero. If signed, the high-order byte of the integer is –1.

Table 9.4. Implicit conversion of integer types.

Original type	Converted type	Method
char	int	High byte is set to zero, or the sign is extended
unsigned char	int	High byte zero filled
signed char	int	Sign is extended
short	int	No difference
unsigned short	unsigned int	No difference
enum	int	No difference

Mathematical operations are not the only actions that cause implicit type conversions. Sometimes the type of conversion can occur during function calls. Within a function, the parameters of a function call are an expression, meaning that an implicit type conversion can occur similarly to conversion for any expression.

Explicit Type Conversions

As you learned in the preceding section, automatic type conversions are the most common method of converting data types, but occasionally you need to force a data type conversion. When you actually cause the type conversion to occur, it is called an *explicit type conversion* or *type casting*.

II

C Programming Basics

The syntax of an explicit type conversion is as follows:

```
( type name ) expression
```

To convert a floating-point to an integer, for example, you can use the following code fragment:

```
int value1;
float value2 = 7.648;
value1 = ( int ) value2;
printf(" value1 = %d, x = %f", value1, value2);
```

In this example, you use two variables, value1 defined as an integer and value2 defined as a floating-point variable. On the third line of the code, the type value1 variable is assigned the value of the float after it is type cast. Then each value prints at the terminal using printf(). If the preceding code fragment is executed, the fractional part of the float variable is dropped in the type conversion.

> **Note**
>
> The values of your variables can change during a type-cast operation, such as when a type float converts to a type int. It is less obvious when an int changes to an exact value for all numbers, such as when int variables are converted to float variables. The resulting value may not be equal to the original value.

Compiling

You use the IDE editor or your own ASCII editor (as covered in previous chapters) to create a source file, or the source module. Obviously, you are not able to execute source modules. They must be compiled and linked into executables. In Chapter 8, "Writing Your First Program," you learned how to compile Turbo C++ programs using the IDE and the command-line compiler. In this section, you learn exactly what happens when a source file becomes an executable.

When you're compiling a source file, it converts into a language the computer can understand. The Turbo C++ compiler accomplishes the following tasks when converting your program to a file that your computer can execute:

- The source file is analyzed and converted into several preprocessing token and whitespace characters

■ The preprocessor directives are executed (see Chapter 8)

■ Additional character and string processing occurs

■ The object file is created (if errors are not encountered)

In the first step, the special characters convert, and statements that take up two or more lines are linked. The tokens are elements that the compiler works with such as constants, operators, and keywords. Whitespace characters are space and tab characters as well as comments, which are removed and replaced with a single space.

In the second step, the compiler's directives such as `#include` and `#define` are included. As you may recall from Chapter 8, the `#include` directive tells the compiler to read in a source file, called a header or include file, before the main source file compiles. Using `#include` enables you to compile many source files at once. The `#define` sets up any macros that you want to use in your program.

In the next step, the compiler analyzes the program to make sure that the syntax and semantics are correct. At this point, any programming errors you may have made are discovered and are displayed as compiler error messages. If the compiler does not discover errors, it creates the object module, ready for linking into an executable module.

In the last step, the linker creates the executable program, or load module. As you may recall, the linker combines the object modules with library files, which come with Turbo C++. The resulting file contains extra machine instructions that cause the computer to perform a setup routine for your program to run.

II

C Programming Basics

Summary

This chapter was the first of many chapters that cover the details of the programming language. Here you learned about how you control program logic and flow, how you declare data types, how to convert a data type, and finally you took a brief look behind the scenes of compiling a program. This chapter covered the following topics:

■ You handle program logic and program flow using several program statements: `if`, `if-else`, `switch`, `do-while`, `while`, and `for`. These statements control conditional branching to make decisions and conditional looping to allow control of repetitive operations.

- The `if` statement makes decisions in a program. When the compiler encounters `if`, it checks a condition and, if true, executes the code associated with the `if` statement.

- The `if` statement, in conjunction with the `else` statement, makes either/or decisions in your program.

- The `switch` statement enables you to check a situation using many predefined conditions.

- The `do-while` statement allows looping operations, checking a condition as the loop completes. The `while` statement allows looping operations, checking a condition before the loop executes. The `for` statement enables you to define the looping counters and conditions on a single line in the program. All looping operations work basically the same.

- Data types declare the type of data and the range of data stored in a variable. You can declare a variable as an integer, floating-point, or a character.

- Using type conversion routines, you can change the data type of a variable. An implicit type conversion is automatic, whereas you force an explicit conversion.

- During the compile operation, the compiler does several things including analyzing the source file, reading preprocessing directives, processing additional characters and strings, and finally creating an object file.

Chapter 10

Introduction to String Constants and String Arrays

In the preceding chapter, you learned how to declare different types of characters, integers, and floating-point variables for use in a C++ program. But what if you want to store several characters or a string of characters in a variable? How are strings processed in a C++ program? What is an array?

The programming language provides the following two methods of maintaining strings:

- String constants
- Character arrays

The purpose of this chapter is to introduce you to the proper use of string constants and character arrays in the C++ language. Sample programs provide you with an understanding of how strings are processed in a C++ program.

Strings are useful in many applications. You use them to manage data such as an address list, to display information such as words or sentences on-screen, or to print words or sentences to the printer.

Constants

Several types of constants are available. They are as follows:

- Integer constants
- Whole number constants
- Floating-point constants
- String constants
- Character constants

As you can determine from the word *constant*, a constant does not change. In the following sections, you examine string constants and their uses.

String Constants

Anything enclosed in double quotation marks is considered a *string constant*. For example:

```
"Que"
"987654321"
"1000 North Main Street"
" "
"*"
```

The preceding examples are string constants. The double quotation marks that surround the string are not contained in the string as stored. Therefore

```
"Que"
```

looks like

```
Que
```

to the compiler. Also note that string constants can contain numbers and noncharacters (such as *, &, ^, and so on), as well as character strings.

> **Note**
>
> Although a string constant can contain a number, mathematical operations on these constants are impossible. For arithmetic operations, use integers or floating-point variables (see Chapter 9, "The Basics of C").

As you saw in earlier program examples, printing string constants is a single operation. In listing 10.1, for example, the string constant defined between the quotation marks on line 7 prints on-screen (`cout` is similar to `printf()`). Notice that variables are not required because data is never stored or processed.

Listing 10.1. STRING1.CPP—Sample program printing a string constant.

```
1.  //  Program: STRING1.CPP
2.  //  Author: David S. Linthicum
3.  //  Purpose: String Constant Demo Program One

4.  #include <iostream.h>

5.  main()

6.  {

7.      printf("Using a String Constant\n"); // Print the string
➡constant
8.      return 0;                            // Function returns 0

9.  }
```

All constants end with a zero in memory (null character). Therefore, in the preceding example, the actual string constant

```
"Using a String Constant"
```

is stored as

```
. . . U s i n g   a   s t r i n g   C o n s t a n t
➡0(null character, not the number 0) . .
```

You cannot see the zero, and you do not need to worry about placing the zero at the end of your string constant. C++ does it automatically.

The zero at the end of a string constant is a *string delimiter*. It makes sure that C++ knows where your string ends in memory. This zero is not the same as a character zero (ASCII 48). It is a null character or null zero (ASCII 0; refer to the ASCII table in Appendix A).

Character Constants

In contrast with string constants, character constants are enclosed in single quotation marks. As with the double quotation marks on string constants, the single quotation marks are not part of the character. For example:

'x' 'X' '0' '^' '=' ',' 'W' '+' '%'

The preceding characters are character constants. A null zero (ASCII 0) is not at the end of the character constant as it is with a string constant because it holds only one position in memory.

Note

Remember that you enclose a character constant in single quotation marks and declare a string constant with double quotation marks. For example:

'X'   "X"

The first 'X' is a single character constant with a length of 1, and the second "X" is a string constant character also with the length of one. The difference is that the string constant includes a null zero at the end of the string because C++ needs to know where the string ends. Therefore, you cannot mix character constants and character strings in your program.

Besides standard ASCII characters, a character constant supports special characters that cannot be represented using your keyboard, for example, the high ASCII characters or escape sequences. For a complete list of ASCII characters, refer to Appendix A at the end of the book.

The sigma (Σ) character (ASCII 228 Hex E4) represents constant characters by enclosing the prefix \x and the hex number from the ASCII table. For example:

```
char sigma = '\xE4';    // Places the sigma symbol into
                        // variable sigma
```

You can use this method to store or print any character represented in the ASCII table by its hex number. In this example, the variable symbol does not contain the four characters (\xE4); it contains only the single sigma symbol.

You also can include a special character in a string using the same method. For example:

```
"The \xE4 is the Greek character sigma"
```

Again, the \xE4 tells the C++ compiler to place the sigma character at that location in the string, and it is the only character stored after *The* and before *is*. The \xE4 is not stored. Using these characters in your program, you can create a variety of special effects, such as line and box drawing, cursor movement, and sound.

A character that is read using a backslash (\) is called an *escape sequence*. Escape sequences are useful in programs. Table 10.1 presents several escape sequences and their meanings.

Table 10.1. Escape sequence characters.

Escape Sequence	Meaning
\a	Alarm
\b	Backspace
\f	Formfeed
\n	Carriage return and linefeed
\r	Carriage return
\t	Tab
\v	Vertical tab
\\	Backslash
\?	Question mark
\"	Double quotation mark
\ooo	Octal number
\xhh	Hexadecimal number
\0	The null zero (ASCII 0)

Listing 10.2 uses escape sequences, for example, to beep the terminal twice and then executes two backspaces. Escape sequences add spice to your application through special effects.

Listing 10.2. STRING2.CPP—Sample program using escape sequence characters.

```
1.   //  Program: STRING2.CPP
2.   //  Author: David S. Linthicum
3.   //  Purpose: String Constant Demo Program Two

4.   #include <iostream.h>

5.   main()

6.   {

7.        char ring = '\a';   // Store the alarm escape sequence to
                              ➥a variable
8.        char bs   = '\b';   // Store the backspace escape
                              ➥sequence to a variable
```

(continues)

Listing 10.2. Continued.

```
9.        cout << ring;       // Send the escape sequence to the
                              ➥terminal
10.       cout << ring;          // to beep the terminal twice

11.       cout << "XX";       // Print two characters

12.       cout << bs;         // Send the escape sequence to the
                              ➥terminal
13.       cout << bs;            // Should move the cursor under
                                 ➥the first 'X' character

14.       return 0;      // Return 0

15.   }
```

Arrays

Arrays are variables that hold strings as well as other types of complex data. Unlike other programming languages that have string variables (Pascal and BASIC, for example), arrays in C++ process string information. Most programming languages support arrays and array processing in one form or another. *Arrays*, also called *tables*, are simply lists of information in memory. Many types of arrays exist; you examine them later in the book. In this section, you learn about character arrays, or arrays that contain a character or string of characters.

Chapter 19, "Using Arrays," covers all arrays in detail. Because character arrays are so important to the basic foundation of C++ programming, however, the basic concepts are presented here. The sample programs presented in the following sections should prove useful in helping you understand arrays and array processing. Make sure you understand each line of code and try each of these programs.

Character Arrays

The developers of the C programming language realized that arrays are the ideal place to store and process string information. Suppose that you want to store and process the name of a city in the United States. Using C++, you simply declare as a character array a variable that can hold a string.

You declare the character array variable in your program as follows to set aside 10 locations for the character array variable `location`:

```
char location [ 10 ];
```

To set aside 20 locations for the character array variable `city`, you declare the variable as follows:

```
char city [ 20 ];
```

The purpose of this declaration is to reserve the memory `locations` for the string that is to be maintained in the character array variable. The size of the array is set by the number inside the brackets [ ]. In the first example, therefore, you declare an array that holds up to 10 characters.

You can store information in the character array variable (as with integer variables) when you declare it. For example:

```
char location [ 10 ] = "Denver CO";
```

Now the string `"Denver CO"` is in the character array. In the actual array, the string looks something like the following:

```
location [ 0 ]   'D'
location [ 1 ]   'e'
location [ 2 ]   'n'
location [ 3 ]   'v'
location [ 4 ]   'e'
location [ 5 ]   'r'
location [ 6 ]   ' '
location [ 7 ]   'C'
location [ 8 ]   'O'
location [ 9 ]   '\0'
location [ 10 ]  ' '
```

Each position in the array uses an addressing method in which the name of the variable and the array position (in brackets) beginning with zero mark the place in memory where a particular character resides. At location [5], therefore, you find the `'r'` character, and at location [6], you find a blank.

This addressing method provides you with a way to manipulate the array character by character. For example:

```
char emp [ 20 ] = "Sara Conner";

// c% tells printf() that the variable is a single character
printf("The employee's initials are %c %c\n", emp [ 0 ], emp [ 5]);
```

If this code program executes, you see

```
The employee's initials are S C
```

because the `printf()` function prints only the character at location 0 (which is S) and the character at location 5 (which is C).

You print character array strings using the standard `printf()` function. For example:

```
char emp [ 20 ] = "Sara Conner";

// s% tells printf() that the variable is a string
printf("The employee's name is %s\n", emp);
```

The output is

```
The employee's name is Sara Conner
```

The \0 or null zero (string-terminating character) after the last character in the array marks the end of the string in memory. The rest of the elements do not contain data but still reserve the allocated areas.

Now that you know the basics, you can look at some programs that use and process arrays. In listing 10.3, an array called `location` is declared with a length of 17 and a string stored in the character array. After it is declared, the entire array prints on-screen using the `printf()` function.

Listing 10.3. ARRAY1.CPP—Demonstrates the basic use of a character array.

```
1.   //  Program: ARRAY1.CPP
2.   //  Author: David S. Linthicum
3.   //  Purpose: Array Demo Program One

4.   #include <stdio.h>
5.   #include <conio.h>

6.   main()

7.   {

8.        char location [17] = "Washington D.C.";

9.        clrscr();

10.       printf("I live in %s \n", location);

11.       return 0;


12.  }
```

The output is presented in figure 10.1.

To see how the string resides within the array, from the Turbo C++ IDE, choose Inspect from the Debug menu and then select the name of the character array variable (in this case `location`). You must take these steps after you set a break point directly after line 8 in the program.

Fig. 10.1.
Output of
listing 10.3.

If you can reach this point, you see an Inspecting window like the one shown in figure 10.2. Notice how each character resides in its own location in the array and how the null zero exists at the end of the string marking the end of the string in memory. In memory, all character arrays basically look like this one.

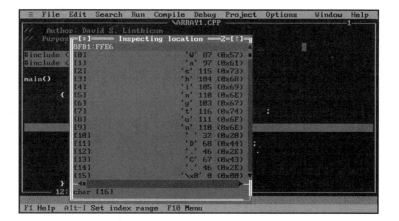

Fig. 10.2.
Inspecting the character array variable location.

In listing 10.4, similar to listing 10.3, the program declares an array and then prints it on-screen. In this program, however, each character is placed into each array element one at a time; then the null zero is stored in the last array element. Remember, the null zero terminates the string. If you do not place the null zero there, C++ does not know where the string is terminated in memory.

If you declare your character array as in listing 10.3, the placement of the null zero at the end of the string is automatic. Of course, this method is not a good way to store string information in an array. You saw in listing 10.3 how to store information at the time of declaration. This program only serves to demonstrate how information inside array elements is manipulated within the program.

Listing 10.4. ARRAY2.CPP—Sample program demonstrating array addressing.

```
1.   //  Program: ARRAY2.CPP
2.   //  Author: David S. Linthicum
3.   //  Purpose: Array Demo Program Two

4.   #include <stdio.h>
5.   #include <conio.h>

6.   main()

7.   {

8.       char location [17];

9.       clrscr();

10.      location[ 0 ]  = ' ';
11.      location[ 1 ]  = 'W';
12.      location[ 2 ]  = 'a';
13.      location[ 3 ]  = 's';
14.      location[ 4 ]  = 'h';
15.      location[ 5 ]  = 'i';
16.      location[ 6 ]  = 'n';
17.      location[ 7 ]  = 'g';
18.      location[ 8 ]  = 't';
19.      location[ 9 ]  = 'o';
20.      location[ 10 ] = 'n';
21.      location[ 11 ] = ' ';
22.      location[ 12 ] = 'D';
23.      location[ 13 ] = '.';
24.      location[ 14 ] = 'C';
25.      location[ 15 ] = '.';
26.      location[ 16 ] = ' ';
27.      location[ 17 ] = '\0';

28.      printf("I live in %s \n", location);

29.      return 0;

30.  }
```

The program generates the following output:

```
I live in Washington, D.C.
```

Listing 10.5 demonstrates how you can replace a character stored inside an array using the array addressing method introduced earlier in the chapter. Here the program first declares and stores a string to a character array variable (location). Then the program uses the

```
variable-name [ location ] = New Value;
```

syntax to store new characters directly into the array at predefined locations using lines 11 through 15 of the program. This syntax has the effect of changing the letters "D.C." to "State" as the program displays using two identical printf() statements on lines 10 and 16.

Listing 10.5. ARRAY3.CPP—Sample program demonstrating array manipulation.

```
1.   //  Program: ARRAY3.CPP
2.   //  Author: David S. Linthicum
3.   //  Purpose: Array Demo Program Three

4.   #include <stdio.h>
5.   #include <conio.h>

6.   main()

7.   {

8.       char location [] = " Washington D.C.   ";

9.       clrscr();

10.      printf("I live in %s \n", location);

11.      location[ 12 ] = 'S';
12.      location[ 13 ] = 't';
13.      location[ 14 ] = 'a';
14.      location[ 15 ] = 't';
15.      location[ 16 ] = 'e';

16.      printf("I live in %s \n", location);

17.      return 0;

18.  }
```

As you can see, the entire meaning of the sentence changes as a result of this program (see fig. 10.3). To find the correct positions in the array, you're going to have to do a little counting. Starting at position 12 should do it.

Fig. 10.3.
Output of
listing 10.5.

You may have noticed something different in the character array declaration statement on line 8 of listing 10.5:

```
char location [] = " Washington D.C.   ";
```

As you can see, no number is between the brackets [ ]. If you leave out the numbers, C++ automatically declares the array to be the size of the string you store into the array in the initial declaration. Leaving out the number saves time because you do not have to count the number of characters in a string. You need to add additional spaces on the end of the array since you're going to need that space to put in additional characters. If the additional spaces were not available and you attempted to overwrite it, you're going to overwrite the null terminator and destroy the array.

Listing 10.6 declares and stores strings in character arrays in two distinct ways. On line 8 of the program, the declaration of the array enables you to place individual characters directly into an array. The resulting array looks similar to a standard string array, except you don't have a null zero at the end of the string.

Figure 10.4, for example, shows the contents of the character array location1. As you can see, the null zero is not at the end of the string. In contrast, figure 10.5 presents the contents of the character array location2, where the null zero is apparent.

This type of character array without a null zero cannot be treated as if it were a string in a program. The elements can be processed individually but not as an entire string.

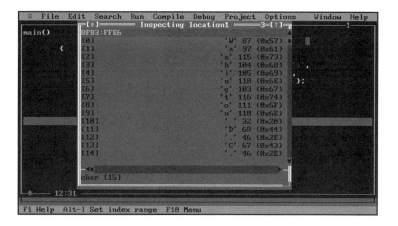

Fig. 10.4.
The character
array variable
location1.

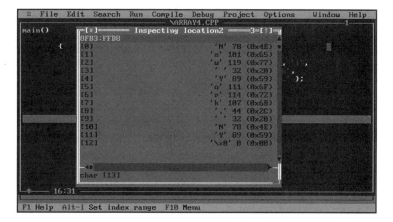

Fig. 10.5.
The character
array variable
location2.

II

C Programming Basics

Listing 10.6. ARRAY4.CPP—Sample demonstrating array declaration methods.

```
1.    //   Program: ARRAY4.CPP
2.    //   Author: David S. Linthicum
3.    //   Purpose: Array Demo Program Four

4.    #include <stdio.h>
5.    #include <conio.h>

6.    main()

7.    {

8.        char location1 [15] = { 'W', 'a', 's', 'h', 'i',
9.                                'n', 'g', 't', 'o', 'n',
10.                               ' ', 'D', '.', 'C', '.' };
```

(continues)

Listing. 10.6. Continued.

```
11.     char location2 [] = "New York, NY";
        printf("Location 1 = %s\n", location1);
        printf("Location 2 = %s\n", location2);
12.     clrscr();


13.     return 0;


14.  }
```

In listing 10.7, the final array demonstration program, you see how arrays are processed using looping statements such as the ones covered in Chapter 9.

Listing 10.7. ARRAY5.CPP—Sample program demonstrating complex character array manipulation using a loop.

```
1.   //  Program: ARRAY5.CPP
2.   //  Author: David S. Linthicum
3.   //  Purpose: Array Demo Program Five

4.   #include <stdio.h>
5.   #include <conio.h>


6.   // Declare an array, and store a string
7.   char str_array1 [ 16 ] = "I am on da move";

8.   // Declare an array
9.   char str_array2 [ 16 ];

10.  // Declare the function
11.  void print_str();

12.  main()

13.  {

14.      // Declare a counter
15.      int count = 0;

16.      // Clear the screen
17.      clrscr();

18.      // Invoke the print_str() function
19.      print_str();

20.      printf("\nCopying : ");
```

```
21.          // Loop 14 times copying a character from one array to
                the other
22.            while (count <= 14)
23.            {
24.                printf(" %c ", str_array1 [ count ] );
25.                str_array2 [ count ] = str_array1 [ count ];
26.                ++count;          //Increment the counter
27.            }

28.        printf("\n Done!\n\n");

29.        print_str();

30.        return 0;

31.  }

32.  // Function prints the contents of the arrays
33.  void print_str()

34.  {

35.        printf("String one =  %s \n", str_array1);
36.        printf("String two =  %s \n", str_array2);

37.  }
```

On lines 7 and 9 of listing 10.7, the program globally declares two arrays—
one with a string and one without. On line 11, a function that main calls
twice is declared globally. This function prints the contents of each array. It
is defined at the bottom of the program on lines 33 through 37. The Looking
function is covered in more detail in chapters 9 and 16.

Inside the main function, both arrays display on-screen, showing the contents
of each before processing begins using the print_str() function. The loop is
entered on line 22. The loop is set up to process each element of the character
arrays by reading a character stored in an element of the primary array
(str_array1) and then storing it in the corresponding element of the second
array (str_array2).

During each loop, notice how the character being processed is displayed on-
screen using the printf() function. This setup shows the user how the processing is progressing and adds interest. The loop executes 20 times, moving
from position zero in the array to position 14, and all of the information
stored in the primary array copies to the second array. After the loop ends,
both arrays match. The program proves this match by printing each on-
screen by calling the print_str() function one last time (see fig. 10.6).

Fig. 10.6.

The output of listing 10.7.

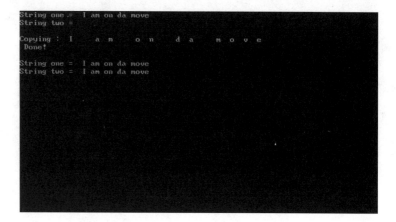

Although you can use other methods to manipulate character arrays, this program simply demonstrates how you can use loops to process each array's elements one element at a time. Many database applications use this sort of array processing with loop operations to search, sort, move, and copy arrays. See chapter 19 for further details on array processing.

Character Arrays versus Character Strings

You may be asking yourself: What is the difference between character arrays and strings? Both character arrays and character strings store information. However, character arrays and character strings have to be treated differently by programmers. Recall from earlier in this chapter, strings do not contain null zero, which is required when processing strings.

In listing 10.6, for example, you declare an array using

```
char location1 [15] = { 'W', 'a', 's', 'h', 'i',
                        'n', 'g', 't', 'o', 'n',
                        ' ', 'D', '.', 'C', '.' };
```

or

```
char location2 [] = "New York, NY";
```

location1 cannot be processed as an array, whereas the variable location2 can. As you progress through the book, of course, you find that knowing the difference between the two types of strings becomes second nature. An elaborate assortment of string processing functions also allows direct manipulation of string variables.

Variables

In this section, you learn about variables: what they are, how they come into existence, and how to use them in a program. Using variables is a big part of learning the C++ programming language and creating programs of your own. Software such as spreadsheet packages (Lotus 1-2-3, for example) or database management systems (FoxPro, for example) can use as many as several thousand variables to track any number of items in the program. Although most of your applications, at least at first, are not going to be that complex, now is a good time to learn the proper use of variables.

As you are creating your program, you can declare variables at any time, for any reason. It is best to declare variables at the beginning of the block of code that is to use them. For example:

```
main()

{

    char location [17] = "Washington D.C.";

    clrscr();

        printf("I live in %s \n", location);

        return 0;


}
```

In this block of code, the variable `destination` is declared inside the function that makes use of it. If you declare variables not used inside your program, the compiler generates warnings. Each variable has its own name, a variable type, and obtains a value.

Managing variables is a lesson in organization. Rookie C++ programmers tend to declare more variables than actually required and with names that have no bearing on the purpose of the variable or its type. Poorly naming your variables does not affect the processing of the program. In a well organized, well-thought-out C++ program, however, variables names are

- Unique

- Given meaningful names

- Easily grouped

Tip
Remember that if you declare variables inside a function such as `main()`, that function is the only one that can use the variable because it is declared locally. If you want a variable to be used by more than one function, you should declare it globally outside of a function, usually at the top of the source file.

You cannot give two variables the same name. If you do, the Turbo C++ compiler cannot differentiate between them.

Variables can have names as short as a letter, as in the following example:

```
int i;
```

Or your variables can have a name as long as 30 characters, as follows:

```
int total_sales_for_FY_1993_in_mkt;
```

All variables must begin with a letter or an underscore (_); then you can use letters, numbers, and underscores to create your variable name. Spaces are not allowed in variable names, and you cannot use the same name as a C++ command or library function.

The following are valid variable names, for example:

```
emp_name    salestotal94    _yesterday       student_age
```

The following are not valid variable names:

```
90_salestotal      emp+name      Fiscal year      printf
```

The first example (`90_salestotal`) begins the variable name with a number (9), which is illegal. The second example contains a plus symbol (+) in the variable name. Because the plus sign is not a letter, number, or underscore, it also is illegal. The third example obviously violates the rule of not having a space in your variable name, and the last example uses a reserved word that is also the name of a library function (`printf()`).

Also remember that C++ is case sensitive; therefore, the following variables, even though spelled the same, look completely different to the C++ compiler:

```
TOTAL     Total    total    tOTAL
```

Generally, C++ programs use lowercase variable names and uppercase letters for macro variables. You can use any variable names you want, of course, but you should try to put some meaning into the way you name your variables.

Consider the following suggested rules:

1. Name declared macro variables using the `#define` statements and uppercase letters. This standard method of naming macro variables can be the easiest way to keep track of them. For more information about macros, see Chapter 12.

Variable names should be descriptive. For example:

```
int totals_FY_sales;
```

is better than using

```
int sales;
```

The second example takes a few more keystrokes, but you will be glad you took the time when you're keeping track of hundreds of variables in your application.

2. When you can, try grouping variables by using special naming standards. If you need to declare several variables used to track employee information, for example, you can use the following:

```
char emp_fname;
char emp_lname;
char emp_address;
char emp_city;
char emp_state;
char emp_zip;
```

Notice how all the variables begin with `emp_`. Now you know that all variables that begin with `emp_` relate to employee information.

3. If you can, declare your variables in groups at the top of your source file or before the block of code that makes use of the variables. Notice how the variables declared in the example in rule #2 group the declaration statements.

4. You should use programming comments to define your variables. You may know what `sales_93` means, but programmers who have to work on your program later may not. Take some time to add comments to your source file where appropriate.

Summary

In this chapter, you learned the ways to store and manage character strings within a C++ program. Using strings, you can manage such information as names, addresses, Social Security numbers, and any other alphanumeric information. At the end of the chapter, you learned how to create, name, and manage variables correctly. The chapter covered the following topics:

II

C Programming Basics

- You create string constants by placing any alphanumeric text between two double quotation marks (" "). In memory, string constants have a null zero at the end of the string. This zero instructs C++ where the string ends in memory. String constants cannot be changed.

- You create character constants by placing any character between two single quotation marks (' '). A null zero is not placed at the end of a character string. You also can use character strings to manage escape sequences that can perform special activities such as beeping the terminal or executing a backspace.

- You declare string arrays to allocate memory for the storage of any string. Each character in the string is stored in an element in an array and can be manipulated as a single element by using a special addressing method. A string array must end with a string terminator (\0). It tells the compiler where the string terminates in memory.

- Character arrays are different from character strings. A character string is not terminated with a null terminator and therefore is processed differently than a character array.

- Variables have characteristics, and correct use of those characteristics is your job as the programmer. Each variable should have a unique name that is legal to the compiler. The name you select for the variable should be meaningful to the purpose of the variable, and whenever possible, variables should be grouped logically and documented inside the source file.

Chapter 11

Understanding Variable Scope

C++, like other programming languages, supports the concept of variable scope, or how variables are recognized and managed in program functions. Managing variables in a C++ program is a challenge. Things are not as intuitive as you may think. You must follow many rules, and you need some experience before managing variables becomes a natural activity.

As you may already know, variables that are local to a particular function are protected from other functions. This concept can be somewhat confusing to a new programmer. This chapter, therefore, is dedicated to explaining variable scope. Here, you learn several aspects of variable management including the following:

- Understanding the concepts of global and local variables

- Defining the scope of a variable

- Using local variables in an application

- Using global variables in an application

- Using automatic and static variables

- Passing variables to functions

The concept of variables, their declaration, and use were touched upon in previous chapters. Mastering variables is a major step to becoming an effective C++ programmer. In the discussion here, several examples make these variable scope concepts clearer. Try each example as it is presented.

Global versus Local Variables

As the name implies, *global variables* are variables that are declared outside any function, and by default, are visible to any function including main(). In contrast, *local variables* are variables declared inside a function and are visible only to that particular function.

In listing 11.1, for example, global variables a, b, and c are declared outside any function and are therefore visible to all functions in this particular application. In the main() function, these variables store values. Other functions can use them in the same way.

Listing 11.1. LISTING1.CPP—Demonstrates the use of global variables in a simple C++ program.

```
1.    //   Program:  LISTING1.CPP
2.    //   Purpose:  Demonstrates the use of global and local
➥variables
3.    // Author:  David Linthicum

4.    #include <stdio.h>

5.    // Declare global variables
6.    int a;
7.    int b;
8.    int c;
      int printme(int d);
9.    main()

10.   {
      // Declare local variables
      int d;
      int e;

      // Put data in the variables
11.       a = 1;
12.       b = 2;
13.       c = 3;

          d = 4;
          e = 5;

      // Display the global variables
14.   printf("\n %i %i %i \n", a, b, c);

      // Display the local variables
      printf("\n %i %i \n", d, d);
      // Call a function to print a local and global variable
      // since d is a local variable to main() this function is not
➥able
```

```
          // to see it.
          // Therefore, you must pass that variable to that function.
          printme(d);

15.       return 0;

16.   }
      int printme(int d)
      {
          // Since a is a global variable it's already available in
          // this function.
          printf("\n %i %i", a, d)'
          return 0;
      }
```

In listing 11.2, similar to listing 11.1, the variables are now declared inside the function main() and therefore are visible inside that function only. Other functions do not recognize these variables and cannot use them.

Listing 11.2. LISTING2.CPP—Using local variables.

```
1.    //   Program:  LISTING2.CPP
2.    //   Purpose:  Demonstrates the use of local variables
3.    //   Author:   David Linthicum

4.    #include <stdio.h>


5.    main()

6.    {

7.        // Declare local variables
8.        int a;
9.        int b;
10.       int c;

11.       a = 1;
12.       b = 2;
13.       c = 3;

14.       printf("\n %i %i %i \n", a, b, c);

15.       return 0;

16.   }
```

In listing 11.3, both local and global variables are used. Note that variable a is visible to all functions in this program, not just main(). Variables b and c are declared locally, however, and are visible only to the function main(). The main() function can alter these variables, but other functions cannot. They are protected.

Listing 11.3. LISTING3.CPP—Using local and global variables.

```
1.   //    Program:  LISTING3.CPP
2.   //    Purpose:  Demonstrates the use of local and global
➥ variables
3.   //    Author:  David Linthicum

4.   #include <stdio.h>
5.   #include <conio.h>

6.   // Declare global variable
7.   int a;

8.   main()

9.   {

10.       clrscr(); // Clear the screen

11.       // Declare local variables
12.       int b;
13.       int c;

14.       a = 1;
15.       b = 2;
16.       c = 3;

17.       printf("\n %i %i %i \n", a, b, c);

18.       return 0;

19.  }
```

You may be thinking to yourself that using global variables is the easiest way to initialize variables because they are available throughout the application. Although this point is true, using global variables can be dangerous. In certain portions of the program, some functions can alter a global variable, thus altering it in all other functions as well.

A sales report user-defined function called `print_sales()`, for example, is responsible for printing out sales information contained in the following variables:

```
// January Sales
int jan_sales;

// Total Sales for the year
int tot_sales;

// Total Sales minus expenses
int net_sales;
```

For the sake of convenience here, each variable is declared globally. Another function called `up_sales()`, which updates sales information to a file, also uses the variable `net_sales`. In this particular function, however, `net_sales` reflects the sales of fishing nets in the sporting goods department.

Now, if the variable `net_sales` is altered in the function `up_sales()`, it is altered globally. When `print_sales()` is invoked, it prints the contents of the variable, which may now be incorrect—altered by another function.

Although this example seems extreme, it does happen quite often. Global variables are visible across many functions, and as you can see in the example, using global variables is dangerous because other functions can inadvertently alter a variable that is used elsewhere. Another reason to avoid global variables is the fact that they consume more memory than local variables. Therefore, it is better to declare variables locally, for use only in your local functions.

Local variables are protected and can be changed only from within the function that declared the variable. A local variable cannot be used, updated, deleted, or otherwise bothered by other functions unless you have set up your program explicitly to do so.

Now look at some additional examples. In listing 11.4, you declare a variable called `sales` globally. In the main function, you store the value of `1000` to this variable and then print it on-screen. After it is printed, a function that uses the same variable is called, but this time the value of `2000` is stored to it. The variable is printed on-screen again when in this function.

After the program returns to the `program` function, the value is printed one last time. Notice how the value stored in the global variable has changed from `1000` to `2000`? Because this variable is not local, the other functions can alter it at will.

Listing 11.4. LISTING4.CPP—Using local and global variables in an application.

```
1.    //   Program:  LISTING4.CPP
2.    //   Purpose:  Demonstrates the use of local and global
➥ variables
3.    //   Author:  David Linthicum

4.    #include <stdio.h>
5.    #include <conio.h>

6.    // Declare global variables
7.    int sales;
```

II

C Programming Basics

(continues)

Listing 11.4. Continued.

```
8.    // Declare functions
9.    void print_sales_again();

10.   main()

11.   {

12.       clrscr(); // Clear the screen

13.       // Set sales to 1000
14.       sales = 1000;

15.       // Print the current value of sales
16.       printf("\n Sales is %i \n", sales);

17.       // Call a function
18.       print_sales_again();

19.       // See what is in sales now
20.       printf("\n Sales is %i \n", sales);

21.       return 0;

22.   }

23.   void print_sales_again()

24.   {

25.       // Set sales to 2000
26.       sales = 2000;

27.       // Print the current value of sales
28.       printf("\n Sales is %i \n", sales);

29.       return;

30.   }
```

In listing 11.5, the program declares a variable called sales locally. In the main function, you store the value of 1000 to this variable and then print it on-screen. After it is printed, a function that uses the same variable is called, but this time the value of 2000 is stored to it. It is printed on-screen again when the function returns (see fig. 11.1).

Notice that the other function must declare the variable again. Because it is not declared globally, it is known only to the function that declares it. After the program returns to the main() function, the value is printed one last time. Notice how the value stored in the variable has not changed from 1000 to 2000. Because this variable is local, the other functions cannot alter it, even if the same variable name is used.

Listing 11.5. LISTING5.CPP—Using local and global variables in an application.

```
1.   //   Program:  LISTING5.CPP
2.   //   Purpose:  Demonstrates the use of local and global
↪ variables
3.   //   Author:  David Linthicum

4.   #include <stdio.h>
5.   #include <conio.h>

6.   // Declare functions
7.   void print_sales_again();

8.   main()

9.   {

10.       clrscr(); // Clear the screen

11.       // Declare local variables
12.       int sales;

13.       // Set sales to 1000
14.       sales = 1000;

15.       // Print the current value of sales
16.       printf("\n Sales is %i \n", sales);

17.       // Call a function
18.       print_sales_again();

19.       // See what is in sales now
20.       printf("\n Sales is %i \n", sales);

21.       return 0;

22.   }

23.   void print_sales_again()

24.   {

25.       // Declare local variables
26.       int sales;

27.       // Set sales to 2000
28.       sales = 2000;

29.       // Print the current value of sales
30.       printf("\n Sales is %i \n", sales);

31.       return;

32.   }
```

Fig. 11.1.
The output from
listing 11.5.

```
Sales is 1000
Sales is 2000
Sales is 1000
```

How to Use Global Variables Sparingly

As you may have gathered by now, it is best to write modular, structured programs that combine many functions, each function performing a particular task. In addition, it is best to define as many variables as possible as local to the functions that use them instead of defining them as global for the reasons cited in the preceding section.

Tip
Declare all global variables at the top of your program. If you use this standard way of defining global variables, you can locate these variables easier as you make changes to your program.

Using many global variables is risky. In some instances, however, using many global variables makes sense, such as when you are defining a variable that is used by most functions in your application. A tax rate or screen size is a good candidate for a global variable that you may want to define once. Other functions can make use of it.

Listing 11.6 demonstrates one possible use of a global variable. In this program, the tax rate is defined at the top of the program and is therefore available to both functions in the program: main() and calc_tax().

Listing 11.6. LISTING6.CCP—Using a global variable in an application.

```
1.    //    Program:  LISTING6.CCP
2.    //    Purpose:  Demonstrates the correct use of global
➥ variables
3.    //    Author:   David Linthicum

4.    #include <stdio.h>
5.    #include <conio.h>

6.    // Global variable and store a value to it
7.    float tax_rate = .20;

8.    // Declare functions
9.    int calc_tax(int gross_sales);
```

```
10.  main()

11.  {

12.        clrscr(); // Clear the screen

13.        // Declare a local variable and store a value in it
14.        int gross_sales = 1000;

15.        // Print the gross sales
16.        printf("\nThe gross sales are %i\n", gross_sales);

17.        // Print the tax rate
18.        printf("The tax rate is      %f\n", tax_rate);

19.        // Print the taxes due using the calc_tax() function
20.        printf("Taxes due is         %i \n",
  ➥ calc_tax(gross_sales));

21.        return 0;

22.  }

23.  int calc_tax(int gross_sales)

24.  {

25.        // Declare local variables
26.        int taxes_due;

27.        // Calculate taxes due
28.        taxes_due = (gross_sales*tax_rate);

29.        return taxes_due;

30.  }
```

An even better way to use a global variable is using the preprocessor to declare a macro, which is used like a global variable in your program. Recall the discussion of using preprocessor macros. When they are encountered in a program, the value set for the macro is replaced automatically in the program. For example:

```
#define TAX_RATE .20
```

This macro may make more sense in listing 11.6 because the macro TAX_RATE cannot be altered in any of the functions, although it is, in a sense, visible to all functions in your program. Remember that a preprocessor macro actually edits the program file before it is submitted to the compiler. For all practical purposes, however, you can use it like a global variable that cannot be altered.

Automatic and Static Variables

What happens to local variables after a function returns? If they have not been declared as static variables, the information is lost. Local variables declared locally in a function are *automatic variables*, meaning that local variables are lost when the function completes. You can use `auto` to declare a variable

```
auto int sales;
```

because local variables automatically are declared as `auto` by default; therefore, using `auto` is optional. All of the following variables are declared as automatic. For example:

```
auto int sales;

auto float perc_tax;

int total_sales;

int systems = 20;
```

Static variables, on the other hand, maintain their value after a function is completed. A variable in a function once declared as static, therefore, maintains a value throughout subsequent executions of the same function. Suppose that in a function you store a 1 to a variable that is declared as a static variable and then change its value to 10 by adding 9 before the function is completed. The next time that function is invoked, the value is already set to 10 when the function begins processing. If the static variable is changed again by adding 9, the value of 19 is stored in the static variable available when the function executes again. You can probably think of many uses for this kind of variable. Listing 11.7 demonstrates this principle.

When the function is complete, a static variable is stored for use the next time that function is called. You declare static variables by placing the keyword `static` in front of the variable. For instance:

```
static int sales = 1000;
static int systems = 500;
```

This value is stored in the static variable only the first time a function executes. If a value is not defined, the compiler stores a zero to a static variable by default.

In listing 11.7, for example, the program calls 20 times a function that prints a variable called `sales`. The `sales` variable is declared in the function `print_sales()` as a static variable where its initial value is stored.

Each time the function is executed, the value in sales is maintained after the function is complete. It is available when the function is called again (see fig. 11.2). Static variables are thus unlike other automatic variables where the value is lost after the function is completed. Notice how the initial value of 0 is stored to the static variable. This value is stored there only the first time the function is called.

Listing 11.7. LISTING7.CPP—Using static variables in an application.

```
1.    //    Program:  LISTING7.CPP
2.    //    Purpose:  Demonstrates the use of static variables
3.    //    Author:   David Linthicum

4.    #include <stdio.h>
5.    #include <conio.h>

6.    // Declare function
7.    void print_sales_again(int counter);

8.    main()

9.    {

10.        clrscr(); // Clear the screen

11.        // Declare local automatic variables
12.        int counter = 1;

13.        // Call the function several time
14.        do
15.        {
16.            print_sales_again(counter);
17.            counter++;
18.        }
19.        while (counter <= 20);

20.        return 0;

21.    }

22.    void print_sales_again(int counter)

23.    {

24.        // Declare local variables
25.        // Only set to 0 the first time the function is called
26.        int static sales = 0;

27.        // Add 1000 to sales
28.        sales = sales+1000;

29.        // Print the current value of sales
30.        printf("Sales in pass %i is %i \n", counter, sales);

31.        return;

32.    }
```

Fig. 11.2.
The output from
listing 11.7.

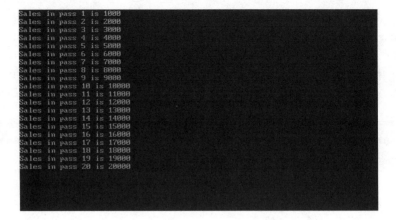

```
Sales in pass 1 is 1000
Sales in pass 2 is 2000
Sales in pass 3 is 3000
Sales in pass 4 is 4000
Sales in pass 5 is 5000
Sales in pass 6 is 6000
Sales in pass 7 is 7000
Sales in pass 8 is 8000
Sales in pass 9 is 9000
Sales in pass 10 is 10000
Sales in pass 11 is 11000
Sales in pass 12 is 12000
Sales in pass 13 is 13000
Sales in pass 14 is 14000
Sales in pass 15 is 15000
Sales in pass 16 is 16000
Sales in pass 17 is 17000
Sales in pass 18 is 18000
Sales in pass 19 is 19000
Sales in pass 20 is 20000
```

Do not confuse local static variables with global variables. A static variable can be altered only by the function that declared it, whereas a global variable can be modified by any function, including `main()`.

How to Pass Variables

Functions are covered in detail in Chapter 13, "Using Functions," of this book. In this section, the concept of passing variables to functions is discussed. C++ enables you to pass variables to functions in one of two ways:

- By copying the value into a function

- By providing the address of a variable

- By reference

- By value

Basically, you copy variables into a function that contains a single value, where an address is passed to functions to tell the function where to find information contained in complex variables such as arrays. Pay special attention to the following sections of the chapter; they might save you many hours of programming time.

Passing Variables by Copy

Passing a variable by copy is the process of calling a function and then passing a variable into that function. Only a copy of the variable is passed to the function; therefore, it cannot modify the original variable, only the copy.

A variable declared locally, for example, can be copied into a function by passing that variable as an argument. You have already seen this process in listing 11.6, where the value in `gross_sales` is passed to the function `calc_tax()`, where it is used to calculate taxes due.

Listing 11.8 demonstrates how a variable is copied into a function to perform a specific action. Here, a function called `count_to()` is declared. Notice that `count_to()` is declared so that this function is set up to receive a value, the variable counter:

```
void count_to(int counter)
```

The function `count_to()` counts to the number being copied to this function. The output of the program is presented in figure 11.3.

Listing 11.8. LISTING8.CPP—Passing values into functions.

```
1.   //   Program:  LISTING8.CPP
2.   //   Purpose:  Demonstrates the use of passing variable to a
➥ function by copy
3.   //   Author:  David Linthicum

4.   #include <stdio.h>
5.   #include <conio.h>

6.   // Declare function
7.   void count_to(int counter);

8.   main()

9.   {

10.      clrscr(); // Clear the screen

11.      printf("Counting to 20\n");
12.      count_to(20);

13.      printf("Counting to 10\n");
14.      count_to(10);

15.      printf("Counting to 15\n");
16.      count_to(15);

17.      return 0;

18.  }

19.  void count_to(int counter)

20.  {
```

II

C Programming Basics

(continues)

Listing 11.8. Continued.

```
21.      int count = 1;

22.      // Count to the number copied into this function
23.      while (count <= counter)
24.          {
25.              // Print the number as it is counted
26.              printf(" %i ", count);
27.              count++;
28.          };

29.      // New line
30.      printf("\n");

31.      return;

32. }
```

Fig. 11.3.
The output from
listing 11.8.

```
Counting to 20
 1  2  3  4  5  6  7  8  9  10  11  12  13  14  15  16  17  18  19  20
Counting to 10
 1  2  3  4  5  6  7  8  9  10
Counting to 15
 1  2  3  4  5  6  7  8  9  10  11  12  13  14  15
```

Remember that only a copy of the variable is passed to the receiving function. In listing 11.8, therefore, if the function count_to() changes the variable count, only the copy of counter changes, not the original version of the variable. This method separates the functions from one another and protects your local variables from being changed by other functions. You can employ various techniques to return a variable from a function, as discussed in Chapter 13.

In addition to passing a single value to a function, you can pass many values as well. Listing 11.9, for example, demonstrates how to pass the copies of two variables into a function. The same rules apply; the only difference is that more than one copy of the variables is passed to the function. And as always, the function cannot change the original variable (see fig. 11.4).

Listing 11.9. LISTING9.CPP—Passing two values into a function.

```
1.   //    Program:  LISTING9.CPP
2.   //    Purpose:  Demonstrates the use of passing two variable to
➡ a function by copy
3.   //    Author:  David Linthicum

4.   #include <stdio.h>
5.   #include <conio.h>

6.   // Declare function
7.   void count_to(int counter, int by);

8.   main()

9.   {

10.        clrscr(); // Clear the screen

11.        printf("Counting to 20 by 2\n");
12.        count_to(20,2);

13.        printf("Counting to 10 by 1\n");
14.        count_to(10,1);

15.        printf("Counting to 15 by 3\n");
16.        count_to(15,3);

17.        return 0;

18.  }

19.  void count_to(int counter, int by)

20.  {

21.        int count = 0;

22.        // Count to the number copied into this function
23.        while (count <= counter)
24.            {
25.                // Print the number as it is counted
26.                printf(" %i ", count);
27.                count=count+by;
28.            };

29.        // New line
30.        printf("\n");

31.        return;

32.  }
```

II

C Programming Basics

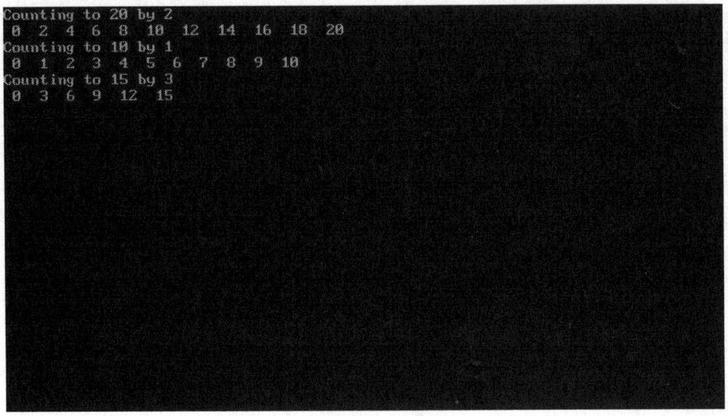

Fig. 11.4.
The output from
listing 11.9.

```
Counting to 20 by 2
 0  2  4  6  8  10  12  14  16  18  20
Counting to 10 by 1
 0  1  2  3  4  5  6  7  8  9  10
Counting to 15 by 3
 0  3  6  9  12  15
```

Passing Variables by Address

Now that you have an understanding of how values are copied into functions, you can explore how the address of arrays and nonarrays are passed to functions. Sometimes this process is called "passing by address" or "passing by reference." Both expressions mean the same thing.

When an address is passed to a function, the function does not copy the item contained in the address to that function. If there are changes made in the function to the variable passed, this changes the variable for the rest of the program to use the new changes. The function knows only where to find the item in memory. This process is illustrated in listing 11.10.

Listing 11.10. LISTING10.CPP—Passing an address to a function.

```
1.   // Program:  LISTING10.CPP
2.   /  Author:  David S. Linthicum
3.   // Purpose:  Calculate the average of 5 grades using an array
➥ passed to a function

4.   #include <stdio.h>
5.   #include <conio.h>

6.   // declare a function
7.   char calc_grade(int scores[]);

8.   // declare grade array
9.   int scores[5];

10.   int main()

11.   {

12.       // Declare local variables
```

```
13.       char grade;
14.       int count = 1;

15.       clrscr();

16.       // Enter grades into an array using a loop
17.       // Loop 5 times for five grades
18.       while (count <= 5)
19.       {
20.       printf("\nEnter the grade %i: ", count);
21.       scanf("%d", &scores[count++]);
22.       }

23.       // Calculate the grade using the array and the function
24.       grade = calc_grade(scores);

25.       // Print the results
26.       printf("\n\nYour grade is %c \n", grade);

27.       return 0;


28.  }


29.  char calc_grade(int scores[])

30.  {

31.       // Declare local variables
32.       float final_grade;      // Final grade
33.       int i;                  // Counter
34.       float total;            // Running total

35.       // Calculate the grade from the array
36.       // Add up all of the scores
37.       for (i=1;  i<=5;i++)
38.          {
39.           total=total+scores[i];
40.          }

41.       // Divide them by the number of scores
42.       final_grade = (total/5);

43.       // Return the correct letter grade based on the final
  grade
44.       if (final_grade >= 90)
45.          {
46.              return 'A';
47.          }

48.       if (final_grade < 90 && final_grade >= 80)
49.          {
50.              return 'B';
51.          }

52.       if (final_grade < 80 && final_grade >= 70)
```

Listing 11.10. Continued.

```
53.               {
54.                     return 'C';
55.               }

56.        if (final_grade < 70 && final_grade >= 60)
57.               {
58.                     return 'D';
59.               }

60.        return 'F';

61. }
```

In this rather complex program, several interesting processes take place. First, on line 7, the function is declared, letting the compiler know that this function is to accept an address to an array:

```
char calc_grade(int scores[]);
```

After the array is filled with information (grades), it then is passed to the function on line 24:

```
grade = calc_grade(scores);
```

The function calculates the grade using the array and then returns a grade. Note that if the function calc_grade() does not receive a copy of the array, it uses the original array by using the address passed to it.

Now that you know how to pass an address of an array into a function, you can examine how to pass the address of nonarrays. Just as you can pass arrays by an address, you can pass nonarrays by an address as well.

By default, nonarrays are passed into a function as a value. However, you can override the default, passing the variable by address. When you're passing a nonarray by its address, you must pass the variable names preceded with an ampersand (&). The receiving function must precede the variable with an asterisk (*) whenever the variable appears. The (&) lets the compiler know that you are passing in the variable by address rather than value. Inside of a function, the (*) must precede the variable name, letting the compiler know you are referencing this variable by an address.

Passing an address rather than a value has the same effect as using an array address. The actual variable, rather than a copy of the value, now is manipulated in the function. As with an array, if the variable is altered in the function, the variable actually changes. The changes, therefore, are visible to the other functions using the variable. There is no need to return the variable from the function.

Look at an example. Listing 11.11 demonstrates how a nonarray is passed to a function. Notice how the variable counter is declared in `main()` as a standard local variable. Then the variable is passed to the function with an ampersand preceding the variable name, instructing the function to use the address rather than the value:

```
do_count(&counter);
```

You declare the function using an asterisk, letting the compiler know that an address is going to be passed into the function as an argument:

```
void do_count(int *counter)
```

Within the function `do_count()`, you must precede all references to the variable with an asterisk. The asterisk lets the compiler know that you are referencing this variable by an address. Any changes that are made in the variable are carried forward when the function is completed, as presented in the output of the program in figure 11.5.

Listing 11.11. LISTING11.CPP—Passing an address to a function using a nonarray.

```
1.   //   Program:  LISTING11.CPP
2.   //   Purpose:  Demonstrates the use of passing nonarray
➡ variable to a function
3.   //   Author:  David Linthicum

4.   #include <stdio.h>
5.   #include <conio.h>

6.   // Declare function
7.   void do_count(int *counter);
8.   void do_count(int *counter)

9.   {

10.       // Set the counter again
11.       *counter = 20;

12.       // Print the contents of counter
13.       printf("The counter is set at %i in do_count() \n",
➡ *counter);

14.       return;

15.   }

16.   main()

17.   {
```

(continues)

Listing 11.11. Continued.

```
18.        clrscr(); // Clear the screen

19.        // Declare local variable
20.        int counter;

21.        // Set the counter
22.        counter = 10;

23.        // Print the contents of counter
24.        printf("The counter is set at %i in main() \n", counter);

25.        // Invoke the function passing the address of counter
26.        do_count(&counter);

27.        // Print the contents of counter
28.        printf("The counter is set at %i back in main() \n",
➥ counter);

29.        return 0;

30.    }
```

Fig. 11.5.
The output from
listing 11.11.

```
The counter is set at 10 in main()
The counter is set at 20 in do_count()
The counter is set at 20 back in main()
```

In general, you have no compelling need to pass variables to a function, but you can do it. Other methods of passing variables include using pointers. Chapter 18, ""Using Pointers," covers the ins and outs of using pointers.

Summary

This chapter discussed how the concept of variable scope is used in Turbo C++ programs. Variable scope refers to how functions perceive variables. It is important that you master the concept of variable scope before you create complex applications. This chapter covered the following topics:

■ You declare global variables outside any function, and they are visible to all functions. You declare local variables within a function, and only that particular function can use them. They are protected from misuse by other functions.

■ Using global variables is risky because other functions can alter their value. They are not protected.

■ Automatic variables are the default for variables declared locally in a function. When the function completes, the information in the variables is lost.

■ Static variables maintain their information even after the function completes. When the function is called again, the variable is set to the value it had when the function ended previously.

■ Passing a variable to a function is tricky. You can pass variables by copying a value to a function or by providing the address of a variable.

■ When a value is copied to a function, only a copy of the variable is passed. Therefore, any changes made to that variable are not carried back to the calling function.

■ When the address of a variable, such as an array, is passed to a function, the information in the variable can be altered by the function that its address is passed to. The variable is not copied. The function is using the address.

■ You can pass array addresses as well as other variable addresses to a function. Using nonarrays, you must follow special rules such as preceding the variable with an ampersand (&) and preceding the variable with an asterisk (*) inside the functions. Pointers provide the same functionality. They are covered in Chapter 18.

■ If you master the use of variables, variable types, and complex variables, you master C++.

II

C Programming Basics

## Chapter 12

Using the Preprocessor

In Chapter 8, "Writing Your First Program," you began your journey into the world of the preprocessor by briefly examining how to use the #include preprocessor directive to include additional source files and the #define directive to define macros. At that point, you needed to know how to use these preprocessor directives just to get started creating C++ programs.

That information may have generated additional questions that you must answer: What exactly is a preprocessor? When are macro variables most useful? What other types of logic can be defined using the preprocessor? What rules should you follow? Here, you learn the details so that you can get the maximum benefit from using the preprocessor.

In this chapter, you explore the concepts of the preprocessor and preprocessor directives. First, you learn what the preprocessor actually is and how you use it. Next, you learn the rules of using preprocessor macros. Then you use the example programs to learn how the preprocessor extends the power of the C++ programming language by providing several handy directives.

The Preprocessor

As you learned briefly in Chapter 8, the preprocessor sees your program before the Turbo C++ compiler does. Some people call the preprocessor the *precompiler* because it alters the way the compiler sees the source code.

Preprocessor directives are statements that the preprocessor reads. Then it makes the appropriate changes to your source file. Using the preprocessor, therefore, you are in a sense editing your source file before compiling it. Don't worry; the changes to your source file are not permanent. Consider the following program, for example:

```
1.    #include <stdio.h>

2.    void main()

3.    {

4.    #include "prthello.hpp"

5.    }
```

The file prthello.hpp contains the following statement:

```
printf("Programming is fun\n");
```

The compiler actually sees the following after it has been through the preprocessor:

```
1.    #include <stdio.h>

2.    void main()

3.    {


4.    printf("Programming is fun\n");


5.    }
```

In this example, when the preprocessor directive

```
#include "prthello.hpp"
```

is read, the preprocessor reads the file prthello.hpp into the source file at the point where the #include directive is located. Then the new but temporary version of the source file is sent to the compiler.

Next time you compile a C program using the Turbo C++ IDE, notice how the Lines compiled message in the Compile Status message box reflects the number of lines in the program you created and the number of lines in the files you have included using the #include directive. You do not have to use a .h or a .hpp file. Any valid DOS file name will do, but .h and .hpp are standard file extensions for header files. The standard convention is to use .H files with .C program files, and .HPP with .CPP.

Keep this example in mind as you read through this chapter. Many new C programmers get confused about the proper use of the preprocessor and avoid using it. Your ability to create powerful C++ programs depends on your ability to use the preprocessor effectively.

Preprocessor Directives

All preprocessor directives begin with a pound sign (#), making them easy to spot inside a C program. Usually, preprocessor directives are at the top of the source file, although they can appear anywhere. You do not place a semicolon at the end of preprocessor directives. Remember that preprocessor directives are not C++ statements. Different rules apply.

Placing Preprocessor Directives

Although you can put the preprocessor directives anywhere in your Turbo C++ program, it is a good idea to place all of your preprocessor directives in column 1 of your program file. This placement provides better code portability because other C and C++ compilers require preprocessor directives to begin in column 1. While it is okay to put preprocesor directives anywhere in your program file, they may not work with all compilers. For example:

```
#include <stdio.h>
#include "myprog.h"
                #define CITY Miami
<better>
#define TRUE 1
```

Although the preceding code fragment compiles under Turbo C++ without a complaint from the compiler, other compilers may generate errors. In addition, programmers generally consider it bad programming practice to place the preprocessor directives in columns other than the first.

II

C Programming Basics

Generally, preprocessor commands reside at the top of the source file, before the program function definitions begin, including `main()`. Many directives read into the source file by the `#include` statement must exist outside the function because the functions and macros they define are global—accessible from all of the program functions. For example:

```
1.    //Preprocessor directives begin

2.    #include <stdio.h>
3.    #include <conio.h>
4.    #define NAME "David"
5.    //Preprocessor directive end

6.    //Program functions begin

7.    int main()
```

```
8.    {
9.        clrscr();
10.       printf("Hello %s !\n", NAME);
11.   }
```

Using the preprocessor, you are able to customize your program by making the compiler react to your preprocessor commands such as #include. The preprocessor is a powerful and handy facility. Now take a look at some additional preprocessor commands that are just as handy as #include.

Using *#include*

Consider the program in the preceding section. In that listing, the preprocessor directive is on line 2 of the program:

```
#include <stdio.h>
```

As discussed earlier in this chapter and in Chapter 8, the #include directive tells the Turbo C++ compiler to include another source file in your main program and reads that file before compiling your application. Usually, these files are called *header files* (*headers* for short) or *include files*. You use the include files that come with Turbo C++ to declare library functions you use in your programs. The printf() function, for example, requires that the stdio.h file be included in the source file.

If you were to edit the stdio.h file using any ASCII editor (such as the IDE), you would see that it is actually a source code file that contains information about many library functions, including printf(). Following are the first 50 or so lines from the stdio.h file so that you can get an idea of what these header files look like:

```
/*  stdio.h

    Definitions for stream input/output.

    Copyright (c) 1987, 1991 by Borland International
    All Rights Reserved.
*/

#ifndef __STDIO_H
#define __STDIO_H

#if !defined( __DEFS_H )
#include <_defs.h>
#endif

#ifndef NULL
```

```
#include <_null.h>
#endif

#ifndef _SIZE_T
#define _SIZE_T
typedef unsigned size_t;
#endif

/* Definition of the file position type
*/
typedef long    fpos_t;


/* Definition of the control structure for streams
*/
typedef struct {
        int            level;      /* fill/empty level of buffer */
        unsigned       flags;      /* File status flags          */
        char           fd;         /* File descriptor            */
        unsigned char  hold;       /* Ungetc char if no buffer   */
        int            bsize;      /* Buffer size                */
        unsigned char  *buffer;     /* Data transfer buffer       */
        unsigned char  *curp;       /* Current active pointer      */
        unsigned       istemp;     /* Temporary file indicator   */
        short          token;      /* Used for validity checking */
}       FILE;                      /* This is the FILE object    */

/* Bufferization type to be used as 3rd argument for "setvbuf" function
 */
#define _IOFBF  0
#define _IOLBF  1
#define _IONBF  2
```

Notice how this file and all header files are made up of function declarations, variable declarations, and macro definitions, which are covered in the next few sections. Do not alter header files that come with Turbo C++. You rely on them to provide you with clean function declarations that are required to use library functions such as printf() or scanf(). If you do alter the file, you might end up reloading Turbo C++ from scratch or chasing some very elusive bugs.

Note that angle brackets (< and >) are placed around files in the default INCLUDE directory (usually in \TC\INCLUDE). If you want to include files in another directory or your local directory, such as files that you have created yourself, then place the file name in quotation marks (" "), as done in the previous example. For example, if #include <stdio.h> tells the compiler to look in the default header files directory (\TC\INCLUDE) for a standard Turbo C++ header file. If you want to use a header that you created and it is not in the default directory, you enclose the header file and path in "" such as #include "D:\MYPROG\HYHEAD.H"."

Macros

The word *macro* represents many things in the computer industry. In Turbo C++, macros represent identifiers defined by using the #define statement. If the preprocessor locates these identifiers, they swap them with a predefined replacement string. With #define, as with #include, the compiler thinks that particular replacement string exists in the source file. The replacement string can be a character, string, or a number. You can use macros with arguments or without. For example, here are some examples of using the #define directive to establish constants for a program:

```
#define TAX_RATE 0.32
#define FALSE 0
#define TRUE 1
#define STRING "Press F1 for additional help"
#define YEAR "1994"
#define PI 3.141592654
```

Macros can save time by doing the following:

- Make it easy for you to alter constant values

- Make your program easier to read

A few simple examples were covered in Chapter 8. In this section, you see several advanced examples of the use of macros in a C++ program. Take some time to get to know macros. They can do a great deal for your program if you use them properly.

Understanding Macro Rules

Like any programming statements, macros must follow certain rules to work correctly:

- Macro definitions are not terminated by a semicolon.

- The name of the macro should adhere to rules you use for any C++ identifier. The macro name, therefore, should not contain special characters and spaces.

- Do not use quotation marks inside quotation marks. If you do, the precompiler does not know where your string begins and ends.

Following are a few friendly suggestions:

- Backspace (\) characters used at the end of a macro definition extend the macro definition to additional lines. Generally, macros should only use one line in a program.

- You usually place macros at the top of the source file, although #define legally can exist anywhere in the file.

- Macros are generally in all uppercase letters, although it certainly is legal to use lowercase letters. Uppercase sets them apart from the other C++ variables.

Using #define

The #define preprocessor command directive signals the beginning of a macro definition. A *macro definition* allows the program to substitute one string for another during normal program operation. Using #define, you can declare any one of the following:

```
printf("In %s the tax rate was %f\n", YEAR, TAXRATE);

printf("In %s the tax rate was %f\n", "1994", 0.40);
```

As you may recall from the discussion of header files, header files include macro definitions. Most C++ programs have at least one include file that accompanies the program file. Using include files enables you to keep all the macro definitions, function, and variable declarations in one file, keeping the program organized.

Listing 12.1 is a simple program demonstrating the use of string macros. On lines 7–10 are the macros that define several strings and characters. The main body of the program uses puts() (output a string) and putchar() (output a character) to display each macro on-screen (see fig. 12.1). Remember that macros are not variables and cannot be seen by the debugger. They alter source code only before sending it to the compiler.

Listing 12.1. MACRO1.CPP—Using string macros.

```
1.   // Program Name: MACRO1.CPP
2.   //    ???Dave: David S. Linthicum
3.   //       Purpose: Demonstrates the use of the object-like macros
```

(continues)

Listing 12.1. Continued.

```
4.   #include <stdio.h>      // Need this file for printf()
5.   #include <stdlib.h>     // Need this file for puts() and putchar()
6.   #include <conio.h>      // Need this file for clrscr()

7.   #define FIRST_NAME  "David "
8.   #define MIDDLE_NAME 'S'
9.   #define LAST_NAME  " Linthicum"
10.  #define STRING "My name is : "

11.  void main()
12.  {
13.       clrscr(); // Clear the screen

14.       // Send each macro variable to the terminal using puts and
➡putchar

15.       puts ( STRING );           //Output a string using puts

16.       puts ( FIRST_NAME );

17.       putchar ( MIDDLE_NAME );       //Output a character using
➡putchar

18.       puts ( LAST_NAME);

19.       //or you may use printf()

20.       printf("\n\n %s %s %c %s ", STRING, FIRST_NAME, MIDDLE_NAME,
➡LAST_NAME);

21.  }
```

Fig. 12.1.
Output from
listing 12.1.

Caution

Remember that you must follow the rules of C when you're defining macros. You enclose a string in double quotation marks:

```
"This is my string"
```

whereas you enclose a character in single quotation marks:

```
'T'
```

The preprocessor does not catch quotation errors, and only when your modified source file is sent to the compiler are such errors actually realized.

Listing 12.2 uses both numbers and a string in its macro definitions. The macros defined on lines 7, 9, and 10 are used throughout the program. If, at some time in the future, the tax rate changes, you need only alter the macro definition for TAX_RATE. You can do the same for YEAR and DEDUCTION—no searching through all your source files, making sure all occurrences of these items change.

Listing 12.2. MACRO2.CPP—Using macros with strings and numbers.

```
1.   // Program Name: MACRO2.CPP
2.   //    ???Dave: David S. Linthicum
3.   //      Purpose: Demonstrates the use of the object-like macros

4.   #include <stdio.h>
5.   #include <conio.h>

6.   // define a string variable for the tax year
7.   #define YEAR "1994"

8.   // define the numeric variables
9.   #define TAX_RATE 0.40
10.  #define DEDUCTION 100.00


11.  int main()

12.  {
13.      int income, net_income, taxable_income;

14.      clrscr(); // Clear the screen

15.      // Get input from the user
16.      printf("Enter your yearly income for %s : ", YEAR);

17.      scanf("%d", &income);
```

(continues)

C Programming Basics

Listing 12.2. Continued.

```
18.         // Calculate taxable income
19.         taxable_income = (income-DEDUCTION);

20.         // Calculate net income
21.         net_income = income-(taxable_income*TAX_RATE);

22.         //Return the results to the user
23.         printf("\n");
24.         printf("Income is:          $ %i\n", income);
25.         printf("Taxable income is:    %i\n", taxable_income);
26.         printf("Taxes withheld:       %i\n", income-net_income);
27.         printf("                    ———");

28.         printf("\n\nYour net income is:  $ %i\n", net_income);
29.         printf("                       ======");

30.         return 0;

31. }
```

If you edit the file and change all of the macros to their macro definitions, the result is the same as using the macros. For example, line 19 looks like the following to the compiler:

```
taxable_income = (income-100.00);
```

and line 21:

```
net_income = income-(taxable_income*0.40);
```

Listing 12.3, an enhanced version of listing 12.2, demonstrates how macros can define a function. This program is tricky, so take some time to study it. On line 12, the following macro appears:

```
#define TAXABLE(m) m - DEDUCTION
```

Notice how the program defines a function TAXABLE(), where m is m minus the contents of DEDUCTION. Therefore, line 22 is as follows:

```
taxable_income = TAXABLE(income);
```

The function, when replaced in the preprocessor, sees the following result:

```
income-100.00
```

A similar macro is on line 13:

```
#define NET_INCOME income - tax_due
```

The compiler sees the following result:

```
income-tax_due
```

Listing 12.3. MACRO3.CPP—Using a macro to define a function.

```
1.    // Program Name: MACRO2.CPP
2.    //    ???Dave: David S. Linthicum
3.    //       Purpose: Demonstrates the use of the object-like macros

4.    #include <stdio.h>
5.    #include <conio.h>

6.    // define a string variable for the tax year
7.    #define YEAR "1994"

8.    // define the numeric variables
9.    #define TAX_RATE 0.40
10.   #define DEDUCTION 100.00

11.   // define a function-like macro
12.   #define TAXABLE(m) m - DEDUCTION
13.   #define NET_INCOME income - tax_due

14.   int main()

15.   {
16.        int income, taxable_income, tax_due;

17.        clrscr(); // Clear the screen

18.        // Get input from the user
19.        printf("Enter your yearly income for %s : ", YEAR);

20.        scanf("%d", &income);

21.        // Calculate taxable income
22.        taxable_income = TAXABLE(income);

23.        // Calculate net income
24.        tax_due = taxable_income*TAX_RATE;

25.        //Return the results to the user
26.        printf("\n");
27.        printf("Income is:           $ %i\n", income);
28.        printf("Taxable income is:     %i\n", taxable_income);
29.        printf("Taxes withheld:        %i\n", tax_due);
30.        printf("                     — — —");

31.        printf("\n\nYour net income is:  $ %i\n", NET_INCOME);
32.        printf("                     ======");

33.        return 0;

34.   }
```

Figure 12.2 presents the output of listing 12.3. Notice how each macro fits
into the program, defining the logic and then the output. Defining functions
with macros is handy, but don't overuse them. Generally, functions defined

in macros are useful for algorithms that constantly change, such as tax rate calculations. For most purposes, you should declare your functions globally.

Fig. 12.2.
Output from
listing 12.3.

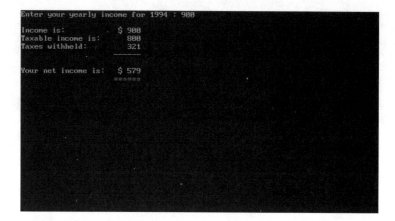

Using macros takes some practice. In the next program that you create, make sure you use a macro. After you've created a few programs, using preprocessor macros becomes second nature.

Conditional Compilation Directives

Several preprocessor directives provide the ability to compile portions of your source file selectively. These directives are called *conditional compilation* directives. Many large software vendors use conditional compilation directives to create a customized version of one particular program for a variety of platforms, such as Windows, DOS, and Unix.

In this section, you learn about the following conditional compilation directives and examine several examples:

- #undef

- #if

- #else

- #endif

- #elif

- #ifdef

- #ifndef

- #line

- #pragma

Using *#undef*

Just as #define defines a macro, #undef removes the defined definition. Its syntax is as follows:

```
#undef macro-name
```

For example:

```
#define WIDTH 18.0
#define HEIGHT 20.0

sq_footage = WIDTH * HEIGHT;

#undef WIDTH
#undef HEIGHT
```

Why do you use #undef? It enables you to use macro names localized in only one portion of the code. You don't have to use #undef on your macros unless you have a specific reason; for example, you need to redefine them later.

Using *#if*, *#else*, *#endif*, and *#elif*

The #if, #else, #endif, and #elif directives enable you to conditionally compile your program using conditional logic similar to the if and else statements of the C++ language. The idea behind the #if directive is that if a constant expression is true, the preprocessor compiles the code between it and the #endif statement. If the condition is false, then the preprocessor skips the code.

The syntax of #if is as follows:

```
#if (constant-expression)
     program statement(s)
#endif
```

For example:

```
1.   #include <stdio.h>

2.   #define NUMBER 20

3.   void main()

4.   {

5.       #if NUMBER > 30
6.           printf("Number is greater than 30\n");
7.       #endif

8.   }
```

The program compiles line 6 if the macro NUMBER is set to a number greater than 30. In this program, it is not. Therefore, line 6 is not submitted to the compiler. Feel free to play around with this. Change lines 6 and 2, then recompile the program to see the results. Notice how your changes affect the output.

The #else directive functions the same as the C++ else statement. The syntax is as follows:

```
#if (constant-expression)
      program statement(s)
#else
      program statement(s)
#endif
```

For example:

```
1.    #include <stdio.h>

2.    #define NUMBER 20

3.    void main()

4.    {

5.        #if NUMBER > 30
6.              printf("Number is greater than 30\n");
7.        #else
8.              printf("Number is not greater than 30\n");
9.        #endif

10.  }
```

The preceding example is similar to the #if example except that now an #else directive lets line 8 compile if the condition on the #if line (line 5) is not met.

The directive #elif (meaning "else if") establishes an if-else-if ladder for multiple compile operations. As with #if, #elif is followed by a constant expression, and the code below #elif compiles based on whether that expression is true.

The syntax of #elif is as follows:

```
#if (constant-expression)
      program statement(s)
#elif (expression 1)
      program statement(s)
#elif (expression 2)
      program statement(s)
#elif (expression 3)
      program statement(s)
      .
      .
      .
#elif (expression N)
      program statement(s)
#endif
```

As you can see, `#elif` works very much like the `switch` statement of C++.
For example:

```
1.   #include <stdio.h>

2.   #define NUMBER 20

3.   void main()

4.   {

5.       #if NUMBER > 30
6.           printf("Number is greater than 30\n");

7.       #elif NUMBER > 20
8.           printf("Number is greater than 20\n");

9.       #elif NUMBER > 10
10.          printf("Number is greater than 10\n");

11.      #else
12.          printf("Number less than 10\n");
13.      #endif

14.  }
```

In the preceding example, the `#if` directive evaluates NUMBER, and if not true,
it moves through a series of checks using the `#elif` directive. If the condition
is true, as it is on line 9, the code directly under that directive compiles.
Again, feel free to change the line number around to recompile and observe
the results.

Just as in standard C++ statements, you can nest these directives as in
listing 12.4.

Listing 12.4. Using conditional compile nesting.

```
1.   #include <stdio.h>


2.   #define IRQ 3
3.   #define DEVICE 1

4.   void main()

5.   {

6.       #if IRQ == 3
7.           #if DEVICE == 1
8.               int irq=3;
9.               int device = 1;
```

(continues)

II

C Programming Basics

Listing 12.4. Continued.

```
10.              #else
11.                  int irq=4;
12.                  int device = 2;
13.              #endif
14.         #else

15.              printf("No devices defined\n");

16.         #endif

17.  }
```

Using *#ifdef* and *#ifndef*

Other preprocessor directives that allow for conditional compilation of your program are #ifdef and #ifndef, which mean "if defined" and "if not defined," respectively.

The syntax for #ifdef is as follows:

```
#ifdef macro-name
     program statement(s)
#endif
```

The programs are only compiled if the macro-name is defined, else the compiler does not even see those lines. Assuming that you have defined the macro previously in a #define statement, the syntax of #ifndef is as follows:

```
#ifndef macro-name
     program statements(s)
#endif
```

Again, assuming the macro name is already defined. Look at the following example:

```
1.   #include<stdio.h>
2.   #define RATE 100.00

3.   int main()

4.   {

5.   #ifdef RATE
6.        printf("The rate is %f\n", RATE);
7.   #endif

8.   #ifndef INCOME
9.        printf("Income not defined\n");
10.  #endif

11.  return 0;

12.  }
```

As you can see in the preceding example, the program checks to see whether the macro name RATE is defined. If so, the code directly under the #ifdef directive compiles. Then the program checks to see whether the macro name INCOME is not defined, and thus the code directly underneath it compiles.

Using #line

The #line directive is used for debugging purposes. The #line directive changes the contents of __LINE__ and __FILE__, which are predefined macro names in Turbo C++. __LINE__ contains the current line number currently being compiled. __FILE__ contains the name of the file being compiled.

The syntax of #line is as follows:

```
#line number "filename"
```

The number is any positive number. The filename (options) is any valid file name. The line number represents the current source line, and the file name is the source file. Generally, you use #line for debugging purposes, but you may find other applications for it.

For example:

```
1.    #include <stdio.h>

2.    #line 25       // Change the line counter
3.    int main()
4.    {
5.         printf("The line is %d\n", __LINE__);
➡// Displays the current line being compiled
6.         return 0;

7.    }
```

In the preceding program, the line currently being compiled is reset to 25 by the #line directive. The printf() function displays the line currently being compiled after the reset has occurred.

Using #pragma

The #pragma directive allows you to perform powerful operations on your code before submitting it to the compiler, such as telling the compiler that in-line assembly code follows, or executing a function when a program terminates. The #pragma directive enables you to define various instructions. It is defined by the ANSI standard (see Chapter 1, "The Basics"), but Borland has expanded its use.

The syntax of #pragma is as follows:

```
#pragma name
```

The name is the name of the #pragma you want to invoke. They are as follows:

inline   Instructs the compiler that in-line assembly code follows in
            the program

saveregs   Prevents a function declared as huge from changing the
            register values

warn   Makes the compiler override warning message options

argsused   Precedes a function and prevents warning messages

exit   Specifies functions called when the program terminates

option   Enables you to specify a command option inside your
            program, instead of the command line

startup   Specifies the functions that are invoked when the program
            is started

hdrfile   Specifies the file that is used to hold the precompiled
            headers

hdrstop   Instructs Turbo C++ to stop precompiling header files

```
1. #include <stdio.h>

2. #pragma startup startme 255

3. main()

4.      {
5.              printf("in the main function\n");
6.              return 0;
7.      }

8. void startme (void)

9.      {
10.             printf("in the startme function\n");

11.     }
```

This program demonstrates how #pragma startup is employed to define a function that executes when the program starts up, in this case startme().

Summary

In this chapter, you learned about the preprocessor, its uses, and most of the preprocessor directives. To control what the compiler actually sees in the source file, preprocessor directives such as `#if` and `#nodef` provide this conditional compilation functionality. Other directives provide various functions. This chapter covered the following topics:

- The preprocessor actually alters the source file before submitting it to the compiler.

- Preprocessor directives are commands that you can use to control what the compiler sees. Several directives are available.

- The `#include` directive reads another source file into the program files. Include files, also called header files or headers, allow various functions, variables, and macros to be defined and read directly into your application.

- The `#define` directive defines macros that replace strings, characters, or numbers in your program before it compiles. This directive is useful in defining variables that often change, such as a tax rate or a price.

- The `#define` directive also can define functions, similar to the way C++ declares and uses functions.

- Conditional compilation directives enable you to control what the compilers actually see through the use of conditional program logic.

- The `#if`, `#else`, and `#endif` directives are examples of how you can conditionally control the compilation of your application. Generally, these conditional compilation directives are most useful when several versions of your program exist, and they compile on different platforms.

- Other preprocessor directives, such as `#line` and `#pragma`, provide specialized operations, such as defining the line number that is currently being compiled or setting a `#pragma` option.

Chapter 13

Using Functions

Functions are the basic component of the C++ language. Many people call C and C++ the languages of "nested functions," because they depend heavily on the use of functions. If you use functions, the language is expandable, which means that you can add functionality such as GUI development to your C++ programs just by adding libraries and functions. This expandability is the attraction of the C language, making it the language of choice to develop graphical user interface (GUI) applications (Microsoft Windows applications, for example) and many other applications that require customization of the language building the application.

Basically, three types of functions are available:

- *C library functions*, which come with Turbo C++, providing general-purpose operations such as printing to the screen or writing to a file (see Chapter 14, "Library Functions—The Basics").

- *Third-party library functions*, which you purchase to enhance the capabilities of the C language. You use these functions in the same way that you use standard C library functions. Generally, they perform specialized tasks that the C library does not support. Third-party functions enable you to do such things as create a graphical user interface application, an application using relational database operations, a program that performs direct device interaction, and many other operations.

- *Custom functions*, or functions that you write yourself to perform a particular task. Generally, these functions are broken out of the main program so that the program is better organized and functional.

In previous chapters, you learned how functions such as `printf()`, `scanf()`, and `clrscr()` already are defined in a C function library. You have also seen how to define your own custom functions and call them from other functions such as `main()`.

In this chapter, you learn the details of how functions structure a program. You also become acquainted with how, when, and where to use them when you're creating your C++ applications. This chapter is a predecessor to your learning the ins and outs of library functions, as explained in Chapter 14, using the C library in Chapter 15, and finally learning the "down and dirty" details of creating your own advanced custom functions in Chapter 17.

This chapter is more conceptual in nature, providing you with a foundation of knowledge that you need to make the best use of functions. You first learn about benefits of functions and then how you declare, define, and use simple functions inside your program. Arguments that you can pass to functions also are introduced, as well as how to pass in complex variable types such as arrays and how you can structure them directly into functions. As always, examples support the concepts presented.

Why Use Functions?

In the C language, subprograms are *functions*. A function is just a way of packaging small portions of program code separate from the rest of the application. Each function performs a particular task and can be called from other parts of the program one or many times.

Following are several reasons for using functions:

- They organize your program

- They enable you to create functions that you or other programmers can reuse

- They reduce the memory consumption of the Turbo C++ compiler

The process of defining program tasks into logical functions makes your application more organized. If you want to maintain a particular accounting function in a business application, for example, you need only examine the function of the program that handles accounting operations. You don't need to search through all the program code.

Functions maximize the reuse of program code, not only among one application, but other applications as well. Because functions are modular, a well-defined function is usable in other applications, similar to the way C++ library functions are used.

Other programmers can even share functions. Many software development organizations have their own store of standard library functions that programmers in the organization use to perform such tasks as displaying the company logo, changing the colors of a screen, or changing printer fonts.

> **Note**
>
> *Third-party library functions*, which are created by other programmers, are functions that you can use in your applications. They are called third party because they were created by someone other than you or the compiler vendor. Generally, you use these functions to perform some types of operations not provided by the standard C++ library. Because these functions are written for you, you need only invoke them in your application. You can purchase these third-party library functions from software vendors specializing in programming, or sometimes certain libraries are available for downloading from a public bulletin board system (BBS).

An example of a third-party library is Baby Driver II from Autumn Hill Software, Inc. This library provides C++ developers with the ability to support text and graphics printing on more than 300 printers.

By executing a function instead of repeating the program statements each time a particular task is carried out, the resulting program requires less memory. In the world of DOS, memory is always in short supply, and creating memory-efficient applications is always the goal of a good DOS programmer.

Creating a Structured Program

In the early days of programming, programmers discovered that repetitive operations in programs were best placed into subprograms. *Subprograms* are a portion of a program that perform a predefined task and can be called over and over again. Repetitive operations such as printing a line of information or writing a file, for example, are good candidates for subprograms. Subprograms are the core of most structured programming languages such as COBOL and C.

II

C Programming Basics

As you may recall from Chapter 1, "Understanding the Basics," a structured program is made up of many subprograms, and when these subprograms are combined, they make up a complete application. Through this *modularization* of a program, you can make the best use of your program code, reusing code whenever possible.

This concept of reusing code is the main advantage of using object-oriented programming. *Object-oriented programming* (as described in Chapter 21, "Introduction to Object-Oriented Programming") builds on the concept of structured programming, enabling you to make even better use of program code. For now, the discussion is focused on structured programming.

A *structured program* is similar to a hierarchy chart that you use to define the chain of command in a company (see fig. 13.1). At the top of the hierarchy, the president of the company provides direction for the departments of the company (Accounting, Sales, and Operations). These departments may have one or many managers and employees working under them, all performing specific tasks for the organization.

Fig. 13.1.
A hierarchy chart
for a company.

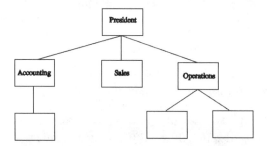

A structured program also has a top position, the function main(). From main(), other functions are called, and they, in turn, can call additional functions. Figure 13.2 presents a conceptual program structure.

Fig. 13.2.
The structure
of a program.

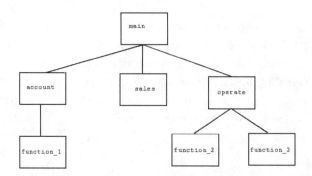

Using Functions

As mentioned in the preceding section, few rules are associated with creating or using functions; however, C++ functions should have the following properties:

- All functions must have a name.

- As with variable names, a function name can have up to 31 characters and must begin with a letter or an underscore. After that, you can use letters, underscores, and numbers to define the function name.

- You follow all function names with a set of parentheses (). They tell C++ that this item is not a variable, but a function.

- You must enclose the program statements that define the function in braces {}. They tell C++ where the function code starts and stops.

In C, you give functions their own name. Other functions such as `main()`, use that name to call the function. In listing 13.1, for example, the function is declared as

```
int any_function();
```

It is called from the function `main()` by naming the function

```
any_function();
```

and thus at the bottom of the program executing the code defined in the function body.

Listing 13.1. Using a function.

```
1.    // A sample structured C++ program
2.    #include <stdio.h>

3.    // Initialize a prototype
4.    int any_function();
```

(continues)

Listing 13.1. Continued.

```
5.    void main()

6.    {

7.          any_function();

8.    }

9.    int any_function()

10.   {

11.         printf("Hello from a function");
12.         return 0;

13.   }
```

Listing 13.2 represents the same program rewritten without a function. As you can see, functions require some additional program statements, but if your function defines a complex task that is performed over and over again, the value of the function is apparent.

Listing 13.2. Not using a function.

```
1.    // A sample C++ program
2.    #include <stdio.h>


3.    void main()

4.    {

5.          printf("Hello from a functionless program");

6.    }
```

In listing 13.3, you can see how functions save programming time by reusing portions of a program over and over again. Here, the program counts from 1 to 10, 20, and 30, respectively (see fig. 13.3). Instead of you having to put the counting logic in the main() function three times, the program calls a function called count_now(), which takes an argument called count_to. count_to specifies when to stop the counting (function parameters are discussed later in this chapter).

Imagine how much longer this program might be if program code had to be placed into the function main() each time the program counts a new block. The extra program code does not affect the way the program actually performs the counting operations, of course, but "wordy" programs make maintenance a nightmare because you must make changes in several locations in the program.

In this example, if changes were required in the counting logic, you would have to change only the function count_now(). Listing 13.3 is an example of using functions effectively to save programming time and making the program more maintainable than if functions were not employed.

Listing 13.3. Making good use of a function in a counting program.

```
1.    // A sample counting program using a function
2.    #include <stdio.h>
3.    #include <conio.h>

4.    // Initialize a function
5.    int count_now(int count_to);

6.    int main()

7.    {

8.        clrscr();

9.        printf("\nCounting to 10\n");
10.       count_now(10);

11.       printf("\nCounting to 20\n");
12.       count_now(20);

13.       printf("\nCounting to 30\n");
14.       count_now(30);

15.       return 0;

16.   }

17.   int count_now(int count_to)

18.   {

19.       // Count from 1 to the variable passed into the function
20.       int counter = 1;

21.       do
22.           {
23.               printf(" %i ", counter);
24.               ++counter;

25.           }
26.       while(counter <= count_to);

27.       return 0;

28.   }
```

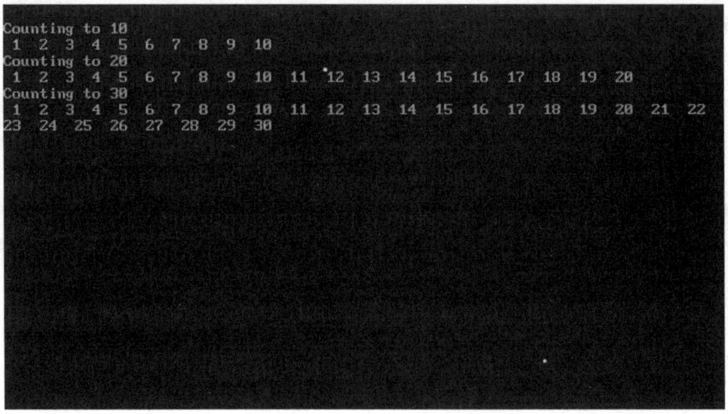

Fig. 13.3.
The output from listing 13.3.

```
Counting to 10
1  2  3  4  5  6  7  8  9  10
Counting to 20
1  2  3  4  5  6  7  8  9  10  11  12  13  14  15  16  17  18  19  20
Counting to 30
1  2  3  4  5  6  7  8  9  10  11  12  13  14  15  16  17  18  19  20  21  22
23  24  25  26  27  28  29  30
```

The same concept applies to C library functions. Instead of writing the function to print information to the screen or to receive input from the user, you simply use a canned function provided by Turbo C++. C library functions are covered in later chapters. For now, concentrate on creating and using functions of your own making. First, you learn how to plan the use of functions in your program, and then you learn the mechanics of using functions.

Planning Your Program

Using functions in programs takes some planning. You need to take time to get the purpose of your application in mind before you start defining the program functions. The best way to start planning is to do the following:

- Define the overall goal of the application program

- Break the application into smaller tasks

- Determine how each piece fits together to make up an application

When you actually begin creating your program, try to look at it as many smaller programs, not just one large program. If, for example, you are writing a program to extract information from an ASCII file, print the information on-screen, and then clear the screen, you may note the following tasks:

- Clear the screen

- Extract the data

- Display the information on-screen

Each of the preceding tasks is a good candidate for a function, but which ones should actually be functions? Remember that the last task can be carried out by a C library function, clrscr(), and, therefore, that task is already a function available to you. You do not need to write it yourself. Creating functions for the first two tasks listed makes sense. Each task is significantly complex enough and should be broken out from the main program.

When you're writing your application, create the functions first and then the main program around the functions. You can test each function as a stand-alone program. Just make sure each function works properly before you combine the functions in the application. This process is called *structured testing*.

> **Note**
>
> Remember that the C++ language is not like the FORTRAN or BASIC languages. You are forced to think in terms of functions. Expert C++ programmers create applications with many small functions, even if the functions are called just once in the application. Therefore, "when in doubt, break it out" into its own function.

Using the *main( )* Function

As you learned in many previous examples, the function main() is the entry point to an application. The main() function is like any other C++ function, but it is always called first as a C++ program executes. Other functions defined in the source file are called from main(); then additional functions are called from those functions, and so on. (See fig. 13.4.) These nestings can continue for many levels.

Declaring Functions

As already well defined, a function performs a predefined operation when called from another function in the program (such as main()). When a function is called, the following actions occur:

- The code contained inside the function executes

- After executing the function, control returns to the calling function

- The program continues processing

You have seen many examples of function declarations in previous chapters. You cannot use a function until it is declared in your program, just as variables are not usable until they, too, are declared.

Usually, you declare functions at the top of the program (see listing 13.1). The function declaration uses the following form:

```
type function_name(type varname, type varname2, ..., type
➥ varnameX);
```

Consider this example from listing 13.3:

```
int count_now(int count_to);
```

Here, the compiler is introduced to a new function named count_now(). The compiler also determines that a parameter or argument with a data type int (integer) is to be passed into this function when it is called. You can specify any C data types, including char, int, arrays, float, and structures, as an argument.

Caution

You cannot declare function arguments the same as you declare variables. For example:

```
    int tax_rate, tax_amount, tax_total
```

does not work as a function parameter. All function parameters must include both type and variable names for all arguments. If you use the preceding variables correctly as a function parameter, therefore, the line should look like the following:

```
    int tax_rate, int tax_amount, int tax_total
```

Function protyping always ends with a semicolon. Functions do not require arguments, and if arguments are not specified, the listing in the parentheses is empty. Consider the following example from listing 13.1:

```
int any_function();
```

Defining the Body of a Function

After you declare your function, letting the compiler know about your function, you also must tell the compiler what the function is going to do. You define the function in the body of its code using the following format:

```
type function_name(type varname, type varname2, ..., type varnameX)
{
    program statements;
    .
    .
    return value;
}
```

A function does not have to be a copy of the declaration. Depending on how the function has been declared, a variable name is not a requirement. You only need to provide a type.

As you can see, the first line is just a copy of the function declaration, without the semicolon. The program statements that execute when the function is called are contained in braces.

In listing 13.3, for example, the body of the count_now() function is defined:

```
int count_now(int count_to)

{

    // Count from 1 to the variable passed into the function
    int counter = 1;

    do
        {
            printf(" %i ", counter);
            ++counter;

        }
    while(counter <= count_to);

    return 0;
}
```

Calling Functions

After you declare and define a function in your program, you must deal with the simple matter of calling the function. Following is the general form for calling a function from main():

```
int main()

{

    program statements;
    function_name(var1, var2, .., varX);

    program statements;

}
```

Consider the following example from listing 13.3:

```
int main()

{
clrscr();

    printf("\nCounting to 10\n");
    count_now(10);
```

```
        printf("\nCounting to 20\n");
        count_now(20);

        printf("\nCounting to 30\n");
        count_now(30);

        return 0;


    }
```

Note how the function count_now() is called several times from the function main(). Remember that using functions this way saves you the time and trouble of entering the code used in the function count_now() three. Also, notice how each time the function is called, a different argument is passed to the function. These arguments control how the function is executed each time it is called. Later, you examine how complex variables such as arrays and data structures are passed into functions.

If a function returns a value (covered next), you can use it as a variable. The general form is as follows:

```
    value = function_name(var1, var2, .., varX);
```

When a value is declared as being equal to a function that returns a value, the function is called and the return value is returned. Remember, you can place a function within any function including library functions or functions you create. For example:

```
    printf("Your total tax bill is %i\n", calc_tax());
```

Returning Values from Functions

You can define functions to not only perform a particular task, but to return a result to the calling function. You do this using the return statement.

The return statement does two things:

- ■ It stops the execution of a function and returns to the calling function
  If return is invoked from main(), the program is stopped

- ■ It returns a value to the calling function

In previous examples, you saw where programs used

```
    return 0;
```

to exit a function and return a value.

Caution

Remember, if you declare a function as void, the compiler does not expect it to return a value. If you include a return in a function declared as void, the compiler generates an error. If you do not provide a return in a function that is not declared as void, you get an error as well.

Listing 13.4 presents a simple function that subtracts one number from another, returning the results to the calling function. Notice how the function is called by using the following:

```
value = difference(enter1, enter2);
```

The arguments (enter1 and enter2) pass information to the function. The function uses this information to calculate the results that are returned to the calling function and placed in the variable value.

Listing 13.4. Using a function that returns a value.

```
1.   // A sample demonstrating how a function returns a value
2.   #include <stdio.h>
3.   #include <conio.h>

4.   // declare a function
5.   int difference(int number1, int number2);

6.   int main()

7.   {

8.        int enter1, enter2;
9.        int value;

10.       clrscr();

11.       printf("\nEnter the first number: ");
12.       scanf("%d", &enter1);
13.       printf("\nEnter the second number: ");
14.       scanf("%d", &enter2);

15.       // Calculate the difference by calling a function
16.       value = difference(enter1, enter2);

17.       printf("\n\nThe result is %i \n", value);

18.       return 0;

19.  }
```

(continues)

Listing 13.4. Continued.

```
20.   // Define the body of the function
21.   int difference(int number1, int number2)
22.   {

23.       int result;

24.       // Do the calculation
25.       result = number1-number2;

26.       // Return the value to the calling function
27.       return result;

28.   }
```

Listing 13.5 makes good use of a function's capability to return a value, in this case, a character. This time the function is declared as a char on line 5 because it returns a character:

```
char calc_grade(int midterm, int final);
```

The program passes two arguments (midterm and final) to the function. The function uses the arguments to calculate the final number grade and then uses program logic to find a grade range and return the appropriate letter grade.

Notice how the function is called on line 19 from printf() and is not stored in a variable, as was the case with the previous example. Using a library function is completely legal:

```
printf("\n\nYour grade is %c \n", calc_grade(midterm, final));
```

Remember: You can call a function from anywhere in your program, even from library functions or a function of your own making. Simply enter the function name and arguments (if required).

Listing 13.5. Using a function to return a letter grade from number grades passed to it.

```
1.    // A sample counting program using a function

2.    #include <stdio.h>
3.    #include <conio.h>

4.    // declare a function
5.    char calc_grade(int midterm, int final);

6.    // declare global variables

7.    int midterm, final;

8.    int main()

9.    {
```

```
10.      char grade;

11.      clrscr();

12.      // Enter midterm grade
13.      printf("\nEnter the midterm grade: ");
14.      scanf("%d", &final);

15.      // Enter final grade
16.      printf("\nEnter the final grade: ");
17.      scanf("%d", &midterm);

18.      // Calculate the grade and print the results
19.      printf("\n\nYour grade is %c \n", calc_grade(midterm,
         ➡ final));

20.      return 0;


21.  }

22.  // Define the calc_grade()
23.  // Used to calculate a final and a midterm grade and return a
         ➡ letter grade
24.  char calc_grade(int midterm, int final)

25.  {

26.      char result;

27.      // Calculate final number grade
28.      int final_grade = ((midterm*.40)+(final*.60));

29.      // Return the correct letter grade based on the final
         ➡ number grade
30.      if (final_grade >= 90)
31.          {
32.              return 'A';
33.          }

34.      if (final_grade < 90 && final_grade >= 80)
35.          {
36.              return 'B';
37.          }

38.      if (final_grade < 80 && final_grade >= 70)
39.          {
40.              return 'C';
41.          }

42.      if (final_grade < 70 && final_grade >= 60)
43.          {
44.              return 'D';
45.          }

46.      return 'F';

47.  }
```

II

C Programming Basics

In listing 13.5, if you return a number instead of a character, C++ will perform the type conversion. Because the function is declared as a character

```
char calc_grade(int midterm, int final);
```

it can return only characters, such as the letter grades in the function `calc_grade()`.

Note

It is interesting to note that if you incorrectly return a value that does not match the declared type of the function, the compiler does not generate an error. However, the results returned from the function are incorrect (usually garbage information). Make sure that you double-check your return values to ensure that they match the data type of the function. Do not use a function declared as a `char` to return a number, or vice versa.

Passing Arguments

In previous examples, you learned some aspects of how arguments can be passed to functions using standard C variables. But what about complex variables, such as arrays and data structures? How are they passed into functions? The following sections show you how to pass complex variables such as these to functions.

Passing Arrays. Chapter 10, "Introducing String Constants and String Arrays," demonstrates how you create arrays, fill them with information, and use them in a C++ program. Arrays are especially useful because they can contain a great deal of information. As with other variables, arrays can be passed into functions. Functions that can receive arrays as an argument, for example, use the following format:

```
function_name(array_name[]);
```

This example is not much different from the previous examples, but remember that arrays can contain more information than `int` and `char` variable types. A pointer is passed into the function to access the information in the array.

Listing 13.6 demonstrates how to use arrays with a function. This program enables you to enter five grades, which are stored in an array. Then the array is passed to the function `calc_grade()`. This function calculates the average of the information contained in the array and determines which letter grade to return, similar to listing 13.5. Note, it also makes sense to use the `switch` statement instead of using the `if` statement when you're determining the letter grade.

Listing 13.6. LISTING6.CPP—Using arrays with functions.

```cpp
1.   // Program:  LISTING6.CPP
2.   / Author:  David S. Linthicum
3.   // Purpose:  Calculate the average of 5 grades using an array
     ➥ passed to a function

4.   #include <stdio.h>
5.   #include <conio.h>

6.   // Declare a function
7.   char calc_grade(int scores[]);

8.   // Declare grade array
9.   int scores[5];

10.  int main()

11.  {

12.      // Declare local variables
13.      char grade;
14.      int count = 1;

15.      clrscr();

16.      // Enter grades into an array using a loop
17.      // Loop 5 times for five grades
18.      while (count <= 5)
19.      {
20.      printf("\nEnter the grade %i: ", count);
21.      scanf("%d", &scores[count++]);
22.      }

23.      // Calculate the grade by passing an array to a function
24.      grade = calc_grade(scores);

25.      // Print the results
26.      printf("\n\nYour grade is %c \n", grade);

27.      return 0;


28.  }


29.  char calc_grade(int scores[])

30.  {

31.      // Declare local variables
32.      float final_grade;      // Final grade
33.      int i;                  // Counter
34.      float total;            // Running total

35.      // Calculate the grade from the array
```

(continues)

Listing 13.6. Continued.

```
36.          // Add up all of the scores
37.          for (i=1; i<=5;i++)
38.             {
39.               total=total+scores[i];
40.             }

41.          // Divide them by the number of scores
42.          final_grade = (total/5);

43.          // Return the correct letter grade based on the final
          ➥ grade
44.          if (final_grade >= 90)
45.             {
46.                  return 'A';
47.             }

48.          if (final_grade < 90 && final_grade >= 80)
49.             {
50.                  return 'B';
51.             }

52.          if (final_grade < 80 && final_grade >= 70)
53.             {
54.                  return 'C';
55.             }

56.          if (final_grade < 70 && final_grade >= 60)
57.             {
58.                  return 'D';
59.             }

60.       return 'F';

61.  }
```

Remember: A function can return only a standard data type, meaning you cannot return an array. Arrays can be altered by a function, but not returned. The array that is passed to the function is not a copy of the array. Unlike local variables that are copied into functions, an array is one and the same. When a function modifies an array, the original array is modified.

Passing Structures. Although structures are not covered until Chapter 20, in this section, you examine how a structure is submitted to a function. See Chapter 20 for additional details on structures. A structure can be passed in as an argument the same way the arrays are passed to a function. Listing 13.7 demonstrates how a structure is created, filled with information, and then passed to a function to process the structure. In this program, you enter a string and a number, which are placed into the structure called student. The structure student is then passed into the function print_emp(), where the contents of the structure are printed on-screen.

Listing 13.7. LISTING7.CPP—Using structures with a function.

```
1.   // Program:  LISTING7.CPP
2.   /  Author:   David S. Linthicum
3.   // Purpose:  Enters information into a structure and prints it
        ➡ using a function

4.   #include <stdio.h>
5.   #include <conio.h>

6.   // declare a structure
7.   struct student
8.   {
9.   char name[25];
10.  int emp_num;
11.  };

12.  // declare a function
13.  void print_student(struct student);

14.  int main()

15.  {

16.      clrscr();

17.      // Set up local storage for the structure
18.      struct student temp;

19.      printf("\nEnter student name   : ");
20.      scanf("%s", &temp.name);

21.      printf("\nEnter student number : ");
22.      scanf("%d", &temp.emp_num);

23.      // Call the function to print the structure
24.      print_student(temp);

25.      return 0;


26.  }

27.  // Function to print information in the structure
28.  void print_student(struct student temp)

29.  {
30.      printf("\nThe student name is %s", temp.name);

31.      printf("\nThe student number is %i", temp.emp_num);

32.  }
```

This program calls a function that prints the information contained in a structure. The structure is passed to the function named print_emp() as an argument. Like the previous array example, this program packs a great deal of information into one variable passed into the function. Arrays that contain character strings and arrays that contain numbers can be passed into functions in the same manner.

Summary

This chapter introduced you to the basics of using functions in your C++ programs. You learned the purpose of functions, as well as the technical details of declaring, defining, and using functions in your program. The chapter covered the following topics:

- You use functions to break a larger program into smaller, more manageable blocks of code. These functions make your programs better organized, and programs that make good use of functions use less memory. You also can share the functions among other applications and programmers.

- Using functions in C++, you can create structured programs. Structured programs separate specific tasks into modules. Each module is called separately.

- Functions should always have a name that adheres to the rules of naming C++ variables.

- Using functions effectively requires planning. Take time to plan out what functions are to be included in your application and how each interacts with another.

- The main() function is the first function called when a C++ program executes. From main(), other functions are called.

- You declare functions at the top of the program; then, you define them later in the source file in the function body.

- Arguments such as data and program control information are parameters that are passed to functions. You can pass all types of variables, including arrays and structures, to functions.

- Some functions return values. These functions usually perform some type of calculation, returning the results when complete.

Chapter 14

Using Library Functions

Now that you have a good background in creating your own C++ functions, you can learn about functions that have been created for you. Over the years, the C language has evolved. As the language was improved, new library functions found their way into most C compilers. As you may recall, library functions are "canned" functions that come with Turbo C++. They include functions that you already learned about in previous chapters. Examples include clrscr(), which clears the screen; printf(), which prints information on-screen; and scanf(), which receives information from the user.

Experienced C++ programmers know that several hundred library functions exist in the Turbo C++ library, and each library function performs a distinctive task. These functions are available so that you don't have to write a program to perform that same operation. Using functions, you can perform the following activities:

- Copy a block of memory

- Manipulate an ASCII file

- Change the screen color

- Change a CPU register

- Make a DOS system call

- Draw a picture

- Make your computer beep

Your job as the programmer is to know what functions are available and to use them where appropriate in the application. However, how do you know what library functions work best where? How can you find information on a particular function? How does your program know how to use a particular function?

The preceding questions are answered in this chapter. Here you expand the knowledge of the function library that you gained from previous chapters, learn how to find information on a particular function, and learn how to implement a library function in your program. In addition, this chapter examines a sampling of library functions and provides examples you can try yourself.

Library functions open a whole new world to beginning C++ programmers. Here the real power of the language comes out. At this point, you should not get overwhelmed with the sheer number of library functions available but make sure that you understand the concepts of library functions, particularly how to find the correct function to solve a problem.

What Is a Library Function?

You can use the Turbo C++ function library to provide routines for common programming tasks, as well as some tasks that are not so common. These functions enable you to perform an operation with just a function call—no need to write the code yourself. Using library functions saves hours—even days—of programming time.

The Turbo C++ function library is divided into the following groups of library routines:

- Graphics: For creating pictures on your computer

- Standard I/O: For the normal I/O operations such as printing to the screen

- Math: For mathematical operations

- Standard routines: For standard program operations

- Text window display: Sends text to the screen

- Variables argument list: For accessing various argument lists from within a program

- Conversion: Routines to convert characters and strings

- Diagnostic: Providing built-in troubleshooting routines

- Inline: Generates code for inline versions

- Interface: For accessing DOS and BIOS routines

- Memory: For manipulating memory by using various memory modules

- Process control: Creating and maintaining processes

- String and memory: Handles strings and blocks of memory

- Time and date: For using time and date operations from your program

- Classification: Classifies characters

- Directory: Manipulates directory and path names

- Miscellaneous: For non-logical operations, *go to* functionality, sound effects, and so on

To use a function in your program, you simply include the correct header file. In Chapter 12, "Using the Preprocessor," you learned that a header file contains the function declarations. The `#include` statement merges the header file with your program.

In listing 14.1, both header files (`conio.h` and `stdio.h`) are read by the compiler. You now have access to all the library functions that each header file supports, such as `clrscr()` in `conio.h` and `printf()` in `stdio.h`. As the file names imply, `conio.h` provides console (screen) input/output control, and `stdio.h` provides functions to control standard input/output. And that is just the tip of the iceberg. Many more header files are available, and each one supports even more functions.

Listing 14.1. Using Turbo C++ library functions.

```
1.    // Program that demonstrates the use of Turbo C++ Library
➥ function

2.    // Include the correct header files

3.    #include <conio.h>  // Include conio.h for the clrscr()
➥ function
```

(continues)

C Programming Basics

Listing 14.1. Continued.

```
4.    #include <stdio.h>  // Include stdio.h for the printf()
➥ functions

5.    void main()

6.    {
7.         // Clear the screen
8.         clrscr();

9.         // Print to the screen
10.        printf("Programming is fun\n");

11.   }
```

Hundreds of library functions are at your beck and call. Groups of library functions are declared in a header file. For example, printf() is declared in stdio.h as well as fprintf() and other functions. The header files define a certain method of how a particular function is called. Some functions are extremely complex, with several arguments that must be passed, and some are simple function calls without parameters. How do you keep track of library functions? It is not easy. In the next section, you learn how to find and use a function you may need in your application.

Finding the Correct Function

Table 14.1 presents all of the available Turbo C++ library functions. Of course, all of these functions cannot be covered in one chapter, or even one book. In this section, you learn how to locate information on a particular function and use that function in your program.

Table 14.1. Turbo C++ Library Functions.

__emit__	_atold	_bios_disk	gettext
gettextinfo	gettestsettings		
_bios_equiplist	_bios_keybrd	_bios_memsize	gettime
getvect	getverify		
_bios_printer	_bios_serialcom	_bios_timeofday	getviewsettings
getw	getx		
_c_exit	_cexit	_chain_intr	gety
gmtime	gotoxy		
_chdrive	_chmod	_clear87	graphdefaults
grapherrormsg	graphresult		
_close	_control87	_creat	harderr
hardresume	hardretn		

_disable	_dos_allocmem	_dos_close	heapcheck
heapcheckfree	heapchecknode		
_dos_creat	_dos_creatnew	_dos_findfirst	heapfillfree
heapwalk	highvideo		
_dos_findnext	_dos_freemem	_dos_getdate	hypot
hypotl	imag		
_dos_getdiskfree	_dos_getdrive	_dos_getfileattr	imagesize
initgraph	inp		
_dos_getftime	_dos_gettime	_dos_getvect	inport
inportb	inpw		
_dos_keep	_dos_open	_dos_read	insline
installuser	installuserfont		
driver			
_dos_setblock	_dos_setdate	_dos_setdrive	int86
int86x	intdos		
_dos_setfileattr	_dos_setftime	_dos_settime	intdosx
intr	ioctl		
_dos_setvect	_dos_write	_enable	isalnum
isalpha	isascii		
_exit	_fmemccpy	_fmemchr	isatty
iscntrl	isdigit		
_fmemcmp	_fmemcpy	_fmemicmp	isgraph
islower	isprint		
_fmemset	_fpreset	_fsopen	ispunct
isspace	isupper		
_fstrcat	_fstrchr	_fstrcmp	isxdigit
	itoa	kbhit	
_fstrcpy	_fstrcspn	_fstrdup	keep
labs	ldexp		
_fstricmp	_fstrlen	_fstrlwr	ldexpl
ldiv	lfind		
_fstrncat	_fstrncmp	_fstrncpy	line
linerel	lineto		
_fstrnicmp	_fstrnset	_fstrpbrk	localeconv
localtime	lock		
_fstrrchr	_fstrrev	_fstrset	locking
log	log10		
_fstrspn	_fstrstr	_fstrtok	log10l
logl	longjmp		
_fstrupr	_fullpath	_getdcwd	lowvideo
lsearch	lseek		
_getdrive	_graphfreemem	_graphgetmem	ltoa
malloc	matherr		
_harderr	_hardresume	_hardretn	max
mblen	mbstowcs		
_lrotl	_lrotr	_makepath	mbtowc
memccpy	memchr		

(continues)

Table 14.1. Continued.

_matherrl	_open	_OvrInitEms	memcmp
memcpy	memicmp		
_OvrInitExt	_read	_rotl	memmove
memset	min		
_rotr	_searchenv	_setcursortype	MK_FP
mkdir	mktemp		
_splitpath	_status87	_strdate	mktime
modf	modfl		
_strerror	_strtime	_strtold	movedata
moverel	movetext		
_tolower	_toupper	_write	moveto
movmem	norm		
abort	abs	absread	normvideo
nosound	open		
abswrite	access	acos	opendir
outp	outport		
acosl	allocmem	arc	outportb
outpw	outtext		
arg	asctime	asin	outtextxy
parsfnm	peek		
asinl	assert	atan	peekb
perror	pieslice		
atan2	atan2l	atanl	poke
pokeb	polar		
atexit	atof	atoi	poly
polyl	pow		
atol	bar	bar3d	pow10
pow10l	powl		
bcd	bdos	bdosptr	printf
putc	putch		
bioscom	biosdisk	biosequip	putchar
putenv	putimage		
bioskey	biosmemory	biosprint	putpixel
puts	puttext		
biostime	brk	bsearch	putw
qsort	raise		
cabs	cabsl	calloc	rand
randbrd	randbwr		
ceil	ceill	cgets	random
randomize	read		
chdir	chmod	chsize	readdir
real	realloc		
circle	cleardevice	clearerr	rectangle
registerbgi	registerbgifont		
driver			
clearviewport	clock	close	registerfarbgi
registerfarbgi	remove		driver
font			

closedir	closegraph	clreol	rename
restorecrtmode	rewind		
clrscr	complex	conj	rewinddir
rmdir	rmtmp		
coreleft	cos	cosh	sbrk
scanf	searchpath		
coshl	cosl	country	sector
segread	set_new_handler		
cprintf	cputs	creat	setactivepage
setallpalette	setaspectratio		
creatnew	creattemp	cscanf	setbkcolor
setblock	setbuf		
ctime	ctrlbrk	delay	setcbrk
setcolor	setdate		
delline	detectgraph	difftime	setdisk
setdta	setfillpattern		
disable	div	dosexterr	setfillstyle
setftime	setgraphbufsize		
dostounix	drawpoly	dup	setgraphmode
setjmp	setlinestyle		
dup2	ecvt	ellipse	setlocale
setmem	setmode		
enable	eof	xecl	setpalette
setrgbpalette	settextjustify		
execle	execlp	execlpe	settextstyle
settime	setusercharsize		
execv	execve	execvp	setvbuf
setvect	setverify		
execvpe	exit	ex	setviewport
setvisualpage	setwritemode		
expl	fabs	fabsl	signal
sin	sinh		
farcalloc	farcoreleft	farfree	sinhl
sinl	sleep		
farheapcheck	farheapcheckfree	farheapchecknode	sopen
sound	spawnl		
farheapfillfree	farheapwalk	farmalloc	spawnle
spawnlp	spawnlpe		
farrealloc	fclose	fcloseall	spawnv
spawnve	spawnvp		
fcvt	fdopen	feof	spawnvpe
sprintf	sqrt		
ferror	fflush	fgetc	sqrtl
srand	sscanf		
fgetchar	fgetpos	fgets	stackavail
stat	stime		

(continues)

II

C Programming Basics

Table 14.1 Continued.

filelength	fileno	fillellipse	stpcpy
strcat	strchr		
fillpoly	findfirst	findnext	strcmp
strcmpi	strcoll		
floodfill	floor	floorl	strcpy
strcspn	strdup		
flushall	fmod	fmodl	strerror
strftime	stricmp		
nmerge	fnsplit	fopen	strlen
strlwr	strncat		
FP_OFF	FP_SEG	fprintf	strncmp
strncmpi	strncpy		
fputc	fputchar	fputs	strnicmp
strnset	strpbrk		
fread	free	freemem	strrchr
strrev	strset		
freopen	frexp	frexpl	strspn
strstr	strtod		
fscanf	fseek	fsetpos	strtok
strtol	strtoul		
stat	ftell	ftime	strupr
strxfrm	swab		
write	gcvt	geninterrupt	system
tan	tanh		
getarccoords	getaspectratio	getbkcolor	tanhl
tanl	tell		
getc	getcbrk	getch	tempnam
textattr	textbackground		
getchar	getche	getcolor	textcolor
textheight	textmode		
getcurdir	getcwd	getdate	textwidth
time	tmpfile		
getdefault	getdfree	getdisk	tmpnam
toascii	olower		
palette			
getdrivername	getdta	getenv	toupper
tzset	ultoa		
getfat	getfatd	getfillpattern	umask
ungetc	ungetch		
getfillsettings	getftime	getgraphmode	unixtodos
unlink	unlock		
getimage	getlinesettings	getmaxcolor	utime
va_arg	va_end		
getmaxmode	getmaxx	getmaxy	va_list
va_start	vfprintf		
getmodename	getmoderange	getpalette	vfscanf
vprintf	vscanf		

getpalettesize	getpass	getpid	vsprintf
vsscanf	wcstombs		
getpixel	getpsp	gets	wctomb
wherex	wherey		
window	_write	write	

Use Your Function Library

Many programmers spend hours of unnecessary programming time writing functions that already exist in the library. If you need to accomplish a particular task in your application, it pays to do a bit of research up front to determine whether a function is available to solve your problem. Many programmers have written BIOS calls by using many lines of in-line assembler code, for example, when a function or two in the dos.h or bios.h header file can perform the same operation with just one program statement. It pays to do your homework.

It often has been said that a good computer programmer is not a person who knows everything, but a person who can effectively find the information he or she needs to know.

You can look up a library function in one of two ways:

- Using the Turbo C++ help system

- Using the documentation

Using Help

Using the help system is by far the best way to locate and get information on Turbo C++ library functions. The IDE help system is an advanced database of related information about all aspects of Turbo C++, including library functions. The help system is always available to you, even from outside Turbo C++, using the help system memory-resident program. If you create your program from the IDE, you simply select Help from the IDE menu and then select the Contents menu command, which displays the Help Contents menu.

From the Help Contents menu, you can see the Function selection (it is highlighted). When you select Functions, a list of function categories appears (see fig. 14.1).

Here you can locate the correct function by the type of operation you want to perform. If you are interested in finding memory and string control functions, for example, you make the appropriate selection: String and memory routines.

Making this selection produces a list of available string and memory routines (see fig. 14.2). In this window, you can select a function—memset(), for example—and a detailed description of the function appears (see fig. 14.3).

Fig.14.1.
Turbo C++ function categories.

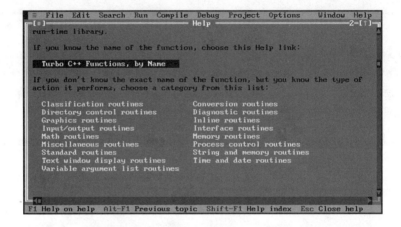

Fig. 14.2.
List of string and memory routines.

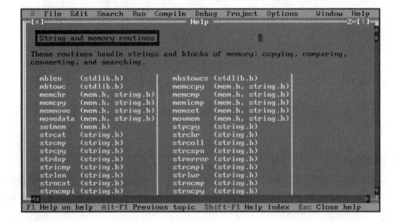

Notice that this window shows you the following:

■ The header files that you must include in the program

■ The function declaration statement

■ Helpful remarks about the function

■ Any value that the function may return

■ Portability from one compiler to another (Turbo C++ to Unix, for example)

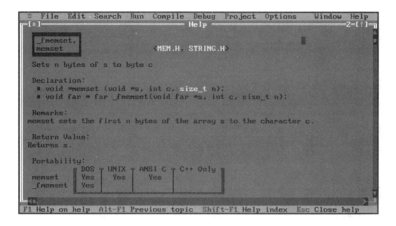

Fig. 14.3.
Details of the
memset( )
function.

Scrolling to the bottom of the memset() help window, you see an example of how to use the function in a program (see fig. 14.4).

```
≡  File  Edit  Search  Run  Compile  Debug  Project  Options    Window  Help
┌─[■]─────────────────────────── Help ───────────────────────2=[↑]─┐
│  See Also:                                                         │
│    Summary of all mem... functions                                 │
│                                          ▌                          │
│  Example:                                                           │
│                                                                     │
│  #include <string.h>                                                │
│  #include <stdio.h>                                                 │
│  #include <mem.h>                                                   │
│                                                                     │
│  int main(void)                                                     │
│  {                                                                  │
│     char buffer[] = "Hello world\n";                                │
│                                                                     │
│     printf("Buffer before memset: %s\n", buffer);                   │
│     memset(buffer, '*', strlen(buffer) - 1);                        │
│     printf("Buffer after memset:  %s\n", buffer);                   │
│     return 0;                                                       │
│  }                                                                  │
│                                                                     │
F1 Help on help  Alt-F1 Previous topic  Shift-F1 Help index  Esc Close help
```

Fig. 14.4.
Example program
using memset().

II

C Programming Basics

You may recall from Chapter 3 that you can copy this sample program to the Clipboard by invoking the Copy example menu command from the Edit menu. Figure 14.5 displays what the program looks like in the Clipboard. From here, you can pass the program directly into your application, or you can create a new application. Using the Clipboard saves having to print out the example and reenter it from scratch.

You gather information on other functions in the same way. You can get information and examples for all the functions listed in table 14.1. The Turbo C++ help system is the best in the business. Make good use of it when you can. It is certainly faster than using the documentation (described next).

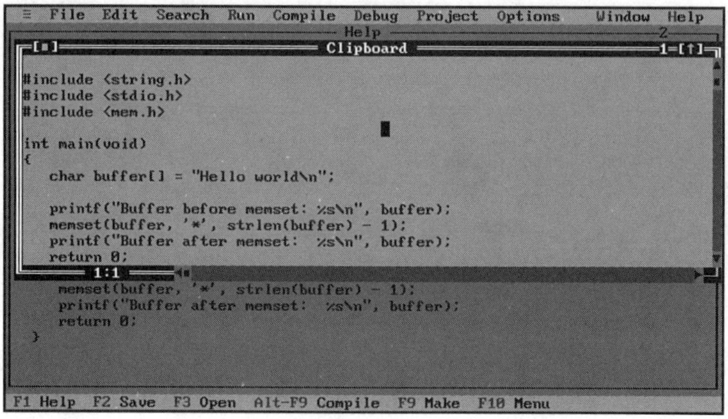

Fig. 14.5.
Example program
in the Clipboard.

```
≡  File  Edit  Search  Run  Compile  Debug  Project  Options      Window  Help
                                    ──Help──────────────────────────────── 2─
┌─[■]─────────────────────── Clipboard ═══════════════════════════════ 1═[↑]┐
#include <string.h>
#include <stdio.h>
#include <mem.h>

int main(void)
{
    char buffer[] = "Hello world\n";

    printf("Buffer before memset: %s\n", buffer);
    memset(buffer, '*', strlen(buffer) - 1);
    printf("Buffer after memset:  %s\n", buffer);
    return 0;
├──────── 1:1 ───────────◄■
    memset(buffer, '*', strlen(buffer) - 1);
    printf("Buffer after memset:  %s\n", buffer);
    return 0;
}

F1 Help  F2 Save  F3 Open  Alt-F9 Compile  F9 Make  F10 Menu
```

Using Your Documentation

Although you can find information on some functions in your Turbo C++
documentation, it does not make a good reference manual. Most general
library functions are described, but many more are not. Refer to this book
or your help system when you're seeking information on library functions.

Including the Correct Files

Functions do not work unless you include the proper header file or files in
your program. In fact, the compiler does not know how to treat a library
function if the header file does not provide the proper declaration statement
for the function. If the header file conio.h is not included in listing 14.1,
for example, the compiler responds with an error message, as shown in
figure 14.6.

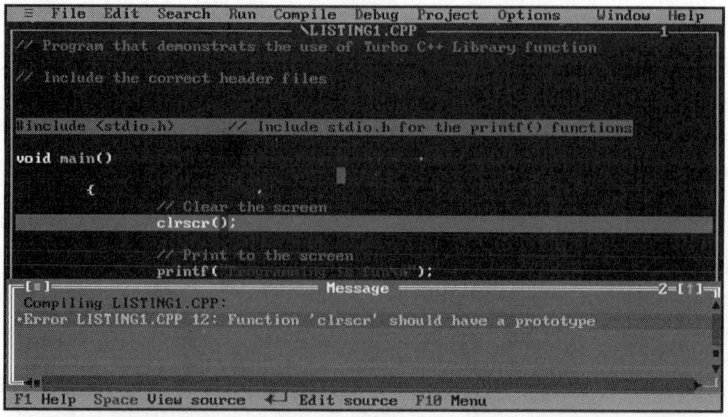

Fig. 14.6.
An error message
appears if the
correct header file
is not included.

```
≡  File  Edit  Search  Run  Compile  Debug  Project  Options      Window  Help
                              ─\LISTING1.CPP─────────────────────────── 1──
// Program that demonstrats the use of Turbo C++ Library function

// Include the correct header files

#include <stdio.h>        // Include stdio.h for the printf() functions

void main()

    {
                          // Clear the screen
        clrscr();

                          // Print to the screen
        printf(
┌─[■]───────────────────────── Message ══════════════════════════════ 2═[↑]┐
 Compiling LISTING1.CPP:
•Error LISTING1.CPP 12: Function 'clrscr' should have a prototype

F1 Help  Space View source  ↵ Edit source  F10 Menu
```

This error message is a good indication that you are using a function that has not been declared previously in a header file. Your help system or your documentation provides information on the proper header files to include in your application to support a required function. You may have noticed in the help system that each function reference includes information on the correct header file to include to gain access to the function being described. Most reference documentation lists header files with functions.

Table 14.2 is a complete listing of header files that come with Turbo C++. Note the function of each and how the names of the files describe the purpose of each. Remember that one header file supports many functions.

Table 14.2. C++ header files.

Header file	Supports
alloc.h	Memory-management functions
assert.h	Debugging
bcd.h	bcd math functions
bios.h	IBM PC ROM-BIOS routines
complex.h	Complex math functions
conio.h	DOS console routines
constrea.h	Screen I/O using streams
ctype.h	Classification/character conversion
dir.h	Directories and path names
direct.h	Directories and path names
dirent.h	POSIX operations
dos.h	DOS and 8086 calls
errno.h	Mnemonics for error codes
fcntl.h	Library routine open
float.h	Floating-point operations
fstream.h	File input and output operations
generic.h	Generic class declarations

(continues)

II

C Programming Basics

Table 14.2. Continued.

Header file	Supports
graphics.h	Graphics functions
io.h	Low-level input/output routines
iomanip.h	Parameterized manipulators
iostream.h	Streams (I/O) routines
limits.h	Ranges of integral quantities
locale.h	Country/language-specific information
malloc.h	Memory management
math.h	Math
mem.h	Memory-manipulation functions (also defined in string.h.)
memory.h	Memory-manipulation functions
new.h	new and newhandler
process.h	spawn and exec functions
search.h	Searching and sorting
setjmp.h	Used by `longjmp` and `setjmp`
share.h	File sharing
signal.h	Signal functions
stdarg.h	Arguments
stddef.h	Common data types and macros
stdio.h	Types and macros needed for the Standard I/O
stdiostr.h	File structures
stdlib.h	Common routines
stream.h	Streams (I/O) routines
string.h	Memory manipulation
strstrea.h	Byte arrays in memory
sys\locking.h	Locking function
sys\stat.h	Opening and creating files

Header file	Supports
sys\timeb.h	Function ftime and timeb
sys\types.h	Time functions
time.h	Time-conversion routines
utime.h	Structure utimbuf
values.h	UNIX System V compatibility
varargs.h	Processing variable argument lists

As you can see, you have quite a selection. Generally, you can use only a few header files over and over again, depending on the type of programming you are assigned to do. Most of the header files listed in table 14.2 may never find their way into your application, but other programmers may find them invaluable.

If your application uses many graphics, for example, then you add

```
#include <graphics.h>
```

into your program more often. Or if PC BIOS (basic input/output system) calls are a part of your application, you add

```
#include <bios.h>
```

into your program file to make BIOS calls.

You can include as many files as you need in your program file, including header files of your own creation defining your own function. As you learned in Chapter 13, "Using Functions," you sometimes can purchase header files to make available functions that perform a certain activity which is not provided by the Turbo C++ library. Generally, you include these files in your application in the same way you include standard Turbo C++ library files.

Using the Library

Chapter 15, "Using the C Library," describes the details of several library functions, including input, output, and conversion functions. In this section, you take a short tour through the world of Turbo C++ library functions, examining a cross section of functions available to you. Real working examples are presented, as well as brief explanations. If you can, try each example.

Function types covered in this section include the following:

- File processing

- String processing

- Mathematical operations

- Date and time operations

- System level functions

- Graphics processing

These functions, of course, are just a few of many hundreds of functions available to you. Refer to your Turbo C++ reference manual or the help system for additional functions and details.

Processing Files

Using files is a common task of computer programs. Several functions are available to manipulate text and binary files (files that only a computer can understand) from your C++ program. File library functions enable you to perform activities such as the following:

- Creating files

- Writing to files

- Reading from files

- Creating and managing complex file structures

Listing 14.2 demonstrates how the function `fprintf()` is employed to write information to a file. First, the file pointer is established (`fp`). Then the file is opened for writing, the information is written to the file, and the file is closed. These file input/output operations are simple.

C++ programs that must read and write from files (mailing list management packages, for example) use similar functions. You can maintain simple and complex file structures from a C++ program using file functions such as `fprintf()`.

```
1.    // Program: FILEOUT.CPP
2.    // Purpose: Demonstrates the use of fprintf() for file I/O
3.    // Author: David Linthicum

4.    #include <stdio.h>
5.    #include <stdlib.h>


6.    main(void)

7.    {

8.         // Establish a file handle
9.         FILE *fp;
           // String going in
           char string[] = "I'm in the file";
           // String coming out
           char stringout[] = "               ";

      {
10.        // Open the file for writing
11.        // If the file cannot be opened, produce an error
12.        if( ! (fp = fopen("temp.txt", "w")))

13.            {
14.                printf("File cannot be opened");
15.                exit(1);
16.            }
17.        // Print a string to the file
18.        fprintf(fp, "Putting this text into the file");

19.        // Close the file
20.        fclose(fp);

           // Open the file again
           if( ! (fp = fopen("temp.bin", "rb")))

       {
       printf("File cannot be opened");
       exit(1);
       }

           // Read and print the contents of the file
➥fread(stringout, sizeof stringout, 1, fp); printf("\n%s\n",
➥stringout);

           // Close the file
           fclose(fp);

21.        return 0;
22.    }
```

Manipulating Strings

You already know how to create and store information to strings. Remember from an earlier chapter that strings are null-terminated arrays of characters, and they are useful to maintain information during program processing.

The library provides several string manipulation functions that enable you to perform virtually any operation on a string such as the following:

- Copying a string

- Reversing the order of a string

- Converting the characters to upper- and lowercase

- Performing operations only on certain portions of the string

Listing 14.3 demonstrates how the strcpy() (string copy) function copies a string into a string variable. Using this function saves having to write a loop to move one string to another, one character at a time. The string function requires the header file string.h.

Caution

Remember that you must use strcpy() or another string function to move one string into another. Many new C++ programmers attempt to use statements such as

```
stringer = "This is a string";
```

which is incorrect. The correct method is

```
strcpy(stringer, "This is a string");
```

You should not treat strings as type char or int.

Listing 14.3. STRCOPY.CPP—Copying a string into a variable using strcpy().

```
1.   // Program: STRCOPY.CPP
2.   // Purpose: Demonstrates the use of strcpy() function
3.   /  Author: David Linthicum

4.   #include <stdio.h>       // Include this for standard I/O
➥functions
5.   #include <string.h> // Include this for string functions


6.   int main()
```

```
7.   {

8.        char char_string[60];

9.        // Copy a string of text to a string variable
10.       strcpy(char_string, "Moving this to a string");

11.       // Print the contents of the string variable
12.       printf(" %s \n", char_string);

13.       return 0;

14.  }
```

Many string functions change the form of a string. In listing 14.4, the
strrev() function reverses the order of a string, and strupr() converts
the entire string to uppercase.

**Listing 14.4. REVSTR.CPP—Using string functions to reverse the
order of a string and convert a string to uppercase.**

```
1.   // Program: REVSTR.CPP
2.   // Purpose: Demonstrates the use of strrev() function
3.   /  Author: David Linthicum

4.   #include <stdio.h>        // Include this for standard I/O
➥functions
5.   #include <string.h> // Include this for string functions
6.   #include <conio.h>  // Include this for console control


7.   int main()

8.   {

9.        // Clear the screen
10.       clrscr();

11.       // Store a string to a variable
12.       char char_msg[] = "David Linthicum";

13.       // Print out the string as stored
14.       printf("\n %s \n", char_msg);

15.       // Use strrev() to reverse the order of the string
16.       strrev(char_msg);

17.       // Print out the string after processed by strrev()
18.       printf(char_msg);

19.       // New line
20.       printf("\n");
```

(continues)

```
Listing 14.4. Continued.

21.        // Use strupr() to convert the string to uppercase
22.        strupr(char_msg);

23.        // Print out the string after processed by strupr()
24.        printf(char_msg);

25.        printf("\n");

26.        return 0;

27.  }
```

Using Math

Virtually any mathematical operation is possible from a Turbo C++ program. For example, using the C library, the following math functions are available:

- Trigonometry

- Hyperbolic functions

- Exponential functions

- Logarithmic functions

In listing 14.5, by including the math.h file, this program makes use of the tanh() function that calculates the hyperbolic tangent of a value passed into it.

```
Listing 14.5. MATH.CPP—Using the math function tanh().

1.   // Program: MATH.CPP
2.   // Purpose: Demonstrates the use of a tanh() math function
3.   /  Author: David Linthicum

4.   #include <stdio.h>      // Include this for standard I/O
➥functions
5.   #include <math.h>       // Include this for math functions
6.   #include <conio.h>  // Include this for console control


7.   int main()

8.   {

9.        // Clear the screen
10.       clrscr();

11.       // Store a value to a variable
12.       double value = -1.0;
```

```
13.        // Prints the hyperbolic tangent in increments of 0.05
14.        do
15.         {
16.          printf("Hyperbolic tangent of %lf is %lf\n", value,
➥tanh(value));
17.           value = value+ 0.05;
18.         }
19.        while(value <= 1.0);

20.        return 0;


21.  }
```

Using Date and Time Functions

From time to time, your application may require that you use date and time information. The time.h header file provides functions to do any of the following:

- Display the current date
- Display the current time
- Make date/time calculations
- Display dates and times for other time zones

In listing 14.6, the program reads the current local date and time from the clock in your computer using the time() function. It then displays the date and time on-screen.

Listing 14.6. TIME.CPP—Using the time() function.

```
1.   // Program: TIME.CPP
2.   // Purpose: Demonstrates the use of TIME()
3.   /  Author: David Linthicum

4.   #include <stdio.h>      // Include this for standard I/O
➥functions
5.   #include <time.h>    // Include this for time functions
6.   #include <conio.h>   // Include this for console control


7.   int main()

8.   {

9.        // Declare a variable that can hold a time
10.       time_t current_time;
```

(continues)

Listing 14.6. Continued.

```
11.     // Store the current time
12.     current_time = time(NULL);

13.     // Print the current time
14.     printf(ctime(&current_time));

15.     return 0;


16.   }
```

Using System-Related Functions

You can add system-related functions to your application through the system functions provided by dos.h or the bios.h header files. Using system-related functions, you can perform operations to do the following:

- Generate sounds

- Control the disk directly

- Control the keyboard directly

- Make BIOS calls (see Chapter 1, "The Basics")

Listing 14.7 demonstrates how to use the sound() function to generate a beep. Notice how a delay() function counts time until the nosound() function turns off the speaker. You can use these functions in any combination to create special sound effects for your application, as may be required to alert the user of an error or something else that needs attention.

Listing 14.7. SYSTEM.CPP—Using the system functions to create sound.

```
1.    // Program: SYSTEM.CPP
2.    // Purpose: Demonstrates the use of a system-related functions
3.    //          Beeps the terminal 3 times
4.    /  Author: David Linthicum

5.    #include <stdio.h>       // Include this for standard I/O
   ➥functions
6.    #include <dos.h>    // Include this for system functions
7.    #include <conio.h>  // Include this for console control


8.    int main()

9.    {
```

```
10.        int delay_time = 300;
11.        int sound_arg  = 500;

12.        // Clear the screen
13.        clrscr();

14.        // Beep the terminal
15.        sound(sound_arg);

16.        // Wait
17.        delay(delay_time);

18.        // Stop the sound
19.        nosound();

20.        // Wait
21.        delay(delay_time);

22.        // Beep again
23.        sound(sound_arg);
24.        delay(delay_time);
25.        nosound();
26.        delay(delay_time);

27.        // Beep again
28.        sound(sound_arg);
29.        delay(delay_time);
30.        nosound();
31.        delay(delay_time);


32.        return 0;


33.  }
```

Using Graphics

Most Turbo C++ programmers consider graphics programming fun. Using the graphics.h, you can perform such operations as

- Altering background and foreground colors

- Drawing shapes such as squares, rectangles, and circles

- Filling portions of the screen with patterns

- Creating animation applications

- Creating business graphics such as line, bar, and pie charts

Tip

For the compiler
to link the graph-
ics functions into
your executable,
you must select
Linker from the
Options menu and
then turn on the
graphics library
option in the
dialog box. If you
don't select this
option, the com-
piler cannot locate
the correct library
(GRAPHICS.LIB)
for the functions
declared in
graphics.h, and
linker errors are
generated.

Listing 14.8 demonstrates how several graphics functions are employed to
change the background color of the screen to blue, draw rectangles, fill part
of the screen with a color, and then after the user presses any key, restore the
screen to a normal state. Before you compile and link the program, you're
going to have to tell the compiler how to locate (GRAPHICS.LIB). In addition,
you'll need to make sure that the BGI file appropriate to your monitor is
available to your graphics program.

Listing 14.8. GRAPHICS.CPP—Using graphics functions.

```
1.    // Program: GRAPHICS.CPP
2.    // Purpose: Demonstrates the use of graphics functions
3.    // Author: David Linthicum

4.    #include <graphics.h>   // Include this for graphics
5.    #include <conio.h>   // Include this for console control

6.    int main()

7.    {

8.        int driver;
9.        int mode;

10.       // Detect the hardware and store it in driver
11.       driver = DETECT;
12.       mode = 0;

13.       // Create the graphic
14.       initgraph(&driver, &mode, " ");

15.       // Set the background color to blue
16.       setbkcolor(BLUE);

17.       // Draw rectangles
18.       rectangle(100, 100, 400, 400);
19.       rectangle(100, 50, 20, 300);
20.       rectangle(50, 10, 20, 50);

21.       // Fill a region
22.       floodfill(200, 300, RED);

23.       getch();        // Wait for the user to press a key

24.       // Restore the screen mode
25.       restorecrtmode();

26.       return 0;

27.   }
```

Summary

This chapter introduced Turbo C++ library functions. Here you began your tour of the many hundreds of library functions that you can use in your application. You learned about the concept of a library function, as well as how to locate function information—such as the correct header files and how to use a particular function correctly—in the help system or documentation. This chapter covered the following topics:

- Library functions come with Turbo C++. They perform particular tasks such as input/output operations or graphics processing. Library functions eliminate the need to write the functions from scratch.

- You may find useful functions in the Turbo C++ help system or documentation. Using the help system, you can locate functions quickly, and examples are available. The documentation that comes with Turbo C++ does not lend itself to the location and identification of library functions.

- Using your references (the help system or reference manual), you learn what header file to include in your application to support a particular library function. Many header files are available, and each one may support numerous functions.

- You can purchase header files and libraries to extend the number of functions provided by the standard Turbo C++ library.

- Library functions provide file input/output processing facilities, math, string manipulation operations, and graphics application support—to name just a few of the categories of functions.

- It is important that beginning C++ programmers know what library functions are, how to locate information on a particular function, and how to use these functions in an application. Functions, if properly used, save many hours of programming time.

II

C Programming Basics

Chapter 15

Using the C Library

The C library is a collection of functions that can be used to simplify programming. Whether your program must interact with a user, read and write to files, or manipulate information, a C library function can accomplish the task.

The extensive set of more than 500 built-in Turbo C++ library functions can appear overwhelming at first. To introduce you to the C library functions gradually, this chapter presents them by topic, according to the typical way a beginning programmer develops applications. First, you learn how to use functions that interact with the keyboard and screen. Second, you learn how to store information to a disk and retrieve information from a disk. Third, you learn about some common library functions that manipulate information.

Interacting with the User: Screen and Keyboard Functions

For a program to be useful, it must interact with the user. This process of *user interaction* consists of two activities: presenting information on-screen to the user and capturing information from the user from the keyboard or the mouse. This may appear confusing at first, because most applications, such as Turbo C++, appear to do both tasks at the same time. However, they are separate tasks and each is controlled by its own set of C library functions.

Figure 15.1 shows how presenting screen information differs from capturing keyboard or mouse information. User 1 is a computer user, much like yourself, using Turbo C++. User 2 is a vending machine user. By inserting a coin in the coin slot, user 2 sets in motion a complex series of mechanical operations. As a result, a product is dispensed at the bottom of the vending machine.

Fig. 15.1.
An illustration of
user interaction.

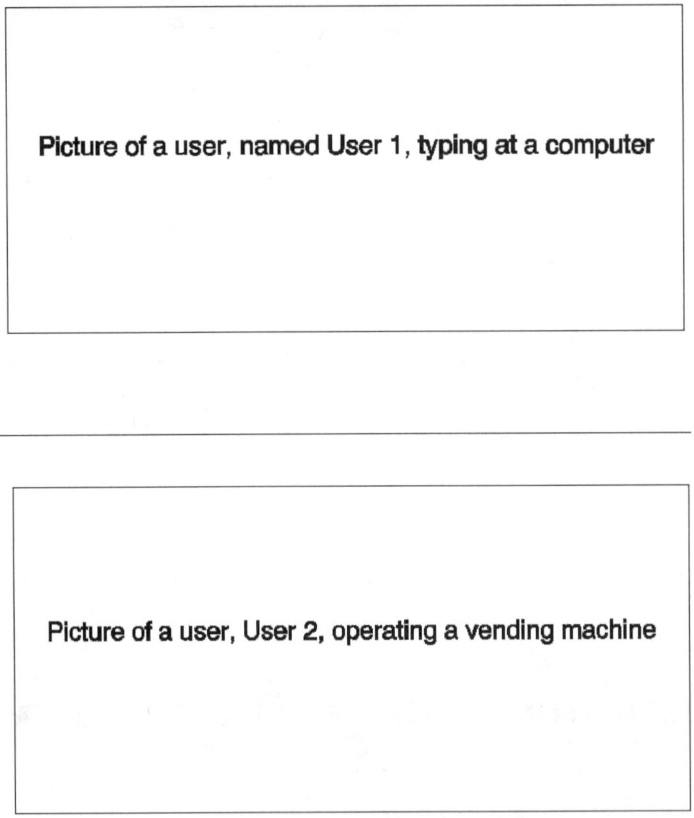

Picture of a user, named User 1, typing at a computer

Picture of a user, User 2, operating a vending machine

Like the vending machine that accepts a coin, your program accepts keyboard entries as input. This input sets in motion a series of operations, which you write. As a result, something is "dispensed" on the screen.

The programmer is responsible for turning the keyboard entries into screen presentations. Nothing happens automatically. This may sound difficult, but it isn't. The Turbo C++ libraries contain a variety of functions for retrieving keyboard entries and displaying information on-screen.

> **Note**
>
> Many C and C++ manuals refer to the screen as the console or monitor. In the context of this chapter, the terms *screen, console,* and *monitor* equally refer to the TV-like device that displays characters to the user.

Character-Based User Interaction

All interaction between the user and the system happens one character at a time. Regardless of how fast a user might type, the system processes only one character at a time. Likewise, information presented to the user, whether it is a single line to prompt for input or a complete screen, is executed one character at a time. The eye cannot detect that the screen is being filled just one character at a time, starting from the top left and continuing to the bottom right, because the computer is operating at a very high speed.

Character-based user interaction is therefore essential to understanding how information is processed in bulk. Programming character-based user interaction is also easier than programming graphics, which makes it a convenient place to start discussing C library functions that deal with user interaction.

Using the *getch( )* and *putch( )* Functions. The two simplest C library functions for screen input and output are getch( ) and putch( ). As you might guess from their names, getch( ) accepts a single keyboard character entered by a user, and putch( ) places a single character on-screen.

> **Note**
>
> The getch() function accepts any keyboard key as valid input. This includes function keys, direction keys, and other nondisplayable keys. A nondisplayable key is one that does not have a screen representation.

The getch( ) function waits until a user presses a key on the keyboard, then returns its value. To test the getch( ) function, enter and run the following code:

```
#include <conio.h>
main()
{
    getch();
    return 0; // return 0 to indicate successful completion
}
```

This program waits for a keyboard key to be pressed. When a key is pressed, the program ends. If you are wondering why the character that was pressed was not displayed on-screen, recall that the keyboard and screen are two separate devices. To display a character, you must use the putch( ) function. The following code shows how to read a character and display it on-screen:

```
#include <conio.h>
main()
{
      char ch;        // declare a placeholder for the character to
                      ➥be read
      ch = getch();   // get the next character that is pressed
      putch(ch);      // put the character just read on-screen
      return 0;       // return 0 to indicate successful completion
}
```

When you run this program, it waits until you press a key. When a key is pressed, the getch( ) function returns the value of the key to the ch character variable. The character variable is then passed to putch( ), which places the character on-screen. Although describing these lines of code may take a while, the computer processes them in a fraction of a second. That is why there is no apparent delay between the time you press a key and the time it takes the next line of code to display it on-screen.

The Value of a Character. All keyboard characters are represented internally to the computer as numbers. The collection of numbers that represent characters is called the *ASCII code*. The ASCII chart is presented in Appendix A.

When a function uses or returns a character, it is using or returning the ASCII integer value that represents the character. For example, the function declaration of getch( ) is as follows:

```
int  getch(void);
```

As the function declaration indicates, `getch( )` takes no arguments (`void`) and returns an integer value (`int`). As the function declaration indicates, `getch( )` takes no arguments and returns an integer value. This return value is the integer representation (the ASCII code) of the character entered by the user.

> **Note**
>
> It is often useful to familiarize yourself with the broader set of C library calls that pertain to a topic.

Characters can be accepted from the keyboard and displayed on-screen with several functions. These functions are similar—but not identical--to the `getch( )` and `putch( )` functions. The following sections describe some of these variations in more detail. The variety of C library functions makes your life as a programmer a little easier.

Using the *getche( )* Function. In the previous example, two C library functions were necessary to display a keyboard character to the screen. The `getch( )` function retrieved the keyboard character that was pressed, and the `putch( )` function presented the character on-screen. You can, however, accomplish both tasks with a single function, `getche( )`. The `getche( )` function echoes characters entered back to the screen. (The additional *e* in `getche( )` refers to *echo*.) To see how this function operates, enter and run the following code:

```
#include <conio.h>
main()
{
    getche();
    return 0; // return 0 to indicate successful completion
}
```

When you run this program, the single function `getche( )` takes the keyboard character that was pressed and displays it to the screen. Now that you know about `getche( )`, however, don't conclude that `getch( )` is an antiquated function. When a user enters a password, for example, you need to get the information but you don't want it displayed on the screen.

Using the *getchar( )* and *putchar( )* Functions. Another variety of the `getch( )` and `putch( )` functions is the `getchar( )` and `putchar( )` functions. The `getchar( )` function differs from `getch( )` in two respects. One, `getchar( )` returns a value only when the Enter key is pressed, whereas `getch( )` returns a value when any key is pressed. Two, getchar( ) enables the system to *buffer* keys (save them in a temporary location) until the Enter key is pressed, then the function returns the value of the first keypress.

The following program uses the getchar( ) and putchar( ) functions:

```
#include <stdio.h>
main()
{
    char ch;
    ch = getchar();
    putchar(ch);
    return 0;
}
```

The header file used in this program is stdio.h, unlike the previous examples, which used the conio.h file. The getchar( ) and putchar( ) functions are part of a different library and therefore require a different header file.

To test the program, try several entries. First press a single key, such as **a**, and then press Enter. The result should look like this:

a
a

The *a* that was originally entered is echoed to the screen, then putchar( ) places the character on the next line. Now try running the program and entering several characters before pressing Enter. If you enter **abcdefghi**, the result is the following:

abcdefghi
a

The first line is an echo of all the characters typed. Then, when the Enter key is pressed, getchar( ) returns (but does not display) the value of the first character in the line. The putchar( ) function places the return value of the getchar( ) function on the next line.

The getchar( ) function is useful when you want the user to be able to correct a character entry. The user can type a character, backspace over the value entered, and enter a new character. Only when the user presses Enter is the value of the character returned to the program.

Where Do Buffered Keys Go? When a key is pressed, its value is stored sequentially in the keyboard buffer, which is a holding spot managed by the system. There is only one keyboard buffer to a system. When a program uses a C library function to retrieve a character, the library function looks into the buffer for the next key to process. The keyboard buffer uses a FIFO (First In-FirstOut) queue, which means the first key pressed (and therefore stored) is the first key processed.

The following program demonstrates the use of the keyboard buffer:

```
#include <stdio.h>
main()
{
    char ch;
    ch = getchar();      // read the first character in the buffer
    putchar(ch);
    ch = getchar();      // read the second character in the buffer
    putchar(ch);
    ch = getchar();      // read the third character in the buffer
    putchar(ch);
    return 0;
}
```

To test the use of the buffer, enter a long set of characters and press Enter. For example, if you type **abcdefghi,** and then press the Enter key, the keyboard buffer is filled with nine characters. The getchar() function is called three times in the preceding program. With each call to the getchar() function, the next character is read in the order that it was entered. The resulting output follows:

```
abcdefghi
abc
```

Try running the program again, but this time enter only one character followed by Enter. If you type **a** and press Enter, for example, the first getchar() function returns the only character in the buffer, which is *a*.

The second call to the getchar() function looks in the buffer and sees that there are no characters, so it waits for another entry. If you enter two or more characters followed by Enter, the subsequent two getchar() functions process the first two of these characters without interruption.If you enter a single character, however, the second getchar() processes the character, then the third getchar() function again waits for user input.

String-Based User Interaction

The greatest limitation of dealing with characters is that most applications must work with words and sentences rather than single characters. Programming an input form, for example, is much easier if functions can display entire lines of screen information to present the input form and retrieve entire lines of keyboard input to process user input. Fortunately, a variety of string-based user interaction functions are part of the C library.

Formatting Screen and Keyboard Interaction. In a typical application, you generally need to manage a variety of variables that are solicited by and presented to the user. Consider, for example, the input form that was mentioned earlier. Although gets( ) and puts( ) might be suitable for presenting a single line of text, they are inadequate for more robust—and often more necessary—formatted screen input and output. This is where the printf( ) and scanf( ) functions are particularly useful.

Using the *scanf( )* and *printf( )* Functions. The principal screen input and output functions are scanf( ) and printf( ). You can use these two functions for simple screen and keyboard management, as well as for complex user input and presentations. The scanf( ) and printf( ) functions have somewhat more complex prototypes than do the other user interface functions, and they are the following:

```
int scanf(const char *format[, address, ...]);
int printf(const char *format[, argument, ...]);
```

In their simplest forms, scanf( ) and printf( ) operate similarly to the puts( ) and gets( ) functions, as you can see in the following:

```
scanf("");
#include <stdio.h>
main()
{
    scanf("")
    printf("You have entered a value.");
    return 0;
}
```

The preceding program pauses for the user to enter some information and buffers the keyboard input until the user presses Enter. The printf( ) function takes a string and presents it to the user. So far, these functions behave similarly to the gets( ) and the puts( ) functions. However, this is the extent of similarity between the two sets of functions.

The following additions to the preceding program demonstrate the more common, and more powerful, uses of scanf( ) and printf( ):

```
#include <stdio.h>
main()
{
    char string[80];
    scanf("%s", string);
    printf("You have entered %s as a value.", string);
    return 0;
}
```

Like the original program, this one waits for a user to enter characters that are collected into the string buffer when Enter is pressed. The program then presents the first word, defined as the set of characters up to the first space or carriage return, in the middle of a sentence.

The significant aspect of this example is that formatting is being done when the user enters information and also when that information is presented. If you run the program and type the sentence

```
"This is a test"
```

The result is

```
"You have entered This as a value."
```

On the input side, the scanf() function uses only the first word. This is done by specifying one formatting code in the format string argument of scanf(). To retrieve the first two strings entered, use two string formatting codes, as in the following:

```
scanf("%s%s", string1, string2);
```

You must provide a corresponding string buffer for every string code you list in the format string argument. This way, when the program starts reading the keyboard buffer based on the scanf() format string, it knows where to place each string specified in the format string argument.

The printf() function also supports multiple format codes in the format code argument. Like the scanf() function, for every format code specified in the format string argument, you must specify a corresponding buffer in the argument list. To present two strings in a sentence, use the following format:

```
printf("The first value is: %s, and the second is: %s\n", string1,
string2);
```

In addition to retrieving and presenting string information, you can use printf() and scanf() to handle various types of numerical and special formatting input and output requirements. That is the topic of the next section.

Using the *gets( )* and *puts( )* Functions. The `gets( )` function retrieves a string of text from the keyboard. The `puts( )` function presents a string of text to the screen. The prototypes for these functions follow:

```
char *gets(char *s)
int  puts(const char *s);
```

> **Note**
>
> A prototype is a description of how a function can be used in your program. The prototype indicates the spelling of the function, the arguments of the function, and its return type.

Both functions take a string pointer rather than a character as an argument. These functions manage entire strings. The line of text entered by the user, up to the Enter keypress, is placed in the keyboard buffer. The `gets( )` function places the contents of the keyboard buffer in the string argument. Then the `puts( )` function can be used to display the string argument to the screen. The subject of pointers in general, and string pointers in particular, are covered in greater detail in Chapter 18, "Using Pointers."

> **Caution**
>
> Be extremely careful when passing a string pointer as an argument to the `gets()` function. If the string pointed to by the argument is not long enough to hold the line of text entered by the user, `gets()` reads past the end of the string buffer and into another program's buffer or into protected memory. This can cause the system to crash. (A program can create many buffers of its own. However, there is only one keyboard buffer — that is, one buffer into which keys pressed by the user are stored.)

Note that the `gets( )` function returns the pointer to the string that was passed as the argument. Why would a function return the same value as the argument that was passed? The answer is that it makes using the function easier. By returning the pointer to the string that was passed as an argument, the `gets( )` function can now be used itself as an argument to yet another function that takes a string pointer. The next example demonstrates how the `gets( )` function is used as an argument.

Look at the following two programs, which use the same functions to read and redisplay a line of text:

```
#include <stdio.h>
main()
{
     char string[80];
     gets(string);
     puts(string);
     return 0;
}

#include <stdio.h>
main()
{
     char string[80];
     puts(gets(string));
     return 0;
}
```

By having the pointer to the string argument as the return value, the gets( ) function can be used in turn as the argument to the puts( ) function. Any function that returns a string pointer can be used as the argument to another function that requires a string pointer as an argument. This is why many string-based functions return the pointer to the string buffer they use.

Using Escape Characters. Escape characters have a special effect on output. They are used, for example, to move to the next line on-screen, tab horizontally, and override values. Table 15.1 lists the escape characters you can use in your Turbo C++ programs.

Table 15.1. Escape Characters.

Escape	Character
\b	Backspace
\f	Form feed
\n	Newline
\r	Carriage return
\t	Horizontal tab
\v	Vertical tab
\\	Backslash
\"	Double quote
\'	Single quote

II

C Programming Basics

Not all these escape characters are relevant to screen display, but their use is the same for all output devices, including the screen output device. The device ignores any escape characters that are not relevant. For example, a form feed, which forces the device to go to the next page, makes sense for a printer but has no relevance for a screen.

You use escape characters by embedding them into text strings, for example:

```
#include <stdio.h>
main()
{
    char string[140] = "The first line\n\  // The end-of-the-line
The second line\n\                    // backslash is necessary
The third line, tab-indented\n\      // to continue the string
Fourth line with a \" in the middle";   // assignment on the next
                                            ➥line

    puts(string);
    return 0;
}
```

The output for this program follows:

```
The first line
The second line
        The third line, tab-indented
Fourth line with a " in the middle
```

The \n escape character causes the subsequent text to be displayed on the next line. \t indents the third line one tab to the right. The \" escape character is necessary when you want to enter double quotation marks as part of a text string. Without the special escape character, the double quotation mark is interpreted by the compiler as the end of the string declaration.

Advanced User Interaction with *scanf( )* and *printf( ).* As listed in the preceding section, the scanf( ) and printf( ) functions can manage a variety of formatting requirements.

The first argument that specifies the format codes of the line to be retrieved is often referred to as the *format specifier*. Among other things, the format specifier tells the function how many arguments to process and in what order, along with each argument's type. The format specifier uses the following basic form:

```
% [width] type_character
```

The [width] specifier determines the number of characters to process for the corresponding argument. type_character stands for the type of argument that is used, such as a string, an integer, or a character. A partial list of type characters available for scanf( ) are listed in table 15.2.

type_character	Expected argument type	Declared as
d	Decimal integer	int
f	Floating-point number	float
c	Character	char
s	Character string	null-terminated string buffer

Table 15.2. Type_character options for printf() and scanf().

The scanf( ) function retrieves functions and uses a pointer to an argument, whereas the printf( ) function uses the argument as declared.

The scanf( ) and printf( ) functions have many more format specifiers. The two functions also differ in many ways. For a complete description of the function specifier options, refer to the Turbo C++ library reference manual or the on-line help.

The format specifier is used to handle special requirements when your program retrieves information from the keyboard using scanf( ) or presents information to the screen using printf( ). For example, to read the first five characters of a keyboard buffer and ignore the rest of the line, use scanf( ) like this:

```
char string[80];
scanf("%5s", string);
```

To read the first two digits entered, use scanf( ) like this:

```
int  i;
scanf("%2d", &i);
```

The argument i is listed as &i because all scanf( ) arguments must be addresses to variables. The function translates the & that precedes a variable to represent the address to the variable. Addresses will be described in greater detail later in this book. For now, precede a variable with the & in the scanf( ) function.

Likewise, to display the first five characters of a string to the screen, use printf( ) like this:

```
char string[] = "ABCDEFGHIJKLMNOP";
printf("%5s", string);
```

Only ABCDE is displayed on-screen. Likewise, to present only the first few digits of a number, use printf( ) like this:

```
int  i = 12345678;
printf("%2d", i);
```

This displays the number 12 on-screen.

One additional format specifier for printf( ) that can be useful in many circumstances is the decimal point, which is referred to as the *precision specifier*. The . has varying effects for the different argument types. For a string argument, the precision specifier determines the number of characters of the string to display. For a float argument, the precision specifier determines the number of integers to the right of the decimal point to display. Table 15.3 lists several combinations of width and precision specifiers and their resulting output.

Table 15.3. Examples using various combinations of width and precision specifiers.	
printf( ) **Example**	**Result**
printf("%10s", "12345")	- - - - -12345
printf("%10.1s", "12345")	- - - - - - - - -1
printf("%1.10s", "12345")	12345
printf("%10f", 123.456)	123.456000
printf("%10.1f", 123.456)	- - - - -123.5
printf("%1.10f", 123.456)	123.4560000000

Managing Files: Using File Functions

The C library comes with a complete set of built-in functions to read from and write to disk files. What may be surprising to first-time users of the C library is that dealing with file management functions is similar to dealing with screen and keyboard functions. The reason for the similarity is that from the C library perspective, disk drive devices look the same as screen and keyboard devices. The C library manages all devices—including any hard disk, disk drive, keyboard, mouse, monitor, and communications ports—in the same way. The secret behind this common method for communicating with any device is a concept called a `stream`.

Streams: The Backbone of Device Communications

A C library stream is very much like its English counterpart—a waterway or current. The name *stream* is appropriate for device communication, because both C library streams and water streams help things get from one place to another, as illustrated in figure 15.2. In the case of the C library, the stream carries bits and bytes rather than ships and boats.

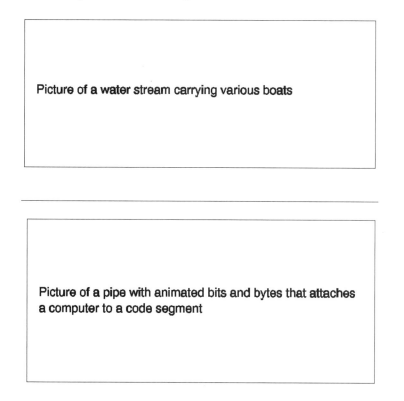

Fig. 15.2.
An illustration of a stream.

Picture of a water stream carrying various boats

Picture of a pipe with animated bits and bytes that attaches a computer to a code segment

Any device that needs to communicate with the C library must be attached by using a stream. The stream sets up a channel for communication between your program and the device. How the bits and bytes then travel to and from the device is the responsibility of the stream.

Although all devices that communicate do so through streams in the C library, some streams get preferential treatment. Specifically, the keyboard and monitor are commonly referred to as the *standard input stream* and *standard output stream*, respectively. Communicating with these devices is the same as with other devices, such as the hard disk, except that the keyboard and monitor have preset streams that the application sets up when you execute the program. To communicate with the keyboard and monitor, you do not need to establish a special stream, because the compiler has done that work for you. Your applications always have a keyboard and monitor stream ready to be used as soon as your application starts executing.

This explains why the preceding section dealing with keyboard and screen communication did not mention streams. Because the keyboard and monitor have dedicated streams that are always available, the creators of the C library decided to give them special functions that are for the exclusive use of communicating with those specific devices. The getch( ), getche( ), getchar( ), and scanf( ) input functions all manage communication between your program and the keyboard using the standard input stream. Likewise, the putch( ), putchar( ), and printf( ) functions manage communication between your program and the monitor using the standard output stream. Because these functions deal exclusively with the standard input and standard output streams, there was no need for the designers of the C library functions to have them specified as arguments.

The standard input stream is often referred to as stdin, and the standard output stream is commonly referred to as stdout.

Communicating with the disk drive requires that you use a special set of stream functions that pertain to the disk drive, and that you manage the streams on your own. Unlike the keyboard and monitor, where only one stream is established for each of these devices, the disk drive can have many streams established simultaneously. Each stream represents a channel to communicate between your program and a single disk file. You can have 10, 20, and even 100 streams open simultaneously.

Basic File Management Functions

The Turbo C++ stream library can be divided into three areas: opening and closing file streams, navigating within file streams, and reading from and writing to file streams. Figure 15.3 illustrates the order in which file stream functions are used.

Using the *fopen( )* and *fclose( )* Functions. To read from or write to a disk file, you must first establish a stream that connects your program with the file with which you would like to communicate. The `fopen( )` function does just that. Its prototype is the following:

```
FILE *fopen(const char* filename, const char* mode);
```

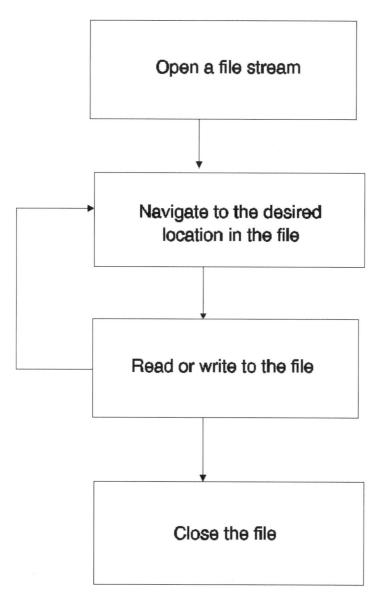

Fig. 15.3.
The order for using file stream functions.

The `fopen( )` function takes two arguments, a *filename* and a *mode*, and returns a pointer to a structure called `FILE`. The two arguments determine what file to open and how to open it. The purpose of the *mode* argument is to tell the `fopen( )` function how to open the file designated by *filename*. You may want to open the file only if it exists, and limit yourself to reading from the file. Or, you may want to create the file if the file does not already exist. The *mode* argument is a flexible and powerful way to determine how `fopen( )` will establish the stream connection to the disk file. The various modes that `fopen( )` supports are listed in table 15.4.

Table 15.4. Mode options for the fopen() function.	
Mode	**Description**
r	Opens a file only for reading.
w	Opens a file only for writing. Creates the file if it does not yet exist, and overwrites the file it does exist.
a	Opens a file for appending; opens a file to write starting at the end of the file. Creates the file for writing if it does not yet exist.
r+	Opens an existing file for reading and writing.
w+	Creates a new file for reading and writing. If a file by that name exists, overwrites it.
a+	Opens a file for reading and writing starting at the end of the file. Creates the file if it does not exist.

The `fopen( )` function returns a pointer to a FILE structure. For now, consider the FILE structure and the stream to be synonymous. This FILE structure is used in subsequent calls to file stream functions to let those functions know which file to operate on.

The `fclose( )` function closes a file stream that was opened by `fopen( )`. The prototype for `fclose( )` is

```
int fclose(FILE *stream);
```

Notice that the `fclose( )` function takes a single argument, a pointer to a FILE structure. Like all file stream functions, the `fclose( )` function knows which file to close based on the FILE pointer argument. After a file is opened, all references to the file are done using the pointer to the FILE structure rather than the file name.

The FILE structure maintains much behind-the-scenes information about the file that it represents. Instead of passing the file name along with a set of overhead information, it is more convenient for the file stream functions to use a FILE structure. When a file stream function wants to know something about the file, it looks it up in the FILE structure that is passed to it as an argument. This way, much information about the file can be efficiently passed between functions that need to operate on the file stream.

The following program outline demonstrates how to use fopen( ) and fclose( ) to establish and close a stream connection to a file:

```c
#include <stdio.h>
main()
{
    FILE *stream;
    stream = fopen("\\autoexec.bat", "r");
         .
         .      // Read information from the file
         .
    fclose(stream);
    return 0;
}
```

Notice that the filename argument used in fopen( ) has a double \. Because the \ character represents the Escape code (such as \t for Tab), you need to use a double \ for the compiler to accept a \ as its own character rather than as part of an escape code.

Using the *fgetc( )* and *fputc( )* Functions. The fgetc( ) and fputc( ) functions read and write single characters to and from a file. Their function prototypes are the following:

```c
int fgetc(FILE *stream);
int fputc(int c, FILE *stream);
```

The only difference between these functions and their keyboard and screen counterparts is that the file stream functions take an extra argument that is a pointer to a FILE structure.

The following example demonstrates how to read text from a disk file:

```c
#include <stdio.h>
main()
{
    FILE *stream;
    char ch;
    stream = fopen("\\autoexec.bat", "r");  // Open file
    ch = fgetc(stream);              // Read the first character
    putchar(ch);                     // Display character to the
                                     ➥screen
    fclose(stream);                  // Close file
    return 0;
}
```

Recall that putchar( ) places a character on-screen. This program opens the AUTOEXEC.BAT file, reads the first character, and places it on the screen. The program then closes the file. Note that all file stream functions use the stream pointer rather than the file name.

The next example demonstrates the use of fputc( ). It also shows that the screen is just another stream that happens to always be available. Recall from the beginning of this section that the screen has its own permanent stream called stdout, which stands for *standard output device*. This stream is available as soon as your program executes.

```
#include <stdio.h>
main()
{
     FILE *stream;
     char ch;
     stream = fopen("\\autoexec.bat", "r");
     ch = fgetc(stream);
     fputc(ch, stdout); // Notice how stdout is used but was never
                              ➥opened
     fclose(stream);
     return 0;
}
```

The fputc( ) function is able to place the first character of the AUTOEXEC.BAT file on the screen using the stdout stream, even though stdout was never opened. The stdout stream is always open and ready to be used.

Using the *fgets( )* and *fputs( )* Functions. Most programs need to read and write lines of text from a file rather than deal with single characters. The fgets( ) and fputs( ) functions read from and write to file streams using entire strings rather than single characters. The prototypes for these functions are

```
char *fgets(char *s, int n, FILE *stream);
int fputs(const char *s, FILE *stream);
```

These functions operate like their keyboard and screen counterparts, gets( ) and puts( ). The one difference is that the fgets( ) function takes an integer value as a second argument. This value tells the fgets( ) function how many characters to read from the file. The fgets( ) function returns either when it has read one less character than the number of characters specified by *n*, the second argument, or when it reaches a newline character.

The purpose of the second argument, *n*, is to provide you with a way to protect your program from accidentally writing beyond the buffer pointed to by *s*. Without the *n* argument, the fgets( ) function continues reading until a newline character or the end of the file is reached. This could be very hazardous if you read a large file with unknown contents. The `fgets( )` function does not check that your buffer is large enough to hold the information it is reading, and would write information passed through the end of the buffer and into another program's or the operating system's memory space. This could cause the system to crash.

By having the *n* argument to limit how many characters the `fgets( )` function reads, you can safely read any file by making sure the buffer passed as the first argument is never smaller than the amount specified by *n*. Never assume you know the contents of a file and therefore set *n* to be a large number, thinking that it will always reach the end of a line before it runs out of buffer space. Someone may use your program to read a longer file, which could cause a system crash.

The following example demonstrates the use of `fgets( )` and `fputs( )`, as well as creating a file using `fopen( )`.

```c
#include <stdio.h>
main()
{
    FILE *stream;
    char buffer[80];

        // Create a temporary file called test1.tmp
        // and place some text in the file

    stream = fopen("test1.tmp", "w+");
    fputs("This is a test of writing to a file", stream);
    fclose(stream);

        // Open the same file for reading
        // Read the file and place the text to the screen

    stream = fopen("test1.tmp", "r");
    fgets(buffer, 10, stream);
    fputs(buffer, stdout);   // Note the use of stdout to display
                             ➥to the screen
    fclose(stream);

    return 0;
}
```

The program operates in two steps. The first step is to create a temporary file, called TEST1.TMP, and place some text in the file. Note the use of the mode parameter for the `fopen( )` function, which creates and opens the file test1.tmp.

The second step is to open the file again for reading and read some text into a buffer. As did the last program, this one uses the stdout stream and the standard stream function fputs( ) to put the text on-screen. The stream functions do not know what kind of device is at the end of the stream to which they are writing. In this program, the fputs( ) function was used to write to a file stream and to the screen using the stdout stream by simply passing the appropriate stream pointer in each case.

You may be wondering why this program did not keep open the file it created and reread what it had just entered into the test1.tmp file. Instead, the program closed the file after it created it and placed some text in it, and then reopened the file to read the text it had just entered. The answer is that when data is placed in a file, the stream increments a pointer that is its placeholder within the file. As data is placed in the file, the placeholder moves forward. In the last program, when the program finishes placing the text in the file using fputs( ), the placeholder is pointing to the end of the file. To reread the text there needs to be a way of getting back to the beginning of a file. That is the subject of the next section.

File Navigation—Using the *fseek( )* Function. When a stream function is used to read from or write to a file, the stream updates an internal pointer that contains the current location for subsequent function calls to the file. The stream naturally goes in only one direction—forward. All stream functions read from or write to files sequentially, starting from the current internal location pointer and moving ahead as the function reads or writes. When a file is opened, the current location pointer is always set to the beginning of the file. To change the internal location pointer of the stream, you must use the fseek( ) function.

The fseek( ) function prototype is

```
int fseek(FILE *stream, long offset, int starting_point);
```

The fseek( ) functions take three arguments: a pointer to a FILE structure, an offset value, and a *starting_point*. The fseek( ) function sets the internal location pointer associated with *stream* to a new position that is *offset* bytes from the file location indicated by *starting_point*. The *starting_point* argument can be set to one of three values, which are listed in table 15.5.

Table 15.5. Starting_point values for fseek( ).	
starting_point value	**Description**
SEEK_SET	Beginning of the file
SEEK_CUR	Current position
SEEK_END	End of the file

Navigation can be forward or backward. To move backward, use a negative value for the offset argument. Table 15.6 lists several variations of the use of fseek( ).

Table 15.6. Examples of fseek( ).	
fseek( ) usage	**Description**
fseek(stream, 0, SEEK_SET)	Go to the beginning of the file
fseek(stream, 0, SEEK_END)	Go to the end of the file (often used for appending information to a file)
fseek(stream, -10, SEEK_CUR)	Go back 10 bytes
fseek(stream, 10, SEEK_SET)	Go to the 10th byte from the beginning of the file
fseek(stream, -10, SEEK_END)	Go to the 10th byte from the end of the file

The following example creates a file and writes some text to it. This example uses fseek( ) to return to the beginning of the file, rather than closing and reopening the file as was done in the preceding example.

```
#include <stdio.h>
main()
{
    FILE *stream;
    char buffer[80];

        // Create a temporary file called test2.tmp
        // and place some text in the file

    stream = fopen("test2.tmp", "w+");
    fputs("This is a test of writing to a file", stream);

        // The file position is now pointing to the end of the
          ➡file
        // so go back to the beginning
```

II

C Programming Basics

```
                    fseek(stream, SEEK_SET, 0);

                        // Read some text from the file
                        // and place the text to the screen

                    fgets(buffer, 10, stream);
                    fputs(buffer, stdout);   // Note the use of stdout to display
                                           ➥to the screen
                    fclose(stream);

                    return 0;
        }
```

**File Input and Output with Formatting—Using the *fscanf( )* and *fprintf( )*
Functions.** Two additional stream functions greatly enhance the ways in
which information is transferred to and from files. These are the fscanf( )
and fprintf( ) functions. The fscanf( ) function reads information from a
stream and the fprintf( ) function writes to a stream. Both functions support
formatting codes.

The prototypes for the fscanf( ) and fprintf( ) functions are

```
        int fscanf(FILE *stream, const char *format[, address, ...]);
        int fprintf(FILE *stream, const char *format[, argument, ...]);
```

These functions are identical to the scanf( ) and printf( ) functions reviewed
earlier, except that they read from and write to file streams.

One of the most common uses of the fscanf( ) and fprintf( ) functions is to
read and write records. A *record* is a collection of information that is associated in some way. For example, a record might be the collection of information your doctor maintains each time you visit. Or a record might be the
collection of information for a single purchase on your credit card. In each
case, a record can store several types of information that collectively represents a common item. The ability to transfer collections of information to
and from files is essential to many programs. All database programs, for example, are based on this premise.

The following example combines several features discussed in this chapter to
demonstrate the powerful capabilities of fscanf( ) and fprintf( ). The program prompts a user for information regarding a purchase order, saves the
information to a file, and then retrieves the information and presents it back
to the user. To make the test realistic, two programs are used. Listing 15.1
prompts a user for a purchase record and saves the information to a file. Listing 15.2 reads a purchase record from a file and presents it back to the user.

Listing 15.1. Purchase record input and storage program.

```c
#include <stdio.h>

main()
{
    FILE *stream;
    char name[40], item[40];
    int  quantity;
    float    price, total;

        // Present prompt request

    printf("\nEnter your first name, item to purchase (single
    ➥word),\n\
quantity, and unit price.  Separate each item with a space.\n\
Press a carriage return when you are done.\n==> ");

        // prompt user for purchase record information

    scanf("%s%s%d%f", name, item, &quantity, &price);

        // Calculate total and present information back to the
        ➥user

    total = quantity * price;
    printf("\nPurchase record for: %s\
        \nItem Purchased: %s\
        \nQuantity: %3d item(s)\
        \nPrice: %5.2f\
        \nTotal Amount Due: %10.2f\n\n",
        name, item, quantity, price, total);

        // save purchase record to test4.tmp
        // using a fprintf()

    stream = fopen("test4.tmp", "w+");
    fprintf(stream, "%s %s %d %f %f",
            name, item, quantity, price, total);
    fclose(stream);
    return 0;
}
```

Listing 15.2. Purchase record retrieval and display program.

```c
#include <stdio.h>

main()
{
    FILE *stream;
    char name[40], item[40];
    int  quantity;
    float    price, total;

        // retrieve purchase record from test4.tmp
```

(continues)

Listing 15.2. Continued.

```
        stream = fopen("test4.tmp", "r");
        fscanf(stream, "%s %s %d %f %f", name, item, &quantity,
        ➥&price, &total);
        fclose(stream);
        printf("\nPurchase record for: %s\
            \nItem Purchased: %s\
            \nQuantity: %3d item(s)\
            \nPrice: %5.2f\
            \nTotal Amount Due: %10.2f", name, item, quantity, price,
        ➥total);

        getchar();
        return 0;
}
```

The program in listing 15.1 uses scanf to read a line of text, such as:

```
Larry Toys 100 39.99
```

The scanf( ) function automatically parses this line into the appropriate four fields: name, item, quantity, and price. After the program retrieves this information from the user, it redisplays the information, using printf( ) to format the record so that the user can read it easily. The program then saves the record to a file in the same way that the user entered it.

The program in listing 15.2 opens the record file and uses the fscanf( ) function to read the entire record. Like scanf( ), fscanf( ) does its own parsing so that when it is done with its retrieval, all variable information is already set. The program then redisplays the record to the user for reference.

These short programs give you a brief glimpse at the power of fprintf( ) and fscanf( ). With just a few lines of code, a program can read a complex set of information, report back to the user, save the information to a file, and retrieve information from a file. That is the power of the C library functions.

Using String Functions

The C library has a set of functions for managing and manipulating strings. A *string* is a consecutive series of characters. The C library uses a *null-terminated string*, which is a string that ends with the null, or 0, character. The null value is literal—there is a physical byte at the end of the string that has a value of zero.

Strings reside in string buffers. A *buffer* is a space in memory that has been set aside by the compiler or by one of the runtime library calls used for memory allocation. Strings are never longer than the buffers in which they reside. Figure 15.4 illustrates the relationship between a buffer and the string it contains. To a C library function that reads a buffer, the buffer illustrated in figure 15.4 reads as follows: "This is a test." The function cannot see past the null terminator, and does not know or care what letters follow the null terminator.

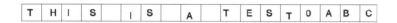

Fig. 15.4.
The relationship between buffers and strings.

The advantage to using null-terminated strings is that you do not need to indicate the length of the buffer that is storing the string for many library functions. The useful information in a string buffer is all the characters before the null value. Therefore, it is safe to pass a pointer to a string buffer, even though the function that receives the pointer does not know how much space is in the buffer. The function assumes that the buffer is at least as long as the null-terminated string that it contains.

Common C Library String Functions

A few of the C library string functions are indispensable. They are listed in table 15.7, along with descriptions. These functions are declared in the header file STRING.H. If you use any of these functions in your code, include the STRING.H header file in your source file.

Table 15.7. Common C library string functions.

String Function	Description
strcpy()	Copies one string into another
strcat()	Appends one string to the end of another
strset()	Sets a specified number of characters in a string to a specific character
strcmp()	Compares one string to another
strupr()	Converts a string to uppercase
strlwr()	Converts a string to lowercase

To get an idea of how strings are managed, take a look at the strcpy( )
function prototype.

```
char *strcpy(char *dest, const char *src);
```

The strcpy( ) function copies a source string into a destination string, overriding whatever was previously in the destination string. Often this function
is used to initialize a string because there are no C library assignment operators for strings such as the = operator (in a later chapter you will see a way to
use C++ assignment operators for strings). Unlike integer values, in which
you can assign a value to a variable, it is illegal to do so with strings. Compare
the two following code sequences:

```
int   i;
i = 100;   // This is legal
char buffer[100];
buffer = "This is a test"   // This is illegal
```

Without an assignment = operator, the only way to assign a value to a string
is to use the strcpy( ) function. It is used as follows:

```
char buffer[100];
strcpy(buffer, "This is a test");
```

In general, the C library string functions use the first argument as the destination. In this case, you are copying the literal string "This is a test" into the
buffer pointed to by buffer.

To append one string to another, use the strcat( ) function. For example, to
append "a test" to the string "This is", use the following code sequence:

```
char buffer[100];
strcpy(buffer, "This is ");
strcat(buffer, "a test");
```

The buffer now contains the full string "This is a test". Sometimes it is
necessary to set each character within a buffer to the identical value. For
example, you might want to initialize a buffer to zeros. To do this, use the
strset( ) function like this:

```
char buffer[100];
strset(buffer, 0);
```

Another common requirement with strings is to determine whether two
strings are equal. The strcmp( ) function compares two string arguments.
The possible results are listed in table 15.8.

Table 15.8. Possible results by using strcmp().	
Example	**Result**
`strcmp("aaa", "bbb")`	-1
`strcmp("aaa", "aaa")`	0
`strcmp("bbb", "aaa")`	1

The last two string functions in table 15.8 are `strupr( )` and `strlwr( )`, which convert entire strings to uppercase and lowercase respectively. Any non-alphabet character that happens to be in the string remains unaffected. Using these functions is straightforward, as follows:

```
char buffer[] = "This Is A Test";
strupr(buffer); // buffer now contains "THIS IS A TEST"
strlwr(buffer); // buffer now contains "this is a test"
```

Using the *sprintf()* Function

The `sprintf( )` function is an output function that uses a buffer as its output target. It operates just like the `printf( )` and `fprintf( )` functions. The only difference is that instead of sending the output to a screen or file stream, the output is sent to a buffer location.

The advantage of using `sprintf( )` over the standard string functions is that it can copy and format many variables into a buffer in a single call. To illustrate this, take the following variables:

```
char buffer1[] = "This";
char buffer2[] = "is";
char buffer3[] = "a";
char buffer4[] = "test";
```

To consolidate them using the standard string functions requires the following steps:

```
char buffer[100];
strcpy(buffer, buffer1);
strcat(buffer, " ");      // requires a space between words
strcat(buffer, buffer2);
strcat(buffer, " ");      // requires a space between words
strcat(buffer, buffer3);
strcat(buffer, " ");      // requires a space between words
strcat(buffer, buffer4);
```

Using the `sprintf( )` functions as an alternative, you can consolidate this into one function call, as follows:

```
char buffer[100];
sprintf(buffer, "%s %s %s %s", buffer1, buffer2, buffer3, buffer4);
```

Like the `printf( )` and `fprintf( )` functions, `sprintf( )` takes a format string and as many arguments as there are format specifiers.

There is another advantage to using `sprintf( )` over the standard C library string functions. The `sprintf( )` function can format many types of variables, including integers, floating-point variables, characters, and long integers. The standard string library functions are designed to work with strings and no other data types. For example, examine the following code:

```
char buffer[100];
char name[] = "Mr. Smith";
int quantity = 10;
sprintf(buffer, "%s purchased %d apples", name, quantity);
```

The contents of the buffer after the call to `sprintf( )` are

```
"Mr. Smith purchased 10 apples"
```

If there is a need for a string that requires special formatting, or one that needs to combine several variables into a single string buffer, `sprintf( )` is likely the easiest way to get the job done.

Data Type Conversion Functions

Sometimes you need a simple function that converts from one data type to another. Rather than wade through format specifiers and `sprintf( )` calls, a set of library functions can manage simple data type conversion efficiently and are easy to use. Table 15.9 lists the common data type conversion functions. These functions are declared in the header file STDLIB.H. If you use any of these functions in your code, include the STDLIB.H header file in your source file.

Table 15.9. Useful data type conversion functions.

Function	Description
`atoi( )`	Converts a string to an integer
`atol( )`	Converts a string to a long integer
`atof( )`	Converts a string to a double
`itoa( )`	Converts an integer to a string
`ltoa( )`	Converts a long integer to a string

The `atoi( )`, `atol( )`, and `atof( )` functions are straightforward to use, because each takes a single string argument and returns an integer, a long integer, and a double float value respectively. To get an idea of how to use these functions, enter and run the following program:

```
#include <stdlib.h>
#include <stdio.h>

main()
{
    int  i;
    long l;
    double    f;

    i = atoi("12345.6789");
    l = atol("12345.6789");
    f = atof("12345.6789");

    printf("i = %d, l = %ld, f = %g", i, l, f);

        return 0;
}
```

The itoa( ) and ltoa( ) functions require a bit of explanation. These functions take an integer or a long integer and convert them to a text string. The prototypes for these functions are as follows:

```
char *itoa(int value, char *string, int radix);
char *ltoa(long value, char *string, int radix);
```

The first argument is the value of the integer or long integer. The second argument is a pointer to a string buffer that will contain the string version of the integer or long integer once it is converted. The radix is another name for the base value to use in converting a number.

Most of the world operates on base 10 numbering system, and this is likely the only value you need to use for this function. Bear in mind that computers are binary machines, and you may one day need to convert the number *128* into a binary string of 1s and 0s. In that case, you could still use the atoi( ) and ltoi( ) functions, but you would use 2 (for base 2) as the value for the radix argument.

Whenever you use a conversion function, be careful to ensure that the buffer you are using is large enough to hold the largest value for that type. It is not recommended that you make assumptions about the possible range of values for your application, because your application may change over time and you may forget your assumptions. Therefore, when converting integer values, never use a buffer that is less than six characters long (the highest number for an integer is 65536, which is five digits, plus one space for the trailing null). For long integers, do not use a buffer of less than 11 characters.

Summary

This chapter covered the highlights of the C library functions. The major areas of the C library functions were reviewed, including keyboard and screen management functions, file management functions, and string manipulation functions.

By now, you should have a sense that there is a C library function that can be helpful to you for many of your programming tasks. Before starting out on a programming task, check the Turbo C++ library function reference. You may be surprised at the number of useful functions that are at your disposal for any given topic.

Also, when you consider using a new function, review the details carefully. As many of the example programs demonstrated, some functions can perform a broad range of tasks. The more you familiarize yourself with the details, the less likely you will end up writing extra code, or duplicating code that is already available to you through the library functions.

In this chapter, you have learned the following:

■ How to read characters entered by the user by using the keyboard, and how to display characters on-screen by using the various versions of the get( ) and put( ) functions

■ How to read strings from the keyboard and write strings to the display by using the scanf( ) and printf(0 functions

■ How to read and write data from and to a file

■ What a stream is

■ How reading and writing to a file is similar to reading from the keyboard and writing to the display

■ What a string is and how to use strings conveniently in your program to manage many characters of data, such as a sentence or paragraph

## Chapter 16

Using Program Logic Control

An intelligent program is a program that makes decisions; decisions about what to present to users, what to do as a result of user input, and what action to take when an error occurs. Program logic controls are the tools with which programmers enable a program to make decisions.

This chapter shows you how to use the fundamental program logic controls of Turbo C++, including the following:

■ `If-Then-Else` logic

■ `Switch` statements

■ `For` loops

■ `While` loops

Conditional Logic-Flow Control

Conditional logic is the staple of program logic control. You use conditional logic regularly in everyday life, such as when you decide, based on your level of fatigue, whether to go swimming. Sometimes the decision-making process is complicated, such as when you have a free afternoon in which you can decide to swim, or play golf, or watch a movie. Maybe you have time to do a combination of these things, which complicates the decision-making process even further.

Conditional logic enables you to represent *decision-tree* logic in a program. A decision tree is a diagram that represents the options from which you can choose when you make a decision. As an example, a choice from among those options can lead to several more options. Eventually you reach a concluding choice that is represented by an action or a conclusion. Figure 16.1 illustrates an example of a decision tree.

Fig. 16.1.
Example of a
decision tree.

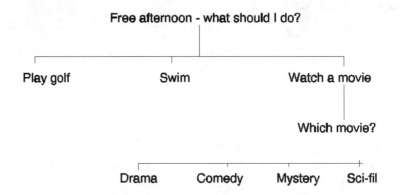

In programming, you use two basic conditional logic statements: the if-then-else statement and the switch statement. These statements are discussed in the following sections.

Using If-Then-Else **Logic Statements**

An if-then-else statement is a way of expressing a simple choice. If a certain condition is met, then an action is taken; otherwise (or else) another preset action is taken.

The syntax for an if-then-else statement is as follows:

```
if ( condition is true )
{
    do action based on true condition
}
else
{
    otherwise execute this action
}
```

To understand the components of the `if-then-else` syntax, consider the following statement:

"If I am happy, I will dance; otherwise I will mope!"

You can translate this statement into a hypothetical program expression by using the following if-then-else expression:

```
if ( happy )
{
    dance();
}
else
{
    mope();
}
```

Within the almost intuitive format of the `if-then-else` statement hides many details. You must be able to answer a number of questions: What is a valid conditional expression? What is a true condition? What is a false condition? If you know the answers to these questions you can skip the next few sections. For those who are new to C and C++, the next few sections provide a brief review of the basics of conditional expressions that apply throughout many areas of C and C++.

True and False Statements. In conditional logic programming, a `true` statement is a statement that evaluates to anything but zero. A `false` statement evaluates to zero. The following simple examples illustrate this point:

```
if ( 1 )  // Evaluates to True
if ( 0 )  // Evaluates to False
if ( 25 )      // Evaluates to True (it is not zero)
if ( -1 )      // Evaluates to True (it is not zero)
```

Conditional Expressions. A *conditional expression* is any C or C++ statement that evaluates to either true or false. Examples of conditional expressions include:

```
if ( 1 + 1 )   // Evaluates to True
if ( 20 / 2 )  // Evaluates to True
if ( 20 - 20 )      // Evaluates to False
```

Conditional expressions can include any relational operator. A *relational operator* compares two values and evaluates to either true or false. Table 16.1 lists the common relational operators and their meanings.

Table 16.1. Common relational operators.	
Relational Operator	**Description**
==	is equal to
!=	is not equal to
<	is less than
>	is greater than
<=	is less than or equal to
>=	is greater than or equal to

Some examples of the uses of relational operators include the following:

```
if ( 10 > 11 )       // Evaluates to False
if ( 10 == ( 9 + 1) )    // Evaluates to True
if ( 10 != 11 )      // Evaluates to True
if ( 10 <= 10 )      // Evaluates to True
```

In addition to numeric values, you can use any C statement that evaluates to either true or false, including using function return values. The following examples illustrate how C functions that return a value can be used in a conditional expression.

```
if ( strlen("ABCD") == 3 )    // Evaluates to False
if ( strlen("ABCD") )    // Evaluates to True - strlen() returns
➡the number 4 which is a value that represents True
```

Another common element of conditional expressions are the logical operators ¦¦ and &&. These symbol pairs represent the words "or" and "and" respectively. Use the ¦¦ and && operators whenever you need to specify more than one condition as part of a condition statement. The following examples show these logical operators included in C++ statements.

```
if ( strlen("ABCD") == 3 ¦¦ 1 )    // Evaluates to True - the
➡second part is true
if ( strlen("ABCD") == 3 && 1 )    // Evaluates to False - both
➡parts must be true and the first is not
```

Nesting If-Then-Else **Logic Statements**

The simple if-then-else format may not be sufficient for some programming statements. *Nested* if-then-else loops enable you to program complex decisions such as those represented by a decision tree. Consider the problem illustrated in figure 16.2. In the top portion of this figure, a problem (which can be stated as "should we marry?") and its solution are represented as a decision tree. The lower portion of the figure shows the problem and its solution represented as a set of nested if-then-else statements. By using nested if-then-else statements, the decision tree of figure 16.2 can be adequately represented in programmatic form.

The program in listing 16.1 uses nested if-then-else statements. The program prompts the user to enter a character (press a key); the program then displays some information based on the key the user presses.

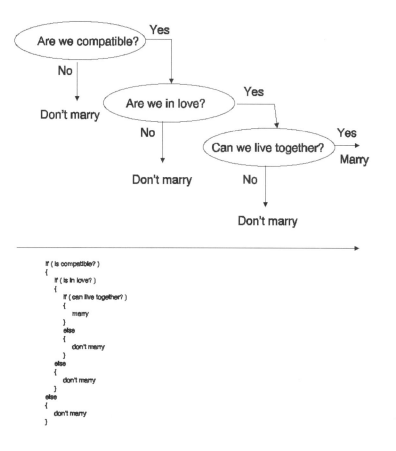

Fig. 16.2.
Using nested if-then-else statements.

II

C Programming Basics

Listing 16.1. Program that uses nested if-then-else **statements to determine type of key pressed.**

```
#include <conio.h>
#include <stdio.h>
main()
{
```

(continues)

Listing 16.1. Continued.

```
            char ch;

            ch = getche(); // get a character

            if ( ch >= '0' && ch <= '9' ) // character is numeric
            {
                printf("\nYou have pressed a number.\n");
            }
            else
            {
                if ( ch >= 'A' && ch <= 'Z' ) // character is an
➥uppercase letter
                {
                    printf("\nYou have pressed an uppercase letter.\n");
                }
                else
                {
                    if ( ch >= 'a' && ch <= 'z' ) // character is a
➥lowercase letter
                    {
                        printf("\nYou have pressed a lowercase
➥letter.\n");
                    }
                    else                   // Some other character was
➥pressed
                    {
                        printf("\nYou have neither pressed a letter or
➥a number.\n");
                    }
                }
            }
            return 0;
        }
```

In the preceding example, a set of if-then-else statements is used to narrow the possible values of the key pressed. The first if-then-else statement checks to determine if the pressed key is between the letters '0' and '9.' (Remember that the getch() function returns the ASCII value of the key pressed; for number keys, the ASCII value is not the same as the key's numeric value.) If this check fails, the key pressed must not be a number. The subsequent nested if-then-else statements keep narrowing the options until the key pressed is matched with a condition, or an appropriate error message is displayed.

Braces ({}) are important components of nested if-then-else statements. Braces define the action that is taken as a result of a true or false condition within a conditional statement. Braces are not always necessary, however. Listing 16.2 shows a revised version of the previous program and uses no braces.

Listing 16.2. Revised program that determines type of key pressed.

```
#include <conio.h>
#include <stdio.h>

main()
{
    char ch;

    ch = getche(); // get a character

    if ( ch >= '0' && ch <= '9' ) // character is numeric
        printf("\nYou have pressed a number.\n");
    else
        if ( ch >= 'A' && ch <= 'Z' ) // character is an
➥uppercase letter
            printf("\nYou have pressed an uppercase letter.\n");
        else
            if ( ch >= 'a' && ch <= 'z' ) // character is a
➥lowercase letter
                printf("\nYou have pressed a lowercase
➥letter.\n");
            else                      // Some other character was
➥pressed
                printf("\nYou have neither pressed a letter or
➥a number.\n");

    return 0;
}
```

II

C Programming Basics

Upon a true condition, the *if* portion of the statement always executes the subsequent *then* portion of the statement, regardless of whether the statement is enclosed in braces. Listing 16.2 does not need any braces for the if-then-else statements, because only a single action is taken as a result of any condition.

To the compiler, a single statement is one line of code or multiple lines of code that are enclosed in braces.

In this program, the compiler views a combined if-then-else sequence as a single statement; therefore, the program can use a complete if-then-else sequence as a single statement that is executed as part of an else clause without the need to enclose the if-then-else sequence in braces.

You also can use a condensed version of the if-then-else sequence, that takes the following form:

```
condition ? expression1 : expression2
```

In this statement, condition is any valid condition expression that evaluates to true or false; expression1 is executed if the condition is true, and expression2 is executed if the condition is false. expression1 and expression2 are any valid C statement that evaluates to a specific C data type. expression1 and expression2 must evaluate to the same data type, such as an integer value.

Programmers typically use this form of the if-then-else logic control to get a return value based on a condition. Unlike the basic if-then-else clause, this form returns a value. For that reason, expression1 and expression2 must evaluate to the same data type. Most programmers do not use nesting in this form of if-then-else statements, because the statements quickly become difficult to read.

Consider the following example of the condensed form of if-then-else statements:

```
#include <conio.h>
#include <stdio.h>

main()
{
    char ch;

    ch = getche(); // get a character

    printf("\nYou have pressed a character that %s a number\n",
            (ch >= '0' && ch <= '9') ? "is" : "is not");

    return 0;

}
```

Notice that the printf() statement uses the condensed version of the if-then-else statement to return a pointer to an "is" or "is not" buffer, depending on whether the user pressed a numeric key. As long as the expression of either condition evaluates to a common data type, this form of the if-then-else statement can return any value.

Using the Switch Statement

Not all decisions can be expressed as either-or options, and therefore the if-then-else form does not always apply. Take for example a windshield wiper, which can have Off, Slow, Fast, and Intermittent options. If you need to program the mechanical steps for operating a windshield wiper, using if-then-else statements can turn into a complex decision tree that is difficult to program and read. The switch statement is designed to handle just this sort of decision tree, where many options are based on a single variable.

The format for a switch statement is as follows:

```
switch ( variable )
{
    case ( value1 ):
        statements;
        break;
    case ( value2 ):
        statements;
        break;
        .
        .
        .
    default:
        statements;
}
```

The *variable* is an expression that evaluates to an integer value that gets tested against each of the value constants. When a match occurs, the statements belonging to the matching value are executed. If no match occurs, the default statements are executed. The different case statements are delineated by break statements. When the program reaches a break statement, the program jumps to the end of the switch statement (a later section of this chapter discusses break statements in detail).

One common use of the switch statement is for checking the value of input against a set of fixed options, such as in a menu program. In any menu, a user can select only certain, specified options. You can use the switch statement to determine which option is selected and to execute the appropriate action based on that selection.

The program in listing 16.3 presents a simple menu and prompts the user for a menu selection. A switch statement is used to determine which menu option the user has selected and to take appropriate action based on that selection. If the user selects an invalid menu option, the program activates the *default switch case* and executes its statements. The default switch case is any value of the variable that does not match any of the case values.

Listing 16.3. Menu program that uses switch statement.

```
#include <conio.h>
#include <stdio.h>

main()
{
    char ch;
```

(continues)

Listing 16.3. Continued.

```
// Present menu

    printf("\n\n\
    Menu\n\
\n\
1. New File\n\
2. Open File\n\
3. Save File\n\
4. Exit\n\n\
Enter menu choice ==> ");

        // Get menu choice

    ch = getche(); // get a character

        // Take appropriate action

    switch ( ch )
    {
        case '1':
            printf("\n\nExecute New File code here\n\n");
            break;
        case '2':
            printf("\n\nExecute Open File code here\n\n");
            break;
        case '3':
            printf("\n\nExecute Save File code here\n\n");
            break;
        case '4':
            printf("\n\nExecute Exit code here\n\n");
            break;
        default:
            printf("\n\nYou have selected an invalid menu
➥option.\n\n");
    }

    return 0;

}
```

Note that the break statement tells the compiler where to stop executing statements that belong to the case that precedes it.

You can extend the capability of the switch statement by combining various values into one case option, or by having one case option execute its own as well as another case option's statements. Listing 16.4, for example, shows the program for a menu that offers a choice of printing one or more files. Because menu option 2 prints its own file as well as the file in menu option 1, the switch statement that processes the menu choices is written so that option 2 prints its own files and then continues to process option 1. This arrangement involves placing the case clause for option 2 above that for option 1 in the switch statement sequence and not ending the option 2 case with a break statement. Subsequently, when the case option 2 statement is completed, processing continues until the program reaches a `break` statement. The next `break` statement is at the end of the case statement for option 1.

Listing 16.4. Menu program that uses combined `switch` statement.

```
#include <conio.h>
#include <stdio.h>

main()
{
    char ch;

        // Present menu

    printf("\n\n\
    Menu\n\
\n\
1. Print File 1\n\
2. Print Files 2 & 1\n\
3. Print File 3, 2 & 1\n\
Enter menu choice ==> ");

        // Prompt user for menu choice

    ch = getche(); // get a character

        // Process menu option

    switch ( ch )
    {
        case '3':
            printf("\nCode to print file 3.\n");
        case '2':
            printf("\nCode to print file 2.\n");
        case '1':
            printf("\nCode to print file 1.\n");
            break;
        default:
            printf("\n\nYou have selected an invalid menu
option.\n\n");
    }

    return 0;

}
```

Using Loop Control Logic

Loop control logic enables you to program repetitive tasks. A *loop* is a set of statements that continue to execute as long as a certain condition is met. Figure 16.3 illustrates the basic flow of a loop control.

Fig. 16.3.
Basic Loop Flow

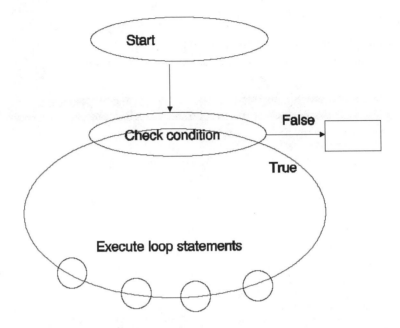

You can use a variety of loop control expressions. Each loop control expression is suitable for a specific type of repetitive task. The common loop control expressions are:

■ `for` loop

■ `while` loop

■ `do` loop

Using the `For` **Loop**

The *for loop* executes a sequence of statements based on a counter. The format for the `for` loop is:

```
for ( initializer; condition; increment )
```

The following program uses the `for` loop:

```
#include <stdio.h>

main()
{
```

```
    int i;

    for ( i = 0; i < 10; i++ )
        printf("This statement has been displayed %d times\n", i);

    return 0;
}
```

In this example, the initializer sets i to 0. The i in this example is checked by
the condition clause with each pass of the loop. When the loop completes a
pass, the loop executes the increment expression, which increments i. The
loop increments i 10 times before the condition i < 10 fails, and the for loop
ceases to execute.

The for loop can take a variety of expressions as its initializer, condition, or
increment. The following example initializes and increments two variables.

```
#include <stdio.h>

main()
{
    int i, j;

    for ( i = 0, j = 10; i < 10; i++, j += 10 )
        printf("This is statement %d.   The value of j is: %d\n", i,
➥j);

    return 0;
}
```

In the above example, the for loop intializes and increments both i and j.
Notice that i and j are neither set nor incremented the same way. Further,
the condition statement uses only i. In fact, the condition statement could
have no connection with variables used in the initializer or increment statements.

The for loop does not necessarily have to iterate through all its values. Further, the condition expression can be any expression that evaluates to true or
false. The next example uses a new C library function, kbhit(), that checks
the keyboard for any key that is pressed. The kbhit() function returns a 0
(false) if no key is pressed or a non-zero value (true) when any key is pressed.
The program in this example causes a line of text to be displayed on-screen
until the user presses a key.

```
#include <conio.h>
#include <stdio.h>

main()
{
```

```
      for ( ; !kbhit(); )
           printf("Press any key to stop this program!\n");

      return 0;
  }
```

This program contains no initializer or increment expressions. In fact, the condition expression !kbhit() looks strange. This expression is a valid for loop, because you do not need to define any expression for the for loop to execute. Until the user presses a key, the condition statement !kbhit() evaluates to true and the subsequent printf() statement continues printing a line of text to the screen. As soon as the user presses a key, the condition statement is set to false and the for loop ceases to execute. Recall that in C++ a nonzero value is equal to true and a zero value is equal to false.

Using the While Loop

The *while loop* is similar to the for loop except that it uses a single condition expression to determine whether to execute its loop statements. The syntax for a while loop is:

```
      while ( condition ) expression
```

When the program enters the while loop it checks the condition. If the condition evaluates to true, the loop expression executes. The loop expression continues to execute as long as the condition is true. When the condition fails the test by evaluating to false instead of true, the while loop ceases to execute.

The following example uses a while loop to display a line of text on the screen until the user presses a key.

```
      #include <conio.h>
      #include <stdio.h>

      main()
      {
          while ( !kbhit() )
               printf("Press any key to stop this program!\n");

          return 0;
      }
```

This program is the same as the previous program example; but in this example, a while loop replaces the for loop. In fact, a while loop is identical to a for loop when the for loop contains neither an initializer nor an increment.

You do not necessarily have to evaluate the condition within the condition statement. If the while loop is being executed so long as a variable is equal to

a certain value, then the variable itself can be used as the condition
statement. Consider this example:

```
#include <conio.h>
#include <stdio.h>

main()
{
    int i;

    i = 0;                  // initialize i

    while ( !i ) {
        printf("Press any key to stop this program!\n");
        i = kbhit();
    }

    return 0;
}
```

In this example, the program uses the i variable alone as the condition. This
program is valid because the i variable is an integer and so evaluates to either
a 0 (false) or a non-0 (true). The i variable is updated with each loop to equal
kbhit(), which places a non-zero value in i if any key is pressed. The loop
ends when a key is pressed.

You may notice that this example uses braces for the while loop, but the last
example did not use braces. Remember that all loops execute a single expression if a condition is met. A single expression is either one statement, or a set
of statements enclosed within braces. Because this program needed more
than one line of code to operate the loop, the braces ensured that all the loop
statements are viewed as a single expression that is executed with each round
of the loop.

Using the Do **Loop**

The *do loop* is similar to the while loop, except that the do loop executes at
least one time before it evaluates a condition. Based on the result of the condition statement, the do loop either executes or ends. The format for a do loop
is:

```
do expression while ( condition );
```

Because the condition is only tested at the end of the loop, the do loop must
execute at least once. The do loop is very useful for many programming
situations. Consider the following example:

```
#include <conio.h>
#include <stdio.h>
```

```
main()
{
    char ch;

    do {
            // Place prompt

        printf("\nPress y to redisplay this prompt ==> ");

            // Get input

        ch = getche();

    } while ( ch == 'y' );    // Check to continue loop

    return 0;
}
```

The code is simplified by the fact that the loop executes the first time without evaluating a condition. This execution enables the first prompt to appear. When the user enters a response to the prompt, the return value is evaluated to determine whether to continue the prompt. Had this program used a while loop, an initial user prompt would have to precede the loop. Having the do loop enables the code to be more efficient and readable.

Using Break **Statements in Loops**

The *break* statement interrupts a loop. The break statement causes the current loop to stop executing and forces the program to continue execution at the next statement after the loop. The condition is not evaluated, nor does the increment expression execute in the case of a for loop.

The break statement is very useful in setting limits to a loop. In some programs, you may be unable to guarantee that the condition will ever evaluate to false and stop processing. You can use a break statement within a loop to ensure that if a preset condition is met, the loop ends regardless of the condition expression.

Consider the previous example program that displays a line of text on the screen until the user presses a key. What happens if the user leaves the terminal and goes home after initiating this loop? No key gets pressed, the loop continues to execute, and a line of text is displayed on the screen until the next day when the user returns. To prevent this situation, you can add a break statement that stops the display after a preset number of loops, even if no key is pressed. The following example illustrates such a program:

```
#include <conio.h>
#include <stdio.h>

main()
{
    int i = 0;

    while ( !kbhit() ) {
        printf("Press any key to stop this program!\n");
        i++;
        if ( i == 100 ) break;   // allow only 100 lines to display
    }

    return 0;
}
```

With each loop execution, the program evaluates the condition to determine if
a key is pressed. If no key is pressed, the loop continues to execute and the line
of text remains on-screen. With each loop iteration, however, the program increments the variable i and tests the variable to see whether it has reached the
value 100. When the value of i reaches 100, a break statement executes to terminate the loop.

A break statement can exit only a loop and a switch statement. A break has no
effect on an if-then-else expression. If you insert a break statement within an
if-then-else expression, you get a compiler error saying that you have a mis-
placed break statement, or you inadvertently exit the loop in which the if-then-
else expression occurs.

Using the Continue **Statement**
The *continue* statement passes control to the beginning of a loop, bypassing any
code between the continue statement and the end of the loop. Consider this
example:

```
#include <conio.h>
#include <stdio.h>

main()
{
    char ch;

    do {
            // Present prompt

        printf("\nEnter a number from 1 to 9 or q to quit ==> ");
        ch = getche();

            // Check input
```

```
        if ( ch < '0' || ch > '9' ) continue;

            // Display number

        printf("\nYou have entered the number %c\n", ch);

    } while ( ch != 'q' ); // check to see if user entered 'q' to
➥quit

        return 0;
}
```

This example program prompts the user to enter a number between 0 and 9. The loop continues as long as the user does not press the letter **q**. Unless the user presses a number, the loop does not bother printing out a status line displaying the character that was pressed. The program checks to determine whether the pressed key is a character between 0 and 9; if the pressed key is not a number, the loop continues to the next round, going straight to the condition statement.

Notice that the program evaluates the loop's condition even after a continue statement is executed. If not for this arrangement, a press of the letter **q** would never get evaluated, and the loop would not exit. The continue statement specifically sends control to the top of the loop, where the condition is evaluated. In the case of a do loop, the top of the loop happens to be at the closing curly brackets (}) where the condition is evaluated.

Using the Goto **Statement**

The *goto* statement unconditionally jumps execution control of your program to a label you specify in the goto statement. The format for a goto statement is:

```
goto Label1;
```

The format for a label is:

```
Label1:
```

When you use a goto statement, your program passes over all the code between the goto statement and the label it points to. When the program reaches a goto statement, the next line of code that executes is the line following the label of the goto statement.

You easily can misuse the goto statement. Goto statements are sometimes used in multiple-nested loops to exit from a deeply-nested loop if a condition is not met.

As a good practice, use goto statements only in those situations where the alternative produces messy and convoluted code. In other words, only use a goto if it actually simplifies your code. One such example is when a critical error occurs. In such circumstances, you may have good reason for using a goto to point to a location that does some last-minute cleanup.

Consider the following sample code:

```
#include <stdio.h>

main()
{
    FILE *stream;
    int result;

    stream = fopen("test.tmp", "w");   // Open file

    result = fputs("test", stream);               // Write to file
    if ( result == EOF ) goto Exit0;
        .
        .
        .

Exit0:
    fclose(stream);                 // Close file

    return 0;
}
```

This program example opens a file and attempts to write some information to that file. If the write fails, you want the program to close the file rather than leave it open. A goto statement causes a jump to the bottom of the program to close the file and exit gracefully.

You may wonder why the program did not exit as soon as it failed to write information to the file. The program doesn't exit at that point because other critical failures may occur within the program. If every critical error handles its own exit, each one can close the file and exit the program. The program in this example is simple and includes minor cleanup. A typical program has extensive cleanup; programming cleanup for every critical error that requires the program to exit is inefficient. Instead, a goto and a label at the end of the program prior to cleanup is a simple way to exit from the program with all the cleanup managed at a single location.

> **Note**
>
> Program cleanup is a general term that refers to the necessary steps a program has to take to end properly. For example, if any files were opened by the program, they must be closed. This is often done at one point within the program and is referred to as program cleanup.

Application Flow Control

Application flow control are functions that change the course of the application to somewhere beyond the application itself. These functions fall under two categories: those that terminate a program, and those that hand execution over to another program.

The functions provided with Turbo C++ that terminate a program are `exit()` and `abort()`. The functions that hand execution over to another program are `system()`, `exec()`, and `spawn()`.

Using Terminating Functions `exit()` and `abort()`

The two functions that cause a program to end abruptly are `exit()` and `abort()`. The `exit()` function terminates a program normally and the `abort()` function terminates a program abnormally.

The `exit()` function typically is used for serious user errors. When such errors occur, the program may choose to terminate rather than risk any further problems, such as system-related malfunctions. The `exit()` can be called with a value that is returned by the program to the operating system. The `exit()` program is called as follows:

```
exit(1);
```

This statement causes the program to return a value of 1 when the program terminates and control is passed back to the operating system.

When an `exit()` function terminates a program, all open files close, output from any C library function that is buffered (held in a temporary storage location) writes to its appropriate destination, and any registered shutdown functions execute. A *shutdown* function is one that is registered by the program using the `atexit()` function. A program is allowed to register up to 32 exit functions using the `atexit()` function. An `atexit()` function is registered as follows:

```
atexit(exit_function1);
```

This statement says that the exit_function1 function is to be called when the program exits. The exit functions execute sequentially, starting from the last one that was registered and going backward in sequence to the first exit function that was registered.

A more severe alternative to the exit() function is the abort() function. The abort() function terminates a program and displays the on-screen message Abnormal program termination. The abort() function returns a 3 to the operating system or its parent process. The return value of 3 has no significance other than being a number that indicates the program terminated abnormally. Save the abort() function for severe internal errors, such as those that may jeopardize the system integrity.

Using Program Execution Functions

Program execution functions are functions that execute another program from within a program. The three types of program execution functions are: system(), exec...(), and spawn...().

The system() function runs a DOS command or program from within a program. For example, adding the line

```
system("dir *.*");
```

displays the directory listing to the screen. This program execution function is convenient if there is a DOS command that displays information or operates as required by your program. For example, if your program required a DOS directory listing, you can use the system() function as shown in the preceding paragraph.

The format for the system() function is:

```
system( const char *command )
```

The value of command can be any string that can be run from the command prompt. The command string, therefore, can include a number of arguments, exactly as they are specified when running the DOS command or program from the command line.

The alternatives to the system() function are the exec...() and spawn...() functions. These functions start other programs, called *child processes*. The program that starts a child process is called the *parent process* in relation to its child process.

The difference between the exec...() functions and the spawn...() functions is that the spawn() functions allow an extra argument, called the *mode*.

The mode determines how the child process operates. Table 16.2 lists the values available for mode arguments.

Table 16.2. Values for the mode argument.	
Mode value	**Description**
P_WAIT	The parent process temporarily stops function-ing until the child process is completed
P_OVERLAY	The child process overlays the memory location of the parent process [this is the default for exec()]

With the exception of the mode argument, the exec() and the spawn() functions are the same.

The following example demonstrates how one program can call another using exec().

```
// Program: child

#include <stdio.h>

main()
{
    printf("This is a child process\n");
    return 0;
}
```

```
// Program: parent

#include <process.h>

main()
{
    execl("child", 0);   // call external program
    return 0;
}
```

The program defined as parent starts a child process called child using the execl() function. Several execl...() and spawn...() variations exist, and each variation offers slightly different options for executing a child process. The version used in the parent program takes a child process name, along with a set of command line arguments that are passed separately. The last argument must be set to 0 to indicate that it is the last one. The parent program does nothing but call the child process. The child program simply displays a line of text to the screen. By executing the parent program, the child program displays a line of text to the screen.

Summary

Most programs require some form of decision logic that determines the flow of the program. This chapter covered many of the fundamental language tools that determine the flow of a program, whether it is by simple conditional logic, loop control or application flow control.

You can combine these language tools in an infinite number of ways to meet virtually any programming need. The challenge is to use these language tools in an efficient way to make your program operate as intelligently as possible.

In this chapter you learned the following:

- An `if-then-else` statement is a way of expressing a simple choice.

- `If-then-else` statements can be nested to represent complex decisions.

- The condensed version of the `if-then-else` statement is: condition ? expression1 (if true) : expression2 (if false).

- A `switch` statement is used when an expression can be evaluated to more than two values, and when a different set of statements must be executed for each of those values.

- The `for` loop is used to execute a set of statements a certain number of times.

- A `while` loop is used to execute a set of statements that are dependent on a condition.

II

C Programming Basics

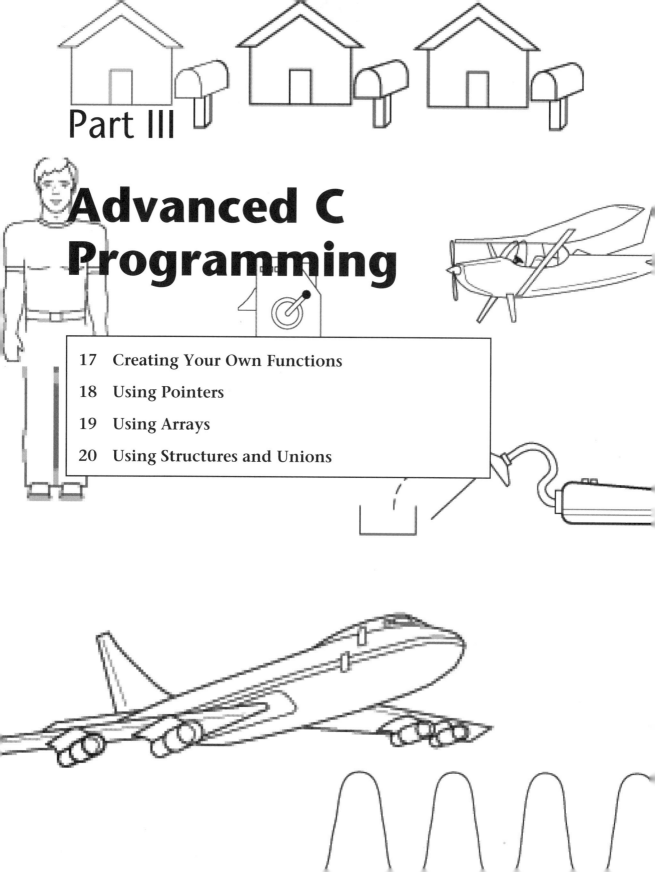

Part III

Advanced C Programming

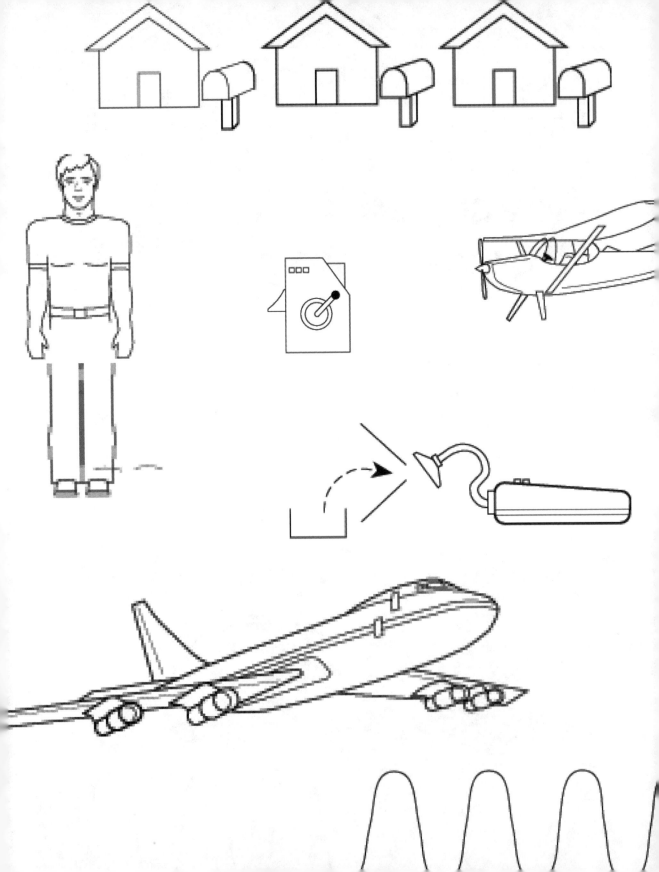

Chapter 17

Creating Your Own Functions

In spite of the vast number of C library functions available in Turbo C++, you need to know how to create functions of your own in order to develop programs. You may need to create a function because the C library lacks a built-in function that meets your specific needs, or you may want to package many C library functions into a single useful function. Using the functions you write is no different than using those provided in the C library.

As well, functions are efficient because they are created once but can be shared and used throughout your program to execute a certain task. You can reduce your coding effort by centralizing common tasks in a set of useful functions that can then be used anywhere in your program where that task is necessary.

This chapter shows you how to create well-written and useful functions for your programs. To accomplish this task, you must know how to design a function. This chapter discusses the various ways that programmers create functions, and shows you how to resolve implementation issues, and how to test and use functions. Creating useful functions is critical to writing applications that are both easy to program and easy to use. This chapter discusses the following:

- How to design and write a function

- How to test your function

- How to use a function that you create

Before jumping into the details of how to write functions, this chapter reviews the process of program design.

Designing a Program

Designing a program is very much like tackling a project. The more organized you are, the better your results. Without a plan of action, you easily can be confused about what functions to write and how to write them. Before writing any program, you need a reasonable understanding of the purpose of the program and how the program is to operate. A good grasp of that information makes the subsequent steps of the design process much simpler.

The Need for Planning

Designing a program is similar to designing a house. First you design a layout plan for the house; next, you create a list of necessary tools and materials and prepare them for use; finally, you begin the actual construction. The construction phase also can be divided into several steps, such as laying the foundation, building the walls and floors, and then finishing the interior.

The process of designing a program is almost identical to this house-building process, as depicted in figure 17.1. First, you must know the "layout" of the program, that is what the program does and how the program is to operate. Next, you review the available C library functions to identify those that may be useful for your program. The C library functions are the tools with which you build your program. When you have selected the appropriate C library functions, you can proceed to write your program.

A program is made up of a series of individual tasks, and when you write a program, you write its tasks. A *task* is a specific action or set of actions, and is represented by a single function. Large tasks are made up of smaller tasks. By having an overall plan and following its steps, you can concentrate on small tasks at first and build them up into larger tasks over time. Because each task is represented by a discrete function, concentrating on small tasks with functions that perform simple operations always is easier than attempting to write larger functions that perform elaborate operations. After you write the smaller functions, you easily can combine them into large functions that perform more complex operations.

Dividing the Work

You may not have realized it, but with each example program you worked with in the previous chapter you actually created a function called main(). The main() function is necessary for every C and C++ program because no C library function starts a program running. To fill this need, you write a function called `main()` and the compiler and linker execute the `main()` function to start the program. The `main()` function, therefore, is the minimal function that you must create to write an operational program.

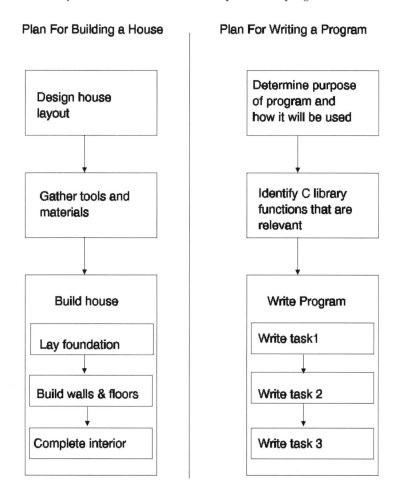

Plan For Building a House   Plan For Writing a Program

Fig. 17.1.
Comparison of program design and building a house.

If you write your whole program in the `main()` function (as is the case with the examples of the previous chapter) you need not create a second function of your own, because you write all tasks into `main()`. If your program is to do anything but the most trivial tasks, however, this approach produces a very long function that is very difficult to read. Writing a meaningful program within the `main()` function alone is nearly impossible.

Consider the discrete tasks that your program must execute. Review the subtasks to see if you can divide them into even simpler groups of tasks. Iterate this process until you have a diagram similar to that shown in figure 17.2. Assign each task to a function. Your program can implement these tasks one by one. Together, these tasks functions constitute your program.

Fig. 17.2.
Diagram of overall task/function design.

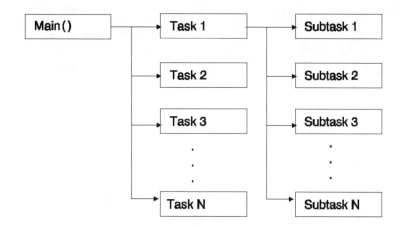

Now that you have reviewed the fundamentals of the overall process of program design and how functions fit into that process, you are ready to begin designing and writing the functions that create the building blocks of your program.

Designing a Function

When you have an outline of your program and know the individual tasks that it must accomplish, you can begin designing your functions. When you design a function, let your work be guided by the following questions:

- What is its purpose?

- How will it be used?

- Where will it be used?

Assume, for example, that you are creating a word processing program. You outline what the word processing program is to do and how it is to operate, and you realize that the program must have an option that enables users to save, for subsequent retrieval, text they have entered into a file. You can write a single function to perform this discrete task. Table 17.1 lists the questions that you may ask yourself when you design the function. Depending on the answers to these questions, you may take very different approaches to writing this function.

Table 17.1. Considerations for designing a `save-text-to-file` function.	
Issue	**Questions**
Purpose	Will the function be used to save only new documents, or will it also save documents that are reopened from the disk?
Usage	Will the function assign a default name to an unnamed file (such as when a user starts a new document), or will it prompt the user for a name?
Calling Issues	Will the function be called as a result of a menu choice? If so, is there any information that must be transferred to the function in order for it to complete its task?

You may think going through these considerations for every function you design is a tedious process. Without question, thinking through each function takes time. The time you spend in thinking through your functions, however, is repaid by the time and effort this preparation saves you when you write the code. Further, a well thought-out function is more likely to be useful and versatile in the long run.

Creating a Function Prototype

A *function prototype* describes how a function is called. To understand the function prototype, compare it to a dictionary entry: the function prototype is similar to the dictionary entry's syntax listing that represents a word's syllables and their emphasis. The syntax tells you nothing about the word's definition, but only how to pronounce the word. Similarly, a function prototype describes how the function is "pronounced" to other functions — in other words, how the function is to be referenced by other programs. The function prototype does not, however, tell anything about what the function does.

III

Advanced C Programming

Naming a Function

Naming a function is an often-overlooked topic. When you write a large program, if your functions have names such as

```
function1()
function2()
function3()
```

the program is going to be very difficult to understand and debug, even with comments. When naming your functions, you can follow a few simple guidelines that help make your code more readable and, therefore, easier to program, enhance, and debug.

The simplest way to name a function is to describe the function's task in English, using a verb-noun combination that best defines the English description. Table 17.2 lists some tasks and the names that may be associated with the functions that accomplish those tasks.

Table 17.2. Examples of function names.	
Function Name	**Description of Task**
SaveFile	Saves a file to disk
PresentMenu	Presents a menu to a user
FindWord	Finds a word in a string
CalculateHeight	Finds the height of an object

A program should not be difficult to read; its code should make general sense to anyone, even a novice programmer.

Don't assume that just because you write your own code you forever will remember the purpose of its functions. Not only does recalling the purpose of every function you design become difficult (especially as your program grows), but most programs end up in another person's hands. That person must decipher your code to add to it or debug it. Choosing descriptive function names not only helps you, it helps everyone who works with your program.

Figure 17.3 illustrates an English description of a complex task that involves other tasks. On the left side of the figure is the English description of the complex task. The right side of the figure demonstrates how, even in code form, the basic program is understandable from the function names.

English Description	Corresponding Functions	**Fig. 17.3.**
"To build a house begin by laying a solid foundation. Once the foundation is complete, place the ground-level flooring down. Build the second-story foundation walls and then the second-story floors. Add a roof. Finish the interior."	LayFoundation(); LayGroundlevelFloor(BuildSupportWalls(); AddFloors(); AddRoof(); FinishInterior();	Translating English descriptions into function names.

Whenever possible, give your functions description. As illustrated in figure 17.3, a function name can work like an English description to convey the task the function performs.

Do not be misled by the cryptic names assigned to many C library functions. C library functions have a long history, and they evolved from contexts in which their names made sense. You have no reason to follow the C library naming pattern if it is not intuitive and readable to you.

Choosing Function Arguments

A *function argument* is a parameter that is passed to the function in order to customize the function. Consider, for example, the following prototype for the puts() function that places a string on the screen, as defined in the Turbo C++ library reference:

```
int puts(const char *s);
```

In this line of code, s represents an argument for the puts() function. The s argument is the string that the puts() function places on the screen. In this example, the s argument customizes the puts() function by allowing any function with its own string to call puts() to place the string on-screen.

When choosing function arguments, you must determine how many arguments and what type of arguments to include in your function. The argument type can be any valid C data type or any data type that you have defined (refer to chapter 10, "Introducing String Constants and String Arrays," for a list of valid C data types and an explanation of how to define your own data types).

The following section discusses how you can determine what number of arguments to include in your function.

Determining the Number of Arguments. When you write a function, you are faced with a tradeoff between making the function flexible (by using many arguments to customize the function) and making a function easy to program and use (by limiting its number of arguments).

Consider the following two function prototypes:

```
void ReadThreeFiles();
void ReadFiles(const char *file1, const char *file2, const char
*file3);
```

The first function has no arguments. The function is easy to use, but you know from the prototype that it can only read three specific files, because it has no way of selecting files to read. The second function takes three arguments — three string pointers. You know from the prototype that this function can be customized to read any combination of three files. The second function is more difficult to write, but because it can read any three files (not just three specific files) it also is more useful.

When you create a function prototype, think of ways you can make the function useful to many parts of the program. Then choose the number and type of arguments that make the function readily customizable by other calling functions to suit their needs. The way in which an argument is declared is the way the argument will be passed to the function.

The three ways of declaring arguments, and corresponding three ways to pass argument information, are as follows:

- By Value

- By Pointer

- By Reference

Passing Arguments by Value. When an argument is passed by *value*, a copy of the original variable is passed to the function. The following example takes a single character variable and passes it to a putchar() function that places the character on the screen.

```
char ch;
ch = 'A';
putchar(ch);
```

The `putchar()` function is not aware of a variable called `ch`. What the function recognizes is a copy of the `ch` variable, that is the value `A`, passed as the function's `ch` argument. That recognition is all the `puts()` function needs to do its job.

Passing by value is useful if the amount of information being passed is not large. For transferring large amounts of information, however, passing by value is inefficient, because it requires that a copy of the information be made each time the information is passed. Passing an argument by pointer avoids this inefficiency.

Passing Arguments by Pointer. An argument that is passed by *pointer* does not get copied. The variable's address is passed, and the function then fetches the value it needs by going to the location pointed to by the argument.

In the previous chapter, you may have noticed that all C library functions that manage strings pass those strings by pointer. Consider again the example of the `puts()` function, whose prototype is:

```
int puts(const char *s);
```

To pass an argument by pointer, you declare the argument by preceding the variable name with an asterisk (*). In this example, the asterisk designates that the string's location, referred to as `s`, rather than the whole string, is passed. The `puts()` function then can get the contents of the string by looking at the location pointed to by its argument.

The reasons for passing strings by pointer are easy to see. Strings often are very long and can contain many hundreds, sometimes thousands, of characters of information. Making a copy of this information when it is needed for various functions is highly inefficient. Instead, using pointers enables the information to be placed in a single location, and that location is then passed to any function that needs to operate on the string. This method uses both space and time efficiently.

When a function uses an argument that is a pointer, the function cannot only read information from, but also write information to the address pointed to by the pointer. The C library function `strcpy()` that copies one string to another, for example, has the following arguments:

```
char *strcpy(char *dest, const char *src);
```

III

Advanced C Programming

When an argument is defined with the const keyword, the value pointed to by the argument is not modifiable, even though it is passed as a pointer.

Both arguments in the strcpy() function are pointers to string buffers. The strcpy() function copies characters at the src location to the dest location.

Declaring a pointer argument is useful if your function must update a variable's information, such as in the case of the strcpy() function. When you are dealing with pointers to variables, however, you must be careful how those variables are referenced. You must use the * to reference the variable correctly, which may at first seem unintuitive. The following example function illustrates this point:

```
void IncrementCounter(int *i)
{
    *i = *i + 1;
}
```

The incrementcounter() function adds one to the argument i. Had the argument i been passed by value (without the *) then a copy of that value would be made and the copy would be incremented instead of the original variable. This is of no use because the whole purpose of the incrementcounter() function is to increment the variable that is passed as the i argument.

By passing the argument as a pointer, the function incrememtcounter() can update the location to store the new incremented value. The penalty for this convenience is that it requires that you deal with pointers, as the single line of the function demonstrates. You learn more about dealing with pointers in chapter 18, "Using Pointers." For now, notice that reading a line of code such as

```
*i = *i + 1;
```

is more cryptic than reading a line of code such as

```
i = i + 1;
```

Although using pointer arguments can add flexibility to a function, they require more attention to ensure that they are used properly. Unless an argument must be passed as a pointer so that its address can be referenced, you can often pass an argument by value and still accomplish your task. The second line of code is more intuitive.

If you want to have the passing argument updated by the function and you do not wish to use pointers, you can use the reference argument type.

Passing Arguments by Reference. Passing an argument by *reference* is the same as passing the pointer to the argument, but with a slight twist: you can use the pointer within your function as if it were the original variable. The term *reference* indicates that the argument is *referred* to as if it is declared internally in the function.

The following example uses the `incrementcounter()` function from the previous example. Using a pointer argument, the function is defined as:

```
void IncrementCounter(int *i)
{
    *i = *i + 1;
}
```

Using a reference argument, the function can be rewritten as:

```
void IncrementCounter(int& i)
{
    i = i + 1;
}
```

The ampersand (&) in front of the argument i tells the compiler to send the location of the variable i instead of the value of i as an argument. The compiler also takes care of translating any reference to i within the `incrementcounter()` function so that the reference to i operates operates on the original variable and not a copy of the variable.

When you use an argument that is passed by reference, you can update the original variable without using pointers. The compiler does all the translating of pointers for you.

Choosing an Appropriate Return Value

A *return value* is the information that the function returns. To understand return values, consider the following C library function, `strlen()`, which determines the length of a string:

```
size_t strlen(const char *s);
```

The return value in this function has the type `size_t`, which is an integer. Because the purpose of the `strlen()` function is to determine the length of a string, its return value is the string length. The `strlen()` function can be used as follows:

```
int MyStringLength;
char MyString[] = "This is my string";

MyStringLength = strlen(MyString);
    .
    .        // do something based on the length of MyString
    .
```

III

Advanced C Programming

A return value must accomplish two things:

- A return value must provide useful information based on the purpose of the function.

- A return value must provide a value that represents an error if the function is incapable of completing its task

Consider the C library function `fopen()` that was used in the previous chapter. `fopen()` is defined as:

```
FILE *fopen(const char *filename, const char *mode);
```

The return value in this function is a valid pointer to a file structure that represents a file if the `fopen()` completed successfully. If `fopen()` uses the specified mode but does not succeed in opening the file, the return value is null (or zero). The `fopen()` function meets both criteria for its return value: if the function succeeds, a useful value is returned; otherwise, a special value that represents an error is returned. The program can test the error value, notify the user, and take appropriate action when the error occurs.

A Prototype Example

To illustrate how to name a function, choose its arguments, and choose a return value, the following paragraphs use these techniques one by one to demonstrate the development of an example program. The specifications for the function are in figure 17.4.

Fig. 17.4.
Specification for a function that displays consecutive letters of the alphabet to the screen.

> **Specifications for a function to display consecutive letters of the alphabet to the screen:**

In this example, the first task is to name the function. One name that describes the purpose of the function is `displayalphabetsequence()`. Long function names can be more descriptive than short names that must be deciphered.

The next step is to decide what arguments are needed for the `displayalphabetsequence()` function. Because the function must be able to take a starting letter as well as how many letters to display, two arguments are necessary. The starting letter and the number of characters are numeric values, so both arguments can be declared as integers.

You could write this function so that it returns a value that represents whether or not the function succeeded. Although this return value is adequate, it tells the calling function only whether or not the function succeeded completely. To make the function more useful, in this example it returns an integer value that represents the number of characters that the function successfully displayed. A zero represents a complete failure, and any other number (short of the number of characters requested to be displayed) represents a partial success.

The full prototype of the function is:

```
int DisplayAlphabetSequence(int offset, int numchars);
```

The offset argument is the corresponding letter of the alphabet when you assign A to 0, B to 1, and so on, which starts the display sequence. The numchars argument is the number of consecutive characters to display, starting from the offset character.

The full function definition and example program can be found in listing 17.1.

Listing 17.1. Displayalphabetsequence() **function definition and example program.**

```
#include <conio.h>
#include <stdio.h>

int DisplayAlphabetSequence(int offset, int numchars)
{
    int i, result;
    char Alphabet[] = "ABCDEFGHIJKLMNOPQRSTUVWXYZ";

        // The following loop executes numchars times
        // to display one character at a time beginning
        // with the offset character

    for ( i = 0; i < numchars ; i++ )
    {
        // Display the i'th character starting from offset

        result = putch(Alphabet[i + offset]);

        // if the putch() function fails exit the loop

        if ( result == EOF ) break;
    }
    return i;
}
```

(continues)

Listing 17.1. Continued.

```
main()
{
    int n;

    n = DisplayAlphabetSequence(3, 10);

    printf("\n\n The number of characters displayed was: %d \n",
n);

    return 0;
}
```

The displayalphabetsequence() function uses a simple loop that displays characters one at a time, beginning with the offset character and continuing for numchars characters. Starting from point i, and going for numchars rounds, the lines between the braces of the for loop are executed. With each execution of the code in the braces, the i counter is incremented by 1. Consequently, the offset value used for the putch() function is one more than the last, and the appropriate character is displayed on the screen. The putch() function uses the Alphabet string and the offset value to select the character to display.

The return value represents the number of times the putch() function was called. Because i is incremented with every loop in which putch() displays the next character to the screen, i represents the number of characters that are displayed on the screen. The return value, therefore, is i.

The main() function calls the displayalphabetsequence() function using an arbitrary set of values for the arguments. You can use any combination of values to test this program and see what happens. After a call to displayalphabetsequence(), the main() function displays a screen message to confirm the number of characters that were actually displayed. This on-screen information is possible only because the displayalphabetsequence() function returns the number of characters it displays, or an error code.

Function Implementation Considerations

After you have designed a prototype of a function, you can write the function code. Your first and most important objective in writing a function is to make the function operate exactly as described in its specifications. The following sections describe several other points you need to consider when writing functions.

Checking Arguments

When a function is declared with one or more arguments, this opens the possibility that the values passed to these arguments are not useful and can lead to the function malfunctioning. You can protect your function from malfunctioning by checking arguments before the arguments are used. If the value in the argument is reasonable then you have the option of exiting the function and returning an error value.

Consider the `displayalphabetsequence()` function from the previous section. Although the alphabet contains only 26 letters, nothing prevents this function from being called using nonsensical values, such as:

```
DisplayAlphabetSequence[12345, 10];
```

This call says that the function is to display 10 characters, beginning with the 12,345th letter of the alphabet. A call such as this call is likely to crash the system, because the `displayalphabetsequence()` function must go well beyond the `Alphabet[]` string to find the 12,345th letter of the alphabet. Now, consider this call to `displayalphabetsequence()`:

```
DisplayAlphabetSequence[10, 12345];
```

This call requests that the function display 12,345 characters beginning with the 11th letter of the alphabet (the first letter is offset 0). Again, because the alphabet contains only 26 letters, this call also is likely to crash the system.

The two preceding examples are not the only possibilities for passing strange values to the `displayalphabetsequence()` function. Negative values also can be passed to the function with unpredictable results.

In short, unless you check the arguments for reasonableness prior to their use, you have no way of guaranteeing that the arguments will work properly within your function.

In the case of the `displayalphabetsequence()` function, checking the following conditions can ensure that the arguments are reasonable:

- `offset` must be between 0 and 25, that is, one of the letters of the alphabet

- `numchars` cannot be larger than 26 - offset, that is, `numchars` cannot be larger than 26 minus the value of `offset`. Therefore, `numchars` cannot cause the sequence to run past the end of the alphabet

III

Advanced C Programming

By checking both offset and numchars before they are used, the function is guaranteed to display only characters from the Alphabet buffer.

The new displayalphabetsequence() function definition, with checks, appears in listing 17.2.

Listing 17.2. Second displayalphabetsequence() **function definition and example program.**

```
#include <conio.h>
#include <stdio.h>

int DisplayAlphabetSequence(int offset, int numchars)
{
    int i, result;
    char Alphabet[] = "ABCDEFGHIJKLMNOPQRSTUVWXYZ";

        // Check arguments

    if ( offset > 25 ||        // offset cannot be more than 25 (0 =
➥A)
        numchars > (26 - offset) ) // numchars cannot run offset
➥passed 26
    {
        printf("One of the arguments is out of range.  Exiting
➥the function.\n");
        return 0;
    }

        // The following loop executes numchars times

    for ( i = 0; i < numchars ; i++ )
    {
        // Display the i'th character starting from offset

        result = putch(Alphabet[i + offset]);

        // if the putch() function fails exit the loop

        if ( result == EOF ) break;
    }
    return i;
}

main()
{
    int n;

    n = DisplayAlphabetSequence(2345, 10);

    printf("\n\n The number of characters displayed was: %d \n",
➥n);

    return 0;
}
```

The preceding `displayalphabetsequence()` function includes a few extra lines that check the boundaries of the arguments. If the argument values are unreasonable, the function displays an error message on the screen and returns 0. Recall that a return value of 0 means that the function has failed completely. When checking arguments reveals an error, remember to return the appropriate error value. Otherwise, the calling function is unaware that an error took place (even with a status message printed to the screen) and may continue processing with the assumption that all went well with the function call.

Choosing What to Include or Exclude

You easily can get carried away and build a function prototype that is completely flexible and does everything for everyone. You must measure the benefit of having such flexibility, however, against the complexity of writing such a function. Sometimes a better approach is to define several function prototypes to manage variations of a task. Other times, you need to make a function more flexible and include all variations of a task within a single function.

No definitive guideline can determine which approach you should use in every circumstance: being overly inclusive (flexible), or exclusive (simple). Writing one flexible function often can be more difficult than writing several small functions, each of which manage a variation of the same task. As a general rule, however, you are wise to avoid writing long complex functions, for several reasons:

- Complex functions are more difficult to write and debug.

- Complex functions are more prone to errors.

- Complex functions are sometimes more difficult to use when a single simple variation of the function is what is most often needed.

To illustrate this last point, take an example of two functions that potentially can be combined into one; in this case, the two C library functions `strcpy()` and `strcat()`. The `strcpy()` function copies one string to another, and the `strcat()` function appends one string onto another. You can combine these two functions into a single function that uses an extra argument to determine which option to use. A prototype for this combined function may look like this:

```
char *strcpycat(char *dest, char *src, int cpy);
```

The third argument, cpy, is an integer variable: if set to 1 a strcpy() is performed; if set to 0, a strcat() is performed. The C library does not include a strcpycat() function because the individual strcpy() and strcat() functions often are need in programs, and combining them would add a level of complexity to each call.

The one circumstance in which a flexible function is most appropriate is when a lot of small variations can be more useful if they are consolidated into a single function. As an extreme example of such a circumstance, imagine using 26 variations of the putch() function, one to display each letter of the alphabet to the screen.

To illustrate the process of adding a variation to a simple function, try revising the displayalphabetsequence() function so that it can display an alphabet sequence in either forward or reverse order. A new prototype for the more flexible version of displayalphabetsequence() is named displayalphabetsequence2() (the 2 is for the dual direction capability):

```
int DisplayAlphabetSequence2(int offset, int numchars, int direction);
```

In this example, you add the third argument to let the function know which direction to use when displaying characters. When the argument is set to 1, the function uses the forward direction, otherwise it displays characters going backwards. When displaying the alphabet in reverse, this function begins with the letter represented by offset and displays the characters going backward in the alphabet. Listing 17.3 is the code for the displayalphabetsequence2() function.

> **Listing 17.3.** Displayalphabetsequence2() **function definition and example program.**

```
#include <conio.h>
#include <stdio.h>

int DisplayAlphabetSequence2(int offset, int numchars, int forward)
{
    int i, result;
    char Alphabet[] = "ABCDEFGHIJKLMNOPQRSTUVWXYZ";

        // Check arguments

    if ( forward == 1 ) // Test arguments if going in the forward
➥direction
        {
```

```c
        if ( offset > 25 ||        // offset cannot be more than 25 (0 =
➥A)
            numchars > (26 - offset) ) // numchars cannot run offset
➥passed 26
        {
            printf("One of the arguments is out of range.  Exiting
➥the function.\n");
            return 0;
        }
    }
    else // Test arguments if going in the backward direction
    {
        if ( offset > 25 ||  // offset cannot be more than 25 (0 = A)
            numchars > offset ) // numchars cannot bo back prior to 0
➥(= A)
        {
            printf("One of the arguments is out of range.  Exiting
➥the function.\n");
            return 0;
        }
    }

        // The following loop executes numchars times

    for ( i = 0; i < numchars ; i++ )
    {
        // Display the i'th character starting from offset

        if ( forward == 1 )
        {
            result = putch(Alphabet[i + offset]);
        }
        else
        {
            result = putch(Alphabet[offset - i]);
        }

        // if the putch() function fails exit the loop

        if ( result == EOF ) break;
    }
    return i;
}

main()
{
    int n;

    n = DisplayAlphabetSequence2(10, 5, 1);

    printf("\n\n The number of characters displayed was: %d \n", n);

    return 0;
}
```

In the program, notice that the check is done twice on the forward argument. The first check is for reasonableness; the second check occurs when the character sequence is being displayed. Remember, if you enable a user to use your function in various ways, you must check the reasonableness of the arguments for each variation.

You must compare the efficiency of writing this new function against the alternative of writing two functions; one such as the original `displayalphabetsequence()` function and a second that display an alphabet sequence backwards. If this function were a complex function, writing the two separate functions would be easier and more useful than writing the single, more complex function.

Using Global Variables in a Function

Beginning programmers often are tempted to use global variables rather than passing arguments to a function. Because global variables are accessible by all your functions, using them might at first sound like an easy way of accessing and manipulating common information. After all, why bother creating function prototypes with arguments that constantly need to be passed, when defining all the variables as global variables is much easier, and all functions can operate on all variables as necessary?

To summarize—do not make this mistake! If all functions have access to the same information, all functions can accidentally corrupt this data as easily as they can operate on it. Additionally, when an error occurs, finding the source is very difficult when all functions are using the same variables. By making variables local and passing them as parameters you are confining both the use and misuse of these variables. Using local variables enables you to detect and rectify errors quickly and easily.

Testing Your Functions

You probably are aware that all functions you create need to be thoroughly tested. Testing functions, similar to other aspects of programming, can be more effective if you use guidelines and a plan. This section shows you how to properly test a function that you create.

In order to demonstrate the various aspects of testing, these sections use an example function, `replacechar()`. This function has the following prototype:

```
int ReplaceChar(const char *string, int offset, char ch);
```

The purpose of this function is to replace a character within a string with the argument ch. The offset argument determines where in the string the ch character is placed. The return value is 1 for success, and 0 for failure. The complete definition for the function is in listing 17.4, along with a main() function that tests the replacechar() function.

Listing 17.4. Replacechar() **function definition.**

```
#include <string.h>
#include <stdio.h>

int ReplaceChar(char *string, int offset, char ch)
{
    // Check arguments

    if ( offset < 0 ||          // Is offset before first character?
         offset > strlen(string) || // Is offset after last character?
         ch < 'A' ||            // Is replacement character valid?
         ch > 'z' )
    {
        printf("Invalid argument.\n");
        return 0;
    }

    // Update character based on offset

    string[offset] = ch;

    return 1;
}

main()
{
    char buffer[40];
    int result;

        // Place original string in buffer

    strcpy(buffer, "Yankee Doodle Went To Town");

        // Display original string

    printf("Original string: %s\n", buffer);

        // Revise string

    result = ReplaceChar(buffer, 0, 'A');

        // Check result and display appropriate message

    if ( result == 1 )  // Function succeeded - display revised string
    {
```

III

Advanced C Programming

(continues)

Listing 17.4. Continued.

```
            printf("Revised string: %s\n", buffer);
        }
        else                    // Function failed - notify user
        {
            printf("Error: string has not been revised\n");
        }
        return 0;
    }
```

The main() function uses the replacechar() function to change a character in the string buffer. The main() function then checks the result variable to determine whether the function succeeded or failed, and displays the appropriate message depending on the result variable's value. You need to check the result of the call and take appropriate action depending on the result, just as you do for a call to any function.

Testing for Accuracy

Testing for accuracy is the most common type of testing. The purpose of this form of testing is to determine that you get the expected result when you use the function. To test the function replacechar() for accuracy, change the line that calls the replacechar() function to read:

```
result = ReplaceChar(buffer, 19, 't');
```

Testing the program produces the following lines of output:

```
Original String: Yankee Doodle Went To Town
Revised String: Yankee Doodle Went to Town
```

Notice that the T of the word To in the first string has been changed in the revised string to a lowercase t.

Testing for accuracy is the most common form of testing because when you write a function, your first concern is that it actually works. You can play with various combinations of offset and ch arguments for further testing of this kind.

Testing For Completeness (or Boundary Checking)

You test for completeness to ensure that you have accounted for all extremes of normal use. This kind of testing specifically focuses on the boundary values of the arguments. Testing for boundary values can mean different things to different functions.

In the case of the `replacechar()` function, the function is complete if it can use all the letters of the alphabet to change any letter of the string. To test this program for completeness, try the following variations of calls to `replacechar()`:

```
ReplaceChar(buffer, 0, 'A');  // Change first letter to 'A'
ReplaceChar(buffer, 25, 'z'); // Change last letter to 'z'
ReplaceChar(buffer, 0, '~');  // Change first letter to '~'
```

The first two variations in this list produce just what you expect; an original string with the revised string. The third variation, however, produces the following lines of output:

```
Original String: Yankee Doodle Went To Town
Invalid argument.
Error: string has not been revised
```

You may be wondering what happened, because the third variation looks just as good as the first two. The purpose of the first two variations of the call to `replacechar()`, however, is not the same as the purpose of the third. The first two variations check for boundary use of the offset argument. The first variation checks to see that the first character in the buffer can be changed; the second tests that the last character in the buffer can be changed. The smallest and largest offsets, therefore, are tested by the first two variations.

The purpose of the third variation is to test the boundary of the third argument, `ch`. This varation checks for what values the `ch` argument accepts. To see why this check fails, look at the check done on the argument `ch` within the `replacechar()` function. Notice that the boundary check is to ensure that `ch` is the ASCII value between A and z. Although this boundary check may appear reasonable, the ACSII table of printable characters extends beyond the letters A through z. The tilde (~) character is four characters past the letter z in the ASCII table.

This check did not necessarily reveal an error; it demonstrated to you the boundary for using the `replacechar()` function. You now have the choice of keeping the original boundary check defined in the function or changing it to reflect the entire list of ASCII printable characters, depending on the needs of your program.

Testing for Usability
You test for usability to determine how well the function meets the changing needs of your program. Frequently, you design a function for a particular task. As your program grows, it may include variations of the same task that require you to redesign or rewrite the function.

As a result of a boundary check used in the previous section, you know that the range of valid characters for the ch argument of the `replacechar()` function is a through z. This range may be sufficient for your original design. At some point, however, you may need to update the function to incorporate all ASCII characters as possible replacement characters.

You also may need the `replacechar()` function to serve the following uses:

■ Have the return value be the character that is replaced

■ Have the function operate on two strings, instead of a string and a character — this function would replace one or more characters of a string starting at an offset into the original string

No definite criteria exists for determining usability. If you find that you must write supplementary code in order to make your function useful, chances are that the function is not as usable as you intended for it to be.

Using Functions

In most circumstances, you use a function to manipulate some information, as do the various function examples in this chapter. The function is called and an argument is modified, as was the case with the `replacechar()` function, or the return value is used, as you saw with the C library `strlen()` function that returns the length of a string. You also can use functions in other ways, such as those discussed in the following sections.

Using Functions as Variables

You can use a function in the same way you use a variable, if the function's return value matches the variable type you need. This use can be illustrated with a simple mathematical example.

Suppose you frequently need to use the average of two numbers. Whenever you need an average, you can write out the full mathematical expression, as shown in the following examples:

```
int  i;
int  a, b, c, d;
a = 20;
b = 30;
c = 40;
d = 50;
i = ((a + b)/2) + 1;           // Average of a and b plus 1
i = ((a + b)/2) + ((c + d)/2);    // Average of a and b plus the average
➥of c and d
```

Alternatively, you easily can write a function to calculate the average of two values. The prototype of the function is:

```
int Average(int a, int b);
```

The importance of this function is that its return value is the average of its arguments. The code for this function is:

```
int Average(int a, int b)
{
    return ((a + b)/2);
}
```

With this function, whenever you need an average, you can use a neat function rather than the more-difficult-to-read mathematical equation. The original math example is now:

```
int  i;
int  a, b, c, d;
a = 20;
b = 30;
c = 40;
d = 50;
i = Average(a, b) + 1;        // Average of a and b plus 1
i = Average(a, b) + Average(c, d); // Average of a and b plus the
➥average of c and d
```

This code not only is easier to read, but also is less prone to error. Because you can write and thoroughly test the average() function at one time, you eliminate the concern of mistyping a bracket or a + sign for each instance that you need your program to calculate an average value. The average() function replaces the individual use of the variables.

Using Functions as Arguments

You also can use functions as arguments. You often can use this convenience often to make coding easier and more readable.

To illustrate this use, consider a new function called sumofaverages() with the prototype:

```
int SumOfAverages(int average1, int average2);
```

The purpose of this function is to calculate the sum of two averages. Although the values of the arguments are integers, the function assumes that they are in fact averages. Look at the code below to see how you can use the average() function defined in the previous example with the new sumofaverages() function.

```
int   i;
int   a, b, c, d;
a = 20;
b = 30;
c = 40;
d = 50;
i = SumOfAverages(Average(a, b), Average(c, d));
```

The program is easy to read, because the functions state their purpose. Note that the `average()` function is used as input to both arguments of the `sumofaverages()` function. This use is allowable because the function `sumofaverages()` takes in integer arguments and the `average()` function returns an integer value.

Do not use a function as an argument value when the function may return an error that is not usable. In this situation, place the function return value in a variable, check the variable, and then use the variable as an argument only if it is valid.

Summary

This chapter covered the various aspects of creating a function. The chapter discussed the many things you must take into account when designing a function, including the function's prototype, choice of arguments, and choice of return value. The chapter also discussed those equally important issues you must consider when writing a function, including checking for valid arguments, ensuring that appropriate return values are sent, and testing the function for accuracy, completeness, and usability.

With all these things to think about when writing a function, you may wonder how entire programs ever get completed! As any programmer will tell you, remembering to take most—if not all—of these concerns into account when you write programs becomes second nature. When you learn any language, fluency comes with practice. The same is true of writing functions, which is the essence of programming in C and C++.

In this chapter, you learned the following:

- Planning is essential to all aspects of programming, whether the task is to design an application or just a single function.

- When you design a program, divide the tasks among various smaller functions, each with its own purpose.

■ If you need to pass arguments to your function, you can declare the arguments so that they are passed by value, by pointer, or by reference.

■ When an argument is passed by value, a copy of the argument is used within the function.

■ When an argument is passed by pointer, the function can access the argument address and therefore read and write to the argument's address location.

■ When an argument is passed by reference, the function can access the argument address and therefore read and write to the argument's address location without having to use the *.

■ Always check an argument value before you use it in a function to ensure that it is reasonable for the function's task.

■ Before using a new function, test it to ensure that the function operates correctly and that the function can account for any value that is passed to its arguments.

Chapter 18

Using Pointers

C pointers have a reputation for being difficult to learn and even more complicated to use. In this chapter, you learn that pointers are no more difficult to use than any of the other programming tools discussed in this book. The pointer is just one more tool you can use to make your programs more efficient and flexible. Pointers are, in fact, one of the reasons that the C language is so powerful.

The program at the end of this chapter incorporates both pointers and memory allocation to demonstrate how you can combine these elements to simplify programming.

This chapter covers the following:

- Pointers

- How to use pointers

- Memory allocation

- How to use the Turbo C++ memory allocation functions

Understanding C Pointers

A *pointer* is an address. We all use the equivalent of pointers in our everyday lives. When you mail a letter, your information is delivered based on a pointer, which is the address on the letter. When you telephone someone you use a pointer — in this case, the telephone number you dial.

A mail address and a telephone number have this in common: they indicate where to find something. They are pointers to buildings and telephones respectively. A C pointer also tells you where to find something. It tells you where to find the data that is associated with a variable. A C pointer is the address of a variable.

Figure 18.1 shows the comparison of a row of houses on a street with a stretch of computer memory. The first house belongs to John, and its address is 100. If you want to find John's house, walk down Main street and look for the number 100 over the door.

Fig. 18.1.
A pointer is comparable to a street address.

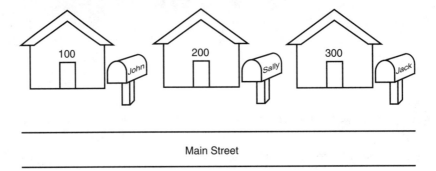

Main Street

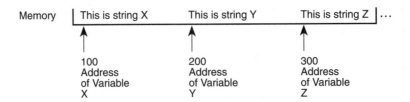

Similarly, computer memory consists of one long "street" of electronic data. Variables are located anywhere along that street. The location of a particular variable along this street of data is indicated by its address. The address of a variable is its mailbox, which is represented by a pointer in the C language. The address enables you to find one variable in among all the others. A C pointer is an address to a specific variable.

Why Use Pointers?
Table 18.1 lists several reasons that pointers are used in C programs. Primarily, you use a pointer to simplify the transfer of information from one location to another. When two functions need to operate on the same set of data, passing along the address of that data is more efficient than passing a copy of the data itself. When the second function receives a pointer, it then can retrieve or update the set of data by going to the address indicated by the pointer.

Table 18.1. Uses of pointers.	
Use	**Description**
Improve Speed	It is faster to pass a pointer to a large set of information than to pass the whole set of information itself
Save Space	Many functions can share a pointer and operate on the same set of data without having to copy it for each function
Flexibility	A pointer can be used to reference different variables as a program executes, thereby enabling certain sophisticated programming techniques
Access to New Space	Using pointers and the C library's runtime allocation functions, a program has access to additional storage space for data

An important use of pointers results from their combination with the C library memory allocation functions. A memory allocation function sets aside new storage space within the computer's memory (RAM) during a program's execution for the exclusive use of that program. Figure 18.2 illustrates the process of memory allocation.

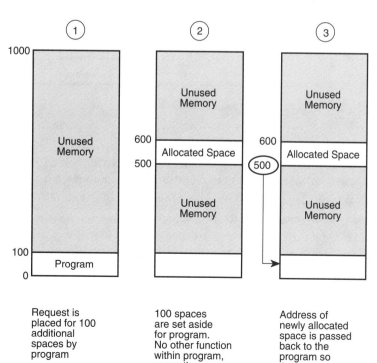

Fig. 18.2.
The memory allocation process.

Request is placed for 100 additional spaces by program

100 spaces are set aside for program. No other function within program, or another program, can directly access the space.

Address of newly allocated space is passed back to the program so that program can access the new space using the address.

III

Advanced C Programming

Your program can request as much memory as it needs to store new information gathered during your program's execution. The program uses C memory allocation functions to request this memory from the operating system. If the allocation function succeeds, it returns a pointer that contains the address of the additional memory. Your program then has exclusive access to this memory and can use it to store any kind of information.

Characteristics of Pointers

A C pointer does not describe the variable it points to. It is an address that directs you to one spot in memory where the value of a variable is stored. Just as a street address says nothing about the kind of building located at the address or how many people live there, the pointer gives no indication of what kind of information is stored at the location or of the value of that information.

Another characteristic of a C pointer is that it can be used as a variable. The pointer can be used as a variable because it has a location of its own in memory and it has a value. The pointer's value is the address of a variable. Figure 18.3 illustrates how a pointer is both a variable and an address.

Fig. 18.3.
The pointer as variable and address.

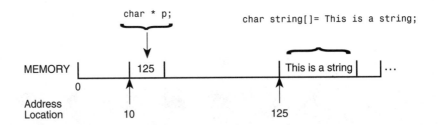

When you refer to p in figure 18.3 as a pointer, you are referring to the fact that it holds the address to the variable string. As a variable, p is an integer with a value of 125. If you did not know that p is a pointer, you would think of p strictly as an integer. In fact, it *is* just an integer, but it is a special type of integer that you can use to reference other locations in memory. In other words, p is an integer whose value is an address. By analogy, the number 100 is just a mathematical unit. If it appears on an address label in front of the words "Main Street," however, the number 100 also is an indicator of a specific house on Main Street. In this context, the number 100 is both an integer and an address; similarly, a pointer is both a variable and an address.

Thinking of pointers as variables can be useful at times. When used as a variable, a pointer can be incremented and decremented. This action often is referred to as *pointer arithmetic*, and it opens vast possibilities for programming complex tasks very efficiently. Pointer arithmetic is covered in greater detail later in this chapter.

Because you can use pointers in many creative ways, you may get somewhat confused in the process. You can avoid some of this confusion if you constantly remind yourself that pointers are just addresses, and an address is simply a particular location in memory. If you're confused about how to use a pointer, picture the pointer as an address label that directs you to a particular house. The "house" in this case is simply a variable.

Using C++ Pointers

You use two unary (a mathematical operator that uses only a single operand) operators, & and *, to associate variables with pointers. Table 18.2 defines these operators.

Table 18.2. Pointer operators.	
Operator	**Purpose**
&	Gets the address of a variable
*	Declares a variable as a pointer
*	Gets the contents of a variable given its pointer

You can see in the table that the * operator has two purposes as a pointer operator. When an operator has more than one purpose it is described as *overloaded*. An overloaded operator is like a word that has two meanings; you determine the word's meaning based on its context. Similarly, the * operator is interpreted by the compiler in different ways, depending on the operator's context. In fact, both the * and & operators have another purpose in C: * is the multiplication operator, and & executes a bitwise or. Fortunately, an operator's context is relatively easy to spot.

Using the * Operator as a Pointer Declaration

You use the * operator to declare a pointer variable. For example, the following are pointer declarations:

```
int *i;   // pointer to an integer
long *l;  // pointer to a long integer
float *f; // pointer to a float
```

A * operator in a declaration indicates that the variable being declared stores an address to the specified data type. The variable *i* in the above declaration stores the address of an integer. The variable f stores the address of a float.

Recall that a pointer is an address and can tell you nothing about the type or content of what it is pointing to. You may be wondering why you need to declare a pointer to a specific data type, such as an integer or a float. Why not declare a general pointer to any data type?

You associate a pointer declaration with a data type because it makes things simpler for the compiler and saves you some programming hassle at the same time.

Each data type has its own storage requirements, and operating on an integer is different than operating on a float. The compiler has to know what storage requirements and operating characteristics it must use for any given type of data. If you do not associate a data type with a pointer, every time your program uses a pointer you have to tell the compiler what type of data is being referenced, so the compiler knows what storage requirements and operating characteristics to use. For the same reasons, if you used a general pointer, you would need to tell the compiler what data type the pointer references. Supplying this information could become very tedious.

Instead of using general pointers, you can assign pointers to a specific data type. This declaration establishes an agreement between you and the compiler. You agree to use the pointer to point only to a specific data type; in turn, the compiler agrees not to ask you for the data type every time it encounters that pointer. The compiler knows to use the storage and operational requirements appropriate to that data type every time it encounters that pointer. This arrangement saves you from a considerable hassle.

Using the & Operator

You use the & operator to return the address of a variable. The & is used in the following way:

```
int i;    // declare a variable i
int *p;   // declare a pointer to an integer p
p = &i;   // assign the address of i to p
```

To understand the & operator, think of it as if it were a function called `gettheaddressof()`. Although no such function exists, you easily could understand the meaning of:

```
p = GetTheAddressOf(i);
```

The & operator replaces the long function name with a simple unary operator. The meaning of this example is the same as that of `p = &i` in the preceding example. Always remember that the & operator actually returns a value. This value is the address of the variable associated with the & operator, which is the variable that immediately follows the & symbol.

Using the * Operator For Dereferencing

The second use of the * operator is to dereference pointers. Recall that a pointer is simply an integer value that happens to be an address. You can use the * operator to get access to the information that is stored in the location pointed to by a pointer. Using the * operator in this way is called *dereferencing.*

Consider the following two statements:

```
int *p;
p = 10;    // statement #1
*p = 10;   // statement #2
```

In statement #1, p is assigned a value of 10. Because p is an address variable, p contains the address 10. Whatever happens to be stored in address 10 can be referenced by p. Generally, you will not know the address location of a variable, since that is determined when the program starts to run. Statement #1 illustrates the effect of using a pointer without the dereferencing * operator. To get an address of a variable, you use the & operator.

Statement #2 uses the * operator as a dereferencing mechanism. This statement updates the location pointed to by p to store the value 10. Because p is just an address, you cannot use it to directly access the information that it points to. Use the * operator as a convenient way to transform the pointer address into the variable itself. When the * operator precedes a pointer, it changes the pointer into the variable that the pointer represents.

Consider the following set of statements:

```
int  i;    // declare an integer variable
int  *p;   // declare a pointer to an integer value
p = &i;    // assign the location of i to the pointer p
```

III

Advanced C Programming

The first declaration tells the compiler to set aside memory for an integer value and give it the label *i*. The second declaration tells the compiler to set aside another variable, called p, that will point to an integer. The third line tells the compiler to associate p with the address of i. The variable p now contains the memory address location of the integer *i*.

You can now reference the variable i in two ways:

```
i = 10;
*p = 10;
```

These references are identical. In computer terms:

```
i == *p
```

where == means *is identical to*. Anything you can do with i, you can do with *p.

Consider the following example.

```
#include <stdio.h>

main()
{
        int i;
        int *p;

        i = 10;
        p = &i;         // assign p the address of i

        printf("The value of i is: %d\n", i);
        printf("The value of *p is: %d\n", *p);

        return 0;
}
```

Both PRINTF() statements display the number 10, because *p is identical to i. The * in front of the pointer p transforms the pointer into the variable it is pointing to.

String Pointers

Declaring an array is one exception to the rule of using the * operator to declare a pointer variable. Chapter 10, "Introducing String Constants and String Arrays," introduced character arrays and strings. This chapter reviews the use of strings and arrays in the context of pointers. A character array is declared as:

```
char buffer[100];    // declares character array
```

This declaration sets aside 100 bytes of space to store information. Although this declaration makes no explicit use of the * operator, buffer actually is a pointer—a pointer to a fixed space in memory that the compiler sets aside. You can consider buffer a single-purpose pointer: it can only point to the original 100 spaces that were set aside when buffer was declared.

Whenever you declare an array, the declaration actually is a pointer. Arrays are covered in greater detail in the next chapter, "Using Arrays." This chapter mentions arrays only to review character arrays and string pointers, because programmers frequently use string pointers.

Another way of declaring a string pointer without a * operator is as follows:

```
char MyString[] = "This is my string";  // string declaration
```

In this example, MyString also is a pointer. MyString is even more restricted than the buffer pointer of the previous example. MyString is a pointer to a single location that can store only the specific value, This is my string. You use this form of declaration to have the compiler set aside a specific block of memory and place a string within it. The MyString variable can be used as a pointer only to the specific string that was declared.

Misusing Pointers

When you declare a pointer, it does not point to anything. Whatever numeric value the pointer may happen to contain at the time it is declared is not meaningful. Consider the following program:

```
#include <stdio.h>

main()
{
    int  *p;

    printf("The pointer p is equal to: %u\n", p);

    return 0;
}
```

This program displays the contents of the pointer p right after the pointer is declared. The contents of p happen to be an address location in memory, since p is a pointer. The compiler has no trouble compiling this program. The pointer is just a number; the number happens to be an address to a specific location in memory. Because the pointer is a number, you can use it as an argument to printf() or any other function or operator, just as you use any integer.

The value displayed in the preceding program is not a predictable number. Further, the value may differ from one run to the next. The value is an unpredictable number because when a pointer is declared, it does not point to anything. Until you tell the pointer to point to a specific variable's address, the pointer may contain any number.

Never use a pointer that has not been assigned.

To assign an address location to a pointer, use the & operator. The & operator returns the location (or address) of the variable that it operates on.

Consider this revised version of the previous program:

```
#include <stdio.h>

main()
{
    int   i;
    int   *p;

    i = 10;        // assign i to equal 10
    p = &i;        // assign the address of i to the pointer p

    printf("The pointer p is equal to: %u\n", p);

    return 0;
}
```

In this program, a new variable i is declared, and i is then assigned a value of 10. The pointer p is then assigned the address of i. Finally, the value of p is printed.

Don't be surprised if you see a number other than 10 displayed on the screen when you run this program, because the program still displays the value of p. The value of p is now a valid address, but the address says nothing about the variable it points to. The value of p is not the value of i. To get to the variable that the pointer references, use the * dereferencing operator.

Do not confuse the value of the pointer address with the value of the variable that it points to. When a pointer is used directly, it is just an integer that happens to be an address. When a pointer is used with the * operator, it is transformed into the variable that it represents.

You now can update the previous program to use the pointer p to print the value of i, as shown in this example:.

```
#include <stdio.h>

main()
{
    int  i;
    int  *p;

    p = &i;         // assign the address of i to the pointer p
    i = 10;

    printf("The content of the address pointed to by p is: %d\n", *p);

    return 0;
}
```

In this program, the printf() function uses *p instead of p. Because *p is the contents of the location pointed to by p, it is identical to i, and the correct value (10) is displayed.

Notice in the preceding program that the pointer p is assigned the address location of i before i is assigned a value. The program still displays *p as 10; why? The answer to that question may be obvious to you, but the next few paragraphs explain it, anyway.

After you have the address of a variable, the value of the variable can change an indefinite number of times without affecting its address. The address always points to the same location, which contains the most recent value of the variable.

In the case of the preceding example, when p is first assigned the address of i, i is unassigned, therefore the content of this location is unpredictable. After i is assigned, the address location remains unchanged, but its contents are updated. Using the street address analogy, 100 Main Street stays where it is, no matter who moves in or out at that address. The value of the pointer p always stays the same after it is assigned the address of i. The contents of that location keep changing as the value of i changes.

Consider another common oversight in which a pointer and the contents to which it is pointing are confused:

```
#include <stdio.h>

main()
{
    int i;
    int *p;
```

```
        i = 10;
        p = i;          // THIS IS NOT CORRECT!

        printf("The value of i is: %d\n", i);
        printf("The value of *p is: %d\n", *p);

        return 0;
    }
```

Notice that p is assigned *i* instead of *&i*. This program cannot compile, because p is declared as a pointer to an integer. Although the pointer p actually is an integer value, p is not an integer in the sense that you can combine it with other integers in mathematical expressions.

Consider the following program that uses an uninitialized pointer. Do not attempt to run this program on your system as it might corrupt memory in your computer:

```
#include <stdio.h>

main()
{
    int i;
    int *p;

    i = 10;
    *p = i;          // THIS IS NOT CORRECT!

    printf("The value of i is: %d\n", i);
    printf("The value of *p is: %d\n", *p);

    return 0;
}
```

Although this program successfully compiles, and the results may appear to be correct in your display, this program contains a bug in the *p = i declaration. The p in the *p = i declaration is uninitialized; it does not yet point to a valid place in memory. An uninitialized variable may point to operating system memory or some other invalid location. The *p = i declaration, therefore, places the value of i to the uninitialized location pointed to by p. You may be lucky and not touch critical memory for a few runs. However, at some point you will be updating system memory and the system may crash.

Always initialize a pointer to a valid address location.

Using Pointer Arithmetic

Because pointers are integers, combining arithmetic operators with pointers makes sense. You need to know how arithmetic operators work with pointers because the combination can make certain complex programming tasks simple and efficient.

In figure 18.4, you see a magnified view of a small segment of a computer's memory. In this segment is a string, THIS IS A STRING, that begins with the hypothetical address of 100. If you initialize a pointer to the beginning of this string, the pointer has the value of 100. In that case, you can assume that 101 is the letter H, 102 the letter I, and so on. Because the address is an integer, it makes sense to be able to use a pointer and some arithmetic to span the contents of a variable, in this case a string.

Fig. 18.4.
The memory map of a string.

In fact, you can use arithmetic operations on pointers in many situations. Suppose you want to cycle through a string to determine which characters are uppercase. The following program is one way of accomplishing this task.

This program first initializes a string called MyString to a particular value. An offset integer variable i is then initialized to 0. This offset becomes the location that the program examines within the string. You use string offsets as follows:

```
MyString[0];   // First character of string
MyString[9];   // Tenth character of string -- offsets start at 0
```

The program starts a loop to examine each character of MyString and determine its lettercase. With each round in the loop, the integer i is incremented by 1. Because i is the offset into the string, each loop examines the next character within the string. The loop stops when the character to be examined is 0. Stopping the loop when you reach a 0 is safe because all initialized strings are *null-terminated*, which means they end with 0. Checking for 0 positively determines that the end of the string has been reached.

The printf() statement displays a line to the screen in the form of:

```
<the next character> <is | is not> uppercase.
```

The printf() uses two parameters; the offset, and either the word is or the words is not. To determine the second parameter, the program tests each character using the condensed version of the if statement (refer to Chapter 16, "Using Program Logic Control") and a function called isupper().

isupper() is defined in the **ctype.h** header file. isupper() checks a character and returns a true value if the character is uppercase, and a false value otherwise. The if statement translates to:

```
return the string "is" if the character is uppercase, otherwise
return the string "is not"
```

The character passed to the isupper() function is the current character that is being examined.

The output of this program is several lines of on-screen text that let you know whether each character within the string is or is not uppercase.

You can simplify this program by rewriting it to use a string pointer and some pointer arithmetic. Consider the following program, which is a revised version of the previous program.

```
#include <stdio.h>
#include <ctype.h>

main()
{
    char MyString[] = "This Is A String";
    char *p;

    p = MyString;        // Assign p to point to MyString

    do printf("%c %s uppercase.\n",
            *p, isupper(*p) ? "is" : "is not");
    while ( *p++ );

    return 0;
}
```

The program in this example uses a pointer to a string instead of a string offset. The program first intializes the pointer p to MyString. The reason the statement reads

```
p = MyString;
```

instead of

```
p = &MyString;
```

is that MyString already is a string pointer. Recall that all string array variables are string pointers.

When p is first initialized, it points to the first character within the string MyString. To get to the next character, you must increment the pointer. You accomplish this increment by using the increment operator ++.

Never use constants to increment or decrement pointers. The compiler figures out the appropriate number of bytes to shift using the ++ and -- operators for each data type and memory model. Only these mathematical operators, therefore, are safe to use with pointers.

The printf() uses *p to point to the current character; *p is the value of the character at the location p. Because p is being incremented with each round of the loop, *p points to the next character each round. The loop ends when *p points to zero (which indicates the end of the string) and the condition of the while loop is false.

This program uses a do loop instead of a while loop, to ensure that the increment operator starts after the first round is completed. When you use a while loop, the increment operator moves the pointer p ahead one location before starting the first round. When printf() is reached in the first round, *p already is pointing to the second character. When you use a do loop, *p remains at the start of the string for the first round.

The previous example demonstrates the versatility of using pointers. The pointer can serve as an address. As an address, it replaces the need for an offset value, because the address can be incremented and point to subsequent characters within the string. The pointer also can be used as the value of the offset into the string, by using the * dereferencing operator.

Using Pointers as Function Arguments

A pointer often is used as an argument to a function. When a pointer is passed as an argument to a function, the function can update information referenced by the pointer. Passing the pointer as an argument enables a function to manipulate information that is stored outside of its domain.

Using pointers as arguments is no different than using pointers in any of the ways described earlier in this chapter. To use pointers as argument, however, you need to know how to read function prototypes that use pointers. With that knowledge, you easily can use pointers as arguments.

Consider the following function that was defined in a previous chapter. This function increments an integer by 1:

```
void IncrementCounter(int *i)
{
    *i = *i + 1;
}
```

The function's significance to this discussion is that even though the argument of the incrementcounter() function is declared as a pointer, you must pass an address to use this function. For example, to call this function use:

```
int i;
i = 10;
IncrementCounter( &i );
```

At first glance, this arrangement may confuse you. Why pass an address of i to the function, when the function argument is declared as a pointer? To see why, refer to figure 18.5.

Fig. 18.5.
Function proto-
types that use
pointer argu-
ments.

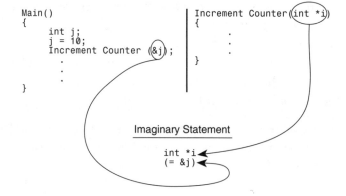

In this figure, the incrementcounter() function declares a pointer. This action is similar to starting an imaginary program with the statement

```
int *i;
```

Next, another function declares its own integer variable to use with the incrementcounter() function. This variable is declared as

```
int j;
```

When you call the incrementcounter() function in figure 18.5, you need to associate the pointer i with the variable **j**. You achieve this association with the expression

```
i = &j;
```

This is why you pass the address to the function. The function is trying to associate a variable with its pointer.

Internally, the increment function is defined with the line

```
*i = *i + 1;
```

Using the * dereferencing operator also makes sense in this function. Because i is declared as a pointer, and * is used to translate a pointer to a variable, you need to use *i to update the variable that was passed as an address.

The following program uses the incrementcounter() function to display a sequence of values on the screen.

```
#include <stdio.h>
#include <conio.h>

void IncrementCounter(int * i)
{
    *i = *i + 1;
}

main()
{
    int  j;

    j = 0;
    while ( !kbhit() ) {            // loop until a key is pressed
        IncrementCounter( &j );  // increment the value of j
        printf("The value of j is: %d\n", j); // display value of j
    }

    return 0;
}
```

Using Void Pointers

A *void pointer* is a pointer that is not assigned to a particular data type. It is declared as:

```
void *v;  // declare void pointer
```

Because pointers are addresses, this pointer is an address to anything. You can use the void pointer to point to an integer or a string buffer.

Because the void pointer does not have a particular data type associated with it, the compiler has no way of knowing how to manage the data that is referenced by the pointer. The statement

```
*v + 10;
```

has no meaning to the compiler, because the compiler does not know whether v points to an integer, float, or a character string. You are responsible, therefore, for telling the compiler what the void pointer is referencing whenever the pointer is used. By telling the compiler this information, you ensure that the compiler correctly handles the void pointer. If you fail to supply the information to the compiler, the results of using the void pointer can be unpredictable.

III

Advanced C Programming

The following program demonstrates one use of a void pointer.

```
#include <stdio.h>

main()
{
     char MyString[] = "This is a string"; // declare and initialize a
string
     void *v;  // declare a void pointer

     v = MyString; // Use the void pointer to point to a string

     printf("The void pointer v points to the string: %s\n", (char *) v);

     return 0;
}
```

The char * in the `printf()` statement is necessary so that the compiler knows to interpret the void printer as a character pointer.

The void pointer in this example is used to point to the `MyString` string buffer. Note that `MyString` is, itself, a pointer and therefore does not need dereferencing in the statement v = `MyString`. The void pointer can be used in other places in the program when a pointer is needed, such as to the `printf()` function.

The void pointer is used more extensively in the next section, when dynamic allocation functions are discussed.

Using Pointers and Dynamic Allocation Functions

A program is assigned by the compiler as much memory as it needs to store the variables that are declared within the program. *Dynamic allocation functions* enable a program to extend beyond its initial memory allocation to gain additional space as the programs is executing. A program can use this additional memory to store any type of data in any amount that can fit in the new allocation. Whenever memory is allocated using a dynamic allocation function, a pointer to the new memory is returned to the calling program, so the program can access the new memory.

Why Use Dynamic Allocation

All the variables you declare within a program get a fixed memory location that is part of the program. This space is set aside regardless of how often, if ever, you use the variables. When programs use only small amounts of data, the data does not occupy much space.

Sometimes, however, your program requires large amounts of memory for short periods of time. Other times, the amount of memory your program requires is determined as a result of user input. Declaring space within the program in these circumstances is inefficient for two reasons:

■ The memory is fixed; when the memory is not being used for its declared purpose, it can't be used at all.

■ No matter how much memory you set aside, it may not be enough, or it may be so large that most of it is wasted most of the time.

Consider the example of a word processing program. The program could declare an internal buffer to store the text that a user enters. To ensure adequate memory, you may declare a buffer such as:

```
char buffer[10000];
```

This declaration enables the user to enter up to 10,000 characters before reaching the limit of memory storage. The buffer is fixed by the compiler and cannot be altered to meet actual memory storage needs. Whether the user needs to enter only 100 characters or as many as 10,100 characters, the memory storage area remains at 10,000 characters. Either way, using declared space for the word processing program makes no sense.

Dynamic allocation functions enable you to choose the amount of memory you need, when you need it. If the memory is too small you can increase it. If you request a lot of memory and decide that most of it is being wasted, you can decrease it. You have complete control over the amount of memory you use.

Using Dynamic Allocation

Dynamic allocation is a three-step process. These steps are:

1. Allocate memory

2. Resize allocated memory

3. Free allocated memory

When you allocate memory, you request that the operating system set aside some memory for the exclusive use of your application. No other application can use this memory while it is allocated. (Although DOS is a single-program operating system, any number of TSRs can run while your program is operating.)

III

Advanced C Programming

To allocate memory, you use the C library function `malloc()`. The `malloc()` function has the following prototype:

```
void *malloc(size_t size);
```

`malloc()` takes one argument, `size_t`, which is the amount of memory that you need in the form of an integer. Because the `malloc()` function cannot predict what you intend to use the memory for, its return value is a void pointer.

You resize memory using the `realloc()` C library function. The `realloc()` function has the following prototype:

```
void *realloc(void *block, size_t size);
```

`realloc()` takes two variables: an allocated pointer and the amount of additional memory that you require. The `realloc()` function returns a void pointer to the new memory.

When reallocating memory, do not assume that the pointer to the new memory is the same as the one for the old memory. Regardless of whether you increase or decrease memory, your original pointer is not valid after the `realloc()` function is called. You must use the return value of the `realloc()` function to get a new pointer to the resized memory.

Always free allocated memory when you are through using it. If you repeatedly allocate memory and forget to free it, you eventually run out of memory; further requests for memory will fail.

You free allocated memory using the function `free()`. The `free()` function prototype is:

```
void free(void *block);
```

The `free()` function takes a pointer to allocated memory and frees that memory for use by another function or application. Again, always free allocated memory when you finish using it.

Memory allocation functions are contained in the alloc.h header file. Include this file in your source code whenever you use any of the allocation functions.

The following program demonstrates the basic use of dynamic memory allocation functions.

```
#include <alloc.h>
#include <stdio.h>
#include <string.h>

main()
{
    char *p;  // declare a string pointer
    int i;        // declare an integer variable

        // allocate memory
        // 128 is the maximum number of characters that
        // the keyboard buffer can hold
    p = (char *) malloc(128);

    gets(p);

        // print the string

    printf("You have entered the string: %s\n", p);

        // strip the excess space wasted

    i = strlen(p);
    p = (char *) realloc(p, i + 1 );  // realloc - include an extra
➥byte for the terminating null

        // print the string

    printf("This string uses the reallocated pointer: %s\n", p);

    free(p);
    return 0;
}
```

This program allocates enough memory to store in a complete keyboard buffer. A keyboard buffer can contain up to 128 characters. Allocating 128 bytes guarantees the amount of allocated memory is large enough to hold the largest amount of information that the user can enter.

Always allocate the maximum amount of space you need to store input from a user. Never assume that the user will not need all the space and therefore will not use it. You always can resize allocated memory when you are certain that its excess space is unnecessary.

Note the casting of the void pointer that is returned by the `malloc()` function. The cast enables the void pointer to be translated into a character pointer. This way the pointer p can be used as a character pointer anywhere the program needs a character pointer. This program uses the p pointer for the `gets()` and `printf()` functions.

As a general practice, cast the return pointer from a malloc() function to the desired data type. The compiler cannot work with void pointers for many operations that pertain to specific data types. Casting the return value enables you to use the allocated pointer in ways that are specific to the data type to which it points.

When a line of text is retrieved into the allocated buffer pointed to by p, the text is displayed on the screen. The program then uses the strlen() function to calculate the actual size of the text and uses the realloc() function to resize the buffer accordingly. This step reduces the size of the buffer to the exact amount of bytes necessary to contain the line of text.

Because you allocate the maximum possible amount of memory the program may require, after you determine the actual memory needs you can free the excess allocated memory. This step ensures that no excess space remains allocated and unusable by other functions and programs.

Finally, the program uses the pointer to reprint the line of text to the reallocated buffer. When you reallocate, you need not concern yourself with the content of the buffer, provided the new buffer is at least as large as the information that you need to maintain. If the system offers as part of the reallocation a memory location other than the original, the contents of the original buffer are moved to fill the new memory. The realloc() function moves only as much information as can fit in the new space.

Putting Things Together—An Example

This example program shown in listing 18.1 combines several C language topics covered in this section. The program is a simple line editor that enables text entry only. As each line is retrieved, the program adds the line to an allocated buffer that is resized to accommodate the new line. The user indicates that the text entry is completed by typing the word **done** on a new line. The program then displays the complete text to the user. This example demonstrates the use of pointers and memory allocation in a realistic program setting.

Listing 18.1. Simple text entry program.

```c
#include <alloc.h>
#include <string.h>
#include <stdio.h>
#include <process.h>

main()
{
    char    NextLine[128];       // buffer for next line of text
    int LineLength;              // integer for NextLine length
    char    *FullText;           // character pointer for allocated
                    //   memory to store full text

        // Initialize FullText pointer

    FullText = (char *) malloc(1);
    if ( FullText == 0 )        // check that allocation succeeded
        exit(1);        // if not, exit program
    FullText[0] = 0;            // Set the buffer to a null string

        // display initial prompt

    printf("\n\nEnter text line by line.\n\
Enter the word 'done' on a new line when you are through.\n\n");

        // start loop that retrieves text line by line

    while(1)
    {
        // get next line of text and its size

        gets(NextLine);
        LineLength = strlen(NextLine) + 1;

        // stop retrieving lines if the user
        // enters a new line that reads "done"

        if ( !strcmpi(NextLine, "done") )
            break;

        // reallocate the FullText buffer to
        // be large enough to hold the existing
        // text as well as the new line, plus an
        // extra carriage return to delineate
        // between lines

        FullText = (char *) realloc( FullText, strlen(FullText) +
➥LineLength + 3);

        // check reallocated buffer
        // exit program if this fails

        if ( !FullText ) exit(1);
```

(continues)

Advanced C Programming

Listing 18.1. Continued.

```
                    // Add a carriage return and then
                    // the new line

                    strcat(FullText, "\n");
                    strcat(FullText, NextLine);
        }

                    // display the complete text

            printf("The complete text entered is:\n%s\n", FullText);

                    // free allocated buffer before exiting

            free(FullText);

            return 0;
        }
```

The program starts by initializing a pointer to a buffer that has one byte. The `malloc()` function returns an error if you attempt to allocate 0 bytes. A prompt notifies the user to begin entering text.

The text is retrieved one line at a time. A while loop whose condition expression is always set to true keeps running until the program uses a break statement to exit the loop. The break statement is triggered when the user enters the word **done** on a new line. To minimize confusion, the test uses a `strcmpi()` function which is not case sensitive; the user can enter **done** in any combination of uppercase and lowercase characters to trigger the break statement.

As each line is entered, its length is calculated. An extra 1 byte added to the end of the LineLength is for the 0 that is at the tail of every null-terminated string, but which is not included in the `strlen()` return value. The length of each new line the user enters is added to the length of the existing text, to calculate the size of the new buffer that is to store the cumulative text. When the buffer is successfully allocated, the new line is added to the existing text using `strcat()`. A carriage return delineates each line from the next and is added to the existing text prior to the new line.

When the user ends text entry by entering **done** on a new line, the program exits the loop and the complete text is displayed back to the user. The program then frees the allocated memory for other functions or programs to use.

The program checks the return value any time it uses the `alloc()` or `realloc()` functions. This check is critical. If you do not check the return values for these functions, and they fail for some reason, you will not have a valid pointer. The pointer will contain an address 0. If you attempt to use this pointer, you are likely to crash the system.

Always check the return value of a call to any critical function.

Summary

Pointers and memory allocation are important language and C library tools that enable you to create well-designed and efficient applications. Although using pointers can become confusing at times, you will find it a straightforward process if you keep in mind the techniques presented in this chapter. As this chapter emphasized, a pointer is an address just like a street address.

The use of pointers and memory allocation are not critical to application design. You can design programs that use neither of these elements. As some examples in this chapter demonstrate, however, using these tools can add flexibility and efficiency to your programs. Further, after you understand them and become accustomed to incorporating them into your applications, you will wonder why you ever bothered to avoid them. Using pointers and memory allocation actually makes your programming easier.

In this chapter, you learned the following:

- A pointer is an address, just like a mailing address, which points to a specific location in memory.

- Pointers are an efficient way to pass large amounts of information to a function, because you only pass the address of the information, rather than the information itself.

- A declaration of a character array is the same as declaring a pointer to a fixed place in memory that is designated by the compiler.

- You must initialize a pointer before its use, or you may get unexpected results when the pointer is used.

- A void pointer is a pointer not assigned to a particular data type and can therefore be used to point to different data types at various places in your program.

III

Advanced C Programming

■ Dynamic memory allocation is memory that is set aside by a program while it is executing.

■ Pointers are used to store the address of dynamic memory when it is allocated for use by a program.

Chapter 19

Using Arrays

As you learned in previous chapters, *arrays* are collections of a common type of data. Common data are easier to manage as a unit than as discrete items. You can group any one type of data into an array. The C++ language enables you to use an array of any data type, provided that all items in the array are of the same type.

The most common type of array is the *string*. As seen in previous chapters, dealing with a string is simpler than managing each character as a separate entity. Similarly, in many situations an array is the most appropriate way of dealing with a set of information. Recognizing when and how to use an array are two key factors in taking advantage of the built-in power of arrays.

This chapter describes:

- What is an array

- How to use arrays

- Using arrays as function arguments

- Using C++ library array functions for searching and sorting arrays

Understanding Arrays

Although an array is a collection of information, not every collection of information constitutes an array. An array is a set of variables that have the following:

- They are of the same type

- They share a common purpose

To a C++ program, a queue of people waiting at the bus stop can be considered an array, as is illustrated in figure 19.1. This array consists of similar elements (people) who share a common purpose (waiting for the bus). You can translate the queue of people into a string array. The first person in the queue is the first element in the array, the second person is the second element in the array, and so on. You then can deal with the array of people as a unit. For example, you can determine the size of the array, or in real-life terms, how many people are standing in line.

Fig. 19.1.
Array representations.

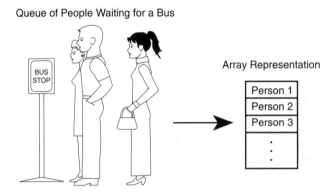

Queue of People Waiting for a Bus

Recognizing Information that Constitutes a Useful Array

You probably can force almost any group of items into an array format, regardless of how dissimilar are the group's discrete elements. To make the most of using arrays, however, you need to learn to recognize which groups of information naturally lend themselves to arrays, and which groups do not (see fig. 19.2).

Walking into a rain forest, you can use an array to keep track of all the living things you encounter, including animals, insects, and plants. Although these living things share something in common (they all reside in one location), the individual elements are too dissimilar to assemble into one category represented by a single array. A count of the array may produce billions of items, but because the plants may vastly outnumber the animals, the count tells you nothing about the animal population within the rain forest. Such a situation may warrant using separate arrays, one for each type of living thing. By having a separate array for animals, fish, and plants, you can get more useful information from your arrays.

In C++ terms, an array can be a collection of only a single type of data. You cannot combine various numbers of integers, floats, and strings into one array. You have no method of declaring such an array, and certainly no C++ language constructs or functions to manage such arrays.

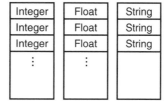

Fig. 19.2.
Valid and invalid
C++ arrays.

All elements in an array must be of the same data type, but each element within the array can have a unique value.

Declaring Arrays

You declare an array by adding square brackets to a variable declaration. For example, the following declares an integer:

```
int i;    // declare an integer
```

To declare an array, add square brackets as follows:

```
int i[]; // declares an array of integers
```

Actually, the preceding array cannot compile. To use an array, you must tell the compiler how many elements you plan to maintain in the array. This information is then used by the compiler to set aside the appropriate amount of memory for the array. In figure 19.3, each box represents an element of the array. When the compiler comes across an array in your code, it sets asides memory space that equals the storage requirement for an element of the array multiplied by the number of elements in the array. To properly declare an array, use the following format:

```
int i[10];     // declares an array of ten integer variables
float f[20];   // declares an array of 20 float variables
```

Declaring an array only ensures that the compiler sets aside the appropriate amount of memory to store all the elements of the array. The array declaration does not fill any of the array elements with any information.

Using Array Subscripts

An array can be dealt with as a unit or as discrete elements. To reference the array, you use the array name. To reference an element within the array, you use a *subscript*. A subscript is a number that indicates the offset into an array, as illustrated in figure 19.4.

III

Advanced C Programming

Fig. 19.3.

Array storage.

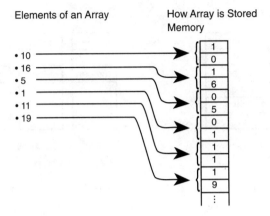

Elements of an Array   How Array is Stored
Memory

Fig. 19.4.

Using subscripts to reference individual items in an array.

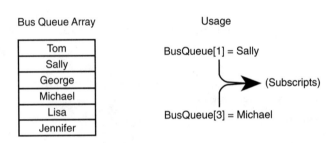

Bus Queue Array   Usage

In figure 19.4, the array BusQueue contains the names of people waiting at a bus stop. Array subscripts always start at 0. To reference the second person in the BusQueue array, therefore, you use the following form:

```
BusQueue[1];    // == "Sally"
```

To reference the fourth person in the array, use:

```
BusQueue[3];    // == "Michael"
```

If BusQueue were an actual program array, you *could* use the the following statement:

```
BusQueue[99];   // == ERROR!
```

This statement references the 100th person in the bus queue. Even though only six people are in the queue, the C++ compiler does not prevent you from using this out-of-bounds subscript. No boundaries exist for checking subscripts. You must ensure that any subscript used is within the bounds of the array.

Similarly, you also can use the following statement:

```
BusQueue[-1];  // == ERROR!
```

In real life, if you are told to look for the 100th person in a bus queue of only six people, you stop after counting the sixth person and let the requester know of the misunderstanding. If you tell a program to look for the 100th person in a bus queue, it calculates how much space one person occupies and then counts 100 of these spaces. When it reaches the 100th space, the program returns whatever is at that location! Similarly, if you tell a program to look for the -1th person, it counts backward one person-space and returns with whatever happens to be in that location. The compiler never makes intelligent decisions about subscripts.

Calculating the Size of an Array

The size of an array is calculated as the size of the data type, multiplied by the number of elements in the array. The size of an array has nothing to do with the data type of the elements that comprise the array. The array size is a static number that always equals the total amount of space allocated for the array.

Consider the following program.

```
#include <stdio.h>

main()
{
    int i[20];
    float f[100];

    printf("The size of an integer is: %d, and the size of i is:
➡%d\n",
                sizeof(int), sizeof(i));
    printf("The size of a float is: %d, and the size of f is:
➡%d\n",
                sizeof(float), sizeof(f));

    return 0;
}
```

This program uses a C++ library macro, `sizeof()`, that returns the size (in number of bytes) of any declared data or data type.

The program displays two lines of text on the screen. The first line indicates the size of a single integer as well as the size of an array of 20 integers. The second line displays similar information about a float and an array of 100 float values.

Notice in the program that an integer uses 2 bytes of storage space and a float uses 4 bytes. This discrepancy illustrates why a C++ array cannot include two

III

Advanced C Programming

different data types: the data types' storage requirements may be different and the compiler cannot know how many bytes to assign each element.

The program demonstrates that an array is the number of elements declared by the array, multiplied by the number of bytes necessary to store a single element of that type. Assigning or not assigning values to the array has no bearing on its size. When you declare an array, its size is fixed as the total amount of memory necessary to store all its elements. As seen from the program, the size of the array, whether or not it is initialized, is the number of elements multiplied by the size of an element.

Initializing Arrays

To initialize an array at declaration, use the following form:

```
data_type array_name[ no_elements ] = { value1, value2, ... };
```

To assign an array a value at declaration, use a set of values separated by commas and enclosed in curly brackets ({}). Here are some examples:

```
int i[5] = {1, 2, 3, 4, 5};
double d[3] = {1.1, 2.2, 3.3};
char string1[7] = {'A','B','C++','D','E','F','G'};
```

The above form of initializing a string at declaration may be unfamiliar to you. The more common form of initializing a character array is:

```
char string2[7] = "ABCDEF";
```

The preceding character array is the proper form for initializing a string. A string in C++ is a null-terminated array of characters. The first "string" declaration is an array of characters, but because it is not null-terminated, it does not constitute a string. If you attempt to use string1 in any of the string functions, such as StrCpy() or StrCmp(), you get no compiler error, because string1 is a valid string pointer. You are likely to get a runtime error or unpredictable results, however, using string1 in any of the string functions. A runtime error is an unexpected result that occurs only when the program is running. If you use string1 with any of the string functions, the functions will look for a null terminator to determine the end of the string. Since string1 has no null terminator, the string function will read memory starting at the location pointed to by string1 and contnue until the function does find a null value. This may be well past the end of the string1 array, and into the memory owned by the operating system.

The form used to initialize the `string2` variable is the proper form for null-terminated strings. This string is only initialized to six characters in order to leave an extra space for the trailing null character, or 0, that follows any string.

The form used for initializing an array when it is declared cannot be used to assign values to the array within your program. The following declaration cannot be used within your program. The following code results in a compiler error:

```
int i[5];
i = { 1, 2, 3, 4, 5 };   // Invalid
```

The compiler error is the result of the second line of code. The reason for the compiler error is that the array `i` is being assigned the values { 1, 2, 3, 4, 5 }. However, this form is only valid when the array `i` is declared. To assign values to `i`, you must assign each element of the array individually.

In general, if you are using an array as a static collection of information, initialize the array at declaration. For arrays whose elements are constantly changing, initialize the arrays at runtime by setting their value to an appropriate initial value.

Using Array Elements

Array elements are the individual variables that have been packaged and labeled into an array. Each element can be considered individually as a separate variable. In most circumstances, when you want to operate on the whole array, you must iterate through the entire array and take the appropriate action for each element of the array.

For example, if you did not initialize an array at declaration, you may want to do so in your code. To initialize an array, assign each element within the array an initial value. The following program, for example, initializes an array within the program code.

```
#include <stdio.h>
#include <string.h>

main()
{
    int Array[5];
    int i;

        // Initialize the array

    for ( i = 0; i < 5; i++ )
```

III

Advanced C Programming

```
                        Array[i] = 10;

                        // Display array values

                    for ( i = 0; i < 5; i++ )
                        printf("Array[%d] = %d\n", i, Array[i]);

                    return 0;
              }
```

The array is initialized at the start of the program using a for loop that
assigns the number 10 to each element within the array. This loop is followed
by another for loop that displays each element's value individually, to ensure
that the initialization succeeded. To initialize Array, you must assign each
element of Array individually.

Though the for loop certainly makes initialization easier, a quicker and simpler alternative exists if every byte of the entire array can be set to the identical value. In many cases, all the array elements must start out initialized to
zero. To initialize all elements to zero, use the C++ library function, memset(),
as in the next program example.

```
        #include <stdio.h>
        #include <string.h>

        main()
        {
              int Array[5];
              int i;

                    // Initialize the array

              memset(Array, 0, sizeof(Array));

                    // Display array values

              for ( i = 0; i < 5; i++ )
                    printf("Array[%d] = %d\n", i, Array[i]);

              return 0;
        }
```

memset() sets an entire memory space to a single value. memset() is declared in
both the string.h and mem.h header files. The prototype for memset() is:

```
        void *memset(void *s, int c, size_t n);
```

The memset() function uses a pointer to a block of memory and sets n bytes to
the value of c. This function provides a very convenient way to initialize a
block of memory when the value of all the array elements must be identical.
The size of the block of memory in the previous example is sizeof(Array).

Recall that this is the total number of bytes allocated for the array. Because the memset() function uses bytes as a unit of measure, using sizeof(Array) is correct.

The memset() function is unaware that it is updating an array. All memset() acknowledges is a block of memory. memset() uses the pointer and the number of bytes to update by setting each byte, one at a time, to the value c. Because memset() does not differentiate between arrays and other blocks of memory, the function can return unexpected results. Consider the next program:

```
#include <stdio.h>
#include <string.h>

main()
{
    int Array[5];
    int i;

        // Initialize the array

    memset(Array, 1, sizeof(Array));

        // Display array values

    for ( i = 0; i < 5; i++ )
        printf("Array[%d] = %d\n", i, Array[i]);

    return 0;
}
```

The output of this program is:

```
Array[0] = 257
Array[1] = 257
Array[2] = 257
Array[3] = 257
Array[4] = 257
```

Instead of a 1 being assigned to each element in the array, each element is equal to 257! The reason for this output is that the memset() function does a byte-for-byte assignment, and places the number 1 in each byte of the memory location pointed to by Array. This action is very different than assigning the individual elements of Array to 1. As mentioned earlier in this chapter, an integer is actually two bytes long. To store a 1 as an integer, you must use integer operations, not byte operations.

When using memset() to initialize an array at runtime, be aware that the value specified will be set for each byte within the array's memory, rather than for each element in the array.

III

Advanced C Programming

Using Arrays - Some Examples

Following are some examples of using arrays.

Example 1 - A Lookup Table. Arrays are often used to store *lookup informa-tion*. Lookup information is a list that is used as a reference. Often the list contains a set of valid values for a particular purpose.

A lookup list is useful for passwords. The example in listing 19.1 uses a lookup list to determine whether the user can proceed, based on whether the user enters a valid code.

Listing 19.1. A lookup list example using an array.

```
#include <stdio.h>

main()
{
    int  ValidCodes[5] = { 1000, 2000, 3000, 4000, 5000 };
    int  i, CodeEntered, IsValidCode = 0;

        // present prompt information

    printf("\nEnter code and press return ==> ");

        // prompt user for a code

    scanf("%d", &CodeEntered);

        // check if code is valid

    for ( i = 0; i < 5; i++ )
        if ( CodeEntered == ValidCodes[i] )
            IsValidCode = 1;

    printf("You are %s to proceed.\n", IsValidCode AUTHORIZED" :
"NOT AUTHORIZED");

        return 0;
}
```

This program uses an integer array that is initialized at declaration to store a list of valid codes. A flag and a counter also are declared. The flag, IsValidCode, is initialized to false, 0. The program assumes that the user has not entered a valid code until the program determines that the code is valid.

The program uses the scan() function to prompt the user for a code. The scanf() function reads a value and converts it to the format indicated by the format code—in this case, the format for an integer value (refer to chapter 15, Using the C++ Library"). After the user enters a number, the program uses a for loop to scan the lookup array and determine whether or not the user-

entered number matches any of the codes in the lookup list. The check uses
an if statement that sets the IsValidCode flag to true, 1, when a match is
found.

When the check for a valid code is complete, the program displays a line to
let the user know whether he or she has an authority to proceed. The
printf() statement uses a condensed version of the if-then-else expression
(see Chapter 16) to return the word AUTHORIZED if the IsValidCode is true, and
the word NOT AUTHORIZED otherwise.

Example 2 - A Summation Program. The next example uses an array to
store a set of user-supplied integer values. The user enters the values one at a
time. When the user finishes, the program sums the values and displays the
total on the screen.

Listing 19.2. Summation program.

```
#include <stdio.h>

main()
{
    int  Items[4];
    int  i, Total = 0;

        // present prompt information

    printf("\nEnter 4 numbers, following each by a return.\n");

        // Get user-supplied numbers to sum

    for ( i = 0; i < 4; i++)
        scanf("%d", &Items[i]);

        // Sum the values

    for ( i = 0; i < 4; i++)
        Total += Items[i];

        // Display the result

    printf("\nThe total of the values entered is: %d\n", Total);

    return 0;
}
```

III

Advanced C Programming

This program uses an integer array of four items. The array is not initialized
either at declaration or when the program is executed before it is used,
because as soon as the program starts, it begins filling the array with the user-
supplied values. In this program, the user input actually is the array
initialization.

The input is controlled by a for loop that uses the `scan()` function to request four integer values. To get the address of an array element for the `scanf()` function, you use the form:

```
&Items[i]
```

This form is valid because `Items[i]` is the same as any integer variable to which you can prefix an & to get its address. Every element in an array is an individual variable. Using the subscript on an array enables you to treat a single element of the array as if it were a discrete variable. Because the & is used to get the address of a variable, it is a valid operator for a subscripted array. A subscripted array is simply a variable that happens to reside in the memory space of an array.

When the user enters the fourth value, the program continues to the next step, summing the values. The program uses another loop to sum the values. The statement uses a += mathematical operator. This operator adds the value of the right side operand to the existing value of the left side operand. The total of these numbers is then saved to the variable on the left side operand. When each element in the array is summed, all values are summed together.

When the summing loop is done, the result is displayed on the user's screen.

Example 3 - A Summation Program with Validity-Checking. An array can be helpful for keeping track of information as it accumulates. The next program uses an array to maintain a list of numbers that the user enters individually. The purpose of the program is to ensure that numbers are entered in sequence. If the user enters a number greater than the previously entered number, the program continues to request another number until the array is filled. If the user enters a number that is less than the previously entered number, however, the program stops and displays an error.

Listing 19.3. Summation program with validity-checking.

```
#include <stdio.h>

main()
{
    int   Items[4];
    int   i, j, Total = 0, LastEntry = 0;

        // get user-supplied numbers to sum

    for ( i = 0, j = 0; i < 4; i++, j++ )
    {

        // present prompt information
```

```
        printf("\nEnter a number that is greater \
than 0 \nand greater than the last number entered ==> ");

        // retrieve current entry

        scanf("%d", &Items[i]);

        // check that current entry is not less than last entry

        if ( Items[i] < LastEntry ) break;

        // make last entry the current one for next loop

        LastEntry = Items[i];
    }

        // sum the values
        // if not all values were entered, then sum only those entered
        // the number of items entered is j

    for ( i = 0; i < j; i++)
        Total += Items[i];

        // Display the result

    printf("\nThe entry completed %s.\n", j == 4 ? "successfully":
➥"unsuccessfully");
    printf("\nThe total of the %d values entered is: %d\n", j,
Total);

    return 0;
}
```

As the user enters a number, the program checks to determine that the number is not less than the previously entered number. This check compares the current entry with a variable called LastEntry. LastEntry is initialized to 0, so a number less than zero fails the validity check of the first loop iteration and causes the for loop to exit.

Applying subscripts enables you to use individual elements of the array. The variable j maintains only the number of valid entries made by the user. With each successful entry, j is incremented. Because j is guaranteed to point to the highest element in the array, it can be used as the boundary of the array in the next loop.

When the user finishes entering the data, j is equal to the number of correct entries. To tally the number of correct entries, the next for loop uses 0 as the lower boundary and j as the upper boundary. If a user entered incorrect data, j can be less than four. Even though some elements in the Items array may never get assigned, those that do get assigned can be used as valid data, because each element of the array is a discrete variable. No element can be affected by the validity of any other element in the array.

The program ends by displaying on-screen whether the data entry was successful, and the number and tally of correctly entered values.

Using Arrays as Arguments in a Function

Arrays generally are associated with large lists of information that need to be used within a program. Often this information must be shared across many functions. To share an array among functions, a program passes the pointer to the array rather than the array's entire contents. Passing the pointer rather than the array's contents makes sharing an array more efficient in terms of time and memory space.

Using an Array Variable as a Pointer. By definition, an array variable is a pointer. When you declare an array as

```
int  Array[10];     // declare an array
```

you actually are declaring a pointer to a sequence of memory that will store integers. Recall from previous chapters that a string declaration was associated with a character pointer. One of the strings used in previous chapters, for example, is as follows:

```
char MyString[] = "This is a string"; // string declaration
```

MyString is a character pointer, even without the * that declares pointers. MyString is an array of characters because it is declared with the square brackets. Every array declaration is a declaration of a pointer to the data type it is associated with. MyString is a declaration of an array to a sequence of characters. This example illustrates why character strings are referred to interchangeably as character arrays.

Now that you see that string declarations also are pointer declarations, recall how these string arrays pass to the string functions. Consider the following lines of code, for example:

```
char MyString[] = "This is a string";
int i;
i = strlen(MyString);
```

The MyString variable is used with the strlen() function, although the strlen() function takes a character pointer as an argument. MyString is a character pointer because it is declared as an array of characters. A variable that represents an array of characters is a character pointer, and so MyString is a character pointer.

You can apply the same concept to any other array. For example, an integer array is declared as:

```
int  Array[5]; // declare integer array
```

The variable array is actual a pointer. It can be used as the argument to a function that takes an integer pointer. Take the following code sequence:

```
int SumIntegerArray(int * AnIntegerArray)
{
    .
    .
    .
}


main() {
    int  Array[5] = {1, 2, 3, 4, 5};
    SumIntegerArray(Array);
    .
    .
    .
}
```

The `SumIntegerArray()` function takes a single argument that is a pointer to an integer; in other words, it takes an integer array. Consequently, the `SumIntegerArray()` function can operate on an array of integers that is declared in another place. The `SumIntegerArray()` function adds the values of all the elements of an array and return the tally.

Things to Consider when Using Arrays as Arguments. When you use an array variable as an argument, the receiving function may not know how many elements are in the array. Without that knowledge, a function cannot use the array. Although the array variable can point to the start of the array, it gives no indication of where the array ends.

The sample function `SumIntegerArray()` that was previously used as an illustration of how to pass a function an array pointer will not work. The `SumIntegerArray()` function is declared as:

```
int SumIntegerArray(int * AnIntegerArray)
{
    .
    .
    .
}
```

Although the `SumIntegerArray()` knows where the array starts, it does not know how many elements are in the array; consequently, it does not know how many elements to sum.

You can use two alternative methods to let a function know the number of arguments associated with an array that is passed as a function argument:

- Place a signal value at the end of the array to indicate that the function is to stop processing there.

- Pass a second argument that indicates the number of elements in the array.

All null-terminated strings use the first method. Strings are arrays of characters. When a string is passed to a function, such as STRLEN(), the function knows it has reached the end of the array when it sees a value of 0 in an element of the array. If, due to a programming error, strlen() fails to encounter a 0 at the end of an array, it continues counting bytes past the string buffer, until it reaches a 0 someplace further along in memory.

Strings always use a 0 to indicate the last element in the array of characters, but 0 is not the only indicator you can use. You can use any value to indicate the final element in your arrays. Programmers have adopted 0 as a standard to lend consistency to library functions and programs, but you are not required to abide by the standard.

A second alternative is to pass the number of elements in an array whenever the array is passed as an argument. The array and the number of elements then become a pair of arguments that must be associated by the function that was called. The SumIntegerArrays() function, for example, can be updated to the following definition:

```
int SumIntegerArray(int * AnIntegerArray, int NoElements)
{
        .
        .
        .
}
```

The second argument, NoElements, is an integer value that tells the SumIntegerArray() function how many elements to process in the array AnIntegerArray.

This alternative is frequently used for noncharacter arrays. The next section illustrates how to use this alternative.

An Example That Uses an Array as a Function Argument. A previous section presented an example program that retrieved some user-supplied numbers and summed the values using a for loop and an array (refer to listing 19.2). The program in listing 19.4 does the same thing, but uses a function to sum the elements in the array.

Listing 19.4. Revised summation program using functions with array argument.

```
#include <stdio.h>

int SumIntegerArray(int * AnIntegerArray, int NoElements)
{
    int  i, Total = 0;

    for ( i = 0; i < NoElements; i++)
        Total += AnIntegerArray[i];

    return Total;
}

main()
{
    int  Items[4];
    int  Total, i;

        // present prompt information

    printf("\nEnter 4 numbers, following each by a return.\n");

        // Get user-supplied numbers to sum

    for ( i = 0; i < 4; i++)
        scanf("%d", &Items[i]);

        // Sum the array using the SumIntegerArray

    Total = SumIntegerArray(Items, 4);

        // Display the result

    printf("\nThe total of the values entered is: %d\n", Total);

    return 0;
}
```

The function SumIntegerArray() takes two arguments: an array pointer and an integer value that tells the function how many array elements to process. This function uses a loop to cycle through the elements of AnIntegerArray the number of times specified by NoElements. With each iteration, the current element is added to the sum of all previous elements maintained by the variable Total.

III

Advanced C Programming

The main program uses a for loop to collect the numbers from a user. The array is then passed on to the `SumIntegerArray()` function and the value of the sum is returned. This value is assigned to the variable `Total` in the `main()` function. The result is then displayed on the screen.

Advanced Array Management: Searching and Sorting

Searching and sorting are integral to using arrays. When you think of an array, you think of a list of items. The most typical function performed on lists is sorting or searching the lists for specific elements.

An often-overlooked set of Turbo C++ library functions are those that actually search and sort lists that are stored as arrays. Many people ignore these functions because their use is not immediately intuitive; using these functions requires a lot of thought and practice. The payback of using these functions, however, can be tremendous. When you have mastered these functions, you easily can program almost all array or list management tasks.

The good part about learning these functions is that when you understand one of them, you can apply that understanding to the remaining functions. The four Turbo C++ library functions that apply to searching and sorting an array are listed in table 19.1.

Table 19.1. C++ Library search and sort functions.

Function	Description
bsearch()	Searches an ordered array for a matching value
lfind()	Searches an array linearly for a matching value
lsearch()	Searches an array linearly for a matching value
qsort()	Sorts an array using the quicksort algorithm

The benefit of using the C++ library functions for searching and sorting is that they are quick. The `qsort()` function is especially quick. Although you can write search and sort algorithms yourself, these libraries were written by expert programmers whose design goal was to make these functions as efficient as possible. Besides being efficient, these functions are ready for your use, so why bother rewriting them!

This section describes how to use the bsearch() and qsort() functions. The other two search and sort functions follow the same format and can be applied in the same way. All sort and search functions are declared in the stdlib.h header file. If you use any of these functions in your program, be certain to include the stdlib.h header file.

The search and sort functions expect that the array being sorted has consecutive valid elements without any gaps. If you pass an array of *x* elements, these functions expect that the elements from 0 to *x* are valid elements without a single gap.

Searching an Array Using BSEARCH()

The bsearch() function uses a binary search algorithm to search an array of ordered values. Binary search algorithms are extremely fast and, therefore, can operate on extremely large lists very efficiently.

The bsearch() library function works only on ordered lists. To search unordered lists, use lsearch() or lfind().

To use the C++ library bsearch() function, you first must spend some time studying the prototype:

```
void *bsearch(const void *key, void *base, size_t nelem, size_t width,
int (*fcmp) (const void *, const void *));
```

You may be starting to think that people are right to avoid these functions, because the prototype alone appears intimidating! With step-by-step guidance, however, using the function is not as bad as it looks to be.

The following example uses a set of working variables to guide you easily through the description of the function. Consider the following variables as part of a program that will call the bsearch() function:

```
int Array[20]; // Array declaration
int n;    // integer of the number of elements in the array
int Key; // integer that will be searched for a match
```

The following paragraphs discuss each of bsearch() arguments in order. As each argument is discussed, the function is filled in using the variables declared above.

Going through the bsearch() argument list from left to right, the first argument is a pointer to a key value. This item is the item that will be checked for a match. The argument is a pointer argument, so it must be passed as an address. You add the first argument as follows:

Advanced C Programming

```
bsearch(&Key, ...
```

The second argument is the base of the array. This argument also is a pointer. This argument is easy to pass, because an array variable is actually a pointer to the base of the array. The second argument can be passed as it is declared. You add this argument as follows:

```
bsearch(&Key, Array, ...
```

The third argument is the number of elements in the array. This argument does not indicate the size of the array. All the bsearch() function learns from this argument is how many elements within the array it is to process when it searches for a match. This number of elements can be all or part of the declared array—however much of the array you want the bsearch() function to use. This number represents the number of elements of the array that the bsearch() function uses, starting from element 0. You add the third argument as follows:

```
bsearch(&Key, Array, n, ...
```

The fourth argument is the width. The width is the number of bytes required for storing an individual element within the array. For an integer array, the width is the size of an integer (which is two bytes). For a float array, the width is four bytes (the size of a float). Use the sizeof() macro, to ensure that the width is precise for the data type being used. You add the fourth argument as follows:

```
bsearch(&Key, Array, n, sizeof(int), ...
```

The final argument is a pointer to a function. Because the bsearch() function does not know how to compare one element of the array with another to determine that it has reached a match, it relies on you to supply that function. You are not expected to write a searching function. The function's only task is to compare two values. The compare function must support a precise prototype and must return specific values based on a comparison in order to operate.

To use the bsearch() function to search Array, you need to define a compare function that takes compares two integers and determines whether they are equal. The function must follow the two rules as described in table 19.2.

Table 19.2. Rules for a compare function.

Domain	Rule
Arguments	Must have two pointer arguments
Return Value	Must return 0 if the two arguments are equal; < 0 if the first argument is less than the second; > 0 if the first argument is greater than the second

You need to define a compare function for Array that can compare two integers. The following function meets that need:

```
int CompareIntegers(const int *i1, const int *i2)
{
    return (*i1 - *i2);
}
```

The CompareIntegers() function meets both specifications of table 19.2. This function uses two arguments that are pointers. Because the function operates only on integers, the value (*i1 - *i2) is equal to zero if both arguments are the same, is less than 0 if *i1 < *i2, and is greater than 0 if *i1 > *i2.

By adding the compare function as the fifth and final argument, you now can call the bsearch() function, as follows:

```
bsearch(&Key, Array, n, sizeof(int), (int(*)(const void *,const void *)
Compare Integers)
```

A cast is needed for the function argument CompareIntegers, to avoid a compiler error. You can use this same cast whenever you pass the CompareIntegers() function as an argument to any of the search and sort library functions.

The program in listing 19.5 shows how the bsearch() function is used.

Listing 19.5. Example of bsearch().

```
#include <stdlib.h>
#include <stdio.h>

int CompareIntegers(const int *i1, const int *i2)
{
    return (*i1 - *i2);
}

main()
{
```

(continues)

Listing 19.5. Continued.

```
int  Array[] = {100, 200, 300, 400, 500};
     int  Key;
     int  *Match;

     while(1) {

          // Present user with a prompt message

          printf("Enter an integer to match ==>");

          // Prompt user for input

          scanf("%d", &Key);

          // If user enters 0 - exit loop

          if ( Key == 0 ) break;

          // Use bsearch() to find a match

          Match = (int *) bsearch(&Key, Array, 5, sizeof(int),
                  (int(*)(const void *,const void *))
➡CompareIntegers);

          // Display appropriate message depending on match result

          if ( Match != NULL ) printf("%d is in the list.\n", Key);
          else printf("%d is not in the list.\n", Key);
     }

     return 0;
}
```

The program begins by presenting the user with a message that prompts the user to enter a numeric value. The value is then retrieved using scanf(). The scanf() function converts the entered value to an integer and stores it in the Key variable. To stop the processing, the user enters a 0 which triggers a break statement. This break statement exits the loop and the program.

Any nonzero entry causes processing to continue. Using the entered value that is stored in Key, the bsearch() function is called. The bsearch() function uses a binary search algorith to searches the array for a match. This algorithm is optimized for sorted lists, and can find a value in very large lists very efficiently.

The return value of the bsearch() function is a pointer to an array item. The return value equals a valid pointer if the search succeeds. If the search fails, the return value equals NULL, which is zero. The return value is checked for a successful match, and an appropriate message is displayed based on the result of the search.

The benefit of using this approach is that when you have set up the CompareIntegers() and bsearch() functions, the rest of the programming is simple. Additionally, you do not need to write an efficient search function—a task that can be complicated and prone to errors. When you use bsearch(), you never need to worry that the search algorithm is incorrect. Further, because the bsearch() function uses an optimized search, you can run this program on lists of hundreds and thousands of entries very efficiently.

Sorting an Array Using QSORT()

Sorting an array can be a difficult task without the qsort() library function. qsort() is a ready-made function that saves you the trouble of writing a sort routine of your own. Further, qsort() happens to be a very fast sort function. Although many algorithms for sorting exist, few can parallel the efficiency of qsort() for general-purpose list sorting.

Using qsort() is basically the same as using bsearch(). The prototype for qsort() is:

```
void qsort(void *base, size_t nelem, size_t width,
          int(*fcmp)(const void *, const void *));
```

The qsort() arguments are the same as those of bsearch(), minus the first value of bsearch()—the key to search for. A sort requires no key, so qsort() uses only four arguments.

The first function is the pointer of the array to be sorted. Because the array variable is a pointer, this argument can be passed by name with no changes necessary. The next argument is the number of elements in the array. This argument is a size_t integer value, and can be passed as a constant. The third value is another size_t integer that represents the width, in numbers of bytes, of a single element in the array. Because the array is a list of integers, this value is the size of an integer.

The fourth and last argument is the compare function. The compare function, as described in the previous section, compares two values. The compare function has a specific prototype for its arguments and must return particular values, based on comparisons of those arguments. (Refer to table 19.2 for a list of the specifications for the compare function.)

The qsort() function uses the user-supplied compare function to compare two values within the array. qsort() uses it own quick sort algorithm to select which two items to compare. The algorithm is designed to minimize the calls to the compare function while sorting is in progress. The whole process of how the sort is conducted is irrelevant to your use of the qsort() function. The function's purpose, in fact, is to provide you with an efficient sort mechanism that relieves you of having to learn about sort algorithms.

Listing 19.6 is a typical sort testing program. This program accepts as many as 50 numbers from the user and sorts the entered numbers in ascending order, using qsort().

Listing 19.6. Example of qsort().

```
#include <stdlib.h>
#include <stdio.h>

int CompareIntegers(const int *i1, const int *i2)
{
    return (*i1 - *i2);
}

main()
{
    int  Array[50];
    int  i, j;

        // Present initial prompt

    printf("Enter number to be sorted or 0 to start sort\n");

        // Loop to retrieve up to 50 numbers in array

    for ( i = 0, j = 0; i < 50; i++, j++ )
    {
        // Prompt for next number

        printf("Enter next value ==> ");

        // Retrieve next number

        scanf("%d", &Array[i]);

        // Stop retrieving when the user enters 0 or less

        if ( Array[i] <= 0 ) break;
    }

        // Use qsort() to sort array

    qsort(Array, i, sizeof(int),
            (int(*)(const void *,const void *))
    ➥CompareIntegers);

        // Display resulting sorted list
```

```
    for ( i = 0; i < j; i++)
        printf("Item %d is %d\n", i, Array[i]);

    return 0;
}
```

The program begins by displaying a message that prompts the user to enter numbers or 0 to quit.

The program then uses a for loop to read a maximum of 50 integer values. At each round in the loop, a prompt requests the next integer, and follows that request with a `scanf()` function that reads and translates the next input into an integer format. When the entry is retrieved, the entry is checked to determine that it is not less than or equal to 0. If the entry is less than or equal to 0 the program exits the loop.

When the program exits the loop, the variable j contains the number of iterations of the loop. Because each iteration of the loop places another value into the array, the variable j is equal to the number of valid entries in the array. This number is very significant. When the array is passed to `qsort()`, `qsort()` must know how many valid elements the array contains. Even though the size of the array may be 50 elements, the array can contain anywhere from 0 to 50 valid entries. Using `qsort()` with the invalid elements of an array can produce unpredictable results.

In the next phase of the program, `qsort()` sorts the array using its own algorithm. `qsort()` uses the `CompareIntegers()` function whenever it needs to compare two elements within the array.

When the sort is completed, the program executes another for loop, this time to display the sorted list. The lower boundary for the sorted list is 0. `qsort()` places the sorted list in the same place as the original list, only in sorted order. The upper boundary is the value j, which is the number of actual items entered by the user. The for loop displays the item number and value for the number of items entered.

Note that `qsort()` requires no additional memory to operate. `qsort()` uses only the amount of memory it thinks it has with your array. If you declare an array of 100 integers, but tell `qsort()` that the array has 50 elements, then `qsort()` operates as if only 50 elements exist. `qsort()` has no way of knowing that the array is declared with memory for 100 elements, and `qsort` uses only the amount of memory occupied by the first 50 elements in this case.

Summary

Arrays are very useful mechanisms for storing lists of information that require frequent maintenance. This chapter introduced the concepts of working with arrays and discussed various ways in which you can use arrays to solve programming problems.

In addition, the chapter described special library functions that provide a powerful mechanism for working with arrays. After you master these functions, they become another tool that can be leveraged to simplify your programming tasks.

In this chapter, you learned the following:

- Arrays are collections of information that share a common purpose and in which each element is the same type.

- Declaring an array requires a variable name followed by the subscript operator [n], where n is the number of elements in the array.

- You can initialize an array when you declare it by using the form {a, b, c, d...}, where a, b, c, and d are values of the array elements.

- To initialize an array programmatically, set each element of the array individually.

- You can initialize an entire array to null values by using the memset() function.

- To sort elements in an array, use the Turbo C++ library function qsort().

- To find an element in an array, use the Turbo C++ library function bsearch(), lfind(), or lsearch(), each of which searches for a value in an array by using an efficient searching method.

Chapter 20

Using Structures and Unions

Structures are similar to arrays in that they are used to group items. Arrays can group only items of the same data type. Structures, however, enable you to combine items of various data types. Structures are most often used to represent objects within your program. An object is anything that has features or characteristics that are definable.

A *union* is also used to represent objects within your program. Unions have the added feature of enabling you to represent the same object in different ways. Similar to structures, each representation of an object that forms a union can consist of a combination of data types.

This chapter shows you how to do the following:

- Define structures and unions to represent objects within your program

- Use the structures and unions that you create

- Use some of the Turbo C++ built-in structures

Understanding Structures

A structure is a way of representing an object within your program. An object is anything with a set of features or characteristics that you can define. One example of an object is an airplane. All airplanes have common features, such as the type and number of engines, total seats, and so on. What distinguishes one airplane from another is the particular combination of specific features. A structure is a convenient way of representing these different airplanes, or any other definable object, within your program.

Figure 20.1 shows how a description of an airplane is represented by a structure. The structure name is `AirplaneDescription`, and contains the variables that represent specific features of an airplane. These features include the number and type of engines, total seats, and the model name of the airplane. One possible combination of values for this structure represents a two-seater, single-engine propeller plane. Another combination of values describes a 500-seater, four-engine jet aircraft.

Fig. 20.1.
This structure is used for describing airplanes.

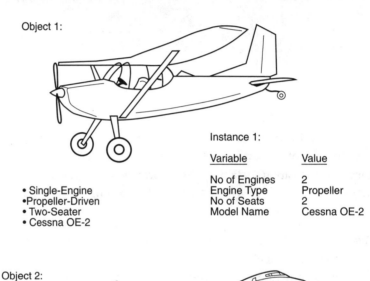

Object 1:

Instance 1:

Variable	Value
No of Engines	2
Engine Type	Propeller
No of Seats	2
Model Name	Cessna OE-2

• Single-Engine
•Propeller-Driven
• Two-Seater
• Cessna OE-2

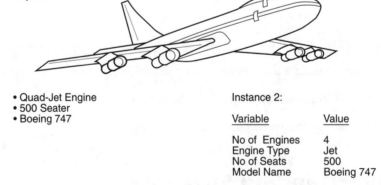

Object 2:

• Quad-Jet Engine
• 500 Seater
• Boeing 747

Instance 2:

Variable	Value
No of Engines	4
Engine Type	Jet
No of Seats	500
Model Name	Boeing 747

The structure of figure 20.1 is useful only for describing airplanes, which is typical of most structures. A structure is generally used to uniquely identify a particular object from a single category of objects. In this case, the AirplaneDescription structure is used to identify a particular airplane among the vast number of those that are available. The structure, however, is not useful for describing cars because the data members of the structure are designed to describe the details of an airplane, which are not relevant to cars. If you want a structure for a car, you must create a second structure that contains data members that describe the features of a car.

The benefit of a structure is that its contents can be managed as a single unit. A complete description of an airplane can be passed to different functions for processing, or saved to a file for future retrieval. It is possible to declare all the variables of AirplaneDescription outside of this structure as individual variables, and manage them yourself whenever you need a complete description of a particular airplane. A structure is easier to use, however, because all the discrete variables are grouped in a convenient package. Then, you can conveniently use this package within your program as a single unit.

Using Structures

Structures are data types, such as int and char. The difference is that the int, char, and other built-in data types have been defined for you. A structure is a data type that you define to suit your programming requirements.

Defining Structures

You declare structures by using the following format:

```
struct tag {
    variable 1 declaration;
    variable 2 declaration;
    variable 3 declaration;
          .
          .
          .
    variable N declaration;
};
```

To declare the function that figure 20.1 discusses, use the following format:

```
struct AirplaneDescription {
    int  NoEngines;
    char EngineType[20];
    int  NoSeats;
    char ModelName[20];
};
```

When you declare a structure, you are only informing the compiler that you intend to use a combination of variables as a unit. You have not yet set aside the memory space for storing any information. To request memory space for storing the values of a structure, declare an instance of your structure within your program by using the following format:

```
struct structure_tag instance_name;
```

The structure_tag is the tag that identifies your structure. For example, to declare an instance of the AirplaneDescription structure, use the following statement:

```
struct AirplaneDescription Airplane1;
```

This statement tells the compiler to set aside enough space to store all the variables that are defined in the AirplaneDescription structure, and give this space a label Airplane1. You can now use the variable Airplane1 to store a complete description of a single airplane. This is certainly easier than requesting space for each individual variable that composes the AirplaneDescription structure!

An extension of this form of declaration combines the structure declaration and the instance declaration of the structure into a single statement, as follows:

```
struct AirplaneDescription {
    int  NoEngines;
    char EngineType[20];
    int  NoSeats;
    char ModelName[20];
} Airplane1;
```

The instance Airplane1 is immediately declared along with the structure AirplaneDescription. This is simply a convenience, which saves you the trouble of later declaring an instance using the struct statement.

Another way exists to declare a structure that is easier to use than the first. The alternative format is as follows:

```
typedef struct {
    variable 1 declaration;
    variable 2 declaration;
    variable 3 declaration;
          .
          .
          .
    variable N declaration;
} tag;
```

Notice that the declaration is now preceded by the word `typedef`, and the tag is at the bottom. The `typedef` tells the compiler that you are registering a data type that can be used in the same way as the built-in data types, such as `int` and `char`. Then, you can use the structure tag as a valid data type as follows:

```
structure_tag instance_name;
```

Using the `AirplaneDescription` structure as an example, you can now declare and use the structure in the following way:

```
typedef struct {
    int  NoEngines;
    char EngineType[20];
    int  NoSeats;
    char ModelName[20];
} AirplaneDescription;
    .
    .
    .

main()
{
    int i;
    AirplaneDescription Airplane1;
    .
    .
    .
}
```

There is no difference between this form of declaration and the previous. The latter form is often used because it is simpler to declare instances of the structure. Notice the identical way in which you can declare an integer and a structure such as `AirplaneDescription`. You can use whichever form of declaring a structure that is easier for you to read. The Turbo C++ compiler manages both forms of the structure declaration identically.

When an instance of a structure is declared, the compiler sets aside enough space to store all the variables of that structure. Figure 20.2 shows the memory layout of a single instance of an `AirplaneDescription` structure. Each variable gets its own storage space as if it had been individually declared. When viewed in memory, there is no difference between declaring either a structure or each of the variables that compose it individually. In both cases, the storage requirements are the same. A structure is used for convenience, to enable you to manage as a single entity several variables that share a common purpose.

III

Advanced C Programming

Fig. 20.2.

This illustration shows memory storage that is laid out for a structure.

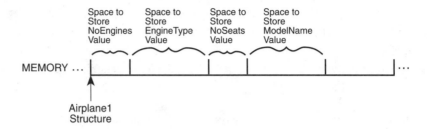

The following example program demonstrates that the sum of the individual variable sizes equals the size of the structure.

```c
#include <stdio.h>

typedef struct
{
    int NoEngines;
    char EngineType[20];
    int NoSeats;
    char ModelType[20];
} AirplaneDescription;

main()
{
    AirplaneDescription Airplane1;

    printf("The size of Airplane1 is %d bytes\n",
➥sizeof(Airplane1));

    return 0;
}
```

The output to the screen reads:

```
The size of Airplane1 is 44 bytes.
```

Recall that the sizeof() macro returns the size of any data type or declared variable in terms of bytes. The AirplaneDescription structure consists of two character buffers that are 20 bytes each, and two integer variables, 2 bytes each. Therefore, the total size of the structure is 44 bytes. Had you declared these variables separately, this exact amount of storage would be used, as well.

Initializing a Structure

You must initialize all the member variables of a structure. This also initializes the structure itself. Similar to arrays, you can initialize the member variables of a structure by using a comma-delimited list.

Consider the following example program:

```
typedef struct {
    int  NoEngines;
    char EngineType[20];
    int  NoSeats;
    char ModelName[20];
} AirplaneDescription;

main()
{
    AirplaneDescription Airplane1 = {1, "propeller", 2, "Cessna 150"};
    .
    .
    .
}
```

The Airplane1 structure is initialized similar to an array. For each member variable of Airplane1, a value is set in curly brackets, with values separated by commas. The sequence of values corresponds to that of variables declared for the AirplaneDescription structure.

The only time that you can set the values of a structure by using comma-delimited values is when an instance of the structure is declared, as in the preceding example. This format is not supported to assign values to a structure elsewhere in your code. The following would not be a valid statement:

```
main()
{
    AirplaneDescription Airplane1;
    .
    .
    .
    Airplane1 = {1, "propeller", 2, "Cessna 150"}; // INVALID STATEMENT!
    .
    .
    .
}
```

An alternative way exists to initialize data in a structure using the C library memset() function. The memset() function sets all the bytes within a memory location to a specific value. You can initialize a structure as follows:

```
main()
{
    AirplaneDescription Airplane1;
    .
    .
    .
    memset(&Airplane1, 0, sizeof(Airplane1));
    .
    .
    .
}
```

The `memset()` function takes three parameters: a memory address, the character you use to initialize the memory location, and the number of bytes to initialize. This is an efficient way of initializing a structure in a single statement within your code. The `memset()` function is generally used to "zero out" a structure: filling it with zeros so that the structure can be identified as unused and ready for input, as opposed to already occupied with data.

Referencing Structure Variables

To reference a structure variable, use the following format:

```
structure.variable
```

For example, to initialize the values of the `AirplaneDescription` structure described earlier in your code, use the following statements:

```
#include <string.h>

typedef struct {
    int  NoEngines;
    char EngineType[20];
    int  NoSeats;
    char ModelName[20];
} AirplaneDescription;

main()
{
    AirplaneDescription Airplane1;

    Airplane1.NoEngines = 1;
    strcpy(Airplane1.EngineType, "propeller");
    Airplane1.NoSeats = 2;
    strcpy(Airplane1.ModelName, "Cessna 150");
    .
    .
    .
}
```

A variable that is part of a structure is used exactly as if it were declared separately, except that it is preceded by the structure name and a '`.`'. Therefore, the `NoEngines` member variable, which is an integer, is assigned by using the standard integer assignment operator; `EngineType`, which is a character buffer, is assigned by using the C library string function `strcpy()`.

Using Pointers to Structures

A structure is similar to any built-in data type, such as `int` or `char`, except that you can define its layout. You can, therefore, use `*` to declare a pointer to a structure, and `&` to return the address of a structure, just as you would any other data type.

To declare a pointer to a structure, use the following:

```
typedef struct {
    int  NoEngines;
    char EngineType[20];
    int  NoSeats;
    char ModelName[20];
} AirplaneDescription;

main()
{
    AirplaneDescription * pAirplane1;  // Declaration of pointer to
                                       // an AirplaneDescription
structure
         .
         .
         .
}
```

In this case, pAirplane1 is strictly a pointer to an AirplaneDescription structure. In this example, no storage space was allocated. You can use the
pAirplane1 pointer to an AirplaneDescription structure whose storage has
been declared elsewhere. If you read Chapter 18, "Using Pointers," this concept should be familiar. The chapter describes the use of pointers for the
built-in data types. It might appear a little unusual at first, but keep in mind
that a structure operates the same as any other data type, except that you
define its layout.

A structure is stored the same as any other data type. Therefore, all pointer
operators work on structures as they do on built-in data types, such as int
and char.

The use of & is also equally applicable to a structure as it is to a data type,
such as int or char. The following code fragment demonstrates this point:

```
main()
{
    AirplaneDescription * pAirplane1;  // Declares a pointer to
                                       // an AirplaneDescription
structure

    AirplaneDescription Airplane1;     // Declares an
AirplaneDescription structure

    int *pInteger1;                    // Declares a pointer to an integer

    int Integer1;               // declares an integer
```

III

Advanced C Programming

```
    pAirplane = &Airplane1;   // Assign the address of Airplane1
                              // to pAirplane1

    pInteger1 = &Integer1;    // Assign the address of integer1
                              // to pInteger1
        .
        .
        .

}
```

The pointer pAirplane1 is assigned the address of the location in memory in which **Airplane1** is stored. pAirplane1 operates the same as a pointer to any other data type. The example code uses an integer pointer and variable to demonstrate that using the pointer to an integer is the same as using a pointer to a structure. Both have a memory location in which the contents of the data type is stored. A pointer is the address of the variable it represents, which can equally be an integer or a structure.

Consider the following example program which demonstrates a typical use of a structure:

```
#include <stdio.h>

typedef struct
{
    char ItemName[20];
    int  Quantity;
    float    Price;
    float    Total;
} Invoice;

main()
{
    Invoice Invoice1;

        // Prompt for invoice data

    printf("Enter your purchase order in the following format:\n\
    Item      Quantity  Price/Unit\n");

    scanf("%s %d %f", Invoice1.ItemName,
            &Invoice1.Quantity, &Invoice1.Price);

        // Calculate total purchase price

    Invoice1.Total = Invoice1.Quantity * Invoice1.Price;

        // Display purchase information to user

    printf("You have purchase %d units of %s at a price of %5.2f\
➥per unit\n\
```

```
        for a total purchase price of %7.2f.\n", Invoice1.Quantity,
    ➥Invoice1.ItemName,
            Invoice1.Price, Invoice1.Total);

        return 0;
    }
```

The program prompts for the name, quantity, and price of an item for purchase. When the user enters these amounts, the program calculates the total. Then, the program displays the total back to the user using the `printf()` function. Note that any time a member variable of the structure `Invoice1` is used, it is prefaced by `"Invoice1"`. This is the variable name of an instance of the `Invoice` structure that is declared at the top of `main()`.

When using this program, it is important to note that working with a structure of variables does not appear very different than had the variables been declared separately outside of a structure. Had the variables been declared separately, the entire code would not require much change. In fact, by simply removing the prefix `"Invoice1"` from each variable, and making sure that the variables are declared at the top of `main()`, everything else would remain the same.

If using the member variables is the same as employing the variables separately, why bother combining them in a structure? The answer is that a structure simplifies the task of managing a collection of information when it needs to be shared by various functions. Using a structure to represent this information enables you to manage the information as a unit. Listing 20.1 is an expanded version of the invoice program that more clearly demonstrates the benefit of grouping information using a structure as compared with declaring the information as separate variables.

Listing 20.1. Use structures to simplify programming.

```
    #include <stdio.h>
    #include <string.h>

    typedef struct
    {
        char ItemName[20];
        int  Quantity;
        float     Price;
        float     Total;
    } Invoice;

    int ValidateEntry(Invoice * AnInvoice)
    {
        char *ValidItems[] = {"flour", "sugar", "salt"};
```

(continues)

Listing 20.1. Continued.

```
int i, nReturn = 0;

        // Check that quantity is between 1 and 10 items

    if ( AnInvoice->Quantity <= 0 ||
         AnInvoice->Quantity > 10 )
    {
        // Display error

        printf("Quantity is not between 1 and 10\n");
        return 0;
    }

        // Check that item is one of the items in stock

    for ( i = 0; i < 3; i++ )
    {
        if ( !strcmpi(AnInvoice->ItemName, ValidItems[i]) )
        {
            nReturn = 1;
            break;
        }
    }

    if ( nReturn == 0 )
    {
        // Display error

        printf("%s is not an in-stock item\n", AnInvoice->ItemName);
    }

    return nReturn;
}

void DisplayInvoice(Invoice& AnInvoice)
{
        // Display purchase information to user

    printf("You have purchase %d units of %s at a price of %5.2f per
unit\n\
for a total purchase price of %7.2f.\n", AnInvoice.Quantity,
AnInvoice.ItemName,
        AnInvoice.Price, AnInvoice.Total);
}

main()
{
    Invoice Invoice1;

        // Loop to retrieve invoice data until
        // user enters "done" for item

    while(1) {

        // Prompt for invoice data
```

```
        printf("\nEnter your purchase order for 1 - 10 items that are
➥in stock\n\
Enter \"done\" as an item to quit.  Use the following format:\n\n\
Item       Quantity  Price/Unit\n");

        scanf("%s %d %f", Invoice1.ItemName,
              &Invoice1.Quantity, &Invoice1.Price);

        // Quit when user enters "done"

    if ( !strcmpi(Invoice1.ItemName, "done") )
        break;

        // Call function to validate values entered

    if ( ValidateEntry(&Invoice1) )
    {
        // Calculate total purhcase price
        // if information entered is valid...

        Invoice1.Total = Invoice1.Quantity * Invoice1.Price;

        // Then display invoice

        DisplayInvoice(Invoice1);
    }
    else
        // Otherwise display an error message

        printf("Invalid entry.  Try again\n\n");
    }

    return 0;
}
```

The program of listing 20.1 prompts the user for a purchase order, then displays it if the information entered is valid. The program uses a separate function for validating a user's entry and also displaying the result back to the user.

The program first declares an invoice structure to maintain the combined information that pertains to a purchase order. This information can now be used collectively by referencing the Invoice1 variable, or individually by referencing one of the member variables of Invoice1. This is very useful when passing the purchase order information to other functions. The program enters a while loop that keeps prompting the user for more purchase orders until the word "done" is entered for the item to purchase.

Within the while loop, the program prompts the user for a purchase order using scanf(). The information is read into the Invoice1 structure. A check is done to determine whether the user wants to exit from the loop by comparing the ItemName member variable of the Invoice1 structure to the word "done". If this test succeeds, and the user wants to exit, a break is called that causes the program flow to continue past the while loop. Then, the program terminates. Otherwise, the next step is executed, which is validating the purchase order information entered by the user.

The information entered is validated by using a function called ValidateEntry. The function returns a 1 (true) if the information entered is correct. Otherwise, it returns a 0 (false). The function takes a pointer to an Invoice structure. Notice that the function declaration for using a pointer to a structure is the same as for any other data type. The address of the Invoice1 structure is passed using the & (address of) operator. (For more information on passing pointer arguments to a function, refer to Chapter 18, "Using Pointers.")

The purpose of the ValidateEntry() function is to verify that the information entered by the user is valid for processing. The function conducts two tests. The first is to determine that the quantity of items ordered is between one and 10. An if statement is used for this test. Notice how the function refers to a member variable of AnInvoice:

```
if ( AnInvoice->Quantity <= 0 ||
        AnInvoice->Quantity > 10 )
```

The -> is used to access a member variable for a pointer to a structure in the same way that '.' is used to access the member variables of a structure itself. No difference exists between -> and '.' except that the former operates on a pointer to a structure, and the latter, on the structure itself.

If the quantity test fails, the program displays an appropriate error message, and returns a 0 (false). Otherwise, processing continues to the next test.

The second test done in the ValidateEntry() function is to ensure that the item selected is in stock. This is done with an array of string pointers initialized to the valid stock items. (For more information on using arrays as lookup tables, refer to Chapter 19.) An internal variable nReturn is set to 0 (false). A lookup (finding a match based on a key) to the valid stock items is done. If a match is found then the nReturn variable is set to 1 (true). This value is returned to indicate to the calling function whether all tests succeeded. Notice that here too a -> is used to reference the ItemName member variable. The AnInvoice variable is declared as a pointer to an Invoice structure, so all member variables referenced within this function must be accessed using -> rather than '.'.

The `validate` function could have taken two separate variable arguments, one for the item name, and another for the quantity. However, it is easier to use a single argument that is a structure which combines all the data entered for a purchase order, than to pass these values as separate items. This difference becomes more dramatic when many items need to be validated. The choice is between using one argument that is a structure or many arguments that represent the individual structure member variables. Obviously, dealing with one structure is easier.

When a call to the `ValidateEntry()` function succeeds, the purchase order information is displayed to the user. A separate function is used for this purpose. The `Invoice` structure is now passed by reference, rather than by pointer, to demonstrate that there is no difference between using a structure data type and a built-in data type. They both can be passed by reference. Notice that within the `DisplayInvoice()` function, the structure is used as if you were declaring it within the function, rather than as a pointer. The member variables of `AnInvoice` are accessed using '`.`' because the `DisplayInvoice()` function treats the `AnInvoice` structure that is passed by reference as if it were an internally-declared structure. This is the same as with all other data types that are passed by reference.

The `DisplayInvoice()` function could have been defined with four arguments, one for each variable of the `Invoice` structure. However, it is evident that the `DisplayInvoice()` function is easier to create and use with the single `Invoice` structure argument.

If the `ValidateEntry()` function returns false, an appropriate error message is displayed. Then, the program flow returns to the top of the loop. Here, the user is prompted for another purchase order.

Using Unions

A union is the same as a structure in that it represents an object. The union extends the concept of a structure by enabling you to represent the same object in varying ways using different groups of variables. By using a union, you can access the same memory area by using different formats. For example, the same memory can be used to store an integer as well as a string.

Declaring a Union

A union has the following declaration:

```
union tag {
      variable 1 declaration;
      variable 2 declaration;
      variable 3 declaration;

              .
              .
              .

      variable N declaration;
};
```

The following is an example of declaring a union, then using it:

```
typedef union {
      int   Integer1;
      char Buffer1[20];
} Example;

main()
{
      Example Ex1;    // declare union
```

Using a union is the same as employing a structure. This includes how to declare a union, access its member variables, and how to use a pointer to a union, and passing unions as arguments as you do for structures. Notice from the preceding example that the typedef statement and declaration follow the same format used for a structure.

Understanding Unions

Although the usage and declaration of a union appear to be identical to that of a structure, the compiler treats the two very differently. Whereas the compiler allocates new space in sequence for each variable declared in a structure, the compiler reuses the same spot in memory for a union. The first variable declaration of a union starts at the same location in memory as the Nth variable declaration.

This might sound absurd at first, but there is a purpose and utility to this variation of a structure. Consider the following example program:

```
#include <stdio.h>
#include <string.h>

typedef union
{
    float     PriceLevel;
    char Category[20];
} ProductClassification;

main()
```

```
    {
        ProductClassification     Product1;

            // Assign price level of

        Product1.PriceLevel = 20.00;

            // Display price level

        printf("Product 1 price level is: $%5.2f\n", Product1.PriceLevel);

            // Assign product category

        strcpy(Product1.Category, "Dry Goods");

            // Display product category

        printf("Product 1 category is: %s\n", Product1.Category);

            // Redisplay product price level

        printf("Product 1 price level is: $%5.2f\n", Product1.PriceLevel);

        return 0;
    }
```

The following is the output of the program:

```
Product 1 price level is: $20.00
Product 1 category is: Dry Goods
Product 1 price level is: $0.00
```

The program uses simple assignments to initialize the value of the PriceLevel member variable of Product1, and displays it on-screen. Then, the program assigns the Category member variable of Product1, and displays that on the screen. So far, the results have been predictable. However, when it goes back to redisplay the PriceLevel member variable of Product1, it has been mysteriously set to 0. To understand the reason for this, refer to figure 20.3.

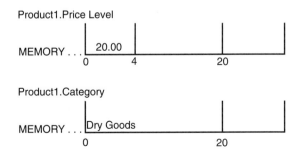

Fig. 20.3.
This figure illustrates a representation of the Product Classification Union.

Unlike a structure, a union only stores as many bytes as necessary for the largest member variable that it contains. In the case of the ProductClassification union, the PriceLevel is 4 bytes long because it is a float. Also, the Category member variable is a 20-byte character array (or buffer). Whereas a structure would set aside 24 bytes to store both these values simultaneously, a union sets aside just 20, and only stores one or the other member variable at a given time.

The previous example uses a union that can be applied to a grocer who needs to review inventory using different classifications, such as a price level or a category of food. At any given time, the grocer only views the inventory based on a single classification, whether it is by price level of all the goods in the store or by category. In this case, there is no need to view two separate classifications simultaneously, because one has little to do with the other.

To see what happens to the Product1 union as the program executes, follow the illustration in figure 20.3. When the example program first assigns a value of 20 to the PriceLevel category, the memory location assigned by the compiler to Product1 resembles the first diagram in figure 20.3.

When the Category member variable is subsequently assigned a value, the compiler uses the complete union location, starting at the beginning of the Product1 memory area, and enters there the value "Dry Goods". This overwrites any previous value assigned to that location, as the second diagram of figure 20.3 illustrates.

When working with a union, the compiler assumes that the use of the member variables are mutually exclusive, and that it can overwrite the space every time you reassign any member variable of the union.

This is the reason the third line of text in the output is an unexpected value. By this time, the term "Dry Goods" has been entered into the location in memory that is referenced by the PriceLevel member variable, as well. Displaying that location in memory as a float produces unexpected results.

Benefits of Using a Union

The primary benefit of using a union is that it is efficient with respect to memory allocation. Whereas a structure allocates space for each individual member variable that it contains, a union only designates sufficient room to store its largest member variable.

The assumption made with a union is that you will never need two member variables at the same time. If you have a task that fits this description, a union is more memory-efficient than a structure.

Using C Library Structures

One of the important reasons for understanding how to use structures is to be able to employ the many useful C library functions that rely on them. Some of the more commonly used functions of this type are reviewed in the next few sections.

Using *getdate()* and the Date Structure

A useful C library function that retrieves the current system date is `getdate()`. The following is the `getdate()` function prototype:

```
void getdate(struct date *datep);
```

The `getdate()` function uses a single argument that is a pointer to a structure referred to as `date`. This structure is defined in the DOS.H header file as:

```
struct date
{
    int  da_year;
    int  da_day;
    int  da_mon;
}
```

Three values always need to be associated with a date: day, month, and year. Therefore, it was easier for the designers of the Turbo C++ library to use a structure for a date rather than having to deal with day, month, and year variables separately.

The `getdate()` function updates the date structure that is passed as an argument. The argument is a pointer to your program's date structure that is defined, so the `getdate()` function can update its address. When the function returns, the value of the day, month, and year have been set in the date structure.

The following contains an example of how to use the `getdate()` function:

```
#include <dos.h>
#include <stdio.h>

int main(void)
{
    struct date d; // declare a date structure
```

```
    // Get the current date

getdate(&d);

    // Display the date in mm/dd/yyyy format

printf("The current date in mm/dd/yyyy format is: %d/%d/%d\n",
        d.da_mon, d.da_day, d.da_year);

return 0;
}
```

This program retrieves the current system date, and displays it on the screen. Notice that the date structure is passed to the `getdate()` function using the `&` operator. The `getdate()` function takes a pointer to the date structure. Therefore, you must pass the address of the date structure to the function. When the date structure is set to the current date, it is then displayed using `printf()`.

Using *gettime()* and the Time Structure

The current system time can be retrieved using the function `gettime()`. The prototype for `gettime()` is defined in dos.h as

```
void gettime(struct time *timep);
```

The `gettime()` function takes a single argument that serves as a pointer to a structure time. The time structure contains all the member variables necessary to describe time. It is defined as

```
struct time
{
    unsigned char  ti_min;
    unsigned char  ti_hour;
    unsigned char  ti_hund;
    unsigned char  ti_sec;
}
```

The time structure uses a separate variable to store the minute, hours, hundredth of a second, and second of time. When passed to the `gettime()` function, the time structure is set to the current system time.

Use `gettime()` as follows:

```
#include    <stdio.h>
#include    <dos.h>

int main(void)
{
    struct  time t;

        // Retrieve system time
```

```
    gettime(&t);

      // Display time

    printf("The current time is: %2d:%02d:%02d.%02d\n",
           t.ti_hour, t.ti_min, t.ti_sec, t.ti_hund);

    return 0;
  }
```

The gettime() function is used to fill a time structure. The gettime() function takes a pointer to a time structure as an argument. Therefore, the address
of the time structure instance t is passed to gettime(). Once the time structure is set to the current system time, it is displayed using the printf()
function.

Using *findfirst()*, *findnext()* and the File Block Structure

A set of C library functions that are indispensable to anyone writing programs that use the DOS directory includes findfirst() and findnext(). These
functions find the first and next files, respectively, that match a given file
specification. The prototype of the findfirst() function is defined in the
dir.h header file as

```
    int findfirst(const char *pathname, struct ffblk *ffblk, int attrib);
```

The first argument is a string that determines the path and file specification
to use for searching among a number of files. Any DOS directory path is valid
for this function, such as

```
    *.*
    *.cpp
    \*.?00
```

This argument is used to confine the search to the specific files that match
the path specification provided.

The second argument is a pointer to a ffblk structure. This structure is the
file block structure, and describes a file. It is defined in the dos.h header file
as

```
    struct ffblk {
      char ff_reserved[21]; /* reserved by DOS */
      char ff_attrib;       /* attribute found */
      int  ff_ftime;        /* file time */
      int  ff_fdate;        /* file date */
      long ff_fsize;        /* file size */
      char ff_name[13];     /* found file name */
    };
```

The member variables are self-explanatory. The file block structure contains all the information necessary to describe a file.

The third argument of the findfirst() function is the attribute of the file for which to search. The possible values of the attributes are defined as constants in the dos.h header file as table 20.1 shows.

Table 20.1. The *findfirst()* function.

Attribute	Description
FA_NORMAL	Any file
FA_RDONLY	Read-only file
FA_HIDDEN	Hidden file
FA_SYSTEM	System file
FA_LABEL	Volume label
FA_DIREC	Directory
FA_ARCH	Archive

By using the attribute argument, you can narrow the file search to a specific type of file, such as a directory or a hidden file.

The return value for the findfirst() function is 0 (false) if a match is discovered, and 1 (true) if no match is found. Although this can appear contrary to what you might expect, it is useful to have the return values set in this way, as the example program later in this section demonstrates.

The findfirst() function is often used in conjunction with the findnext() function. This, too, is declared in the DIR.H header file as

```
int findnext(struct ffblk *ffblk);
```

The findnext() function can only be used after a ffblk structure is filled by a call to the findfirst() function. The only argument findnext() requires is a pointer to a ffblk structure. It implicitly uses the pathname and attrib arguments of the original call to findfirst() to continue the search for matching files using the same specifications. If another subsequent match is found, the ffblk structure is filled with the appropriate information, and findnext() returns a 0. Otherwise, findnext() returns a 1 if no subsequent matching file is found.

The following example program displays the current directory for all matching files:

```
#include <dir.h>
#include <stdio.h>

main()
{
    ffblk    ffblk;
    int  done = 0;

        // Display heading

    printf("My directory listing\n\tFile\t\tSize (in bytes) \n");

        // Initiate directory list

    done = findfirst("*.*", &ffblk, 0);

        // Start loop to go through directory

    while (!done)
    {
        // Display listing of last file retrieved

        printf("\t%s\t%ld\n", ffblk.ff_name, ffblk.ff_fsize);

        // Get next file

        done = findnext(&ffblk);
    }

    return 0;
}
```

The example program first displays a header line of text that indicates what information is about to be displayed. The program then uses `findfirst()` to fill a file block structure with the first file that matches the `*.*` specification, which is any file in the directory. No specific path is given. Therefore, the current directory is assumed. The return value is placed in a variable called `done`. The variable `done` is set to `true` (1) if no match is found. Otherwise, it is set to `0` (`false`) if a match is discovered.

The program continues in a loop as long as Done is not equal to `true`—that is, providing there is any subsequent file in the directory. If there is a match, both the file name and size are displayed on the screen.

With each iteration of the `while` loop, a call to `findnext()` is executed that fills the file block structure, and returns a value to the Done variable. As long as there is another file in the directory, `findnext()` returns 0, and the while loop continues. In this way, the program displays the entire directory, similar to the DOS directory command.

III

Advanced C Programming

Using an Array of Objects

A structure describes a single object of a category of them. To describe a list of objects of a given category, use an array of them. Using an array of objects is the same as using an array of any other data type. Due to its significance for programming many tasks, using array structures is covered separately here.

Most computer users are familiar with the notion of a database. It is a set of rows, each of which contains information in a set pattern. Every row in a database is, in fact, a structure. An entire database is an array of structures. The significance of knowing how to work with an array of structures is that you can then work with databases that you create and control.

Programming many popular tasks requires the knowledge of how to manipulate lists of information that can be represented as a database. For example, maintaining an inventory list, or a register of employees, are basically database-oriented tasks that are most efficiently represented within a program as an array of structures.

Fortunately, using an array of structures should be familiar. An array of structures is similar to any other array. To demonstrate this, listing 20.2 uses an array of structures to modify the previous program of this chapter that displays purchase orders. This version takes up to 10 purchase orders, and calculates the total price for each. Then, the total price of the complete order is calculated.

Listing 20.2. This purchase order program uses an array of structures to update its information.

```
#include <stdio.h>
#include <string.h>

typedef struct
{
    char ItemName[20];
    int  Quantity;
    float    Price;
    float    Total;
} Invoice;

int ValidateEntry(Invoice * AnInvoice)
{
    struct {
        char ItemName[20];
        float Price;
```

```
        } ValidItems[] = {"flour", 2.50,
                   "sugar", 3.00,
                   "salt", 1.50};

    int i, nReturn = 0;

        // Check that quantity is between 1 and 10 items

    if ( AnInvoice->Quantity <= 0 ||
         AnInvoice->Quantity > 10 )
    {
        // Display error

        printf("Quantity is not between 1 and 10\n");
        return 0;
    }

        // Check that item is one of the items in stock

    for ( i = 0; i < 3; i++ )
    {
        if ( !strcmpi(AnInvoice->ItemName, ValidItems[i].ItemName) )
        {
            nReturn = 1;
            AnInvoice->Price = ValidItems[i].Price;
            break;
        }
    }

    if ( nReturn == 0 )
    {
        // Display error

        printf("%s is not an in-stock item\n", AnInvoice->ItemName);
    }

    return nReturn;
}

void DisplayInvoice(Invoice& AnInvoice)
{
        // Display purchase information to user

    printf("\t%s\t%d\t%5.2f\t%7.2f\n", AnInvoice.ItemName,
➡AnInvoice.Quantity,
        AnInvoice.Price, AnInvoice.Total);
}

main()
{
    Invoice Invoices[10];
    int  i, j;
    float    Total;

        // Display instructions

        printf("\nEnter your purchase order for any of the 10 items
➡that are in stock\n\
```

(continues)

Listing 20.2. Continued.

```
Enter \"done\" as an item to quit.  Use the following format:\n\n\
Item     Quantity\n");

        // Loop to retrieve invoice data until
        // user enters "done" for item or until
        // 10 items are entered, whichever comes first

    for ( i = 0; i < 10; i++ )
    {
        // Prompt for invoice data

        scanf("%s %d", Invoices[i].ItemName, &Invoices[i].Quantity);

            // Quit when user enters "done"

        if ( !strcmpi(Invoices[i].ItemName, "done") )
            break;

            // Call function to validate values entered

        if ( ValidateEntry(&Invoices[i]) )
        {
            // Calculate total purchase price
            // if information entered is valid...

            Invoices[i].Total = Invoices[i].Quantity *
➥Invoices[i].Price;
        }
        else
        {
            // Otherwise display an error message

            printf("Invalid entry.  Try again\n\n");

            // Decrement counter to reuse current invoice structure

            i--;
        }
    }

        // Display heading for summary listing

    printf("\n\nThe complete listing of this purchase order is:\n\n\
\tItem\tQuan\tPrice\tTotal\n\n");


    for ( j = 0, Total = 0; j < i; j++ )
    {
        DisplayInvoice(Invoices[j]);
        Total += Invoices[j].Total;
    }

    printf("The total amount of this purchase order is: %5.2f\n",
➥Total);

    return 0;
}
```

Various changes have been made from the original program in listing 20.1. In this version, the ValidateEntry() function now uses an internal array of structures to maintain a list of items in stock as well as their prices. The array of structures enables you to specify a more useful lookup table, as each item can be associated with useful information. In this case, the stock item is associated with a price that is fixed for that item. Note how information in this lookup table is initialized.

The second change is that the main() program uses a loop to ensure that, at most, only 10 iterations of the loop are executed. The reason is that the entire purchase order is maintained in an array of Invoice structures that is declared at the top of main(). The Invoices array only declares space for 10 Invoice structures.

When the user finishes entering items, the program displays the resulting list of items purchased as a complete invoice. The invoice is, in fact, a database listing, because it consists of rows of information that have a set format. The total price of the invoice is also calculated and displayed. This is possible because the entire invoice is maintained in memory.

Summary

This chapter introduced the various ways that structures can be used to facilitate programming. The basic use of a structure is to group various elements into a single entity to simplify managing them. This use of structures can be extended to cover many areas of programming tasks that require keeping track of objects or groups of information.

The following topics were covered in this chapter:

■ How to recognize structures

■ How to define, declare, initialize, and use structures to manage groups of information

■ How to translate into structures actual objects so that they can be represented within a program

■ How to use pointers with structures

■ How to define, declare, initialize, and use unions

III

Advanced C Programming

■ How to recognize differences between unions and structures

■ How to use structures of C library functions

■ How to use an array of structures to implement an application with database functionality

Part IV

C++ and Object-Oriented Programming

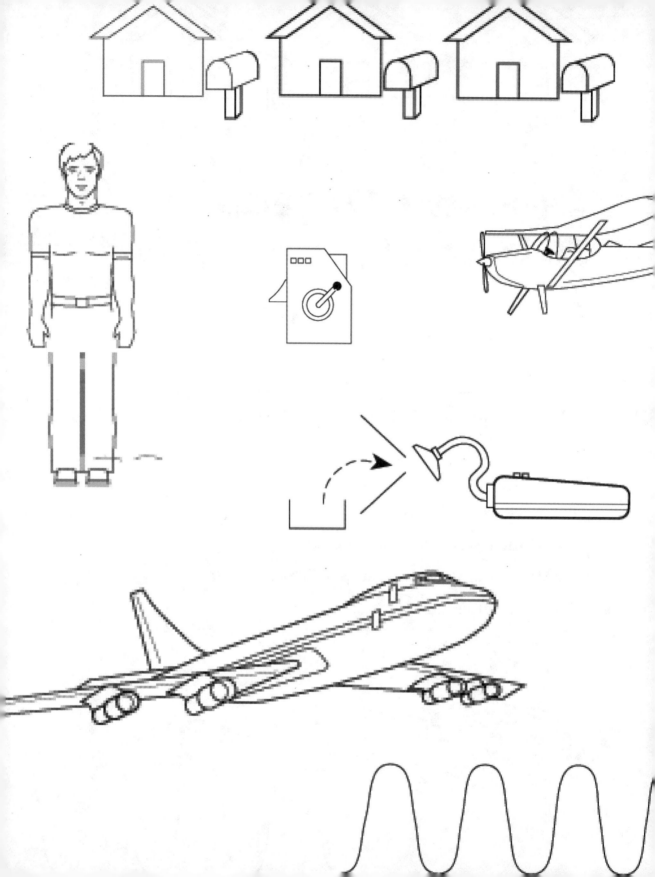

Chapter 21

Introduction to Object-Oriented Programming

Now that you understand the concepts of both structured programming and data structures, you can learn about another method that combines these two concepts: object-oriented programming. Object-oriented programming has received a great deal of press lately, and has the attention of most organizations involved in software development. Certainly, it is the most significant change in the way that programmers develop software since the introduction of structured programming years ago.

As you might recall from the initial discussion in Chapter 1, object-oriented programming is supported with the release of the C++ programming language and therefore is supported in Turbo C++.

Today, C++ is the standard object-oriented programming language, but others exist such as Smalltalk, Actor, and Eifle. More than 90 percent of object-oriented applications developed today use the C++ language. You can begin creating object-oriented applications immediately. No additional software, header files, or libraries are required.

Object-oriented programming, or OOP, is a new method of programming and a new way to think about this task. OOP adheres to an *object-oriented model* that defines how your application is constructed, and the concepts behind its operation. The object-oriented model provides better paradigms and tools for doing the following:

- Modeling your applications as close to actual objects and situations as possible

- Creating reusable software components

■ Creating extensible libraries for reuse

■ The ability to modify and extend the implementation of the objects

In this chapter, you are introduced to the world of object-oriented concepts and OOP. Here is the place in which you begin your journey toward using object-oriented programming concepts in your own Turbo C++ applications. The details about how OOP is implemented in Turbo C++ are explained in upcoming chapters.

Take some time to learn the concepts presented here. Even if you are an experienced structured programmer, you will benefit from learning about the basics of OOP before diving into your first object-oriented application. The better you understand OOP conceptually, the easier it is to implement in your application.

Why Use Object-Oriented Programming?

OOP saves programming time because of a feature of OOP called *inheritance*. Inheritance provides the ability to maximize the reuse of existing programming code. By far, this concept is the most compelling reason to use OOP. Inheritance enables you to inherit characteristics (methods and data) from other objects, and use them in your program as if you created them yourself. A *method* is function, and *data* is information contained or encapsulated in an object.

After objects are defined, they can be stored in a library for use by other objects, applications, or programmers. This is similar conceptually to structured programs, reusing code by invoking functions. Just as you can purchase function libraries to extend the programming language, you are able to buy object libraries for the same reason. Other OOP concepts include class, object, encapsulation, messages, libraries, and polymorphism.

Object-Oriented versus Structured Programming

In the previous chapters, you learned that a structured program contains data that is passive. Information is passed from one function to another by using an external subroutine (see figure 21.1). Functions call other functions on a continual basis.

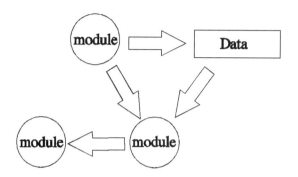

Fig. 21.1.
Information is
passed from one
function to
another in a
structured
program.

Object-oriented programming enables you to define objects that contain data structures, in much the same way data structures are implemented in structured programs. The difference is that methods are included in an object to control how the data it contains is manipulated.

A method can be defined as a small structured program within an object. These methods define how the object behaves. Figure 21.2 shows a model of a class. A class defines an object. Notice how the methods surround the data contained in that object. The concept of sealing data and methods into an object is known as *encapsulation*. (This concept is explained later.)

The definition of both a class and an object might confuse you. A *class* is the blueprint for an object. An *object* is an instance of a class. In other words, a class is how an object is defined, and an object is created when the program is invoked from the class definition.

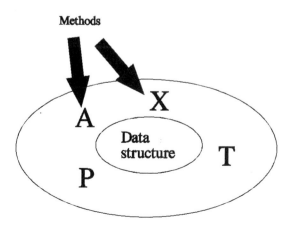

Fig. 21.2.
The methods
surround the data
contained in an
object.

You can mix structured and object-oriented concepts in your application. However, it generally is a better idea to make your program adhere to object-oriented programming concepts as much as possible. In the next section of this chapter, the concepts of object-oriented programming are discussed in greater detail.

Object-Oriented Programming Concepts

Now that you know some basics of OOP, you can study its concepts. This chapter covers these OOP concepts:

- Class

- Object

- Encapsulation

- Inheritance

- Messages

- Polymorphism

It is very important that you understand these concepts so that you can implement them in your application.

Class

A *class* is a software implementation of an object type. It defines methods that apply to each object a class defines. For example, a Student class can include data, such as the following:

```
student_name

student_address

student_number

student_phone

student_state

student_zip
```

A class also defines the permissible operations that control how the preceding data is manipulated inside an object defined by our class. Our `Student` class could include operations or methods, such as *suspend*, *graduate*, and *change* phone number. The details of the method of operations are defined in the class. Figure 21.3 depicts a model of the `Student` class previously defined.

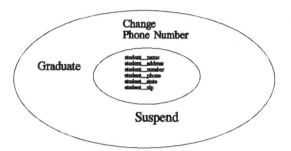

Fig. 21.3.
This illustration is a model of the `Student` class.

Object

An *object* by definition is an instance of a class. It is sometimes defined as the runtime version of a class. An object represents things that actually exist or are conceptual in nature. For example, you may create an object that represents a physical concept such as an employee, company, or car; or, an object may represent something abstract such as equations or economics (see figure 21.4).

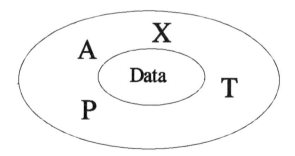

Fig. 21.4.
You can use an object to store data and methods used to retrieve it.

Almost anything can be an object, such as the following:

■ A bill

■ A company

■ An icon on a screen

- A window

- A data item

- A device

An object can contain other objects. These objects can contain additional ones, as well. For example, you can define an object from the Student class from the previous example (see figure 21.5).

Fig. 21.5.

The Student Object.

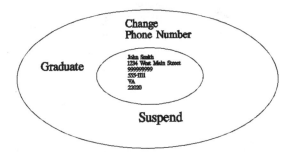

Notice how actual data is now contained inside the objects. The methods that surround the data control how other external processes access the data on a student(s).

If another message is received, instructing the Student object to change the phone number, the method responsible for performing that operation executes and alters the phone number (see figures 21.6 and 21.7). Remember, the object controls how the data contained within it is altered, not external modules as in most structured programs.

Fig. 21.6.

A message is sent to change the student's phone number.

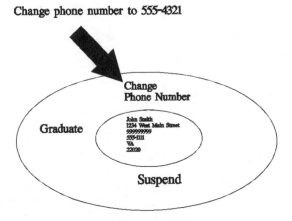

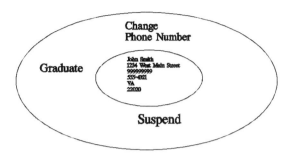

Fig. 21.7.
The illustration shows the object after the phone number is changed.

Inheritance

Now that you understand the concepts of class and object, you can explore the most powerful aspect of OOP, inheritance. *Inheritance* is the capability of creating an object or class that has all of the characteristics (functions, data, behavior, and properties) of a parent object, or an existing object that is used to create a new one.

For example, figure 21.8 shows how information is inherited from an object. Notice how methods denoted by A, X, P, T are inherited by the child object below it. Also notice, a new method Z has been added to the new object.

You can inherit characteristics from an object. Then, you can add additional characteristics, if needed. Therefore, you can use someone else's object as a starting point for your own. The idea is finding the correct object from which to inherit. Remember, you can use objects that you create, or those that are purchased (such as Borland's Object Windows Library that comes with Borland's C++ Application Framework). Objects stored for reuse by other applications and programmers are called class libraries. They are discussed later.

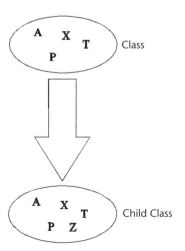

Fig. 21.8.
Information is inherited from an object.

For example, figure 21.9 shows how inheritance is fully exploited. A new file dialog box with many "bells and whistles" is created from an existing dialog box object. The programmer need only create a new object from this existing one, and add the additional characteristics needed, such as radio buttons, text fields, colors, and graphics.

Using inheritance correctly can save virtually hundreds of programming hours, and makes the best use of OPC—Other People's Code.

Fig. 21.9.
You can use inheritance to create a custom file dialog box.

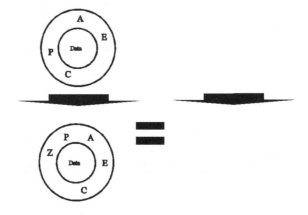

Inheritance by Example

You can further explore this OOP concept of inheritance by creating an example. Pretend that you are in the auto business, and you need to produce several types of vehicles. Using object-oriented concepts, you define a standard generic vehicle (see figure 21.10) that has the characteristics you want for all of your vehicles. The following includes these characteristics:

- A frame

- Four tires

- A body

- A medium-powered engine

If you have ever owned a car, you know that several items are missing. This is just a generic car object. No one is going to drive it yet. From this generic object, you inherit the generic properties of a car, and use them as a basis for the different types of vehicles you are going to sell.

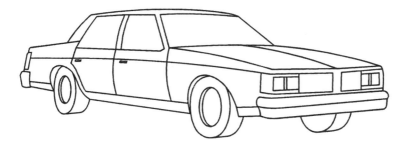

IV

Object-Oriented Programming

In this example, you would like to build sports cars and trucks. Using the characteristics of our generic car, two new objects are created, truck and sports car. Therefore, each new object has all the characteristics of the generic car object from which it was derived: frame, four tires, body, and an engine.

The truck object can modify itself to include larger tires (just a small change to the tire characteristic inherited), a cab, and a truck bed. However, it uses the same engine and body that is passed down from the generic vehicle object.

The sports car object can modify itself to include high performance tires, a streamlined body, and a larger engine. Neither the truck nor the sports car has to be constructed from scratch. Therefore, they take less time to construct.

If some items change in the generic car, the object that inherits from it is altered as well. For example, if the Environmental Protection Agency (EPA) changes the emission requirements (and thus, engines) installed in cars, you would only need to make that engine change in the generic car. The new engine characteristics are inherited from the generic object into both the sports car and the truck objects. No need to modify those objects directly. Can you see the advantage that OOP provides? Changes only need to be implemented in one (generic) object, and they are automatically implemented in the other objects, as well.

What if a customer that you frequently serve came to you and asked that you construct a tow truck based on the current truck you are now selling? You would only need to derive from the truck object, then add all the characteristics required to make a tow truck, such as the car lift. This is also depicted in figure 21.11. Notice how the truck object is created from the generic vehicle object. Then, note that the tow truck object is created from the truck object.

This is a good example of an object hierarchy. Notice how all objects benefit from the one directly above each. Figure 21.11 depicts the class hierarchy as described in our example. Notice how each object relates to one another.

Fig. 21.11.
This car object hierarchy shows how features are added to a generic vehicle to create a tow truck.

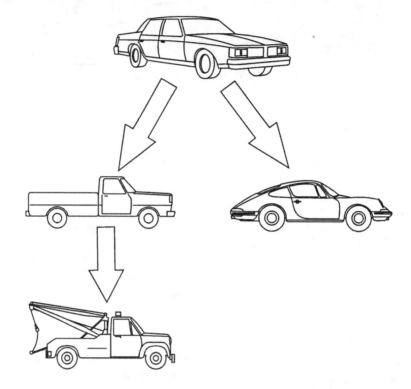

Multiple Inheritance

You have learned that one object can inherit characteristics from another. An object can also inherit characteristics from multiple objects. This concept is known as multiple inheritance. Multiple inheritance enables a new object to benefit from data and methods contained in more than one object, creating a kind of "super object," with the properties of all the involved objects combined. Figure 21.12 presents how our inheritance model uses multiple inheritance to combine the characteristics of two objects into one.

In the preceding example, if two objects referred to as truck and furniture, respectively, are inherited by a new object, the resulting one would be a furniture truck (see figure 12.13).

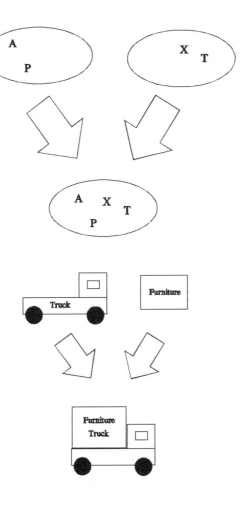

Fig. 21.12.
The model uses
multiple inherit-
ance to combine
the characteristics
of two objects.

Fig. 21.13.
Combining a truck
object with a
furniture object
creates a furniture
truck.

Encapsulation

As already mentioned, packing data and methods in an object is referred to as
encapsulation. An object hides the data from other objects that might exist in
your application. This process is known as *information hiding.* Encapsulation
affords data control and protection: Using the methods that control how data
is manipulated within it, an object can protect its data from other objects. If
the data could be modified by any other object or non-object process, it
could easily corrupt.

Encapsulation hides the details of the characteristics from other objects. Requests are made to objects in the form of a message. (This concept is covered
later.) Then, the object responds without revealing how the operation is performed.

The concept of encapsulation enables you to create objects that have a personality. You define the behavior of the object. It is easy to modify programs by using encapsulation because these objects usually stand alone, and do not affect other objects in the system. If an object is altered, only the methods and data structures contained in it are affected.

A review of the basic definitions discussed thus far would be helpful. An *object* encapsulates a data structure and methods of data control. The data structure is the core of the object, and defines the data that is maintained within the object. *Methods* manipulate data in the objects. Other objects must use methods to make an object perform an operation. *Encapsulation* provides the restriction of access, and protects the data from corruption.

Polymorphism

Another useful feature of OOP and languages that support it is polymorphism. As with inheritance, this feature enables you to reuse code. *Polymorphism* is a concept that allows you to create several versions of the same method or operator. The method or operator is programmed to function differently. The word polymorphic means "take many forms."

A method can be implemented differently in one object and any other objects that inherit from it. For example, consider the Student object that was previously introduced. If a new object is created that handles postgraduate students, it inherits all of the data and methods defined in the original object.

As you know, both postgraduate and undergraduate students are not graduated from a university in the same way. The method Graduate is present in both objects. However, it graduates students differently, depending on the method contained in either of the two objects, the UnderGraduate or the PostGraduate.

Therefore, if a message is sent to the UnderGraduate object to graduate Karen, the method *graduate* is invoked. She receives the undergraduate diploma, and updates her transcripts accordingly. If a message is sent to the PostGraduate object to graduate Celeste, the method graduate is also invoked. However, this method overrides the one for graduating an undergraduate student, and alters the procedure. Celeste receives a graduate rather than an undergraduate degree, and her transcripts are updated accordingly (see fig. 21.14). Although each method differs in the operation, both accomplish the same function. This is the idea behind polymorphism.

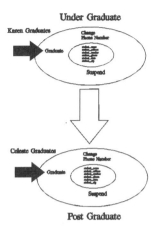

Fig. 21.14.
Polymorphism enables you to reuse code.

Message Passing

Objects communicate with one another by using messages. A message is a request that causes an operation to be invoked. A message is like a telephone call between objects. One object communicates with another object to make that object perform some predefined action. This action is comparable to the way you communicate with other people by using the telephone or a fax machine. You send messages and expect actions to occur, just as objects send messages to other objects for the same reason. Within the C++ language, a message is sent to an object by naming the object and method, similar to a calling function. Recall from figure 21.6 that a message is sent to a method in an object. Then, the object acts on the message by performing an operation.

Objects continually communicate by using messages in a typical object-oriented application. Figure 21.15 depicts how objects send messages to each other.

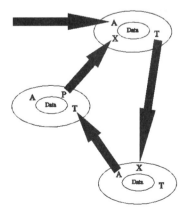

Fig. 21.15.
Objects communicate through messages.

A message is a request to carry out an indicated operation for a particular object, then return a result. Messages can come from other objects, or from outside sources, such as a mouse or a keyboard.

Objects vary in complexity. Some contain several hundreds of possible methods that can be invoked by another object using a message. Other objects do not need to know the internal complexity of an object. They only need to know how to communicate with an object, and how it returns information.

A Windows application is a good example of how messages are employed to communicate among objects. The user presses a button to dispatch messages to other objects that carry out a particular function. If you press the Exit button, a message is sent to the object responsible for closing the application. If the message is valid, the internal method is invoked. Then, the application is closed.

Using Constructors and Destructors

In the C++ languages, there are special functions responsible for creating and destroying objects in the normal execution of an object-oriented program. Constructors allocate memory for all the data fields and methods defined in an object. Destructors are called when an object is no longer needed. Then, the memory is freed.

A *constructor* is a special type of member function (method) that sets up and initializes an object. The programmer is responsible for ensuring that all data members in a particular object are initialized. If they are not, undesirable results occur because the correct amount of memory has not been allocated for the data. This can stop your program, or cause the dreaded hard lock. When this happens, you're going to have to turn off or reset your computer. Using a constructor is important to your object-oriented application. If a constructor is not defined in the program, the application generates a constructor by default (see Chapter 26 for further information).

A *destructor* reverses the operation of the constructor. It, too, is a type of member function. However, it destroys an object. Also, it frees up the memory allocated for that object. The data and the methods are no longer available to other objects in your application. If the destructor did not free up the memory that was allocated for an object, the memory would not be available for use by other objects. Additionally, if the destructors were not invoked in an object that is created several times in the execution of a program, you would eventually run out of memory. Then, your application would stop. If a destructor is not defined in the program, one is generated by default (see Chapter 26 for further information).

In C++, the constructor and destructor names are distinguished from all other member functions. They are named after the class to which they belong (see following complete class listing). Constructors are called as simple functions:

```
// constructor
List();
```

A destructor is called with the tilde preceding its name.

```
// destructor
~List();
```

The code fragment below is a simple class referred to as List, which uses a few member functions or methods. Note how the destructor and constructor are invoked from the class definition.

```
class List
{

    Node *Nodes;

public:
    // constructor
    List();

    // destructor
    ~List();

    // add an item
    void Add_to_List(Point *New_Item);

    // Print the report
    void Report_List();

};
```

As you can see, constructors and destructors have many of the same properties that standard member functions have. They are defined in the same way. So what makes constructors and destructors unique from other member functions? Consider the following characteristics of constructors and destructors:

■ Turbo C++ automatically invokes constructors and destructors.

■ Although constructors and destructors resemble functions, they do not return values.

- Objects do not inherit constructors and destructors. Each object defines its own constructor and destructor.

- Constructors are not called in the same way that you do for standard functions. They only serve one function: to create an object.

In upcoming chapters, you learn how constructors and destructors are implemented in an object-oriented program. This section has served as an introduction.

Object-Oriented Design

As you can see from our preceding discussion, object-oriented programming is a different way of thinking about how an application is implemented. OOP requires that you do some additional planning for your application. Using OOP, modules are no longer placed into a structured hierarchy. A good object-oriented application is defined by well placed, well-thought-out objects. Therefore, the success of your object-oriented program is determined by how well it is designed and programmed.

For a well-designed object-oriented application, you should do the following before attempting to write your OOP:

- Identify the objects that are to be included in your OOP.

- Define that data that the objects are to contain.

- Determine the behavior of the objects by defining the methods contained in each one, and the data element on which each operates.

- Determine how the objects are to communicate with one another in your application.

- Place the objects in a hierarchy in which the benefits of inheritance are maximized.

Object-oriented analysis and design (OOA/OOD) are techniques, notations, and procedures employed to analyze and design an object-oriented application. Many books have been written defining formal methodologies that one can employ to do this. Computer Aided Software Engineering (CASE) tools exist that automate the analysis and design process. These tools use advanced diagraming programs in connection with a database on the objects that you are designing.

Object-oriented applications require more planning than structured programs. If you must not only program but also design your applications, it makes good sense to use a popular object-oriented analysis and design method.

The details of object-oriented analysis and design are beyond the scope of this book. The very basic concepts previously presented should give you a good idea of how object-oriented applications are designed before a single line of code is written. During your first OOP efforts, think about what objects are to be utilized, and what each contains. Also, consider how your objects are implemented in your application. A little planning in the beginning saves many hours of programming time.

Using Class Libraries

Now that you know the benefits of inheritance in an object-oriented application, consider how Class libraries are used in OOP to store useful objects. A *Class library* is a set of objects stored for use by other objects in other applications or by other programmers. You simply need to inherit from an object contained in a Class library. Then, all the data and methods defined in that particular object can automatically be used from your new object (see figure 21.16).

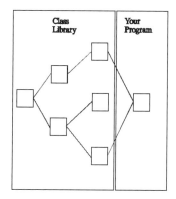

Fig. 21.16.
You can inherit data and methods from objects in a Class library.

For example, if Ben from down the hall creates a really unique object that displays the company logo in the upper right-hand corner of the screen, Ben can place that object in a Class library. Now that the object is in the Class library, Ben can use it in the future when creating other applications. Additionally, other programmers can use Ben's object as well when they need to perform the same or similar activities.

Remember that others cannot only inherit the characteristics of Ben's object, but they can modify, delete, and add data and methods that might be required. Even if a lot of work needs to be performed to make the new object (created from another one) work in a way that meets a new requirement, it is usually better than starting from scratch. If you inherit from an object that in turn has been inherited from additional objects, the characteristics from all of them are present in your new object. You can also use multiple inheritance to take the best characteristics from more than one object (see figure 21.16). Objects passed down from a library can be altered by the object that inherits them in contrast to structured programs that are taken as they are written.

Some organizations have several thousand objects in their Class library, each performing a unique activity. This situation saves the company money because it does not have to pay a programmer to write a program, or part of one that has already been created by someone else. Class libraries can be purchased. Generally these libraries provide specialized functions, such as Windows development, database operations, or communication functions. The same concepts apply, and the objects can be used in the same way as objects you or someone else in your organization defines.

Summary

his chapter covered object-oriented programming concepts. Object-oriented programming is a combination of structured programming techniques and data structures. It has been receiving a great deal of attention recently. Many new applications are being developed using object-oriented programming (OOP) languages, such as C++. Turbo C++ completely supports the object-oriented programming model.

OOP uses several object-oriented concepts, such as class, object, message, inheritance, encapsulation, methods, and polymorphism to control how an object-oriented program is implemented.

This chapter covered the following topics:

■ OOP is gaining acceptance in the software development world because it supports the object-oriented concepts of inheritance. This feature enables a programmer to inherit the characteristics (methods and data) from other objects. These save the programmer from having to write the code that is now inherited. The maximization of code reuse is a major benefit of OOP.

- OOP is a new way of thinking about programming. It is different in many ways from structured programming concepts. Objects are self-contained entities. Data and the processes are maintained within an object. In structured programming, data is passive, and the processes and data are usually separated.

- A class is the blueprint of an object. It defines the data structure of an object, and the methods, or how the object is going to behave. Methods are small structured programs.

- An object is a runtime version or an instance of an object. It takes a portion of memory, and acts on messages sent to it. Live data is encapsulated in an object. Other objects and processes must use the methods that surround the object to manipulate the data.

- The concepts of inheritance enable you to inherit characteristics from other classes/objects. You can inherit from objects that you create, or from class libraries that you purchase.

- You can inherit from more than one object. This concept is known as multiple inheritance.

- Encapsulation is the process by which an object contains both data and the methods used to gain access to it.

- Objects communicate using messages. Messages are dispatched by other objects, devices, and processes. At any given time in an object-oriented program, several messages can be transmitted to objects.

- Polymorphism is the concept of a method performing differently, depending on the object in which it is contained. An inherited method can override the functions of the original method.

- Constructors are used to create an object. They allocate memory for data. Destructors destroy an object, and free up the memory.

- Careful planning and application design are necessary when creating an object-oriented application. Well designed objects are the basis of a bug-free, effective, object-oriented program.

Chapter 22

Using C++ Classes

A class is a means of representing objects within your program. It is similar to a structure in that both enable you to group variables in a convenient package that can be more easily managed as a single unit. A class extends this notion further by enabling you to manipulate the variables it contains, and limit access to them. This gives you more control over how the group of variables is managed.

This chapter expands the description of a class from the previous chapter, and discusses the following concepts:

- How to declare a class

- The various components that compose a class

- How you can use classes

Understanding C++ Classes

A class is a thorough way of describing an object. A class enables you to describe not only features of an object but actions, as well. For example, you might describe a person as someone with arms, legs, and a head. This information can be represented in a structure, as figure 22.1 illustrates. However, a person can also talk, walk, and sing. These are active features that cannot be represented in a structure using only variables.

Fig. 22.1.

Using a class, you can thoroughly describe an object.

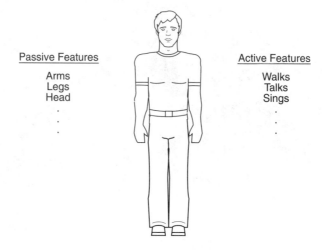

Passive Features

Arms
Legs
Head
.
.
.

Active Features

Walks
Talks
Sings
.
.
.

Perhaps you want to depict an action. Then, the computer must execute code that represents the action in some way. For example, to represent a person walking, the computer might display an animated graphical sequence that renders a picture of a person strolling across the screen. A class is a special form of structure that enables you to represent actions associated with an object, along with its features.

A class enables you to represent features as well as actions of an object by supporting two types of components. The first type can only represent features and are called *data members*. The data members of a class only store pieces of information that together describe passive characteristics of an object.

The second type can represent an action that can be done to or by the object and are called *member functions*.

A class can more thoroughly and accurately describe an object within your program by enabling you to combine data members and member functions that correspond to the features and associated actions, respectively, of an object. This is the basic premise of C++ classes. By encapsulating passive features as well as active characteristics of an object into a single package, you can use the class as a more complete reference to an object. Figure 22.2 illustrates this concept.

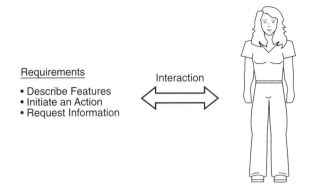

Fig. 22.2.
This illustration
shows the
relationship
between a class
and the object that
it represents.

Requirements
• Describe Features
• Initiate an Action
• Request Information

Interaction

Class Definition of a Person:

Data Functions   Member Functions

Head   Walk
Arms   Talk
Legs   Sing
.   .
.   .
.   .

Figure 22.2 compares a real person with its class representation. In both
cases, you can find out information about the person through observation.
In the case of a real person, you visually see features. In the case of a class,
this information is stored in its data member variables. Both the real
person and the class representation can execute an action, such as walking
or talking. In the case of a class object, you request it to "walk" or "talk" by
initiating its corresponding member function.

Obviously, a class cannot completely describe a person. The class representation will always lack many passive and active features of a person.
Additionally, a person has intelligence, whereas a class is a programmed set of
information and actions. As a representation, however, a class is a better form
for describing a human than any other method available to a programmer.

Most objects are more than static pieces of information. A class, therefore,
offers an extremely versatile way of accommodating an object's features. It
provides more than just a convenient way of grouping the passive features of
an object into an easy-to-use package; it also enables you to include in the
package actions that are done by or to the object. This combination of features and actions of a class is often referred to as encapsulation. A class encapsulates not only the features of an object, but its capabilities, as well. Using
classes can simplify programming, since anything to do with an object can
be included in a neat and self-enclosed package.

Declaring C++ Classes

You declare a class with a format that is similar to a structure, as follows:

```
class class_name
{
    data member 1; // represents features
    data member 2;
    data member 3;
        .
        .
        .
    data member N

    member function 1;    // represents actions
    member function 2;
    member function 3;
        .
        .
        .
    member function N
};
```

The name of a class is preceded by the word "class." This tells the compiler that it is a special form of a structure that supports data members as well as member functions. The data members represent features, and member functions stand for actions.

Member functions of a class are sometimes referred to as class methods.

You can declare data members and member functions in any combination and order. There is no requirement to declare any of the data members or member functions. The following is a valid declaration:

```
class Useless
{
};
```

The Useless class does not contain information, and does nothing. It might be used as a placeholder when you start programming. Then, you can expand it as the need for the class grows. You can declare a class with all data members or member functions, depending on your requirements for representing an object.

Data members are declared in a class as variables. A data member can be any type of variable, including the standard C data types (such as int and char), an array, a pointer, a structure, a union, or even another class.

You can declare member functions within a class as functions. The general rules regarding function declarations apply to class member functions as well, such as how to declare and pass arguments, and how to use the return value.

The following is a sample class declaration that describes a person:

```
class Person
{
    // Data Members

    char HairColor[20];
    int  Height;        // in inches
    int  Weight;        // in pounds

    // Member Functions

    void Walk();
    void Talk();
    void ChangeHairColor(char * NewHairColor);
    void Person::Walk()
{
   //to be defined
}
    void Person::Talk()
{
   //to be defined
}
    void Person::ChangeHairColor(char * NewHairColor)
{
   //to be defined
};
main()
{
    Person Person1;
    .
    .
    .
}
```

The Person class represents some features about a person, such as hair color, height, and weight. These variables store values that represent specific details of a feature. For example, by setting the data member variable Height to 65, you are using the Person class to describe someone who is 65 inches tall.

The Person class also represents several actions that a person can do, such as talking, walking, and changing the hair color. These are declared as functions. In this case, the function names describe the actions that they represent. The first two member functions represent the action of walking and talking, respectively.

Obviously, the Walk() and Talk() member functions do not mean that the computer object referred to as Person walks or talks. The member functions Walk() and Talk() operate within the class, and can execute a parallel action in the computer that describes a person actually walking or talking.

For example, if the Person class is a picture of a person on the screen, the Walk() function might cause the picture to move along the screen in the form of a person walking. The Talk() member function might accomplish a similar task.

The ChangeHairColor() is different from the other member functions because the action it represents is associated with a feature. The ChangeHairColor() function represents a person changing the hair color from one shade to another. The single argument, NewHairColor, represents the new shade.

The reason the ChangeHairColor() function uses an argument is to better reflect the real-life action of a person changing the hair color. The NewHairColor argument represents the choice of shade that is used to dye the hair. Within the ChangeHairColor function, the NewHairColor argument is used to update the data member HairColor when the action is executed. When you execute the ChangeHairColor() function with a color Blond, you are representing the real-life action of a person dyeing the hair blond.

To declare an instance of the class Person, you use the following format:

```
class_name instance_name;
```

This sets aside the space to store all the information necessary for a single instance of a class Person. There is no need to set aside space for member functions because they are not information that is stored. They are ways of expressing actions in your program that apply to a particular class. The only difference between member functions and general functions is that member functions are limited to operating within the context of the class in which they are defined. You can use general functions in any context.

Defining Member Functions

In the preceding section, a class Person was defined with three member functions as follows:

```
class Person
{
    // Data Members

    char HairColor[20];
    int  Height;        // in inches
    int  Weight;        // in pounds

    // Member Functions

    void Walk();
    void Talk();
    void ChangeHairColor(char * NewHairColor);
};
```

The three member functions, `Walk()`, `Talk()`, and `ChangeHairColor()`, need to be defined. Declaring class member functions is similar to declaring C library functions: The declaration is simply the prototype of the function. The actual function itself must be defined elsewhere so that the compiler knows what code to execute when the function is called.

To define a member function, use the following syntax:

```
class_instance_name::member_function_name(argument_list)
{
    .
    .        // add code here to represent an action
    .
}
```

Class member functions are generally declared outside of the class itself. (The next chapter shows how to define a class member function in the class declaration.) The member function defines the actions to take when it is called. For example, the following is a sample listing of the function definitions of the class Person:

```
void Person::Walk()
{
    .
    .        // code that represents walking
    .
}
void Person::Talk()
{
    .
    .        // code that represents talking
    .
}
```

When the member function is called, it refers to the definition of the function to determine what action to take. The definition of a class can be anywhere in your code, as long as it follows the class declaration.

You can also define member functions that do not represent an action. You can use these member functions for special data manipulation that pertain only to the class data members. No limit exists on the number of member functions that a class can contain.

Accessing Class Members

To access a class member, use the same method as that for accessing structure variables. You use the `'.'` operator to reference the data member or member function of a class, as follows:

```
class Person
{
    // Data Members

    char HairColor[20];
    int  Height;      // in inches
    int  Weight;      // in pounds

    // Member Functions

    void Walk();
    void Talk();
    void ChangeHairColor(char * NewHairColor);
};
void Person::Walk()
{
   // to be defined
}

void Person::Talk()
{
   // to be defined
}

void Person::ChangeHairColor(char * NewHairColor)
{
   // to be defined
}
main()
{
    Person Person1;

    Person1.Height = 65;      // Set height of Person1 to 65"
    Person1.ChangeHairColor("blond"); // Change hair color to blond
    .
    .
    .
}
```

The following is the general syntax for referencing either a data member or a member function of a class:

```
class_instance_name.member
```

In this example, the Height of Person1 is assigned a value of 65 using the following statement:

```
Person1.Height = 65;      // Set height of Person1 to 65"
```

Notice how the data member Height is referenced by associating it with the instance Person1. The Person1 instance of class Person now represents some-one who is 65 inches tall. You can only use the variable Height in connection with an instance of a class Person. You cannot reference this variable on its own. The following reference to the data member `Height` would cause a compiler error:

```
Height = 65;
```

In the preceding line of code the data member `Height` is used without any connection to the instance `Person1` to which it belongs. The compiler assumes that the reference to `Height` is to a global or local variable, and when it finds no declaration of a local or global variable named `Height` it generates a compiler error.

The example also executes the `ChangeHairColor()` member function by passing an argument literal "blond." This represents an action—that of `Person1` changing the hair color to a shade of blond. Notice that accessing a member function is the same as accessing a data member.

This example code does not actually compile. It is used here to illustrate how to reference data members and member functions. If you attempt to compile this example, the compiler would tell you that you cannot access `Height` and `ChangeHairColor()`. The reason is that by default, all members of a class are inaccessible to code outside the class. For this type of code, you must deliberately make the class member accessible. The next section discusses this subject.

Understanding Private, Protected, and Public Keywords

You can declare data members and member functions as private, protected, or public members. Figure 22.3 illustrates the differences among these three member types.

A private data member or member function can only be referenced by another member function of the same class. No function outside of the class can access a private member.

It is important to remember that all members of a class are by default private. When you declare a class, all its data and function members are private unless you indicate otherwise to the compiler.

To enable access to members of a class, declare them as public. A public class member is one that anyone can access directly with use of the instance name.

The protected declaration is described in greater detail in the subsequent chapters whose topics relate more closely to it. For this chapter, it is sufficient to note that a protected member is inaccessible outside its class, as is a private member.

Fig. 22.3.
You can declare
data members and
member functions
as private, pro-
tected, or public.

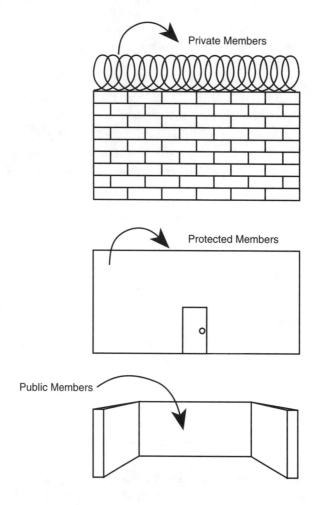

To declare a member private or public, use the following format:

```
private:
member
public:
member
```

The following example program shows how to use the private and public
declaration keywords:

```
class Person
{
     // Private Data Members

private:
     char HairColor[20];

     // Public Data Members
```

```
public:
    int  Height;        // in inches
    int  Weight;        // in pounds

    // Private Member Functions

private:
    void Walk();

    // Public Member Functions

public:

    void Talk();
    void ChangeHairColor(char * NewHairColor);
};
```

In this example, the data members Height and Weight are public, as well as
the member functions Talk() and ChangeHairColor(). These members can
be accessed by any other function or statement with the use of the instance
name. The data member HairColor and member function Walk() are declared
private. Therefore, they are inaccessible, except to the member functions of
the class Person.

Note from this example that a private keyword affects all members that are
declared after it until another public (or protected) keyword is declared. The
same rule applies to the public and protected keywords.

In the last section, a short example program that used the class Person did
not compile. The reason was that the program attempted to access class
members of Person that were by default private. The following is a revised
version of the program that compiles correctly:

```
class Person
{
    // Private Data Members

private:
    char HairColor[20];

    // Public Data Members

public:
    int  Height;        // in inches
    int  Weight;        // in pounds

    // Private Member Functions

private:
    void Walk();

    // Public Member Functions
```

```
    public:

        void Talk();
        void ChangeHairColor(char * NewHairColor);
    };

    main()
    {
        Person Person1;

        Person1.Height = 65;       // Set height of Person1 to 65"
        Person1.ChangeHairColor("blond"); // Change hair color to blond
    }
```

In this example, the Height data member of Person can be assigned because Height is declared public. The code in the main() function can therefore access Height directly. The same applies to the member function ChangeHairColor(), which can also be accessed by the main() function because it is declared public. The main() function of this example still cannot access the data member HairColor nor the member function Walk(), because they are declared private. An attempt to access them would cause a compiler error.

Using Private and Public Keywords

You might be wondering why a class assumes its members are private by default. A more general question is, why have private members at all?

The purpose of the access keywords private, protected, and public is to enable you to control how a class is used. The access control keywords are much of the reason C++ classes are useful. To see why, consider the illustration in figure 22.4, which depicts a bank and a vault. When you deposit money in the bank, it is placed into a vault. No one questions that it is your money in the vault. However, only bank employees can manage the money in the vault directly on your behalf. This setup protects your money from accidental or unauthorized access.

A class assumes that it is a vault for the information that it maintains. Unless you specify otherwise, "vault" protects the members that compose the class from authoriized access. To get access to a private data member, you must go through a member function that is deliberately declared public. By ensuring that the public member functions are the only ones that an external function can access, you can control how the private data members are used. With a class, you have complete control over how other code interacts with the members of your class.

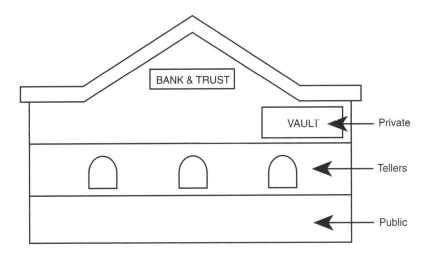

Fig. 22.4.
The drawing illustrates how private and public keywords function.

The private and public access keywords enable you to ensure that the members of a class are used in a particular way. The program in listing 22.1 demonstrates this concept.

Listing 22.1. You use private and public keywords to make sure members of a class are used a certain way.

```
1.    #include <stdio.h>
2.    #include <string.h>

3.    class Person
4.    {
5.    // Private data member
6.    private:
7.    char HairColor[20];

8.    // Public data members
9.    public:
10.   int  Height;
11.   int  Weight;

12.   // Private member functions
13.   private:
14.   void Walk();

15.   // Public member functions
16.   public:
17.   void Talk();
18.   void ChangeHairColor(const char *NewHairColor);
19.   const char *GetHairColor();
20.   };
```

(continues)

Listing 22.1. Continued.

```
21.  void Person::Walk()
22.  {
23.  // Not yet defined
24.  }

25.  void Person::Talk()
26.  {
27.  printf("Yap, yap, yap, yap, yap...\n");
28.  }

29.  void Person::ChangeHairColor(const char *NewHairColor)
30.  {
31.       // Check if new hair color is valid

32.  if ( !strcmpi(NewHairColor, "green") )
33.       {
34.       printf("%s is not a real hair color\n", NewHairColor);
35.       return;
36.  }

37.       // If new hair color is valid, update hair color

38.  strcpy(HairColor, NewHairColor);
39.  }

40.  const char *Person::GetHairColor()
41.  {
42.  return HairColor;
43.  }

44.  main()
45.  {
46.  Person Person1;

47.       // Set Person1 data members

48.  Person1.Height = 65;
49.  Person1.ChangeHairColor("Blond");

50.       // Display new settings

51.  printf("Person1 is %d\" tall and has %s hair\n",
52.            Person1.Height, Person1.GetHairColor());

53.       // Attempt to reset hair color

54.  Person1.ChangeHairColor("green");

55.       // Redisplay Person1 settings

56.  printf("Person1 is still %d\" tall and still has %s hair\n",
57.            Person1.Height, Person1.GetHairColor());
```

```
58.        // Make Person1 talk

59.    Person1.Talk();

60.    return 0;
61.    }
```

Listing 22.1 defines a class referred to as Person. Lines 5 through 11 declare features of a person that are maintained by the class, and include the hair color, height, and weight of a person. Lines 12 through 19 declare member functions that are actions which are applicable for this class.

The variable HairColor is a private data member; this means that there is no access to this variable from outside the class. To access the value of the HairColor variable, you must use special member functions. They are ChangeHairColor() and GetHairColor(), declared in lines 18 and 19, which set and retrieve the HairColor variable, respectively. Line 49 shows how to indicate a change of hair color using the public member function ChangeHairColor() for the person represented by Person1. Line 51 and 52 display the known features of Person1 to the screen, including the newly set hair color.

Notice that you have no direct option to set the HairColor variable directly. If you attempt to do so in your code, the compiler generates an error stating that you do not have access to the HairColor variable. This variable is completely locked to the outside, except through the member functions that control it.

The benefit of having exclusive access to HairColor strictly through member functions is to prevent the intentional or accidental corruption of the HairColor data member. For example, the member function ChangeHairColor(), which is defined starting on line 29, checks to make sure that the new hair color is not green. Green hair is not a valid hair color for a person described using this class.

On line 54, an attempt is made to change the hair color for the person represented by Person1 to the color green. The only way to represent a change of hair color is with the ChangeHairColor() member function. Therefore, the ChangeHairColor() function detects that green is not a valid change of hair color, and rejects the attempted update. This is reflected in the following line when the features of Person1 are again displayed, and the hair color is still described as blonde.

The HairColor variable is completely safeguarded by declaring it as a private variable. A program cannot intentionally or unintentionally set this variable to data that the class does not filter, and therefore validate.

A corollary to this protection is that when you do need access to HairColor, such as when you want to retrieve its value, you need a member function to do so. The GetHairColor() public member function, declared on line 19, and defined on line 40, does just that. Notice that the GetHairColor() simply returns a pointer to the HairColor variable. The pointer is returned as a **const** value; this protects the pointer from being used to update the **HairColor** variable directly.

In contrast to the HairColor member variable, the Height and Weight variables are declared as public data members of the class Person (lines 10 and 11 of listing 22.1). These variables identify the height and weight, respectively, of a person represented by class Person. They can be freely accessed. Line 48 assigns a value of 65 to the data member Height, which represents the height of the particular person described by Person1. Notice there are no checks done for this assignment. There is no control over data members that are defined public. They can be freely accessed, as if they were members of a structure, or individually declared variables.

To determine whether to declare a data member public or private, consider how it is to be used. If the data member can be assigned an invalid or corrupt value, it is a good candidate to declare as private. A set of functions can then be defined to safely set and retrieve the data member.

One additional statement in listing 22.1 is worthy of mention. Line 59 shows how to represent the action of talking associated with the class Person. To do so, the member function Talk() is executed for Person1. The Talk() member function is defined starting on line 25. The Talk() function simply displays a line of text to the screen that indicates someone is talking. If this were a multimedia application, the Talk() function could just as well have the computer generate the sound of a voice talking. The point is that to get Person1 to talk, simply call its member function by that name.

Understanding the *this* Pointer

One of the more confusing aspects of C++ is understanding how a member function knows which instance of a class called it. This is important because the member function must know whose instance data should be updated. Consider the example in listing 22.2 that illustrates this problem.

Listing 22.2. This program illustrates the special this **Pointer.**

```
1.    class FlagPole
2.    {
3.    private:
4.    int  Height;

5.    public:
6.    void SetHeight(int NewHeight);
7.    };

8.    void FlagPole::SetHeight(int NewHeight)
9.    {
10.   Height = NewHeight;
11.   }

12.   main()
13.   {
14.   FlagPole Pole1, Pole2;

15.   Pole1.SetHeight(20);
16.   Pole2.SetHeight(20);

17.   return 0;
18.   }
```

You can declare a FlagPole class with a single data member to describe its height, and a single member function that sets the Height data member. The main() function declares two instances of FlagPole called Pole1 and Pole2. Line 15 sets the height of Pole1, and line 16 sets the height of Pole2.

Using SetHeight() might appear intuitive to the reader of the program. Nevertheless, how does the SetHeight() function itself know in one case that the Pole1 instance called it, and in the other, that the Pole2 one called it? As the SetHeight() definition on line 8 shows, there is no information sent to the SetHeight() member function that would indicate who called it. Yet, the Height data member of Pole1 is properly set in line 15, and likewise for Pole2 in line 16 (by calling the same SetHeight member function in either case).

The answer is that there is, in fact, a pointer that is sent to the SetHeight() member function. It is a special pointer that is implicitly declared for every class. Also, it is implicitly passed whenever a member of a class is used. The implicit pointer is referred to as this, and is a part of every class.

The this pointer is the address of the instance of a class. Figure 22.5 illustrates how every class contains an implicit pointer called this that points to itself. In the case of the Pole1 instance of the FlagPole class, the this pointer is the address in memory of the place in which Pole1 information is stored. The this pointer of Pole2 is the address of the place in which Pole2 information is stored.

Fig. 22.5.
this points to
the memory in
which each of
two instances of a
class is stored.

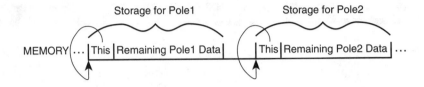

Whenever a member function of a class is executed, it is implicitly passed a
this pointer, as figure 22.6 illustrates. The this pointer is the address of
whichever instance of the class called the member function. In this way, the
member function knows who called it. The member function has the address
of the class instance that called it. Therefore, it can update the correct data
members in each case.

Fig. 22.6.
This drawing is an
illustration of the
implicit this
pointer passed to
member functions.

Statement Used to Call
Member Function: ⟹ Statement Implied:

```
Pole1.SetHeight(20);        SetHeight(this = address of Pole1, 20);
```

The this pointer is completely transparent to your program. The compiler
and linker make sure that the this pointer is passed behind-the-scenes
whenever and wherever it is needed. There is no need for you to maintain
any information for the this pointer.

It is useful to know how to use the this pointer. This is especially helpful in
the event that you want to pass the address of the class (from within it) to
another function. The only way to reference the address of the class from
within a member function is to use the this pointer variable that is implicitly
declared for every class. Consider the following code fragment:

```
class A
{
        void MemberFunction1();
}

void GeneralFunction1(class A *p)
{
        .
        .
        .
}

void A::MemberFunction1()
{
        GeneralFunction1(this);
        .
        .
        .
}
```

Notice how `MemberFunction1()` calls `GeneralFunction()`. `GeneralFunction()` takes a pointer to class A as an argument. Therefore, the pointer to class A must somehow be available to `MemberFunction1()`. It is in the form of the `this` pointer.

Comparing C++ Structures and Unions with C++ Classes

A C++ structure is a class whose members are implicitly public. Other than this point, a C++ structure is identical to a class.

To illustrate the similarity between a class and a structure, consider the following example program. It was used earlier in this chapter, and failed to compile:

```
class Person
{
    // Data Members

    char HairColor[20];
    int  Height;        // in inches
    int  Weight;        // in pounds

    // Member Functions

    void Walk();
    void Talk();
    void ChangeHairColor(char * NewHairColor);
};

main()
{
    Person Person1;

    Person1.Height = 65;     // Set height of Person1 to 65"
    Person1.ChangeHairColor("blonde"); // Change hair color to blonde
}
```

It was noted that this program would not compile because a class declares all its members private by default. Also, the `main()` function is illegally attempting to assign a value directly to a private data member. However, by changing the type class to `struct`, all members are implicitly public, and the program compiles without any errors. The new class declaration becomes a structure declaration as follows:

```
struct Person
{
    // Data Members
```

```
        char HairColor[20];
        int  Height;          // in inches
        int  Weight;          // in pounds

        // Member Functions

        void Walk();
        void Talk();
        void ChangeHairColor(char * NewHairColor);
};
```

Notice that the C++ structure supports data members as well as member functions. Using a C++ structure is no different than employing a C++ class. In fact, a C++ class is simply a specialized C++ structure whose default access declaration for its members is private. A structure can also use the private keyword for any member to override its default access.

A C++ union also assumes that all its members are public by default. In keeping with the definition of a C union, only one data member of a C++ union can be active at a time. For example, the following is a C++ union:

```
union Person
{
    // Data Members

    char HairColor[20];
    int  Height;          // in inches
    int  Weight;          // in pounds

    // Member Functions

    void Walk();
    void Talk();
    void ChangeHairColor(char * NewHairColor);
};
```

In this case, only one of the data members HairColor, Height, or Weight is valid at any time. As seen by the preceding example, unions are in all other ways identical to classes.

Benefits of Using C++ Classes

Many benefits of using C++ classes have been described and illustrated in this chapter. They are summarized in table 22.1.

Table 22.1. Using C++ classes affords many benefits.

Benefit	Description
Safer to Use	A class can declare data members as private to prevent unauthorized access to the data member variable. This not only prevents inadvertent misuse of the data member; it also filters access to the data member through member functions that can then validate the way in which the data member is accessed.
Easier to Use	It is simpler to call a class member function to operate on internal data member variables than to manage them as one unit, and the functions that operate them as separate items. A C++ class adds to the convenience of a C structure by enabling operations to the structure to be built-in. In this way, each member function implicitly operates on the data members of its own class, with less confusion and administrative hassle to the programmer.
Easier to Share	Member functions are implicitly connected with the data members on which they operate. Therefore, there is often little need when using classes to deal with variables. In a well-defined class, the access to information can be almost exclusively limited to using the member functions alone. This hides the complexity of how the class operates. Also, it enables any programmer to more easily focus on the higher-level actions that pertain to a class rather than how those actions are defined. The class packages a complex set of operations into an easy-to-use unit which can more easily be shared by others (who do not need to understand how the information within the class is managed).

The program in listing 22.3 illustrates the benefits of using C++ classes. The program is one that was first used in chapter 20 to store a complete purchase order entered by a user, and redisplay the information when the entry was completed.

Listing 22.3. This program illustrates using a class to enter and display an invoice.

```
1.   #include <stdio.h>
2.   #include <string.h>

3.   typedef struct {
4.   char ItemName[20];
5.   int  Quantity;
6.   float    Price;
7.   float    Total;
8.   } InvoiceRow;
```

(continues)

Listing 22.3. Continued.

```
 9.   class Invoice
10.   {
11.   private:
12.     InvoiceRow Rows[10];      // declare 10 items max for invoice

13.     float    Total;          // used to keep total invoice price
14.     int  CurrentRow;     // used to keep track of next row to use

15.     int  ValidateEntry(); // only used by EnterInvoiceData()

16.   public:
17.     void Initialize();
18.     void EnterInvoiceData();
19.     void DisplayInvoice();
20.   };

21.   void Invoice::Initialize()
22.   {
23.     CurrentRow = 0;          // start at row 0
24.   }

25.   int Invoice::ValidateEntry()
26.   {
27.         // Declare valid list of in-stock items and their prices

28.   struct {
29.         char ItemName[20];
30.         float Price;
31.   } ValidItems[] = {"flour", 2.50,
32.                 "sugar", 3.00,
33.                 "salt", 1.50};

34.     int i, nReturn = 0;

35.         // Check that quantity is between 1 and 10 items

36.   if ( Rows[CurrentRow].Quantity <= 0 ||
37.         Rows[CurrentRow].Quantity > 10 )
38.   {
39.         // Display error if incorrect quantity

40.         printf("Quantity is not between 1 and 10\n");
41.         return 0;
42.   }

43.         // Check that item is one of the items in stock

44.   for ( i = 0; i < 3; i++ )
45.   {
46.         if ( !strcmpi(Rows[CurrentRow].ItemName,
      ValidItems[i].ItemName) )
47.         {
48.             nReturn = 1;

49.             // Update price of item to that selected
```

```
50.              Rows[CurrentRow].Price = ValidItems[i].Price;
51.              break;
52.        }
53.  }

54.  if ( nReturn == 0 )
55.  {
56.       // Display error if item not in stock

57.       printf("%s is not an in-stock item\n",
     Rows[CurrentRow].ItemName);
58.  }

59.  return nReturn;
60.  }

61.  void Invoice::DisplayInvoice()
62.  {
63.  int  i;

64.       // Display heading for summary listing

65.  printf("\n\nThe complete listing of this purchase order is:\n\n\
66.  \tItem\tQuan\tPrice\tTotal\n\n");

67.       // Display summary listing of invoice

68.  for ( i = 0; i < CurrentRow; i++ )
69.       printf("\t%s\t%d\t%5.2f\t%7.2f\n", Rows[i].ItemName,
     Rows[i].Quantity,
70.            Rows[i].Price, Rows[i].Total);

71.       // Display total amount of invoice

72.  printf("The total amount of this purchase order is: %5.2f\n", Total);
73.  }

74.  void Invoice::EnterInvoiceData()
75.  {
76.  int i;

77.       // Display instructions

78.       printf("\nEnter your purchase order for any of the items 1
     through 10 items that are in stock\n\
79.  Enter \"done\" as an item to quit.  Use the following format:\n\n\
80.  Item     Quantity\n");

81.       // Loop to retrieve invoice data until
82.       // user enters "done" for item, or until
83.       // 10 items are entered, whichever comes first

84.  for ( CurrentRow = 0; CurrentRow < 10; CurrentRow++ )
85.  {
86.       // Prompt for invoice data
```

(continues)

Listing 22.3. Continued.

```
87.          scanf("%s %d", Rows[CurrentRow].ItemName,
         &Rows[CurrentRow].Quantity);

88.              // Quit when user enters "done"

89.          if ( !strcmpi(Rows[CurrentRow].ItemName, "done") )
90.              break;

91.              // Call function to validate values entered

92.          if ( ValidateEntry() )
93.          {
94.              // Calculate total purchase price
95.              // for current row
96.              // if information entered is valid...

97.              Rows[CurrentRow].Total = Rows[CurrentRow].Quantity *
         Rows[CurrentRow].Price;
98.          }
99.          else
100.         {
101.             // Otherwise, display an error message

102.             printf("Invalid entry.  Try again\n\n");

103.             // Decrement counter to reuse current invoice structure

104.             CurrentRow--;
105.         }
106. }

107.         // Calculate total invoice price
108.         // when entry is completed

109. for ( i = 0, Total = 0; i < CurrentRow; i++ )
110.     Total += Rows[i].Total;
111. }


112. main()
113. {
114.         // Declare new invoice

115. Invoice Invoice1;

116.         // Initialize data members

117. Invoice1.Initialize();

118.         // Retrieve invoice data

119. Invoice1.EnterInvoiceData();
```

```
120.      // Display invoice data

121. Invoice1.DisplayInvoice();

122. return 0;
123. }
```

The program in Listing 22.3 prompts a user for purchase order information. As the user enters each item and its quantity, the program validates that it is in stock. Then, the program calculates the line item total cost. When the user is finished entering line items, the program calculates the invoice total. The invoice details are then displayed to the user.

This program demonstrates the many benefits of C++ classes. If you study the code in the main() function, and ignore the rest of the program, you see four statements that are easy to read. Line 115 declares an instance of an Invoice class. This class contains all the data members that are necessary to store a complete invoice. The class also holds the member functions that are used to gather and display invoice data.

Line 117 is used to initialize any data for the new invoice. This is necessary to set whatever internal variables are used to starting values that make sense to the class. Line 119 executes a member function that retrieves the invoice data from the user. Once the user is finished entering the invoice data, line 121 displays it back to the user in a table format that is easy to read.

The one feature that stands out when you focus on just the main() function is that the Invoice class is very easy to use. The member functions state their purpose. To retrieve invoice data, use the EnterInvoiceData() member function. To display the invoice entered, use the DisplayInvoice() member function. If you want to keep track of 100 invoices, for example, an extension to this program to facilitate this number would not be difficult. Simply declare an array of 100 Invoice classes. Then, read them in, one at a time, using the EnterInvoiceData() to manage the complex task of entering invoice data. The Invoice class manages all the administrative and functional details associated with these tasks. You simply need to know the name of the Invoice instance. Then, you can tell it to execute the appropriate task for itself.

Another implicit benefit is that you have no direct access to any of the invoice data. Therefore, you cannot accidentally corrupt it. The invoice data is internally managed. It is declared private so that no function that is external to the class can access the invoice data. No function, other than the Invoice class member functions, can manipulate the invoice data. This protects the invoice data from unwarranted access. It also forces all entry of data through the class member function `EnterInvoiceData()`. This member function adds a validity check using the `ValidateEntry()` member function from each line item entered.

The Invoice class is self-contained; therefore, it is easier for someone who is unfamiliar with the details of invoice processing to incorporate these tasks into another program. By providing just the class and the names of the public member functions, any programmer can include the necessary code to prompt a user for invoice data, and use a neatly formatted table to display it to a user. This makes classes easier to share.

The class itself is defined using the rest of the program. Notice that the invoice is maintained in the class as an array of structures (line 12 of Listing 22.3). A data member can be any data type, including structures, and even other classes. To keep the class self-contained, you can declare variables within it to maintain both the total amount of the invoice (line 13) and the current row that is being processed (line 14). The latter variable is also used to store the total number of rows entered when the user finishes entering data.

This example illustrates yet another attribute of C++. If a class is well-written, it is generally simple to improve and reuse. This is what was done with the `Invoice` class. In the last chapter, a simpler version of the `Invoice` class was first developed. In this chapter, the functionality of the `Invoice` class was augmented, without having to start over.

Another interesting feature of this program is that a member function is declared as private, namely the `ValidateEntry()` function (line 15). The reason for declaring `ValidateEntry()` private is that it is only used by another member function. The `ValidateEntry()` member function checks that the current row just entered contains an in-stock item, and that the quantity is within the bounds established by the class (in this case, between one and 10). Since the entire invoice data entry is managed by a single member function, `EnterInvoiceData()`, all validation occurs internally.

When a function can only be used internally, it is best to declare it as private so that it is not accidentally called at an inappropriate time. In this case, no damage can be done by calling `ValidateEntry()` at any time. However, in another class, calling a member function at unexpected times (when it is only used internally in specific instances) might cause the system to crash. It is best to keep all functions private except those that are necessary to operate the class. In this way, you protect the class from inadvertent use of data members or member functions.

The rest of the details of listing 22.3 are described at the end of Chapter 20.

Summary

This chapter discussed how classes are used to better represent objects. By enabling you to represent the features of an object as well as the actions that pertain to it, a class can be used to describe almost anything within a program.

In this chapter you learned:

- How C++ classes represent features and actions pertaining to an object, and that this is useful to more completely describe an object within a program

- How C++ classes are declared using data members and member functions

- How data members represent features, and member functions stand for actions

- How member functions are defined

- How data members and member functions are accessed.

- How the private, protected, and public access keywords enable you to protect data within the class, and how this lets you control the way in which external functions use the class

- When to declare data members and member variables as private or public

- How and when to use the this pointer

- How a structure, a union, and a class differ, and how you can use each

- The various benefits of using a C++ class, including how a C++ class makes it easier and safer to use and share programs that manage an object and its associated tasks

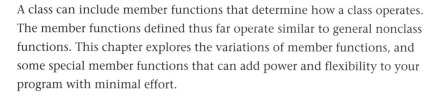

Chapter 23

Using Member Functions

A class can include member functions that determine how a class operates. The member functions defined thus far operate similar to general nonclass functions. This chapter explores the variations of member functions, and some special member functions that can add power and flexibility to your program with minimal effort.

This chapter describes the following:

- Various ways of declaring member functions and their arguments, and the purpose of each variation

- Using constructor and destructor member functions

- Using friend member functions

Using Member Functions in Different Ways

A member function is often declared and used in much the same way that general nonclass functions are declared and used. Both take a set of arguments, manipulate information, and return a value when the function is done. Thus far, you have studied only one unique capability of a member function: it can access private data members of the class to which it belongs.

There is a rich set of variations to declaring member functions that can enhance the flexibility of your programs with a minimal amount of coding effort. This chapter discusses these variations.

Using Default Arguments

A typical function, whether it is a general function or a class member function, takes the form of the following:

```
return_value function_name(arguments);
```

The following is an example of a function:

```
int GetInformation(char *AboutWho);
```

The purpose of the GetInformation() function is presumably to get information about the person or object specified by the AboutWho argument. In C++, you can set default values to the argument variables of member functions so that if the calling function does not specify a value, a default one is used. Consider the following variation of GetInformation():

```
int GetInformation(char *AboutWho = "Mr. Smith");
```

When it is called with an argument, the GetInformation() function uses the argument. However, if the GetInformation() function is called with no argument, the information pertaining to Mr. Smith is used. The reason is that Mr. Smith is the default value.

Consider the following example program:

```
#include <stdio.h>

class Useless
{
public:
    void DisplayNumber(int i = 10);
};

void Useless::DisplayNumber(int i)
{
    printf("The number is: %d\n", i);
}

main()
{
    Useless   U;   // declare instance of class Useless

        // Display a default number

    U.DisplayNumber();

        // Display a specific number

    U.DisplayNumber(100);

    return 0;
}
```

You declare the class useless with a single public member function that displays a number to the screen. This number is the argument passed to the DisplayNumber() member function. If no number is provided, the argument uses a default value of 10. Notice that the default value is set only once: When the member function is declared. You can set the default value for an argument either at the time the member function is declared, or when it is defined. However, you cannot set the default in both the function declaration and in its definition, even if they have the same value.

In the main() program, an instance of the Useless class is declared. Its member function DisplayNumber() is called once without any argument, and a second time with an argument. The first time the default value 10 is displayed. The second time, the value of the argument, 100, is displayed.

You can set as many arguments as you want to default values. The only limitation is that an argument with a default value cannot be followed by one that does not have a default value. The following example class contains a valid member function with multiple arguments that have a default value:

```
class Useless
{
public:
    void DisplayNumber(int i = 10, int j = 100, int k = 1000);
};
```

In this case, the member function can be called in a variety of ways, as the following code demonstrates:

```
class Useless
{
public:
    void DisplayNumber(int i = 10, int j = 100, int k = 1000);
};

void Useless::DisplayNumber(int i, int j, int k)
{
    .
    .    // function not declared yet
    .
}

main()
{
    Useless U;

    U.DisplayNumber(); // i = 10, j = 100, k = 1000
    U.DisplayNumber(5); // i = 5, j = 100, k = 1000
    U.DisplayNumber(5, 50); // i = 5, j = 50, k = 1000
    U.DisplayNumber(5, 50, 500); // i = 5, j = 50, k = 500
}
```

An additional argument is specified in each call to the `DisplayNumber()` member function. Notice that the default values are always applied in sequence from left to right. There is no way of skipping over a default argument. When a value is specified, it is applied to the argument to the far left. You cannot specify only the second argument in a list containing three of them. If you need to specify a second argument, you are forced to specify a value for the first as well. In the preceding example, there is no way to specify a value only for `j` without also designating one for `i`.

You can even use functions as default values. The following shows how a function is used as a default value:

```
int Get10()
{
    return 10;
}

class Useless
{
public:
    void DisplayNumber(int i = Get10());
};
```

In this example, a function `Get10()` returns the value `10`. The `Get10()` function is used to set the default value of `DisplayNumber()` to 10.

Several limitations exist to setting default values. You cannot set the default value of an argument to a data member. For example, the following is illegal:

```
class Useless
{
    int  j;
public:
    void DisplayNumber(int i = j); // ILLEGAL!
};
```

You cannot set a default value for one argument that is followed by another that does not have a default value. For example, the following is also illegal:

```
class Useless
{
public:
    void DisplayNumber(int i = 10, int j); // ILLEGAL!
};
```

If you need to set default values for the arguments of a member function, place these arguments at the end of the argument list. In a list of arguments, you can have some that have default values set, and others that do not, as follows:

```
class Useless
{
public:
    void DisplayNumber(int i, int j = 10); // OK
};
```

The program in listing 23.1 demonstrates a practical use of having arguments set to default values.

Listing 23.1. It is practical to set some arguments to default values.

```
1.   #include <stdio.h>

2.   class Image
3.   {
4.   int  Rotation;      // Declare rotation as degrees (0 - 360)
5.   public:
6.   void SetRotation(int NewRotation = 0);  //  Sets rotation to a
➥ fixed amount
7.   void DisplayRotation();      // Displays current rotation
8.   void Rotate(int ByDegrees = 90);   // Rotates by additional
➥ degrees specified
9.   };

10.  void Image::SetRotation(int NewRotation)
11.  {
12.  Rotation = NewRotation;
13.  }

14.  void Image::Rotate(int ByDegrees)
15.  {
16.  Rotation += ByDegrees;
17.  }

18.  void Image::DisplayRotation()
19.  {
20.  printf("Current rotation is: %d\n", Rotation);
21.  }

22.  main()
23.  {
24.  Image Image1; // declare instance of Image class

25.      // Initialize and display rotation

26.  Image1.SetRotation();
27.  Image1.DisplayRotation();  // Should be 0

28.      // Rotate image by default amount, and display

29.  Image1.Rotate();
30.  Image1.DisplayRotation();  // Should be 90

31.      // Rotate image by 10 more degrees, and display

32.  Image1.Rotate(10);
33.  Image1.DisplayRotation();  // Should be 100

34.      // Set rotation to 222, and display

35.  Image1.SetRotation(222);
```

(continues)

Listing 23.1. continued.

```
36.   Image1.DisplayRotation();   // Should be 222
37.   return 0;
38.   }
```

The program in listing 23.1 declares a class object that represents a computer image. For this example, the only feature that is tracked is the current rotation of the image. As figure 23.1 illustrates, 0-degree rotation represents an image displayed in portrait mode, 90 degrees is landscape, and so on. This feature is stored in the data member `Rotation`.

Fig. 23.1.
The class object illustrated has four different image rotations.

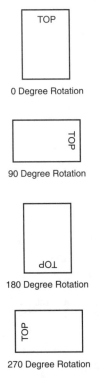

0 Degree Rotation

90 Degree Rotation

180 Degree Rotation

270 Degree Rotation

The class object enables a user to set the rotation using `SetRotation()` that is declared on line 6. This member function takes a single argument that is the new rotation value. If no new rotation value is provided, the `SetRotation()` member function assumes that the user wants to initialize the image rotation back to 0 degrees. By using a default value, the `Set...` function increases its usefulness.

You can, of course, set the new rotation value to 0 by specifying this as the argument to `SetRotation()`. However, the default is an internally set number that reflects a default state that might not always be known. In this case, it happens to be 0.

Lines 26 and 27 initialize the state of the rotation, and display its value on the screen. If this were a real application, the display might have been the actual image itself.

Another function that is useful in managing images is the `Rotate()` member function, which rotates an image using a relative offset. If the image is portrait (0 degrees), adding a rotation of 90 degrees causes it to display in landscape (90 degrees). Adding an additional 90 degrees causes it to display upside-down (180 degrees). Refer to figure 23.1 for an illustration of these rotations.

The `Rotate()` member function takes a single argument that determines the relative offset of rotation in terms of degrees. It assumes a 90-degree rotation unless otherwise specified. This is done by setting the default value of its argument to 90. This is an instance in which the default value might not be readily known outside the class. The default value represents a rotation that is meaningful to the class. When no rotation value is specified as an argument, the image is turned 90 degrees by using the `Rotate()` member function. Rotating an image by 90 degrees has the effect of turning it sideways.

Line 29 rotates the image by the default amount. This line calls the `Rotate()` function with no arguments, so that the image is now at 90 degrees. Line 30 displays the image rotation.

Line 32 rotates the image by another 10 degrees because, in this case, an argument is provided to the `Rotate()` function. Line 33 displays the image rotation that is now up to 100.

Line 35 uses the same `SetRotation()` member function used earlier to initialize the image rotation. Only this time, the line resets the image to a specific rotation value of 222 degrees. Line 36 displays the image rotation.

Note the continuous use of default argument values. For the `Image` class, the default values are significant because a user of this class might not know what a logical value of an argument should be. The default value for `SetRotation()` is `0`, whereas for `Rotate()`, it is 90. The default argument values provide a way of including extra functionality into the class without much effort.

The default argument also simplifies the usage of member functions. `Rotate()` is most often used to rotate an image by 90 degrees. Therefore, setting the default to 90 saves a programmer the trouble of declaring this value, possibly incorrectly at times, for each call to the `Rotate()` member function. The default value guarantees a consistent use of the `Rotate()` member function when it is used in its default state.

Using an Inline Member Function

The inline member function operates similar to a macro: the code that defines this type of function is repeated, rather than called, each time it is used.

Consider the following example program:

```
#include <stdio.h>

class Sum
{
    int Total;
public:
    void SumValues(int i, int j, int k)
        { Total = i + j + k; }
    void DisplayTotal();
};

void Sum::DisplayTotal()
{
    printf("The total is: %d\n", Total);
}

main()
{
    Sum Sum1; // declare instance of Sum class

        // Add values

    Sum1.SumValues(1, 2, 3);

        // Display Total

    Sum1.DisplayTotal(); // Displays 6

    return 0;
}
```

This program uses a class to add three values. Then, the program stores the total using a member function SumValues(). The total can then be displayed whenever it is needed using the member function DisplayTotal().

The member function SumValues() is inline because you declare and define it within the class declaration. When SumValues() is called, for example from within main(), the program does not call the function SumValues(). Instead, it replaces the call with the code of SumValues(). When SumValues() is called, it is as if the following statement replaced the word SumValues():

```
Total = i + j + k;
```

Inline functions are used either for very short function definitions, or ones that are called millions of times (in situations in which the inline code operates quicker than calling the function). It is also used to simplify coding if the amount of code necessary to define a member function is brief. The inline function is efficient because its declaration and definition *are* combined into a single statement.

In a typical application, an inline function is often used to return the value of a private data member that cannot be accessed except through a member function. This type of member function simply returns a value. Therefore, it is convenient to avoid the longer definition format of class member functions in favor of the shorter inline format. The following example program uses inline functions to enable controlled access to the private data members of a class:

```
class Useless
{
private:
    int  Integer1; // declare integer
    char Buffer1[20]; // declare string buffer

public:
    int  GetInteger1()
              { return Integer1; }
    const char * GetBuffer1()
              { return Buffer1; }
    .
    .
    .
}
```

This example declares a class Useless that has two private data members, Integer1 and Buffer1. There is no direct way to access these data members. A set of public member functions, therefore, are declared and defined to enable other functions to retrieve these values, but not to modify them. All that is required of these member functions is the return value of a private data member. Therefore, it is simpler to define these functions inline than use the longer format of defining them outside the class.

Notice that the declaration of GetBuffer1() includes the keyword const for the return value. The return value of GetBuffer1() is a pointer; therefore, the calling program can modify the data stored at the location of Buffer1 with a pointer to its storage address. By using the const keyword, the compiler prevents the return pointer from being used to modify the Buffer1 variable.

To prevent a pointer from being used to update the information it represents, declare it using the const keyword.

You can also declare a function inline even when it is defined outside the class declaration by preceding its definition with the keyword inline. This method is useful when defining an inline function that is several statements long. Having a definition within the class declaration can make the class difficult to read. Instead, you can define the member function outside the class declaration, and use the keyword inline. This tells the compiler that the function should be treated as if it were declared within the class declaration. Whenever an inline function is used, the compiler replaces it with its complete definition, rather than executing a call to the function.

The following example program is an alternative version to the preceding version. This version declares the SumValues() member function as inline, except that this function is now defined outside the class.

```c
#include <stdio.h>

class Sum
{
        int Total;
public:
        void SumValues(int i, int j, int k);
        void DisplayTotal();
};

inline void Sum::SumValues(int i, int j, int k)
{
        Total = i + j + k;
}

void Sum::DisplayTotal()
{
        printf("The total is: %d\n", Total);
}

main()
{
        Sum Sum1; // declare instance of Sum class

                // Add values

        Sum1.SumValues(1, 2, 3);

                // Display Total

        Sum1.DisplayTotal(); // Displays 6

        return 0;
}
```

The keyword inline that precedes the SumValues() member function definition tells the compiler to treat the function as if it were defined within the class.

Static Member Functions

A static member function is a fixed function that can be called without an instance of a class. Unlike non-static member functions, the static member function does not receive a `this` pointer when it is called because it is not tied to any instance. It cannot, therefore, not access any data members because they are only allocated a storage space when an instance of a class is declared. A static member function, however, can be called without an instance of a class.

The following example program illustrates how you declare and reference a static member function:

```
class Useless
{
public:
     static void NoOperation() {};
};

Useless::NoOperation();
```

Notice that the `NoOperation()` member function is called with the `Useless` class reference, rather than the typical instance reference. Also, the `NoOperation()` member function is referenced using the `::` operator, rather than the `'.'` operator. The reason is that the `'.'` is used to access a member of an instance of a class. The `::` operator is used to access a member of the class itself. The `NoOperation()` function is static. Therefore, it is not a member of any instance, but belongs to the class in general.

A static member function cannot access any data members because it cannot be associated with an instance of the class. The following is illegal:

```
class Useless
{
     int  Integer1;
public:
     static void NoOperation()
          { Integer1 = 10; }; // ILLEGAL!
};
```

A static member function is often used to initialize data for all future reference by the class. It is not tied to any instance; therefore, it can be called at the start of a program to initialize values that are later used by all other instances of the class.

Listing 23.2 illustrates the use of the static member function to initialize a value for all future instances of a class.

Listing 23.2. This revised image rotation example uses static member functions.

```
1.   #include <stdio.h>

2.   int  DefaultRotation;

3.   class Image
4.   {
5.   int  Rotation;      // Declare rotation as degrees (0 - 360)
6.   public:
7.   static void    SetDefaultRotation(int DefaultValue)
8.        { DefaultRotation = DefaultValue; }
9.   void SetRotation(int NewRotation = DefaultRotation);  // Sets
➥ rotation to a fixed amount
10.  void DisplayRotation();       // Displays current rotation
11.  void Rotate(int ByDegrees = 90);   // Rotates by additional
➥ degrees specified
12.  };

13.  void Image::SetRotation(int NewRotation)
14.  {
15.  Rotation = NewRotation;
16.  }

17.  void Image::Rotate(int ByDegrees)
18.  {
19.  Rotation += ByDegrees;
20.  }

21.  void Image::DisplayRotation()
22.  {
23.  printf("Current rotation is: %d\n", Rotation);
24.  }

25.  main()
26.  {
27.       // Initialize default rotation for all
28.       // future instances of the Image class

29.  Image::SetDefaultRotation(10);

30.  Image Image1; // declare instance of Image class

31.       // Initialize rotation and display rotation

32.  Image1.SetRotation();
33.  Image1.DisplayRotation();  // Should be 10

34.       // Rotate image by default amount and display

35.  Image1.Rotate();
36.  Image1.DisplayRotation();  // Should be 100

37.       // Rotate image by 10 more degrees and display

38.  Image1.Rotate(10);
```

```
39.    Image1.DisplayRotation();   // Should be 110

40.        // Set rotation to 222 and display

41.    Image1.SetRotation(222);
42.    Image1.DisplayRotation();   // Should be 222

43.    return 0;
44.    }
```

The program in listing 23.2 manages the rotation of images, similar to that of listing 23.1. The difference is that this version enables the program to begin by initializing a global value that is to be used by all instances of the class Image.

Recall that the Image class represents a graphics image on the screen. In this case, the Image class simply manages the rotation of the image, and nothing else. When you declare an instance of an Image class, the starting rotation is set using a call to the SetRotation() member function with no arguments (refer to line 28). When SetRotation() is called with no arguments, it uses a default value (line 9) that is set to the global value DefaultRotation (line 2). In this way, you use the DefaultRotation variable to initialize all instances of the Image class with a starting rotation.

This method of using a variable rather than a fixed value for setting the default rotation state of new instances of the Image class adds flexibility to the program. Now different programs can use the Image class; each can set its own default starting rotation for all instances of the Image class.

You use a static member function referred to as SetDefaultRotation() to set the DefaultRotation variable. This function is defined and declared in lines 7 and 8. The only purpose of this function is to set the DefaultVariable variable for all future instances of the Image class. It is, therefore, declared static because it belongs to the class rather than to any particular instance.

The first action the main() function takes when it starts the program is called SetDefaultRotation() (line 25). This establishes the default state for all future instances of the Image class. Note that the rotations of the Image1 instance are offset by 10 because the SetDefaultRotation() is set to 10 at the start of the program.

Using *const* With Member Functions

A const keyword is useful when you want to restrict access. When applied to a pointer, it means that no function can update the variable referenced by the pointer. The const keyword can also be applied to a member function. It has a different effect, depending on how it is used.

You can use the `const` keyword in two places in a member function declaration, as follows:

```
class Useless
{
    const char* Function1();
    char *Function2() const;
}
```

An example of an incorrect use of `const` is as follows:

```
char* const Function3();
```

The difference between the declaration for `Function1()` and `Function2()` is the place in which you put the `const` keyword. For the declaration of `Function1()`, you place the `const` keyword in front of the return value. With this form, the `const` keyword is applied to the return value. You cannot use the return character pointer of `Function1()` to update the data that it references.

The `Function2()` declaration uses the `const` keyword after the function name. This `const` applies to the `this` pointer that is implicitly passed to all member functions of a class. The `const` keyword restricts access to the data members of the instance that called the function so that they cannot be updated.

Consider the following example program:

```
class Useless
{
    int  Integer1;

public:

    void Function1() const
        { Integer1 = 10; }   // ILLEGAL!
}
```

The definition of `Function1()` is illegal because this function is declared with the `const` keyword that follows the function name. The `this` pointer that is implicitly passed to `Function1()` is, therefore, a `const`, rendering all data members of the `Useless` class inaccessible for updates. The `Function1()` definition attempts to update a data member. The compiler will not successfully compile this code.

You can still reference data members within a function that is declared with the `const` keyword, as long as the data members are not being updated. For example, the following code is valid:

```
class Useless
{
```

```
        int  Integer1;

    public:

        int  Function1() const
                { return Integer1; } // VALID!
    }
```

In this example, the `Function1()` definition also uses the `Integer1` data member. However, it is only using the current data member as a return value without updating the `Integer1` data member itself. Therefore, the code is valid, and successfully compiles.

A `const` keyword is frequently used when you want to protect a function from inadvertently corrupting the data member variables. This protection is particularly relevant when the topic of inheritance is discussed in Chapter 27, "Using Inheritance."

Special Member Functions

Two member functions are implicit in every class whether they are declared or not: the constructor and the destructor. The constructor is called whenever a new instance of a class is declared. The destructor is called whenever an instance of the class is destroyed.

Using Constructors

A constructor is a special member function that is called whenever an instance of a class is declared. The constructor member function always has the function name that is identical to the class to which it belongs. If no constructor is specifically declared by the class (which is the case for all the class examples discussed thus far), an implicit one is used.

A constructor is called only once when you declare a new instance of the class. This provides an opportune place to do any initialization routines.

The following two class declarations are identical, although one declares a constructor, and the other one does not. The first version of the class declares the constructor explicitly:

```
    class Useless
    {
    public:
        Useless() {};
        void DoNothing1();
    }
```

Notice that the constructor does not return a value. Once a class has been created, for each instance of it, the constructor is executed once.

The second version of the same class contains an implicit constructor:

```
class Useless
{
public:
     void DoNothing1();
}
```

Although there is no constructor member function defined with the name Useless(), it is assumed by the class to exist. The implicit Useless() constructor does nothing. No difference exists between this class and the example one that preceded it. Both have the identical class declaration. The only difference is that for the second class declaration, the compiler assumes the constructor member function is defined, even though none is declared.

A constructor member function cannot have a return value. It can, however, have a set of arguments, as does any other member function. These arguments can be set to default values, if necessary. Listing 23.3 demonstrates the use of a constructor.

Listing 23.3. Another image rotation program demonstrates using constructors.

```
1.    #include <stdio.h>

2.    class Image
3.    {
4.    int  Rotation;       // Declare rotation as degrees (0 - 360)
5.    public:
6.    Image(int StartingRotation = 0);   // constructor
7.    void DisplayRotation();       // Displays current rotation
8.    };

9.    Image::Image(int StartingRotation)
10.   {
11.   Rotation = StartingRotation;
12.   }

13.   void Image::DisplayRotation()
14.   {
15.   printf("Current rotation is: %d\n", Rotation);
16.   }

17.   main()
18.   {
19.   Image Image1, Image2(90), Image3(180); // declare three
➡ instances of Image class
```

```
20.   Image1.DisplayRotation();
21.   Image2.DisplayRotation();
22.   Image3.DisplayRotation();

23.   return 0;
24.   }
```

The program in listing 23.3 is a slightly scaled-down version of the one in listing 23.1. The program demonstrates how to create a class referred to as Image to represent an image in a program.

Recall in listing 23.1 that to initialize the Rotation data member, it was necessary to call the member function SetRotation(). In this example, the use of a constructor replaces the need to call an extra function to initialize data member variables. All constructors are called by the name of the class to which they belong. In this case, the constructor is the member function referred to as Image().

The Image() constructor is declared within the class at line 6. The Image constructor takes a single argument that is used to customize the initialization. If the user does not enter a value when the instance of the class is created, the agrument is set to a default value.

To use the constructor, declare an instance of a class and pass the argument necessary for the constructor. Line 19 starts the main() function by declaring three Image objects. The first Image object uses the default value for the constructor. The first Image object, therefore, does not have to pass any arguments, even though the Image constructor is declared with one. The reason is that the one argument that the constructor accepts uses a default of 0. Without any explicit value, the constructor assumes a value of 0 for its argument. The other two Image class instances use an argument for their construction.

With each new instance of the Image class, the constructor, as defined starting on line 9, is executed. For Image1, a value of 0 is passed to the constructor; for Image2, a value of 90; and for Image3, a value of 180.

The definition of the Image constructor begins on line 9. The definition follows the same pattern for defining member functions:

```
class_name::member_function_name()
```

class_name and member_function_name are always the same with a constructor. This might appear strange at first. When looking through large source files, however, it is handy to have this definition stand out because the constructor is often vital to the operation of a class.

The Image class constructor simply assigns the value passed as an argument to the Rotation data member variable (refer to line 11). To see that the three Image instances accepted the constructor argument correctly, lines 20-22 call the DisplayRotation() member functions for each Image object to display the value of the Rotation data member. The output should reflect the different rotations of each of the Image instances.

One of the convenient uses of a constructor is to employ it to copy an existing instance to one that is being declared. Listing 23.4 illustrates how this is done, and demonstrates its use.

Listing 23.4. You can use a constructor to copy an existing instance to one you are declaring.

```
1.    #include <stdio.h>

2.    class Image
3.    {
4.    int  Rotation;      // Declare rotation as degrees (0 - 360)
5.    public:
6.    Image(int StartingRotation = 0);   // constructor
7.    Image(Image& AnImage);   // constructor
8.    void SetRotation(int NewRotation = 0);   //  Sets rotation to a
➥ fixed amount
9.    void DisplayRotation();       // Displays current rotation
10.   };

11.   Image::Image(int StartingRotation)
12.   {
13.   Rotation = StartingRotation;
14.   }

15.   Image::Image(Image& AnImage)
16.   {
17.   Rotation = AnImage.Rotation;
18.   }

19.   void Image::SetRotation(int NewRotation)
20.   {
21.   Rotation = NewRotation;
22.   }

23.   void Image::DisplayRotation()
24.   {
25.   printf("Current rotation is: %d\n", Rotation);
26.   }

27.   main()
28.   {
```

```
29.  Image Image1(90); // declare instance of Image class

30.       // Display rotation of Image1

31.  Image1.DisplayRotation();

32.       // Create a second instance of an
33.       // Image class using Image1 as a reference

34.  Image Image2(Image1);

35.       // Display rotation of Image1

36.  Image2.DisplayRotation();

37.  return 0;
38.  }
```

Listing 23.4 declares another version of the Image class, this time with two constructors, one on line 6 and the other on line 7. This is acceptable, and is called overloading. Chapter 26 covers in greater detail overloaded member functions.

The first constructor of line 6 is the same as the one in listing 23.3. This constructor accepts a starting rotation value, and assigns it to the Rotation data member. The definition of this constructor begins on line 11.

The second constructor of line 7 takes a single argument that is a reference to the Image class. You can create a new instance of the Image class using this constructor. After you do so, you must pass to the constructor another Image class. This might appear strange. However, it has an exceptionally useful purpose. By taking in a reference to another instance of the Image class, this constructor is building a new instance of the Image class. The constructor does this using an existing instance as a reference. Whatever values are in the existing instance are used for the instance that you are creating.

To see how this works, refer to line 34 of listing 23.4. First, Image1 is created by using the constructor that sets the rotation data member. Then, Image1 is used as an argument to create Image2. The constructor used is the second one that is defined on line 15. This constructor takes the value of the Rotation data member of Image1, and assigns it to the Rotation data member of Image2.

The output for both Image1 and Image2 instances of the Image class are identical. The reason is that Image2 has been created using Image1 as its model. Once the Image2 class has been declared, either one of the Image class instances can be updated separately, and they will not affect each other.

Using Destructors

A destructor is a member function that is called when the class is destroyed. All classes have an implicit destructor, even though one is not declared (as is the case with all the example programs discussed thus far). The implicit destructor does not do anything. However, you can declare and define an explicit destructor member function to suit the requirements of a class.

You can declare a destructor using the following format:

```
~class_name();
```

The name of the destructor is the same as the class name to which it belongs. It is distinguished from a constructor by the ~ that precedes its name. A destructor cannot take any arguments.

A destructor is most often used to clean up information when the class is destroyed. One common item that requires cleanup is allocated memory. When memory is allocated, and not freed, it remains inaccessible to anyone. If a class allocates new memory, a common place to free this memory is in the destructor.

The following example demonstrates how a destructor operates:

```
#include <stdio.h>

class Example
{
public:
        ~Example();
};

Example::~Example()
{
        printf("The class is now being destroyed\n");
}
main()
{
        Example Example1;

        return 0;
}
```

This program does nothing except print the line:

```
The class is now being destroyed.
```

If you finish using an object in your program and want to free the memory occupied by the object you create while a program is running, use the destructor member function to destroy the object.

If you examine the code, you do not find any explicit call to the destructor. Similar to the constructor, the destructor is called implicitly when the object to which it belongs is destroyed.

When the `main()` function (and program) terminates, it attempts to erase the `Example` class. Prior to being destroyed, the `Example1` instance calls its destructor. In this case, the destructor of the `Example` class is explicitly defined to print out a line of text. Therefore, the program prints a line of text because the destructor is called when the `Example` class is being destroyed.

Using Friend Member Functions

There are times when a general function needs access to the private data members of a class. In such circumstances, you can declare the function a friend of the class. To do this, declare the function within the class, and precede it with the keyword `friend`. The following example illustrates the use of the friend function.

```
#include <stdio.h>

class Example
{
    int Integer1;
public:
    friend void SetInteger1(Example& E, int i)
        { E.Integer1 = i; }
    friend int GetInteger1(Example& E)
        { return E.Integer1; }
};

main()
{
    Example Example1;

        // Set private data member of Example1

    SetInteger1(Example1, 10);

    // Display private data member of Example1

    printf("The value of Integer1 is: %d\n",
    GetInteger1(Example1));

    return 0;
}
```

This program declares a class referred to as `Example`, which contains a private data member and two friend functions, `SetInteger1()` and `GetInteger1()`. The private data member `Integer1` is generally not accessible by a function. However, since `SetInteger1()` and `GetInteger1()` are declared as friend functions, these can access the private members of the `Example` class.

It is important to note that the friend function is not really part of the `Example` class. When an instance of the `Example` class is declared, the friend function is not a member function. It does not implicitly receive the `this` pointer to tell the function on which instance of the `Example` class to operate. You, therefore, need to pass the instance of the `Example` class on which the `SetInteger1()` and `GetInteger1()` functions must operate.

The program uses the functions `SetInteger1()` and `GetInteher1()` to set the value of the `Integer1` private data member, and display the value on the screen.

To illustrate the point that friend functions are not members of a class, try the following example program:

```
#include <stdio.h>

class Example
{
     int Integer1;
public:
     friend void SetInteger1(Example& E, int i)
          { E.Integer1 = i; }
     friend int GetInteger1(Example& E)
          { return E.Integer1; }
};

main()
{
     Example Example1;

          // Set private data member of Example1

     Example1.SetInteger1(Example1, 10);      // ILLEGAL!

     // Display private data member of Example1

     printf("The value of Integer1 is: %d\n",
          GetInteger1(Example1.Example1));   // ILLEGAL!

     return 0;
}
```

This example program attempts to use the `SetInteger1()` and `GetInteger1()` functions as if they were members of the `Example` class. This program does not compile. You receive a message that `SetInteger1()` and `Example1` are not members of the class `Example`, and cannot be called using the `'.'` operator.

A friend function is used when you want to maintain the protection of data members of a class, but need to make an exception for a few functions. Instead of changing the access of the data members of the class to public so that every function can access them, you can keep them private. Thus, you can open the data members to only the few functions that need to access them. In this way, the data members are still protected from inadvertently being modified. Also, the functions that need direct access to the private data members can have it by being declared a friend of the class.

Summary

The member functions of a class can be used in a variety of ways to customize the way in which they are used. This chapter reviewed the common ways in which a member function can be customized. In this chapter, you learned

- How to use default values for member function arguments so that they are easier to employ, and to correctly initialize the function if the calling function does not do so.

- How to use inline functions to simplify coding.

- How to use static member functions to initialize data for all future instances of a class.

- How to prevent a member function from updating the data members of a class by declaring the function with a const keyword.

- How to use constructors and destructors to initialize and clean up information that is particular for each instance of the class.

- How to use a constructor of a class to copy one instance of a class into another.

- How to safeguard the data members of a class by keeping them private, and still give access to them by declaring those functions a friend of the class.

Chapter 24

Reviewing C++ Scope

This chapter reviews an important aspect of using C++ objects, and that is scope. *Scope* is the domain in which a C++ object is valid. A variety of important rules govern a C++ object. Knowing how C++ objects operate can help you avoid confusing problems.

This chapter covers these topics:

- Rules of C++ scope

- Understanding how C++ scope operates

- Using and possible mishandling of C++ objects

C++ Scope Rules

The scope of an object refers to the place in a program in which an object can be accessed. The accessibility of a C++ object depends on the place in which it is declared within a program. Its point of declaration can limit its use or conflict with other objects that have the same name.

C++ enables four levels of scope, as table 24.1 lists. These levels of scope correspond to the place in a program in which a C++ object is declared.

Table 24.1. These are the types of C++ scope and their descriptions.	
Scope	**Description**
Local	Declared and used within one set of curly brackets (a block)
Function	Declared and used within a single function
File	Declared and used within a single file
Class	Declared and used within a single class

C++ enables you to declare different objects using the same name. Therefore, understanding the rules of scope can help avoid accidentally using the wrong object. There also can be instances when you want to specifically reuse an object name. Knowing the rules of scope enables you to use this concept as a way to control how C++ objects are accessed in your program.

The term C++ object and C++ variable are sometimes used interchangeably in this chapter. A variable is one form of a C++ object that is commonly used in programs. The term *object*, when used by itself in this chapter, refers to variables as well as to objects. For a background on the general use of scope in a program, refer to Chapter 11, "Understanding Variable Scope." This chapter discusses scope as it applies specifically to C++.

Using Local Scope

A C++ object with local scope is any object declared within a set of curly brackets. A local object can only be used within the outermost set of curly brackets in which it is declared.

The code within a set of curly brackets is often referred to as a *block*.

Consider the following program:

```
void main()
{
        // define first block

    {
        int  a;    // declare variable a in first block
    }

        // define second block

    {
        a = 1;     // use variable a in second block
                   // INVALID!
    }
}
```

This example program defines two blocks. In the first block, a variable is declared; in the second block, it is used. This example program does not compile successfully. Variable **a** is automatically assigned a local scope in the first block because it is declared there. A local scope variable can only be referenced within the block in which it is declared. In this case, it is the first block.

When the program attempts to access variable a in the second block, it does not "see" the variable a of the first block. The reason is that the second block cannot access variables declared in the first one. No variables of the name a are declared in the second block. Therefore, the example program fails to compile.

A variable that is declared within a block is automatically assigned local scope to that block.

Note that the `main()` function is declared as

```
void main()
```

This tells the compiler that the return value of the `main()` program is void. The compiler does not expect any return value. Also, the compiler does not give a warning when the `main()` function does not use a return statement. Avoiding a return statement is not a good practice. The reason is that every function should return a value that indicates whether the function succeeded in its task. However, for short example programs used here, and elsewhere in the book, the `main()` is sometimes declared void for simplicity.

Consider this next example program:

```
void main()
{
        // define first block

    {
        int  a;    // declare variable a in first block

        // define second block

        {
            a = 1;     // use variable a in second block
                       // OK!
        }

    }

}
```

This program compiles successfully, even though the variable a is declared in one block, and used in another. The reason is that a local variable is visible within the outermost block in which it is declared. The first block wholly contains the second. Therefore, all local variables within the first block are visible in the second.

Figure 24.1 illustrates how C++ scope rules apply to local objects. The blocks in this illustration are compared to valleys. In the first case, an object in the first valley (block) cannot be seen from the second valley (block). The reason is that the two valleys (blocks) are completely separated. This illustration is analogous to the first example program in which two blocks are declared at the same program level, and the variable a is declared for the first block. Variable a is not "visible" in the second block.

Fig. 24.1.
This illustration shows scope rules as they apply to local objects.

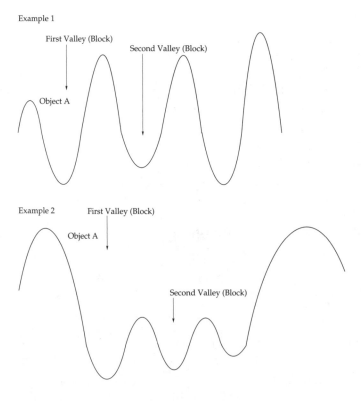

In the second example, the second valley (block) is within the first valley (block). Therefore, an object declared in the first valley (block) can be seen in the second. This illustration is analogous to the second example program in which one block is enclosed by an outer block. A variable declared in the outer block is "higher up" and, therefore, "visible" from within the inner block.

A local object is visible within its own block, and any nested block within its own block.

A local object's visibility can be interrupted if another object by the same name is redeclared in a nested block. Consider the following program:

```
#include <stdio.h>

void main()
{
        // define first block

    {
        int  a = 10;  // declare and define variable a to 10

        // display value of a

        printf("The value of a in the first block is: %d\n", a);

        // define second block

        {
            float    a = 20;  // declare and define variable a
    to 20

            // display value of a

            printf("The value of a in the second block is:
    %f\n", a);
        }
        }
}
```

This example program uses a single variable a twice. In the first, outer block, it is declared as an integer with the value 10. In the second, inner block, it is declared as a float with the value 20. The output for this program is

```
The value of a in the first block is: 10
The value of a in the second block is: 20.000000
```

C++ object names can be reused in different blocks. As the above example program demonstrates, this is valid even for concentric blocks in which the outer block variable is still visible. When an object is redeclared, the new declaration is visible within its block; any object declared with the same name outside the block is shut out. In the above example program, this is the reason that the inner block can declare the object a as a different type of object than the one in the outer block.

Once an object has been redeclared, the new declaration takes effect within its own block, and any block declared within its boundaries, as well. An object can be redeclared to any other valid one. These concepts are demonstrated in the program in listing 24.1.

Listing 24.1. An object can be redeclared to other valid objects.

```
1.    #include <stdio.h>

2.    void main()
3.    {
4.         // define first block

5.    {
6.         int  a = 10;  // declare and define variable a to 10

7.         // display value of a

8.         printf("The value of a in the first block is: %d\n", a);

9.         // define second block

10.        {
11.             float    a = 20;  // declare and define variable a
to 20

12.             // display value of a

13.             printf("The value of a in the second block is:
➥%f\n", a);

14.        // define third block

15.             {
16.                 class Example
17.                 {
18.                 public:
19.                     int GetValue() { return 30; }
20.                 } a;

21.             // display value of a

22.                 printf("The value of a in the third block is:
➥%d\n", a.GetValue());

23.             }
24.        }

25.        // redisplay value of a

26.        printf("The value of a in the first block is still:
➥%d\n", a);
27.    }
28.    }
```

The output for listing 24.1 is

```
The value of a in the first block is: 10
The value of a in the second block is: 20.000000
The value of a in the third block is: 30
The value of a in the first block is still: 10
```

Listing 24.1 might be confusing because the same object name is reused several times. Three blocks are declared within the program at lines 5, 10, and 15. Within each of these blocks, the object name a is used for a different object type. On line 6, it is used to declare an integer variable. On line 11, it is used to declare a float. On line 20, it is used to declare an instance of the class example.

Notice that the compiler does not place any limitation on the type of object to which the name a is assigned and reassigned. Once an object name is reassigned for a block, it is as if the former assignment does not exist for that block. The assignment for the object a is valid for the block in which it is declared, and any block that is bounded by the one in which a is declared. However, when the block ends (by the curly bracket that signifies closing), the variable a reverts to its former declaration.

This can be seen by the last line of output, which follows the second and third blocks. Even though the object named a has been reassigned as a float and an instance of a class, those assignments only apply to the block in which they are declared. Once the block ends with the curly bracket that signifies closing, the reassignment ceases to exist for the remainder of the program.

The last part of the output is executed on line 26, and is within the scope of the first block. It, therefore, uses the integer declaration of a as line 6 shows. The other declarations of a are not visible to the program at this point because the blocks in which the reassignments were declared are now out of scope, and therefore unavailable.

Also, note from listing 24.1, and from the other examples in this section, that a local object can be declared in any place that a statement can be used. A local object does not need to be declared at the top of the block in which it resides. This is clearly illustrated in the next example program:

```
#include <stdio.h>

void main()
{
    int i;    // declare an integer object i

    i = 10;   // use i

    int j;    // declare another integer object j

    j = 11;  // use j

    float f;  // declare a float object f
```

```
    f = 12.12; // use f

        // Display values that were declared and assigned

    printf("The object are: i = %d, j = %d, f = %f\n", i, j, f);
}
```

This example program declares three variables at different points within the function main(). The program manages all three variables correctly because each is a valid statement.

You can declare an object anywhere a statement can be used. You can only use an object at a point in the program after it has been declared. You cannot use the same name for two objects within the same block.

Using Function Scope

Function scope refers to a declaration that is guaranteed to be visible with a function. A function is, strictly speaking, just a block, because it is delineated by curly brackets. However, it is a block that can be called because it is given a label, that is, the function name.

Only one type of statement is valid for an entire function, regardless of the place in the function in which it is referenced. This is the goto label.

Labels are specifically designed to jump code from one place to the next. Therefore, it is necessary to make the label visible from anywhere within the function. Consider this next example program:

```
void main()
{
        // define first block
    {
        goto Label1;
    }

        // define second block
    {
Label1:
    }
}
```

Although the above example program does not do anything, it does compile! This is significant because the goto statement in the first block points to a label in the second block. This is the only case in which the view within a block is extended outside its scope, and into another.

A label can be seen from anywhere within a single function. However, the view of a label does not extend from one function to another, as the next example demonstrates.

```
void DoNothing()
{
Label1:
}

void main()
{
    goto Label1;
}
```

This example produces a compiler error:

```
Undefined label 'Label1' in function main()
```

The reason for this error is that `Label1` is declared in the function `DoNothing()`. When the `main()` function attempts to jump to `Label1` using a `goto` statement, the compiler searches anywhere in `main()` for that label. Even though the label is defined, it is in another function that is outside the scope of `main()`. Therefore, it cannot be found, and the compiler generates an error.

Using File Scope

A *file object* is one that is visible within all blocks of a file. It is often referred to as a *global object*.

File objects can also be referred to as global objects.

To understand global objects, consider the diagram in figure 24.2. Unlike local objects, file objects are visible from any block. They are at a different level of declaration. To understand this concept, consider an analogy. A file object is visible to all blocks just as a blimp can be seen from any valley. A file object can be used from within any function and block of code within the file.

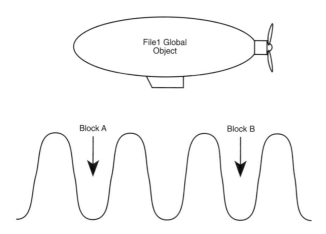

Fig. 24.2.
Global objects are visible from within all blocks of a file.

You can declare a file object by doing so outside of any function. It can be declared anywhere within a file. The only limitation is that you must declare it at a location preceding the one in which it is used. File objects are commonly declared at the beginning of a file. In this way, anyone looking at the file immediately knows what file objects can be referenced from within it.

Consider the following example program:

```
#include <stdio.h>

int a;    // declare a file (global) object

void main()
{
    a = 10;   // assign the file object

    // display the value of a

    printf("The value of a is: %d\n", a);

}
```

The object a is declared as an integer at the beginning of the file. Therefore, it is considered a file or global object. As a file object, it can be referenced within any function or block in the file. In this example, it is assigned a value which is displayed in the main() function.

When both a global and local object are declared with the same name, the local object is used within its block. Consider the next example:

```
#include <stdio.h>

    // declare and assign a global object

int   a = 10;

void main()
{
        // display global object a

    printf("The value of the global object a is: %d\n", a);

        // start a new block of code
    {
        // redeclare and assign a as a local object

        float a = 20;

        // display local object a

        printf("The value of the local object a is: %f\n", a);
    }
}
```

The output for this program is

```
The value of the global object a is: 10
The value of the local object a is: 20.000000
```

The global object a is used as long as there is no other assignment of an object a locally. Declaring a block enables the object name a to be reused. When object a is redeclared and assigned, the local object and its value is seen, rather than the global object.

A global object name can be redeclared differently to make it a local object.

As part of the flexibility of C++, objects can sometimes be redeclared in a way that is valid, but can cause confusion. One case is noted here so that you can be aware of its possibility, and avoid it. The cause of the confusion is that a C++ object can be used within the same block as two different objects! Consider the following example program:

```
#include <stdio.h>

    // declare a global object

int   chameleon;

void main()
{
        // assign global object

    chameleon = 10;

        // display global object

    printf("The value of the global object chameleon is: %d\n",
➡chameleon);

        // redeclare and assign chameleon as a local object

    float    chameleon = 20;

        // display local object chameleon

    printf("The value of the local object chameleon is: %f\n",
➡chameleon);

}
```

The output for this example is

```
The value of the global object chameleon is: 10
The value of the local object chameleon is: 20.000000
```

In this example program, the object Chameleon is used within the same block of the main() function as both a global and a local variable. When it is first used, the only object of which the compiler is aware is the global one.

The reason is that it is the only one that has so far been declared. The first display of chameleon is, therefore, the value assigned to the global object.

A C++ global object name can be redeclared locally. The second local declaration of the object Chameleon is for a different type of object (a float variable). Even though the main() function is a single block of code in which the global object Chameleon has already been used, C++ still lets you redeclare the object Chameleon locally.

After reaching the local declaration of the object Chameleon, the compiler uses the new declaration for all subsequent references within the block. The subsequent display of the object Chameleon reflects the new declaration and assignment.

Although using the same object name twice in a block as two different objects is valid, it can be very confusing. Discussing the issue should help you avoid problems that stem from reusing the same object name. If you reuse an object name to represent different objects, you might come across situations in which your program compiles. However, the value assigned might not be the one you expect. The reason for this discrepancy might be that you are inadvertently using the wrong declaration of the object. To avoid confusion, it is best not to give local and global objects the same name.

You can reuse a global object name locally, even after the global object has been referenced. However, to avoid confusion, it is best to give global and local objects different names.

You can access a global object even after you redeclare the same name as a local object by using the :: operator. The following example program demonstrates how to use the :: operator to specifically reference a global object.

```
#include <stdio.h>

    // declare a global object

int   chameleon;

void main()
{
        // assign global object

    chameleon = 10;

        // display global object

    printf("The value of the global object chameleon is: %d\n",
➡chameleon);
```

```
        // redeclare and assign chameleon as a local object

    float    chameleon = 20;

        // display local object chameleon

    printf("The value of the local object chameleon is: %f\n",
➥chameleon);

        // redisplay global object chameleon

    printf("The value of the global object chameleon is still:
➥%d\n", ::chameleon);
    }
```

The output for this example is

```
The value of the global object chameleon is: 10
The value of the local object chameleon is: 20.000000
The value of the global object chameleon is still: 10
```

This example is identical to the last one, except for the final line of the `main()` function. The program first declares a global object Chameleon. The value of the object is displayed. The object name Chameleon is then redeclared as a local object, and displayed as such. Next, the final line of the `main()` function redisplays the value of the global object using the `::` operator. This operator tells the compiler to ignore the local redeclaration of the chameleon object, and refer to the global one instead.

The `::` operator is called a *scope resolution operator*. It is used to resolve what version of an object or function is intended when there are more than one of either of these by the same name. In this case, it resolves the confusion between the global and local objects that are both named Chameleon. When it is used in a block of code to reference an object, the `::` operator overrides a local declaration, and searches for a global declaration by that object name.

The `::` operator cannot be used to refer to a local object that is declared in an outer block when an object by the same name is declared in an inner block. The following example program illustrates this point:

```
#include <stdio.h>
main()
{
    int  a;  // declare object in outer block

    {
        float a; // declare same object name in inner block

        ::a = 1; // attempt to update outer block object
            // INVALID::
    }
}
```

In this example, the object a is declared in both an inner and an outer block of code. The program does not compile because the object a is referenced using the :: global override operator. Even though there is an outer object a, the :: operator can only reference a global object. The program fails because this operator does not see one. The outer block object a is also a local object, and does not count as a global one, even relative to the inner block of code. A global object is one that is declared outside any function.

Using Class Scope

All members within a class object belong to the class. To access objects of a class from outside requires special operators. In some cases, the class member objects are inaccessible from outside the class. Although prior chapters have already covered some of this information, it is helpful to review these rules. The following are the basic rules for accessing members of a class:

- A class member can only be used directly by a member function of the same class.

- A public member of a class can be accessed by an external function by using the '.' operator.

- A public member of a pointer to a class can be accessed by an external function by using the -> operator.

- A public member of a class can be referenced using the :: operator to resolve ambiguities.

The first two points are illustrated by the following example program:

```
#include <stdio.h>

class Useless
{
public:
    int Integer1;
    GetInteger1() { return Integer1; }
};

void main()
{
        // Declare an instance of the Useless class

    Useless Useless1;

        // Set value of Integer1

    Useless1.Integer1 = 100;

        // Display value of Integer1
```

```
        printf("The value of Integer1 is: %d\n",
→Useless1.GetInteger1());
}
```

The class Useless is first declared with a public member integer variable called Integer1, and a public member function called GetInteger1(). Notice that the GetInteger1() member function can access the Integer1 member variable directly because they both belong to the same class.

When an instance of the Useless class is declared in the main() function, referred to Useless1, the program must use the '.' operator to access any of its members. First, the '.' operator is used to assign a value to the Integer1 member variable of Useless1. In the printf() statement, the '.' operator is used to access the GetInteger1() member function of Useless1. The '.' operator is used for accessing both member variables and member functions.

To access a member of a pointer to a class, use the -> operator. The following example program demonstrates how to use the -> operator:

```
#include <stdio.h>

class Useless
{
public:
    int  Integer1;
};

void main()
{
    Useless Useless1; // Declare an instance of the Useless class
    Useless * pUseless1; // Declare a pointer to an instance of a
Useless class

        // Assign the address of Useless1 to pUseless1

    pUseless1 = &Useless1;

        // Assign a value to Integer1 using the pointer

    pUseless1->Integer1 = 100;

        // Display value of Integer1

    printf("The value of Integer1 is: %d\n", pUseless1->Integer1);
}
```

This program declares a class, Useless, with a single public member variable, Integer1. The main() function declares an instance of class Useless referred to as Useless1. Additionally, a pointer to a class instance of Useless is declared as pUseless1. The address of Useless1 is assigned to the pointer pUseless1. Notice that the method of assigning pointers is the same for class objects as for any other type of object. In C++, all data types are objects, including integers as well as classes. Also, the operators used for managing objects and pointers to them are the same for all objects.

The program then assigns a value to the `Integer1` member of the class instance `Useless1` using a pointer. The `->` operator is used to reference `Integer1` in this case, rather than the `'.'` operator. The reason is that `pUseless1` is a pointer. The value of `Integer1` is then displayed by using a `printf()` function, in which the `Integer1` member variable is again referenced using the `->` operator. The reason is that `Integer1` is referenced by a pointer to the `Useless1` instance.

The final rule of accessing a class member concerns using the `::` operator. The form for using this operator is

```
class_instance_name::member_function
```

A subsequent chapter that discusses inheritance also covers the purpose of using the `::` operator in this way.

You can also use the `::` operator within a class to access a global object. In the last section, the `::` operator was used to access a global variable from within a block that has a local variable declared by the same name. In this section, the use of the `::` is demonstrated to access a global function from within a class that has a member function by the same name.

Consider the following example program:

```
#include <stdio.h>

int GetNumber() { return 50; }

class Number
{
public:
    int GetNumber() { return 100; }
    int GetGlobalNumber() { return ::GetNumber(); }
};

void main()
{
    Number Number1; // declare instance of Number class

        // Display global number

    printf("The global number is: %d\n", GetNumber());

        // Display class number
```

```
        printf("The class number is: %d\n", Number1.GetNumber());

            // Display global number using class member function

        printf("The global number (using the class member function)
➥is: %d\n", Number1.GetGlobalNumber());
    }
```

The output for this example is

```
The global number is: 50
The class number is: 100
The global number (using the class member function) is: 50
```

This example program has two functions that are referred to as `GetNumber()`. The first is declared as a global function at the beginning of the file. The second is declared as a public member function of the Number class, and is defined inline. The global `GetNumber()` function returns the number 50, while the class `GetNumber()` function returns the number 100.

The Number class contains a second public member function referred to as `GetGlobalNumber()`. This function returns the number returned by the global `GetNumber()` function. To call the global `GetNumber()` function within the Number class, a special operator is needed. Otherwise, the Number class function by that name is called. The `::` operator is, therefore, used in the definition of the `GetGlobalNumber()` function to let the compiler know that the global `GetNumber()` function should be used, rather than the one defined in the class.

In general, when a function is called within a class, the compiler first searches for a function by that name which belongs to the class. If it finds a matching function name, the compiler uses it. The only way to tell the compiler to ignore the class scope, and use instead a global function by that name, is to prefix the function by the `::` scope resolution operator. This operator lets the compiler know that it should ignore the class scope, and search instead for a global function by that name.

Understanding C++ Scope

The rules of C++ scope can be best learned and applied if the concept of scope is clearly understood. In the last section, the scope of an object was defined as its visibility within a program. This section clarifies the reason this is so.

Figure 24.3 illustrates how local (auto) objects are placed in memory. A local object begins its existence when a block opens. At this point, it is given space on the stack to store its value. In figure 24.3, the local variables a, f, and string are placed on the stack starting from the stack pointer position. When space for the local objects has been allocated, this memory can be used for the duration of the block, except for these local objects.

Fig. 24.3.
Local objects are placed in memory.

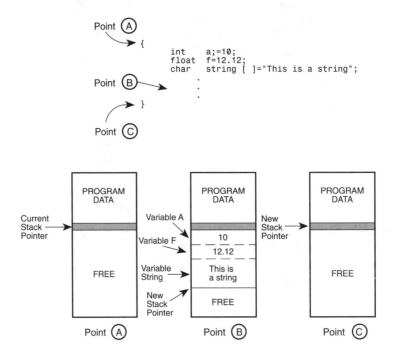

The space allocated by adjusting the stack pointer is temporary memory. Stack memory is, in fact, defined as temporary memory because it is set aside only when it is needed. The start of a block prompts the program to check whether there are any local objects declared within the block. Then, the program sets aside stack memory for those objects, as needed.

As figure 24.3 illustrates, setting aside memory is nothing more than adjusting the position of the stack pointer to a location further down in memory that provides enough space to contain all the locally declared objects. The stack pointer only remains at this location until the block ends. At the close of the block (Point C), the stack pointer returns to the position to which it was pointing at the beginning of the block. The memory that was employed to contain the local objects is now considered freed for other functions or blocks to use.

When a program sees a nested block, it adjusts the stack pointer down to provide enough space to store the local objects of this block. The space that is allocated for a nested block begins in the place in which the outer block's stack memory ends. Figure 24.4 illustrates how nested block objects appear in memory.

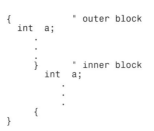

```
{              " outer block
  int  a;
     .
     .
     .
  }            " inner block
    int  a;
      .
      .
      .
    {
}
```

Fig. 24.4.
Nested blocks get their own space in stack memory.

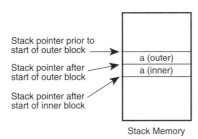

Stack pointer prior to
start of outer block ──→   a (outer)

Stack pointer after ──→   a (inner)
start of outer block

Stack pointer after ╱
start of inner block

Stack Memory

IV

Object-Oriented Programming

One of the significant features noted in figure 24.4 is that the nested block gets its own space in stack memory. Even though the object name a is used in both the inner and outer blocks, in terms of stack memory, both objects get their own unique space in which to contain their respective values.

This explains the reason a program does not confuse two objects with the same name. Even though to the programmer, the inner and outer block objects are referenced by the same name, to the program itself, each object has its own unique location in memory, and its own distinct internal name. The internal name is the object's address in memory, and this always remains distinct. Internally, there is no confusion between the two objects because they are situated at different points in memory. Therefore, they carry distinct "names."

When you give objects the same name, remember that to the program they represent two completely different objects that have no connection. You might choose to call the objects by the same name for convenience or clarity in your particular program. Internally, however, these objects are managed as separate entities, as if they were named uniquely.

Global objects are allocated at the start of a program, and remain in memory for its duration. They remain at the same location; therefore, they can be used from within any block or function in a program. The memory used to store global objects is only freed at the conclusion of the program.

Using and Mishandling C++ Scope

There are times when calling different objects by the same name is a convenience. Therefore, the rules of C++ scope enable you to do this. Generally, it is best to name objects so that their purpose is evident. This section provides some common ways to use object scope, as well as the manners in which it can be mishandled.

Assigning Objects and Functions the Same Name

In C++, you cannot give a global object the same name as a function. For example, the following program does not compile:

```
int twin;  // Declare a global variable

int twin() { return 10; };  // Declare a function

main()
{
    .
    .
    .
}
```

You can declare a local object using the same name as a function. However, accessing the function from within the block in which the local object by the same name is declared requires the :: operator. Consider the following example program:

```
#include <stdio.h>

    // Declare and define function

int twin() { return 10; };

void main()
{
    int twin = 20;  // declare local variable

        // Display value of local variable twin

    printf("The value of the local object twin is: %d\n", twin);

        // Display value of the function twin()
```

```
        printf("The value of the function twin is: %d\n", ::twin());
}
```

The output for the preceding program is as follows:

```
The value of the local object twin is:20
The value of the function twin is: 10
```

This program declares a function named `twin`. The same name is used again
to declare a local object, which is a variable. The local variable `twin` "hides"
the function `twin()`. The reason is that you can only reference the name twin
without any special operators as the local variable `twin`. The local object
name always takes precedence.

To reference the function from within the block of code defined by `main()`,
use the `::` operator, as is done in the preceding example. The `::` operator is
often referred to as the scope resolution operator because it resolves to which
object or function by that name you intend to refer. When you use the `::`
operator to precede an object or function name, you are referring to the
object or function that is declared globally.

Referring to a function and an object by the same name can add confusion to
your program. It can cause a compiler error if you forget to use the `::` operator when accessing the function—a move which indicates that the function
does not exist. Even when the program compiles correctly, having a function
and object with the same name makes reading and understanding the flow of
the program confusing.

Passing Global Objects as Parameters

C++ enables you to pass the value or pointer to a global object as an
argument to a function, as in the following example program:

```
#include <stdio.h>

int AnInteger; // Declare global variable AnInteger

    // Define function to display the value of an integer

void DisplayInteger(int i)
{
    printf("The value of the integer is: %d\n", i);
}

void main()
{
        // Assign a value to the global variable AnInteger

    AnInteger = 10;
```

```
                          // Use DisplayInteger() function to display
                          // the value of the global variable i

                      DisplayInteger(AnInteger);
             }
```

The `DisplayInteger()` function in this example is called, using the global variable `AnInteger` as an argument. This is valid, and the program compiles and runs as expected.

Although passing a global object as an argument to a function is valid, it is not recommended. An object should only be declared for the duration that it is needed. If an object is only needed temporarily, it should be declared local.

Certain circumstances exist when a value is needed for the duration of a program. For example, the command line flags that are used to indicate how the program should operate when it is called might be necessary at different points of its operation. If they are to be referenced throughout the program, these must be declared globally. However, it is not good practice to pass these values as an argument to a function. As global objects, they should be referenced directly.

Assigning Function Arguments and Global Objects the Same Name

You can name an argument of a function using the same term that you employ for a global object, as in the following example:

```
#include <stdio.h>

int AnInteger; // Declare global variable AnInteger

    // Define function to display the value of an integer

void DisplayInteger(int AnInteger)
{
    printf("The value of the integer is: %d\n", AnInteger);
}

void main()
{
        // Use DisplayInteger() function to display a value

    DisplayInteger(100);
}
```

In this example, the argument to the `DisplayInteger()` function is declared with the same name as the global variable `AnInteger`. This, too, is valid in C++, and the program compiles and runs as expected, displaying the value `100` on the screen.

It is not good programming practice to name a parameter the same as a global object. When you declare an argument of a function, it is as if you had done so at the start of the function block. It is, therefore, governed by the same rules as a local (auto) object. As such, when you give a global object and a local argument the same name, the latter hides the former. You cannot access the global object directly within the function. You still can use the global scope resolution operator :: to access the global object by the same name. However, this only adds a level of complexity to your program that is unnecessary and sometimes confusing.

For clearer and less confusing programs, it is best to have global objects and arguments assigned unique names.

Assigning Members in Two Classes the Same Name

One of the powers of C++ classes is its capability to encapsulate all the functionality of an object. In many circumstances, you can describe the functionality of various objects using similar names. Consider the program in listing 24.2 that reuses the same member names in two different classes.

Listing 24.2. Different classes can contain the same member names.

```
1.   #include <stdio.h>
2.   #include <string.h>

3.   class Circle
4.   {
5.   char Color[20];
6.   public:
7.   void AssignColor(char *AColor)
8.        { strcpy(Color, AColor); }
9.   void DisplayColor()
10.       { printf("The circle color is: %s\n", Color); }
11.  };

12.  class Square
13.  {
14.  char Color[20];
15.  public:
16.  void AssignColor(char *AColor)
17.       { strcpy(Color, AColor); }
18.  void DisplayColor()
19.       { printf("The square color is: %s\n", Color); }
20.  };

21.  void main()
22.  {
23.  Circle Circle1;  // Declare an instance of Circle

24.  Square Square1;  // Declare an instance of Square
```

(continues)

Listing 24.2. Continued.

```
25.      // Assign a color to Circle1
26.  Circle1.AssignColor("Blue");
27.      // Assign a color to Square1
28.  Square1.AssignColor("Green");
29.      // Display the color of Circle1
30.  Circle1.DisplayColor();
31.      // Display the color of Circle1
32.  Square1.DisplayColor();
33.  }
```

This program defines two classes, one to represent a circle, and the other, a square. The only feature that is tracked in this example is the color of the object.

In both classes, the names of the members are identical. To track the color, both objects use a character buffer referred to as `Color`. To assign a color to the object, both the Circle and Square classes have a member function called `AssignColor()` that is defined. To display the color value for either class, a member function `Display Color()` is used. This program compiles and runs as expected. The assignment for each class is properly made, and the color for each is displayed correctly.

With global and local objects, you should not reuse the same name because this adds confusion. However, in this case, it actually simplifies reading and using the Circle and Square classes. When defining different classes that are related, or that contain similar features and perform actions that are alike, it is common practice to use identical names for data members and member functions. Using matching names for data members and member functions helps to represent similar features and functionality in the different classes.

By using the same member names in different classes that behave similarly, you can use the different class objects in the same way. For example, to assign a color to an object, you only need to be aware that the member function `AssignColor()` is used. This applies to both the Circle and the Square class. In a real application, you might have many more objects that behave as do the Circle and Square classes, such as a Rectangle or Line class. Having the same member function, `AssignColor()`, defined for all these related classes makes it simpler to use any of them.

Having the same name for functions that accomplish the same task for different classes makes sense. To program the Square and Circle classes, you know that AssignColor() has the same effect of assigning the value of the argument to the internal Color data member. From a usage perspective, assigning a color to a Circle or Square, or any other similar class object, means the same thing. Having the same member function simply means that you can use the corresponding programming vocabulary to describe the equivalent action to similar class objects. This makes working with similar classes easier to deal with because only one set of vocabulary is required.

Assigning Class and Global Objects the Same Name

Another combination of objects that C++ enables you to declare with the same name includes classes and global objects. This makes sense because a class is just another C++ object, similar to an integer. It is mentioned separately to highlight certain points regarding sharing a name between a class and an object.

Consider the following example program:

```
int Circle;  // Declare a global variable Circle

class Circle // Declare a class Circle
{
public:
    char Color[20];
};

void main()
{
    Circle Circle1;  // Declare an instance of Circle class
            // INVALID!
    .
    .
    .
}
```

This program declares a class and a global variable using the same name, Circle. If the main() function did not contain a line that attempts to declare an instance of the class Circle, the program would compile. C++ enables both the class and the integer variable to be declared with the same name Circle. However, if you attempt to use the name Circle to reference the class, the compiler does not 'see' the class Circle. The reason is that it is hidden by the global integer variable Circle. Using the scope resolution operator :: to access the class does not work in this case because the integer Circle is itself a global variable.

In this case, you can access the class Circle by using the class keyword, as follows:

```
int Circle;  // Declare a global variable Circle

class Circle // Declare a class Circle
{
public:
    char Color[20];
};

void main()
{
    class Circle Circle1;  // Declare an instance of Circle class
                      // OK
    .
    .
    .
}
```

The class keyword tells the compiler that the Circle object that is referenced in this statement, refers to the class Circle rather than the global variable Circle.

Although you can declare a class and a global object with the same name, and use the class keyword to resolve the ambiguity to the compiler, this practice is also not recommended. Whenever the name of one object can be confused with another, it is best to rename either so that the name better describes the unique purpose. In this way, reading and using the objects will be clear and meaningful, rather than confusing.

Loop Variable Declarations

One of the most common reasons for redeclaring a variable name is to use it in a loop. The following example illustrates how this is done:

```
#include <stdio.h>

int counter = 10; // Declare global variable counter

void main()
{
        // Reuse variable counter in a loop

    for ( int counter = 0; counter < 5; counter++ )
        printf("The value of counter is: %d\n", counter);

        // Display value of counter again

    printf("The value of counter after the loop is: %d\n",
➥counter);

        // Display value of global counter again

    printf("The value of global counter is: %d\n", ::counter);
}
```

This example declares a global variable counter, and initializes its value to 10. In the `main()` function, the `for` loop then redeclares the integer variable counter for its own internal purpose, and displays the value of counter with each iteration of the loop. The complete output of this example is

```
The value of counter is: 0
The value of counter is: 1
The value of counter is: 2
The value of counter is: 3
The value of counter is: 4
The value of counter after the loop is: 5
The value of global counter is: 10
```

When the `for` loop declares the variable counter, it is a local variable. The `for` loop body is considered a single block in which local variables are only visible within the loop. Therefore, the counter declaration is considered the `for` loop block and therefore is considered a local variable to the `main()` function. The sixth line of output reflects this. In the sixth line of output, the counter variable is used without any scope operator, and reflects the value of the `for` loop counter variable, which is 5 at the close of this loop.

The counter variable is declared local to the `main()` function. Therefore, it persists as the only visible object with the name "counter." To reference the global variable counter, you must use the global resolution operator `::`, as is done in the last line of `main()`. The output, which is 10, reflects the value of the global counter variable rather than the local one.

Remember that when you declare a variable for a loop, you are declaring a local variable for the entire block of code in which the loop resides. If the variable shares the same name as a global object, the same rules and recommendations apply (similar to a common case involving the sharing of global and local object names).

Summary

The rules of C++ scope are flexible. This gives a great degree of latitude to programmers so that they can creatively use these rules to their benefit. However, along with the flexibility can come confusion. For example, you might use a shared object name, and mistakenly refer to the non-intended object. This chapter reviewed the rules of C++ scope, and also some of the common uses of, and ways to mishandle, these rules.

The issues that this chapter covered included the following:

■ How to know the C++ scope rules, including local, function, file (global), and class scope.

■ How to use the global resolution operator : : to reference a global object or function when a local object is declared by the same name.

■ How C++ local objects are declared in memory, and how C++ enables names to be shared.

■ How to use C++ shared names to simplify programming, as when you define members of similar classes with identical names to refer to the same features or actions of these classes.

■ How to avoid confusing programs by not declaring global and local objects, and function parameters with identical names.

Chapter 25

Using Overloaded Functions and Operators

The term *overloaded* in C++ means that a single function or operator can be defined in several different ways. This capability is similar to the notion that the English language supports several meanings of the same word. You implicitly know the meaning of a word that has multiple definitions by the context in which it is used; similarly, the compiler in C++ knows which version of the function or operator you intend to use by the context in which it is employed.

This chapter covers the many details and variations of creating and using overloaded functions and operators. In this chapter, you learn how to declare, define, and use

- Overloaded global functions
- Overloaded class member functions
- Overloaded operator functions
- Overloaded friend operator functions

Understanding Overloading

To overload a function or operator refers to giving it multiple definitions. This notion is taken for granted in spoken languages. For example, the word *RUN* has several meanings, as figure 25.1 shows.

Fig. 25.1.
The Word RUN has
several different
meanings.

run (rŭn) *v*. **1.** To move swiftly on foot with both feet leaving the ground
during each stride. **2.** To put or be in operation.

You know which definition of the word RUN is referred to by the context in
which the word is used. For example, these two sentences have different meanings for the word RUN:

"If you want to get there fast, you need to run now."

"The baseball player hit a two-run double yesterday."

You cannot confuse the preceding first and the second statements. One is referring to a fast-pace walk, and the other, to baseball. It is easy to distinguish
between the two by the context in which they are used in a sentence.

An overloaded function works on the same principle. The compiler knows which
version of the function or operator you intend to use based on the arguments by
which it is called. The *arguments* of an overloaded function are its context, and
how the compiler distinguishes one version of a function from another.

Using Overloaded Functions

An *overloaded function* is one that is defined by the same name more than once.
To distinguish one version from another, each definition of the function must
have a different set of arguments. For example, the following are different overloaded functions:

```
void DoNothing();
void DoNothing(char *string);
void DoNothing(int i, float f);
```

Each of these versions of the `DoNothing()` function can be used in the same
program. The compiler knows which version of the `DoNothing()` function you
intend to use based on the arguments by which it is called. For example, table
25.1 lists several calls to `DoNothing()`, and indicates which version of this function the compiler selects.

Table 25.1. The compiler picks among several versions of calls to `DoNothing()`.	
How `DoNothing()` **is Called**	**Version of** `DoNothing()` **Used**
`int i = 10; // declare integer`	`void DoNothing(int i, float f);`
`float f = 12.2; // declare float`	

How DoNothing() **is Called**	**Version of** DoNothing() **Used**
DoNothing(i, f);	
char string[] = "This is a string";	void DoNothing(char *string);
DoNothing(string);	
DoNothing();	void DoNothing();

When the compiler sees an overloaded function, it reviews all the versions of this function that have been declared in the program. Then, it finds the version that matches the number and type of arguments that are used. This is how the compiler knows which version of an overloaded function to call.

The compiler finds a match for an overloaded function based on three criteria:

■ Number of arguments

■ Type of arguments

■ Order of arguments

All three criteria are significant. For example, the following pairs of overloaded functions are not identical:

```
void DoNothing(int i, int j);
void DoNothing(int i);   // NOT THE SAME
                         // different number of arguments

void DoNothing(int i, float f);
void DoNothing(float f, int i);   // NOT THE SAME
                                  // different order of arguments

void DoNothing(int i, int j);
void DoNothing(int i, float j);   // NOT THE SAME
                                  // different types of arguments
```

Each of the pairs of overloaded functions above are valid. However, they are not identical. When the compiler sees each of the preceding pairs of functions that are declared, it translates them into two different versions of the function DoNothing(). When the DoNothing() function is then used in a program, the compiler can distinguish one version of the function from the other.

The return value of a function is not a criteria for distinguishing one version of an overloaded function from another. The following pair of functions produces a compiler error:

```
void DoNothing();
int DoNothing();    // INVALID OVERLOAD
```

Overloaded functions must have a unique context. A change of return values is not a unique context in C++. Only the three distinctions listed in the previous fragment: number, order, and type of arguments, determine a context for an overloaded function.

You can define overloaded functions as regular functions or member functions of a class.

Overloading Global Functions

In C++, you can overload any function that you are able to define globally. For example, the following program demonstrates how a global function can be overloaded:

```
#include <stdio.h>

void DisplayNumber()     // Declare with no arguments
{
    printf("The number is: 10\n");
}

void DisplayNumber(int i)  // Declare with a single integer argu-
ment
{
    printf("The number is: %d \n", i);
}

void main()
{
    int i = 20; // declare and initialize an integer variable

        // Display a default number

    DisplayNumber();

        // Display a user-defined number

    DisplayNumber(i);
}
```

The output for this program is

```
The number is: 10
The number is: 20
```

In this program, the function `DisplayNumber()` is declared twice. The first time, it is declared with no arguments, and the second, with a single integer argument. When the `main()` function uses `DisplayNumber()` for the first time, it is used with no arguments. Therefore, the version of `DisplayNumber()` with no arguments is called. The second time `DisplayNumber()` is used in the `main()` function is with a single integer argument. The only version of `DisplayNumber()` function that matches this argument list is the second one. Therefore, the second `DisplayNumber()` function is called.

One of the common uses of overloaded function is to execute the same sequence of instructions for different data types. Consider the program in listing 25.1.

Listing 25.1. Overloaded Functions are used to Create Blank Spread sheets.

```c
1.    #include <stdio.h>

2.    // Define several versions of a function
3.    // to display a blank spreadsheet with
4.    // customized column headings

5.    void CreateSpreadsheet(int i, int j, int k)
6.    {
7.         // Display custom headings

8.    printf("\n\t%d\t%d\t%d\n", i, j, k);

9.         // Display rows

10.   printf("Row 1:\nRow 2:\nRow 3:\n\n");
11.   }

12.   void CreateSpreadsheet(char a, char b, char c)
13.   {
14.        // Display custom headings

15.   printf("\n\t%c\t%c\t%c\n", a, b, c);

16.        // Display rows

17.   printf("Row 1:\nRow 2:\nRow 3:\n\n");
18.   }

19.   void CreateSpreadsheet(char *a, char *b, char *c)
20.   {
21.        // Display custom headings

22.   printf("\n\t%s\t%s\t%s\n", a, b, c);

23.        // Display rows

24.   printf("Row 1:\nRow 2:\nRow 3:\n\n");
25.   }
```

(continues)

Listing 25.1. Continued.

```
26.   void main()
27.   {
28.       // Create blank spreadsheet with character column headings

29.   CreateSpreadsheet('L', 'M', 'N');

30.       // Create blank spreadsheet with string column headings

31.   CreateSpreadsheet("Item", "Quantity", "Total");

32.       // Create blank spreadsheet with numeric column headings

33.   CreateSpreadsheet(1, 2, 3);
34.   }
```

The output for this program is

```
            L       M       N
Row 1:
Row 2:
Row 3:


            Item    Quantity        Total
Row 1:
Row 2:
Row 3:


            1       2       3
Row 1:
Row 2:
Row 3:
```

This program is designed to create a blank spreadsheet. To simplify the program, the spreadsheets are three columns by three rows. The CreateSpreadsheet() functions defined on lines 5, 12, and 19 each take a different set of arguments to customize the column headings. On line 5, the CreateSpreadsheet() function accepts integers as column headings. On line 12, the CreateSpreadsheet() function accepts characters, and on line 19, it accepts strings as column headings.

By having the same function declared several times using different arguments, you can create a blank spreadsheet in a number of ways. This gives added flexibility to the function named CreateSpreadsheet().

Overloaded functions should not be confused with scope issues. In listing 25.1, all versions of CreateSpreadsheet() are declared as global (file) functions, and can be used anywhere. As the main() function in listing 25.1 illustrates, the various versions of `CreateSpreadsheet()` can be used in the same block. This is in contrast to objects that are redeclared in another scope in which, for a given block of code, only a single version of an object is visible at a time.

Overloading Member Functions

You can declare a class with overloaded member functions. An overloaded member function is governed by the same rules that control the global overloaded functions. The scope of overloaded member functions remains within the class, just as with any other member function.

The following example illustrates the use of overloaded class member functions:

```
#include <stdio.h>

class Item
{
public:
    void Display()           // Display no item
        { printf("The item is: NOTHING\n"); }

    void Display(int i) // Display integer item
        { printf("The item is the integer: %d\n", i); }

    void Display(char *string)    // Display a string item
        { printf("The item is the string: %s\n", string); }
};

void main()
{
        // Declare an instance of Item

    Item Item1;

        // Display a string item

    Item1.Display("This is a string");

        // Display no item

    Item1.Display();

        // Display an integer item

    Item1.Display(100);
}
```

The output for this example is

```
The item is the string: This is a string
The item is: NOTHING
The item is the integer: 100
```

In this example, the class Item is declared with three versions of the Display()
member function. Each version of the Declare() member function is used to
display a different type of argument, such as a string or an integer. If no argument is used, a default text line is displayed on the screen.

In the main() function, each of these versions of the Display() member function is used. The compiler has no trouble identifying which version of the
Display() member function to call because the arguments passed can easily
be distinguished. The compiler matches the argument used for each call to
the Display() in the main() function, and searches for the appropriate declaration of Display() that matches. If the compiler cannot find a correct match,
the program fails.

Avoiding Ambiguities

With all the flexibility that C++ provides in function overloading, automatic
type conversion, and default parameter passing, several pitfalls are worth noting. The pitfalls are generally caused by a pair of overloaded functions that can
be confused with each other in a particular circumstance. These ambiguities are
equally applicable to global as well as member functions. The following examples illustrate the most common ambiguities of overloaded functions.

Misusing Default Argument Values

One of the common oversights is to declare a pair of overloaded functions
so that when the default arguments are used in a function declaration, both
functions appear identical. The following example illustrates this point:

```
#include <stdio.h>

void Display(char c, int n = 10)   // Displays the c character n
times, 10 by default
{
    for(int i = 0; i < n; i++)
        putchar(c);

    putchar('\n');
}

void Display(char c)               // Displays a single character
{
    printf("%c\n", c);
}

void main()
{
        // Display a character 25 times

    Display('B', 25);
```

```
                // Display a character 10 times by default using the
     first Display(),
                // OR, a single character using the second Display()

        Display('A');
    }
```

This example defines two versions of a function named `Display()`. The first version takes two arguments, a character and an integer. The purpose of the first `Display()` function is to display a character the number of times indicated by the second argument. To make this function convenient to use, the second argument is given a default value of `10`. This means that if the second argument is not used, the character displays ten times on the screen.

The second version of the `Display()` function is used to display a single character on the screen. It takes a single argument that is a character.

When it calls `Display()` for the first time, `main()` uses two arguments, the letter `B` and the number `25`. This argument list matches the first declaration of `Display()`. Thus, the compiler knows to call the first `Display()` function. This function displays the letter `B` twenty-five times on the screen.

When the `main()` function calls `Display()` a second time with only a single argument that is a character, the compiler becomes confused. The compiler looks at the first declaration of `Display()` and realizes that it can apply because it can use the default value for the integer argument, and be left with a single character argument. It looks at the second declaration of `Display()` and sees that it, too, can apply. The reason is that because the second `Display()` declaration only takes a single argument that is a character.

Both versions of `Display()` can apply, in this instance. However, the compiler cannot choose on its own which one is the correct version of `Display()` to call. This program fails, and produces a compile error indicating that there is an ambiguous call to an overloaded function.

What is especially confusing in this case is that the compiler does not look for potential ambiguities. Had the second call to `Display()` not been made in the `main()` function, the program would have compiled correctly. It is only when the second call to `Display()` is made with a single argument (that is a character) that the compiler attempts to use the different versions of `Display()`. After trying the different versions of `Display()`, and realizing that each one can apply, only then does the compiler produce the error. When the compiler tries the different versions of `Display()`, and realizes that each one can apply, only then does it produce the compile error.

Misusing Reference Arguments

A simple oversight that involves using a copy and a reference to an argument can also cause a compiler error. Consider the following example program:

```
#include <stdio.h>

int Triple(int i)   // Triples the value
{
    return 3 * i;
}

int Triple(int& i)  // Triples the value
{
    return 3 * i;
}

main()
{
        // Display the triple value of a number

    printf("The triple value of 10 is: %d\n", Triple(10)):
}
```

In this example, the overloaded function `Triple()` is used to multiply a value by three. The value is passed as an argument to the `Triple()` function.

The example fails to compile. The reason is that when the compiler attempts to match the use of `Triple()` in the `main()` function, it sees that two versions of the Triple() function can apply. The reason is that a reference to a value is passed in the same way as is a copy of a value. Therefore, when a value is used as an argument, both versions of `Triple()` can apply. The compiler cannot decide on its own which one to use. Thus, it produces an error, and fails to compile the program.

Misusing Type Promotion or Type Conversion

Another form of ambiguity is caused when two versions of an overloaded function appear the same when a type conversion or type promotion is necessary.

Type promotion refers to upgrading from one data type to another related type. Consider the following statements:

```
float f;

f = 10;    // Assign a value to f
```

In this case, the integer value of `10` is upgraded by the compiler to a float value of `10` so that it can properly be assigned to the float variable `f`. Internally, a float value and an integer value are stored very differently. Therefore, the upgrade is necessary for the assignment to take place. This is referred to as a type promotion because both a float and an integer are similar, but not identical, data types.

A *type conversion* is simply a stronger kind of type upgrade in which the values are not necessarily similar. However, the compiler still thinks it can convert the data usefully. The following is an example of a type conversion.

```
char c;

c = 42;    // Assign a value to c
```

In this case, an integer is used for an assignment to a variable that is declared as a character. An integer is not similar to a character from the outside. However, internally, an integer and a character are not very different. Everything is stored internally as a set of binary numbers. Therefore, a character, which is a single byte of information, can easily be converted to and from an integer.

When the integer 42 is assigned to the character variable c in the preceding example, the compiler can make the translation, and convert the integer 42 into the character '*'. This is referred to as type conversion.

The compiler automatically does a type promotion and conversion when it sees that it can do so successfully. This is the situation in which a type conversion can be confusing—when it is used in conjunction with overloaded functions. The next example illustrates such a case.

```
#include <stdio.h>

void Display(float f)    // Display the value of a float
{
    printf("The value of the float is: %f\n", f);
}

void Display(double d)    // Display the value of a double
{
    printf("The value of the double is: %f\n",d);
}

void main()
{
    int i = 10;  // Declare and initialize an integer
    float f = 12.12;  // Declare and initialize a float
    double d = 15.15;  // Declare and initialize a double

        // Display the float variable f

    Display(f);
```

```
        // Display the double variable d

    Display(d);

        // Display the integer variable i

    Display(i);
}
```

The preceding example uses the overloaded function `Display()` to display either a float value or a double. The difference between the two is that a double has the capability to store a much larger number than can a float. However, they can both store fractions.

The `main()` function declares three variables: an integer, a float, and a double. When the function `Display()` is called for the first time, it is passed a float variable as an argument. Even though technically a float can be upgraded to a double, and both versions of `Display()` can apply, the direct match with no conversion takes precedence over a match that requires a conversion. Thus, there is no ambiguity in the call. The second call to `Display()` using a double argument also matches a version of this function without any conversion. Therefore, there is no ambiguity to confuse the compiler.

When the third call to `Display()` is made in the `main()` function, it is passed an integer variable. The compiler now has a choice: it can use the first version of `Display()`, and upgrade the integer value from an integer to a float. Alternatively, it can use the second version of the function, and upgrade the integer value to a double. Both are valid upgrades. However, the compiler cannot decide on its own. It fails to compile this program, and produces an error.

Using Overloaded Operators

In C++, you can define various ways in which operators are used just as you can overload functions. Defining operators follows a similar pattern as overloading functions: you declare the operator and arguments that are to be used. Then, you define a function that executes that version of the redefined operator. However, there are many more details to cover when defining operator functions.

Table 25.2 lists the four basic types of operators.

IV

Table 25.2. There are four types of operators.	
Type	**Description**
Binary	Uses two arguments, such as + and -
Unary	Uses a single argument, such as ++. —, and the unary -
Relational	Uses two arguments, and returns a relational value indicating true or false, such as == and !=
Assignment	The = operator that assigns one value to another

Overloaded operators are generally associated with classes. They apply to a class in the same way as built-in operators apply to built-in data types. For example, the following statement is valid:

```
int i = 10;
int j = 20;
int k;

k = i + j;
```

The + operator is used to add the integer variables i and j. In fact, the + operator is inherently overloaded because you can use it to add floats, doubles, and integers. In each case, the compiler knows how to manage the data internally. The reason is that the + operator is overloaded so that you can apply it to the various types of data.

When you declare classes, the operators are not applicable in the same way that they are with built-in types. Consider the following example program:

```
class A
{
    .
    .
    .
};

void main()
{
    A a1, a2, a3;
    .
    .
    .
    a3 = a1 + a2;
}
```

The + operator cannot be used in this case because the compiler has no idea how to add the a1 instance to the a2 instance of class A. The class A is not a built-in type. Therefore, the two instances could potentially be added any number of ways of which the compiler is totally unaware.

To remedy this, and to make C++ easy to use with classes, C++ enables you to declare operator functions that tell the compiler how to apply operators to the classes that you define. In this way, you can define operators for your own classes. The user would intuitively associate with every operator the function that you intend, especially as each applies to your class.

Of course, once you can define operators, you can make them perform in any way. However, to make classes intuitive, it is best to apply the conventional understanding of how an operator is used to your own classes.

To declare an operator, you use the following syntax:

```
return_value operator@(arguments);
```

The return value can be any valid built-in or user-defined data type, and follows the general rules for return values of any other function. A specific return value is necessary in certain situations. In others, certain types of return values should be avoided. An upcoming discussion covers these.

The declaration of the function must include the word operator. The @ character is the place in which you put the operator, such as + or -. You can declare the arguments in the same way as you would for general functions, with certain limitations for some operator functions. The next sections discuss these.

The full declaration of an overloaded operator function resembles this:

```
class A
{
    .
    .
    .
    A operator+(A a1);
}
```

In this example, the class A defines an overloaded + operator function. The + function takes a single argument that is a copy of class A, and it returns a copy of class A. With this declaration, you can add two instances of the class A.

When you define an operator function, you must observe the following rules:

■ The number of operands cannot change. For example, a binary operator, such as +, takes two operands. When you redefine the + operator, you must use two operands.

- The precedence of operators cannot change. For example, C++ defines unary operators as having precedence over binary ones. You cannot redefine any operator so that it can change its precedence.

- An overloaded operator cannot be defined as static. A static function applies to a class, and an operator function must apply to an instance of a class. Therefore, an operator function cannot be declared as static.

- You cannot overload certain operators. These operators are ., .*, ::, ?:, #, and ##. These operators are used internally by C++ for a definite purpose, and cannot be overloaded.

There are enough distinguishing details of each type of function overloading that table 25.2 lists to warrant covering each kind separately.

Binary Operator Overloading

Any binary operator can be overloaded. A *binary operator* is any operator that requires two values for its use. The most common binary operators are + and - because each needs two values. Table 25.3 lists the complete set of binary operators that you can define.

Table 25.3. These binary operators can be overloaded.	
Operator	**Description**
+	Addition
-	Subtraction
+=	Inclusive addition
-=	Inclusive subtraction
/	Division
*	Multiplication
/=	Inclusive division
*=	Inclusive multiplication
%	Remainder

A binary operator function takes a single argument. Although this might appear confusing, this rule makes sense when you begin to work with overloaded functions because a binary operator uses two operands. The operand to the left is passed implicitly to the operator function. The one on the right must be declared and passed.

Consider the following example which illustrates several interesting points regarding binary operator functions.

Listing 25.2. This program illustrates binary operator function overloading.

```
1.   #include <stdio.h>
2.   #include <string.h>

3.   #define MAX_INGREDIENTS  200

4.   class Soup
5.   {
6.   char Ingredients[MAX_INGREDIENTS];

7.   public:
8.        // Constructor

9.   Soup() { Ingredients[0] = 0; }

10.       //  Member function to display ingredients

11.  void DisplayIngredients()
12.       { printf("The ingredients for the soup are: %s\n",
➥Ingredients); }

13.       // Overloaded operator function += to add new ingredients

14.  void operator+=(char *NewIngredient);
15.  };

16.  void Soup::operator+=(char *NewIngredient)
17.  {
18.  int NewLength;  // Declare an integer value to store total
➥length of Ingredients

19.       // Calculate total length of Ingredients if NewIngredient
➥is added
20.       // Use three extra for blank space, comma, and trailing 0

21.  NewLength = strlen(NewIngredient) + strlen(Ingredients) + 3;

22.       // If it is over the maximum amount of buffer space,
➥don't add it

23.  if ( NewLength > MAX_INGREDIENTS ) return;

24.       // Add new ingredient to the list

25.  if ( Ingredients[0] == 0 )              // if Ingredient list
➥is empty
```

```
26.        strcpy(Ingredients, NewIngredient);  // just place new
➥ingredient in list
27.  else                          // otherwise,
28.  {
29.        strcat(Ingredients, ", ");          // append a comma-
➥delimiter
30.        strcat(Ingredients, NewIngredient); // then append new
➥ingredient
31.  }
32.  }

33.  void main()
34.  {
35.  Soup MySoup;  // Declare instance of Soup class

36.        // Display soup ingredients

37.  MySoup.DisplayIngredients();

38.        // Add some ingredients

39.  MySoup += "Potatoes";
40.  MySoup += "Celery";

41.        // Display soup ingredients again

42.  MySoup.DisplayIngredients();
43.  }
```

The output to this program is

```
The ingredients for the soup are:
The ingredients for the soup are: Potatoes, Celery
```

The program in listing 25.2 declares a single class called Soup. The purpose of this class is to maintain the information necessary for cooking a soup.

The class contains a single data member called Ingredients that is a character array (buffer). This buffer holds all the ingredients necessary for the soup.

The Soup class also defines three member functions. The first is a constructor, and is declared and defined inline on line 9. When an instance of the class is declared, a constructor is called once. Its purpose is generally to initialize data within the class. In this case, it initializes the Ingredients buffer so that it contains a 0 in the first byte of the buffer. For a null-terminated string, this is the same as setting it to empty.

The second member function is DisplayIngredients() declared and defined inline on line 11. The purpose of this function is to display the Ingredients data member on the screen. This lets the user know which ingredients have so far been added to the soup.

The third member function declared for the Soup class is an overloaded +=
operator on line 14. The += operator is the inclusive add operator, which
generally implies that the operand on the right is added and included in the
one on the left. In this case, the operand on the right is declared as the argument, which is the new ingredient that is added to the Soup class.

There are various points to note regarding the declaration of the += overloaded
member function for the Soup class. The operand to the left is implicitly passed
in all binary operator functions. In the statement on line 39 that uses the +=
operator, the implicit this pointer, to MySoup, is automatically passed. Therefore, it is not needed as an argument when declaring the += member function.

The argument does not need to be any particular type. In this case, because
the += operator for the Soup class is used to add ingredients, a character
pointer for an argument is most convenient. Also, note that no particular
return value needs to be declared. In this case, the void type is used to make
the function simple.

The += member function is defined outside the class function starting on line
16. The syntax for defining an operator function is basically the same as that
for defining any member function outside the class. The only point here is
that the word operator must be maintained in the declaration line.

The += operator function first checks that the length of the new ingredient
string, when added to the existing list of ingredients, does not exceed the maximum buffer size for the data member Ingredients, which is MAX_INGREDIENTS.
If the new ingredient can be added, another check is performed to see if it is
the first one. If it is not the first ingredient, a comma-delimiter and a space are
placed between ingredients to make the output more readable.

The output of listing 25.2 reflects the two calls to DisplayIngredients(). The
first call is immediately after the MySoup instance is declared, and no ingredients were added. The second call is after two ingredients are added. This describes the simple use of a binary operator.

One of the more useful features of binary functions is that you can string
them together in a sequence, provided they are defined correctly. Using the
soup class, you might have the following sequence:

```
Soup Soup1, Soup2, Soup3;  // Declare 3 instances of the Soup class
     .
     .
     .
Soup3 = Soup1 + Soup2;  // Add two instances and place them in a
third instance
```

In this sequence, two instances of the class Soup are added to form a third one. If you examine the logic that the + operator must follow to make this work, you come up with the following explanation. The + operator must take an operand on the right, add it to the current operand (on the left). Then, the operator returns a copy of the combined classes, which is necessary so that it can be implicitly used. For example, in the above instance, the combination of Soup1 and Soup2 are assigned to another class, Soup3. You also need a temporary combined class in the sequence:

Soup1 + Soup2 + Soup3

The pair of classes to the left will be combined first using the normal order of precedence of operators. The combined pair of classes needs to be placed in a temporary class so that it can be used in the next operation, which is adding the combined Soup1 and Soup2 to the Soup3 instance. As with the normal use of +, you cannot change the value of the operands. Therefore, a temporary value is necessary when adding objects in sequence.

The next listing implements an overloaded function to manage the + operator for the Soup class. The + operator for the Soup class will serve the purpose of combining all ingredients of one soup with another. Remember that the operand to the left is the one passed as the implicit this pointer, while the operand to the right is passed explicitly through the argument. This makes a difference in the sequence of ingredients that are added together using their respective Soup classes.

Listing 25.3 is an extended version of the previous listing, adding an overloaded + operator to the Soup class.

Listing 25.3. An overloaded function is used to manage the + operator for the Soup class.

```
1.
2.    #include <stdio.h>
3.    #include <string.h>

4.    #define MAX_INGREDIENTS  200

5.    class Soup
6.    {
7.    char Ingredients[MAX_INGREDIENTS];

8.    public:
9.        // Constructor
```

(continues)

Listing 25.3. Continued.

```
10.   Soup() { Ingredients[0] = 0; }

11.      //  Member function to display ingredients

12.   void DisplayIngredients()
13.       { printf("The ingredients for the soup are: %s\n",
➥Ingredients); }

14.       // Overloaded operator function += to add new ingredients

15.   void operator+=(char *NewIngredient);

16.       // Overloaded operator function + to combine Soup classes

17.   Soup operator+(Soup& ASoup);
18.   };

19.   void Soup::operator+=(char *NewIngredient)
20.   {
21.   int NewLength;  // Declare an integer value to store total
➥length of Ingredients

22.       // Calculate total length of Ingredients if NewIngredient
➥is added
23.       // Use three extra bytes for blank space, comma and
➥trailing 0

24.   NewLength = strlen(NewIngredient) + strlen(Ingredients) + 3;

25.       // If it is over the maximum amount of buffer space,
➥don't add it

26.   if ( NewLength > MAX_INGREDIENTS ) return;

27.       // Add new ingredient to the list

28.   if ( Ingredients[0] == 0 )              // if Ingredient list
➥is empty
29.       strcpy(Ingredients, NewIngredient);  // just place new
➥ingredient in list
30.   else                          // otherwise,
31.   {
32.       strcat(Ingredients, ", ");          // append a comma-
➥delimiter
33.       strcat(Ingredients, NewIngredient); // then, append new
➥ingredient
34.   }
35.   }

36.   Soup Soup::operator+(Soup& ASoup)
37.   {
38.   Soup TempSoup;  // Declare temporary soup class to return

39.       // Add ingredients of both the left and right operands
```

```
40.          // to TempSoup

41.   TempSoup += Ingredients; // Add ingredients of the left
➥operand
42.                          // (it is implicitly the this pointer)

43.   TempSoup += ASoup.Ingredients;  // Add ingredients of the
➥right operand

44.   return TempSoup;          // return temporary Soup class
45.   }

46.   void main()
47.   {
48.   Soup MySoup1, MySoup2, MySoup3;  // Declare three instances of
➥the Soup class

49.          // Add ingredients to MySoup1 and MySoup2

50.   MySoup1 += "Carrots";
51.   MySoup2 += "Zuchini";

52.          // Combine MySoup1 and MySoup2 and add add the result

53.   MySoup3 = MySoup1 + MySoup2;

54.          // Display MySoup3 ingredients

55.   MySoup3.DisplayIngredients();
56.   }
```

The output for listing 25.3 is

```
The ingredients for the soup are: Carrots, Zuchini
```

The new overloaded + operator for the Soup class is declared on line 17, and
defined on line 36. Notice that the declaration takes as an argument a reference to a Soup class, and returns a copy of this class. The + operator is used to
add two instances of the Soup class together. Therefore, the right operand
must be a class. The right operand must accept a class instance. The reason is
that this operand is reflected in the argument of the + function. A reference
to a Soup class (rather than a copy of it) was selected as the argument type for
the right operand for efficiency.

The return value of the + operator function is a temporary copy of the Soup
class that is declared in the + member function. This temporary class is necessary as a return value so that the result of the + operation (which is the return
value) can be used in sequence with other operators. Some of these others
include another +, or the = operator, both of which require a Soup class reference as an operand.

In this case, the actual definition of the + operator starting on line 36 turns out to be uncomplicated. The + operator is defined as combining the ingredients for the Soup class. Therefore, the ingredients for the right and left operands are inclusively added to the temporary Soup class declared internal to the function. Notice that the left operand, which is implicitly passed as the this pointer, is used first in conformance with the normal precedence order of the + operator. This order ensures that the ingredients of the left operand appear before the ingredients of the right one.

The main() function of listing 25.3 declares three instances of the Soup class, and adds ingredients to the first two. The first two Soup instances are then added together, and assigned to the third. The result is displayed, and is as expected.

Unary Operator Overloading

Unary operator overloading works very similarly to binary operator overloading, except that no arguments are necessary. A unary operator uses a single operand which is passed an implicit **this** pointer. Therefore, no argument is necessary in a unary function declaration. Table 25.4 lists the unary operators that can be overloaded in Turbo C++.

Table 25.4. These unary operators can be overloaded.	
Operator	**Description**
+	Unary +
-	Unary -
*	Pointer Dereference
&	Address of
~	One's complement
++	Increment
—	Decrement

A unary operator is declared the same way as a binary operator function, except that a unary operator is defined with no arguments.

Consider the class defined in the previous section with a unary operator +. For the purposes of this example, the + operator in this case clears the contents of the Ingredients data member, and return a reference to the class.

Although this is not the normal association with the + operator, you can define operators any way you want. The use of the unary + operator to clear the ingredients list, rather than add to it, is used to illustrate how a class distinguishes between a unary and a binary + operator. Listing 25.4 contains the new version of the Soup class.

Listing 25.4. The unary + operator is used to clear the Soup class.

```
1.   #include <stdio.h>
2.   #include <string.h>

3.   #define MAX_INGREDIENTS  200

4.   class Soup
5.   {
6.   char Ingredients[MAX_INGREDIENTS];

7.   public:
8.        // Constructor

9.   Soup() { Ingredients[0] = 0; }

10.       //  Member function to display ingredients

11.  void DisplayIngredients()
12.       { printf("The ingredients for the soup are: %s\n",
➥Ingredients); }

13.       // Overloaded operator function += to add new ingredients

14.  void operator+=(char *NewIngredient);

15.       // Overloaded operator function + to combine Soup classes

16.  Soup operator+(Soup& ASoup);

17.       // Overloaded operator function (unary) + to clear
➥Ingredients

18.  Soup& operator+()
19.       { Ingredients[0] = 0; return *this; }
20.  };

21.  void Soup::operator+=(char *NewIngredient)
22.  {
23.  int NewLength;  // Declare an integer value to store total
➥length of Ingredients

24.       // Calculate total length of Ingredients if NewIngredient
➥is added
25.       // Use three extra for blank space, comma, and trailing 0

26.  NewLength = strlen(NewIngredient) + strlen(Ingredients) + 3;
```

(continues)

Listing 25.4. Continued.

```
27.        // If it is over the maximum amount of buffer space,
➥don't add it

28.   if ( NewLength > MAX_INGREDIENTS ) return;

29.        // Add new ingredient to the list

30.   if ( Ingredients[0] == 0 )                // if Ingredient list
➥is empty
31.        strcpy(Ingredients, NewIngredient);  // just place new
➥ingredient in list
32.   else                          // otherwise,
33.   {
34.        strcat(Ingredients, ", ");           // append a comma-
➥delimiter
35.        strcat(Ingredients, NewIngredient); // then, append new
➥ingredient
36.   }
37.   }

38.   Soup Soup::operator+(Soup& ASoup)
39.   {
40.   Soup TempSoup;  // Declare temporary soup class to return

41.        // Add ingredients of left and right operands
42.        // to TempSoup

43.   TempSoup += Ingredients; // Add ingredients of left operand
44.                            // (it is implicitly the this pointer)

45.   TempSoup += ASoup.Ingredients;  // Add ingredients of right
➥operand

46.   return TempSoup;           // return temporary Soup class
47.   }

48.   void main()
49.   {
50.   Soup MySoup1, MySoup2, MySoup3;  // Declare three instances of
➥the Soup class

51.        // Add ingredients to MySoup1 and MySoup2 and add the
➥results

52.   MySoup1 += "Carrots";
53.   MySoup2 += "Zuchini";

54.        // Combine MySoup1 and MySoup2 and add it to MySoup3

55.   MySoup3 = MySoup1 + MySoup2;

56.        // Display MySoup3 ingredients

57.   MySoup3.DisplayIngredients();
```

IV

Object-Oriented Programming

```
58.        // Clear MySoup3 using the unary + operator

59.   +MySoup3;

60.        // Display MySoup3 ingredients again

61.   MySoup3.DisplayIngredients();
62.   }
```

The output for listing 25.4 is

```
The ingredients for the soup are: Carrots, Zuchini
The ingredients for the soup are:
```

The only additional parts added to the Soup class are lines 18 and 19, which declare and define the overloaded unary + operator for this class. The purpose of the unary + operator is to erase the ingredients. This is done on line 19 by setting the first byte of the Ingredients buffer to 0. For null-terminated strings, this effectively erases the contents. The return value is a reference to the instance of the Soup class itself. The reason for this return value is so that the unary + operator can be used in sequence with other operators that require a reference to the Soup class in the same statement.

One important point to notice concerning the Soup class is that it now has two overloaded + operator functions. The way it knows which one to use is the context in which the overloaded + operator function is employed in a statement. On line 55, in which MySoup1 is combined with MySoup2, the + operator has two operands. The first (the left operand MySoup1), is passed implicitly and the second is passed as an argument. The compiler searches for an overloaded + operator function with a single argument in this case. This is the binary + operator that is declared on line 16.

The next use of the + operator is on line 59. In this statement, only one operand is found. It is passed as the implicit this pointer. There are no other operands, so the compiler looks for an overloaded + operator function that has no arguments. This is the unary + operator function declared on line 18.

In this way, the compiler can tell the difference between a unary and binary overloaded operator function.

Logical and Relational Operator Overloading

Logical and relational operators are really binary operators that are limited in what return values they can use. Logical and relational operators are used to compare two items, and return a value that represents the result of the comparison. Therefore, an overloaded logical or relational operator must be defined to conform to this standard.

Table 25.5 lists the common return values for logical operators. Table 25.6 lists common return values for relational operators.

Table 25.5. Logical operators can have these return values.	
Return Value	**Use**
1 or any non-zero number	True
0	False

Table 25.6. Relational operators can have these return values.	
Return Value	**Use**
1 or any positive number	Left operand is greater than right operand
0	Operands are equal
-1 or any negative value	Left operand is less than right operand

Table 25.7 lists the logical and relational operators that can be overloaded in Turbo C++.

Table 25.7. These unary operators can be overloaded.	
Operator	**Description**
==	Logical equals
!=	Logical not equals
>	Relational greater than
<	Relational less than
>=	Relational greater than or equals
<=	Relational less than or equals

Using the Soup class of the previous section, it is straightforward to add an overloaded == operator member function which determines whether two Soup instances are equal. The equality is based on whether the ingredients are the same for both Soup instances. Listing 25.5 provides the additional code necessary for the == operator member function.

Listing 25.5. The = operator function determines whether two Soup **instances are equal.**

```
1.    #include <stdio.h>
2.    #include <string.h>

3.    #define MAX_INGREDIENTS  200

4.    class Soup
5.    {
6.    char Ingredients[MAX_INGREDIENTS];

7.    public:
8.        // Constructor

9.    Soup() { Ingredients[0] = 0; }

10.       //  Member function to display ingredients

11.   void DisplayIngredients()
12.       { printf("The ingredients for the soup are: %s\n",
➥Ingredients); }

13.       // Overloaded operator function += to add new ingredients

14.   void operator+=(char *NewIngredient);

15.       // Overloaded operator function + to combine Soup classes

16.   Soup operator+(Soup& ASoup);

17.       // Overloaded operator function (unary) + to clear
➥Ingredients

18.   Soup& operator+()
19.       { Ingredients[0] = 0; return *this; }

20.       // Overloaded operator function ==

21.   int operator==(Soup& ASoup)
22.       { return !strcmp(Ingredients, ASoup.Ingredients); }
23.   };

24.   void Soup::operator+=(char *NewIngredient)
25.   {
26.   int NewLength;  // Declare an integer value to store total
➥length of Ingredients

27.       // Calculate total length of Ingredients if NewIngredient
➥is added
28.       // Use three extra for blank space, comma, and trailing 0

29.   NewLength = strlen(NewIngredient) + strlen(Ingredients) + 3;

30.       // If it is over the maximum amount of buffer space,
➥don't add it
```

(continues)

Listing 25.5. Continued.

```
31.  if ( NewLength > MAX_INGREDIENTS ) return;

32.       // Add new ingredient to the list

33.  if ( Ingredients[0] == 0 )              // if Ingredient list
➥is empty
34.       strcpy(Ingredients, NewIngredient);  // just place new
➥ingredient in list
35.  else                        // otherwise,
36.  {
37.       strcat(Ingredients, ", ");          // append a comma-
➥delimiter
38.       strcat(Ingredients, NewIngredient); // then, append new
➥ingredient
39.  }
40.  }

41.  Soup Soup::operator+(Soup& ASoup)
42.  {
43.  Soup TempSoup;  // Declare temporary soup class to return

44.       // Add ingredients of left and right operands
45.       // to TempSoup

46.  TempSoup += Ingredients; // Add ingredients of left operand
47.                    // (it is implicitly the this pointer)

48.  TempSoup += ASoup.Ingredients;  // Add ingredients of right
➥operand

49.  return TempSoup;          // return temporary Soup class
50.  }

51.  void main()
52.  {
53.  Soup MySoup1, MySoup2, MySoup3;  // Declare 3 instances of the
➥Soup class

54.       // Add ingredients to MySoup1, MySoup2 & MySoup3

55.  MySoup1 += "Carrots";
56.  MySoup2 += "Zuchini";
57.  MySoup3 += "Carrots";

58.       // Compare MySoup1 & MySoup2, and print result

59.  if ( MySoup1 == MySoup2)
60.       printf("MySoup1 and MySoup2 are equal\n");
61.  else
62.       printf("MySoup1 and MySoup2 are NOT equal\n");

63.       // Compare MySoup1 & MySoup3, and print result
```

```
64.  if ( MySoup1 == MySoup3)
65.      printf("MySoup1 and MySoup3 are equal\n");
66.  else
67.      printf("MySoup1 and MySoup3 are NOT equal\n");
68.  }
```

The output for this program is

```
MySoup1 and MySoup2 are NOT equal
MySoup1 and MySoup3 are equal
```

The == operator function is declared and defined inline on lines 21 and 22. For the Soup class, the most reasonable comparison of two instances would determine whether their respective ingredients are the same. To accomplish this, a C library strcmp() is used to compare the Ingredients data member of the two Soup instances. The negative value for strcmp() is returned.

The reason for returning the negative value is that for logical operators, a value of 1 indicates true, and 0, false. Table 25.5 lists these values. The strcmp() function returns a 0 for true (equality), and a non-zero value for false (non-equality). Therefore, the return of strcmp() must be reversed to get the effect necessary for the == operator.

Notice in this and other operator definitions that the instance of Soup that is passed as an argument appears internally as a friend. The private data members of the Soup class that are passed as an argument are directly accessible within the operator function.

Assignment Operator Overloading

The assignment operator = is unique because it is the only operator that is automatically defined for every class. However, many reasons exist to override the default definition for the assignment operator.

By default, the assignment operator does a bit-by-bit copy of the right operand to the left operand. On line 53 of listing 25.3, the following statement is used:

```
MySoup3 = MySoup1 + MySoup2;
```

Even though the assignment operator was not declared for the Soup class, the assignment statement worked. The default assignment operator copied every bit of the combined MySoup1 and MySoup2 classes, and placed the result in MySoup3. The latter class, therefore, contained valid Ingredient information.

There are times when the default assignment operator is not useful.

- If a class contains allocated pointers, the default assignment does not work correctly. With a bitwise copy, only the pointer variable is duplicated, rather than the information that is pointed to. Once the class is copied, there is no guarantee that the information at the address of the pointer will remain there for the duration of the assigned class. In this case, a customized assignment operator is more suitable so that new memory can be allocated. Then, the allocated information can be copied into memory location that is controlled by the assigned class.

- If a class has certain data members that require copying, and others that need special treatment, the default assignment operator does not work. The default operator copies all bits of a class. Therefore, all data members are copied. A customized assignment operator function is required to ensure that only the appropriate data members are copied, and the remaining ones set to appropriate values.

When defining your own assignment operator, keep the following points in mind.

- The assignment operator function should take a single argument that is a reference to the class. An assignment operator uses two instances of a class: the instance on the right that is copied to the one on the left. Although a copy of the instance on the right can also be used, it is inefficient.

- The assignment operator function should return a reference to the left operand class. This is to ensure that the result of the assignment operation can be used in sequence with other functions that require a copy or reference to the class.

- The assignment operator function should ensure that the right class reference is copied to the left one, rather than the reverse, in keeping with the normal use of the assignment operator within C++. Although you can actually define the assignment operator to perform in the reverse, or even execute an unrelated sequence of steps, this can simply cause confusion. It would disconcert the person using the class who sees an assignment operator declared, and assumes that it works as do all other assignment operators.

- The assignment operator cannot be declared a friend member function.

Using Friend Operator Functions

A *friend operator function* is one that is declared using the `friend` keyword. This keyword works the same as in other function declarations: It enables the function to access the private data members of a reference to the class that is passed as an argument.

The most significant distinguishing feature of the friend operator class is that any operand that is needed for the operator function must be declared and passed. The friend function does not get an implicit `this` pointer passed for the left operand. Therefore, the friend function must declare it explicitly.

Having all operands passed as arguments to the friend operator class is exactly what makes this kind of operator function useful. In a non-friend operator function, the left operand is passed implicitly, assuming that it is the class object. For example, in the previous section in which the += operator was defined for the Soup class, the operator definition assumed that the left operand was a Soup class object. When the += operator was used, it was always with the following format:

```
MySoup += "Carrots";  // Add ingredient to the Soup class
```

Although the right operand can be any data type, the left one always has to be a Soup class object. Suppose that you wanted to use the += operator in the following way:

```
"Carrots" += MySoup;  // Add ingredient to the soup class
```

The compiler searches for a += function definition that has a string pointer as the left argument, and a reference to a Soup class as the right one. The += operator function of the prior listings does not match this argument list. Therefore, this operator function is not used.

Supporting non-class references as the left argument for operator functions requires a friend operator function. The friend operator function can declare both its arguments. As such, you can use any combination of left and right arguments for the += operator.

Listing 25.6 illustrates how the friend += operator is defined to support a string buffer as a left argument.

Listing 25.6. This program uses a friend += operator function.

```
1.   #include <stdio.h>
2.   #include <string.h>

3.   #define MAX_INGREDIENTS  200

4.   class Soup
5.   {
6.   char Ingredients[MAX_INGREDIENTS];

7.   public:
8.       // Constructor

9.   Soup() { Ingredients[0] = 0; }

10.       //  Member function to display ingredients

11.  void DisplayIngredients()
12.      { printf("The ingredients for the soup are: %s\n",
➥Ingredients); }

13.      // Overloaded operator function += to add new ingredients

14.  void operator+=(char *NewIngredient);

15.      // Overloaded friend operator function += to add new
➥ingredients

16.  friend void operator+=(char *NewIngredient, Soup& ASoup)
17.      { ASoup += NewIngredient; }

18.      // Overloaded operator function + to combine Soup classes

19.  Soup operator+(Soup& ASoup);

20.      // Overloaded operator function (unary) + to clear
➥Ingredients

21.  Soup& operator+()
22.      { Ingredients[0] = 0; return *this; }

23.      // Overloaded operator function ==

24.  int operator==(Soup& ASoup)
25.      { return !strcmp(Ingredients, ASoup.Ingredients); }
26.  };

27.  void Soup::operator+=(char *NewIngredient)
28.  {
29.  int NewLength;  // Declare an integer value to store total
➥length of Ingredients
```

```
30.        // Calculate total length of Ingredients if NewIngredient
➥is add
31.        // Use three extra for blank space, comma, and trailing 0

32.  NewLength = strlen(NewIngredient) + strlen(Ingredients) + 3;

33.        // If it is over the maximum amount of buffer space,
➥don't add it

34.  if ( NewLength > MAX_INGREDIENTS ) return;

35.        // Add new ingredient to the list

36.  if ( Ingredients[0] == 0 )              // if Ingredient list
➥is empty
37.        strcpy(Ingredients, NewIngredient);  // just place new
➥ingredient in list
38.  else                      // otherwise,
39.  {
40.        strcat(Ingredients, ", ");         // append a comma-
➥delimiter
41.        strcat(Ingredients, NewIngredient); // then, append new
➥ingredient
42.  }
43.  }

44.  Soup Soup::operator+(Soup& ASoup)
45.  {
46.  Soup TempSoup;  // Declare temporary soup class to return

47.        // Add ingredients of left and right operands
48.        // to TempSoup

49.  TempSoup += Ingredients; // Add ingredients of left operand
50.                    // (it is implicitly the this pointer)

51.  TempSoup += ASoup.Ingredients;  // Add ingredients of right
➥operand

52.  return TempSoup;        // return temporary Soup class
53.  }

54.  void main()
55.  {
56.  Soup MySoup;  // Declare instance of the Soup class

57.        // Add ingredients to MySoup

58.  "Carrots" += MySoup;
59.  "Zuchini" += MySoup;
60.  "Cucumbers" += MySoup;

61.        // Display ingredients of MySoup

62.  MySoup.DisplayIngredients();
63.  }
```

The new += friend operator function is declared and defined inline on line 16 and 17. Notice that the first argument of the function declaration is a pointer to a character array (buffer), and the second is a reference to a Soup class. The function definition merely calls the original += operator definition with the arguments reversed.

The new friend += operator function enables you to add ingredients using a character string as the left operand. This is done in lines 58, 59, and 60. The output of the program in listing 25.6 is

```
The ingredients for the soup are: Carrots, Zuchini, Cucumbers
```

The ingredients are added one at a time, from left to right, the same as if the non-friend += operator function had been used. The only difference here is that the left operand is a string rather than a reference to a Soup class.

Summary

Overloading functions is one way to make your class easier to use. A function can be used in more places and in more ways by having its function name associated with a single purpose, and declared for several varieties of argument lists. This makes overloaded functions useful.

Overloaded operators enable you to make a class functional with operators that are familiar to every programmer. For example, a + operator is always associated with adding. By defining a relevant + operator for your class, it can be used in a way that does not require much education or training. The reason is that everyone knows what a + operator does. The challenge is to make the + operator add to your class something relevant that can be recognized by someone else.

This chapter covered many details and rules regarding function and operator overloading. In this chapter you learned the following:

- Overloaded functions are similar to a word in English that has many meanings. The function can be used with the same name, and its functionality depends on the context in which it is used.

- The context of an overloaded function is determined by the number of arguments that it is called by their order and their type.

IV

- You declare and define overloaded functions similar to the way you do so for non-overloaded functions. What makes an overloaded function more useful is that you can declare it more than once.

- Operators can also be overloaded for a class, using a special syntax. To declare an operator function, use the keyword operator followed by the actual operator character to be overloaded.

- Operator function overloading must follow certain rules. An operator function cannot change the precedence of operator priority. Also, an operator function must be used with the same number of operands as is normally associated with the operator, and cannot be declared static.

- The number of arguments for a non-friend operator function is one less than the number of operands for that operator. The left operand is passed implicitly as the `this` pointer.

- The assignment operator is implicitly defined for all classes. The default assignment operator does a bitwise copy to the assigned class.

- The assignment operator can also be overloaded. It is necessary to overload the assignment operator when you do not want a bitwise copy for the assignment. The reason is that some data members need to be initialized, or there is a data member that is a pointer.

- A friend operator function is declared with an argument for each operand. The left operand is not passed implicitly. Therefore, it must be declared as an argument.

- Friend operator functions can be helpful when you do not want the left operand to be a reference to the class.

Chapter 26

Using Constructors and Destructors

IV

Object-Oriented Programming

C++ offers a unique approach to creating objects. When you define an object, you can also specify certain tasks that should take place when the object is created and destroyed. These tasks will happen, regardless of how the object is created and destroyed. These tasks are called constructors and destructors, and are defined implicitly as part of every C++ class.

You have the opportunity to override the implicit, or default, constructor and destructor functions so that tasks that are customized for your class are called when your class is created and destroyed. This chapter shows you the following:

- How constructors and destructors work

- How to customize and use constructors

- How to customize and use destructors

- How to use the specialized C++ allocation and deallocation keywords `new` and `delete`

Understanding Constructors and Destructors

When an instance of a C++ object is declared, the program sets aside the proper amount of memory in which to store the object information. Figure 26.1 shows the amount of space set aside for several C++ objects. This space is retained for the duration that the C++ object is used. When the object is no longer used, the space set aside for its data is freed for another object.

Fig. 26.1.
Space is set aside
for selected C++
objects.

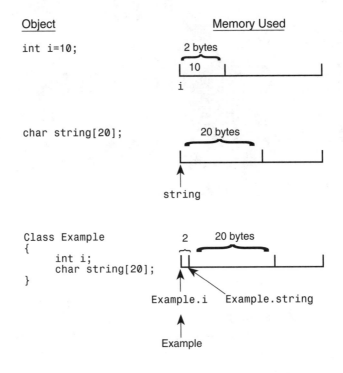

In addition to setting aside space when an object is created, a special function is executed. This function is called a *constructor*. Also, immediately before the freeing of an object's space (when it is no longer used), another special function is executed. This function is called a *destructor*. Figure 26.2 illustrates the sequence of events when an object is created and destroyed.

In C++, every object has a constructor and destructor function implicitly defined for it. The reason you might not have noticed this before is that you do not need to define these special functions for them to work. The compiler builds a constructor and destructor function for each object if none is defined. These are called the default constructor and destructor functions. They add nothing to the creation and destruction of an object. They are created so that if you want to, you can override them to execute specialized tasks when an object you define is created or destroyed.

To override a constructor or destructor function, you merely have to define them. You can define either one of them without the other, or both. As soon as a compiler sees a user-defined constructor or destructor function, it uses the one you define, instead of creating a default one.

Events When an Object is Used:

Create Object:

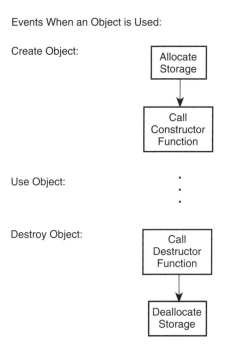

Fig. 26.2.
This drawing
illustrates the
sequence of
events when an
object is created,
then destroyed.

Use Object:

Destroy Object:

If you do not need a constructor or destructor, the compiler builds a default one for you that does nothing. Otherwise, if you declare either one, the compiler calls your customized constructor or destructor function when it creates or destroys your object.

Defining a constructor and destructor is similar to declaring and defining any other function. You can use all the C library calls within these functions just as you could in any other function. However, there are certain limitations as well as some guidelines that make your constructor and destructor functions more useful. The next sections cover these.

Using Constructors

A constructor is built by default for every class that is defined. The default constructor does nothing. To add specialized functionality when an instance of a class is created, you must define a constructor.

A customized constructor is useful in many situations. Constructors are commonly used to perform the following tasks:

■ Initialize data members to values that are useful. In many classes one or more data members need to be set to initial values. The most useful place to do this is in the constructor function. This way, whenever an instance of the class is created, the appropriate data members are initialized.

■ Allocate extra storage space for a class. In some situations, you might need to allocate extra space in which to store additional information in a class. For example, a class that contains a list in the form of an array is a good candidate for allocating space. It can be used for the array data member when the class is created. You can declare an array of values relevant to the class with a maximum number of elements. However, a more flexible method is to tell the class how many elements you need when it is created. The constructor can then dynamically allocate the appropriate space necessary to store the list of array values. In this way, only the correct amount of space is allocated for each instance of the class.

To override the default constructor which does not execute any code, you need to declare and define a constructor function. When the compiler sees a constructor defined for your class, it automatically uses your constructor rather than the default one. The next section describes how to override a constructor function.

Overriding the Default Constructor

A constructor can be defined for any class. You do this by declaring within the class a function that has its name. In other words, the constructor function is a function that is the name of the class. The following example code illustrates how a constructor is defined:

```
class DoNothing     // declare a class
{
    .
    .     // place private members here
    .
public:
    DoNothing();    // declare constructor using name of class
    .
    .   // place public members here
    .
}
```

Notice that a constructor is just a function that shares its name with the class in which it is defined. You cannot use the name of the class for any other purpose. If the compiler sees a member function with the name of the class, it automatically uses it as a constructor.

A constructor function shares many features with other class member functions. A constructor can be called with any number of arguments. The arguments of a function can be set to default values. A constructor function can call any C library function, as well as call or access any other private or public member of the class. A constructor can be declared inline, or defined outside a class. You can even overload the constructor by declaring various constructor functions. You do this by declaring several member functions with different arguments that all have the same name as the class in which they are declared.

The following special rules apply to a constructor. However, they do not apply to other class member functions.

- A constructor cannot have a return value. If you declare a constructor with a return value, you get a compiler error.

- A constructor cannot be declared as static. A constructor is called when an instance of a class is declared. Therefore, it does not make sense to have a static constructor that is called for the class itself, rather than an instance of it.

- You cannot stop a constructor from being called. When an instance of a class is declared, a constructor is called. If the arguments of the instance declaration match those of one of the constructors that you define, that constructor is called.

- Once a single constructor is defined for a class, the compiler does not create a default constructor with no arguments. Therefore, if you define a constructor with one or more arguments, you cannot use the default constructor with no arguments to create an instance of the class.

- A constructor cannot be declared as virtual. Chapter 28 provides more detail on virtual functions.

The following example program demonstrates how a constructor is defined and used:

```
#include <stdio.h>

class Circle
{
     int Radius;  // data member to hold radius of circle
public:

     Circle() { Radius = 10; }  // Declare inline constructor
                    // to set radius to 10
```

```
            void DisplayRadius()  //  Member function to display radius
                 { printf("The radius of the circle is: %d\n", Radius); }
        };

        void main()
        {
            Circle Circle1;  // Declare instance of Circle class
            Circle Circle2 = Circle();  // Declare another instance of Circle class

                // Display radius of Circle classes

            Circle1.DisplayRadius();
            Circle2.DisplayRadius();
        }
```

The output for this program is

```
        The radius of the circle is: 10
        The radius of the circle is: 10
```

This example program illustrates several points regarding constructors. The Circle class is defined with one data member, Radius, that contains the radius of the circle. The Circle class also has two member functions defined: a constructor, and a member function to display the radius.

The first member function is called Circle, which is the name of the class. This makes the Circle() function a constructor. It is declared inline as is any other function. Declaring a constructor inline is not necessary. However, in this case, the constructor is declared inline because it is brief. Note that there is no return value for the constructor function.

The purpose of the Circle constructor is to initialize the data member Radius to the value of 10. This is typical of constructor functions. They are often used to initialize data members upon the creation of an instance of the class. In the case of the Circle class, the radius always starts out with a value of 10. This saves the programmer the trouble of always setting this value when the Circle class is created.

An instance of the Circle class is declared using two different methods in the main() function. In the first case, the Circle class is declared using the implicit default constructor. When you use this method of declaring an instance of a class, the compiler searches for a constructor with no arguments. This can be the default constructor if no constructor functions have been declared for the class. However, if any constructor function is declared for the class, at least one of the constructor functions must accept no arguments using this class declaration syntax.

The second method used for creating an instance of the `Circle` class uses an explicit call to a constructor with no arguments. This is not a call to the default constructor. This is a direct call to one of the constructor functions that have been explicitly declared. In this case, the call is to the constructor with no arguments, which also happens to be the default constructor.

The only other member function declared for the `Circle` class is `DisplayRadius()`. This simply displays the value of the radius of the class.

Consider the following alternative constructor to the previous example:

```
#include <stdio.h>

class Circle
{
    int Radius;  // data member to hold radius of circle
public:

    Circle(int ARadius) { Radius = ARadius; }  // Declare inline constructor
                                // to set radius to the value of
                                // the constructor argument

    void DisplayRadius()  //  Member function to display radius
        { printf("The radius of the circle is: %d\n", Radius); }
};

void main()
{
    Circle Circle1;  // Declare instance of Circle class
                    // INVALID!
    Circle Circle2 = Circle();  // Declare another instance of Circle class
                        // INVALID!
    Circle Circle3(8);  // Declare a valid instance of Circle class
}
```

This example program uses a more flexible method of creating an instance of `Circle`. Instead of fixing the radius of the class to `10`, the class constructor is defined so that it can accept a radius at the time it is created. This is done by declaring the constructor with an integer argument. The value of the argument is assigned to the `Radius` class.

This program fails to compile. The reason is that the first two statements that attempt to create an instance for the `Circle` class are invalid. In the case of `Circle1`, it is declared using the default constructor method. However, the default constructor is not valid because an explicit constructor is defined that takes an integer argument. The constructor with no arguments is therefore not a valid form of a constructor function, and cannot be used for creating an instance of the `Circle` class.

The Circle2 instance is also not valid because it attempts to call a constructor using no arguments. There is no constructor defined that accepts no arguments in this instance. Therefore, this statement fails to compile.

The Circle3 class is valid because it calls a Circle constructor using a single integer argument. In this case, the Circle3 class starts with a value of 8.

It is not good practice to define constructors for a class without leaving one that does not require any arguments. As in the previous example program, this renders invalid the default constructor method of declaring an instance of the class.

A better method of gaining flexibility while retaining the default constructor is to declare one constructor that accepts no arguments. Alternatively, you can provide default values for the arguments of a constructor. In this way, the constructor function can be called with no arguments, and the constructor function will use the default values. The following example program demonstrates how this is done:

```
#include <stdio.h>

class Circle
{
        int Radius;  // data member to hold radius of circle
public:

        Circle(int ARadius = 10) { Radius = ARadius; }  // Declare inline
        ➥constructor
                           // to set radius to 10

        void DisplayRadius()  //  Member function to display radius
             { printf("The radius of the circle is: %d\n", Radius); }
};

void main()
{
        Circle Circle1;  // Declare instance of Circle class
        Circle Circle2(8);  // Declare another instance of Circle class

            // Display radius of Circle classes

        Circle1.DisplayRadius();
        Circle2.DisplayRadius();
}
```

The output for this example program is

```
The radius of the circle is: 10
The radius of the circle is: 8
```

In this example, a single constructor is used as the default constructor as well as one that can accept a value to customize the radius of the Circle class. This is done by declaring the Circle constructor function with an integer argument that takes a default value of 10.

When Circle1 is declared, the compiler searches for a constructor that accepts no arguments. It finds a match because the Circle constructor can use 10 as the default value, and not require any arguments.

The Circle2 instance is declared with an explicit call to the constructor with a single argument. Once again, the compiler can find a matching constructor function. The value of each instance of Circle is then displayed appropriately.

When declaring constructor functions, be aware of overloading them in a way that they can overlap. Avoid the ambiguities noted in the previous chapter for defining overloaded functions.

Using the Copy Constructor

The copy constructor is used if you want to create an instance of a class using the data of another instance of the same class. The copy constructor implies the start-up events that figure 26.3 illustrates.

Startup Sequence of Events for Copy Constructor:

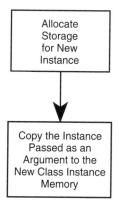

Fig. 26.3.
The copy constructor assigns one instance of a class to another.

The copy constructor is identical to assigning one instance of a class to another. The syntax for the assignment, though, is in the form of an instance declaration. Consider the following example program:

```
#include <stdio.h>

class Circle
{
    int Radius;  // data member to hold radius of circle
public:

    Circle(int ARadius = 10) { Radius = ARadius; }  // Declare inline
    ➥constructor
                        // to set radius to 10

    void DisplayRadius()  // Member function to display radius
        { printf("The radius of the circle is: %d\n", Radius); }
};

void main()
{
    Circle Circle1;  // Declare instance of Circle class
    Circle Circle2(&Circle1);  // Declare another instance of Circle class
        // Display radius of Circle classes

    Circle1.DisplayRadius();
    Circle2.DisplayRadius();
}
```

The output for this example program is

```
The radius of the circle is: 10
The radius of the circle is: 10
```

The declaration of the Circle2 instance uses the copy constructor function. The copy constructor must take a single argument that is a reference to an instance of the same class. This instance is used to initialize the data in the class that is created.

If you notice in the above example, there is no specific constructor defined for the Circle class that takes a single argument that is a reference to this class. The program still compiles, and runs as expected. The reason is that Turbo C++ defines a default copy constructor for every class. Similar to the default constructor itself, the default copy constructor can be explicitly defined.

The copy constructor is really the same as the assignment operator. The purpose of each is to copy the value of one instance of a class into another. The copy constructor simply does the copy during the process of creating a class. The reason the copy constructor is available, even though it is not declared explicitly, is that every class comes with an assignment operator, which is used for the default copy constructor.

Recall from the previous chapter that the assignment operator is implicitly defined for every class. The default assignment operator does a bitwise copy of the right operand to the left one. Both operands must be an instance of the same class for the default assignment operator to work.

The default copy constructor is simply the assignment operator repackaged. When the compiler sees an instance of a class declared with an argument that is a reference to another instance, it can translate this into an assignment statement. For example, the copy constructor used for Circle2 can be restated, as follows:

```
Circle Circle2 = Circle1;
```

This statement is the same as the original one that declared Circle2 using the copy constructor. This also explains the reason that the copy constructor needs a reference to an instance of the same class as an argument. Translating a copy constructor to an assignment statement requires that there is a left and right operand of the same class type. In the case of the copy constructor, the left operand is the class that is created, and the right is the class reference passed as an argument. Translating the copy constructor into an assignment statement is, therefore, possible.

The reasons for overriding the default copy constructor that uses a bitwise copy is the same as for overloading the = operator. You would explicitly define a copy constructor in these situations:

- If a class contains allocated pointers, the default copy constructor will not work correctly. With a bitwise copy, only the pointer variable is copied, rather than the information that is pointed to. Once the class is copied, there is no guarantee that the information at the address of the pointer will remain there for the duration of the assigned class. In this case, a customized copy constructor is more suitable so that new memory can be allocated. Thus, the information copied into memory location is controlled by the class that is created.

- If a class has certain data members that require copying, and others that need special treatment, the default copy constructor will not work. By default, all bits of a class are copied. Therefore, all data members will be copied. To ensure that only the appropriate data members are copied, and the remaining ones set to appropriate values, requires that a customized copy constructor be defined.

The advantage of a `copy` constructor over an assignment operator is that the `copy` constructor creates the class. Then, this constructor copies the data from the class passed as an argument. The assignment operator simply copies the right operand class to the left operand class. The latter class must be declared prior to the assignment for the assignment operator to work.

Sequence of Constructor Calls

In most cases, the calling sequence of constructors is not important. However, when one class is embedded in another, it is imperative to know the calling sequence. Consider the following example program:

```
#include <stdio.h>

class InnerObject  // Declare class that is to be embedded in another
➥class
{
public:
    InnerObject()  // Constructor
        { printf("Constructing InnerObject\n"); }
};

class OuterObject  // Declare class that has another embedded class
{
    InnerObject MyInnerObject;  // Data member that is a class
public:
    OuterObject()
        { printf("Constructing OuterObject\n"); }
};

void main()
{
        // Declare instance of OuterObject

    OuterObject MyOuterObject;
}
```

The output of this program is as follows:

```
Constructing InnerObject
Constructing OuterObject
```

Figure 26.4 illustrates the sequence of calls for this example. The `OuterObject` class in this example contains a data member that is an `InnerObject` class. When an instance of the `OuterObject` is declared, it first allocates storage for its data members. One of its data members, `InnerObject`, is a class. The data member class, in this `InnerObject`, must therefore be created. When the `InnerObject` class is created, its constructor is called.

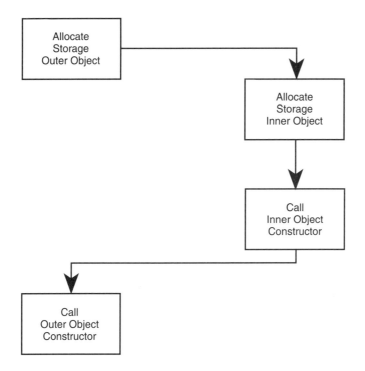

Fig. 26.4.
Illustration of
Sequence of
Constructor Calls
for an Example
Program.

When an instance of a class is declared, all the necessary arrangements are
first made for the data members. Then, the constructor for the class is called.
This explains the reason that the InnerObject constructor is called before the
OuterObject one in the preceding example.

This calling sequence of constructors is very useful. By having the data members fully created by the time the constructor of a class is called, it is safe to
access the data member class. Using the preceding example as an illustration,
the OuterObject constructor can safely access member functions and data members of the InnerObject data member class. The reason is that the InnerObject
class is fully constructed by the time the OuterObject constructor is called.

The sequence of constructor calls for multiple classes that are data members is
the order in which they appear. Consider the next example in listing 26.1:

**Listing 26.1. The sequence of constructor calls is called in the order
in which they appear.**

```
1.    #include <stdio.h>

2.    class GlobalObject  // Declare class that is to be used as a global
➥object
```

(continues)

Listing 26.1. Continued.

```
3.   {
4.   public:
5.   GlobalObject()  // Constructor
6.        { printf("Constructing GlobalObject\n"); }
7.   };

8.   class InnerObject1  // Declare class that is to be embedded in
➥another class
9.   {
10.  public:
11.  InnerObject1()  // Constructor
12.       { printf("Constructing InnerObject1\n"); }
13.  };

14.  class InnerObject2  // Declare class that is to be embedded in
➥another class
15.  {
16.  public:
17.  InnerObject2()  // Constructor
18.       { printf("Constructing InnerObject2\n"); }
19.  };

20.  class OuterObject  // Declare class that has another embedded one
21.  {
22.  InnerObject1 MyInnerObject1;  // Data member that is a class
23.  InnerObject2 MyInnerObject2;  // Another data member that is a class
24.  public:
25.  OuterObject()
26.       { printf("Constructing OuterObject\n"); }
27.  };

28.  GlobalObject MyGlobalObject;

29.  void main()
30.  {
31.       // Declare instance of OuterObject

32.  OuterObject MyOuterObject;
```

The output for listing 26.1 is

```
Constructing GlobalObject
Constructing InnerObject1
Constructing InnerObject2
Constructing OuterObject
```

Listing 26.1 illustrates several points regarding class constructors and the creation of objects. The program declares four classes. Each of the classes has only a single constructor function defined that prints out a status message that it is executing.

The first class constructor that is called is the GlobalObject. Although no GlobalObject class is declared in the main() function, there is one declared globally on line 28. When a global object that is a class is declared, its constructor is called. Therefore, the status message of its constructor is displayed on the screen. This illustrates the fact that global objects are created before the main() function is called.

The main() function is then called; it declares an instance of the OuterObject class on line 32. The OuterObject class has two data members, each of which is a class itself. An instance of both these classes is declared on lines 22 and 23.

As noted earlier, the data members of a class are created before the constructor of a class is called. This example illustrates a new point: The data members are created in the order that they are declared. In this case, the InnerObject1 is declared before InnerObject2. Therefore, InnerObject1's constructor is called first. Then, the constructor for InnerObject2 is called. Finally, the constructor of OuterObject is called.

Avoiding Circular Constructors

One of the pitfalls of having data members wholly constructed prior to the constructor of a class that you are calling is that you can accidentally create a sequence of constructor calls that goes into a never-ending loop. This section describes two common ways of getting into a circular loop of constructor calls.

One way of creating a circular loop of constructor calls is to declare a temporary class object of the same class that you are creating within the constructor. This is illustrated in the following example:

```
class DoNothing
{
        .
        .
        .
public:
    DoNothing();  // Declare constructor
    .
    .
    .
};

DoNothing::DoNothing()    // Define constructor
{
    DoNothing Temp;  // Declare a temporary instance
    .
    .
    .
}
```

In this example, the DoNothing constructor attempts to create a temporary instance of a DoNothing class, presumably for some internal purpose.

However, the temporary instance of the DoNothing class also creates a temporary duplicate of itself within its constructor. This does not stop, because each temporary instance of the DoNothing class again calls a constructor which, in turn, creates a temporary DoNothing class.

Do not declare an instance of the same class that is created within the class constructor. This causes the program to go into an infinite loop.

Another slightly more difficult loop to detect is the one that results when you have each of two classes attempting to create the other's class within the origin (or creator) class constructor.

```
class A
{
public:
      A();   // declare constructor for A
};

class B
{
public:
      B();   // declare constructor for B
};

A::A()
{
      B TempB;   // declare a temporary instance of B
      .
      .
      .
}

B::B()
{
      A TempA;   // declare a temporary instance of A
      .
      .
      .
}
```

This example program shows the two classes A and B with only their constructors declared and defined. The constructor for class A creates a temporary instance of class B. The constructor for class B creates a temporary instance of class A. What happens if an instance of either A or B is declared? One class creates within its constructor an instance of the other in its constructor, which is continuously reversed. This puts the constructor sequence in an infinite loop.

Avoid situations in which each of two classes creates in its constructor an instance of the other.

Using Private Constructors

In general, constructors are declared as public member functions so that any other function can create the class object using its constructor. However, you can declare a constructor private or protected. In this case, the constructor cannot be accessed by any other function except the class's own member functions.

A constructor function can call any other member function in its class. Similarly, any member function can call the constructor of a class to which it belongs. One of the reasons for making a constructor private is to provide member functions with a specialized way of creating a copy of the class to which it belongs. Consider the following example:

```
class Circle
    int Radius;  // Contains radius of circle

        // Declare private constructor

    Circle() {}

public:
        // Declare public constructor

    Circle(int ARadius)
        { Radius = ARadius; }
};
```

In the class declaration of `Circle`, there are two constructors. The first constructor is private, and takes no arguments. The second class is public; it forces any non-`Circle` function to declare an instance of the `Circle` class using an argument that represents the radius of the circle to be created.

In this case, there is good reason to make the first constructor private. It does not initialize the `Radius` data member. Therefore, if any function can use this constructor, it will likely cause problems when other member functions of Circle are called that expect a valid `Radius` value. (The `Circle` class defined in the preceding example is incomplete, and would presumably include member functions for displaying and manipulating a `Circle` object.) Instead, the class includes a constructor that forces the calling function to specify a value. This value is passed as the constructor argument so that the `Radius` data member is initialized.

Having a default constructor that does not require any initialization can be useful for purposes internal to the class. Only class members can use this

constructor. Therefore, it can be used safely internally because all the limitations
of the constructor are known.

Initializing an Array of Class Objects

Similar to any object in C++, you can declare an array of class objects using array subscripts. The syntax is

```
class_name instance_name[#];
```

The # represents the number of instances of the class to create. However, if the class constructor requires an argument, you must declare an array of classes using an array of constructor argument values. The following program demonstrates how to do this.

```
#include <stdio.h>

class Circle
{
    int Radius;  // data member to hold radius of circle
public:
    Circle(int ARadius)    // Declare inline constructor
        { Radius = ARadius; }

    void DisplayRadius()  //  Member function to display radius
        { printf("The radius of the circle is: %d\n", Radius); }
};

void main()
{
        // Declare an array of instances of Circle class

    Circle CircleArray[10] = {1, 2, 3, 4, 5, 6, 7, 8, 9, 10};

        // Display the radius for each instance

    for ( int i = 0 ; i < 10; i++)
        CircleArray[i].DisplayRadius();
}
```

The output for this program example is

```
The radius of the circle is: 1
The radius of the circle is: 2
The radius of the circle is: 3
The radius of the circle is: 4
The radius of the circle is: 5
The radius of the circle is: 6
The radius of the circle is: 7
The radius of the circle is: 8
The radius of the circle is: 9
The radius of the circle is: 10
```

In this example, the class `Circle` is defined with a constructor that requires a single integer argument. A single instance of this argument is declared by passing the integer value in parentheses, as in the following statement:

```
Circle Circle1(10);   // Declare instance of Circle class
```

To declare an array, you must use the square brackets that indicate to the compiler the number of instances of the object to create. The constructor arguments for an array declaration are then passed in curly brackets as the preceding example shows.

Using Destructors

Destructors are the counterparts to constructors. They are called immediately before an instance of a class is about to be destroyed. Also, destructors are called implicitly before a class is destroyed.

The compiler provides for every class a default destructor that does nothing. To specify what happens in the destructor, you need to define a customized destructor function. A customized destructor is used to clean up any outstanding data before a class is destroyed. A destructor is most often used to deallocate memory that was designated in the constructor of the class, or during one of the operations executed by its member function.

To override the default destructor which does not execute any code, you need to declare and define a destructor. When the compiler sees a destructor defined for your class, it automatically uses your destructor rather than the default one. The next section describes how to override a destructor function for a class.

Overriding the Default Destructor

You can define a destructor for any class. You do this by declaring a function within the class that has the same name as the class itself, and is preceded by a tilde ~. The following example code illustrates how a destructor is defined:

```
class DoNothing      // declare a class
{
    .
    .      // place private members here
    .
public:
    ~DoNothing();  // declare destructor using name of class
    .
    .      // place public members here
    .
}
```

In this case, the destructor is a function that shares its name with the class in which it belongs, and is preceded by a ~. A function declared in this way is automatically assumed to be the destructor.

A destructor function shares many features with other class member functions. A destructor function can call any C library function. Also, it can call or access any other private or public member. A destructor can be declared inline, or defined outside a class. Unlike a constructor, a destructor can be declared virtual.

The following special rules apply to a destructor function. (They do not apply to other class member functions):

- A destructor function cannot have any arguments. A destructor is called implicitly before a class is destroyed; therefore, it is called without any arguments.

- Only one destructor can exist per class. Although you can explicitly define a destructor for a class, thereby overriding the default one, you cannot overload destructor functions. The reason is that a destructor function cannot have any arguments. The only way to distinguish overloaded functions is by the arguments of a function. A destructor must be declared with no arguments; therefore, you can declare only one destructor per class.

- There is no return value for a destructor function.

- However, only a class can be declared static. This state cannot apply to a destructor because it only is relevant with respect to an *instance* of a class. Therefore, declaring a destructor as a static function makes no sense.

- You cannot stop a destructor from being called. When an instance of a class is about to be destroyed, a destructor is always called. If you defined a destructor, it is called. Otherwise, the default destructor is called.

The following example program demonstrates how a destructor is defined and called:

```
#include <stdio.h>

class DoNothing
{
public:
    ~DoNothing()  // Declare a destructor inline
```

```
                { printf("Destructing the DoNothing object\n"); }
        };

        main()
        {
                // Declare instance of DoNothing

            DoNothing DoNothing1;
        }
```

The output for this example program is

```
        Destructing the DoNothing object
```

The example program defines a DoNothing class that contains a single destructor function. The destructor function is the same as the DoNothing class, except that it is preceded by the ~ character. The ~ is what distinguishes a destructor from a constructor.

The destructor is declared inline in the preceding example. You could declare it outside the class by using the following definition:

```
        DoNothing::~DoNothing()  // Declare a destructor outside the class
        {
            printf("Destructing the DoNothing object\n");
        }
```

Notice that the destructor was called even though no reference to the destructor function can be found in main(). The reason is that the destructor is called implicitly before an object is destroyed. In the main() function, the DoNothing object is destroyed immediately before it goes out of scope, at the end of the main() function.

Destructors do not have to be called. They are automatically called when a class object is being destroyed.

Sequence of Destructor Calls

Similar to the constructors, it is generally unimportant to know the precise instance when a destructor is called. However, when you are using embedded classes that interrelate, knowing the sequence of destructor calls can help avoid an accidental reference to a class that is destroyed.

Listing 26.2 illustrates how destructors are called in situations in which interrelated and global objects are declared.

Listing 26.2. This program shows the sequence of destructor calls.

```
1.   #include <stdio.h>

2.   class GlobalObject  // Declare class that is to be used as a
➥global object
3.   {
4.   public:
5.   ~GlobalObject()  // Destructor
6.       { printf("Destructing GlobalObject\n"); }
7.   };

8.   class InnerObject1  // Declare class that is to be embedded in
➥another class
9.   {
10.  public:
11.  ~InnerObject1()  // Destructor
12.      { printf("Destructing InnerObject1\n"); }
13.  };

14.  class InnerObject2  // Declare class that is to be embedded in
➥another class
15.  {
16.  public:
17.  ~InnerObject2()  // Destructor
18.      { printf("Destructing InnerObject2\n"); }
19.  };

20.  class OuterObject  // Declare class that has another embedded class
21.  {
22.  InnerObject1 MyInnerObject1;  // Data member that is a class
23.  InnerObject2 MyInnerObject2;  // Another data member that is a class
24.  public:
25.  ~OuterObject()
26.      { printf("Destructing OuterObject\n"); }
27.  };

28.  GlobalObject MyGlobalObject;

29.  void main()
30.  {
31.      // Declare instance of OuterObject

32.  OuterObject MyOuterObject;
33.  }
```

The output for listing 26.2 is

```
Destructing OuterObject
Destructing InnerObject2
Destructing InnerObject1
Destructing GlobalObject
```

Listing 26.2 defines four classes, each with a destructor explicitly defined.
The destructor displays a status message indicating that it is executing.

The sequence of calls is exactly the reverse of the constructor calls generated by the example that listing 26.1 shows. The destructors are called in the reverse sequence of when the objects were created. In this case, the `OuterObject` was created last; therefore, its destructor is called first. The two data members of `OuterObject` that are classes are created in sequence. Therefore, their destructors are called in reverse sequence. Finally, the `GlobalObject` is created first, before the `main()` function begins. Therefore, the `GlobalObject` destructor is called last.

The general rule is that destructors are called in the reverse order in which their objects are created.

Using the `new` and `delete` Functions

There is an alternative way of creating an object other than by declaring an instance of it in your program. The alternative is to allocate the object explicitly. By allocating an object, you explicitly state when you want the object both created and destroyed.

Allocating an object differs from using an object declaration in two main areas, as figure 26.5 illustrates. The first is when the object is declared. When you declare an object, it is created at the point at which it is declared. That point defines the scope of the object. The object is only visible within its scope; it is destroyed when it goes out of scope. That is, the object is only visible within its own block and subblocks; it is destroyed at the end of the block in which it is declared. By comparison, allocating an object does not give it any scope. It can be declared anywhere, and accessed from any other place.

Declaring an Object	Allocating an Object
• Scope is determined by point of declaration	• Scope extends beyond block in which the object is allocated
• Storage taken from stack	• Storage taken from heap

Fig. 26.5.
Note the comparison between declaring and allocating an object.

The second difference is the place in which information is stored. For a declared object, the storage for its information comes from the stack. The storage for the allocated objects is the heap.

The two ways of allocating an object are to either use the C library allocation functions, or the special C++ function referred to as new. To destroy an object allocated using the C library allocation functions, you must employ a C library deallocation function. To deallocate an object allocated by the C++ new function, use the C++ special deallocation function referred to as delete.

The advantages of using the C++ new and delete functions, as compared to the C library allocation functions, are as follows:

- The new and delete functions call the constructor and destructor of the class object that is created, in addition to allocating space for its data. The C library allocation functions merely designate space for the object data. Using the new and delete functions is easier because the storage and constructor/destructor issues are dealt with using a single function call.

- The return value of new is a pointer to the object type that is created. By comparison, the C allocation functions return a void pointer. In order for it to be useful, the pointer needs to be cast to the data type that is created.

- The new and delete functions do not take arguments. Therefore, they are easier to use than their C library counterparts. All space and allocation requirements are handled for you automatically.

The general way you use the new and delete functions is as follows:

```
class DoNothing
{
    .
    .
    .
}

main()
    DoNothing *DoNothing1 = new DoNothing;
    .
    .
    .
    delete DoNothing;
}
```

This sample code illustrates several important points. The new function allocates space for an object, and calls its constructor. The return value of a new function is a pointer to the newly allocated space. Recall that accessing member functions of a pointer to a class requires the -> operator rather than the '.' operator.

The other important point to note in the preceding sample code is that the `delete` statement is called at the end of the `main()` function. Objects allocated with `new` are not destroyed on their own. If you do not deallocate them using the `delete` function, they remain in memory, and occupy space that cannot be used by other functions and programs. As with any allocated space used by your program, you should only keep the object for as long as you need it. Then, deallocate the space so that another function or program can use it.

The program in listing 26.3 illustrates how you can control when an object is created and destroyed using the `new` and `delete` functions.

Listing 26.3. This program shows how to use `new` and `delete`.

```
1.    #include <stdio.h>

2.    class InnerObject1  // Declare class that is to be embedded in
➥another class
3.    {
4.    public:
5.    InnerObject1()  // Constructor
6.         { printf("Constructing InnerObject1\n"); }
7.    ~InnerObject1()  // Destructor
8.         { printf("Destructing InnerObject1\n"); }
9.    };

10.   class InnerObject2  // Declare class that is to be embedded in
➥another class
11.   {
12.   public:
13.   InnerObject2()  // Constructor
14.        { printf("Constructing InnerObject2\n"); }
15.   ~InnerObject2()  // Destructor
16.        { printf("Destructing InnerObject2\n"); }
17.   };

18.   class OuterObject  // Declare class that has another embedded class
19.   {
20.   InnerObject1 *MyInnerObject1;  // Data member that is a
➥pointer to a class
21.   InnerObject2 *MyInnerObject2;  // Another data member that is
➥a pointer to a class
22.   public:
23.   OuterObject();  // Constructor
24.   ~OuterObject();  // Destructor
25.   };

26.   OuterObject::OuterObject()  // Define constructor
27.   {
28.   printf("Constructing OuterObject\n");
29.   MyInnerObject2 = new InnerObject2;
30.   delete MyInnerObject2;
```

(continues)

Listing 26.3. Continued.

```
31.  }

32.  OuterObject::~OuterObject()  // Define destructor
33.  {
34.  printf("Destructing OuterObject\n");
35.  MyInnerObject1 = new InnerObject1;
36.  delete MyInnerObject1;
37.  }

38.  void main()
39.  {
40.       // Declare instance of OuterObject

41.  OuterObject MyOuterObject;
42.  }
```

The output for listing 26.3 is

```
Constructing OuterObject
Constructing InnerObject2
Destructing InnerObject2
Destructing OuterObject
Constructing InnerObject1
Destructing InnerObject1
```

Listing 26.3 defines three classes, each of which has an explicit declaration for its respective constructor and destructor functions. For the InnerObject1 and InnerObject2 objects, the constructor and destructor functions are declared inline, and merely display a status message indicating that they are executing.

The OuterObject class is declared with two data members that are pointers to the InnerObject1 and InnerObject2 classes (lines 20 and 21). A pointer is unlike a declaration in that nothing is automatically produced when an instance of OuterObject is created. The pointer is an address variable. These pointers are used to hold the address of InnerObject1 and InnerObject2 classes, respectively, when they are allocated. InnerObject1 and InnerObject2 classes can be allocated and deallocated at any time. Also, the address of the allocated class can be placed in the data member pointer variables.

When the OuterObject class is declared on line 41, the first step taken by the program is to allocate space for two pointer variables. No constructors are called yet for InnerObject1 or InnerObject2 because no declaration for these classes has yet been made.

The next step taken when OuterObject is declared is to call the OuterObject constructor. The OuterObject constructor is defined starting on line 26. The first three lines of output are a result of the three statements that constitute the OuterObject constructor function.

The first statement in the constructor displays a status message that OuterObject is being created. The second statement of the constructor uses new to allocate an InnerObject2 class object. A new function is used; therefore, the InnerObject2 constructor is called. This produces the second output line stating that InnerObject2 is being created. The third statement of the OuterObject constructor calls the delete function that deallocates the InnerObject2 instance. This frees up the space that is used for the InnerObject2 instance, and calls the InnerObject2 destructor.

When the OuterObject goes out of scope, as is the case when the main() function ends, the OuterObject destructor is automatically called. The destructor for the OuterObject class is defined starting on line 32. The last three lines of output correspond to the three statements that compose the OuterObject destructor function.

Notice that when the new function is used, it returns a pointer to the class type that is created. This is the reason the result of new can be directly assigned to the appropriate pointers on lines 29 and 35.

The return value of a failed call to a new function is 0. This should always be checked to ensure that the new function successfully allocated the intended object, and that it can be safely referenced using the return pointer.

Summary

Constructors and destructors are used to control how a class is initialized and destroyed. The advantage of using constructors and destructors is that they are automatically called when a function is created and destroyed. This convenience enables you to customize classes in a way that is easy to program and use.

This chapter highlighted many important features and issues regarding constructors and destructors. Some of these include

- Every object includes a default constructor and destructor. The default constructor and destructor functions do not execute any statements.

- To customize the way an object is created or destroyed, you must override the default constructor and destructor. Then, when a class is created and destroyed, the customized constructor and destructor are used, rather than the default ones.

■ A constructor shares many features with other functions. A constructor can be declared with arguments. It can also be overloaded, and declared inline. However, a constructor cannot have a return value. Also, you cannot declare it static, or stop it from being called.

■ A destructor shares some features with other functions. A destructor can be called inline. Also, it can call C library, and other class member functions. However, a destructor cannot have any arguments, and can only be declared once per class. You cannot declare a destructor static. A destructor cannot have a return value. Also, you are unable to stop the destructor from being called when the object is destroyed.

■ The calling sequence of constructors is the order in which objects are declared.

■ The calling sequence of destructors is the reverse order in which objects are declared.

■ You can control how and when objects are created and destroyed using the C++ `new` and `delete` functions. The `new` function allocates space for an object, and calls its constructor. The `delete` function calls the destructor of an object, then deallocates space for the object.

Chapter 27

Using Inheritance

In C++, you can make an object assume the features and actions of another object through inheritance. To do this, you declare an object as inheriting another C++ object in a particular way. The data members and member functions of the parent object are then accessible to the newly created (child) object. Inheritance is one of the basic extensions added to C by the C++ language specification; it is what makes C++ an object-oriented language.

This chapter demonstrates how to use the C++ inheritance capability, showing you the following things:

- How inheritance operates
- Benefits of using inheritance
- Use of base and derived classes
- Use of multiple inheritance

How Inheritance Operates

Inheritance is the process of deriving one object from another, previously-defined, object. In C++, the previously-defined object is the *parent* and the new object being created is the *child*. A child object can become a parent object by being the basis of yet another child object.

One of the goals of C++ is to provide ways of representing real-world objects within a programming language. Inheritance is one way C++ meets this goal: it enables a programmer to define base objects with certain features and actions. Other objects can then be derived from the base object, and the derived objects automatically inherit all the features and actions of the base objects from which they are descended. The derived objects can then extend their own features and actions to become the base objects to yet other derived objects (see figure 27.1).

Fig. 27.1.
Inherited objects.

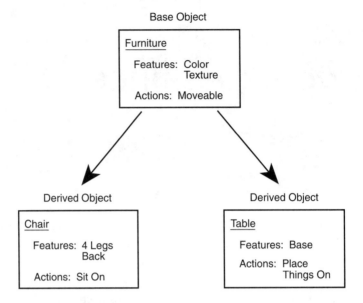

In figure 27.1, the base object is called *Furniture*. This is a C++ object that represents furniture. All furniture shares some common features, such as Color and Texture. Instead of creating an object for each individual type of furniture with these features, a base object is created that contains the shared features of all furniture.

Then, when you need to describe a particular type of furniture, such as tables or chairs, you can derive these specific types of furniture from the base object Furniture. In figure 27.1, the derived object Chair extends the features of Furniture by adding the features Legs and Back. These new features are added to the base object Furniture features, Color and Texture. Together, the base object and derived object features better describe a chair.

The hierarchical method that is enabled by the inheritance capability makes it efficient and easy to describe complex objects in C++. Rather than describe every individual object as a discrete unit that carries all the characteristics of that object, you can determine common characteristics of several objects and define them in a *base object*. This base object is the cornerstone of other objects that share the same base characteristics. By deriving new objects from a base object, you have no need to redeclare all the base object features. Those features are maintained by the base object and are available automatically to any derived object.

Aspects of Inheritance

Inheritance can be divided into two parts:

- Derivation

- Classification

All objects can be derived. *Derivation* refers to the ability to define a base (or parent) object and derive child objects from that object. A child object carries with it all the features that are defined for it specifically, as well as those defined for the base object.

Classification is the process of looking at complex objects and filtering the common features of several objects that can be defined in a base object. It is the process of taking a series of linear objects and creating a hierarchy based on common features. You, the programmer, have to decide what is a base object and what is a derived object. Learning how to classify objects is something that takes practice and experience. However, it is fundamental to creating useful hierarchies of objects.

The process of classification is part art and part science. The science part is straightforward: look for common features and characteristics of several objects and combine them into a base object. Then use the base object to derive other objects that share the features of the base object. In real life, there are many ways of combining objects, each of which is valid and may have advantages and disadvantages. This part is an art and has no fixed method. As you learn this art, remember that the decision about which hierarchy to use must take into consideration the intended use of the objects.

Consider an unordered series of books on a bookshelf, as illustrated in figure 27.2. To order these books, you can divide them by type of book. This is Classification 1 in figure 27.2. This type of classification is useful for small libraries, such as a personal library, where it is probably not difficult to get to a book if you know the type of book you want.

For larger groups of books, this type of classification may not be as useful. You might try organizing the books by title or author. With that type of classification, anyone who knows the title or author can easily find the book. However, it does not allow someone to browse easily for books of a certain type.

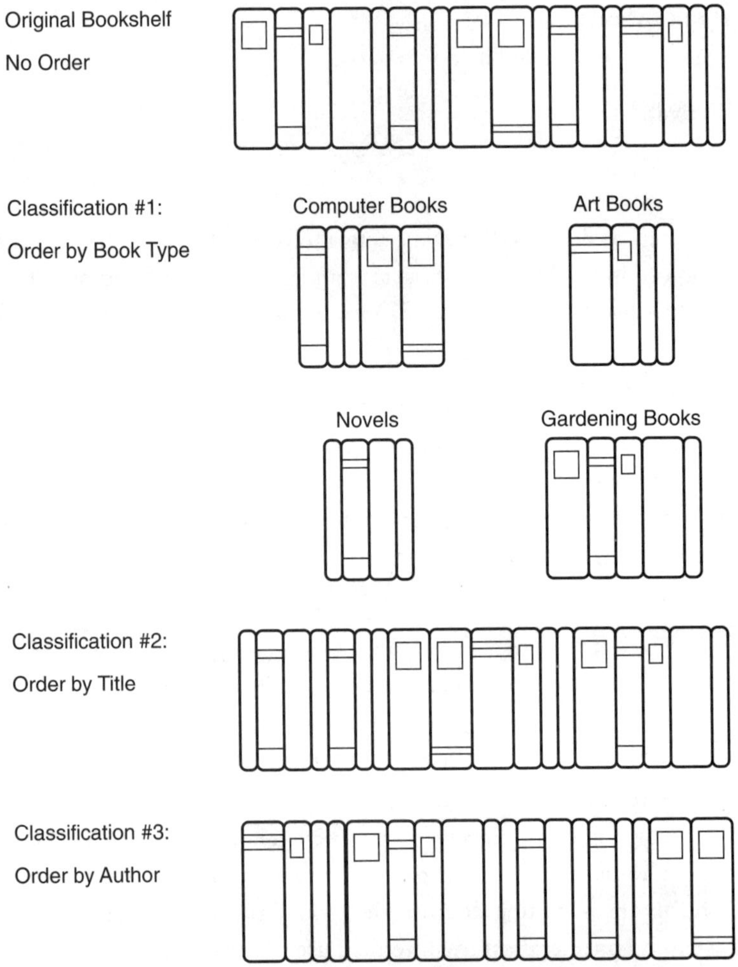

Fig. 27.2.

A Classification 1
type of book order.

Original Bookshelf

No Order

Classification #1:

Order by Book Type

Computer Books

Art Books

Novels

Gardening Books

Classification #2:

Order by Title

Classification #3:

Order by Author

The most thorough classification hierarchy for books is no doubt one of the library classification methods, such as the one used by the Library of Congress. In that hierarchy, virtually every topic and type of book has a slot in which it is placed in sequence. Any new book that arrives is easy to place properly because the classification codes take into consideration all possibilities. However, such a classification system would be inconvenient and unnecessary for a home library, in which only a few types of books are generally found. The first classification of figure 27.2 is probably more appropriate for most home libraries.

For any group of objects, more than one way exists of creating a hierarchy of those objects—which is the process of classification. The process must blend the science of looking for common features to combine into base objects and the art of choosing which features to combine to make the object hierarchy efficient and effective for its intended use.

Benefits of Inheritance

There are a variety of benefits to using inheritance. The first is efficiency. Most real-world objects are not simple. You can represent real-world objects in a program by using a long list of features for every object represented. Doing that, however, is highly inefficient, because objects often share common features. By using inheritance, you can classify the various objects used in your program according to a logical hierarchy based on how those objects are used. The features and actions associated with each category can then be dealt with as a unit, which is simpler than dealing with the entire range of objects and their individual, specific features.

Another reason for using inheritance is that after you have classified and defined objects, you can reuse them in any combination as a basis for other objects. If you need to represent a new object that is similar to one or more existing objects, you can easily establish the new object within your program. To do so, derive the new object from existing objects that have the necessary common features. You can then extend the new object by any particular set of features that pertain to just that object. In this way, you are reusing existing objects in a way that will make extending your program easier.

Inheritance is generally associated with classes. The remainder of this chapter deals with inheritance of classes, which is the most typical use of C++ inheritance, although inheritance is also applicable to other C++ objects such as structures and unions.

Use of Base and Derived Classes

In C++, the most common use of inheritance is to derive a class, using a base class as a starting point. The *base class* provides the data members and member functions that define the object's key features and actions. The *derived class* need only define the incremental features and actions using additional data members and member functions.

A class is be derived from a base class using the following syntax:

```
class derived_class : [access mode] base_class
{
    .
    .
    .
};
```

To declare a class using a base class, simply add to the derived class declaration the : operator followed by the name of the base class. Then, any data member and member function that is defined for the base class becomes available to the derived class. The [access mode] option determines the extent to which the base class members are accessible to the derived class.

Consider the following code fragment:

```
class Base
{
      int   Integer1;
};

class Derived : Base
{
      int   Integer2;
};
```

Ignoring access issues, which will be dealt with shortly, the data member Integer1 that is declared for the class Base is accessible by the class Derived. The reason is that the derived class is declared with the base class as its base. Therefore, members of base class are accessible by the derived class. However, the reverse is not true. Base class has no knowledge of, and therefore no access to, the members of the derived class.

The above example illustrates the way derivation is declared in general. This particular example will not allow the class Derived to access the Integer1 data member of the class Base, even though Base is a base class of Derived, because of access limitations. Access limitations of derived classes is a major component of inheritance and is the topic of the next section.

Base Member Access from Derived Classes

Class members can be defined as *public*, *protected*, or *private*. The protected access mode was not discussed earlier in this book because it applies to inheritance. In addition to base class *members* having an access mode, a base class itself can be inherited as either public or private. The access rights of a base class member from a derived class are therefore affected by two things:

- ■ The access mode of the members of the base class. The access mode of members of a class can be private, protected, or public. The default access mode of class members is private.

- ■ The base class access option used in the declaration of a new class to inherit members of a base class. The access options for inheriting a base class are private and public. This inheritance access option is private by default.

The combination of how a base class member is declared and what access option is used to inherit a base class determines how the base class member appears to the derived class. Figure 27.3 lists the possible options.

Base Member Access ⟍ Inheritance ⟍	Private	Protected	Public
Private	Not Accessible	Accessible as Private Member	Accessible as Public Member
Public	Not Accessible	Accessible as Protected Member	Accessible as Public Member

Fig. 27.3.
Accessibility of base class members by derived class.

As illustrated by figure 27.3, a private base class member is not accessible by the derived class. A *private member* remains inaccessible to any other function or class outside of the one in which it is declared, even to derived classes. A *public member* of a base class is always accessible; therefore, being accessible to derived classes is not especially noteworthy.

The data member access that is affected by inheritance is the protected access mode. When a base class member is declared as *protected*, it means that it is private to the base class and to any class derived from the base class. A derived class can therefore access a protected base class member like one of its own.

Consider the following example program.

```
class Base
{
private:
    int  Integer1;
protected:
    int  Integer2;
public:
    int  Integer3;
};

class Derived : public Base
{
public:
    void AccessInteger1() { Integer1 = 10; }  // INVALID!!
    void AccessInteger2() { Integer2 = 20; }  // VALID
    void AccessInteger3() { Integer3 = 30; }  // VALID
};
```

In this example, the base class is declared with three integers, one declared as private, one as protected, and one as public. The class `Derived` inherits `Base` class as a public base class. The public and protected data members of `Base` are therefore accessible directly from within the class `Derived`.

The `Derived` class defines three member functions. The `AccessInteger1()` member function is invalid. It attempts to access `Integer1` of the Base class, which is private. A derived class cannot access the private members of a base class, even if the inheritance access mode is public. Therefore, `AccessInteger1()` is not valid.

The other member functions of `Derived` are valid because they access a public or a protected member of the base class. A derived class can access a protected member of a base class, and of course a public member is accessible even outside of a derived class.

The purpose of a protected member is to expand the privileges of a private class member. A *private class member* can only be accessed within the class in which it is declared. A *protected class member* is accessible to any derived class as well. However, both private and protected members are not accessible to any outside classes or functions. To an outside function, a protected member of a class is considered private.

The access mode of a protected class member can be changed when it is inherited. In the above example, the base class is inherited as public, and accordingly the protected members of `Base` remain protected within `Derived`. However, if the inheritance access mode is private, any base class members that are protected turn private within the derived class. Consider the next example program:

```
class Parent
{
protected:
    int  Integer1;
};

class Child : private Parent
{
    void AccessInteger1() { Integer1 = 10; }  // VALID
};

class GrandChild : public Child
{
    void AccessInteger1() { Integer1 = 10; }  // INVALID!!
};
```

In this example, there are three levels of classes:

■ The topmost class in this hierarchy is Parent; it has one integer data member that is defined with the protected access mode. It is used as a base class for Child.

■ Child inherits Parent using the private access mode, which means that any protected member of Parent turns into a private member for Child. Class Child can still access Integer1 because it is still private and accessible within class Child. When class Child inherits class Parent as private and turns Integer1 from protected to private, Integer1 is thereby shut out from subsequently inherited classes of Child. As the table in figure 27.3 shows, a private data member of a base class is inaccessible to a derived class.

■ Class Grandchild inherits all data members of Child. However, in the above example, Integer1 appears as a private data member of class Child from within class Grandchild. Therefore class Grandchild cannot access the data member Integer1.

The purpose of the inherit access mode is to moderate how a protected class member appears within the derived class. This affects how the class member will be accessed by subsequently inherited classes.

Listing 27.1 is a program that makes use of the inheritance to simplify managing several objects. It demonstrates how certain aspects of inheritance can be used to your advantage. The purpose of the program is to track geometrical objects. Because geometrical objects share similar features, a hierarchy is useful. This hierarchy is implemented in the form of inherited classes in listing 27.1.

Listing 27.1. An example of base and derived set of classes.

```
1.    #include <stdio.h>
2.    #include <string.h>

3.    class GeoObject
4.    {
5.    char Color[20];   // Data member to track color of object

6.    protected:
7.          // Member function to set color
```

(continues)

Listing 27.1. Continued.

```
8.   void SetColor(char * AColor)
9.       { strcpy(Color, AColor); }

10.      // Member function to get color

11.  const char* GetColor()
12.      { return Color; }
13.  };

14.  class Square : public GeoObject
15.  {
16.  int  SideLength;
17.  public:
18.      // Constructor definition

19.  Square(char * AColor, int ASideLength)
20.      { SetColor(AColor); SideLength = ASideLength; }

21.      // Member function to display features

22.  void DisplayFeatures()
23.      { printf("The square is %s and has a sidelength of %d\n",
24.              GetColor(), SideLength); }
25.  };

26.  class Circle : public GeoObject
27.  {
28.  int  Radius;  // Data member to track radius of circle

29.  public:
30.      // Constructor definition

31.  Circle(char * AColor, int ARadius)
32.      { SetColor(AColor); Radius = ARadius; }

33.      // Member function to display features

34.  void DisplayFeatures()
35.      { printf("The circle is %s and has a radius of %d\n",
36.              GetColor(), Radius); }
37.  };

38.  void main()
39.  {
40.      // Declare instance of a square and circle

41.  Square MySquare("Red", 10);
42.  Circle MyCircle("Blue", 15);

43.      // Display features of square and circle instance

44.  MySquare.DisplayFeatures();
45.  MyCircle.DisplayFeatures();
46.  }
```

The output of listing 27.1 is as follows:

```
The square is Red and has a sidelength of 10
The circle is Blue and has a radius of 15
```

Listing 27.1 defines three classes in a hierarchy that is illustrated in figure 27.4. A base class GeoObject is used for all geometrical objects. The GeoObject class is defined starting on line 3. For simplicity, it maintains a single feature that represents the color of the object. Because any object needs a color, the Color data member can be used regardless for what class the GeoObject will become a base to. The GeoObject class also defines two member functions for setting and retrieving the color of the objects on lines 8 and 11, respectively.

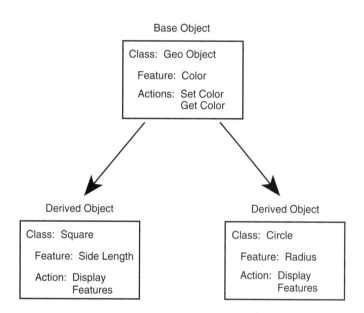

Fig. 27.4.
An hierarchy of geometrical object classes.

The access mode of the data member Color on line 5 is defined as private (the default access mode for a class is private). Similarly, the member functions SetColor() and GetColor(), defined on lines 8 and 11, are inaccessible from outside of the class because they are defined as protected. This in typical of base classes. Base classes are often defined for the exclusive use of derived classes. In this case, only the Circle and Square derived classes can access the member functions of class GeoObject, because these member functions are declared as protected.

Not even the derived classes can access the Color data member, because it is private. A base class should protect its members from derived classes, just as it needs to protect them from outside functions. The better protection that is built in through access mode limitations, the more robust and safe the class will be to use. Part of the objective of C++ is to give access to only the pieces of data that are necessary to another function. If a data member is not intended to be used by either an outside function or a derived function, it is best to protect that data by making it private. This way, only the class to which the private data member belongs can access it. Any other function, whether a derived class function and certainly an outside function, cannot modify and indirectly corrupt that data member.

The Square and Circle classes each add a feature that pertain to their own respective classes but not to any other class. The Square class declares an integer that represents the length of a side of the square on line 16.

The values for the Color and SideLength variables are set in the Square class constructor. The constructor is useful for initializing an object's features, as was discussed in Chapter 26. The constructor for the Square class, which is declared and defined inline starting on line 19, accesses the SetColor() member function of the base class as if it were declared for its own class. This is valid because protected and public base class members are accessible by derived classes as if they were declared local to the class.

The Square class includes one more member function called DisplayFeatures(). This function displays the features of the square that the class represents, including its color and the length of its side.

The Circle class, which is defined starting on line 26, also inherits the GeoObject class. It therefore can use the SetColor() and GetColor() member functions just like the Square class. The circle class adds its own internal data member (on line 28) called Radius to keep track of the radius of the circle it represents. It too has a DisplayFeatures() member function that displays the color and radius of a circle that it represents.

The program of listing 27.1 illustrates how the shared feature color can be safely placed in a base class and used strictly by derived classes. This is done by setting the access mode of the member functions SetColor() and GetColor() to protected. No outside function, other than derived classes, can use these data members. The GeoObject class is therefore only useful as a base class for derived classes that represent specific geometrical objects.

Calling the Constructor of a Base Class

A constructor is called every time an instance of an object is created. In the case of a derived object, the base object constructor function is always called when an instance of the derived object is created. For a derived object, you may also need to call a specific constructor function of the base object, if one is defined. C++ enables you to do so with a specialized syntax. The following example illustrates how to do this:

```
class Base
{
    .
    .
    .
};

class Derived
{
public:
        // define constructor
    Derived() : Base() {}
    .
    .
    .
}
```

In this example, the base constructor function is called from the derived constructor function using a : operator. This operator can only be used to call a base constructor function when a derived constructor is being defined. It is not valid anywhere else.

Having a derived class call a base class constructor can be very convenient. Because a constructor is called automatically, the constructors for base and derived classes can add a lot of flexibility without having to make any explicit function calls. For example, the program of listing 27.1 can be rewritten so that some explicit function calls are replaced with an implicit call to a base class constructor. Listing 27.2 shows the revised program.

Listing 27.2. Example of a using a base class constructor from a derived constructor declaration.

```
1.    #include <stdio.h>
2.    #include <string.h>

3.    class GeoObject
4.    {
5.    char Color[20];  // Data member to track color of object
```

(continues)

Listing 27.2. Continued.

```
6.    protected:
7.         // Constructor
8.    GeoObject(char * AColor)
9.         { strcpy(Color, AColor); };

10.        // Member function to get color

11.   const char* GetColor()
12.        { return Color; }
13.   };

14.   class Square : public GeoObject
15.   {
16.   int  SideLength;
17.   public:
18.        // Constructor definition

19.   Square(char * AColor, int ASideLength) : GeoObject(AColor)
20.        { SideLength = ASideLength; }

21.        // Member function to display features

22.   void DisplayFeatures()
23.        { printf("The square is %s and has a sidelength of %d\n",
24.                GetColor(), SideLength); }
25.   };

26.   class Circle : public GeoObject
27.   {
28.   int  Radius;  // Data member to track radius of circle

29.   public:
30.        // Constructor definition

31.   Circle(char * AColor, int ARadius) : GeoObject(AColor)
32.        { Radius = ARadius; }

33.        // Member function to display features

34.   void DisplayFeatures()
35.        { printf("The circle is %s and has a radius of %d\n",
36.                GetColor(), Radius); }
37.   };

38.   void main()
39.   {
40.        // Declare instance of a square and circle

41.   Square MySquare("Red", 10);
42.   Circle MyCircle("Blue", 15);

43.        // Display features of square and circle instance

44.   MySquare.DisplayFeatures();
45.   MyCircle.DisplayFeatures();
46.   }
```

The difference between the program in listing 27.2 and the one in listing 27.1, both of which accomplish the same end, is that the GeoObject class now has a constructor. The GeoObject constructor function is declared and defined on line 8. It replaces the function SetColor() of listing 27.1, because the SetColor function was only used in the constructor functions of the derived classes. In listing 27.2, the GeoObject constructor function can take care of assigning a color to an object when an instance of a geometrical shape is being created.

The derived classes Square and Circle automatically call the GeoObject constructor function. For class Square, its constructor is declared and defined on line 19. Notice how the : operator is used to invoke the base class constructor. Also notice that an argument that is passed to the Square class is passed along to the base class GeoObject constructor.

The Circle class constructor, which is declared and defined on line 31 also uses the : operator to invoke the base class constructor in the same way that the Square class does.

Although in this case not much has been gained, when the base class constructor is lengthy, having it invoked automatically when the derived class constructor is called is a convenience.

Keep the following points in mind when dealing with base and derived class constructors:

- Any of the available base class constructor functions can be used when calling it implicitly from a derived constructor function. You are not limited to calling the default base constructor. You may have different derived constructor functions, each of which calls a different base class constructor function.

- You can use any or all of the derived class constructor arguments as arguments for the base class constructor. As listing 27.2 illustrates, you can pass along an argument of a derived class constructor to a base class. You can use any or all derived class arguments for values that are passed to the base class constructor. In many class hierarchies, the derived class constructor passes all its arguments to a base class constructor and uses none of the arguments for its own purpose. In other class hierarchies, none of the arguments used for the derived class are passed along to the base class. It all depends on the way the classes are set up and the requirements of the derived class.

■ You can pass a constant value as an argument to a base class constructor. You are not limited to passing just variables. If necessary, you can fix the value of a base class constructor argument using a constant.

Sequence of Constructor Calls to Inherited Classes

When a sequence of constructor functions is called using a base class, the base class constructor always gets called first. If the base class is itself a derived class, then its base class constructor gets called first. The following example program demonstrates the sequence of calls for a set of derived classes.

```
#include <stdio.h>

class A
{
public:
    A() { printf("Constructing class A\n"); }
};

class B : public A
{
public:
    B() : A() { printf("Constructing class B\n"); }
};

class C : public B
{
public:
    C() : B() { printf("Constructing class C\n"); }
};

void main()
{
    C c1;
}
```

The output for this program is as follows:

```
Constructing class A
Constructing class B
Constructing class C
```

In this example, the class C is based on the class B which is based on the class A. For each class, only a constructor is defined as a member function. The derived class B calls the constructor of its base class A. The derived class C calls the constructor of its base class B.

The sequence of constructor calls is illustrated by the output of this program. A derived class always calls its base class constructor first and then its own constructor. This ensures that all data members are set up by the base class constructor before the derived constructor has a chance to access them.

In this case, an instance of C is declared. The base class of C is B, and so the B constructor is invoked. However, the constructor of B invokes its base class constructor of A before its own. Therefore, the sequence of constructor calls is first A, then B, and finally C.

Having the sequence of constructors called in this way can open interesting possibilities. For example, a base class constructor can initialize or modify a data member in the class hierarchy that is then modified by a subsequent derived class constructor. With a long set of hierarchical constructor calls, the data members can be set and reset, essentially fine-tuning the features represented by the data members, so that by the time the final derived class is created the features of the object it represents is well-defined. The example in listing 27.3 illustrates this point.

Listing 27.3. Adjusting data members in sequential constructor calls.

```
1.    #include <stdio.h>
2.    #include <string.h>

3.    class StandardTable
4.    {
5.    protected:
6.    char Base[20];   // Stores the type of base for a table
7.    public:
8.          // Constructor

9.    StandardTable() { strcpy(Base, "Four Legs"); }

10.         // Member function to display type of base

11.   void DisplayBase()
12.        { printf("The base type is: %s\n", Base); }
13.   };

14.   class OvalTable : public StandardTable
15.   {
16.   public:
17.        // Constructor

18.   OvalTable() { strcpy(Base, "Single-pedestal"); }
19.   };

20.   class FancyOvalTable : public OvalTable
21.   {
22.   public:
23.        // Constructor

24.   FancyOvalTable() { strcpy(Base, "Double-pedestal"); }
25.   };
```

(continues)

Listing 27.3. Continued.

```
26.   void main()
27.   {
28.         // Declare instance of FancyOvalTable

29.   FancyOvalTable MyFancyOvalTable;

30.         // Display base type

31.   MyFancyOvalTable.DisplayBase();
32.   }
```

The output for listing 27.3 is as follows:

```
The base type is: Double-pedestal
```

Listing 27.3 includes three classes that represent table objects that are joined in a linear hierarchy as depicted in figure 27.5. For simplicity, the Table object maintains a single feature, which is the type of base used for the table. A real object class would include many more data members that represented common features in the StandardTable class, such as type of tabletop, color, texture, finish, and so on.

Fig. 27.5.

An hierarchy of table object classes.

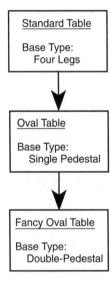

The topmost object in the hierarchy is the standard table, represented by the class StandardTable on line 3. For this example, a standard table is one that, unless otherwise stated, has four legs. This is represented by the value assigned to the Base data member in the StandardTable constructor on line 9.

The next level of specific type of table is the oval table, represented by the class OvalTable on line 14. This object class may share many features of a standard table. However, for this example the base of a table that is oval must be single-pedestal. This is represented in the constructor of OvalTable on line 18, where the value "single-pedestal" is assigned to the data member Base.

The final level in this hierarchy is the fancy oval table, represented by the class FancyOvalTable on line 20. Tables belonging to this class must have a double-pedestal, which is represented in the constructor on line 24 by assigning the value "double-pedestal" to the data member Base.

When an instance of FancyOvalTable is declared in the main() function on line 29 the constructors are called starting from the highest object in the hierarchy. The StandardTable constructor assigns a value of Four Legs to the data member Base (line 9). Then the OvalTable constructor is called, assigning a value of Single-pedestal to the data member Base (line 18). Finally, the FancyOvalTable constructor is called, and it assigns the value of Double-pedestal to the data member Base (line 24). This is what is displayed in the output when the DisplayBase() member function is called.

The constructors can manipulate data members that refine their values to better reflect the more specific nature of the class for which the constructor is called. As a constructor is called in a hierarchy of classes, it can add or change values of its own or any base class's data member that is above it in the hierarchy of derived classes. This affords a high degree of customization for data members that can happen behind-the-scenes and automatically when an instance within the hierarchy is created.

One more point worth noticing in this program is the call to DisplayBase() member function on line 31. Even though DisplayMember() is declared and defined for the class StandardTable, it can still be called with the class FancyOvalTable, which is two levels down the hierarchy of derived classes (as depicted in figure 27.5). Functions of any base class are accessible from derived classes as if they were defined for the derived class itself. This is why DisplayBase is called as if it were declared for the class FancyOvalTable itself.

Use of Multiple Inheritance

In C++, you can derived a class from more than one base class. This is called *multiple inheritance*. There are two ways to get multiple inheritance, as depicted in figure 27.6. The first way, discussed in the prior section, is that when you have a sequence of classes in a linear hierarchy (such as in the first diagram in figure 27.6), the bottom class cumulatively inherits the members of all the preceding classes in the hierarchy.

Fig. 27.6.

The types of multiple inheritance.

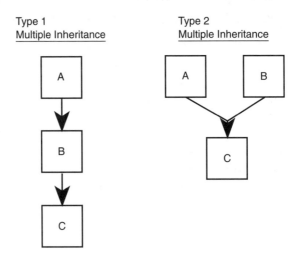

This section discusses the second type of multiple inheritance: the one in which a single class inherits members from two disparate types of classes.

Multiple inheritance is a preferable way of representing an object in many cases. Consider a class called Color and another called Shape. The Color class represents the color of an object, and the Shape class represents the shape of an object. The two have nothing in common. However, virtually every real-world object could use members that belong to both these classes.

For example, consider the object Ball, which represents a real-world ball. It has a color and a shape. Figure 27.7 depicts how the class Ball could use the classes Color and Shape. The class Ball utilizes the features of the classes Color and Shape to represent the color and shape of the ball.

To implement multiple inheritance, you must extend the use of the : operator when declaring a class. For example, in the case of the `Ball` class, you would declare it as follows:

```
class Ball : Shape, Color
{
    .
    .
    .
};
```

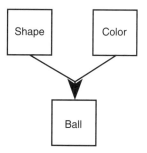

Fig. 27.7.
An illustration of a ball class using multiple inheritance.

The base classes in a multiple inheritance class declaration are listed in sequence after the : operator. The only requirement is that you separate the base classes by a comma. The base classes can also be individually modified by an access mode. Consider the following example:

```
class Ball : public Shape, private Color
{
    .
    .
    .
};
```

In this case, the base class `Shape` uses the public inheritance access mode, and the base class `Color` uses the private inheritance access mode. Protected members of `Shape` will be accessible to classes derived from `Ball`, but protected members of `Color` will not be accessible to classes derived from `Ball`. Recall that the private inheritance access mode changes protected members of a base class to private, which cannot be accessed by classes further down the hierarchy of derived classes.

Listing 27.4 is a practical implementation of the class `Ball`, using the classes `Shape` and `Color` as base classes.

Listing 27.4. Implementation of ball class using multiple inheritance.

```
1.   #include <stdio.h>
2.   #include <string.h>

3.   class Shape
4.   {
5.   protected:
6.   char Description[20];  // Description of the shape
7.   public:
8.       // Constructor

9.   Shape(char *ADescription)
10.      { strcpy(Description, ADescription); }
11.  };

12.  class Color
13.  {
14.  protected:
15.  char Shade[20];  // Shade of color
16.  public:
17.      // Constructor

18.  Color(char * AShade)
19.      { strcpy(Shade, AShade); }
20.  };

21.  class Ball : public Shape, Color
22.  {
23.  int  Diameter;  // Contains diameter of ball
24.  public:
25.      // Constructor

26.  Ball(int ADiameter, char *AColor)
27.      : Color(AColor), Shape("Round")
28.      { Diameter = ADiameter; }

29.      // Member function to display features

30.  void DisplayFeatures()
31.      { printf("I am a ball.  I am %d inches in diameter. \
32.  \nMy shape is %s and my color is %s.\n", Diameter, Descrip-
     tion, Shade); }
33.  };

34.  void main()
35.  {
36.      // Declare instance of Ball

37.  Ball MyBall(10, "Green");

38.      // Display features of MyBall

39.  MyBall.DisplayFeatures();
40.  }
```

The output for listing 27.4 is:

```
I am a ball.  I am 10 inches in diameter.
My shape is Round and my color is Green.
```

Listing 27.4 implements the classes Shape and Color in lines 3 and 12 that maintain a string to represent a shape and a color. The class Ball, which is defined starting on line 21, includes several interesting points. The declaration of Ball on line 21 uses a public inheritance mode for Shape. However, this only applies to Shape. It does not apply to Color. In fact, the Color class is defined with a private inheritance mode because that is the default inheritance mode for classes if none is provided.

> **Note**
>
> When you declare several base classes, you must declare an inheritance access mode for each base class. The inheritance mode used for one class does not apply to the subsequent class. If no specific access mode is defined for a base class, the class is assumed to be inherited by using the private access mode.

The constructor for the class Ball is declared and defined starting on line 26. Multiple base class constructors are called in sequence separated by a comma. In the example, the base classes are called in a different order from the way in which they were inherited. You can call base classes in any order. Base class constructors are called in the sequence that they are invoked, from left to right.

By invoking the base class constructors, the Ball constructor function sets the values for shape and color. The Shape constructor is invoked using a constant as an argument. The Color constructor is invoked using an argument that is passed to the Ball constructor function.

You can use any combination of values as arguments to base constructors. You do not even have to call the base constructors if that is not relevant and if there is a default constructor that can be invoked for the base class. The default constructor, or a defined constructor with no arguments, is necessary because every instance of a class, even a base class, executes a constructor function. If a base class constructor is not explicitly called or invoked, then the default one or the one that is declared with no arguments is called.

The Ball class includes a single additional member function called DisplayFeatures() that displays the features of the ball that it represents. It can directly access the Description data member, which belongs to the Shape class, as well as the Shade data member, which belongs to the Color class, as if they belonged to the Ball class itself. Any base class member that is accessible by a derived class is used as if it were declared internal to that class.

The main() function simply declares an instance of the Ball class and displays its features using the DisplayFeatures() member function.

Scope Issues with Multiple Inheritance

One problem particular to multiple inheritance is resolving name conflicts among base classes. When two or more base classes are used in which a particular member name is declared for each base class, which member does the derived class use? This problem is resolved in different ways for the two types of multiple inheritance depicted in figure 26.7.

Resolving Name Conflicts In Multiple Linear Base Classes. Name conflicts can result in linear base classes when one member name is used by two or more base classes along the linear hierarchy. The following is an example of this situation:

```
class A
{
     int  Integer1;
};

class B : A
{
     int  Integer1;
};

class C : B
{
};
```

In this example, class C inherits a data member Integer1 from class B, which itself inherits a data member called Integer1 from class A. The general rule is that the member closest in proximity to the point of use is the one used. For example, the Integer1 data member that belongs to class B is closest to class C. Any direct reference to Integer1 within class C defaults to the data member declared for class B.

You can override the default scope by using the :: scope resolution operator. To reference another member along the hierarchy, preface the member with the class to which it belongs and the :: operator. For example, to access the Integer1 data member from the class C, reference it as follows:

```
A::Integer1
```

This lets the compiler know that the version of Integer1 you want to access is not the default one but another specific one instead.

The program in listing 27.5 illustrates how to access the same member from different base classes along a hierarchy.

Listing 27.5. Accessing members with same name from different base classes.

```
1.   #include <stdio.h>

2.   class Integers
3.   {
4.   public:
5.        // Member function to display the integer numbers 1 & 2

6.   void Display1() { printf("The integer 1 is: %d\n", 1); }
7.   void Display2() { printf("The integer 2 is: %d\n", 2); }
8.   };

9.   class Floats : public Integers
10.  {
11.  public:
12.       // Member function to display the float numbers 1 & 2

13.  void Display1() { printf("The float 1 is: %f\n", (float) 1); }
14.  void Display2() { printf("The float 2 is: %f\n", (float) 2); }

15.       // Member function that uses base class Display1

16.  void DisplayInteger1() { Integers::Display1(); }
17.  };

18.  void main()
19.  {
20.       // Declare instance of class Floats

21.  Floats MyFloat;

22.       // Use default to display the number 1

23.  MyFloat.Display1();

24.       // Use scope resolution operator to display
25.       // the base class Display2() of MyFloat

26.  MyFloat.Integers::Display2();

27.       // Call to Integers::Display1 using
28.       // a Floats member

29.  MyFloat.DisplayInteger1();
30.  }
```

The output for listing 27.5 is as follows:

```
The float 1 is: 1.000000
The integer 2 is: 2
The integer 1 is: 1
```

The two classes of listing 27.5, Integers and Floats, both have member functions named Display1() and Display2(). Display1 displays the number 1, and Display2() displays the number 2. For the Integers class, these numbers are displayed as integers, and for the Floats class these numbers are displayed as floats.

In the main() function, the first call from MyFloat to the function Display1() on line 23 is resolved by using the function closest to the Floats class. In this case, the Floats class has the member function Display1() defined, and so that is the one that is used. The first line of output is therefore from the Display1() member function defined for the Floats class.

To override the default access of a name, you must tell the compiler which class member you intend to access. On line 26, the compiler is told to look for the Display1() function that belongs to the Integers class. This is done using a prefix to the Display1() function that specifies the Integers class should be used followed by the :: scope resolution operator. Had the direct method for accessing Display2() been used, the Display2() function defined for the Floats class would have been used. With the override call, the Display2() function that is defined for the Integers class is called instead. This produces the second line of output.

The third output line comes from the call to DisplayInteger1() on line 29. This is a member function of the Floats class that overrides a call to the Display1() member function. DisplayInteger1() is defined for the Floats class on line 16. A call to Display1() from within the Floats class would normally call the Display1() function defined for Floats, because that is the closest matching member name. However, the call to Display1 is prefaced by a specific reference to the Integers1 class name followed by the :: operator to point to the Display1() member function defined for the Integers class. The compiler is thereby told which version of Display1() function to use in the hierarchy.

> **Note**
>
> To access a member in a specific class along a set of base classes in a hierarchy, prefix the member with the class name and the :: scope resolution operator.

Resolving Name Conflicts in Multiple Nonlinear Base Classes. Resolving name conflicts in multiple nonlinear base classes uses the same approach as the one used in linear base classes. The only difference is that base classes of a derived class are all at the same level. Unlike linear base classes, the compiler cannot pick one member over another with the same name from two base classes, because both are equally close to the derived class.

Consider the following example.

```
class A
{
    int  Integer1;
};

class B
{
    int  Integer1;
};

class C : A, B
{
};
```

Class C uses both class A and class B as base classes. Class A and class B are therefore at the same level with respect to class C. A reference to Integer1 in class C is ambiguous and will cause a compiler error because the compiler has no reason to pick the Integer1 of class A over the Integer1 of class B.

In cases where a reference to a member name is ambiguous, you must always specify which class you are referring to. This is done using the prefix of the class name and the :: scope resolution operator.

The program in listing 27.6 demonstrates how to access ambiguous names in a case of nonlinear multiple base classes.

Listing 27.6. Accessing members with same name from different base classes.

```
1.   #include <stdio.h>

2.   class Integers
3.   {
4.   public:
5.       // Member function to display the integer numbers 1 & 2

6.   void Display1() { printf("The integer 1 is: %d\n", 1); }
7.   void Display2() { printf("The integer 2 is: %d\n", 2); }
```

(continues)

```
 Listing 27.6. Continued.

 8.    };

 9.    class Floats
10.    {
11.    public:
12.         // Member function to display the float numbers 1 & 2

13.    void Display1() { printf("The float 1 is: %f\n", (float) 1); }
14.    void Display2() { printf("The float 2 is: %f\n", (float) 2); }
15.    };

16.    class Numbers   // Class defined for all numbers
17.    : public Integers, public Floats
18.    {
19.    };

20.    void main()
21.    {
22.    Numbers MyNumber;

23.         // Display the integer value 1

24.    MyNumber.Integers::Display1();

25.         // Display the float value 2

26.    MyNumber.Floats::Display2();
27.    }
```

The output for listing 27.6 is as follows:

```
The integer 1 is: 1
The float 2 is: 2.000000
```

Listing 27.6 defines the classes Integers, Floats, and Numbers. The Integers and Floats classes are independent and do not interrelate. The are joined as base classes for the new class Numbers. Because a derived class views the members of its base classes as if they were declared internal to the derived class itself, the Numbers class now has two copies of Display1() and Display2() member functions.

In this example, a call to Display1() or Display2() from the Numbers class has no default and would be ambiguous. The functions defined for the Integers and Floats classes are at the same level of access, or scope, relative to the Numbers class. Therefore, any access to these member functions must be done using a specific reference. On line 24, the reference to Display1() is preceded by the class name `Integers` and the `::` operator. Therefore the `Display1()` function defined for the `Integers` class is called. On line 26, the call to `Display2()` is preceded by the class name `Floats` and the `::` operator, and so the `Display2()` function defined for the `Floats` class is called.

Any direct call to `Display1()` or `Display2()` would cause a compiler error, such as the following:

```
MyNumber.Display1()
MyNumber.Display2()
```

In this case, the compiler would see two versions of `Display1()` that it could use relative to the `Numbers` class. Because it cannot decide on its own which version to use, it would produce a compiler error.

Summary

This chapter discussed one of the basic principles of C++: inheritance. Inheritance enables you to combine features of objects into base classes that can then be used for more specific derived classes. A derived class inherits the features of its base class automatically. By creating a hierarchy of base and derived classes, you can simplify how real-world objects are represented in your program.

This chapter demonstrated the following things:

- Inheritance is the basis of creating a hierarchy of objects that interrelate. Features of a base class can be passed on to derived classes using inheritance.

- A real-world set of objects can often be better represented by a hierarchy of objects.

- The benefits to using inheritance are more efficient management objects and enhanced reuse of object components as a basis for new objects.

- You can limit access of base class members from derived classes, using the class inheritance access option. Private members of a base class always remain private and are inaccessible even from derived classes. Public members of base classes are always public and therefore accessible from any other function, including from derived class functions. Protected members of a base class are inaccessible to functions outside of the class but are accessible to derived classes.

■ A protected member of a base class becomes a private member of a derived class if the base class is inherited using the private access mode.

■ Base class constructors are called when an instance of a derived class is created.

■ You can specify which base class constructor a program calls in the declaration of the derived class constructor.

■ The base class constructor is always called first in a linear hierarchy of classes.

■ Several classes can be inherited at a time by a single derived class.

■ To access a member of a specific base class when the member is defined for more than one base class, you prefix the member with the intended base class name followed by the :: scope resolution operator.

Part V

Advanced C++ Object-Oriented Programming

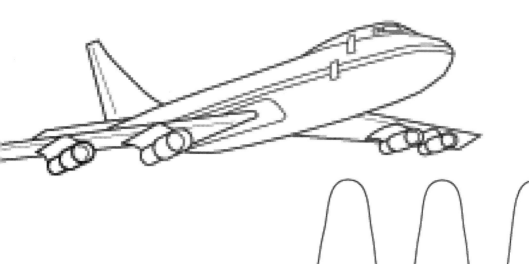

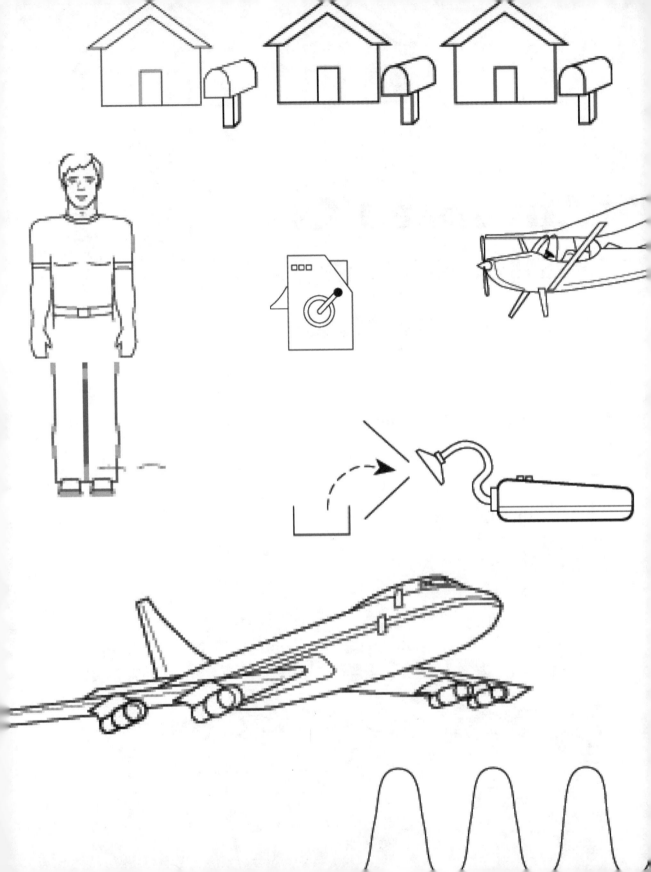

Chapter 28

Using Virtual Functions

The basic concept of virtual functions is relatively easy to learn because virtual functions do not have many associated rules. However, virtual functions often pose a challenge for programmers new to C++ to implement correctly and usefully. This is because virtual functions have no similarity with other programming concepts. Their uniqueness is what makes the concept of virtual functions one of the most powerful aspects of C++.

This chapter shows you the following things:

- How to use virtual functions
- How to use abstract classes and pure virtual functions
- How to use virtual base classes

Understanding Virtual Functions

A *virtual function* is one that is defined with the virtual keyword for a base class as well as a derived class. Virtual functions are, therefore, only relevant to classes that are inherited. When a call to a virtual function is made, the program looks to see what object the call is being used for and determines whether to use the base class or derived class version of the virtual function.

This may sound similar to the definition of overloaded functions, which was discussed earlier in this book. Although there are some similarities between virtual function and overloaded functions, there are even more differences. Whereas the choice of overloaded functions is determined by the context in which they are used, the choice of virtual functions is determined by the object type that references the function.

In Chapter 25, overloaded functions were compared to an English word that has many meanings. When the word is used, you know its meaning by the context of the sentence in which it is used. Like such a word, an overloaded function is determined by the context (the type, number, and order of arguments) in which it is used.

Virtual functions do not have a context like overloaded functions do. In fact, virtual functions are declared identically for a base class and for a derived class. The way the program knows which version of the virtual function to use is by the object type that called it. This is comparable to having two people of different nationalities saying the same word, as illustrated in figure 28.1.

Fig. 28.1.
Illustration of virtual function analogy.

In both diagrams of figure 28.1, a person is using the word *bell*. Because the word is the same and no context is provided, you can determine the intent of the word by who said it. If an English person is using the word, you know he is referring to an object that rings. If a French person is using the word, you know he is referring to something beautiful. Similarly, a program looks to the object that uses a virtual function to determine which version of the function to use.

Table 28.1 notes the differences between a virtual function and an overloaded one.

Table 28.1. Differences between virtual and overloaded functions.

Overloaded Functions	Virtual Functions
Overloaded functions are declared differently.	Virtual functions are declared identically.
Overloaded functions can be general functions or class members.	Virtual functions can only be class members.
The compiler determines which version of the overloaded function is intended by the type, number, and order of arguments used with the call to the function.	The runtime program determines which version of the virtual function to use based on which object called the function.
The choice of which overloaded function to use is made at compile time.	The choice of which virtual function to use is made at runtime.
Overloaded functions are implemented at the same level (for example, within the same class or as global functions).	Virtual functions are only implemented in a class hierarchy.

Using Virtual Functions

A *virtual function* is a nonstatic function that is declared in a base class and is preceded by the word *virtual*. The following is an example of a virtual function:

```
class Base
{
    virtual void Function1();
    .
    .
    .
}
```

Function1() is virtual by merely being declared as such. It will not have any effect unless the class Base is derived. Virtual functions are only useful in the context of inheritance.

To get a clear sense of how virtual functions differ from standard overloaded or redeclared functions, consider listing 28.1 and listing 28.2, which are identical except for the single word *virtual* in the second listing.

V

Advanced Programming

> **Listing 28.1. Standard redeclared member function.**

```
1.    #include <stdio.h>

2.    class Base
3.    {
4.    public:
5.    void DisplayMessage()
6.              { Message(); };
7.    void Message()
8.              { printf("Message from Base class\n"); }
9.    };

10.   class Derived : public Base
11.   {
12.   public:
13.   void Message()
14.             { printf("Message from Derived class\n"); }
15.   };

16.   void main()
17.   {
18.   Derived Derived1;

19.   Derived1.DisplayMessage();
20.   }
```

The output for listing 28.1 is as follows:

```
Message from Base class
```

The logic flow for the `main()` function of listing 28.1 is as follows:

Step 1: Declare an instance of the class `Derived`, called `Derived1`.

Step 2: Call the member function `DisplayMessage()` of `Derived1`.

Step 3: There is no member function called `DisplayMessage()` for the `Derived` class, so look for one in its parent class `Base`.

Step 4: There is a member function called `DisplayMessage()` declared in the `Base` class, so execute it.

Step 5: While executing the `DisplayMessage()` member function of `Base`, a call to a member function `Message()` is made.

Step 6: Look for the `Message()` member function that is closest in proximity to the place from where it was called, which in this case is the `Base` member function `Message()`. Execute the `Base` member function `Message()`.

The two most significant aspects to note in this sequence of logic are these:

- The entire flow of logic takes place while the program is compiling. After it is finished compiling, the executable program knows exactly which version of Message() to call in Step 6.

- The choice of which version of Message to use in Step 6 is easy to make. Because the Base class member function DisplayMessage() is calling the Message() function, its own class member function Message() is used, and not the Derived class Message() member function. In fact, the Base class does not even know that it has been derived. Recall from Chapter 27 that a derived class inherits its base class members but a base class does not know of its derived class members. Therefore, when a call to Message() is made in Step 6 from within another Base class function, it can only use one of its own member functions.

The next example is identical to the one in listing 28.1 except that the Base class member function Message() is declared as virtual. The output result changes.

Listing 28.2. Virtual redeclared member function.

```
1.    #include <stdio.h>

2.    class Base
3.    {
4.    public:
5.    void DisplayMessage()
6.            { Message(); };
7.    virtual void    Message()
8.            { printf("Message from Base class\n"); }
9.    };

10.   class Derived : public Base
11.   {
12.   public:
13.   void Message()
14.           { printf("Message from Derived class\n"); }
15.   };

16.   void main()
17.   {
18.   Derived Derived1;

19.   Derived1.DisplayMessage();
20.   }
```

The output for listing 28.2 is as follows:

```
Message from Derived class
```

The `Message()` member function of the `Derived` class is now being used! The logic for this program is similar to that of the prior example, except for a couple of important points pertaining to step 6. The logic flow for the `main()` function of listing 28.2 is as follows:

Step 1: Declare an instance of the class `Derived`, called `Derived1`.

Step 2: Call the member function `DisplayMessage()` of `Derived1`.

Step 3: There is no member function called `DisplayMessage()` for the `Derived` class, so look for one in its parent class `Base`.

Step 4: There is a member function called `DisplayMessage()` declared in the `Base` class, so execute it.

Step 5: While executing the `DisplayMessage()` member function of `Base`, a call to a member function `Message()` is made.

Step 6: Look for the virtual `Message()` member function that is closest in proximity to the class object that this function is being used for. In this case, an instance of the `Derived` class is being used. Check to see whether a `Message()` function has been declared for the `Derived` class. It has, so the `Derived` class `Message()` member function is used.

The two most significant aspects to note in this sequence of logic are these:

■ The logic of Step 6 takes place at runtime. With virtual functions, the only way to know which version to use is based on the class object it is being used for, not defined for. This is only known when an instance of an object is declared and used, which happens at runtime.

■ The choice of which version of the `Message()` member function to use in Step 6 is determined based on the fact that it is being called on behalf of a `Derived` class object. Because it is being called on behalf of a `Derived` class object, the `Derived` class object member functions get preference. Therefore, the `Message()` member function of `Derived` class is used.

In listing 28.2, a base class member function calls a derived class' member function. With virtual functions, a base class can "peek" into the derived classes to see whether a virtual function has been redeclared. This is in fact the whole purpose of virtual classes.

Virtual functions are used primarily as placeholders in base classes. When a base class is defined, there are often actions that need to be done but are dependent on what type of derived class object is used. The next example illustrates this point.

The diagram in figure 28.2 illustrates a hierarchy of geometrical objects. Geometrical objects all share many of the same properties, such as area and circumference. However, the calculations used for many of these common properties is different, depending on the object in use. These properties can still be maintained by a base class using the virtual functions that are redefined in the derived classes that represent the different particular shapes.

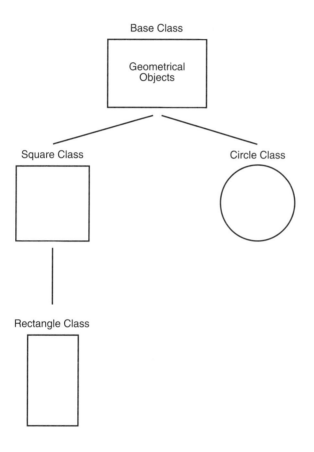

Fig. 28.2.
Hierarchy of geometrical objects.

Listing 28.3 is an example of a base class that represents geometrical objects. For simplicity, the base class displays only the circumference of an object. To calculate the circumference of an object to display, the base class uses a virtual function. This way, whenever a derived class is used, its own circumference member function will be used instead of the base class circumference function. This example illustrates many of the aspects that make virtual functions useful.

Listing 28.3. Virtual function to calculate circumference of a geometrical object.

```
1.   #include <stdio.h>

2.   class GeoObject
3.   {
4.   public:
5.        // Virtual member function to get circumference

6.   virtual int Circumference() { return 0; };

7.        // Member function to display circumference

8.   void DisplayCircumference()
9.        { printf("The circumference is: %d\n", Circumference()); }
10.  };

11.  class Circle : public GeoObject
12.  {
13.  int Radius;   // Maintains radius of circle
14.  public:
15.       // Constructor

16.  Circle(int ARadius) { Radius = ARadius; }

17.       // Redeclare virtual base function Circumference

18.  int Circumference() { return 2 * 3.14159 * Radius; }
19.  };

20.  class Square : public GeoObject
21.  {
22.  protected:
23.  int SideLength;   // Maintains length of the side of the square
24.  public:
25.       // Constructor

26.  Square(int ASideLength) { SideLength = ASideLength; }

27.       // Redeclare virtual base function Circumference

28.  int Circumference() { return 4 * SideLength; }
29.  };

30.  class Rectangle : public Square
31.  {
32.  int TopLength;   // Maintains length of top of rectangle
33.  public:
34.       // Constructor

35.  Rectangle(int ASideLength, int ATopLength)
36.       : Square(ASideLength)
37.       { TopLength = ATopLength; }

38.       // Redeclare virtual base function Circumference
```

```
39.    int Circumference() { return (2 * SideLength + 2 * TopLength); }
40.    };

41.    void main()
42.    {
43.        // Declare instances of geometrical objects

44.    Circle MyCircle(5);
45.    Square MySquare(10);
46.    Rectangle MyRectangle(20, 2);

47.        // Display the circumference of each object

48.    MyCircle.DisplayCircumference();
49.    MySquare.DisplayCircumference();
50.    MyRectangle.DisplayCircumference();
51.    }
```

The output for listing 28.3 is as follows:

```
The circumference is: 31
The circumference is: 40
The circumference is: 44
```

Listing 28.3 declares a base object that represents all geometrical objects called GeoObject. This class is defined starting on line 2. The class contains no data members of its own. It declares a virtual function called Circumference that returns a value of 0 if used directly. However, the purpose of the member function is not that it should be used directly but as a placeholder so that derived classes can redeclare it using the circumference calculations that are applicable to the derived class.

The GeoObject class defines another function, called DisplayCircumference(), that displays the value of the circumference of an object. To get the value of the circumference, DisplayCircumference() calls the function Circumference(). If Circumference() were defined as a standard member function, then DisplayCircumference() would always call the Circumference() member function of its own class. However, because Circumference() is declared virtual, the Circumference() function that is actually called in DisplayCircumference() is that of the derived class. Which derived class version of Circumference() is called depends on which instance of a derived object is used to call DisplayCircumference(). This is described shortly.

The other three classes defined in listing 28.3 are Circle, Square, and Rectangle. Each class maintains the information that is necessary to calculate the circumference of that particular shape. A Circle class maintains a radius data member. A Square class maintains the length of a single side. These are the minimal pieces of information necessary to calculate the circumference of a circle and a square, respectively.

The Rectangle class uses the Square class as a base class. Because a rectangle object is an extension of a square object, this is reasonable. The Square class already comes with a data member to maintain the value of one of its sides, and so the Rectangle class only needs to add one more data member to maintain the length of the top. The circumference of a rectangle is calculated using the length of its two different sides.

The circumference for each derived class is calculated using a function called Circumference(). Because the topmost class in this hierarchy is the GeoObject class, as is illustrated in figure 28.2, and it declares Circumference() as virtual, all Circumference() declarations in derived classes are automatically virtual.

You do not need to use the term virtual in a derived class after a function has been declared virtual in the base class. The virtual attribute is inherited by any function in a derived class that is declared identically as a virtual function in a base class.

The different instances of the shape classes are created in the main() function on lines 44, 45, and 46. When the DisplayCircumference() function is used for each instance, the base class DisplayCircumference() function is called. It in turn calls the virtual function Circumference() of each the appropriate derived classes based on the instance object that calls DisplayCircumference().

On line 48, an instance of the Circle class calls DisplayCircumference(). Even though DisplayCircumference() is only defined for the GeoObject class and is inherited by the Circle class, when DisplayCircumference() calls the member function Circumference() it looks for one defined for the Circle class, rather than the one defined for its own GeoObject class. Because the Circumference() function is declared virtual, the DisplayCircumference() function knows to look for the Circumference() function of the object that called it. In this case, an instance of a Circle class called DisplayCircumference(), so the Circumference() member function of the Circle class is called.

By looking at the calling object, rather than where the function is defined, the program determines at runtime which version of the Circumference() function to call. Even when the Circumference() function is redeclared twice, as in the case of the Rectangle class that inherits the Square class which inherits the GeoObject class, DisplayCircumference() still knows which object instance called it and uses the Circumference() member function of the calling object.

Using Pure Virtual Functions and Abstract Classes

A *pure virtual function* is one that is declared with no purpose at all except to be a placeholder for derived classes. A pure virtual function has the following declaration:

```
virtual return_value function_name(arguments) = 0
```

A pure virtual function is one that equates to 0. No code or space is set aside for this function. It is used as a placeholder so that derived classes can redeclare it. A class that contains a pure virtual function is called an *abstract class*. You cannot declare an instance of an abstract class because it is missing a function definition of the pure virtual function. Therefore, only an instance of a derived class that is based on an abstract class can be created.

Consider the following example:

```
#include <stdio.h>

class Shape
{
public:
            // Pure virtual function

    virtual void Draw() = 0;
};

void main()
{
    Shape Shape1;
}
```

This example program will not compile. The Shape class, which is a base class for rendering general shapes, has a pure virtual function called Draw(). The pure virtual function Draw() is not a valid function; it cannot be called directly. Draw must be redeclared by a derived class in order for it to be used by the Shape class or any derived class. Therefore, when an instance of Shape is declared in the main() function, the program does not know how to deal with the Draw() function, and the compiler generates an error saying you cannot declare an instance of an abstract class.

An abstract class is different from a class in which a virtual function is defined to do nothing. Consider the next example program:

```
#include <stdio.h>

class Shape
```

```
{
public:
            // Virtual function declared to do nothing

    virtual void Draw() {};
};

void main()
{
    Shape Shape1;
}
```

This example will compile because the Shape class is not an abstract class and therefore you can declare an instance of it. The Draw() function in this case is declared and defined; it is defined to do nothing. However, it is defined, and therefore it is not a pure virtual function, which means that the Shape class is not an abstract class.

Abstract classes are used to ensure that they are never created on their own. Creating an abstract class is a way of protecting a base class from accidentally being used as a wholly functional class. Instead of declaring and defining placeholder virtual functions, an abstract class declares a pure virtual function that requires a derived class to define it. The pure virtual function cannot be used on its own. The base class is thereby protected from accidental use of its virtual function that is declared only to be used as a placeholder.

Listing 28.4 uses a pure virtual function to determine the speed of a vehicle depending on the type of vehicle used.

Listing 28.4. Use of an abstract class to describe a vehicle.

```
1.    #include <stdio.h>

2.    class Vehicle
3.    {
4.    public:
5.            // Declare pure virtual function to determine speed

6.    virtual int Speed() = 0;

7.            // Declare pure virtual function to determine
8.            // type of vehicle

9.    virtual const char *Type() = 0;

10.           // Base member function to represent the vehicle traveling

11.    void Travel()
```

```
12.          { printf("A %s travels at %d mph\n", Type(), Speed()); }
13.    };

14.    class Car : public Vehicle
15.    {
16.    public:
17.          // Redeclare speed of vehicle to that of a car

18.    int Speed() { return 55; }

19.          // Redeclare type of vehicle to that of a car

20.    const char *Type() { return "car"; }
21.    };

22.    class Bicycle : public Vehicle
23.    {
24.    public:
25.          // Redeclare speed of vehicle to that of a bicycle

26.    int Speed() { return 15; }

27.          // Redeclare type of vehicle to that of a bicycle

28.    const char *Type() { return "bicycle"; }
29.    };

30.    void main()
31.    {
32.          // Declare instances of vehicles

33.    Car MyCar;
34.    Bicycle MyBicycle;

35.          // Render vehicles traveling

36.    MyCar.Travel();
37.    MyBicycle.Travel();
38.    }
```

The output for listing 28.4 is:

```
A car travels at 55 mph
A bicycle travels at 15 mph
```

The program of listing 28.4 defines a pure virtual class called Vehicle, which is defined starting on line 2. Vehicle is used as a base class for other classes that represent particular types of vehicles. Vehicle class is declared with two pure virtual functions, Speed() and Type(), declared on lines 6 and 9 respectively, which determine the speed and type of vehicle that is defined by the derived class. Because the Speed() and Type() functions are defined as virtual and equate to 0, they are pure virtual functions that cannot be used. They *must* be redefined by a derived class. This makes the class Vehicle an abstract class.

The Vehicle class does not have any purpose on its own. It has a Travel() member function declared and defined on line 11 that represents the vehicle traveling. However, this function cannot be used without a derived class because the function Travel() depends on the member functions Speed() and Type(). The Speed() and Type() functions are pure virtual functions that can only be used when redefined in a derived class.

Both conceptually and practically, the functions Speed() and Type() have no value for the class Vehicle. Conceptually, a vehicle has neither a type nor a speed. It does not have a type because it represents all vehicles. It has no speed because it does not represent a specific type of vehicle. Therefore, the concept of traveling using a super category of vehicle does not make sense. Without knowing which type of vehicle you are referring to, you cannot know what to travel in and how fast to travel. This is represented in the Travel class by the fact that the Speed() and Type() functions are declared pure virtual functions. These functions cannot be used, unless they are redefined by a derived class that represents a particular type of vehicle.

The Car and Bicycle classes are derived classes from the base class Vehicle. They represent particular types of vehicles. For this example, they add nothing but redefinitions to the pure virtual functions Speed() and Type(). Now that the Speed() and Type() functions are redefined in a derived class, the base class Travel() function defined in Vehicle can be used.

In the main() function, the Travel() function is called by an instance of a Car class and by another instance of a Bicycle class. In each case, the appropriate Speed() and Type() member functions are used that pertain to the class instance. When an instance of a Car class calls the Travel() function, the Travel() function uses the Speed() and Type() member functions declared for the Car class. When an instance of a Bicycle class calls the Travel() function, the Travel() function uses the Speed() and Type() member functions declared for the Bicycle class.

The Vehicle class can never be used on its own, but it serves as an excellent abstract class that organizes the concept of traveling for all vehicles. This is done using the Travel() member function that calls pure virtual functions to represent the speed and type of vehicle used for travel of the derived classes.

Using the Scope Resolution Operator

The scope resolution operator :: can be used for two purposes: to let a function know which specific class version of a virtual function to use, and to override what it would otherwise use by default. To use the scope resolution operator, preface the call to a member function by the class name of the member function that you want to reference followed by the :: operator as follows:

```
class_name::member_function()
```

Consider the program of listing 28.2. Without any overrides, the Base class function `DisplayMessage()` will call the `Message()` function of the calling object. If the calling object is a derived class, such as the `Derived` class defined in listing 28.2, then the `Message()` function of the `Derived` class is used. To get the `DisplayMessage()` function to always call the `Message()` function of its own class, even though it is declared as virtual, use the scope resolution operator. Listing 28.5 demonstrates how to do this.

Listing 28.5. Use of the :: operator to override the default virtual function.

```
1.    #include <stdio.h>

2.    class Base
3.    {
4.    public:
5.    void DisplayMessage()
6.              { Base::Message(); };
7.    virtual void   Message()
8.              { printf("Message from Base class\n"); }
9.    };

10.   class Derived : public Base
11.   {
12.   public:
13.   void Message()
14.             { printf("Message from Derived class\n"); }
15.   };

16.   void main()
17.   {
18.   Derived Derived1;

19.   Derived1.DisplayMessage();
20.   }
```

The output for listing 28.5 is as follows:

```
Message from Base class
```

On line 6, the call to the virtual function `Message()` is prefixed using the `Base` class name and the :: scope resolution operator. This lets the program know that even though the `Message()` function is a virtual function called by an instance of the `Derived` class on line 10, use the `Base` class version of the `Message()` function in any case and ignore the fact that the `Derived` class has it redefined.

The class name followed by the scope resolution operator can be used anywhere within a class hierarchy to point to member functions in its own class and any class higher than it in the hierarchy. You cannot use this method to point to a member function of a specific class that is lower in the class hierarchy.

Using Virtual Base Classes

One of the conditions not discussed in Chapter 27 along with multiple inheritance is the problem of multiple base classes. Consider the diagram in figure 28.3. Both class B and C inherit class A. Using multiple inheritance, class D inherits class B and C. Class D inherits members of class A twice, once from its base class B and the other from its base class C.

Fig. 28.3.
Duplicate base classes in a class hierarchy.

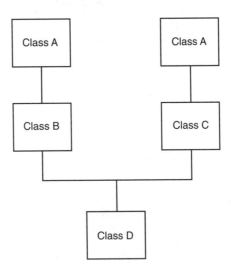

You can use the scope resolution operator whenever a member of class A is referenced, to tell the program whether you are referring to the instance of class A that is derived from B or the instance of class A that is derived from C. This is done in the following example.

```
class A
{
public:
        int Integer1;
};
```

```
class B : public A
{
};

class C : public A
{
};

class D : public B, public C
{
};

void main()
{
    D d1;

    d1.B::Integer1 = 10;
    d1.C::Integer1 = 10;
}
```

The reference to Integer1 in the main() function is always prefixed with the
base class name and :: operator to let the program know which version of
Integer1 to use, the one inherited from the base class B or the one inherited
from the base class C.

Another alternative is more appropriate in many circumstances: use virtual
base classes. *Virtual base classes* are the same as any other class with one exception: when a virtual base class appears more than once in a derived class
using multiple inheritance, only one version of the class is used. If you declare the base class A in the above example as a virtual base class, only one
version of the class A is inherited by class D, even though both classes B and C
use class A as a base class and are inherited by class D.

To declare a base class virtual, use the keyword *virtual* in the derived class
declaration. The following program revises the previous example to use only
one base class of A for the declaration of class D.

```
class A
{
public:
    int Integer1;
};

class B : public virtual A
{
};

class C : public virtual A
```

```
    {
    };

    class D : public B, public C
    {
    };

    void main()
    {
        D d1;

        d1.Integer1 = 10;
    }
```

The derived classes B and C declare the base class A as a virtual base class. If any duplicate base class A shows up through the hierarchy, the program can use only one instance of class A.

The main() function can now reference a data member of class A through class D without letting the program know through which base class the reference to class A is made. Because there is only one class A in this case, no scope resolution operator is necessary. This direct reference to a data member of class A would have generated a compiler error in the previous example.

When programs become more complex, you will have a tendency to use more complex and interrelated classes. When this occurs, the use of virtual base classes is very significant. Virtual base classes enable you to streamline how a derived class views its hierarchy of base classes. When using virtual base classes, you can set your derived class so that only one base class of a class type is inherited.

The next problem is one that demonstrates the use of virtual base classes. It also points out how several classes can be interrelated so that each class serves a purpose and adds an incremental value to the network of classes. Essentially, each class becomes an object or aspect of an object that can be combined with other objects to form more complex objects.

The purpose of the program in listing 28.6 is to build a vehicle using several components, such as seats and wheels. Each component has its own features, and, in this case, color. To simplify the design of the final product, all components of a single vehicle are the same color. The vehicle class can then be used to build a car or a bicycle. The hierarchy of classes is depicted in figure 28.4.

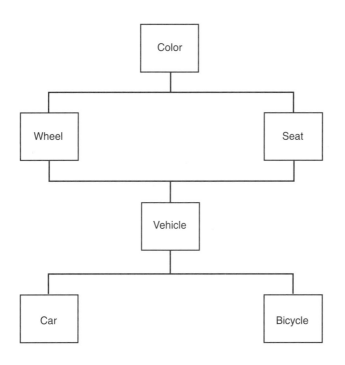

Fig. 28.4.
Hierarchy of
classes used for
listing 28.6.

Listing 28.6. Multiple inheritance and virtual base classes.

```
1.   #include <stdio.h>
2.   #include <string.h>

3.   class Color
4.   {
5.   protected:
6.   char Shade[20]; // Stores shade of object
7.   public:
8.        // Member function to set color of an object

9.   void SetColor(char *AShade) { strcpy(Shade, AShade); }
10.  };

11.  class Wheel : public virtual Color
12.  {
13.  protected:
14.  int NoWheels;  // Stores the number of wheels
15.  public:
16.       // Constructor

17.  Wheel(int HowMany) { NoWheels = HowMany; }

18.  };

19.  class Seat : public virtual Color
```

(continues)

Listing 28.6. Continued.

```
20.  {
21.  protected:
22.  int NoSeats;   // Stores the number of seats
23.  public:
24.      // Constructor

25.  Seat(int HowMany) { NoSeats = HowMany; }
26.  };

27.  class Vehicle : public Seat, public Wheel
28.  {
29.  public:
30.      // Constructor

31.  Vehicle(int Wheels, int Seats, char *AColor)
32.      : Wheel(Wheels), Seat(Seats)
33.      { SetColor(AColor); }

34.      // Display features of vehicle

35.  void DisplayFeatures()
36.      { printf("The vehicle has %d wheels\n\
37.  The vehicle has %d seats\nThe vehicle is the color %s\n",
38.           NoWheels, NoSeats, Shade); }
39.  };

40.  class Car : public Vehicle
41.  {
42.  public:
43.      // Constructor

44.  Car(int Wheels, int Seats, char *AColor)
45.      : Vehicle(Wheels, Seats, AColor) {}

46.      // Display features a car

47.  void DisplayFeatures()
48.      { Vehicle::DisplayFeatures();
49.        printf("The vehicle is a car\n\n\n"); }
50.  };

51.  class Bicycle : public Vehicle
52.  {
53.  public:
54.      // Constructor

55.  Bicycle(int Wheels, int Seats, char *AColor)
56.      : Vehicle(Wheels, Seats, AColor) {}

57.      // Display features a bicycle

58.  void DisplayFeatures()
59.      { Vehicle::DisplayFeatures();
60.        printf("The vehicle is a bicycle\n\n\n"); }
```

```
61.  };

62.  void main()
63.  {
64.        // Create an instance of a Car and Bicycle classes

65.  Car MyCar(4, 4, "Red");
66.  Bicycle MyBicycle(2, 1, "Blue");

67.        // Display features of MyCar and MyBicycle

68.  MyCar.DisplayFeatures();
69.  MyBicycle.DisplayFeatures();
70.  }
```

The output for listing 28.6 is as follows:

```
The vehicle has 4 wheels
The vehicle has 4 seats
The vehicle is the color Red
The vehicle is a car


The vehicle has 2 wheels
The vehicle has 1 seats
The vehicle is the color Blue
The vehicle is a bicycle
```

The member functions of the various classes defined in listing 28.6 can get confusing. This is not unusual for complex networks of classes. Much of the work is done using constructors and virtual functions.

In this example, two objects are created, one on line 65 and one on line 68. They are an instance of a `Car` class and an instance of a `Bicycle` class. All the work for setting the features of these two objects are completed within the constructors. The sequence of constructors for building an instance of the `Car` class is called in the order depicted in figure 28.5. When an instance of the class `Car` is declared, the base class `Vehicle` invokes the constructors of its base classes up the hierarchy of classes. By the time the instance of the `Car` class is created, the number of wheels, number of seats, and color have been set.

In the statement on line 33, which is part of the constructor of `Vehicle`, the `Vehicle` class can use `Setcolor()` as a single-inherited member function, even though the class `Vehicle` inherits the class `Color` twice, once from the class `Wheel` and another time from the class `Seat`. This is possible because the `Seat` and `Wheel` classes inherit `Color` as a virtual base class. For this example, the entire vehicle and all its components get one color.

Fig. 28.5.
Sequence of
constructor calls
when creating an
instance of the
class car.

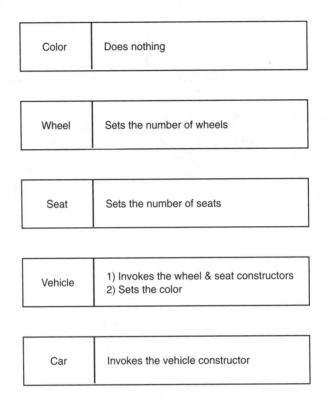

Anything derived from Vehicle inherits all its features, including those that Vehicle inherited from other classes. The class Car defined on line 40 inherits data members to track its color, number of seats, and number of wheels. When the class Car displays its features, it calls the Vehicle class DisplayFeatures() function first, so that all the features of the parent class are displayed before it adds its own features. In this way, all the features up the chain of hierarchy of classes get displayed.

This example illustrates how virtual base classes affect a real-world objective. In this case, the real-world objective is to have all the components of a Car or Bicycle class be the same color. This is done by making sure that all the component classes, each of which uses its own Color class, inherits the Color class as a virtual base class. In this way, when the program combines the hierarchy of base classes together, only one Color class is used in the final derived class.

Summary

Virtual functions are yet one more tool in the toolbox of C++ features that enable you to program a hierarchy of classes in which a base class can effectively access the member functions of a derived class.

This chapter demonstrated the following aspects of virtual classes:

- Virtual functions only apply to base classes that are derived.

- Virtual functions are declared by a derived class identically with a base class member function that is declared with the keyword *virtual*.

- The program determines which version of the virtual function to use at runtime, based on which object type is being used.

- Virtual functions are used primarily as placeholders in base classes. When a base class is defined, there are often actions that need to be done but that are dependent on what type of derived class object is used. These functions are declared virtual in the base class and then redefined in derived classes.

- A pure virtual function is one that is equated to 0. It has no purpose except as a placeholder for a derived class to redefine. A pure virtual function cannot be called directly.

- An abstract class is one that contains one or more pure virtual functions. An instance of an abstract class cannot be declared.

- A base class can be declared virtual. When two or more instances of the same virtual base class are derived, only one instance of the base class is used.

V

Advanced Programming

Chapter 29

Using C++ Streams

C++ streams build on the flexibility of C++ and provide you with a comprehensive way to deal with all forms of input and output. In Chapter 15, "Using the C Library," the topic of streams was covered for the standard C library. C++ streams extend this foundation by providing a broad range of capabilities for information transfer in a package that is manageable, flexible, and very powerful.

This chapter shows you the following things:

- What C++ streams are

- How C++ stream classes operate

- How to format data using C++ streams

- How to extend the capabilities of the C++ streams

Understanding C++ Streams

C++ streams are conceptually similar to C library streams. A *stream* is anything that will funnel information from one location to another. The advantage of using C++ streams is that they include embedded functionality because C++ streams are based on classes. A *C++ stream* is a class object whose purpose is to manage the flow of information.

C++ streams share many features with C library stream functions:

- C++ and C library streams manage information flow

- C++ and C library streams are device independent—the same functions can be used to transfer information to and from a console, keyboard, or other device

- C++ and C library streams include specialized streams for standard input, output, and error devices

There are several advantages to using the C++ streams over their counterpart C library functions:

- C++ streams include type-safe information transfer. The same functions apply to many different data types. This is accomplished by built-in overloaded C++ stream functions that handle various common data types.

- C++ streams include embedded functionality. Because C++ streams are based on classes, much of the administrative management, such as tracking handles and errors, is handled internal to the class.

- C++ streams are extendible. Unlike standard C library stream functions, a C++ stream class can be extended to provide custom features. You can add to the existing ways of formatting data with C++ streams. You can even overload the C++ stream functions themselves to include special processing.

- C++ streams are standardized. More than C library stream functions, the C++ streams are designed to operate similarly across the various stream types. With C++ overloading in stream classes, the same function that is used for outputting information to a buffer is used for outputting information to a file or console. Operators are also overloaded to provide identical methods for transferring information across stream types.

C++ streams are based on a hierarchy of multiple-inherited classes. By sharing a common set of base classes, C++ stream classes share common functions. This makes C++ streams easier to learn, because what applies to one stream type will often apply identically to other stream types.

Basic Features of C++ Streams

One of the benefits of C++ streams is that a lot of commonality exists between using a C++ stream for a console device and using a stream that manages an in-memory buffer. This section reviews the features of C++ streams that are shared by all stream types.

Insertion and Extraction Overloaded Operators

The most important functions of C++ streams are the insertion (<<) and extraction (>>) overloaded operators. As their names imply, the *insertion operator* (<<) places information onto a stream and the *extraction operator* (>>)gets information from a stream. The following is an example of how these operators are used:

```
stream << "This is a test";  // Write a character array to a stream

int  i;
stream >> i;   // Read an integer value from a stream
```

You can view the insertion operator as a large funnel, as depicted in figure 29.1. The insertion operator works very much like a real funnel, by channeling information in the direction of the apex of the funnel.

Output Stream

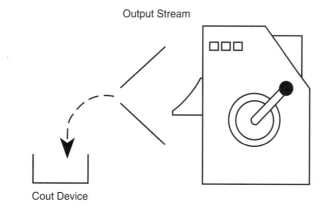

Cout Device

Fig. 29.1.
C++ stream input
and output.

Input Stream

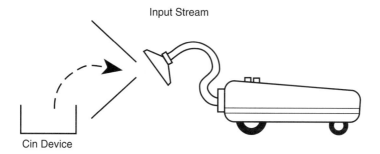

Cin Device

All streams support the insertion and extraction operators. These functions can be used the same way to read data from a keyboard, as well as from a file or a buffer. As long as a stream is declared and opened properly, you can safely use the insertion and extraction operators to write and read information from any stream.

All streams support the << insertion and >> extraction operators.

Concatenation of Sequences

Another common feature of C++ streams is the ability to concatenate a sequence of insertion and extraction operators. For example, to write several objects onto a stream, use the following format:

```
stream << Object1 << Object2 << Object3 ... ;
```

Objects are written one at a time starting from the left. They are placed on the stream in direct succession. Consider the following example:

```
stream << "This " << "is " << "a " << "test.";
```

This stream now contains the value:

```
This is a test.
```

The insertion and extraction operators can be concatenated in a single statement to implement compound read-and-write statements.

Compound Stream Statements

Compound C++ stream statements are very common. They enable you to append one transfer of information after another, where each transfer can be of a different data type. The process is an extension of the basic transfer process. The compound process can be thought of as one transfer machine passing data to another transfer machine and picking up new information as it moves along the assembly line, as depicted in figure 29.2.

Fig. 29.2.
Concatenated C++
stream output.

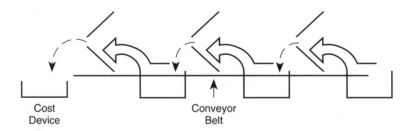

Cost
Device

Conveyor
Belt

To understand how this process operates, you must first look at how the stream operators are defined. Consider the *standard insertion operator*. It is defined as follows:

```
stream& operator<<(stream& stream, data_type)
```

The *insertion operator* is defined as an overloaded << operator function. It takes two arguments: a stream and a data type. There are a variety of overloaded << operator functions, one for each data type. In addition, you can overload this operator for a customized data type that you create. The return value is a reference to the stream itself.

Recall that a binary operator, such as the insertion operator, uses a left- and right-hand argument. The left-hand argument is the value to the left of the operator, and the right-hand argument is the value to the right of the operator. The function returns a value just like any other function.

When the program sees a C++ stream statement that combines several insertions, it starts with the left-most insertion operator. The left-hand argument is the value to the left of the << argument. It uses the right-hand argument as the data that requires transferring using the stream. The process, as can be seen by the << operator function prototype, returns the value of the stream.

The return value, which is a stream, now becomes the left-hand argument for the next << insertion operation. This continues until all the insertion operators are used in sequence. In this way, the compound C++ stream is in sequence, from left to right. The compound input sequence operates the same way except that information is being *extracted* from left to right.

You cannot mix insertion and extraction operators in one statement. For example, the following statement is invalid:

```
stream << "This is a test" >> buffer;      // INVALID!!
```

You cannot use an insertion operator and an extraction operator in the same statement.

You can use a variety of data types within a single C++ stream statement. The following example demonstrates this point:

```
int   i = 10;
float    f = 11.11;
double   d = 12.12;
char     buffer[] = "This is a test";

stream << i << f << d << buffer;    // OK
```

This example is valid even though several different data types are written to the stream using the same statement. The insertion and extraction operators are overloaded functions that can accept a variety of data types. Because each insertion or extraction operation is handled one at a time, each one can be different.

You can use multiple data types in a stream statement.

Three Kinds of Streams

In spite of the similarity across all C++ stream classes, there are differences among the main categories of streams. Fortunately, for simple use of C++ streams, the differences are limited to how the various types of streams are created. The actual use of the different stream types to transfer information is very similar across stream types.

The C++ stream classes can be divided into three main categories:

- User-interaction streams, such as those that control the console and keyboard

- File input and output streams

- In-memory information transfer streams

The stream classes are based on a complex hierarchy of interrelated classes, a portion of which is depicted in figure 29.3. Each type of stream class that is commonly used is at the bottom of the hierarchy. The base classes provide many of the features that are shared by the various derived classes. This is what enables the different stream types to share common features.

Fig. 29.3.
C++ stream
class hierarchy.

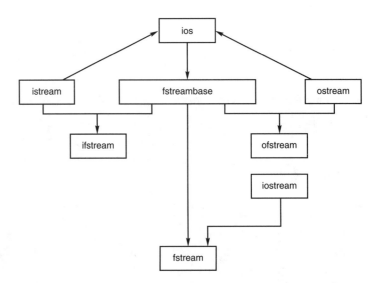

You do not have to memorize the actual hierarchy in order to utilize streams. Once you know the most common streams to use for any of the stream categories, you can focus on that category and not have to deal with the base class streams. Many of the base class streams within the hierarchy are not classes that can or should be directly instantiated.

This section reviews the basic features of creating an instance of each of these three categories of stream classes. The next section will discuss the more complex features and uses of streams that are applicable to all the streams.

C++ User Interaction Streams

The C++ stream that handles user interaction devices, such as the keyboard and monitor, is called the standard I/O stream. (The term *I/O* refers to input/output.) There are four standard I/O streams, as listed in table 29.1. To use any of the standard C++ streams, include the header file IOSTREAM.H in your source file.

Table 29.1. Standard C++ I/O streams.	
Stream Name	**Description**
`cin`	Standard input device, such as the keyboard
`cout`	Standard output device, such as the monitor
`cerr`	Standard error device, often assigned to the same device as the cout stream
`clog`	Buffered version of `cerr`

Consider the following example program that uses the standard output device.

```
#include <iostream.h>

void main()
{
    cout << "This is test.";
}
```

The output for this example program is as follows:

```
This is a test.
```

This example demonstrates the use of the output stream `cout` and the `<<` insertion operator. The insertion operator is used the same way for this as well as all other stream types.

To use an input stream, you apply the same principles except using the extraction operator. Consider the following example program.

```
#include <iostream.h>

void main()
```

```
{
    int  i;

    cin >> i;
}
```

In this example, the program waits for a value that is an integer. The extraction operator is taking information from the input stream cin, and placing it in the variable i.

Because all standard I/O streams are always open, they are available anywhere within a program, and you can combine the use of the various I/O streams. Consider the next example program.

```
#include <iostream.h>

void main()
{
    int  i;   // Declare an integer variable

    cin >> i; // Get an integer value from the user

        // Display the integer value back to the user

    cout << "The value of the integer entered is: " << i;
}
```

If you entered a value of 100 at the prompt for the variable i, the output of this program is as follows:

```
The value of the integer entered is: 100
```

This simple example demonstrates the elegant way in which streams are utilized. When you are familiar with the direction of the insertion and extraction operators, the code is very simple to read. Information always flows towards the apex of the operator. The << operator flows information from the right-hand operator to the left hand stream. The >> operator flows information from the left-hand stream to the right-hand variable.

The << insertion operator is concatenated in the output statement so that the output is a compound of two insertion operations.

File Input and Output Streams

The C++ file input and output streams are based on the C library buffered file system. However, the C++ streams are often simpler to use, are more flexible, and provide a broader range of capabilities. The three main C++ classes that manage file streams are listed in table 29.2. To use the C++ file streams, include the header file FSTREAM.H in your source code.

Table 29.2. C++ classes that manage file input and output.	
Class Name	**Purpose**
ifstream	Handles file input
ofstream	Handles file output
fstream	Handles both file input and file output

The most common method of creating an instance of these streams is to provide the constructor a name of a file to use. Consider the following examples.

```
ifstream in("input.txt");     // Create a stream for file input

ofstream out("output.txt");   // Create a stream for file output
```

There are two ways to open files using the C++ file classes. One way is to provide a filename and specifications in the constructor call when you create an instance of the file stream class. The following example demonstrates this method:

```
#include <fstream.h>

void main()
{
        // Create a file called test.out for output

    ofstream out("test.out");

        // Write a line of text to the file

    out << "This is a test.";
}
```

This program creates a file called TEST.OUT and writes a line of text to it. By using the constructor that accepts a name of a file, you automatically open the file for use. The file is automatically closed when the out instance is destroyed. Because out is a local object, it is destroyed when it goes out of focus at the end of the main() function. The TEST.OUT file is therefore automatically closed when the main() function ends.

The other way to open a file is to create an instance of a C++ file stream class with no information in the constructor. This simply creates an instance of the class. To open the file, use the open() member function, which accepts a name of a file as an argument. To close the file, use the close() member function. This provides a greater degree of flexibility for you to manage when the file is opened or closed. The following program demonstrates the use of open() and close() member functions with the C++ file stream classes.

```
#include <fstream.h>

void main()
{
        // Create a C++ file output stream object

    ofstream out;

        // Open the file test.out using the open member function

    out.open("test.out");

        // Write a line of text to the file

    out << "This is another test.";

        // Close the file

    out.close();
}
```

In this example, an instance of the C++ output stream class ofstream is created using the default constructor. No file is associated with the stream at the time the instance of the output stream class is created. You can choose when to open and close the file, using the open() and close() member functions. After the file has been opened, you can write to the file using all the standard C++ stream operators and functions.

This example explicitly calls the close() function to close the file when it is not needed any more, which was not actually necessary in this particular case. The fstream classes automatically close the file associated with an instance of a class when the instance of the class is destroyed. In this case, the out class is destroyed when it goes out of focus at the end of the main() function. Even though the open() function was used to open the file, the file would still automatically be closed when the class instance is destroyed. However, it is a good practice to close files explicitly when they are not needed.

The constructor and the open() function of the fstream classes can optionally take arguments for the mode in which the file is opened, and also for the access privilege that is assigned to the file. The prototypes for the various relevant constructors and functions are these:

```
ifstream(const char *filename, int mode = ios::in, int access =
filebuf::openprot);

ofstream(const char *filename, int mode = ios::out, int access =
filebuf::openprot);

fstream(const char *filename, int mode, int access =
filebuf::openprot);
```

```
ifstream::open(const char *filename, int mode = ios::in, int access
= filebuf::openprot);

ofstream::open(const char *filename, int mode = ios::out, int
access = filebuf::openprot);

fstream::open(const char *filename, int mode, int access =
filebuf::openprot);
```

In each of these functions, the mode constructor argument is used to determine how the file is opened, and the access constructor argument determines the access privileges assigned to the file when it is opened. Table 29.3 lists the options for the mode argument.

Table 29.3. Options for the mode argument.

Mode Option	Purpose
ios::in	Read only
ios::out	Write only
ios::ate	Place the file position at the end of the file when it is opened
ios::app	Append data to the end of the file when data is written to the file
ios::trunc	Clear the contents of the file if the file exists when it is opened
ios::nocreate	Open a file that exists. Do not create the file if it does not exist
ios::noreplace	Create a file and open it. Do not open a file if the file already exists
ios::binary	Open a file for binary data transfer. Files are opened in text mode by default

You can combine the mode options by using a bitwise OR operator. For example, to open an existing file for input, use this mode:

```
ios::in ¦¦ ios::nocreate
```

In the functions listed, for the input stream constructor and open() functions, the mode argument is assigned a default value of ios::in. This makes these functions easier to use, because you can use them with just the file name. The output stream constructor and open() member functions assign a default value of ios::out for the mode argument.

The mode values are declared as part of the ios base class. This makes them accessible to a variety of derived classes that need them. The mode values therefore are accessed by using the ios class name followed by the :: scope resolution operator. This tells the compiler to look in the ios class for the values associated with these mode options.

The access mode is set for all functions to default to the value of filebuf::openprot. The access values are defined in another base class called filebuf. The default value openprot means that read-and-write access rights exist for the file. The *access rights* differ from the mode in that access rights determine the limitation of the file, while the mode determines the method used to access the file, with the instance being declared even if the rights extend beyond the mode. The default access value should be used except in special circumstances that are beyond the scope of this book.

Listing 29.1 demonstrates a typical sequence of events using the C++ stream classes.

Listing 29.1. C++ stream input and output.

```
1.    #include <fstream.h>
2.    #include <iostream.h>

3.    void main()
4.    {
5.    int  i;   // Declare an integer value

6.          // Prompt the user for an integer

7.    cout << "Enter an integer value and press return: \n";
8.    cin >> i;

9.          // Create an output file and
10.         // write the value of the integer and some text
11.         // to a file

12.   ofstream out;
13.   out.open("test.out");
14.   out << i;
15.   out.close();

16.         // Reopen the file, read the contents of the
17.         // file and display it to the screen

18.   char buffer[80];   // Declare buffer to hold data

19.   ifstream in("test.out");
20.   in >> buffer;       // Read file contents into buffer
21.   cout << buffer;            // Display contents of buffer to screen
22.   }
```

This program demonstrates the sequence of writing to and then reading from a file. The program has several interesting features worth noting. It starts by prompting the user for an integer value using the standard C++ I/O streams (on lines 7 and 8). Then it creates an instance of an output stream class (on line 12). This version of the constructor is used to prevent the file from being opened when the instance of the output stream class is created. Because this stream will not be destroyed until the end of the `main()` function, and the file should be closed, the standard constructor for the `ofstream` class is used that does not open the file.

The output file is opened on line 13, and the value of *i* is written to the file on line 14. Writing to a file is identical to writing to the standard C++ output stream `cout`. The insertion and extraction operators are overloaded for all input and output stream classes. When data is written to a file, it takes into consideration the mode of the file. In this case, the standard text mode is being used, so the text that represents the value of *i* is written to the file, rather than the binary value of *i*. If you open the file and read it using an editor, you will see the number written out as ASCII text. The output file is explicitly closed on line 15.

The next segment of code reopens the file using an input stream class. The contents of the file are in ASCII text mode, so the default open mode is used. The information can now be read as either an integer value or as text. The extraction operator determines how the program will read the value of the file based on the arguments used for the extraction statement.

In this case, a character buffer is used on line 20. The contents of the file are therefore read as text. The contents could equally have been read as an integer value. The following example code could be used to replace lines 18 through 21 of listing 29.1 with the same results.

```
18.  int  j;

19.  ifstream in("test.out");
20.  in >> j;          // Read file contents into variable j
21.  cout << j;             // Display contents of j to screen
```

The overloaded extraction operator determines the program reads the contents of the stream based on the data type used for storing the data. In the original program, a character buffer is used in the extraction statement, so the overloaded extraction operator reads the file as ASCII text. In the revised version of lines 18 through 21, an integer value is used with the extraction statement on line 20. The correct extraction operator is used to convert the text file contents into an integer value. This is just one demonstration of the flexibility of using C++ stream classes.

In-Memory Streams

The in-memory C++ stream class is used as a replacement for the `sprintf()` buffer formatting function. The C++ in-memory stream class is called `strstream`. To use this class you must include the header file STRSTREA.H in your source file.

A C++ in-memory stream class applies the stream capability to a buffer. The flexibility of the formatting and functions that are available for the other stream classes can be used with buffers as well. A simple example demonstrates the use of the in-memory stream class.

```
#include <strstrea.h>
#include <iostream.h>

void main()
{
    int i = 10;    // Declare and assign a value to an integer
variable

        // Declare instance of C++ buffer stream class

    strstream buffer;

        // Place formatted text in the buffer

    buffer << "The value of i is: " << i<< '\0';

        // Display the contents of the buffer

    cout << buffer.str();
}
```

The output for this example is as follows:

```
The value of i is: 10
```

This program demonstrates how to declare an instance of the C++ in-memory stream class. After the declaration has been made, using it is identical to using any other stream. The insertion operator is used just like any other C++ stream class. The only unique function is the `str()` member function, which returns the buffer associated with the instance of the in-memory stream class. Whenever you need to access the actual string of the stream, use the `str()` member function.

In this example, a length of the buffer was never assigned. By using the default constructor for the `strstream` class, the stream dynamically manages its own memory. This is an extremely important aspect of the `strstream` class and one of the advantages to using it over conventional C buffers.

You can declare a size limitation to the buffer that is used by the `strstream` class. To do this, use an alternative constructor when declaring an instance of the `strstream` class. The alternative constructor has the following prototype:

```
strstream(char *buffer, int size, int mode);
```

This version of the `strstream` constructor uses an external buffer to store the information of the stream. It is an external buffer; therefore, you must provide the size of the buffer, so that the `strstream` class does not write beyond the limits of the buffer.

You can also specify the mode of using the buffer with the alternative `strstream` constructor. Only the `ios::out`, `ios::ate`, and `ios::app` modes as listed in table 29.3 are supported for the `strstream` class. If the buffer is not a null-terminated string, `ios::ate` and `ios::app` do not apply. Because both the `ios::ate` and the `ios::app` modes require that the class position itself at the end of the stream, unless the buffer is null-terminated there is no way of determining where the end of the buffer is.

Formatting Stream Input and Output

If all you could do was read and write simple variables, the C++ stream operations would not be that useful. In fact, the C++ stream classes support a variety of sophisticated features that can help format input and output without a lot of programming.

Using Format Flags

C++ streams include the ability to format information using format flags. A *format flag* is a value that is set using the stream class member function `setf()` that changes the way information is formatted for transfer to and from the stream. A format flag is reset using the stream class member function `unsetf()`.

Turbo C++ supports a variety of format flags (listed in table 29.4).

Table 29.4. C++ stream format flags.	
Flag	**Purpose**
skipws	Used to skip white spaces during a read using the extraction operator. A *white space* is a set of characters generally used to separate words, including the spaces, tabs, carriage returns, line feeds, and form feeds
left	Output information so that it is left-aligned

Table 29.4. Continued.	
Flag	**Purpose**
right	Output information so that it is right-aligned
internal	Affects only floating point numbers. It causes padding characters to be inserted after a sign or base indicator and before the value itself
dec	Input data is in decimal format
oct	Input data is in octal format
hex	Input data is in hex format
showbase	For any numeric output, causes the base indicator to be shown
showpoint	For floating point numbers, causes the decimal point to be shown on output
uppercase	Causes all characters that appear in numeric output to be in uppercase
showpos	For numeric output, causes the + sign to appear for positive numbers. Generally, the + sign is ignored for positive numbers
scientific	For floating point numbers, causes the use of scientific notation for output

The following example demonstrates the use of format flags.

```
#include <iostream.h>

void main()
{
        // Set format for output stream

    cout.setf(ios::uppercase);

        // Display some data

    cout << 1e10 << '\n';

        // Reset format for output stream

    cout.unsetf(ios::uppercase);

        // Display some data

    cout << 1e10 << '\n';
}
```

The output for this program is as follows:

```
1E10
1e10
```

Several points are illustrated by this example program. Formatting flags are set
using the setf() stream class member function and reset using the unsetf()
member function. The format flags themselves are defined as part of the stream
class. Therefore they must be referenced using the class name in which the flags
are defined followed by the :: scope resolution operator. In this example, the
uppercase flag is referenced as ios::uppercase. The flags are defined in the ios
stream class.

To reference a format flag, preface it with the ios class name followed by the
:: scope resolution operator. For example, to reference the left format flag,
use ios::left.

You can combine many flags in a single call to setf() by using the bitwise OR
operator. Consider the next example which uses a combination of three flags
to format output.

```
#include <iostream.h>

void main()
{
        // Set format for output stream
    cout.setf(ios::uppercase | ios::hex | ios::showbase);

        // Display some data
    cout << 1000 << '\n';

        // Reset format for output stream
    cout.unsetf(ios::uppercase | ios::hex | ios::showbase);

        // Display some data
    cout << 1000 << '\n';
}
```

The output for this program is as follows:

```
0X3E8
1000
```

In the first statement of the main() function, the three flags that are set are
uppercase, hex, and showbase.

- The *uppercase flag* causes output of characters that are part of a numeric output to be displayed in uppercase

- The *hex flag* is used to display numbers in hexadecimal format

- The *showbase flag* causes the output to show the base type, such as octal or hexadecimal, when displaying a number

The combined flags cause the number 1000 to display as 0X3E8, which is the hexadecimal equivalent of 1000. When these format flags are reset in the unsetf() function, the number 1000 displays as expected.

The format flags provide an easy way to format all subsequent information transfer for a stream. After a format flag has been set, it remains in effect until it is explicitly unset. You can then continue to transfer information with the format flag controlling the format of information for the duration of the use of the stream.

Using Format Functions

In addition to format flags, there are three important format functions that are members of the stream classes: width(), precision(), and fill(). Their use is described in table 29.5.

Table 29.5. C++ stream format member functions.

Function	Purpose
width(int)	Sets the minimum number of spaces used to output the subsequent data
width()	Returns the current setting for the minimum width
precision(int)	Sets the minimum number of digits used after the decimal point for displaying floating point numbers
precision()	Returns the current setting for the minimum precision
fill(int char)	Sets the character to use when blank spaces are necessary in an output. By default, the space character is used
fill()	Returns the current setting for the blank space character

The program in listing 29.2 demonstrates the use of the format functions.

Listing 29.2. Use of format functions.

```
#include <iostream.h>

void main()
{
        // Display the current settings for format functions

     cout << "The current width setting is: " << cout.width() <<
'\n';
     cout << "The current fill setting is: " << cout.fill() <<
'\n';
     cout << "The current precision setting is: " <<
cout.precision() << '\n';

        // Set the width option and display data

     cout.width(20);
     cout << "Test" << '\n';

        // Set the fill option and display data

     cout.width(20);
     cout.fill('*');
     cout << "Test" << '\n';
}
```

The output for listing 29.2 is as follows:

```
The current width setting is: 0
The current fill setting is:
The current precision setting is: 0
                Test
****************Test
```

Listing 29.2 uses the fill() and width() member functions of a stream to set the width and blank fill characters that are used in the output of information to the cout stream. The format member functions are called like any other member functions, using the . operator for the stream to which they are applied. In this case, the stream that they are being applied to is the cout output stream.

You can combine format member functions by calling more than one prior to the use of a stream. As listing 29.2 illustrates, width and fill settings are combined to give the output a special effect. You can also combine format flags along with format member functions to generate a particular output format.

C++ stream class format flags and member functions have several limitations:

■ The format flags and member functions remain set for the duration of the stream rather than for the subsequent output

- The format flags and member functions must be set prior to the stream data transfer. They cannot be called as part of a stream data transfer

- The format flags and member functions cannot be extended or customized

To overcome these limitations, the C++ stream classes include manipulators, which is the topic of the next section.

Using Manipulators

Manipulators are functions that can be embedded in a stream statement to format data or alter the effect of the information flow. The advantage of using manipulators is that you can add your own manipulator functions that do custom formatting. Table 29.6 lists the manipulators that are built into C++ streams. You must include the header file IOMANIP.H in your source file to use any of the stream manipulator functions.

Table 29.6. Built-in C++ stream manipulators.

Manipulator	Purpose
dec	Formats next item in the stream to a decimal value
hex	Formats next item in the stream to a hexadecimal value
oct	Formats next item in the stream to an octal value
ws	Jumps over white spaces in an input stream
endl	Inserts a newline character in an output stream
ends	Inserts a \0 character in an output stream
flush	Flushes output streams

setbase(int)	Sets the base value for output of numeric data
	    0 - default
	    8 - octal
	    10 - decimal
	    16 - hexadecimal
	All other values are ignored

resetiosflags(long)	Resets the flags identified in the argument
setiosflags(long)	Sets the flags identified in the argument
setfill(int)	Sets the fill character for blank spaces
setprecision(int)	Sets the precision of floating point output
setw(int)	Sets the minimum width of the next value for output

The manipulators can be used as part of a stream statement. Consider this example:

```
#include <iostream.h>
#include <iomanip.h>

void main()
{
    float f = 12.34;

    cout << "The value of f is: "
        << setprecision(8) << setw(10)
        << f << endl;
}
```

The output for this example program is as follows:

```
The value of f is: 12.3400000000
```

Notice that some computers may display slightly different values for the least significant digits.

The functions setprecision(), setw(), and endl() are embedded in the stream statement. Using manipulators is an efficient way to effect a change in the way data is formatted in a stream.

By using the setiosflags() manipulator, you can directly access the format flags within a stream statement. Consider the next example, which uses the format flags to set the formatting of a floating point number:

```
#include <iostream.h>
#include <iomanip.h>

void main()
{
    float f = 123.456789;

    cout << "The value of f is: "
        << setiosflags(ios::uppercase | ios::right |
ios::scientific | ios::showpos)
        << setprecision(4) << setw(20)
        << f << endl;
}
```

The output for this example program is as follows:

```
The value of f is:          +1.2345E+02
```

In this program, the format flags were set as part of the stream statement using the iossetflags() manipulator. The manipulators offer a straightforward method for customizing the format of information transferred by a stream.

Customizing Manipulators. The stream classes come with only a handful of manipulators. Although these are very useful, the built-in manipulators often do not meet all the formatting needs of a program. With C++, you can implement your own manipulators to affect the way information is passed in a stream.

To create a manipulator, you must define a manipulator function with the following prototype:

```
stream& manipulator_name(stream &stream)
{
    .
    .
    .
    return stream;
}
```

The manipulator function must take a single argument that is the stream and return the same stream. A manipulator works with the same principle as an overloaded operator function. The function takes as an implicit first argument the stream.

You can define either an input manipulator or an output manipulator. However, the same manipulator cannot operate as both an input and output manipulator. You can, however, define an overloaded set of functions with the identical purpose, one for input and the other for output.

Consider the next example, which uses a manipulator to format a memo:

```
#include <iostream.h>
#include <iomanip.h>

ostream& memo(ostream& stream)
{
    stream << endl
           << "MEMO" << endl << endl
           << "To:" << endl
           << "From:" << endl << endl;

    return stream;
}

void main()
{
    cout << memo << "Contents of the memo";
}
```

The output for this example program is as follows:

```
MEMO

To:
From:

Contents of the memo
```

This example illustrates how a custom manipulator can be used to set up the output of a document. In this case, the memo manipulator is used to present a memo format in a way that is easy to use. The stream value used as the argument and return value of the memo manipulator function is the output stream. The output stream is the class `ostream` and the input stream is the class `istream`. The memo manipulator function returns the stream reference. This enables the custom memo manipulator to be embedded in a chain of stream operations.

Another possible use of a manipulator is to combine several format manipulators into a single manipulator with a descriptive name. In this way, the descriptive name can be embedded in a stream statement that will then become easier to read and maintain. Consider the next example program, which uses an input manipulator:

```
#include <iostream.h>
#include <iomanip.h>

ostream& MessageTerminator(ostream& stream)
{
    stream << endl << endl
        << "**************" << endl
        << "This is the end of the message.";

        return stream;
}

void main()
{
        // Write the contents of a message and use the
        // MessageTerminator() manipulator to end the message

    cout << "Contents of a message" << MessageTerminator;
}
```

The output for this example program is as follows:

```
Contents of a message

**************
This is the end of the message.
```

Summary

This chapter introduced the hierarchy of C++ stream classes. The C++ stream classes provide a new way of managing the information flow of a program. Whether you are reading and writing to a file, using the keyboard and console, or just reading and writing information to a buffer, there is a C++ stream class that can add simplicity, flexibility and power to your program.

Although this chapter only introduced the C++ stream classes, many topics were discussed, including the following:

- C++ streams share many features with C library stream functions. Both are basically device-independent, and both have special streams for standard input from the keyboard and standard output to the monitor.

- Using the C++ streams has several advantages over using their C library counterpart functions: C++ streams include type-safe information transfer, include embedded functionality, are extendible, and are more standardized across stream types than the C library stream functions.

- The most important functions of C++ streams are the insertion << and extraction >> overloaded operators. The << insertion operator places information onto a stream and the >> extraction operator gets information from a stream.

- All streams support the << insertion and >> extraction operators.

- The insertion and extraction operators can be concatenated in a single statement to implement compound read-and-write statements.

- You cannot use an insertion and extraction operator in the same statement.

- You can use multiple data types in a stream statement.

- There are three main categories of C++ stream classes: user-interaction streams, such as those that control the console and keyboard; file input and output streams; and in-memory information transfer streams.

- There are four standard I/O streams. The two most significant ones are cout (the output stream to the standard display) and cin (the input stream from the standard input device).

- All standard I/O streams are always open and are therefore available for use anywhere within a program.

- There are two ways to open files using the C++ file stream classes. The first is to provide a filename and specifications in the constructor call when you create an instance of the file stream class. This opens the file immediately for use. The alternative is to create an instance of the class using the default constructor and call the open() and close() member functions to open and close a file.

- There are two ways to create an in-memory C++ stream class. The first is to use the standard constructor, in which the buffer is maintained internally and its size is managed internally by a dynamically allocated buffer. The alternative is to use a constructor and pass an external buffer along with its size, which will then be used by the class.

- Format flags can be used to format data in a stream. A format flag is a value that is set using the stream class member function called `setf()`, which changes the way information is formatted for transfer to and from the stream. A format flag is reset using the stream class member function `unsetf()`.

- Three format functions are members of the stream classes: `width()`, `precision()`, and `fill()`. They are used to format the stream data as well.

- Manipulators are functions that can be embedded in a stream statement to format data or alter the effect of the information flow. The advantage of manipulators is that you can add your own manipulator functions that do custom formatting.

V

Advanced Programming

Chapter 30

Using the Container
Class Library

The Turbo C++ container class library is a pre-written set of classes designed
to manage collections of information. You can use the container class
libraries as they are, or extend them to suit the needs of your particular
application.

This chapter explains the following things:

- The container class hierarchy

- How to use the String, Date, and Time information classes

- How to use the Array and SortedArray container classes

- How to use the Dictionary and Association classes

- The differences among, and ways to use, the Queue, Deque, and
  PriorityQueue container classes

Understanding C++ Container Classes

The greatest impediment to understanding Turbo C++ container classes is the
fact that the Turbo C++ documentation barely covers the topic. This is surprising only because the Turbo C++ container classes are incredibly powerful
and therefore extremely useful. What you would otherwise have to do programmatically on your own to manage collections of information, which
almost all programs do, is programmed for you by Borland.

The *container classes* are a set of pre-built classes that manage collections of information. There are many classes in this library because there are many types of collections. For example, one type of collection is a simple array. In a simple array, you need to keep track of a set of data of the same type. However, you might want to keep the set of information in sorted order. Then you would need a collection of sorted data items. Whenever an item is entered into the array, the array would automatically place the data item in its proper location. These two array types, the regular array and the sorted array, are managed by two different container classes.

Similarly, many container classes share common features. For example, every container class needs to allow a programmer to determine the number of items in the container. This and other common functions are placed in abstract classes that are used as base classes for other derived container classes. The abstract classes serve as seed classes for common member functions that apply to many container classes.

The Turbo C++ container class libraries include a variety of classes that manage sets of information that have different characteristics. The classes are built by using a complex hierarchy of classes, as shown in figures 30.1 and 30.2. Many of these classes are base classes or virtual base classes that are not intended to be used directly. These classes are mainly used to derive the other end-user classes in the hierarchy and to provide general functionality that can be shared across many derived classes.

Fig. 30.1.
Collection container classes.

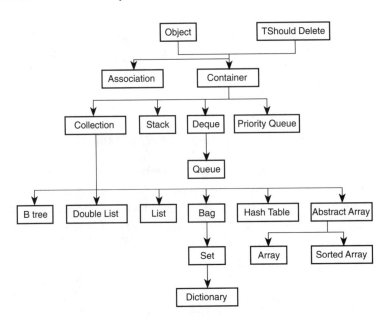

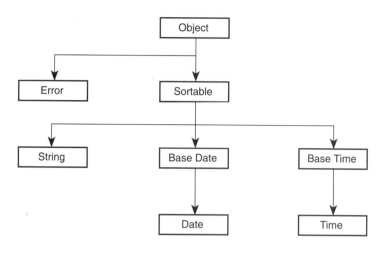

Fig. 30.2.
Information
container classes.

Table 30.1 lists the container classes with a brief description of each.

Table 30.1. Container classes.	
Class Name	**Description**
AbstractArray	Base class for Array and SortedArray. Used for common array functionality such as setting the upper and lower bounds of the array.
Array	A collection of objects with no order. Multiple objects can be added.
Association	Stores a single pair of objects. Often used as an object for a list or an array container class.
Bag	Unordered container that can have multiple copies of an object.
BaseDate	Base class for the Date class.
BaseTime	Base class for the Time class.
BTree	Balanced tree list. Maintains a set of objects in a balanced set of trees to make searching for particular objects very efficient.
Collection	Abstract class that is used to maintain a group of items. Items do not have to be of the same type. Used as a base class for other container classes.
Container	Abstract class that is used as a base class for anything that manages multiple objects.
Date	Class that manages dates.

(continues)

Table 30.1. Continued.

Class Name	Description
Deque	Specialized version of the Queue class that allows insertions or processing from either side of a Queue.
Dictionary	Used to maintain a list of Association objects.
DoubleList	Class that maintains a doubly-linked list. List can be traversed forward and backward.
Error	Facilitates error handling. This class is not designed to be used as a stand-alone class.
HashTable	Manages a hash table for any class that requires one. This class is not designed to be used as a stand-alone class.
List	Maintains a linked list of objects. Objects can be traversed in the forward direction only.
Object	Abstract class that is used as a seed class to represent functionality common to all container classes.
PriorityQueue	Maintains a queue that has an associated priority for each object.
Queue	Maintains a standard FIFO (first-in-first-out) list.
Set	Maintains a group of objects in which an object can only appear once.
Sortable	Abstract class for any object that can be sorted. Used as a base class for String, BaseTime, and BaseDate.
SortedArray	Same as Array class except that objects in the array are maintained in sorted order. The sort order is dictated by the object type maintained by the SortedArray.
Stack	Maintains a list of objects based on the order of insertion.
String	Special object class for managing null-terminated strings.
Time	Special object class for managing a time structure.
TShouldDelete	Base class for managing object ownership for derived classes.

One benefit of using the container classes, aside from simplifying managing collections of data, is that they are directly linked to the C++ stream classes. All the container classes can use the stream insertion and extraction operators. This makes using the container classes an even more compelling option when dealing with collections of information than creating collection classes of your own.

This chapter shows how to use some of the container classes. Many classes share similar features, as the examples illustrate; therefore, when you understand how to apply several of the container classes, you should be able to use the remaining classes with little difficulty.

Information Classes

Three classes within the container class library do not manage collections of information: the String, Date, and Time classes. As their names indicate, they manage string, date, and time information respectively, all of which are single items of data.

The String Class

The String class manages string information in a class structure. Much of the common functionality required to manage a string is encapsulated in the String class so that working with strings is easier using this class. To use the String class, include the strng.h header file in your source file.

Two constructors are defined for the String class. Their prototypes are these:

```
String(const char* = "");

String(const String&);
```

The first constructor enables you to declare an instance of the String class using a specific string or no string at all. If no string is given, the constructor uses a default string with no characters. This is different from no string at all. All String class instances must have an associated string. If no string is given, the class creates a string, one without any characters.

The second constructor is the copy constructor, which allows you to declare one String instance using another String instance as an example. The copy constructor copies the source String value into the target String instance.

Use of the String class is very straightforward, as demonstrated in the following example.

```
#include <iostream.h>
#include <strng.h>

void main()
{
    String String1("This is a test");

    cout << String1;
}
```

The output for this program is as follows:

```
This is a test
```

The String class, like all container classes, supports the standard stream insertion operator, as shown in this example. All container classes support both the insertion and extraction operators.

Several useful, built-in member functions are included in the String class; two are listed in table 30.2.

Table 30.2. String class member functions.	
Member Function	**Description**
`String& operator=(const String&)`	Copies the contents of the argument string.
`operator const char*() const;`	Returns a pointer to the null-terminated string managed by the String class.

Several other member functions are available to the String class using the hierarchy of classes: the relational operators ==, !=, and <.

The following is an example of how the String class can be used to simplify string management.

```
#include <iostream.h>
#include <strng.h>

void main()
{
        // Declare String instances

    String String1("ONE"), String2("TWO");

        // Test the equality of String1 and String2

    cout << String1 << " and " << String2 << " are " <<
        ((String1 == String2) ? "absolutely " : "not ") <<
        "equal" << endl;

        // Test which string is greater

    cout << String1 << " is " <<
        ((String1 < String2) ? "less than " : "not less than ")
<<
        String2 << endl;
}
```

The output for this program is as follows:

```
ONE and TWO are not equal
ONE is less than TWO
```

This example demonstrates the way strings are managed using the String classes. You can create strings so that the String class internally manages the string buffer, and you can compare strings easily. You can also output strings to any of the available streams.

Although the String class is useful, it lacks some common features you might expect from a String class, such as operators that add two strings together or find a substring in a string. You can create your own string class by using the String class as a base and adding only the functionality you require. Although this is not always a simple thing to do, it is certainly simpler than having to create a string class with no base upon which to build.

The Date Class

The Date class is designed to simplify the use of dates within a program. The Date class supports the internal clock date as well as a user-defined date. To use the Date class, include the header file ldate.h in your source file.

There are two constructors for the Date class. Their prototypes are these:

```
Date();

Date(unsigned char month, unsigned char day, unsigned year);
```

The first constructor, which is the default constructor, is used when you want to use the Date class that contains the system (internal) date. The second constructor is used for a date that is specified. The month argument is a number from 1 to 12, the day argument is a number from 1 to 31, and the year argument is a number from 1 to 65535. Both kinds of dates are managed the same way. The constructor is used only to determine which date will be managed by the instance of the Date class.

The Date class does not include any sophisticated date manipulation member functions. Table 30.3 lists the member functions available for the Date class. The Date class is primarily useful as a simple means of tracking a date and printing it to a stream.

V

Advanced Programming

Table 30.3. Date class member functions.

Member Function	Description
`Date(const  Date a Date);`	Copy constructor that assigns the instance a copy of a Date.
`Date();`	Constructor that assigns the instance the internal system date.
`Date(unsigned char month, unsigned char day, unsigned year);`	Constructor that assigns the instance a user-assigned date.
`unsigned Day();`	Returns the day of the month.
`unsigned Month();`	Returns the month as an integer between 1 and 12.
`void SetDay(unsigned char);`	Sets the day value of the date.
`void SetMonth(unsigned char);`	Sets the month value of the date.
`void SetYear(unsigned);`	Sets the year value of the date.
`unsigned Year();`	Returns the year as an integer value.

The following example demonstrates a typical use of the Date class.

```
#include <iostream.h>
#include <ldate.h>

void main()
{
        // Declare instances of Date

    Date Date1, Date2(1, 1, 1993);

        // Display the dates

    cout << "Date1 is: " << Date1 << endl <<
        "And Date2 is: " << Date2 << endl;

        // Determine which one is greater

    cout << Date1 << " is " <<
        ((Date1 < Date2) ? "less than " : "not less than ") <<
            Date2 << endl;
}
```

The output for this program is as follows:

```
Date1 is: August 23, 1993
And Date2 is: January 1, 1993
August 23, 1993 is not less than January 1, 1993
```

This example illustrates two important points about the Date class. The first point is that output to a stream is always in the following form:

Month DD, YYYY

The second point is that you must supply the full year for the second constructor type when declaring a user-defined instance of the Date class. The starting point is year 0 of the common era. To instruct the Date class to use the year 1993, you must specify 1993 in the constructor.

As with all the container classes, you can use the comparison operators. In this example, the comparison operator is used to determine which of two dates is greater.

The Time Class

The Time class is used to simplify the use of time structures in a program. It is very similar conceptually and practically to the Date class. The Time class, like the Date class, can be automatically set to the internal system time or to a user-defined time. To use the Time class, include the header file ltime.h in your source file.

There are three constructors for the Time class. Their prototypes are as follows:

```
Time();

Time(const Time&);

Time(unsigned char hour, unsigned char minute = 0, unsigned char
second = 0, unsigned char hundredths = 0);
```

The first constructor is used to set the instance of the Time class to the internal system time. The second constructor is the copy constructor, which is used to set the current instance to the time associated with another instance of a Time class. The third constructor is used to set the instance of the Time class to a user-specified time.

The Time class does not include any sophisticated time manipulation member functions. It is primarily useful as a simple means of tracking a time and printing it to a stream. Table 30.4 lists the member functions for the Time class.

Table 30.4. Time class member functions.

Member Function	Description
`Time();`	Constructor that assigns the instance the internal system time.

`Time(unsigned char hour,`
`unsigned char minute = 0,`
`unsigned char second = 0,`
`unsigned char hundredths = 0);`
	Constructor that assigns the instance a user-assigned time.

`Time(const Time&);`	Copy constructor.
`unsigned hour() const;`	Returns the hour.
`unsigned hundredths() const;`	Returns the hundredths of a second.
`unsigned minute() const;`	Returns the minute.
`unsigned second() const;`	Returns the second.
`void SetHour(unsigned char);`	Sets the hour.
`void SetHundredths` `(unsigned char);`	Sets the hundredths of a second.
`void SetMinute(unsigned char);`	Sets the minute.
`void SetSecond(unsigned char);`	Sets the second.

The following example demonstrates a typical use of the Time class.

```
#include <iostream.h>
#include <ltime.h>

void main()
{
        // Declare instances of Time

    Time Time1, Time2(10, 30);

        // Use copy constructor for new Time instance

    Time Time3(Time2);

        // Display the times
```

```
        cout << "Time1 is: " << Time1 << endl <<
             "Time2 is: " << Time2 << endl <<
             "Time3 is: " << Time3 << endl;

             // Determine which one is greater

        cout << Time1 << " is " <<
             ((Time1 < Time2) ? "less than " : "not less than ") <<
             Time2 << endl;
    }
```

The output for this program is as follows:

```
Time1 is: 11:03:59.38 am
Time2 is: 10:30:00.00 am
Time3 is: 10:30:00.00 am
11:03:59.38 am is not less than 10:30:00.00 am
```

This example illustrates several important points regarding the Time class. The default format for displaying the time on a stream is this:

HH:MM:SS.HS

HH is the hour using 24-hour (military) time. MM is the minute, SS is the second, and HS is the hundredth of a second. To display the time using another format, you have to derive a class of your own using the Time class as a base and override the function printOn().

The Time2 instance in the example is declared by using only arguments. The first two arguments specify the hour and minute of the instance. The remaining arguments are set to zero using the default value of the constructor. In fact, the only value you need to specify with the user-specified Time constructor is the hour. The remaining values will default to zero, which indicates the start of the hour.

The Timer Class

The Timer class is essentially a stopwatch class. It is used to determine elapsed time. It is not associated with the container class directly (it is not even on the class hierarchy diagrams in figures 30.1 or 30.2). Nonetheless, it is a built-in class that has a utility in many applications. To use the Timer class, include the header file timer.h in your source file.

Use of the Timer class is straightforward. Declare an instance of the Timer class, start the stopwatch, stop the stopwatch, and get the elapsed time. Table 30.5 lists the available member functions.

V

Advanced Programming

Table 30.5. Timer member functions.	
Member Function	**Description**
`Timer()`	Constructor.
`void reset()`	Resets the stopwatch.
`static double resolution()`	Returns the precision of the timer in terms of seconds. This is hardware-dependent.
`void start()`	Starts the stopwatch.
`int status()`	Returns a 1 if the stopwatch is running, 0 if it is stopped.
`void stop()`	Stops the stopwatch.
`double time()`	Returns the elapsed time.

The following example demonstrates the use of the Timer class.

```
#include <iostream.h>
#include <timer.h>

void main()
{
        // Declare instance of Timer class

    Timer StopWatch;

        // Use StopWatch to time a task

    StopWatch.start();

    for(int i = 0; i < 10000; i++ )
    {
        int * ex = new int[100];
        delete ex;
    }

    StopWatch.stop();

        // Display elapsed time of first task

    cout << "The first task took " <<
        StopWatch.time() <<
        " seconds to execute." << endl;

        // Use StopWatch to time another task

    StopWatch.reset();  // Don't forget to reset timer
                // if it is being reused
    StopWatch.start();
```

```
        for(i = 0; i < 10000; i++ )
        {
        }

        StopWatch.stop();

            // Display elapsed time of second task

        cout << "The second task took " <<
             StopWatch.time() <<
             " seconds to execute." << endl;
    }
```

The output of this class on a 486 33 Mhz machine is as follows:

```
The first task took 0.096467 seconds to execute.
The second task took 0.009621 seconds to execute.
```

This program demonstrates the basic use of the Timer class. The values in the output for this program obviously depend on the hardware being used. When using the Timer class, keep in mind that you must reset it when reusing the same instance for various purposes. If you forget to reset the instance, the timer will keep incrementing its internal variable that tracks elapsed time.

Using Arrays and Sorted Arrays

In Chapter 19, the topic of arrays was discussed, using standard array structures. This section describes an alternative to using arrays that can greatly simplify many programming tasks. An *Array class* is a simple collection of information. A *SortedArray class* is a collection of information that is sorted, based on the type of information that is being maintained by the array.

The Array and SortedArray container classes are designed to maintain objects that are part of the container class library. For example, you can declare an array of String objects, or of Date and Time objects. If you need to maintain an array of objects for an object that is not already a part of the container class library, you must derive the new object from the class Object. This will make the new object readable by other container classes.

Arrays

An *array* is a simple collection of data. It is widely used in programming because it imposes little or no restrictions on how information is maintained in the list. An array starts as an empty list. As data is added to the array, it places the information basically in the order it was entered, although this is not guaranteed. To use the Array container class, include the array.h header file in your source file.

The Array class includes a single constructor. Its prototype is as follows:

```
Array(int upper, int lower = 0, sizeType growby = 0);
```

The first two arguments of the Array constructor represent the upper and lower bounds of the array. For example, the values 2 and 0 for the first two arguments represent an array of 3 items, with the first item in the array slot 0 and the third item in the array slot 2.

The lower bound value defaults to 0, though it does not need to be set that way. You can have the upper and lower bounds set at 20 and 10 respectively, which will create an array of 11 items whose lowest index is 10 and highest is 20.

The upper bound is not necessarily fixed, nor is the number of items that an Array class can contain. If the third argument is set to 0, then the upper and lower bounds are fixed. Otherwise, the instance of the Array grows dynamically. When new items are added to the array beyond the upper bound limit, the array grows by the number of items equal to the value of the third argument of the constructor. This enables you to maintain a large array without the hassle of managing the memory associated with fluctuating lists.

Table 30.6 lists the member functions and their descriptions for the Array class.

Table 30.6. Array class member functions.

Member Function	Description

`Array(int upper,`
`int lower = 0,`
`sizeType growby = 0`
	Constructor.

`virtual void add(Object&);`	Adds an object that is derived from the Object class in the first available slot.
`void addAt(Object&,` `int index);`	Adds an object that is derived from the Object class at a given index.
`sizeType arraySize() const;`	Returns the size of the array, which equals: upper - lower + 1.
`void destroy(int index);`	Removes and deletes an object at a given index.

Member Function	Description

`virtual void detach`
`(Object&,`
`DeleteType = NoDelete);`
	Searches for a matching object and detaches it from the array. If more than one match is in an array, only the one at the lowest index is detached.

`virtual void detach` `(int index,`	Removes the object at a given index.

`DeleteType = NoDelete);`
`virtual void flush`
`(DeleteType = NoDelete);`
	Removes and optionally deletes all the objects in an array.

`int lowerBound() const;`	Returns the lowest index that is usable.
`int upperBound() const;`	Returns the largest index that is usable.
`Object& operator[]` `(int index) const;`	Returns a reference to the object at a given index.

The following is an example of using the Array class.

```
#include <strng.h>
#include <array.h>

void main()
{
        // Declare three String objects

      String * String1 = new String("First string");
      String * String2 = new String("Second string");
      String * String3 = new String("Third string");

        // Declare an instance of the class Array

      Array MyArray(1, 0, 1);

        // Add items to the array

      MyArray.add(*String1);
      MyArray.add(*String2);
      MyArray.add(*String3);

        // Display array contents

      cout << MyArray;
}
```

The output for this program is as follows:

```
Array {
     First string,
     Second string,
     Third string }
```

Many interesting points are illustrated in this simple example. Starting from the top of the program, the following issues must be dealt with whenever you use the Array class:

- Items that are used in the Array or any other container class must be instances of another container class derived from the Object abstract class. In this example, the items to be added to the Array class are instances of the String class.

- The String items used in this example are created using the C++ dynamic allocation function new but are never deleted. The Array class, like most of the container classes, by default owns the objects that are added to it. The Array class therefore deletes the objects that it maintains when the instance of the Array class is itself destroyed. In this example, the MyArray instance is destroyed when it goes out of focus at the end of the main() function. (There are ways of changing the ownership of a container class, but this is beyond the scope of this book.)

- The MyArray instance of the Array class is declared with the arguments 1, 0, and 1. This means that the array starts with space for two items and will grow one object at a time as necessary. In this example, because three objects are added to MyArray, MyArray grew dynamically by one extra item.

- Items are added to the Array class by using the add() member function. You do not need to specify where in the array items get added. This is handled by the Array class internally. The add() member function takes a reference to an item. You must therefore use the * dereferencing operator when adding the String items to MyArray.

- The insertion operator is overloaded for all container classes. This provides at least a default way of displaying the data maintained in any of the container classes. You can override this operator using a derived class of Array to present the list of items using the insertion operator in a way that is more suitable to your program.

Sorted Arrays

You can use a special version of the Array class that automatically maintains its items in sorted order. Because all objects of an array must be derived from the Object class, and all Object-derived classes have associated relational operators, any Object-derived class can be sorted. The sorted array class is called *SortedArray*. To use the SortedArray class, include the sortarry.h header file in your source file.

The member functions for the SortedArray class are identical to the ones for the Array class listed in table 30.6. The add() and detach() member functions are redefined to specially handle the list so that it maintains its sorted order.

The following is a variation of the Array example that demonstrates the automatic sorting capability of the SortedArray class.

```
#include <strng.h>
#include <sortarry.h>

void main()
{
        // Declare three String objects

    String& String1 = *new String("E");
    String& String2 = *new String("B");
    String& String3 = *new String("C");
    String& String4 = *new String("A");
    String& String5 = *new String("D");
    String& String6 = *new String("F");

        // Declare an instance of the class SortedArray

    SortedArray MySortedArray(1, 0, 1);

        // Add items to the array

    MySortedArray.add(String1);
    MySortedArray.add(String2);
    MySortedArray.add(String3);
    MySortedArray.add(String4);
    MySortedArray.add(String5);
    MySortedArray.add(String6);

        // Display array contents

    cout << MySortedArray;
}
```

The output for this program is as follows:

```
SortedArray {
      A,
      B,
      C,
      D,
      E,
      F }
```

The String items added to the `MySortedArray` class were added in no particular order. Using the default version of the insertion operator, the values of the `MySortedArray` instance are printed in sorted order. The values are actually maintained internally in sorted order, as they are added to the SortedArray class.

This example also demonstrates another way of declaring and using objects as items to be added to a container class. Because the container classes generally require a reference to an object when they are added to the container, one way of declaring an object is by using the object's reference variable in the declaration. The String instances are declared with this method in this example.

The String objects are allocated by using the standard C++ `new` allocation function. However, they are placed in a reference (rather than a pointer) String variable so that the variable can be used directly in an `add()` function. The `add()` function takes the reference variable directly. The String declarations therefore add the `*` dereferencing operator on the right side of the declaration, so that the value returned is a reference rather than a pointer.

Using the Association and Dictionary Classes

A *Dictionary class* contains a collection of objects that are Associations. An *Association object* is one that associates two objects. The two classes, Dictionary and Association, are therefore related and are explained together in this section.

The Associated Class

The Associated class connects two objects into a single reference. For example, a dictionary entry is an association because it connects a word with a meaning. You can only have one pair of values associated in an Associated class. To use the Associated class, include the assoc.h header file in your source file.

There are two constructors for the Associated class. Their prototypes are these:

```
Associated(Object& key, Object& value);

Associated(const Association&);
```

The first constructor takes two arguments that are both references to Object-derived classes. The first argument is the key for the association. Any searches or relational operations are done using the first argument. The second argument is the value associated with a key. The value can be any Object-derived class as well. This enables a great degree of flexibility as to what can get associated. Because any structure can be made into an Object, virtually any two items can be connected using the Associated class.

The second constructor is the copy constructor. Given one instance of an Association class, you can create a carbon copy in a second instance.

The Association class has only a few relevant member functions, as listed in table 30.7.

Table 30.7. Associated class member functions.

Member Function	Description
Association(Object& key, Object& value);	Constructor.
Association(const Association&);	Constructor.
Object& key() const;	Returns a reference to the key object.
Object& value() const;	Returns a reference to the value object.

V

Advanced Programming

The following is an example of using the Association class.

```
#include <assoc.h>
#include <strng.h>
#include <ltime.h>

void main()
{
        // Declare items to be inserted into a container class

    String* String1 = new String("Time to wake up.");
    Time* Time1 = new Time(7);

        // Declare instance of an Association class

    Association MyAssociation(*Time1, *String1);

        // Display MyAssociation

    cout << MyAssociation;
}
```

The output for this program is as follows:

```
Association { 7:00:00.00 am, Time to wake up. }
```

As this program illustrates, the Association class can relate two disparate objects, in this case a Time and a String object. The Association class, like all container classes, supports a default version of the insertion operator, so that displaying the contents of a class for information purposes is simple.

Using an Association class by itself is rarely necessary. If all you need to maintain are two objects, then it is easier to do so without an Association class. The Association class becomes very powerful when used in conjunction with another container class that can maintain a large number of Association objects. One of the container classes with which the Association class is often connected is the Dictionary class.

The Dictionary Class

The Dictionary class is a special type of container class that only manages a collection of Association objects. Like a dictionary, it maintains a list of a pair of items and lists an item only once. Unlike a dictionary, it does not maintain the list in any particular order. To use the Dictionary class, include the header file dict.h in your source file.

A Dictionary class always starts as an empty container. You then add one Association object at a time. The constructor for the Dictionary class has the following form:

```
Dictionary(unsigned hashvalue = DEFAULT_HASH_TABLE_SIZE);
```

The *hash value* is a number that is used internally to better manage a fluctuating list of entries. How these values are used is beyond the scope of this book. The only point to remember is that using a prime number improves the efficiency of how items in the Dictionary class are internally managed. You can use the default value in most cases.

The Dictionary class has only a few relevant member functions, as listed in table 30.8.

Table 30.8. Dictionary class member functions.

Member Function	Description
Dictionary(unsigned hashvalue = DEFAULT_HASH_TABLE_SIZE);	Constructor.

Member Function	Description
`virtual void add(Object&);`	Adds an item to the Dictionary class. The Object can only be an Association or derived class object.
`void destroy(Object&);`	Removes and deletes the object within the Dictionary.
`virtual void detach (Object&,`	Removes and optionally deletes an object from the Dictionary.
`DeleteType = NoDelete);` `virtual Object& findMember (Object&) const;`	Searches for a matching object in the Dictionary. Returns NOOBJECT if the search fails.
`virtual void flush (DeleteType = DefDelete);`	Removes and optionally deletes all the objects in the Dictionary.
`virtual countType getItemsInContainer() const;`	Returns the number of items in the Dictionary.
`virtual int isEmpty() const;`	Returns a nonzero value if the Dictionary is empty.
`Association& lookup (const Object&) const;`	Returns the Association object whose key Object value matches the one provided as the argument. If no object matches, returns the value NOOBJECT.

V

Advanced Programming

The following is an example of using the Dictionary class.

```
#include <dict.h>
#include <assoc.h>
#include <strng.h>
#include <ldate.h>

void main()
{
        // Declare a set of names

    String* Name1 = new String("Carol");
    String* Name2 = new String("Bob");
    String* Name3 = new String("John");
    String* Name4 = new String("Jill");

        // Declare a list of birthdates

    Date* Date1 = new Date(2, 4, 1960);
    Date* Date2 = new Date(6, 30, 1958);
    Date* Date3 = new Date(12, 1, 1962);
    Date* Date4 = new Date(8, 16, 1955);

        // Declare a list of Associations
```

```
Association* Association1 = new Association(*Date1, *Name1);
Association* Association2 = new Association(*Date2, *Name2);
Association* Association3 = new Association(*Date3, *Name3);
Association* Association4 = new Association(*Date4, *Name4);

    // Declare an instance of a Dictionary

Dictionary BirthDates;

    // Add birthday Association items

BirthDates.add(*Association1);
BirthDates.add(*Association2);
BirthDates.add(*Association3);
BirthDates.add(*Association4);

    // Display the birthdates

cout << "The following birthdays are being maintained: " <<
    endl << BirthDates;
}
```

The output for this program is as follows:

```
The following birthdays are being maintained:
Dictionary {
    Association { February 4, 1960, Carol },
    Association { December 1, 1962, John },
    Association { August 16, 1955, Jill },
    Association { June 30, 1958, Bob }, }
```

Much of the above example is spent setting up the Dictionary. First, a set of name strings is declared. This is followed by a set of dates. The names and dates are associated using a set of declared Associated classes. Finally a Dictionary class instance is declared, and the Associated class instances are added to the Dictionary class. The Dictionary class is displayed using the default insertion operator to the default output stream.

What makes the Dictionary class so powerful is that all the work of dynamically managing the information in memory is done on your behalf. From a programmer's perspective, it does not matter where this information is being stored.

Using Queues, Deques, and Priority Queues

Queues, in their various forms, are successions of items in which a particular sequence exists for adding and removing objects in the list. A queue-based list has a front and a back. The different queue classes manage how the information is added and removed from the Queue, as shown in figure 30.3.

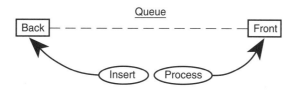

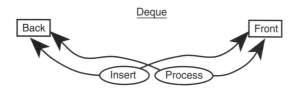

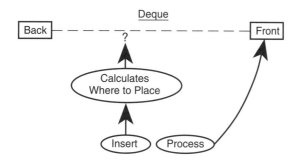

Fig. 30.3.
Different queue-based classes.

As figure 30.3 illustrates, a regular Queue adds items to the back end of a list and processes items at the front end of the list. This is often referred to as an FIFO list, which stands for *first-in-first-out*. Because items are placed in a lineup, the first item that is entered into the list is processed first.

The second type of Queue is a Deque. This is a flexible Queue; you can add or process items from either the front end or the back end of the list. You cannot process items from the middle of the list. A Deque allows you to create variations on the FIFO list, such as the FILO list (*first-in-last-out*). In fact, you can mix and match how items are entered and removed with each item.

A Priority Queue class implements an FIFO class that is based on a priority. Each item added to the Priority Queue is prioritized. The front and back of the list are therefore the highest and lowest ranking items respectively.

The Queue Class

The Queue class manages a special type of list in which only one item from the list can be accessed at a time. This item is always the first item entered in the list. When the first item is processed, it is removed from the list, and the next item in the order of insertion becomes the first item in the list. This type of list is called a FIFO list: *first-in-first-out*. The first item inserted in the list is always the first one that can be accessed. To use the Queue class, include the header file queue.h in your source file.

The Queue class has a default constructor that does not take any arguments. Table 30.9 lists the member functions available for the Queue class.

Table 30.9. Queue class member functions.

Member Function	Description
`Queue()`	Constructor.
`virtual void flush (DeleteType = DefDelete);`	Removes and optionally deletes all the objects in the queue.
`Object& get();`	Removes the next item to be processed, which is the item at the front of the queue.
`virtual countType getItemsInContainer() const;`	Returns the number of items in the queue.
`virtual int isEmpty() const;`	Returns a nonzero value if the queue is empty.
`void put(Object&);`	Adds an object to the queue, which is always placed at the back end of the queue.

The following is an example of using the Queue class.

```
#include <iostream.h>
#include <queue.h>
#include <strng.h>

void main()
{
        // Declare strings

    String* String1 = new String("First string entered");
    String* String2 = new String("Second string entered");
    String* String3 = new String("Third string entered");

        // Declare an instance of a Queue class

    Queue MyQueue;

        // Add strings to the Queue

    MyQueue.put(*String1);
```

```
            MyQueue.put(*String2);
            MyQueue.put(*String3);

                // Display contents of a Queue

            cout << MyQueue << endl;

                // Display Queue as items are processed

            while ( !MyQueue.isEmpty() )
                cout << MyQueue.get() << endl;
        }
```

The output for this program is as follows:

```
    Queue {
        Third string entered,
        Second string entered,
        First string entered }

    First string entered
    Second string entered
    Third string entered
```

The String objects are entered into the Queue using the member function
put(). This always places the next item in the back of the queue. This is demonstrated by the default output, which should be read as if the list were being
displayed from left to right. The first item in the default output is actually the
item at the end of the list. The last item in the default output is actually the
right-most item, which is the first item in the list.

The order of the list is confirmed by displaying the items one at a time as
they come off the list, using the member function get(). Because get() returns the next item in the list to be processed, it can be used within an insertion statement. In the second round of output, the order of the strings is
correctly displayed, the first string entered being displayed first.

Notice the use of the isEmpty() member function. This is a useful function to
iterate through a list without having to deal with indices.

The Deque Class
The Deque class is the base class for the Queue class discussed above. The
Deque class allows you to access objects in the list at either end. You cannot
access items in the middle of the list. To use the Deque class, include the
header file deque.h in your source file.

The Deque class includes a default constructor that takes no arguments. Table
30.10 lists the member functions of the Deque class.

Table 30.10. Deque class member functions.

Member Function	Description
Deque	Constructor.
virtual void flush (DeleteType = DefDelete);	Removes and optionally deletes all the objects in the queue.
virtual countType getItemsInContainer() const;	Returns the number of items in the queue.
Object& getLeft();	Removes and returns the left-most object from the list.
Object& getLeft();	Removes and returns the right-most object from the list.
virtual int isEmpty() const;	Returns a nonzero value if the queue is empty.
Object& peekLeft() const;	Returns the object at the end of the list.
Object& peekRight() const;	Returns the object at the front of the list.
void putLeft(Object&);	Places an object at the end of the list.
void putRight(Object&);	Places an object at the front end of the list.

The following is an example of using the Deque class.

```
#include <iostream.h>
#include <deque.h>
#include <ltime.h>

void main()
{
        // Declare times

    Time* Time1 = new Time(1);
    Time* Time2 = new Time(2);
    Time* Time3 = new Time(3);
    Time* Time4 = new Time(4);
    Time* Time5 = new Time(5);

        // Declare a Deque class

    Deque MyDeque;

        // Add items
```

```
      MyDeque.putRight(*Time1);
      MyDeque.putLeft(*Time2);
      MyDeque.putRight(*Time3);
      MyDeque.putLeft(*Time4);
      MyDeque.putRight(*Time5);

         // Display Deque

      cout << MyDeque;
   }
```

The output for this program is as follows:

```
Deque {
     4:00:00.00 am,
     2:00:00.00 am,
     1:00:00.00 am,
     3:00:00.00 am,
     5:00:00.00 am }
```

The default list should be read from left to right, where the left item is the last item in the list and the right item is the first item in the list. Figure 30.4 illustrates the list as it grows with each new item.

After 1st Item:	1:00:00.00 am	First item placed at the right side.
After 2nd Item:	2:00:00.00 am	Second item placed at the left side (tail) of the list.
After 3rd Item:	2:00:00.00 1:00:00.00 3:00:00.00	Third item placed at the rigth side (front) of the list.
After 4th Item:	4:00:00.00 2:00:00.00 1:00:00.00 3:00:00.00	Fourth item placed at the left side (tail) of the list.
After 5th Item:	4:00:00.00 2:00:00.00 1:00:00.00 3:00:00.00 5:00:00.00	Fifth item placed at the right side (front) of the list.

Fig. 30.4. Deque as each item is added.

As each item is added, it is placed either at the left or at the right of the list, depending on whether it was added using the putLeft() or putRight() member function. A Deque object can only grow at either end; it cannot add an item in the middle of the list.

The PriorityQueue Class

The PriorityQueue class is a special version of a Queue that manages items in a particular priority. Based on the priority of items, it sets up a Queue such that the item with the highest priority gets processed next. You cannot skip priority order when processing the list. To use the PriorityQueue class, include the header file priortyq.h in your source file.

The priority of an object is based on its ranking using the internally-supported relational operator of the object being maintained by the PriorityQueue. For example, if a String object is being maintained, then String1 is ranked higher than String2 if the following statement evaluates to true:

```
String1 > String2;
```

For the String, Date, and Time classes, the rankings are evaluated based on their internally-defined relational operators. For Strings, a string comparison determines which is greater. For Date objects, later dates evaluate higher than earlier dates. The same applies to Time objects. You can create your own Object-derived classes with special evaluation operators that suit the needs of your application.

The PriorityQueue class only has a default constructor that takes no arguments. Table 30.11 lists the member functions for the PriorityQueue class.

Table 30.11. PriorityQueue class member functions.

Member Function	Description
PriorityQueue()	Constructor.
virtual void flush (DeleteType = DefDelete);	Removes and optionally deletes all the objects in the queue.
Object& get();	Removes the next item to be processed, which is the item at the front of the queue.
virtual countType getItemsInContainer() const;	Returns the number of items in the queue.
virtual int isEmpty() const;	Returns a nonzero value if the queue is empty.
void put(Object&);	Adds an object to the queue, which is always placed at the back end of the queue.

The following is an example of using the PriorityQueue class.

```
#include <iostream.h>
#include <priortyq.h>
#include <ldate.h>

void main()
{
        // Declare date objects

    Date* Date1 = new Date(1, 1, 1980);
    Date* Date2 = new Date(7, 4, 1776);
    Date* Date3 = new Date(1, 2, 1980);
    Date* Date4 = new Date(6, 16, 1962);
    Date* Date5 = new Date(8, 23, 1993);

        // Declare an instance of a PriorityQueue

    PriorityQueue MyPriorityQueue;

        // Add Date items to the queue

    MyPriorityQueue.put(*Date1);
    MyPriorityQueue.put(*Date2);
    MyPriorityQueue.put(*Date3);
    MyPriorityQueue.put(*Date4);
    MyPriorityQueue.put(*Date5);

        // Display the queue

    cout << MyPriorityQueue;
}
```

The output for this program is as follows:

```
PriorityQueue {
    July 4, 1776,
    June 16, 1962,
    January 1, 1980,
    January 2, 1980,
    August 23, 1993 }
```

The Date class determines its order based on the chronological date. Later dates are evaluated higher when compared to earlier dates. For a PriorityQueue, this means that later dates are assigned a higher priority.

The dates in the above example were added to the queue in no particular order. However, when the queue is displayed, the earlier dates are placed last. Reading the output as if it were written from left to right, the earliest date appears in the queue as the last item. As the dates get later in chronological time, they appear closer to the front of the queue. The PriorityQueue places the items in the correct order when they are placed in the queue.

Summary

This chapter reviewed some of the common uses of container classes. The container classes are an invaluable set of prewritten classes that manage groups of items in a practical and easy-to-use way.

This chapter demonstrated the following things:

- The container class library is based on a complex hierarchy of classes, many of which are abstract classes that only serve as seed classes for the other container classes.

- All container classes support stream operations to the standard input and output devices.

- Several container classes manage information rather than lists: the String, Date, and Time classes.

- All classes derived from the abstract class Object support certain common member functions, including relational operators.

- Items added to a container class must be derived from the class Object.

- Container classes by default own the objects that they manage. When the container class is deleted, so are the objects it maintains.

- The String, Date, and Time classes are useful in simplifying the management of strings, dates, and times in programs.

- A Timer class exists that is not part of the container class but is nonetheless useful as a stopwatch. The Timer() class enables you to calculate easily the elapsed time between tasks.

- Array and SortedArray classes can grow dynamically based on the number of items added to the array.

- The Association class is used to relate two items, both of which must be derived from the Object class.

- The Dictionary class is used to manage a collection of Association classes.

- The Queue, Deque, and PriorityQueue classes are used to manage queues of items. A queue is characterized by the fact that it can only access an item that is either at the front or rear of the queue. In the case of Queue and PriorityQueue, you can only access items at the front of the queue.

Chapter 31

Using Templates

Templates extend the functionality of C++ by enabling you to customize objects. A *template* is a pattern or form of an object that can be applied to various specific object types. This chapter introduces the topic of templates, discussing the three main areas of template use with C++:

- Function templates
- Class templates
- Template container classes

Understanding Templates

A template is a form of an object. A form of an object is a general pattern that applies to an object, without necessarily specifying which object type is being referred to. A template is analogous to a factory assembly line that can produce a variety of objects. If fitted with one set of material, the assembly line produces stereos. When fitted with another set of material, the factory line produces televisions. The C++ template is a factory assembly line for producing C++ objects.

One of the difficulties with any language, including C, is that you must specify the type of object with which you are working. For example, you cannot write a program that references objects without first telling the compiler the type of objects being referenced. The following example program does not compile in C++.

```
void main
{
    i = j + 10;
}
```

Although there is nothing wrong with the syntax of this example, the compiler does not know what type of objects are being referred to by the variables i and j. The reason this is necessary for the compiler is that the storage and manipulation requirements of different objects are unique. For example, an integer occupies two bytes and is added using one form of CPU arithmetic. A class with an overloaded + operator uses a completely different set of storage requirements and its addition is governed by the overloaded + operator function, which most likely is completely different than the standard + arithmetic operation.

The purpose of a template i is to define a pattern of operations suitable for a variety of object types. The object type becomes one of the variables for the template. The template can then be used to generate structures or classes for any specific object type. By assigning the object type variable, the compiler generates the appropriate structure or class for that object type, using the template as a guideline.

Using Function Templates

A *function template* is a function prototype that does not specify the object types of at least one of its arguments. Instead, the object type is replaced by a template argument that is a placeholder for the object type to be used. When the program is compiled, the compiler looks for how the function is being used and then builds the necessary version (or versions) of the template function as needed by the program.

A function template has the following general form:

```
template <class Type> function_declaration
```

The function template starts out with a keyword template followed by the words <class Type>. This tells the compiler that the word *Type* is used as a variable that refers to a generic object type. When the variable name Type is then used anywhere else in the template function, it is referring to the generic object type of the template function. The generic object type is replaced by the specific object type at compile time.

The following is an example of a prototype declaration of a template function:

```
template <class Type> Type Function1(Type arg1, Type arg2);
```

This prototype declares a function called Function1() that takes two arguments. Both these arguments are not specified in the prototype. In fact, the arguments can be any valid object type, because the function is declared as a template. The function can now be used with a variety of object types. Consider the following uses of the function Function1().

```
template <class Type> Type Function1(Type arg1, Type arg2)
{
    .
    .      // Function1() defined here
    .
}

void main()
{
    int i, j; // Declare integer variables

    float a, b;    // Declare float variables

        // Use Function1() with integer values

    Function1(i, j);

        // Use Function1() with float variables

    Function1(a, b);
}
```

This example program declares a template function called Function1() and uses the function with either integer arguments or float arguments.

When the compiler sees the template function, it does not build anything until the function is actually used in the program. When the function Function() is used for the first time, it is called with two integer arguments. The compiler looks at the template function, sees that the arguments are declared with variable object types, and builds a corresponding function that uses integers as arguments. The compiler generates the following actual function out of the template function:

```
int Function1(int arg1, int arg2)
{
    .
    .      // Function1() defined here
    .
}
```

The object type int is used anywhere that the object type variable Type was declared in the template prototype.

When the function Function1() is used the second time with float arguments, the compiler generates the following actual function out of the template function:

```
float Function1(float arg1, float arg2)
{
    .
    .      // Function1() defined here
    .
}
```

This time the object type variable `Type` found in the template prototype is replaced by the object type `float`.

The compiler generates as many functions as necessary to match all the instances where `Function1()` is used with a unique object type. This spares the programmer from declaring various overloaded or unique versions of the function `Function1()`, each specifying a different object type to use. With templates, the compiler does all this work for you.

Listing 31.1 provides an example of how a template function can be used to simplify programming.

Listing 31.1. Function template example.

```
1.   #include <iostream.h>

2.        // Define template class to assign one array to another

3.   template <class Type> void AssignArray(Type *Target, Type
    ➥Source, int Items)
4.   {
5.        // Declare loop for number of items to copy

6.        for(int i = 0; i < Items; i++)
7.        {
8.        // Copy items from array to another using index i
9.        // The type of object being copied is determined
10.       // at compile time based on Type

11.       Target[i] = Source[i];
12.  }
13.}

14.  void main()
15.  {
16.       // Declare one assigned and another empty integer array

17.  int i[5] = {1, 2, 3, 4, 5}, j[5];

18.       // Declare one assigned and another empty float array

19.  float a[4] = {1.1, 2.2, 3.3, 4.4}, b[4];

20.       // Declare one assigned and another empty character array

21.  char c[3] = {'A', 'B', 'C'}, d[3];

22.       // Use the AssignArray() function to copy the values of
23.       // the assigned arrays to the empty arrays

24.  AssignArray(j, i, 5);
25.  AssignArray(b, a, 4);
```

```
26.   AssignArray(d, c, 3);


27.       // Display the values of the newly filled arrays

28.   cout << "Integer array j: " << j[0] << "," << j[1] <<
29.        "," << j[2] << "," << j[3] << "," << j[4] << endl;

30.   cout << "Float array b: " << b[0] << "," << b[1] << "," <<
      31.   << "," << b[3] << endl;

32.   cout << "Character array d: " << d[0] << "," << d[1] << "," <<
      33.   << endl;
34.   }
```

The output for this program is:

```
Integer array j: 1,2,3,4,5
Float array b: 1.1,2.2,3.3,4.4
Character array d: A,B,C
```

Listing 31.1 defines a template function called AssignArray that assigns the values of one array into another. Normally, you must define a separate function to manage each individual array type. If you want to use a function like AssignArray() to work with a pair of integer, float, and character arrays without using templates, you must declare and define three functions as follows:

```
void AssignArray(int *Target, int *Source, int Items);
void AssignArray(float *Target, float *Source, int Items);
void AssignArray(char *Target, char *Source, int Items);
```

The compiler is then able to use the AssignArray() function using these different object types as arguments. The alternative, and the simpler solution, is to use the single function prototype AssignArray() and declare it as a template function. This is done in listing 31.1 on line 3.

The template declaration is defined once using a generic object type, declared in this case as the variable Type. When AssignValue() is used in the program with a specific object type, a specific version of the AssignValue() function is generated by the compiler to match the argument type with which it is being called. On line 24 of listing 31.1, the AssignArray() function is called with a pair of integer arguments. The compiler generates an appropriate AssignArray() function as follows:

```
void AssignArray(int *Target, int *Source, int Items)
{
    for(int i = 0; i < Items; i++)
    {
        Target[i] = Source[i];
    }
}
```

V

Advanced Programming

On line 25 of listing 31.1, when the `AssignArray()` function is used with float values, the compiler generates another (overloaded) version of the function as follows:

```
void AssignArray(float *Target, float *Source, int Items)
{
    for(int i = 0; i < Items; i++)
    {
        Target[i] = Source[i];
    }
}
```

Finally, on line 26 of listing 31.1, when the `AssignArray()` function is used with character array arguments, the compiler generates yet another version of the `AssignArray()` function as follows:

```
void AssignArray(char *Target, char *Source, int Items)
{
    for(int i = 0; i < Items; i++)
    {
        Target[i] = Source[i];
    }
}
```

With each use of `AssignArray()` that is called with new argument types, the compiler builds another overloaded version of the `AssignArray()` function. Although you could do this on your own, it is simpler to allow the compiler to do this work for you.

Certain limitations exist with template functions that you must keep in mind when considering this form of function definition. As is illustrated in the example of listing 31.1, the type of function that can benefit from a template definition is one that has the identical actions for each data type being used. For example, the `AssignArray()` function could not be used with the following call:

```
AssignArray(d, a, 3);
```

In this case, the variable d is a character array, and the variable a is a float array. The template specifically declares that the first two arguments are the same object type, even though it does not matter what argument type that may be. The above use of the `AssignArray()` function produces the following compiler error:

```
Could not find a match for AssignArray(char *, float *, int)
```

Do not use any statements within the template function that conflict with any of intended object types with which it must operate. Consider the following version of the `AssignArray()` function of listing 31.1.

```
3.    template <class Type> void AssignArray(Type *Target, Type
➥Source, int Items)
4.    {
5.         // Declare loop for number of items to copy

6.         for(int i = 0; i < Items; i++)
7.         {
8.         // Copy items from array to another using index i
9.         // The type of object being copied is determined
10.        // at compile time based on Type

11.        strcpy(Target[i], Source[i]);
12.    }
13.}
```

Line 11 now uses the strcpy() function to copy the items in the array. The function strcpy() can only be used with character pointer arguments. This conflicts with the intended use of the template function for object types such as integers and floats. When this function is used with a pair of integer arguments, the compiler builds a version of the AssignArray() function using the integer data types. However, the strcpy() function cannot be used with integers, so the compiler produces an error.

Template functions are extremely useful if the function itself can be defined in a way that is valid for all intended data types had the function been declared specifically for each data type separately.

Using Class Templates

A *class template* is a class that can be used with different data types. Like a function template, a class template uses a variable that represents a generic data type to be used with the class. The prototype for a class template is as follows:

```
template <class Type> class_declaration...
```

The class can then be used with various data types. When the class is used with a specific data type, the compiler generates a version of the class using the specific data type. The variable Type is then replaced by the compiler with the specific data type that is used in the class instance declaration. The following is an example of a class template prototype:

```
template <class Type> class DoNothing
{
public:
     MemberFunction(Type t);
     .
     .         // Define other class members here
     .
}
```

To call this class from within a program, use the following syntax:

```
void main()
{
      DoNothing<int> MyDoNothing1;

      DoNothing<char> MyDoNothing2;
}
```

The DoNothing class is called using angle brackets to let the compiler know what data or class type to use as the Type variable declared in the class template definition. The compiler would have no other way of knowing what to use as the data or class type for the Type variable in the class template definition. This example program generates two separate versions of the class DoNothing. The first version of the DoNothing class takes the form:

```
class DoNothing
{
public:
      MemberFunction(int t);
      .
      .       // Define other class members here
      .

}
```

The second version of the class DoNothing takes the following form:

```
class DoNothing
{
public:
      MemberFunction(char t);
      .
      .       // Define other class members here
      .

}
```

Each version of the DoNothing class uses a different type of argument for the MemberFunction() function. The compiler generates a new version of the function for each data or class type that is used for the variable Type in the class template definition.

You could declare several template variables. For example, the DoNothing template class can be defined to take three template variable, as follows:

```
template <class Type1, class Type2, class Type3> class DoNothing
{
public:
      MemberFunction1(Type1 t1);
      MemberFunction2(Type2 t2, Type3 t3);
      .
      .       // Define other class members here
      .

}
```

The template variables are used to determine what version of the class to generate at compile time. In the above example of the DoNothing class template definition, you could call this class with the following different variations:

```
// Instance of DoNothing class using variation #1

DoNothing<int, int, int> DoNothing;

// Instance of DoNothing class using variation #2

DoNothing<float, int, char> DoNothing;

// Instance of DoNothing class using variation #3

DoNothing<char, float, float> DoNothing;
```

The compiler sees three different versions of the class DoNothing at compile time because each instance is called with a different set of template variables. The compiler uses the template variables to generate three different versions of the DoNothing class as follows:

```
// Compiler-generated class for version #1

class DoNothing
{
public:
    MemberFunction1(int t1);
    MemberFunction2(int t2, int t3);
    .
    .    // Define other class members here
    .
}

// Compiler-generated class for version #2

class DoNothing
{
public:
    MemberFunction1(float t1);
    MemberFunction2(int t2, char t3);
    .
    .    // Define other class members here
    .
}

// Compiler-generated class for version #1

class DoNothing
{
public:
    MemberFunction1(char t1);
    MemberFunction2(float t2, float t3);
    .
    .    // Define other class members here
    .
}
```

V

Advanced Programming

The order of template variables is maintained by the compiler. The order in which the types are declared in the angle brackets when an instance of the DoNothing class is declared is the order in which they are assigned to the template class variables, as declared in the class template definition. The first template variable in the angle brackets is assigned to the template variable Type1, the second to Type2, and the third to Type3.

The same considerations that apply to the template functions apply to the template classes. The compiler is simply generating a class on your behalf, replacing the template variables with the ones you provide at the time you declare an instance of the class. You must think of the class as if you declared and defined the class explicitly with the template variables already replaced. Whatever you can do with the template types if they were declared explicitly, you can do with template classes declared implicitly. However, whatever is invalid as an explicit call is not going to become valid by a template declaration.

Listing 31.2 provides an example of a class template.

Listing 31.2. Template class example.

```
1.    #include <iostream.h>

2.    // Define a template class to manage an array of items

3.    template <class Type> class GenericArray
4.    {
5.    protected:
6.    Type * List;    // Declare variable to contain array

7.    public:
8.        // Constructor

9.    GenericArray(int Items)
10.        { List = new Type[Items]; }   // Allocate items

11.        // Destructor

12.    ~GenericArray()
13.        { delete List; }      // Deallocate items

14.        // Member function to get an item

15.    const Type& GetItem(int Item)
16.        { return (Type&) List[Item]; }

17.        // Member function to set an item

18.    void SetItem(Type& t, int Item)
19.        { List[Item] = t; }
```

```
20.   }

21.   void main()
22.   {
23.        // Declare GenericArray as a list of integers

24.   GenericArray<int> IntArray(10);

25.        // Assign values to the IntArray

26.   for(int i = 0; i < 10; i++ ) IntArray.SetItem(i, i);

27.        // Declare GenericArray as a list of characters

28.   GenericArray<char> CharArray(3);

29.        // Assign values to the CharArray

30.   for(i = 0; i < 10; i++ ) CharArray.SetItem((char) i + 65, i);

31.        // Display array values for IntArray

32.   cout << "Values for IntArray:" << endl;
33.   for ( i = 0; i < 10; i++ ) cout << IntArray.GetItem(i) << endl;

34.        // Display array values for CharArray

35.   cout << "Values for CharArray:" << endl;
36.   for ( i = 0; i < 10; i++ ) cout << CharArray.GetItem(i) << endl;
37.   }
```

The output for listing 31.2 is as follows:

```
Values for IntArray:
0
1
2
3
4
5
6
7
8
9
Value for CharArray:
A
B
C
D
E
F
G
H
I
J
```

V

Advanced Programming

Listing 31.2 defines a template array class called GenericArray. The GenericArray class can work with any data or object type (unlike the container classes that can only work with Object-derived objects). This is accomplished by declaring the type of object that is being maintained by the array to be a template variable, in this case Type on line 3. Any time a member function needs to operate on the object type, it uses a Type object so that it is compatible with any user-defined object type.

The GenericArray class defines a constructor that takes a single integer argument on line 9. An internal array, declared as a pointer to the object type represented by the template variable Type, is allocated, using the C++ new allocation function. This is necessary because the new allocation function is generic as well. Regardless of the object type that will be used, a new allocation operator is safe to use.

Because memory has been allocated by using the new allocation function, it must be explicitly deleted. This is done in the destructor, defined on line 12. The C++ delete deallocation function, like the new function, operates on any object type, and so is safe to use in this class. Remember that the class must be defined in such a way that it will operate correctly regardless of the object type with which it is used.

The two other member functions defined for the GenericArray class are GetItem() and SetItems(). These functions, defined on lines 15 and 18 respectively, enable a user to get and set a specific item in the array.

At this point, the compiler has yet to create a class called GenericArray. Unless it is actually used, the template is not a formal declaration of a class. It is simply a pattern to be used to generate real classes. This can only be done when the program declares an instance of the class, letting the compiler know what object type to use to generate the real class.

This is done first on line 24 in the main() function. This statement declares an instance of GenericArray, using an integer as an object type for the class. This is denoted by the type integer in angle brackets. At this point, the compiler builds a version of the GenericArray template class into a real class that is defined as follows:

```
class GenericArray
{
protected:
Type * List;   // Declare variable to contain array

public:
```

```
        // Constructor

GenericArray(int Items)
      { List = new int[Items]; }   // Allocate items

        // Destructor

~GenericArray()
      { delete List; }     // Deallocate items

        // Member function to get an item

const int& GetItem(int Item)
      { return (int&) List[Item]; }

        // Member function to set an item

void SetItem(int& t, int Item)
      { List[Item] = t; }
}
```

As with the template functions, the template variable Type is replaced with
the int keyword. The compiler generates this class internally. You will not see
this class anywhere in a listing. It is maintained by the compiler as one of the
valid versions of the GenericArray class. When you view the template class as
a real class with the int keyword, rather than with the Type template variable,
it is simpler to read. The GetItem() and SetItem() member functions are self-
explanatory. In fact, the entire class is legible. To see how a template class
operates, it is useful to remove the template variables and create at least one
version of the class yourself using the nontemplate format. After all, that is
exactly what the compiler will do on your behalf.

Line 26 assigns values to the array items of IntArray, using the SetItem()
member function.

The program then declares another instance of GenericArray, this time using
a different object type as the template variable Type. This is done on line 28,
where an instance of the GenericArray class is declared using the char keyword. This prompts the compiler to create yet another version of the
GenericArray class that looks as follows:

```
class GenericArray
{
protected:
Type * List;   // Declare variable to contain array

public:
      // Constructor

GenericArray(int Items)
```

V

Advanced Programming

```
            { List = new char[Items]; }  // Allocate items

            // Destructor

        ~GenericArray()
            { delete List; }    // Deallocate items

            // Member function to get an item

        const char& GetItem(char Item)
            { return (char&) List[Item]; }

            // Member function to set an item

        void SetItem(char& t, int Item)
            { List[Item] = t; }
        }
```

This time the template variable Type is replaced with the keyword char. This is the second version of the GenericArray class that is maintained by the compiler. After you make the change to a real class, the class is easier to read. The GetItem() and SetItem() member functions are intuitive. This is useful because the template class must be able to work with any object type that the user chooses.

Line 30 assigns character values to the items in the CharArray array. This is done using a for loop, and assigning i+65 to the array item at index i. The number 65 is the ASCII offset to the letter *A*. By using i+65 as the item for index i, the letter *A* is placed at index 0, *B* placed at index 1, and so on.

The arrays are displayed using a for loop that cycles through the array indices, using GetItem() to return a value that is passed to the C++ output stream. The GetItem() member function returns a reference to whatever object type the instance of GenericArray is maintaining. For IntArray, it returns a reference to an integer value. For CharArray, it returns a reference to a character value. The C++ output stream automatically supports output of the built-in data types int and char. Therefore, returning a reference to these data types means that they can be used in a C++ output stream.

Using the template classes has several benefits. The one that has already been mentioned is the economy of programming effort. By declaring a template class, you can define a single class that generates many versions of the class using specific object types, as is necessary by the program itself.

Another benefit to using template classes is that each version of the class that is created with a template class is predictably the same. All member functions operate identically because they are defined within the same class template. This is efficient for debugging, maintenance, and upgrading.

Template Container Classes

Turbo C++ includes a set of templates that implement container classes similar to the container classes discussed in Chapter 30. One of the limitations of the standard container classes is that all data objects of the container classes must be derived from the class Object, which is the base class of all container classes. This excludes all built-in data types that are typically necessary for applications. For example, you cannot declare a container class array of integers or floats. Turbo C++ has an alternative set of container classes that are based on template classes that work with any data object, built-in or user-defined.

The template-based container classes are called BIDS—Borland International Data Structures. These structures are a complex set of interrelated classes and structures whose full explanation could easily fill a book. This section introduces the BIDS library and demonstrates how to use one of the template classes.

The BIDS library can be divided into two main categories:

- Direct storage templates: template classes that directly store the objects that the class maintains

- Indirect storage templates: template classes that store pointers to the objects that the class maintains

Because the BIDS library is template-based, any object type can be used. You can use a BIDS library to declare an instance of an integer array, a float array, or a String container class array. BIDS library classes are extremely flexible.

Numerous BIDS classes exist to choose from. Rather than a single template that manages a collection of objects, templates exist for every type of storage method. For example, there are templates for direct and indirect standard arrays, linked lists and doubly-linked lists. Additionally, there are templates for stacks, deques, queues, and bags. Each of these templates manages objects using the same principles described in Chapter 30 for the container classes. The main difference is that BIDS classes are template-based and therefore applicable to any object type.

One of the basic BIDS templates is the vector template. This template stores information as a linear vector of objects. There is no particular limitation as to how objects are stored or retrieved. The direct storage vector template is called `BI_VectorImp`, and the indirect storage version is called `BI_IVectorImp`.

V

Advanced Programming

To create an instance of the BIDS vector template, you must declare the instance using the object type to be stored in angle brackets. The following are some examples of vector declarations.

```
BI_VectorImp<int> IntVector(10); // Declare an array of 10 integers

BI_VectorImp<float> FloatVector(2); // Declare an array of 2 floats

BI_VectorImp<String> StringVector(5); // Declare an array of 5
String objects
```

Using the vector template member functions is similar to using the container class member functions. Many function names are shared between the libraries, such as the add() and detach() member functions. However, many member functions will be particular to the BIDS library template classes.

Unfortunately, no single reference guide to the BIDS library classes is published by Borland. The only way to get a full list of available member functions is to refer to the header file in which a particular template is defined. Although this is very inconvenient, it does serve the purpose of illustrating how the BIDS classes are interrelated and how template classes in general are implemented.

The following is an example of an array of objects maintained by the BIDS vector template.

```
#include <iostream.h>
#include <vectimp.h>
#include <strng.h>

void main()
{
        // Declare a vector of integers

    BI_CVectorImp<int> IntVector(5);

        // Assign values to the IntVector items

    for ( int i = 0; i < 5; i++) IntVector[i] = i;

        // Declare a vector of String objects

    BI_CVectorImp<String> StringVector(4);

        // Assign values to the StringVector items

    StringVector.add(String("This"));
    StringVector.add(String("is"));
    StringVector.add(String("a"));
    StringVector.add(String("test"));

        // Display the values of IntVector

    cout << "The values of IntVector are:" << endl;
```

```
        for( i = 0; i < 5; i++ ) cout << IntVector[i] << endl;

            // Display the values of StringVector

        cout << "The values of StringVector are:" << endl;
        for( i = 0; i < 4; i++ ) cout << StringVector[i] << endl;
    }
```

The output for this program is as follows:

```
The values of IntVector are:
0
1
2
3
4
The Values of StringVector are:
This
is
a
test
```

The version of the vector template class used in this example is called
BI_CVectorImp, which is the counted vector class. This class includes such
member functions as add() that enable the class to internally maintain the
vector. When an object is added to the vector using the add() member function, it is placed in the next available slot. Alternatively, you can place an
object at any available slot of the vector directly.

This example program demonstrates a few of the capabilities of the vector
class. The same vector template is used to create an instance of the vector
class for Integer as well as String objects. This itself is an advantage over the
standard container classes, which could store only items derived from the
Object class. Additionally, whatever functionality is available for the integer
vector is available for the String vector as well. This allows you to select one
or two standard template classes, study them well, and apply them regularly
to a variety of situations where different object types are necessary.

One of the major functions lacking in the BIDS classes that is available in the
standard container classes is direct support for C++ streams. The BIDS classes
cannot be used directly with C++ streams. For example, you could not use the
following statement in the previous example:

```
cout << IntVector;   // Invalid!!
cout << StringVector;   // Invalid!!
```

To use the C++ streams directly, you must derive a class based on the vector
template class and define an insertion operator. However, you can use the
C++ streams for any item that is maintained by a vector class that supports
C++ streams. The above example uses this method to display the IntVector as
well as the StringVector classes.

V

Advanced Programming

The above example uses the direct storage version of the vector class. The integer and String objects are copied into storage that is dynamically allocated by the vector. When the vector is destroyed, the memory used to store the vector items is destroyed along with it.

Summary

Templates provide flexibility for you, allowing you to declare a single function or class and then use it for various object types. The compiler generates a version of a template for each object type that it is used in the program.

In this chapter, the following points about templates were made:

- You can define function templates by declaring a function with the template keyword, followed by a list of template arguments, followed by the function declaration.

- Template functions determine the type of function to build based on the object type of the function arguments.

- The template arguments are used by the compiler as variables. When the template function is used, the arguments used are assumed by the compiler to match the template arguments. The compiler then generates a version of the functions for each set of unique template variables for which the template function is used.

- Class templates are declared by specifying the template keyword, followed by a list of template arguments, followed by the class declaration.

- When an instance of the class is declared, you must specify the object types for each template argument. These types are then used by the compiler to generate a class that has the template argument's types replaced by the actual data types used in the instance declaration.

- The compiler generates a class for each unique set of template types used in an instance declaration of a class template.

- Turbo C++ comes with a set of template classes, called the BIDS library, that implements container classes as templates.

- The advantage of using the BIDS library is that the container classes can store any built-in or user-defined data types.

- The flaw of the BIDS classes is that they do not directly support C++ streams.

Part VI

Reference

ASCII Codes

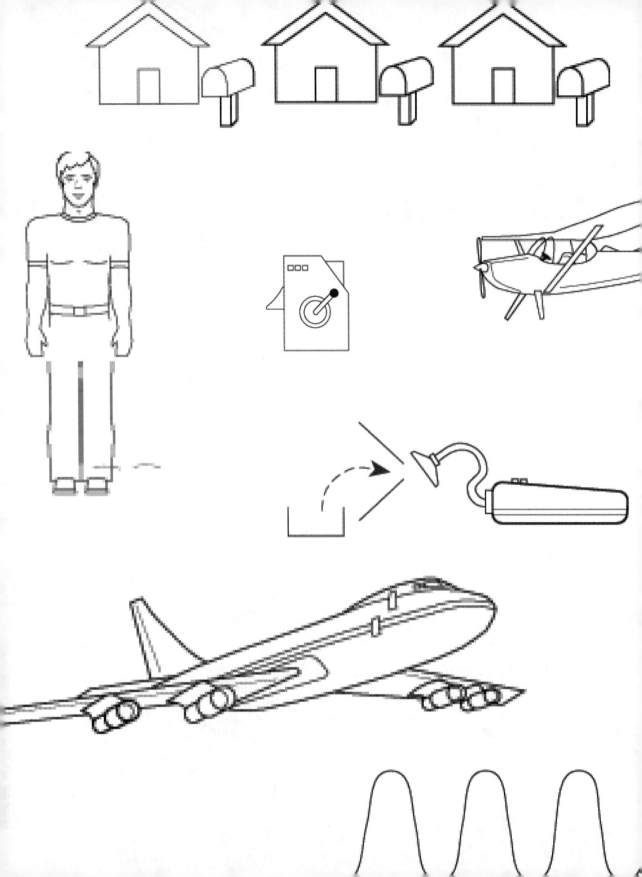

Appendix A

ASCII Codes

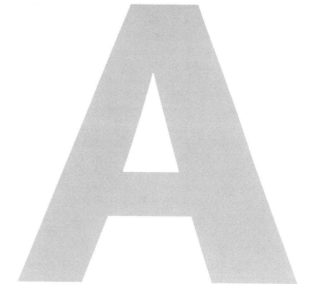

ASCII (American Standard Code for Information Interchange) is a widely used standard that defines numeric values for a common set of alphabetic characters.

Dec X_{10}	Hex X_{16}	Binary X_2	ASCII Charater
000	00	0000 0000	null
001	01	0000 0001	☺
002	02	0000 0010	☻
003	03	0000 0011	♥
004	04	0000 0100	♦
005	05	0000 0101	♣
006	06	0000 0110	♠
007	07	0000 0111	●
008	08	0000 1000	■
009	09	0000 1001	○
010	0A	0000 1010	■
011	0B	0000 1011	♂
012	0C	0000 1100	♀
013	0D	0000 1101	♪
014	0E	0000 1110	♪♪
015	0F	0000 1111	☼
016	10	0001 0000	►
017	11	0001 0001	◄
018	12	0001 0010	↕
019	13	0001 0011	‼
020	14	0001 0100	¶
021	15	0001 0101	§
022	16	0001 0110	▬
023	17	0001 0111	↨

Dec x_{10}	Hex X_{16}	Binary X_2	ASCII Charater
024	18	0001 1000	↑
025	19	0001 1001	↓
026	1A	0001 1010	→
027	1B	0001 1011	←
028	1C	0001 1100	∟
029	1D	0001 1101	↔
030	1E	0001 1110	▲
031	1F	0001 1111	▼
032	20	0010 0000	Space
033	21	0010 0001	!
034	22	0010 0010	"
035	23	0010 0011	#
036	24	0010 0100	$
037	25	0010 0101	%
038	26	0010 0110	&
039	27	0010 0111	'
040	28	0010 1000	(
041	29	0010 1001	)
042	2A	0010 1010	*
043	2B	0010 1011	+
044	2C	0010 1100	,
045	2D	0010 1101	-
046	2E	0010 1110	.
047	2F	0010 1111	/
048	30	0011 0000	0
049	31	0011 0001	1
050	32	0011 0010	2
051	33	0011 0011	3
052	34	0011 0100	4
053	35	0011 0101	5
054	36	0011 0110	6
055	37	0011 0111	7
056	38	0011 1000	8
057	39	0011 1001	9
058	3A	0011 1010	:

Dec x_{10}	Hex X_{16}	Binary X_2	ASCII Charater
059	3B	0011 1011	;
060	3C	0011 1100	<
061	3D	0011 1101	=
062	3E	0011 1110	>
063	3F	0011 1111	?
064	40	0100 0000	@
065	41	0100 0001	A
066	42	0100 0010	B
067	43	0100 0011	C
068	44	0100 0100	D
069	45	0100 0101	E
070	46	0100 0110	F
071	47	0100 0111	G
072	48	0100 1000	H
073	49	0100 1001	I
074	4A	0100 1010	J
075	4B	0100 1011	K
076	4C	0100 1100	L
077	4D	0100 1101	M
078	4E	0100 1110	N
079	4F	0100 1111	O
080	50	0101 0000	P
081	51	0101 0001	Q
082	52	0101 0010	R
083	53	0101 0011	S
084	54	0101 0100	T
085	55	0101 0101	U
086	56	0101 0110	V
087	57	0101 0111	W
088	58	0101 1000	X
089	59	0101 1001	Y
090	5A	0101 1010	Z
091	5B	0101 1011	[
092	5C	0101 1100	\
093	5D	0101 1101	]

VI

Reference

Dec x_{10}	Hex X_{16}	Binary X_2	ASCII Charater
094	5E	0101 1110	^
095	5F	0101 1111	–
096	60	0110 0000	`
097	61	0110 0001	a
098	62	0110 0010	b
099	63	0110 0011	c
100	64	0110 0100	d
101	65	0110 0101	e
102	66	0110 0110	f
103	67	0110 0111	g
104	68	0110 1000	h
105	69	0110 1001	i
106	6A	0110 1010	j
107	6B	0110 1011	k
108	6C	0110 1100	l
109	6D	0110 1101	m
110	6E	0110 1110	n
111	6F	0110 1111	o
112	70	0111 0000	p
113	71	0111 0001	q
114	72	0111 0010	r
115	73	0111 0011	s
116	74	0111 0100	t
117	75	0111 0101	u
118	76	0111 0110	v
119	77	0111 0111	w
120	78	0111 1000	x
121	79	0111 1001	y
122	7A	0111 1010	z
123	7B	0111 1011	{
124	7C	0111 1100	¦
125	7D	0111 1101	}
126	7E	0111 1110	~
127	7F	0111 1111	Delete

Index

W–Z

GO AHEAD. PLUG YOURSELF INTO PRENTICE HALL COMPUTER PUBLISHING.

Introducing the PHCP Forum on CompuServe®

Yes, it's true. Now, you can have CompuServe access to the same professional, friendly folks who have made computers easier for years. On the PHCP Forum, you'll find additional information on the topics covered by every PHCP imprint—including Que, Sams Publishing, New Riders Publishing, Alpha Books, Brady Books, Hayden Books, and Adobe Press. In addition, you'll be able to receive technical support and disk updates for the software produced by Que Software and Paramount Interactive, a division of the Paramount Technology Group. It's a great way to supplement the best information in the business.

WHAT CAN YOU DO ON THE PHCP FORUM?

Play an important role in the publishing process—and make our books better while you make your work easier:

- Leave messages and ask questions about PHCP books and software—you're guaranteed a response within 24 hours
- Download helpful tips and software to help you get the most out of your computer
- Contact authors of your favorite PHCP books through electronic mail
- Present your own book ideas
- Keep up to date on all the latest books available from each of PHCP's exciting imprints

JOIN NOW AND GET A FREE COMPUSERVE STARTER KIT!

To receive your free CompuServe Introductory Membership, call toll-free, **1-800-848-8199** and ask for representative **#K597**. The Starter Kit Includes:

- Personal ID number and password
- $15 credit on the system
- Subscription to CompuServe Magazine

HERE'S HOW TO PLUG INTO PHCP:

Once on the CompuServe System, type any of these phrases to access the PHCP Forum:

GO PHCP   **GO BRADY**
GO QUEBOOKS   **GO HAYDEN**
GO SAMS   **GO QUESOFT**
GO NEWRIDERS   **GO PARAMOUNTINTER**
GO ALPHA

Once you're on the CompuServe Information Service, be sure to take advantage of all of CompuServe's resources. CompuServe is home to more than 1,700 products and services—plus it has over 1.5 million members worldwide. You'll find valuable online reference materials, travel and investor services, electronic mail, weather updates, leisure-time games and hassle-free shopping (no jam-packed parking lots or crowded stores).

Seek out the hundreds of other forums that populate CompuServe. Covering diverse topics such as pet care, rock music, cooking, and political issues, you're sure to find others with the same concerns as you—and expand your knowledge at the same time.

Complete Computer Coverage

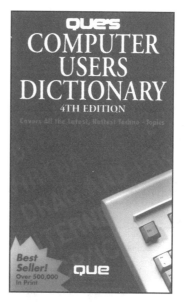

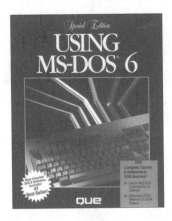

Que Has WordPerfect 6 Books
for All Types of Users!

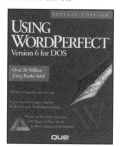